THE CAT FROM HUÉ

THE CAT

FROM HUÉ

A VIETNAM WAR STORY

John Laurence

PUBLICAFFAIRS   NEW YORK

Book design and composition by Mark McGarry, Texas Type & Book Works.
Set in Monotype Dante.

Library of Congress Cataloging-in-Publication data
The cat from Hué / by John Laurence.
p. cm.
ISBN 1-891620-31-2
1. Vietnamese Conflict, 1961–1975—Personal narratives, American. 2. John Laurence
I. Title
DS557-7.L376 2001
959.704′3′092—dc21

10 9 8 7 6 5 4 3 2

For the fine memories of Bill Wilson and Robert Smith,
and for all who follow in their steps.

AUTHOR'S NOTE

What follows is true. All the events described here actually happened. Details have been taken from film and still photographs that were shot at the scene, from audiotapes recorded during the events, and from notes, maps, descriptions and sketches written in notebooks at the time. Also from letters home, interviews during and after the war, and from contemporary accounts by other reporters, writers and historians. Some descriptions are taken from memory, but knowing the fallibility of memory over time, I have trusted only those for which there is supporting evidence. No actions have been invented.

Quotes are described two ways. Spoken words that appear in *full* quotation marks (i.e., "Hello there, cat"), were recorded on film, tape or in a notebook at the time, or were recalled and written down soon after the event. Where words are quoted in *single* quotation marks (i.e., 'Cease fire! Cease fire!'), no record exists other than in my knowledge of the conversation or remark having taken place, or in written notes to myself of the substance of what was said rather than the words. I have tried to recreate those words and conversations honestly and accurately.

In a few cases where I had no precise record of the weather or physical terrain—that is, other than when they were important to the event or when I had a specific recollection of them—some descriptions of the sun, rain, wind, clouds, heat and light are portrayed as they usually were in that location at that time of day and year.

The actual names of the people involved in these events are used throughout, except in a few cases where noted to avoid embarrassment. I apologize for any errors of fact, interpretation or omission.

J.L.

The world's an orphans' home. Shall
we never have peace without sorrow?
without pleas of the dying for
help that won't come? O
quiet form upon the dust, I cannot
look and yet I must. If these great patient
dyings—all these agonies
and woundbearings and bloodshed—
can teach us how to live, these
dyings were not wasted.

MARIANNE MOORE

"In Distrust of Merits" (1944)

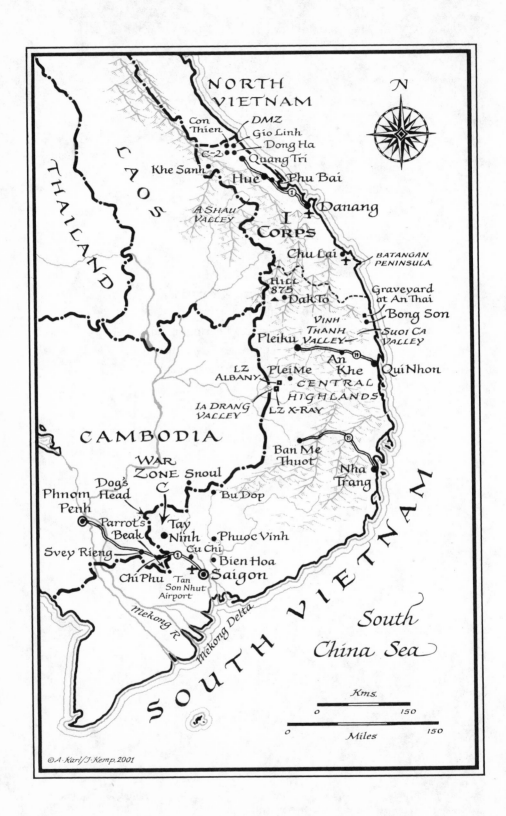

PART ONE

HUÉ 1968

There is no need to sound my reputation.
I have a sense of right and wrong, what's more—
heaven's proudest gift. Call no man blessed
until he ends his life in peace, fulfilled.
If I can live by what I say, I have no fear.

AESCHYLUS
Agamemnon

FEBRUARY 19, 1968

The whole war was in the room. Light came in through a hole in the roof made by a mortar—monsoon light, murky and dim, filtered by low heavy clouds the color of stone. The floor was littered with wreckage from the explosion: sharp-edged fragments of a metal shell, pieces of plaster ripped off the walls, splinters of wood from a shattered table, and a pool of blood that was slowly becoming a dark stain on the once shiny surface of the tiled floor now scorched black by the explosion and covered with a film of fine dust. The air was cold and wet. Nothing moved.

I sat on the floor with my back to a wall, eating a can of C ration food with a white plastic spoon. Beyond the wall, a few hundred yards up the line, a machinegun rattled, stopped, rattled again. The bullets hissed in flight and the hisses gathered in a long steady *sssshhhhuuuusssssshhhhh* that caromed off the walls and buildings and the great chunks of broken stone of the old Hué Citadel and reverberated around the city. Grenades burst—muffled blasts— one at a time, punctuating the flow of riflefire. A mortar banged—first the pop of the tube, then, a few seconds later, the crash of the shell. Rifles cracked, sixteens and AKs, fast and slow fire.

Thank God I'm not up there, I thought. I had arrived at the house an hour before and had asked the Marines to take me forward, but they said nothing was going up during the fight. 'Later,' they said, 'we'll take you up later, when we go up with this stuff.'

At the house next door, a teenage Marine carried wooden cases of ammunition from inside the house to a pebble-covered driveway outside and heaved them one by one onto a small flatbed vehicle called a mechanical mule. The young Marine wore a dark green T-shirt, fatigue trousers, flak jacket and helmet and was sweating hard in the humid air. As soon as the battle up ahead was finished, he and the other Marines in his squad would load their mules and drive the ammo and other supplies to the front, then turn around and come back for more, bringing with them the wounded and dead. The military supply line was an endless conveyor—from factories in the States to the riflemen at the front—a long human chain moving men and materials forward for the infantry: replacements, rifle ammunition, machinegun bullets, hand grenades, mortar shells, rockets, tank gun canisters, high explosives, food, water, gas, tank parts, batteries, mail, medicine, morphine, IV fluid, bandages, body bags—all the paraphernalia required by a U.S. Marine infantry battalion of 650 men to sustain itself in extended combat. In this case it was 1st Battalion, 5th Marines. The battalion was trying to take a tall brick watchtower in the Citadel, had been for days, but the advance was slow.

An animal appeared in an open doorway at the back of the room. It was visible at first only in silhouette, a black shape against the bleak light outside. The creature was dirty, disheveled, its greasy fur sticking out at odd angles. Silent, curious, its nose twitched above its head and turned from side to side in a slow arc, sniffing the scent of food from my C ration can. It appeared to be a kitten, maybe eight weeks old, about the size of my hand.

Not much chance of a scrawny cat surviving this place, I thought. *Lucky it hasn't already gone in a cooking pot.* The kitten stared at the can of food and sniffed the air above its head.

"Hello, there, cat," I said. Anything new or unusual, any distraction, anything that took your mind off where you were and what you were doing was worth the diversion.

The kitten paid no attention. '*Chào ông,*' I said, trying to get the tones right, figuring it might know a little Vietnamese. The kitten turned its head a fraction to one side and looked at me as if I were demented.

'Too young to know the language. I get it,' I said, smiling. The kitten sniffed the air.

When I had finished eating, I reached into a pocket of my fatigue jacket, opened a waterproof plastic case, shook out a cigarette, and lit it. The metal lid of the lighter snapped shut, making a sharp metallic *click*. Instantly the kitten turned and dashed out the doorway.

Spooked, I thought.

No wonder. All of Hué was spooked. The venerable old city of shaded gardens and pastel yellow villas and slender graceful people had endured twenty days of unrelieved fright, twenty days of riflefire and shellbursts and sleepless nights and empty stomachs and mad subhuman screams and slow-moving death that spread from house to house and street to street like a plague, crawling on khaki-covered knees and elbows across garden walls and narrow alleys and bursting through doorways with weapons blasting, constantly maneuvering closer for a kill. Hué was thunderstruck by violence. After being spared most of the misery of two Indochina wars over the past twenty years, the citizens of Hué were now condemned to suffer the worst of it all at once.

I got up and walked to the doorway. The air in the garden behind the house was heavy with moisture. A light afternoon rain had lifted, leaving a fine cold mist in the air. The garden was tangled with tall vines and fat leafy plants that had flowered in kinder times but were now struggling to survive against an encroaching wild of weeds. Everything was green and gray. Beneath the foliage, a stream gurgled. Invisible insects screeched. A waist-high wooden barrel full of rainwater stood next to the doorway beneath a drainpipe that ran down from the roof. The kitten was perched on the edge of the barrel, its front paws and hind legs together, drinking in fast tiny laps. As soon as I appeared in the doorway, it looked up and saw me, then jumped to the ground and ran into the garden and out of sight.

I took a breath and looked around. The house was part of a compound of one-story buildings made of stucco and wood with orange tile roofs. Five houses were arranged in a neat semicircle with a courtyard and circular driveway in front. The style was graceful, harmonious with the surroundings, practical and elegant, peaceful.

Must have been one big family, I thought—maybe twenty to thirty people—grandparents and great-grandparents with their children and their children's children. I imagined what it would have been like three weeks before on the first day of Tet. It was Vietnam's biggest holiday, a celebration based on tradition, rebirth and renewal. Tet marked the beginning of the lunar year, in this case, Nhâm Thân, the year of the monkey. I pictured the family, some visiting from far away, enjoying themselves in this compound, observing their ancient rituals: tending the family gravesites, honoring their ancestors, making offerings to the *Ong Tao*, decorating the house with bright-colored flower blossoms and lanterns and handmade prints, baking *bánh chung* cakes and other delicacies, catching up on family news, exchanging stories of babies born and sons gone off to war. I imagined the elders sitting with their children and sharing observations, the young children laughing in excitement at the sparkle of skyrockets, playing perhaps with a litter of newborn kittens.

Then, in the cool early hours of New Year's Day, as the city slept, the war burst upon Hué and its people with the convulsions of a volcano. The night exploded in brilliant light. Fierce white flashes of military flares illuminated the sky. The slow red rush of machinegun tracers flew above the rooftops. The earth rumbled with the shock waves of long-range rockets. Shells shrieked over the city and cracked open the earth and everything on it.

In the turmoil, thousands of North Vietnamese and Viet Cong soldiers trotted through the streets in their dark close-cropped hair with rifles and rocket launchers on their shoulders. They seized the city's main installations —government buildings, bridges, the airfield, police stations, communications facilities—and started digging in to defend them. The few hundred South Vietnamese and U.S. soldiers on duty in Hué were surprised by the swift-moving attack and forced to withdraw to their headquarters, where they were quickly surrounded. Scores of others were killed or captured. At least half of the government soldiers were away on leave because of the holidays. Intelligence reports that the North Vietnamese and Viet Cong were preparing an offensive throughout South Vietnam did not suggest it would come during the three-day Tet holiday. Many civilians had no adequate bomb shelters, no trenches, no safe places to hide. Families gathered behind the doors of their houses and held one another in their arms. Mortar, rocket and artillery shells flew out of the sky and crashed onto the rooftops and streets.

And the one large family of Vietnamese who lived in the compound where I now stood staring into the garden survived the twenty days of fire and smoke and ferocious noise, adjusted to the new conditions of danger and shortages, and made their accommodation with the crisis. Each day they searched for food to eat, gathered water and wood, fought back their fear, consoled the children, tried to cheer each other, and lived their diminished lives with daily, individual acts of dignity and fortitude—*they survived*—until this afternoon of the twentieth day when the mortar crashed through the roof of their home and exploded in a flash of flame and heat. Arriving at the compound an hour ago, a few minutes after the explosion, I saw the family being taken away, their pale brown bodies piled in the back of a Marine truck, broken and bleeding and making no sound at all, their arms and legs limp and twisted, faces frozen in expressions of pain and disbelief—the dead and dying family, together still at Tet.

From the doorway at the back of the house, I stared into the tangle of tropical trees and vines in the misty garden. I was lost in thought, my vision out of focus. Gradually, I became aware of something moving in the interior of the brush. My sight sharpened. A shadowed presence deep inside the foliage took shape. *A Vietnamese soldier!* He was crouched on one knee on the ground with a rifle in his hands, an AK-47. Now I saw him in sharp focus: mustard-brown uniform, ammunition vest, green bamboo helmet, black hair sticking out the sides. A North Vietnamese Army regular. Slowly, with deliberate care, he stood up in the thicket of vines and raised the rifle to his shoulder and pointed the end of the barrel at me. Movement in the garden ceased. There was absolute silence. I couldn't move, even to breathe. I felt trapped, paralyzed by the fear of what was about to happen, as in a bad dream. A thought flashed into consciousness. *So you've made it all this way and it ends like this.*

Time slowed and stopped. My concentration on the soldier was total, no sense of anything but the danger, my perceptions heightened, all other reality suspended.

The soldier's eyes came away from the rifle sights and looked out at me from inside the shadow of his helmet. *How young he is!* The barrel of the rifle dipped. Then, in one slow continuous move, he turned his head and looked behind him and swung his shoulders around with the rifle in his hands and twisted his hips and then his legs and stepped back into the brush and disappeared into the green and gray foliage.

The garden was still. I took what felt like my first breath. A pulse beat in my temples. Time started to move. An insect chirped. I hadn't heard anything for what had seemed like an hour but could only have been a few seconds. The air felt cold, damp.

Why didn't he shoot? Because I didn't have a gun? Because I was looking for the cat? Maybe I wasn't worth it? He might have been after someone more important, an officer perhaps. It didn't make sense.

His presence was still there, lingering, as if some part of him remained in the mist. Nothing tangible, only the essence of our encounter, but nearly physical. I was aware of the narrow separation between life and death in this place, between extinction and survival, and the immediate closeness of both. It was being defined in Hué so often these days that everyone seemed to take it for granted, saw it as just another part of the landscape: everybody ended up with one or the other, nothing you could do about it. But I was taking it personally.

I stepped back from the doorway, crossed the room and sat down against the wall. Out of breath, mouth too dry to swallow, I picked up my helmet and put it on. The noise of fighting at the front sounded more menacing.

Hey, man, you must have imagined him. Surely it was just a phantom. Couldn't be anything else. Otherwise he would have shot you. You must be seeing things. Short-timer's syndrome. Who knows? Or was it a premonition? Something up there waiting for you? God knows. I tried hard not to think.

The kitten appeared in the open doorway again and sat. Its tiny ears turned toward me.

"Puss-puss-puss," I whispered between my lips. No reaction. I tried a number of different animal calls without effect.

Spunky cat, I thought. The kitten seemed to sense danger. I must have looked and smelled like the Marines in the house next door. Faded green combat fatigues, boots, helmet, flak jacket—for all it mattered to the cat I was one of them. It couldn't know I was no danger at all, just an unarmed civilian, a noncombatant, a reporter. The kitten was drawn to the food by a desperate hunger, but its fear of me was greater.

I unfastened the straps of my rucksack, lifted out a can of C ration meat and opened it with a small metal tool called a P-38. I pried back the lid and held out the can a few inches above the floor, offering it. The kitten raised its nose high over its head and caught the scent. Then it stood up and stiffened its muscles, straightened its four legs to their full height, arched its back and danced a few feet toward me, sideways. *So, it's a skitter cat*, I thought, surprised by its jerky movements. It reminded me of a book from childhood.

The kitten crossed a third of the room and sat on its back legs, straining its neck toward the food. I held out the can again and called, "puss-puss-puss." The kitten danced a few inches closer and stopped. As much as I coaxed, it would not come nearer than the center of the room. It sat, tense and alert, watching over its shoulder, measuring its route out the doorway to the safety of the garden.

I could see the animal more clearly now. Its face, legs and paws were mostly black. There were a few spots of soft white on its flanks. A splash of orange on its forehead, from the bridge of its nose to the space between its ears, gave it a distinctive, offbeat look. Its short, slender tail appeared to be light brown or orange and had a crook at the tip. Its pale blue eyes were dull, distracted.

"So, you're a *lucky* cat," I said.

Most Vietnamese do not have the same affection for cats that many Westerners do, but I knew that some of them thought an orange, black and white cat—a calico cat—brought good luck to itself and its owner. The Vietnamese called it "a cat of three colors" and believed it to be rare, to be prized. I looked at the kitten with new respect. It looked at me and the food but did not move.

Like most line troops and combat reporters, I was superstitious. I'd do almost anything to get an edge against the fear, the vulnerability that went with me into the field. Each time I went out I wore the same old set of GI fatigues I had first bought on the black market in 1965, scrubbed in Stone Age Vietnamese laundries until they were bleached and threadbare and tattered and safe. Like a few other field reporters, I never polished my boots. Over time they had become scuffed and worn and encrusted with layers of dirt and mud from all over—from Con Thien to Can Tho, from Pleiku to Bong Son—a record of where I'd been, my ID as an old hand in this place. I wore a lucky hat, a floppy Australian bush hat that had been a gift from Dan Rather. The hat was a size too small but it was certified good luck so I wore it under my helmet. I also carried coins, charms, four-leaf clovers, religious medals and all kinds of talismans in my pockets, wallet, around my neck. The one thing I did not carry was a weapon.

Of all the superstitions, going into battle without a weapon was the most important. I believed that those of us who took no part in the killing were less vulnerable to becoming casualties ourselves. It was part of my personal war ideology—a loose-knit, undefined mix of humanism, morality, religion, ethics, law, pacifism, survival strategy, common sense and, above all, pathological superstition. My hope was that we noncombatants got special protection, were somehow given immunity, as if at the center of all the carnage in Vietnam some higher being watched over innocent reporters and spared us from the physical effects of the violence we were covering. I was wrong of course; no one was safe. Reporters and photographers were killed and wounded in the same proportion as the frontline troops they accompanied. (On this same day in Hué, just up the line, three print journalists were seriously wounded in the fighting. Two of them were later given medals for helping evacuate wounded Marines.) Whatever the evidence, I needed something to believe, something to balance against the fear. My reasonable expectation of survival (or denial of the alternative) made it possible to do the job. Somewhere at the center of my being I felt protected, insured, sometimes even blessed. Somehow I was going to survive this.

The cat of three colors was down on its luck. The skin was so tight on its tiny frame its ribcage showed through the fur. "No wonder you haven't been gobbled up," I said, smiling. "There wouldn't be anything to eat."

The kitten's eyes squeezed together in a peculiar squint and blinked rapidly, as if irritated or infected. Small black insects buzzed around its ears. Its fur appeared to be infested with fleas. And yet, despite its discomfort, the kitten tried to hold its head with the confidence of a healthy cat, sitting with pride, staring at me and my offer of food as if it were not afraid.

This is some kind of spunky cat, I thought, admiring its elegant grace. At the same time, the kitten looked as vulnerable as I felt. This was my last assignment of a long second tour and Hué was the worst place ever. I had been in the war too long, seen too much, been scared too many times. Long overdue to leave, I was jumping at shadows too.

I pushed the can of food to the center of the room, left it and moved back to the wall. The kitten skittered up to the can, sniffed it, looked around and sat, but did not eat.

A tall, thin-faced Marine walked into the room. "If you want to get up to the CP," he said, biting off the words, "we've got a mule goin up any minute."

His voice was cold, impersonal, no sign of friendliness. The bitterness surprised me. Marines in the field were scrupulously polite. I did not know yet that the North Vietnamese mortar attack that had destroyed the Vietnamese family in the compound had also killed two Marines from the supply squad, two of his buddies.

"Thanks," I said, "thank you much," grateful to be moving on. The presence of the North Vietnamese soldier in the garden had not gone away.

I stood up and heaved the pack on my back, set the helmet straight on my head and walked out of the room. At the front doorway I turned and looked back at the kitten. It sat by the can of food in the center of the room, watching me.

"Good luck, cat," I said.

FEBRUARY 3, 1968

(Sixteen days earlier)

Racing at maximum speed toward Hué on the fourth day of the battle, bouncing in the back of a flatbed truck filled with Marines, hurtling over holes in the road the size of small shell craters, watching a blur of silent villages sweep by in the background, I felt the first hit of the feeling that came with close combat—a concentrated charge of excitement and fear, my fright-flight-fight instinct engaged in all its intensity, an organic speedball of adrenaline, noradrenaline and cortisol pumping through my system and powering the tension I now took for granted, so familiar I never imagined I might be addicted.

Keith Kay crouched on the metal bed in the back of the truck and struggled to keep his balance. One of his big hands held a thirty-pound film camera steady on his right shoulder while the other gripped a wooden slat at the side of the truck. Kay's shoulders were wide and muscled like a running back's and the weight of the camera and brace fell on them naturally, as if they were an extension of his body. His hair was long and black and blew in the slipstream of the cab. A bright patch of premature white the size of a silver dollar made a spot on the side of his head, a mark of the war. The dominant expression on his dark broad-nosed face was determination, a hard scowl that seemed to say, *How the hell did you get us into this?*

Kay and I were partners. He shot the film and I wrote the narration for the stories we covered for CBS News. We had worked together for the past six months in violent, out-of-the-way killing grounds like Khe Sanh and Con Thien, dropping in on the Marines for a few hours or a few days, asking them questions and recording their answers, trying to get a sense of what was going on in the war from the young men who were trapped in its most tortured places. When we had enough film to tell a story, we hitched a ride back to the rear and shipped it home to be shown on *The Evening News with Walter Cronkite.*

The truck was a six by six with low metal sides and horizontal slats to keep cargo from falling out—in this case about fifteen Marines and four

reporters and photographers. The truck charged along the two-lane black-
top that covered the twelve miles of flat coastal plain between Phu Bai and
Hué, stopping for nothing. It was one in a convoy carrying more than a hundred heavily armed Marines with orders to break through the North Vietnamese death grip on Hué and reinforce the small American garrison inside.
The day before, on the same road, a Marine convoy trying to get into Hué
had driven into an ambush and had lost some of its men. The survivors
fought their way through with multiple dead and wounded. Today the road
was empty.

Route 1 was part of a long busy highway that connected Saigon in the
south with Hanoi in the north during Vietnam's brief periods of peace. The
road had a violent history. Farther north, on the other side of Hué, it was
known as *la rue sans joie* (the street without joy). The French had named it
during their war with the Vietnamese and for good reason: families who
lived in the area were determined to be free of foreign domination and
fought the French with unremitting ferocity. Nowadays, Marines who knew
the history of the place called the entire road from Danang north "street
without joy" and tried to avoid it.

The truck carried a Marine colonel who had been ordered into Hué to
take over U.S. military operations in the city. He wore a worried expression.
A small garrison of American troops, mostly Army soldiers, had been fighting for four days and nights to hold their headquarters, the size of a small
city block, against repeated assaults, sniper attacks and mortar fire. Now the
men in the compound were exhausted, running out of ammunition and
suffering a growing toll of dead and wounded.

Colonel Stanley Smith Hughes was a combat hero of World War II, a
much decorated veteran. He commanded more than two thousand men, the
First Marine Regiment, but they were scattered across the northern military
region known as I Corps and not all of them were under his control. Heading into Hué with one of his rifle companies, Hughes appeared to be distracted, uncertain, with no clear idea about the dimensions of the fight
ahead.

Keith Kay put his right eye to the viewfinder of his Arriflex-BL, focused
the lens with the fingers of his left hand, and switched on the camera with
the other. Sixteen millimeter film rolled past the shutter with a whirring
sound and recorded the solemn expressions on the faces of the colonel and

the men around him. Crowded close together with their flak jackets touching, green camouflage helmets bobbing on their heads, the young Marines bounced up and down on the back of the speeding truck like a tough gang of teenagers on a trampoline.

They looked at us with wonder. An hour earlier the Marines had welcomed us at Phu Bai with the reception they usually gave to civilian visitors —respectful and correct, occasionally light-hearted, friendly. Outwardly, they seemed pleased to have us with them.

'You guys know something we don't?' one of them asked, smiling.

'Yeah, what's going on in Hué?' another said. Their voices were mildly apprehensive.

'You know as much as we do,' Kay said with measured nonchalance, climbing onto the truck with his camera.

They were fascinated by the camera and what it could do, though the idea of being photographed during what was about to happen—*God knows what's about to happen*—was outside their experience and therefore strange. They kept a polite distance from us, presumably because the old man was in the truck and looked so serious, but also because they were worried about what was waiting up the road. The Marines had not expected civilians to be going into Hué with them and weren't sure how to behave. They looked at us with the curiosity they reserved for those rare occasions when something genuinely new and interesting was happening, distractions from the usual boring routine of infantry work.

Why Kay and I chose to go with them when we could have stayed behind was beyond their comprehension. As the convoy left Phu Bai, they waved good-bye to more than a dozen other reporters and photographers who had decided not to make the journey. That made sense to them. Details of the ambush the day before were still coming in and the North Vietnamese appeared to be everywhere in Hué, anxious to fight. They held all but two small pockets of the city—the headquarters of the American and South Vietnamese armies, one in the Citadel, the other across the river. The Marines in the truck knew that the odds of this convoy getting through safely were poor. Kay and I had decided to go along anyway because the battle was such a big story, the biggest story of the war, and we wanted to get in and report it. It was our job. Besides, if the Marines were going in, we thought their firepower and fighting ability would give us protection. Being with them gave us some confidence we would survive, but it was never a sure thing.

Two other civilians were in the truck: Jeff Gralnick, an associate producer for CBS News who volunteered to record sound when Kay's Vietnamese sound technician chose to stay behind, and our friend Dana Stone, a still photographer for United Press International. Gralnick sat on the floor of the truck holding the microphone in the air with one hand and adjusting the sound level of the amplifier with the other. He kept his sight on the VU meter moving on the instrument panel of the amplifier, concentrating hard.

As we approached Hué, shooting started just as the lead trucks in the convoy lurched across a low bridge over a canal. Automatic riflefire exploded, first a few short bursts and then dozens of bullets snapping all at once—*crackcrackcrackcrackcrackcrackcrackcrack*—the closer sounds of tiny metal slugs whizzing overhead—*fffssst, fffssst, fffssst*—buzzing and spinning angrily. Then a thunderous volley of sharper-pitched .223-caliber bullets split the air as Marines returned fire with their M-16s from all the trucks in the convoy. The riflefire was punctuated by occasional deep, hollow explosions —B-40 rocket-propelled grenades—fired by North Vietnamese gunners and by M-79 grenade rounds from the Americans. All the weapons together blasted the air with percussion and shock that produced a continuous roar of noise as loud and sharp as the sound of close lightning.

Our truck sped faster now, all the Marines firing on full automatic into the brush and buildings on both sides of the road, shouting to one another into the wind of the roaring racket.

'That's our people down there!' a radio operator screamed. An officer took the handset of the radio, shouted his call sign, and listened for a reply, his free hand covering his open ear. When he heard the voice at the other end, he yelled, 'Cease fire! For Christ's sake, cease fire! Cease fire!'

Houses, trees and tracer rounds flashed by the speeding trucks in a blur of shapes and colors. Officers shouted at their sergeants who screamed at the men, 'Cease fire, God damn it!'

Without warning, an older noncommissioned officer—a crag-faced sergeant major with a wide stub of a neck—pushed Colonel Hughes roughly down on his stomach onto the metal bed of the truck and hurled himself on top—flak jacket, web belt, helmet and all. Seeing them fall, other Marines flopped down on each side of Hughes, completing a protective embrace.

The colonel was stunned, unable to see the fight, unable to command. *We're not going to make it with the old man flat on his face*, I thought.

With nowhere to hide and no job to do, I watched. My physical perceptions were ultra alert. Colors looked brighter, sounds sharper, my reflexes quicker. Everything appeared with precise clarity. And yet the speeding, fast-moving fight unfolded in slow motion, like a macabre ballet. Outgoing machinegun tracers flew away from the trucks in a slow-moving stream of soft lights, throwing up sprays of sparks when they hit something hard. The noise was overpowering—a furious pandemonium of popping, cracking, blasting—a weapon itself. As the truck sped along the road, the sights and sounds spun wildly out of control—fleeting images, gunfire, shouts, powder smells—holding me in the grip of overwhelming powerlessness, a feeling of being on the border of madness myself, not knowing nor being able to change or caring what might happen next.

Kay struggled to hold the camera steady against the shuddering motion of the truck, rolling film, watching the fight through the viewfinder, fully absorbed in his camerawork. Gralnick tried to record the sound on film, but the noise was beyond the tolerance of the equipment and constantly pegged the VU meter above the redline.

Then, as suddenly as the firing started, it ceased. The convoy stopped. Marines jumped off the back of the truck, hitched up their gear and walked warily toward the gates of the U.S. military compound in Hué. The convoy had arrived. Men from the regimental headquarters group helped the colonel get to his feet. His breath was short, his legs unsteady. Gently, they led him into the compound, a long two-story concrete building that faced north, the symbol of the U.S. presence in Hué, headquarters of the Military Assistance Command, Vietnam—MACV. The front of the building was pocked and spattered with shell holes.

The arriving Marines were greeted by men from the company which had arrived the day before on the convoy that was ambushed. They made dark suggestions about what was waiting for the new arrivals in the streets.

'Welcome to Hoo-way,' one of them said.

'Gooks got the whole city,' another said. 'All's we got is this here and the ARVNs got a little bitty piece of the Citadel over there.'

'Jes make sure you got your next of kin form filled in fore ya go out there,' another said.

'Yeah, we lost a whole platoon yesterday and this mornin.'

The Marines looked north across the dark stagnant river that divided the city. Oil-black smoke curled up from the battlefires inside a great walled fortress on the other side—the Citadel. Red brick embattlements rose out of the ground and reached toward the wet heavy clouds hanging above. The Citadel looked like a bastion from the Middle Ages, a Crusader castle. Every thirty seconds or so, riflefire snapped.

A small, skinny Frenchwoman with dark blond hair tied in a long ponytail ran toward us, shouting and smiling. She threw her arms around my neck and pulled herself up on her toes and kissed me hard on both cheeks. Then Kay, then Dana Stone. 'Oh, God, I'm glad to see you guys,' she said, cursing, excited. 'You know, ah love zeez fuckeeng Marines. Zay save my life!'

Catherine Leroy, barely five feet tall, was a freelance photographer with a reputation for daring in combat. She told us she had come to Hué on the second day of the battle on a bicycle. She was travelling with Francois Mazure of Agence France Presse, the French news agency, and they were captured almost immediately by the North Vietnamese. At best, she expected to be taken prisoner, at worst to be shot. Surprisingly, an NVA officer allowed her to take pictures of his troops in one neighborhood of the city, dramatic color stills that showed them in control of the streets, the soldiers smiling and waving flags like liberators. It would make a sensational picture story for *Paris Match,* the French magazine, and LIFE, the American one. When they had made their photographs, Leroy and Mazure were released. Safe now, she was in an expansive mood.

'You know, Jack, I was never scared so much in my life,' she said. 'I tell you the truth. Really. Personally, I don't ever think I am going to be so glad to see these fucking Marines.' She laughed like a child and we laughed with her.

The drivers of the convoy trucks said they had to get back to Phu Bai before dark so they could make another run tomorrow. They offered to take us back with them if we wished, or they would carry our film. Kay's exposed film was so important that Gralnick volunteered to hand-carry it to Saigon and write the voice-over narration of the convoy to Hué himself. (Gralnick's ambition was to become a network TV correspondent, and reporting a big breaking story would surely help his chances.) Kay told him to get ready to do an on-camera bridge for the piece and positioned him with his back to the Citadel so that the smoke appeared behind him in the shot. Gralnick took the microphone and ad-libbed a few sentences about the battle while Kay recorded his image on film and I did the sound. A few minutes later, Gralnick took the film, got into one of the trucks and rode away.

It was afternoon and we were tired. 'Glad we're not going back today,' Kay said. 'I'm not ready for another ride like that.' We worried about Gralnick getting back to Phu Bai. When no news came in over the Marine radio net, we assumed he had made it through safely.

An Army captain introduced himself to Kay, Dana Stone and me and invited us into the mess hall of the compound. 'You can drop your gear here,' he said in a serious commanding way. He stood over a space for three bedrolls on the floor.

'Anybody know how to fire a weapon?' he said.

Kay, Stone and I looked at each other. 'We're civilians,' Kay said. 'We don't carry guns.'

'That's not what I asked you,' the captain said. 'I'm responsible for security here and I need people to guard the perimeter. Everybody I can get, especially at night.' Kay, Stone and I looked at each other and smiled.

'The NVA hold those buildings on two sides of us,' the captain said, pointing, 'south and east, and they probe us at night.'

He looked at Stone. 'How about you?' Stone's face was innocent. He was five and a half feet tall, thin as wire, and had reddish hair that was rarely combed. Stone's jawline was square and sharp and it gave some maturity to his boy's face. He wore rectangular glasses with dark plastic frames that slipped down his nose and that he pushed back in place with the forefinger of his hand every minute or so. Stone had been in Vietnam nearly two years and knew the war zones and the people in them as well or better than anyone in the country. He knew the Marines in I Corps especially well. He had many friends among them and they loved his modest Yankee personality (he was from Vermont), his backcountry accent and mischievous sense of humor. His abilities as a tracker in the field got him the nickname "Supergrunt." Stone was an inventive practical joker. His fiendish pranks were already legends in Danang.

The captain led the way to an empty room on the edge of the perimeter that had been converted into a firing position. Sandbags were stacked around an open window with no glass. Old ammo boxes and shell casings were scattered across the floor. The room was damp. The captain pointed out the window to the wall of a building about fifty yards away. The side of the wall was etched with bullet holes. He handed Stone a carbine—a lightweight, short-barreled rifle—and told him to aim for a powder burn the size of a frying pan on the wall.

'Let's see if you know how to hit anything,' he said.

In one smooth movement, Stone flipped off the safety with his thumb, put the carbine to his shoulder, took aim and fired the clip at the wall, one quick shot after another: *crack-crack-crack-crack-crack-crack*. All the shots hit the center of the powder burn.

Immediately gunfire began cracking around the compound. Soldiers and Marines on the other sides of the perimeter had heard the rapid shots from Stone's carbine and started shooting as well, putting out a heavy base of automatic weapons fire toward the south and east. The North Vietnamese heard this volley as incoming and apparently thought it was a prelude to a ground assault by the American troops they had just observed arriving. They returned the fire. AK-47 rounds ripped into the compound and ricocheted off the walls. Grenades exploded. Men screamed. Everyone ran for cover.

The captain seized the carbine from Stone's hand and gave him a fast angry glare, then turned and ran down the corridor shouting, "Cease fire! Cease fire!"

I leaned back against the sandbags and lit a cigarette. Kay did the same. No one spoke. After a minute the shooting slackened, then stopped. Stone looked at us with eyes of perfect innocence. "Well," he said, "*he told me* to shoot the spot on the wall, didn't he?"

FEBRUARY 4, 1968

The next morning, in the cold deceptive calm of dawn, when senses still swam in the safe oblivion of sleep and the war seemed far away, I got up and put on my boots. Everyone else was asleep. I walked out of the MACV building and crossed the courtyard to the street outside, then two blocks north toward Le Loi Boulevard and the campus of Hué University. Nothing moved, not even the air. Pools of rainwater sat on the wet pavement. Power cables and telephone lines dangled over the deserted streets. Chunks of concrete and masonry, blasted off buildings by tank cannon, rested in awkward lumps across sidewalks and alleys, blocking the way. The hollow shell of a burned-out truck—a six-by like the one we came in on—lay abandoned by the side of the street. Wet crumpled pieces of clothing, paper, cooking utensils, furniture, bicycles, rags and other rubble were strewn over the ground. The neighborhood looked like it had been hit by a hurricane. The wreckage formed the landscape of a giant junkyard that included the bodies of several North Vietnamese soldiers lying in the streets, stiff and swollen in their faded khaki-brown uniforms, their cold gray skin the color of ash.

I walked carefully in the dark light. Farther up the street, near the river, the buildings of the university were smashed. Pale yellow walls and orange-tiled roofs were scarred by shellfire. Parts of the roofs had collapsed from exploding mortar shells. Windows were shattered, classrooms sacked, the chemistry lab looted. Textbooks were strewn across the floors, Marine graffiti scrawled on the walls: 'Fuck Communism,' 'GOOK DIE' and the more subtle "Class dismissed."

The university complex had been captured two days earlier by Golf 2/5, one of two rifle companies which fought their way into Hué on the first day of the battle. The other company, Alpha 1/1, had eighty of its men killed or wounded trying to reach the Citadel. Higher headquarters had ordered Alpha 1/1 on a suicide mission to reinforce ARVN headquarters. This was the fifth day of the battle, a Sunday, and the Marines were now fully entrenched in the university grounds. They had set up communication lines between buildings, mortar pits, a headquarters area, observation posts, fields of fire, sniper positions, tank parks, a kitchen, sleeping areas, latrines. 1/1 and 2/5 made up a large, lethal, tightly organized combat force. Nearby, a U.S. Navy doctor and team of corpsmen were operating an emergency first aid station for battle casualties. A helicopter landing zone, the first LZ of the operation, had been set up along the south bank of the river to evacuate wounded, though only the most committed medevac pilots dared to fly through the flurry of incoming fire from the Citadel that met them on the way in. At night, Navy boats fought their way up the river to bring in supplies and take out wounded. At one side of the LZ, alone on an isolated patch of grass in a riverside park, a row of American bodies—the first of the Hué battle dead—waited in dark green waterproof bags for the long journey home.

The camp came awake. Marines got up and went to work, quietly, without tension. They cooked C ration breakfasts, fixed equipment and clothing, wrote letters home, looked through old newspapers and magazines. All of them cleaned their rifles. After months in the bush fighting snipers, the young men seemed out of place in the enclosed spaces of the city, unsure how to carry themselves, awkward, like country boys on their first trip to a big city. Only a few of the older noncommissioned officers who had been in Korea had experienced street fighting. Sergeants walked through the camp explaining how the squads would line up for the attack that would start soon.

The Marines were mostly young—eighteen- and nineteen-year-olds with short hair and boyish faces but with the demeanor of older more cautious men, matured by trauma. Their manner was pleasant, convivial, no sign of anger. War seemed to make them more humane, more gentle, at least with one another, as if everybody involved in this violent undertaking was trying to behave his best, not knowing what might be coming next.

I wandered through the classrooms inspecting the damage, taking notes, talking with the men about the fighting, trying to get a sense of what the story was, what was going on beneath the outward appearance of ordered combat. The Marines were pleased to have a visitor and asked me as many questions as I asked them. For almost a week they had received no firsthand news from outside the narrow dimensions of their isolated world. We stood in a corridor while I told them what I knew about the Tet Offensive: that the Viet Cong and North Vietnamese had attacked and in some cases overrun all but a few of the forty-four provincial capitals in South Vietnam; that the U.S. embassy in Saigon had been attacked in force but was narrowly held by the Marine guards and military police; that fighting was still going on in Saigon and several other places. Their eyes flashed a measure of awe at the audacity of the NVA soldiers they had already come to respect for their sacrifice in battle.

'They's grunts like us,' a Marine said, 'no doubt about it.'

'Least we get to go home after thirteen months,' another said.

'*If* we make it.'

'Yeah, imagine what it'd be like if we were one of them. Out there in the bush for years and years, waitin for your number to come up.'

'Here for the duration.'

'Maybe that's why they're tryin to get it over with.'

I told them what happened in Danang on the first night of the offensive: thirty to forty VC killed trying to take the I Corps headquarters, nearly succeeding, getting tangled up by the complexity of their attack and maneuver plan. It was too complicated, too intricate, like a double reverse two yards from the goal line. Next morning, the bodies were laid out in a long row beside a busy road near the Danang River. Most of them were very young. Passersby on bicycles stopped and looked at the unmoving row of bodies without expression.

I told the Marines that on the second night of the offensive, just outside Quang Tri City, Keith Kay and I had watched from a water tower while a battle was fought for control of the provincial capital. Tracers filled the night air. It looked like a furious fight. At the same time, I heard later, soldiers from the 1st Cavalry Division landed in their helicopters by chance in the midst of a North Vietnamese battalion moving up to reinforce the attack on Quang Tri. The Americans drove the North Vietnamese away with a large number of dead and injured. The city was held.

'There are stories like that all over,' I said. 'Nobody really knows what the big picture is. The ARVN seem to be holding in most places. But the casualties are pretty high, theirs *and* ours.'

'Man, ain't that somethin?' one of the Marines said, 'I thought we's winnin the war.'

'Yeah, that's what they been tellin us.'

'If you believed that bullshit, you'd believe anything.'

'Just a minor fuckup in intelligence.'

'Charlie's tryin to win the whole thing, ain't he?'

I told them it was the heaviest fighting of the war, but they already knew that.

Sounds of shooting, close and loud, broke the stillness. Young men who were relaxed a moment before now moved with urgent purpose. Everyone had a job and went to do it. I dropped to one knee. My impulse was to move closer to the sound of shooting to find out what was happening. *I wish Keith were here to film this.* I stood up and walked quickly along a second floor corridor toward the southwest corner of the complex, near the point of contact. Men ran in various directions, some of them shouting. Explosions burst. At the end of the corridor, I stood near the corner of the building and looked down a wide stairway to the ground floor. At the bottom, a Marine officer stood just inside an open doorway facing west and looked out around the corner of the doorway to the left. Outside, a North Vietnamese machinegun fired up the street in front of the building from south to north. Marines crouched on their knees in the small space between the building and the street, ready to run across. Red-orange tracers flashed brightly up the middle of the street a foot above the ground, short rapid bursts of fast-moving light like pulses of a laser.

Lieutenant Colonel Ernest Cheatham leaned out the doorway and examined the cramped battlefield in front of him. Most of his troops bent over low or lay prone behind trees and walls. Cheatham, the commanding officer of 2d Battalion, 5th Marines, spoke in a steady voice into the black plastic handset of a field radio beside him. He was trying to get one of his platoons to fire and maneuver across the street, but the machinegun was holding them up. No one dared to cross. Looking out the doorway, Cheatham listened to a group of junior officers and NCOs who stood around him, listening to the radios, monitoring the fight. They provided a running flow of information to the colonel: movements of the battalion's men, intelligence as it came in, casualty figures, supply problems, anything that affected the well-being of the battalion and the outcome of the fight. Sometimes they made suggestions.

'They've got that RPD in that building down there,' one of the NCOs said, referring to the NVA machinegun. 'No way we're gonna hit it.'

'We need something big,' a major said.

'Yeah, tac-air.'

'Forget it,' Cheatham said. 'Air strikes are out.'

Cheatham stood a giant among them—a dark Achillean figure with a full round face and the oversized goggles of a tank commander pushed back on his helmet. His eyes were alert, intense, no doubt or hesitation in them—the look of a hard professional warrior. Standing six feet four inches tall, he pointed at the buildings across the street with big gloved hands and shouted orders at the men with bold gruff barks.

'Get your people out that way,' Cheatham called to an officer outside the building. 'That way, to the left. Take 'em on the flank.'

I began to get the picture. More would become apparent in the days that followed. Hué was war fighting at its most ferocious. In this case, it was an urban brawl between two armed and largely adolescent tribes, both new to the territory and intent on taking it, a street fight of fast action and merciless bloodletting. There were no rules. Lives were taken without thought— snuffed, wasted, zapped. Marine officers, educated in the practice of modern combat arms, tried to bring maximum force upon any weak points they discovered in their enemy's resistance. They pounded them with firepower, tried to crack open the line, then drive their own men through the breach and envelop the North Vietnamese from their sides and rear. The Marines at greatest risk, the line infantrymen who called themselves grunts, were ordered to apply the force. One or two at a time, they ran forward a few yards and tried to take cover without being hit. Sometimes they made it. Men behind tried to spot enemy fire coming from buildings ahead and return it. When someone was hit, two other Marines ran forward, tried to suppress the fire, and pulled the wounded man back later. Sergeants and corporals fought beside the grunts, leading at times, commanding at others. All this took place in a storm of fire and smoke, noise and concussion. Rifles, machineguns, grenades, rockets and mortars exploded in concert. At the end, the more violent powerful gang drove the other off and claimed what was left. The losers withdrew with their casualties and lived to fight another day. The winners got the ruins. So it was in Hué.

A young Marine ran across the street wobbling under the weight of his helmet, flak jacket, field pack, M-60 machinegun and ammunition. From the left, a long burst of machinegun fire followed behind him down the middle of the street. A few seconds later, another Marine dashed across. He carried two bandoleers of .30-caliber bullets for the M-60 across his chest. Both of them made it safely to the other side. Sprawled on their stomachs, they set up at the corner of a high concrete wall for cover and tried to fire the M-60 left-handed back down the street at the NVA machinegun. They had a narrow field of fire with the wall to their right and friendly troops on the other side of the street to the left. They worked with steady concentration, like mechanics, positioning the weapon, arming and aiming it, getting the first round of the belt loaded into the chamber. As soon as the young Marine fired, the M-60 jammed. Quickly, he cleared the chamber, banged the hard plastic butt of the weapon on the ground, reloaded, aimed and fired. One round went off with a muffled *pop* but no more. The young Marine cursed. His movements were rushed and jerky now, his eyes fierce. He swore, banged the butt of the gun on the ground, relaid the belt in the chamber, slapped the breach shut, chambered a round, and fired again. Again the M-60 jammed.

A third Marine ran across the street at the same point. Red tracers from the NVA machinegun flashed at his knees. The Marine stumbled in the middle of the street and fell heavily, as if tackled at the ankles. He did not cry out. Trying to pull himself out of the line of fire on his elbows, he reached back with each movement of his upper body and dragged his wounded legs, one at a time, with him. He moved only a few inches. The two Marines next to the wall dropped the machinegun and crawled into the street on their forearms and pulled the wounded man with them back to the far wall. They left a ribbon of blood on the black pavement marking where they had been, a thin red line. Throughout the rescue, the North Vietnamese machinegunner fired along the same line just above the Marines' heads without moving the inch or two it would have taken to strike all three of them. *Why doesn't he adjust his fire?* I wondered.

Watching from a rectangular hole in the wall where a second floor window had been, thirty feet above the street, I had the impression of watching a war movie, spectacular and close and vivid. But there were no cuts, no close-ups, no dialogue, no music, just the one wide shot framed by the window. I had seen battles before but none so clearly. Others had been obscured by jungle bush or hedgerows or rice paddy walls and usually involved a much greater volume of fire, incoming and outgoing. This was exceptionally simple: a street, a North Vietnamese machinegun, and three young Americans trying to cross. The Marines were extremely brave, not so much because they overcame their fear to attempt the mission (everyone in Hué was doing that), but because their behavior was so straightforward, so calm in the face of such visible danger. *Who would run through a stream of machinegun bullets? And go back into it to rescue someone?* That the Marines were trained to do so made it no less courageous. Or futile, with a weapon that was jamming.

Keith isn't going to believe this, I thought. *I wish he were here to film it. No one's got a scene this close before.* Despite the volume of war coverage on American TV, combat as close as this was not often captured on film. Most scenes were shot from farther away. I was determined to show people at home, especially the families, what was happening to their young men, what the price was for having them here.

As I watched out the second-floor window, a group of Marines struggled into the room carrying a cannon—a big, bulky gun nearly twelve feet long and weighing almost five hundred pounds—a 106 millimeter recoilless rifle. The weapon was awkward, virtually all barrel with a loading breech at the end. The men worked with great energy to balance the gun across a wooden table, wrestling with it, aiming it finally out a corner window at the machinegun. A major commanding the group ordered everybody out of the room. No one knew what to expect. A 106 is not supposed to be fired from indoors. The officer shouted, 'Fire,' and the gunner pulled the lanyard and the long gun exploded with the sound of thunder, a shattering *BOOOOOOOM!* that rocked the floors and ceilings and knocked plaster off walls and brought a shower of debris down on the gun and the men around it. The blast shook the entire building. For a few seconds no one moved. Everyone seemed to be in shock. Dust fell slowly through the air. Then silence. Scared but not hurt, standing in shrouds of fine white dust, Marines started to point at one another, 'Oh, man, look at your sorry ass,' laughing at the sight of themselves, slapping their thighs, swearing, 'Sheee-it,' forgetting where they were for a moment, as silly as the high school kids they had been so recently.

A few seconds later Marines in other parts of the building began to shout, 'Hey, Charlie, how's that for a wake-up?'

And, turning on the men who fired the gun, 'Hey! Whose side you ass-holes shootin for? Us or them?'

After a while someone noticed that the machinegun had stopped firing.

FEBRUARY 4, 1968

(the same day)

I walked back through the blasted buildings of the university and out onto the wet desolate streets past the wreckage of the truck and the Vietnamese soldiers' bodies until I came back to the MACV compound. Stone was gone, his rucksack stowed neatly on the concrete floor. Cathy Leroy was gone too, somewhere up the line with the Marines. Sounds from the fight I had just left cracked the air.

Kay was asleep.

'C'mon, man,' I said, shaking him by the shoulder, 'there's a war on.'

He was slow to wake. His bloodshot eyes blinked open, the lashes stuck with nighttime ooze. He looked around the mess hall. Other forms slept, motionless.

'Where the hell are we?'

'Hué. Remember? We came in on the convoy yesterday.'

'Oh, yeah. How'd I let you talk me into this one?'

'I promised you a good story.'

'I'm supposed to be on R and R.'

'You *are* on R and R, haven't you noticed?'

Kay laughed and fumbled for a cigarette, withdrawing a straight Camel from a crumpled pack and tamping an end hard against his thumbnail. I leaned over and lit it for him with my metal lighter.

'There's a hell of a fight up the street at the university,' I said. 'Real close. Easy to cover. If we hurry we can still get it.'

'When's breakfast around this place?' Kay grumbled.

'You missed it,' I said. 'They had juice, bacon and eggs, pancakes and sausages, toast, home fries, all you could eat. But it's over now. C'mon, man, we'll scrounge something when we get back.'

'I need a cup of coffee. How d'ya expect me to start work without coffee at least?'

I went to the kitchen, found an open case of C rations and lit a heat tab under a canteen cup of water. When it boiled, I stirred in a packet of instant coffee and another of chocolate powder and gave the hot concoction to Kay. He pushed himself up on one elbow and after a couple of sips he smiled and lit another Camel. I told him about the Marines trying to take out the machinegun, the wounded man in the street, firing the 106 out the window. He listened without comment.

'We might still be able to get some good shots,' I said.

Kay finished the drink and gathered up his camera gear and followed me out the MACV compound into the street. Nothing was moving outside. We stayed close to the buildings and ran across the intersections. By the time we got to the university, the shooting had stopped. *Damn*, I thought.

Kay filmed the damaged buildings, the burned-out truck and the bodies of the North Vietnamese soldiers in the street. We located the battalion command post in the university grounds and found Lieutenant Colonel Cheatham talking to his company commanders, young captains with thin faces and tired eyes. Cheatham was holding an old tourist map of the city, the best he could get for an operations map, and was pointing out details with his big fingers.

"So you've gotta dig these rats outta their holes," he said. "Got it?" The company commanders nodded their heads but their expressions were solemn.

When Cheatham finished, I asked if he would give us an interview. He agreed without hesitation. His manner was friendly and accommodating, relaxed, assured. Kay looked around for a good location to do the interview. He asked Cheatham to stand outside in front of a tank. The light was flat, without shadows. Kay put the heavy Arriflex on his shoulder and switched it on and I adjusted the sound level on the amplifier, listening on a pair of plastic headphones as I asked the questions.

Cheatham explained in his deep, husky voice that two of his companies, Hotel and Foxtrot, were going to try to take a couple of large buildings across the street and clear the next two blocks forward. They would be going west, across the same road where the machinegun had been firing earlier. The buildings on the other side were held by the North Vietnamese and the walls were thick. On Cheatham's left flank, Alpha and Bravo companies of 1/1 were trying to do the same.

"What kind of fighting is it going to be?" I asked, holding the microphone under his chin.

"It's house to house and room to room," he said matter-of-fact, a positive tone in his voice.

"Kind of inch by inch," I said.

"That's exactly what it is," said Cheatham. His face was round and full, and his cheeks had long creases like dimples.

"Did you ever expect to experience this kind of street fighting in Vietnam?"

"No I didn't," he said, "and this is my first crack at street fighting. I think this is the first time the Marines have been street fighting since Seoul in 1950."

"And a little bit in Santo Domingo," I reminded him. (Marines had been sent to the Dominican Republic in 1965.)

"And a little bit there, yes, right." As he spoke, a column of Marines walked behind him into the attack.

Lieutenant Colonel Cheatham was clear and concise on camera, honest, unpretentious. His disposition had a naturally confident quality that was common among Marine combat officers. Some of the warrant officers, NCOs and enlisted men had it too, but not all of them. Like others in his profession, Cheatham appeared to accept that part of his job was to tell the press from time to time what was going on in his area of responsibility. At the moment, Kay and I were the only press in the immediate area. Cheatham seemed to trust us to get it right.

"What's going to happen to civilians who might get caught in there?" I said. It was a tough question and Cheatham acknowledged it with a snap of his eyes.

"Well, we're hoping that we don't run into any civilians in there right now. If they are . . ." he paused, "I'm pretty sure they are civilians that we would consider bad guys right now. We have certain areas in there that we have blocked off, that we know there are friendly civilians, and we aren't gonna take those under fire."

"And the others?"

"The others—if there's somebody in there right now, they're Charlie as far as we're concerned."

Which meant death. Few Marines would take the time to distinguish between a North Vietnamese soldier and a South Vietnamese civilian when one or the other of them appeared suddenly in the Marine's gunsights and a moment's hesitation might cost him his life. Vietnamese families who tried to escape the violence by hiding in the ground beneath their homes or by running away during a firefight were at great risk. The graffiti written on the classroom walls of the university suggested that Cheatham's battalion had suffered too many losses elsewhere in Vietnam to go softly on the local population here.

I worried about the well-being of civilians; not only the ones in Hué. I asked the question to remind Cheatham that the fate of civilians was a sensitive issue outside the narrow scope of his command, that Kay and I intended to report whatever we saw, and that the world outside was watching.

'Do you mind if we go in there with your people?' I asked.

'No, not at all,' Cheatham said, 'just be careful.'

Kay and I joined a platoon of Marines from Fox company moving in a column along a street of residential houses. We chose a place in the column between squads and tried to keep the same distance apart as the others, five to six feet. The line of men moved slowly most of the time, then fast for a few seconds, then slowly again. The sound amplifier hung from a thin leather strap around my neck and was connected to the back of Kay's camera by a five-foot-long insulated wire cable. Each time he started to walk or run, his camera took up the slack in the cable and pulled the amplifier forward, suddenly tightening the strap around my neck and snapping my head forward with a jerk.

"I feel like a monkey on a string," I complained.

Kay turned around and smiled. "I'm going to get you a little red hat and a tin cup."

The men around us in the platoon laughed. They wore dark green and black camouflage helmets and flak jackets, and carried rockets, machine-guns, grenade launchers and M-16 rifles.

'Who y'all with?' one of them said.

'CBS News,' Kay said.

'Who's that? *Walter Cronkite?*'

'That's the man.'

'No shit?'

'No shit.'

The Marine turned and spoke to the men behind him, 'Do you believe *that*? We're gonna be on the *news*.'

'Man, I didn't think we's *newsworthy*, did you?' another Marine said, laughing.

'My ass ain't worth *shit* out here,' another said. 'And you know that ain't news.'

'That's a *fact*, man.'

The platoon went forward, west, in among the houses and gardens of the neighborhood around the university, walking slowly, carefully.

'You guys must be fuckin *crazy* to come out here.'

'No more crazy than you," I said.

'Hey, man, we don't have anything to say about it. You guys have a *choice.*'

'Not as much as you think.'

'They must be payin you a lotta money to do this.'

'Yeah,' Kay said, 'we get an extra $25 a week.'

'Is that all?'

'Yup. CBS calls it *combat pay.*'

'Ain't that a joke.'

'Well, it pays for a good meal when we get back to Saigon,' I said.

'I'd give anything for a good breakfast right now,' Kay said. 'My stomach's going to give away our position.'

'Shit,' one of the Marines said, 'I'd tell 'em to *shove* their combat pay. Hundred dollars a month.'

Some of the Marines in the column shook their heads trying to make sense of us.

'Well you're sure as hell welcome to come with us,' one of them said. 'Just make sure you tell 'em back home what's *really* going on out here.'

'Yeah, man, tell it like it *is.*'

'We're trying,' Kay said softly.

The point man and his fire team turned left off the paved street and walked between two single-story houses into the bamboo gardens behind the homes. The rest of the platoon followed. The houses looked empty and there were no civilians in sight. Maneuvering around low garden walls, the point turned right, facing west, and came to a street bordered by a high gray wall of mortar and stone. Tall, mature plane trees rose from the ground on both sides of the street, casting gray shade across it. A large building three stories high with cavernous rooms stood in the dim shadows beyond the trees on the other side of the street. The building looked like a government headquarters of some kind, heavy and imposing, with thick walls. It was the Treasury. Nothing moved in or around it. Twenty meters from the street, the platoon spread out along a line parallel to the street and got into fighting positions using the houses and garden walls and trees for cover. It was unusually quiet.

The point man ran across the street and shooting started at once—heavy automatic fire from several directions to the front and left. Everyone hit the ground and lay flat except Kay, who stood with his back to the wall of a house that screened him from the incoming fire on the left. Standing, he filmed Marines crawling forward on their elbows and knees. Their helmets bobbed on their heads as they hurried to find cover. Their eyes were worried.

The squad formed a line behind a low garden fence made of cement about two and a half feet high. Single aimed shots buzzed over the fence and struck the soft ground around them. At the far end of the fence an NCO stood up behind a concrete post and looked around the edge, trying to spot the incoming fire. He was a big man in his twenties and he waved his left arm in a broad sweep, shouting to the Marines in the squad to spread out and move laterally toward the left. A Marine popped up on one knee from behind the fence and fired a long burst from his rifle toward the front. As soon as he dropped down, another Marine got up and sprayed the front for a few seconds and got down. Marines shouted warnings at one another but the pandemonium of riflefire overrode their voices. All I heard were fragments of sentences, a few words at a time. No plan of action was apparent. The squad stayed low in the cover of the garden fence. The smell of burnt gunpowder hung in the air with the smoke of the riflefire.

Screened by the building, Kay stood a few feet away rolling film. He was absorbed in the work, concentrating on images in his viewfinder, framing and focusing the lens, taking no notice of the danger.

I looked over the top of the fence, just my helmet and eyes exposed. About twenty feet forward, ahead of the line, a Marine stood up and ran toward the cover of the high stone wall parallel to the street. Reaching it, he crouched on one knee and looked back at the rest of the squad.

"Get your head down!" Kay shouted at me. I heard his voice over my shoulder but I did not obey.

Word came down the line that the platoon leader wanted the men to move forward. Orders were shouted from man to man. At the leader's command, the squad was to run forward through a gap in the fence and get behind the big wall. One Marine close to me looked confused. Bullets hissed into the position and struck the ground but no one was hit.

The squad on the left flank fired bursts of automatic rifle and machine-gun fire and someone shouted "Go!" over the bedlam and a young Marine got up and ran toward the wall. From the left, riflefire followed him. The Marine got to within ten feet of the cover of the wall when he toppled over abruptly and fell onto the ground, collapsing in a tangled lump of arms, legs and equipment. He did not move. No one shouted for a corpsman.

I lowered my head. At the same instant an incoming bullet struck the top of the garden fence and drove cement chips onto my helmet, ripping into the cloth cover. The bullet struck the fence and ricocheted away an inch from where my face had been a moment before. I looked over at Kay who stood at the far wall.

"Now will you keep your head down?" he shouted, grinning from behind the camera.

The North Vietnamese soldier had fired his rifle in the same moment I had dropped my head. We had made our decisions simultaneously: he saw me and took aim and squeezed the trigger of his AK-47 as I made the decision to get down, unaware of his intention. The bullet struck the fence a fraction of a second later. I didn't know what impulse, what reflex, what inspiration caused me to move at that moment. It may have been coincidence or luck or the natural order of things, maybe an act of a benevolent God, a small miracle.

After sixteen months in Vietnam, I became accustomed to miracles. They happened every day. I had come to expect them. In a place where the line between life and death was so fine and was being crossed so often, I had come to believe in miracles as regular wartime experience, part of the daily routine, as real as anything else. Under the circumstances, it was the natural order. Whenever my camera team and I escaped some danger (an ambush, a bad shelling, a helicopter crash)—or whenever some good fortune happened (a kind act, an unexpected lift in a plane or a helicopter, a turn of fortune)— what others would consider common luck, I called our "daily miracle." The remark was casual, offhand, lighthearted, as if miracles could be taken for granted. The American and European camera crews in the bureau did not believe in my daily miracles, though they were polite enough not to say it openly. With the exception of the French, none of them wanted to work with me anymore because they considered me too dangerous. But my Vietnamese colleagues understood completely. They seemed to know about miracles, to believe in them, as I did. In those moments of inexpressible relief, when something as simple and precious as our lives or our sanity or our dignity had been rescued, even when only a basic comfort like a hot meal or a cold drink or a dry place to sleep was provided, they looked at me and nodded their heads and said, "Yes, Jack, daily miracle," and smiled.

The Marines in the squad behind the fence were moving forward one by one toward the wall. We had been with them about an hour, no more.

"I think we've got enough," Kay said. He set his camera and shoulder brace on the ground beside him and took out a cigarette and lit it. Looking at me, he made a pantomime with both hands of eating a meal. We had the film we needed for this scene in the story.

"Then let's go," I said.

It was a familiar exchange. Whether it took a few hours or several days, as soon as we had enough combat footage (known in the New York–inspired jargon of TV news as *bang-bang*), we got out of the field as fast as possible. The earlier we started back to a city with an airfield, the better the chance of getting the film to Saigon the same day for shipment to the United States. Trying to get back to base from remote parts of the country could take a full day, even two. At times it took longer to travel to and from the story than to cover it.

No one wanted to spend any more time than necessary being shot at. It was not because of laziness or cowardice or lack of commitment to the story; it was really about survival. TV film editors in the States used only a fraction of the footage we sent them, usually 10 percent or less. Often, they got more combat footage than they had time to show on the air. So, as soon as Kay and I had enough film to tell the story, we tried to get away from the fighting as quickly as we could. Sometimes it was not possible. One of the best and brightest CBS News correspondents in Vietnam, George Syvertsen, said, "No sense getting killed for something that's going to end up on the cutting room floor," smiling as he said it. It was a clever remark, measured by George's fine sense of irony, but it wasn't only a joke. Later, in Cambodia, as the North Vietnamese and Khmer Rouge advanced toward Phnom Penh, Syvertsen led two CBS camera teams out of the capital and down a deserted provincial road that a British reporter, a supposed friend, had told him was safe. They drove into an ambush that took all their lives.

Kay and I said good-bye to the squad behind the fence.

'Good luck, you guys, we're going back,' I called.

'See?' one of them said, 'You *do* have a choice.'

'Hey, next time I'll remember that,' Kay called back. To withdraw, we would have to expose ourselves to incoming fire.

'You need somebody to carry the camera?' a Marine shouted, keeping low, his face smiling.

'Yeah,' another said. 'Plenty of volunteers around.'

'How 'bout a RTO?' the radio operator suggested, 'keep you in touch with what's going on.' Everyone laughed.

'See you guys later,' Kay said.

'Just you be sure and tell it like it is.'

'You bet.'

'See you around.'

Kay and I ran in a low crouch back between houses to the rear. Riflefire cracked behind us as some of the Marines gave cover. It bothered me to leave them so soon. I hadn't had time to get their names and hometowns.

The troops rarely objected to our dropping in and out of their locations and taking pictures of them, even for a short time. But it made *us* feel guilty, especially after a firefight or a heavy shelling, when we'd just begun to get acquainted and were becoming friendly with them, the way you do quickly with people you meet in a war. We usually had to leave in a hurry, knowing we probably wouldn't see them again. Most of them seemed grateful to have us around for a few hours, particularly in fearful places like Con Thien and Khe Sanh and now Hué. We'd get a quick picture of what was happening, talk to the Marines and Navy men about it, give them a chance to express their feelings, share some of their hardship (if only briefly), and put what they said and did on film for our producers at home to make into a story. Having a TV crew around added another dimension to their lives, changed it in a subtle way, modifying the usual routine of their difficult existence, verifying some small part of their experience, maybe even validating it, if only for the folks at home. Millions of Americans felt profound sympathy for the men in the field—especially their friends and family, particularly when they saw them on television.

Kay and I walked back to the MACV compound and dropped our gear on the concrete floor and sat on pieces of C ration cardboard. Kay described each sequence he had shot on film and I wrote it in my notebook: empty street scenes, bodies, smashed buildings, interview with Lieutenant Colonel Cheatham, the patrol, the firefight, the Marine who was shot.

'I'm sure I was rolling on him when he went down,' Kay said.

'Do you think he's dead?'

'Yeah. No doubt about it. Poor bastard.'

Our coverage of the battle of Hué existed on two rolls of exposed film, about eight hundred feet, and now the problem was how to get it shipped to the United States to be processed, screened, edited and broadcast. The film and the narration I would write to go with it had to be shipped from Saigon.

The next step was to get out of Hué and back to Phu Bai, the division head-quarters, and then to Danang, the corps headquarters, and then down to Saigon. A helicopter was our best chance on the first leg out of Hué.

Dana Stone and Cathy Leroy were up on the line. There were no other reporters around. I found the regimental commander, Colonel Hughes, sitting on the back steps of the compound. He was speaking on a field radio to his commanding officers in Phu Bai. Hughes seemed fully in command now, confident and decisive, and I was surprised how much he had changed in less than a day.

'Did you get up to the line?' he asked.

'Yes, sir,' I said.

'How's it going up there?'

'Very slow. Foxtrot is trying to get across the street into that big government building west of the university. Lot of incoming from the south and west. We've lost a few men.'

'Did you get what you needed?'

'Yes, sir. The men are very brave.'

'Yes, I know.' Hughes thought for a moment. 'Take care of yourselves today. We'll get you out in the morning. If you need anything let us know.'

I went back to the mess hall and started cooking a meal while Kay changed the exposed film in the magazine and put in a fresh roll and then wrote out the cameraman's dope sheet with details of what was on the film. We called the story "Hué Battle—Day Five."

FEBRUARY 5, 1968

At dawn, a resupply helicopter rushed toward the landing zone by the side of the river, banked sharply south, then landed in a wind-whipped clatter of rotor blades, machinegun fire, screaming men and hissing air. The chopper crew and Marines on the ground hurried to carry out boxes of ammunition and medical supplies and threw them on the ground. In less than a minute it was done. Kay and I ran through the cyclone of wind and men and equipment and up the back ramp onto the big green twin-rotor Sea Knight just as it lifted off the grass and into the air and turned its heavy metal belly toward the Citadel, gaining speed as bright-colored tracers tore the early morning air around it. Heading away, the helicopter raced low over the south bank of the black river while a door gunner fired long bursts from his M-60 at the Citadel on the other side. Inside, the CH-46 was empty except for the crew and Marines who were leaving Hué because their tours of duty were almost over or because they had essential work to do in the rear or because they were being evacuated for medical reasons. A few of the wounded did not wear bandages. Their injuries were visible only in their eyes. They gazed with fixed stares straight ahead out the windows of the helicopter and into the gray mists. The healthy Marines who were going home looked sorry, as if they were leaving something behind.

The helicopter skimmed over the surface of the river. When it was a mile away from the Citadel it rose up swiftly through the clouds and into the sunlight. The light was dazzling. I reached into the bottom of my pack, pulled out a pewter flask, unscrewed the metal cap and drank. The Courvoisier was bitter. I passed the flask to Kay, who drank some and gave it to the Marine next to him. He looked surprised by the offer, holding the flask in his hand without drinking, but after a few seconds he put it to his mouth and drank. Then the flask went around and most of the Marines in the cabin took a small swig in turn and passed it on. It was one of our rituals. I carried the flask in my pack and saved the cognac until the worst was over and we were on our way out. The flask went around twice, then it was empty.

One by one, the Marines unsnapped their flak jackets and took off their helmets. A PFC gave me a thumbs-up as if to say thanks, that's better. The rotor blades beat steadily into the wind and the monotonous drone of the engines drowned attempts at conversation. Gradually the noise of the helicopter and the rushing wind supplanted the sounds of gunfire fresh in our minds. The air above the clouds felt clean and warm and fresh.

Flying away safely from Hué was great magic. No other feeling compares to the power of escape from a war zone. After days of nervous tension— hyperalert for snipers, rockets, ricochets, mortars, grenades, booby traps, friendly fire, loss of life, loss of face—after our long intimate proximity with death and the primitive instincts that go with it, suddenly the terror fell away. It was replaced by feelings that come only after the passing of great danger. Our overactive adrenaline pumps shut down. Heartbeats returned to normal. Muscles relaxed. Our brains were flushed with an intoxicating, exhilarating sense of safety from harm, of well-being, a physical euphoria that blended with the exquisite emotional relief at having made it out alive.

Drinking the cognac helped unwind the tightness in our minds and bodies and sharpen the sense of relief. It was to become part of the memory of the experience of flying safely out of Hué, an unconscious chemical imprint that, drinking cognac years later, would recall the original euphoria, though it never equaled it, no matter how much I drank.

Twenty minutes later the Sea Knight landed at Phu Bai airfield and we said good-bye to the crew and the Marines. Kay asked the traffic controller for a ride to Danang, but the Air Force sergeant said nothing was scheduled the rest of the day. Everything he had coming in was going north or west. Kay and I were disappointed. Not only would we have to spend the night in the military passenger terminal—a cavernous tin-and plywood-hanger with concrete floors and the prospect of limitless boredom—but another full day would be lost getting the story on the air. The battle of Hué was big news and the film needed to get out and on the air as soon as possible. Kay, better at accepting fate, sat against the wall of the terminal and smoked a cigarette.

Time passed.

Late in the afternoon, the traffic controller said he had an unscheduled C-130 that was going to Danang. My heart felt joy. 'But it's gotta make one stop and drop off a load of gas on the way,' he said.

'Where's that?' Kay said.

The sergeant looked at his tackboard. "Khe Sanh."

Kay and I looked at each other. Could a ride to Danang be worth a stopover in the most dangerous place in the world?

'No way, man,' said Kay.

'Well, I'm going,' I said, not knowing why. *What the hell*, I thought, *it's a chance to get back to Danang by nightfall*. I was tired.

Kay argued as vigorously as possible, then gave up. He handed me the two rolls of exposed film. The traffic controller read out the tail number of the C-130 (it was something like YD 481) and pointed to it on the tarmac. I walked out on the runway where the four-engine cargo plane was being loaded with black rubber fuel bladders the size of small trucks. An Air Force noncom standing by the plane supervised the loading, checking a list. I asked if I could go with them to Danang as a passenger, and he looked at me with an expression he might usually have reserved for lost children or injured animals. 'Sure,' he said, 'if the skipper says okay.'

I got aboard and strapped myself into a seat near the back of the cargo hold, closed my eyes and started to fall asleep. A few minutes later the engines began to turn the propellers and I looked up to see Kay at the open doorway at the back of the plane. *So, he's changed his mind and decided to come*, I thought. Kay walked toward me. He was not carrying his camera or field pack. His face was set in anger.

"If you don't get off this God damn plane right now," he said, "I'm gonna drag you off." His jaw was fixed. I got up, grabbed my pack and climbed down the steps. Before we reached the edge of the runway, we were both apologizing.

"I just didn't want all my footage wasted because you got yourself zapped in Khe Sanh," he said.

'Oh, that was all,' I said. I reached into the pack and gave him back the film.

We waited near the runway and watched YD 481 take off and turn west toward the mountains.

An hour passed. At twilight, we noticed three Americans dressed in civilian clothes making a preflight check on an old C-47. The two-engine cargo plane was painted silver and had no markings. Kay and I walked out on the runway to ask if they were going to Danang. One of them said, 'Yeah, eventually.' We explained that we had footage from Hué and needed to get back as soon as possible. The leader of the team, a man in his mid-thirties wearing a short-sleeved white shirt with khaki trousers, told us to get aboard and strap in.

The plane warmed up. Just before takeoff, the team leader came down the aisle and said in a calm voice, 'Just don't take any pictures and don't write about what you're gonna see. Understood?' Kay and I nodded our heads. It was not possible to tell whether he was State Department or CIA, but we assumed Agency.

Danang was less than fifty miles south of Phu Bai, but when the C-47 took off it turned north toward Hué. When it got over the city, the plane circled above the clouds at about eight or nine thousand feet. Flares fell below, making bright glowing pulses in the cloudy dark. The American team leader opened the rear side door of the plane, pushed a portable field radio part way outside and spoke into the handset. Shouting above the noise of the engines, he called to someone on the ground. (A number of American diplomats and intelligence agents, including the senior U.S. government representative in Hué, were trapped by the fighting, and it was hoped they were barricaded in safe houses, waiting for help. This mission appeared to be an attempt to make radio contact with them in order to plan a rescue.) Again and again, with disciplined patience, the team leader called on the radio and listened for an answer, as if he knew personally the people he was calling. Circling above the city, the wind outside rushing past the open doorway of the plane, he spoke into the night with slow mechanical repetition for more than two hours. No answer came.

Danang was quiet when we arrived back at the press center. The hour was late. Kay bought two beers at the dining room bar and brought one to me and put it on the card table in the CBS room where I sat typing. While he wrapped the film for shipment, I wrote the voice-over narration as fast as I could on my portable typewriter, asking him questions about the length and content of certain shots as I went along. Kay called the Air Force at the airbase and was told a courier jet would be flying to Saigon at midnight and would take our film if it was ready. Typing quickly, I tried to capture some of the mood of the Marines and the location and the danger, the deadly seriousness of it, adding specific details like the platoon's assault on the wall and the death of the Marine who ran forward alone. The words and pictures would give only an impression of what was going on, a sense of the mood rather than a straight factual account of the battle. In the time it took for the film to reach the States, viewers already would have read more detailed accounts of the battle in newspapers, written by reporters far removed from the scene of the fighting but with better access to communications. Our story would enhance earlier versions, possibly clarify them, maybe contradict some of them. Being on film and natural sound, our work could be more vivid, more realistic than some of the printed accounts. The last line of narration paraphrased the quote from Lieutenant Colonel Cheatham: "It is inch by shattered inch in the five-day battle for Hué." We had not bothered to do an on-camera stand-up.

The story was broadcast on *The Evening News with Walter Cronkite* two days later. The foreign editor of CBS News, Robert Little, a veteran of old-school journalism and not particularly generous with praise, sent Kay a cable congratulating him for his photography, saying it was the closest, most dramatic combat film he'd seen from any war.

The next day, I called the Air Force information officer at the Danang airbase and asked him to check on YD 481, the C-130 that flew from Phu Bai to Khe Sanh without me or Kay aboard. Waiting at the press center, I got out the files of Air Force missions flown to Khe Sanh and looked up the figures for military personnel killed, wounded or missing. The numbers for recent weeks were surprisingly high. Calculating the figures, I estimated that the odds of making the round-trip to the Marine combat base at Khe Sanh without being hurt or killed were roughly one in two, or about 50 percent. Later in the day, the Air Force officer called back to say that YD 481 was missing in the hills near Khe Sanh and was presumed to have been shot down. There were no survivors. 'Any particular reason you want to know?' he asked.

FEBRUARY 19, 1968

When I left Hué on February 5, I hadn't imagined the battle would last another three weeks. Nor did I much care. My second tour of duty for CBS in Vietnam was over and I was tired. It was time to go home. But the fighting in Hué was exhausting the resources of CBS News. Almost all of the correspondents and camera crews based in Southeast Asia had gone into Hué once (a few had refused) and did not want to go back a second time. Keith Kay had already left the country. I had stayed on to help the bureau cover the continued fighting in Saigon and to make another trip to Khe Sanh. Weary, overextended, I was persuaded by the bureau chief finally that if I made one more trip to Hué, I could go home.

By the twentieth day of the battle of Hué all anyone could think about was staying alive. Foul-smelling smoke drifted up from the burned-out shells of houses and buildings and garbage and blackened the low clouds hanging over the Citadel. Much of the city was demolished. Dead bodies lay in the streets. Food was scarce, nerves frazzled. The noise of battle was loud and incessant. Artillery shells, mortars, rifle bullets, machinegun tracers, tank cannon, hand grenades, gas grenades, rocket-propelled grenades, rocket artillery, recoilless rifles and even shells from the long heavy guns of U.S. Navy destroyers in the South China Sea whooshed overhead with shrieking whistlescreams and burst upon the pulverized remains of the city. The noise was regular and violent, so loud it shattered people's eardrums, played havoc with their sanity. Madness was in the air.

The Americans and North Vietnamese were like two exhausted boxers in the final round of an ugly fight that had already been decided, trying to hang on long enough to get in a few last shots without getting killed, waiting without hope for someone to stop it. Each day the Marines advanced a few more meters across the burned ground and each day the two sides sent back another load of battle dead. Thousands of people had been killed.

And yet, after twenty days, the Marines in Hué seemed to have adjusted to the noise and smoke and death. To most of them, it had become normal, a background to the blighted landscape. When shells came in, some of them no longer bothered to duck.

I left the kitten in the room where the mortar came through the roof and walked out the door to the courtyard of the compound. The Marines were ready to take the camera crew and me to the front. The Vietnamese kitten was on its own. I had enough on my mind without having to worry about a cat. I was too short, in other words, I had too little time left in-country, counting the days until I could leave. Only a few more days, maybe a week. This was going to be my last time in combat. I tried to appear relaxed but my insides were churning. I had all the symptoms of short-timer's syndrome: general anxiety about being around guns, heart-stopping insecurity at the sound of close battle, and the specific fear that having survived this tour and all the life-threatening incidents the war could devise, one of these final few hours would be fatal. I had been scheduled to go home ten days earlier but here I was, being a good soldier, doing one more story for the *Evening News*. The network executives had said, 'Jack, we really, really need you to cover this one,' appealing to my sense of duty (which was actually *their* sense of duty) to stay on. CBS News executives, accustomed to giving their corre-spondents orders, rarely asked for favors. I was so flattered to be asked per-sonally to help them out that I agreed. After nearly a year and a half of combat, the idea of getting killed or wounded *after* my tour was officially over was terrifying. I was working on borrowed time.

The Vietnamese camera team waited in the courtyard on the back of a mule. Duong Van Ri, the photographer, was anxious to get to the front and cover the fighting, but Pham Tan Dan, the sound technician, was not. It was a fair reflection of their personalities. Ri was tall and skinny with arms like chair legs and a cheerful disposition. He had apprenticed as a sound techni-cian with Kurt Volkert, a German photographer who taught him to shoot film, and this was his first combat assignment with the camera. He seemed to fear nothing. His happy brown eyes showed his delight at the prospect of making hundreds of dollars a week working for CBS. (Ri kept two homes in different parts of the country and supported two wives and families. His appetite for sex got him the nickname Boom-Boom.) He smiled as I approached the mule and made room for me to sit next to him.

Pham Tam Dan, who pronounced his given name "Zahn," was as short and heavy as Ri was tall and thin. Dan smiled much of the time, a humble life-loving smile that made him pleasant to be with. In combat he was steady, reliable, hardworking and dependable, even though he hated war. Dan was thirty-two years old, the oldest one on our team, and was devoutly spiritual. He accepted whatever happened to him, pleasant or not, with equanimity, giving the impression of being at peace with his surroundings in all conditions. Usually Dan worked with Keith Kay, but Kay was taking a break from the Tet Offensive and was home in Hong Kong with his wife and children. Kay, Dan and I had been around I Corps since the previous August, in and out of battle, and now Dan too looked like he'd had enough.

The Marine driver put the mule into gear and drove up a paved deserted street with trees and houses on both sides. Nothing else moved. Passing under an archway, we entered the Citadel, a dark forbidding fortress surrounded by a moat with brick walls twenty feet high and fifty feet thick. The Citadel was an enclosed city within Hué that had been built one hundred fifty years before in the time of Vietnamese emperors. It was modeled on the Forbidden City of Beijing.

Gunshots cracked ahead, close. Riding in back of the mule, I caught my breath. Dan's head snapped around. Ri put the camera on his shoulder. The driver kept going forward as if nothing had happened. I knew from experience that war sounds in cities are deceptive. Buildings distort distance and direction so that a rifleshot two hundred yards away sounds like it might be coming from around the corner. And a shot around the corner sounds like it's next to you. Knowing was no help. I was thoroughly spooked. To my eyes, snipers lurked in every bush and building. Land mines were buried in the road. Booby traps with trip wires were strung along the trails. Each time a mortar round exploded, even far away, I feared the next one would land on us.

True danger is more apparent at the moment of entering or leaving a war zone. Long duty in dangerous places modifies your sense of peril, immunizing you against the paralysis of fright. For a year and a half I had survived the environment, ducked in and out of battle, put a brave face on the fear. But now that I was close to getting away, I was starting to think normally again, making the slow mental adjustment from war to peace, starting to consider home life and its simple pleasures. How sweet a thought that was: to be at home, at peace . . . How seductive, too fragile to hold for long, too risky to contemplate seriously. Only when the prospect of survival was offered could you appreciate the true menace of the war, the absolute finality of what was happening, how swiftly your dream of making it home safely could be carried away on the wind of one explosion.

The mule arrived at the battalion command post. The Marines occupied a residential villa built in French colonial style with wide walls, wooden shutters that closed over the windows and a small garden outside. The villa was big enough to accommodate twenty to thirty Marines on the command staff who worked mostly in silence in the noise of the nearby guns, listening to their radios, monitoring the rifle companies on the line, updating their maps. A tank drove down the street past the villa and turned the corner in a hurry.

I checked in with a master sergeant named Nuanez and sat on the floor of the entrance hall with my back to a wall waiting to talk with the battalion commander when he was not busy. Ri and Dan went outside to film some tanks they had seen in the streets. A tan and orange dog wandered through the CP, its eyes wild with fear. Each time it heard an explosion, it let out a howl, a high-pitched cry of anguish, full of terror. The dog had given birth recently but she had no milk and her nipples sagged, stretching the loose skin around her ribcage. She was a small dog, a Vietnamese mongrel with a long tail that hung behind her. She limped on three legs, carrying the fourth under her, wandering from room to room, whining. No sign of her pups.

"Somebody oughta shoot that crazy dog," an old Marine said, his voice hard.

The dog came over and I took her to my chest, speaking softly, cradling her head. Foam bubbled around her mouth. The short hairs of her light brown fur were full of fleas. I ran my hand across her back a few times and she began to relax. Reaching for a canteen on my web belt, I poured water into the cupped palm of my hand and held it under the dog's nose. She lapped the water and looked at me with mad woeful eyes. Outside, artillery shelling came more rapidly and the dog limped away, wandering through the rooms of the house again as if searching for something. I put my head against the wall and went to sleep.

I awoke to a commotion by the doorway. Three men walked into the villa demanding to see the battalion commander at once. Two of them spoke Italian and the third spoke French. They also spoke some English but it was not fluent and at least two of them always seemed to speak at the same time. They were wearing workaday sports jackets that were not particularly fashionable and sharply pointed leather shoes with splashes of mud on them. They carried commercial airline bags over their shoulders that made them look as if they'd just got off a flight from Naples or Marseilles. I figured them for newspaper journalists. Sergeant Nuanez came out to greet them and said with a calm voice, 'The major's real busy right now. We got a war on, you know.' The Europeans spoke in loud insistent voices, repeating the names of their newspapers and the words "deadline" and "Danang," pointing for emphasis to the watches on their wrists. The sergeant's mouth smiled but his eyes were cold. 'I'll see what I can do,' he said.

A few minutes later an officer appeared and introduced himself as Major Robert H. Thompson, commanding officer of 1st Battalion, 5th Marines. Thompson looked weary. He told the visitors in a soft voice he was from Corinth, Mississippi, and he had been directing the American side of the battle in the Citadel for more than a week. (South Vietnamese soldiers were fighting a few hundred yards away in another part of the Citadel.) Thompson's battalion had arrived in Hué eight days ago, he said, on Sunday, and made contact with the North Vietnamese Tuesday morning.

'The resistance is getting stiffer,' Thompson told them. 'It's most difficult because of such close contact. We get an occasional gunship but no other air support. Charlie's dug way down into the buildings and they're too strong for our light mortars.'

The Europeans asked questions in fast excited voices, talking over one another, asking where the rifle companies were located exactly, how many casualties each unit had suffered, how many replacements had come in, how many of his Marines were still able to fight. The questioning was very detailed in a military way and Thompson answered them truthfully.

This is insane! I thought. *These guys can be on a plane to Hong Kong tonight and on the phone to Hanoi in a few hours. This kind of information would be priceless to the other side.*

'Excuse me,' I said. 'We can't report this kind of stuff. It's against the ground rules. Especially with a battle in progress. What do you need that kind of detail for, anyway?' The Europeans scowled at me, as if to say, mind your own business, you're not the information officer. The sergeant told them the major had to get back to work now, and that was all the time he could spare. The reporters put their notebooks in their flight bags and demanded a ride to the rear as soon as possible. Major Thompson listened to them politely and told the sergeant to give them his jeep and driver.

"Anything to help our friends in Europe," he said, but they missed the sarcasm. After they had left, I had the impression he and the sergeant were glad to see them go.

Thompson returned to work and I went back to the protection of the wall and sleep. Ri and Dan appeared saying they had filmed a couple of tanks as they moved into position up the street. Hours passed. It was dark when I heard my name being called and woke up.

'Sir,' a voice said softly. 'The major's got a few minutes to talk to you now.'

The noise of shooting had stopped and the house was silent, near midnight. Ri and Dan were asleep on the floor. I got out my notebook and walked into the main room of the villa, a wide space that ran the length of the house and was crowded with the sleeping forms of Marines, packs, weapons, boxes of ammunition, C ration cases. Major Thompson sat at a long wooden table with his chin resting in the palms of his hands and his eyes staring at a maze of military symbols on a map of the Citadel in front of him. Dull yellow light from candles and a kerosene lantern cast a soft glow around the table. A line of portable two-way field radios was arranged in a neat row on another table nearby and monitored by a young Marine who listened to periodic situation reports from the rifle companies a few blocks away. All quiet. A group of younger officers, company commanders, listened as the major briefed them for another push forward in a few hours.

Thompson shook hands and apologized for the long wait. He offered a cup of coffee. 'It's the most hospitality I have to give you,' he said.

He had deep dark pouches under his eyes as if he was keeping awake on caffeine and adrenaline. He was polite and friendly but deeply tired. He talked about the slow advance against unyielding North Vietnamese opposition that characterized the twenty days of fighting so far.

"It's tough for us because the contact is so close," Thompson said in his Mississippi drawl. "We get a gunship occasionally, but no air support, except for one day when the weather cleared." He spoke in the clipped, straightforward style of a briefing officer.

"Our mortars are no good in this kind of fighting because they won't crack these buildings. It's very tough, the most difficult situation an attacking force could encounter, toe to toe."

"What are your casualties like?" I asked, "And how's morale?"

Thompson thought for a few seconds and then spoke, choosing his words with care. "To keep pushing the troops without air support would mean taking too many unnecessary casualties," he said.

That's new, I thought. I had never heard a Marine officer talk about taking too many casualties—Marines *always* take a lot of casualties. Then he said,

"Morale-wise, I don't think we're hurting. The troops are still a bunch of tigers."

One of the company commanders winced. I kept writing in my notebook. The silence was awkward.

'How long have you been over here?' Thompson said, changing the subject.

The question surprised me. 'Oh, uh, second tour, seventh or eighth month, I think. Supposed to go home pretty soon,' I said.

'Gettin short, huh?'

'Yeah, I hope this is my last time in the field.'

'Well,' said Thompson, 'see you don't get shot tomorrow. Hate to lose a civilian on his last day in the field. We had three reporters hit down the street here today.'

He looked at me with a fatherly, career officer's concern that said, 'Don't worry, we're all in this together.' He might have seen a trace of panic in my face when he mentioned the three wounded journalists.

'Say, do you have a safe place to sleep?' he said, turning to one of the sergeants. 'Top, see that Mr. Laurence gets a good spot to sack out, will you? We'll take him and his camera crew up to the line in the morning.'

Sergeant Nuanez led the way to a corner of the command post. The window sills were stacked with sandbags and the openings blacked out with hanging blankets. He pushed a sleeping Marine to one side to make room for me.

Nuanez leaned toward me so that no one else would hear him. "This place is worse than Seoul," he said in a whisper, pronouncing it *Sool*. He was old and grizzled-looking enough to have been there, the folds of his neck leathery, his breath cold. "Takin too many casualties. Grunts are getting tired."

Master Sergeant Nuanez was giving me his own private briefing. No matter that it contradicted the major's official version. He didn't bother to say, 'This is off the record' or 'Don't quote me, but . . .' He had nothing to lose by telling the truth.

"Never seen so much, uh, shell shock, ya know?" He spoke the words with his breath.

Shell shock? My mind flashed with images of hollow-eyed trench warfare, too long in the line, *1914–1918*.

'Thanks, Top,' I said. 'I'll check it out.' He slipped away without another word, silent as a shadow. I took off my boots and pulled a poncho around me, squeezed the backpack into shape for a pillow, put the helmet on its side to protect one side of my head and said a prayer. The floor was cold.

A few yards away, against the wall, two teenage Marines wrestled in a narrow wooden bed.

"It's my turn on top," the voice a loud whisper.

"No it's not. You were on top last night."

Giggling, maneuvering for position in the bed, the Marines wrestled playfully. Then an older Marine rasped harshly at them in a voice that was a gurgle of gravel and salt. "You dumb faggots shut up and go to sleep," he said. "There's reporters aroun."

FEBRUARY 20, 1968

From the beginning of the battle the days were cold and dark. Monsoon rain fell on the city in a slow drizzle that kept everything but the barrels of the guns cool and wet. Fog crept in before first light and cast a blanket of mist across the blasted houses, broken walls and fractured trees of no-man's-land. Low clouds cut the light and trapped the lingering smoke from burning rubble and campfires. The Citadel was enveloped in a wet gloom that gathered early and haunted the morning like the memory of a bad dream.

At dawn, most of the Marines in the command post were asleep—unconscious and unmoving—wrapped in silent green ponchos like body bags. Major Thompson sat at the map table, the candles extinguished, his head resting on folded arms, asleep. One by one the Marines began to move. A few feet away, two teenage PFCs leaned over on their sides to face each other and lit cigarettes, resting on their elbows.

'Hey, what day is this?' one said.

The other Marine thought for a moment, 'Must be the twentieth.'

'Hey! It's my birthday!'

'Every day's your birthday.'

'No. I mean it. Today really *is* my birthday,' his adolescent voice raised just above a whisper, sincere.

'You say that every day: *'today's my birthday,''* imitating his friend's voice. 'You're crazy, man.'

'Listen,' the first Marine said. 'I signed up on my birthday, right? When I was seventeen. The dude said I could get out on my twenty-first birthday. And today's my birthday. So, I'm supposed to get out, right?'

'You crazy fucker, you ain't never gettin out. Besides, you told me your birthday's in August.'

'Hey, man, I'm not gonna *live* that long! What good am I to the Marine Corps if I'm dead, huh? I tell you they should let me out like they said. It's my birthday!'

'So how old are you?'

'Oh, 'bout twelve and a half.'

'See? You're crazy.'

The room came to life with slow-moving figures who stretched and yawned, aching with fatigue. Sleeping on the floor was painful. The cold damp got into muscles and made them stiff. No one complained. It was far better than sleeping on the line outdoors. I rolled up my poncho, strapped it to my pack, dug out a canteen cup and went outside to look for Dan and Ri. The rain had stopped in the night but the low clouds were still in place. There was no sign of the dog from the day before. Ri and Dan squatted on their haunches in the Vietnamese way, their knees level with their chins, their feet flat on the ground. They cooked noodle soup on a wood fire, chatting softly. When they saw me, they smiled and offered to share breakfast. I boiled a cup of water for coffee. Ri asked when we were going to see some fighting.

'We'll get a good story,' I said. 'But we stay with the major.'

Ri was anxious to prove himself as a combat photographer but I wasn't willing to risk my life recklessly for his reputation.

'No chances,' I said. 'Okay?'

Ri frowned and turned back to his soup. Dan smiled.

An hour later when heat from the sun was melting the morning mist, Major Thompson announced he was ready to move up to the front to inspect the lines. He looked rested and spoke in a positive, energetic way. A team of scouts appeared at the CP to direct us through the streets to the forward positions. One scout was short and thin with intense black eyes that caught every movement around him. The other scout was taller and wore a bandanna made from parachute silk around his neck. They checked their ammunition clips and loaded rounds into the chambers of their M-16s and clicked them on safe. Other Marines were assigned to guard the flanks. The group pushed off with the scouts on point, Thompson and his radio operator next, followed by Ri, Dan and me, and Sergeant Nuanez at the back. This was as safe as it got for visitors to the line but I was nervous.

The column walked single file along a deserted street lined with trees that were charred like dead matchsticks, past abandoned houses, shuttered and silent. Every building was gouged by bullets. The sturdier, more prominent buildings that had been defended were reduced to skeletons, their roofs collapsed. The carcass of a water buffalo, black and bloated, lay on its side in the shallow dirt beside the road. Nothing moved. No signs of life. Every breath smelled of garbage, smoke, sewage and rotting flesh.

At the front it was quiet, the big guns silent. The column stopped at a small building the size of a garden shed that was being used as a command post by Delta Company. The CP was screened on the left by a towering wall of brick and stone blocks, part of the original Citadel fortifications. The hollow windows of the little building were covered with blankets. Thompson went inside.

Marines in the line were slumped behind mounds of brown dirt, tree stumps and low stone walls, waiting. One or two slept. Ahead of them was a blackened wasteland of burned-out houses, broken trees, piles of bamboo, sheets of corrugated tin roofing pierced by bullets and shrapnel, and acres of twisted smoking debris that looked like the photographs of World War I. The thick southeast wall of the Citadel, the Marines' objective, rose in the distance, two hundred yards away. Hidden in the rubble between the Marines and the wall were the North Vietnamese.

The line was thin, the men several yards apart. *Why are they spaced out so far? I wondered. For better security? Or because they've lost so many people?* Their faces were dark with dirt and smoke and brick dust. They looked vulnerable, innocent. One Marine stared at Ri and Dan with disbelief, his jaw loose, eyes disoriented, as if the presence of two young Vietnamese men inside the company lines was too incredible to comprehend. His eyes were angry. His careless movements gave the appearance of being beyond fear, beyond caring in a conscious way anymore about survival, his mind in a primitive state of automatic response, worn down by the war to a point that the notion of a bad wound was no more than another option to be considered, even a possible escape from the horrors of the Citadel.

When they saw us, some of the Marines relaxed. They welcomed us, asked where we were from and how long we'd been over here. I told them I was from New England originally, had been in-country since last August, that it was my second tour, the first in '65 and '66.

'Must have been different, then,' one of them said.

'Very much so,' I said. 'Not so much heavy fighting.'

'Positively *peaceful*,' another said.

'Yes, by comparison,' I said, looking at the scene around them. 'Hué used to be a nice place.'

'Where are you guys from?' they asked Ri and Dan.

'They're from here,' I said. 'Been over here all their lives.' The Marines laughed. 'Yeah, some home you got here,' one said.

Ri went to work filming the scene. I asked a lieutenant where the North Vietnamese were.

"Out there," he said, pointing over the heads of the Marines.

"How far?"

"We don't know yet, not till we try to move up. Then they hit us. It's the same every day. We made fifty meters yesterday." The lieutenant told me about their losses. 'Seventy-five percent in some units,' he said. I was shocked at the figure.

Ri found a place in the line where we could do interviews without being exposed to fire. We ran over to a squad of Marines who stood behind a ten-foot wall, one of them watching through a gap. I introduced myself and asked them how it was going. They answered in soft, clear voices, matter-of-fact, as if describing a school field trip.

"The gooks are really dug in there," one of them said.

"They're in bunkers, tunnels, spider holes, you name it," said another.

"They got *all kinds* of heavy weapons."

"What are casualties like?" I asked, the camera rolling.

"Many think we're hurtin real bad right now," said a young PFC named Gary Bolten. He wore glasses and had a southern drawl. "We lost Second Platoon, they was wiped out. And, First Platoon, they lost a lot of people. We'll probably have to withdraw today to regroup."

"How do you feel yourself?" I hated to ask that question, *How do you feel?* But Bolten looked worried and it was a way to probe his private thoughts.

"I'm scared, I guess." He grinned with embarrassment. He was honest about the fear, brave to admit it. As he finished speaking, automatic fire rattled from the right front, far away.

Ri said this would be a good place to do an on-camera open. He lined up a shot of an American flag on a pole above a watchtower that had been blasted by fire. He said he would do a pullback with the lens to reveal me standing behind the wall with the watchtower in the background. I tried to think of an opening line for the story that did not contradict the picture. 'I'll wing it,' I said. With Ri's camera rolling on the flag, I held the microphone and said, "The American flag flies on the Citadel wall, but there is no breeze to blow it. . . . And the job is far from done for Delta Company. The last two hundred yards are the toughest."

What I could not say without breaking the agreed rules of self-censorship for journalists was that Marine losses were so great that the 1/5 barely existed as an efficient fighting battalion. Delta Company was a seasoned unit of combat veterans commanded by a bright, able captain named Myron Harrington, the only officer in the company who had not been killed or wounded. He had taken his company into the battle of Hué with one hundred twenty Marines. Now he had about thirty. Unit for unit, Marine casualty rates in the Citadel approached those of the French and British at Verdun and the Somme. Companies were down to the size of platoons. Platoons were reduced to rifle squads. Squads were the size of fire teams. Some squads no longer existed. North Vietnamese casualties were higher. All the killing and wounding had occurred in less than one week of fighting.

We thanked the Marines in the line for talking to us and went back to the company command post. Ri loaded the exposed film into a container and put a fresh magazine on his camera. Waiting outside the CP for the major to finish his meeting, I suddenly had nothing to do. My nerves began to unravel. There had been no big explosions all morning. The silence was strange.

'All we need is an interview with the major, and we're finished,' I said to Ri and Dan. 'But let's not do the interview here, okay?'

Ri was disappointed. 'Maybe we get bang-bang later?'

'We don't really need any,' I said. 'It's a good story already. I want to get out of this place.'

Dan smiled approval. Ri looked ahead, alert, his camera on his shoulder, ready to film anything that happened.

Thompson came out of the building and said he was going back to the rear, that the camera crew and I could stay here or go back with him as we wished. I said we would go with him.

'Saddle up!' Nuanez shouted and the group began its procession back to the battalion command post, single file. First the scouts, then the antisniper team, and then the major walked away from the CP and back toward the rear, followed by the radio operator, me, Ri, Dan, and the rest of the Marines. I felt relief to be going back, my first steps on the way home.

We stopped to do an interview when we were safely away from the front line. Thompson stood with his shoulders straight and spoke in a confident voice.

"This is really a formidable, fortified position," he said. "I just can't imagine any one being more difficult than this right here. So, we'll get it sooner or later. It'll just take a little time."

An artillery shell shrieked overhead and exploded nearby, causing the ground to shake. I ducked, disappearing from Ri's picture frame for a second. Thompson did not blink, just paused a beat and continued.

"Hopefully, the weather will improve and we can get the maximum amount of air support and the support that we really want," he said. "And I don't think it'll be tough at all."

His confidence seemed extraordinary. Ten hours earlier, struggling to stay awake at his map table in the battalion CP, he had looked like a casualty. Now he spoke with the measured assurance of one who had just finished a training course at Quantico. Not only Thompson and Ernie Cheatham, the commander of 2/5 south of the river, and Mike Gravel, CO of 1/1, but most of the Marine officers in Hué were confident, self-assured, determined. They also seemed calm, almost serene, not at all nervous. I couldn't figure it out. Calling it good public relations with the press was too simple, though it may have been a factor. No one else could act so well-composed in these circumstances. It wasn't tranquilizers either; their minds were too quick. I couldn't tell whether it was their individual characters, their officer's training, combat experience (or lack of it), vanity, or the deepest part of their traditional Marine Corps identity that generated such behavior. Among themselves, they called it command presence.

The column moved on. The point scout came to a narrow dirt road that our route had to cross. The road was perfectly straight in both directions. The surface was elevated about two feet above the surrounding terrain to keep it from flooding. The scouts ran across one at a time, bent low, followed by the antisniper team and other Marines, running fast. Thompson walked calmly across the road without looking to the side, his head up and shoulders back, the picture of self-control. The radio operator followed a few steps behind. I wanted to run across quickly but the radioman was in the way so I walked, the third slow man in a column.

A bullet came down the road from left to right, fast and close, leading me by an inch. I heard the compressed air as the round went by, buzzing on a straight line down the middle of the road, head high, the sound of a big fat bumblebee in a hurry. The bullet passed close enough for me to feel a faint breeze on my forehead at the pressure of its passing. I heard no sound of the shot from the rifle of the sniper.

Safely on the other side of the road, Dan looked at me for a moment with an expression of incredulity. Then his face broke into a flowering Buddha smile. "Daily miracle," he said, laughing with his eyes.

The near miss with the sniper pushed me over the edge of self-control. Every time a shell burst I ducked for cover, even when no one else did. It was involuntary. All my concentration was needed just to give the appearance of holding the fear in check. By the time Ri, Dan and I got back to the battalion supply point where the mortar round had come through the roof the day before, all I could focus on was the idea of getting somewhere safe. Inside, my heart was cold, cold as stone, all compassion drained out of it. We had our film story in the can and I wanted to be out of Hué.

The supply point was busy. Marines were unloading C ration cases and water cans from trucks that had come up from the rear. Working hard, they stacked them in the courtyard and transferred them onto mules for delivery to the front. The sun was hidden by clouds but the air was warming. Heavy firing came from the direction we had left but no one paid attention.

I asked the corporal in charge if anyone was going to the rear.

'The lieutenant needs to talk with the doc at the aid station,' he said, 'so he'll be going down that way in a while.' He looked at me closely.

'Why don't you guys take it easy and we'll let you know when he's ready,' he said. In combat, veterans can often tell by your eyes what's going on in your mind.

I told Ri and Dan what was happening and looked around for a place to sit down in safety. The same room I had used the day before was empty. I went inside and sat against the wall. I wasn't physically tired—the walk up to the line had not been far—but I was exhausted by what had happened with the sniper. To be safe, we needed to get another half mile or so down the road to the medical aid station and the helicopter landing zone next to it. It was not safe to walk it by ourselves.

The kitten appeared in the doorway and turned its head from side to side, surveying the room. Then it walked straight toward me, all feline nonchalance, no fear. I had forgotten about our meeting the day before.

"So, you're still around, huh, cat?" I said. I hadn't expected it to survive.

The kitten walked up and sniffed one of my boots. It sat casually, as I held out my hand, and sniffed my fingers.

"Want some C rats?" I said, smiling. The kitten looked at me with indiff-erence. 'Bet you couldn't handle a real rat.'

There was nothing illogical about talking to a cat. It kept me from think-ing about myself.

All that was left to eat was a can marked "beef slices." I opened it with the P-38 and cut the precooked meat into small pieces. I held them out, one at a time, on the tips of my fingers. The kitten snatched the food with its teeth and swallowed without chewing.

"Guess you really are hungry." I gave it the meat as fast as it swallowed. If I left my fingers extended an instant too long, it bit me with small sharp teeth.

'Glad *you* like this stuff. Nobody else does.'

I cut up the rest of the food and set the can on the floor. The kitten gob-bled it greedily. When it had finished eating it licked the juice from the can until it was clean. Its eyes blinked involuntarily, the fleas on its head crawling under its eyelids. One eye was half closed and red.

I took the towel from around my neck and soaked a corner of it in water from a canteen, then held the kitten behind the shoulders and washed some of the fleas and dirt from its face. The kitten did not resist. I scrubbed the top of its head with the wet corner of the towel and dug the dirt and fleas out of its ears with my fingertips. Then I washed the filth off its mouth and rubbed its chin and whiskers clean. There was no time to clear away the infestation of fleas and lice on its body; that would take a bath.

'There,' I said, 'is that better?'

The kitten sat next to the empty can, licked the fur on its foreleg and completed washing its face. The corners of its mouth seemed to be turned up in a permanent smile. When it finished cleaning itself, the kitten moved closer and licked the back of my hand.

The Marine corporal walked into the room.

'Better get your people together,' he said. 'The lieutenant's leavin in a couple of minutes.'

He looked at the kitten. 'Looks like you got a friend there. He don't come near any of us.'

'Who does it belong to?' I stood up and strapped on my gear.

'Don't know,' the corporal said. 'Must've belonged to that family got blown away yesterday.' He said nothing for a second. 'Better get going.' He turned and walked out of the house.

I went to the doorway and paused, looking down at the kitten next to the empty C ration can. An emotion stirred.

"So long, cat," I said, repressing the feeling. "Hope you make it."

Ri and Dan waited outside. We climbed into the back of a jeep and squeezed in next to the camera gear and packs. The driver, a clean-faced teenager with black PFC bars on the lapels of his fatigue collar, sat at the wheel. The front seat of the jeep was empty, the lieutenant still in the house. A radio in the jeep hissed softly. Minutes passed.

My confidence was coming back. I figured that if we made it safely to the aid station, we would have the rest of the afternoon to find a ride to Phu Bai. Helicopters had been coming in and taking off from the LZ all morning, bringing in supplies and replacements, taking away wounded and dead. If we got to Phu Bai by six o'clock, I knew a helicopter squadron that flew back to its base in Danang every day just before sunset. Danang was relatively secure. The press center had hot food and cold beer and air-conditioned rooms with beds and clean linen. China Beach and the South China Sea would be waiting in the morning.

The driver went into the house to find the lieutenant. *Going home now,* I thought. *Finally getting out of this place.* The back of the jeep felt secure. Dan smiled. Ri looked around, camera ready.

I thought about the kitten. *Poor devil will probably starve. If the fleas and lice don't finish it first.*

An idea appeared. *Why not take it out of here? Down to Danang, or Saigon even.*

Nah, another part of me answered. *Too much trouble. Too far to travel. Not worth it.*

The lieutenant emerged from the doorway of the house, map under his arm, talking with another Marine.

A sudden surge of inspiration struck me, an inexplicable impulse, a compulsion stronger than my self-will.

What the hell? I said to myself. *Why not?*

I climbed out of the jeep and called to the lieutenant, 'Wait one, will you?' and hurried into the house. The kitten sat next to the empty C ration can washing itself, contented. I rushed forward and seized it.

"Come on, cat," I said. "Stick with me."

Waiting by the side of the jeep, the lieutenant smiled as I got in with the kitten in my hand. I stuffed it into the top left pocket of my fatigue jacket and snapped the flap around its head. Its face appeared, eyes frightened.

'You taking that thing?' the lieutenant said, swinging himself into the jeep.

'Why not?' I said, embarrassed. 'It doesn't have a family.' I suspected it would not be the last question about the cat I'd hear.

The driver put the jeep in gear, backed around in the courtyard, and drove down the road to the rear, fast.

What was I doing? I didn't know. The compulsion to take the cat was so strong I didn't care. I was determined now to save it, to protect its new life. It gave me something to worry about instead of myself. Besides, if I didn't look after it, no one would. Its chances of survival were practically zero. Also, I was heading home, could afford a small gesture of charity. The farther we got from the front, the more my small evanescent spark of compassion glowed.

The driver hit the brakes hard and the jeep skidded to a stop outside the medical aid station. A pair of Quonset huts with curved tin roofs stood side by side facing the road. A Vietnamese family waited outside one of the entrances. The cat was off the jeep first, thrown out by me. From my jacket pocket, the kitten had injected its needle-sharp claws through the heavy fabric of the coat, the fatigue shirt, the undershirt and finally into my skin. Then it had scratched vigorously, drawing blood, digging a trench in my chest. When it tired of scratching, it chewed into the button snap of the flap on the pocket, trying to unfasten it.

"Cat's more trouble than it's worth," I said as the kitten landed on the ground.

"Meeow! Meeow!" Ri and Dan shouted, pointing and laughing. The kitten sniffed the dirt at the side of the road.

"Keep an eye on it, will you?" I said, walking to one of the Quonset huts. I didn't understand what amused them so much about the cat.

The air inside the aid station was hot, humid and stuffy. Several Marines sat on the concrete floor near the entrance, their arms and shoulders limp, their faces impassive. Farther inside, four stretchers were rigged on benches for operating tables, empty at the moment.

A second lieutenant from the Marine press office in Danang, a friendly young officer with a stubby red mustache, introduced me to the U.S. Navy doctor in charge. Drinking coffee from a plastic cup, the surgeon said that the fighting had been light so far today and all his physical injury cases had been medevac'd to the field hospital in Phu Bai. But, he said, so many combat casualties had come through in the past week, he wondered how much longer the division could keep 1/5 in the line.

'We've got some serious cases of combat fatigue,' he said quietly, almost under his breath. He nodded toward the Marines near the door.

'Some of them have lost buddies,' he said. 'They see people they know, wounded, carried through here. A couple of them are in shock. Not much we can do for them except keep them sedated. But this is not the right place for them. They can hear the shells and that's not good for recovery. They really should be given a long rest, somewhere quiet.'

I felt sorry for the Marines but my priority was to get out of Hué.

'Any chance of a chopper?' I said.

The redheaded lieutenant answered. 'Nothing scheduled all afternoon. Might be something late, but don't count on it. Clouds are pretty low.'

It was not my practice to press the issue in situations like this. If a chopper came in, wonderful, another daily miracle. If one did not, so be it, nothing we could do. This time, though, I was more anxious than usual to get out. The prospect of another night in Hué worried me. I told the press office lieutenant we had a strong story about the situation at the front and needed to get it on the air as soon as possible. I said I felt a responsibility to Major Thompson and his men to tell people in the States what they were going through. I mentioned some of the details. The lieutenant said he understood and would do what he could.

I went back to the entrance where three Marines sat on the cement floor. They were silent, unmoving, barely breathing, their faces empty, eyes staring at the walls. It seemed as if their consciousness was suspended, their minds somewhere else. Something in their expressions spoke of sorrow and depression, of deep scalding trauma, of nerves that had snapped. I sat opposite them with my back to a wall.

Not knowing what to do, I got out a canteen, took a sip of water and offered it to the Marine across from me. He looked up out of a daze and took it, drank some and passed it back. His hands and arms moved without strength, listless. The third Marine moved closer.

'You been up there?' he asked, motioning toward the front.

'Yes.'

'Did you see a guy named Lawhorn?'

'I don't know,' I said. 'What's he look like?'

'Colored dude, with Delta Comp'ny.'

I thought for a moment. 'I don't know. I was with Delta this morning. It was pretty quiet. They might get pulled out of the line today. They don't have many people left.'

'Man, I hope you're right,' he said and leaned back against the wall.

One of the Marines sat on the floor with his legs straight in front of him, staring forward. The weariness in his eyes went beyond ordinary exhaustion. He was about nineteen or twenty, round-faced and tanned with normal features and light fuzz where a beard would be. He was not wearing a utility hat or helmet and there was no sign of his weapon or field pack. His green-gray fatigues were dirty, his dark hair longer than Marines wear it anywhere but in extended combat. His boots, mud-caked and split, told as much of the story as the empty look in his eyes.

'How's it going?' I said.

He did not move, did not acknowledge me. He stared unblinking into the distance. Though he looked at the wall his gaze went beyond the Quonset hut, beyond the red brick battlements of the Citadel, beyond Vietnam and its vicissitudes of violence and pain, to somewhere far away, private and safe.

'What happened to him?' I asked the others.

The Marine who had asked about Lawhorn said, 'Don't know. He's from Second Platoon, that's all I know.'

Shell shock. Battle fatigue. Combat shock. In World War II, traumatized Marines were said to have the thousand-yard stare. In World War I, British officers with shell shock were evacuated to the rear, mainly to special hospitals in England and Scotland. Enlisted men with the same condition were shot for cowardice or desertion.

The Marine had lived in the line for days, his body embedded in the earth until it had become part of it, moving on his stomach like a snake, falling asleep exhausted and waking up tired. His senses had absorbed fire and blast, cries of the wounded from no-man's-land, the silences. Most of the men around him had been hit but he had not. He had seen his friends' bodies pierced by flying steel, their blood draining away in the dirt, and so finally the fuses of his modest self-control snapped. Some internal regulator switched off his external senses from the unbearable reality of the Citadel, shut down his nervous system, located a quieter, safer place in the dreamy interiors of his mind, and left him alone. He was finished with the war. His mind had taken refuge in another reality.

Everyone who went through close combat in the war was like him to some degree: more or less isolated, cut off from reality, lost in other worlds, at least in the mind. The war just got to him sooner. Who's to say he was less sane than anyone else? His condition had nothing to do with mental stability or strength of character or courage or cowardice or being a good Marine. My guess was that it had more to do with his tolerance for insanity.

Outside the medical aid station, Ri and Dan sat by the road, their legs crossed, their faces smiling—silent Buddha statues. No kitten. I looked behind the Quonset hut and the trees by the road.

"Where's the cat?" I said.

Ri and Dan covered their mouths with their hands and giggled, like children sharing a secret joke. Tears formed in Dan's eyes. He pointed to the second Quonset hut, chuckling.

I opened the door and looked inside. The one long room was hot and noisy and crowded with Vietnamese soldiers and civilians. The smell was of fish sauce and cigarette smoke and old sweat. A doctor in a green operating gown stood at the far end of the room. Soldiers with bandages sat on the floor chatting with their relatives. As I entered, the talking stopped and everyone looked around. I was the only non-Vietnamese among them. At the edge of my vision I saw the kitten run behind a stretcher. I moved toward it, stepping over wounded soldiers, apologizing. Some of the Vietnamese giggled, discreetly. The kitten peeked from behind the stretcher, saw me coming, then hopped farther away. I stumbled over someone on the floor and nearly fell. The Vietnamese laughed. The kitten escaped. More laughter, louder now, more open. I felt like one of the fools in a silent film. The soldiers and their families were pointing at me and the kitten and speaking rapidly to one another and laughing hard at the same time. I chased the kitten into a corner. It was trapped now and froze in place, back to the wall, waiting for me. I feinted to one side and lurched to the other, falling on my hands and knees, sprawling across the floor and reaching out with one hand just in time to seize it. Wild laughter came from the crowd.

"Okay, cat," I said, holding it tight. "From now on you stay with me."

Outside, Ri and Dan looked at the tiny head peeking out of my snapped-down coat pocket and laughed.

"Meeow! Meeow!" they said, pointing. The cat began to scratch my chest. I found a piece of cardboard and put it under the jacket pocket.

When it was quiet, I said, "What's the Vietnamese word for cat?"

"Cat?" they said and looked at one another.

"Yeah, cat," I said, "C-A-T."

"Oh, *le chat!*" Ri said in French.

"Right. How you say in Vietnamese?"

"Vietnamese say, *May-oh*," he said. Both of them chuckled. They repeated the word several times, using a different musical tone and stress for each syllable.

I asked Dan to write the word in my notebook. He took my pen and wrote in fine thin letters, *M È O.*

"Okay," I said, "that's it. The cat's name is Mèo." I pronounced it *Mee-oh*.

"No, no, no!" they cried. "Must say *May-oh*."

"*Mao*," I said, sounding the name of the Chinese leader.

"No, no! *May-oh*."

They said it again slowly, drawing out the tones, and waited for me to try, patiently, teaching a child.

When I got the tones right and said "*May-oh*," they cheered, clapped their hands together, smiled brightly. Then they giggled.

The cat now had a name: "Mèo," pronounced *May-oh*.

The Marine lieutenant with the red mustache came out of the aid station and called us together. He said he was taking a truck down to the river to meet a Navy boat that would soon be bringing in a load of replacements. When it was finished, he said, the boat would go back down the river to the rear. 'It's your best bet to get out of Hué today,' he said. Ri, Dan and I agreed to go along. It would take longer, but it would get us out. After a few minutes, a large flatbed truck pulled up at the aid station, took us and our gear aboard, and started down the road toward the river. The kitten got through the cardboard and started to dig a foxhole in my chest. I dropped it on the metal floor of the truck. The tailgate was up and too high and smooth for it to climb. Again, the thought occurred that the kitten was more trouble than it was worth.

We arrived at the river and stopped at a muddy landing point. There was no pier or dock, just a dirt road that ran down to the water's edge. The river was narrow and black. To the left, it disappeared into a sharp right-hand bend. To the right, it ran into the main channel of the Huong Giang River, dividing the city. A short spur off the main road connected the landing point with the road back to the aid station. Both sides of the road were occupied by single-story Vietnamese houses. People came out to watch. Other than Ri and Dan, they were the first Vietnamese I had seen outdoors all day. The Marine driver parked the truck on sloping ground in front of the landing point. Across the river, a dense growth of wild palm trees and tropical brush grew down to the riverbank.

Short bursts of sharp AK fire came from the other side of the river. The lieutenant ran for the cab of the truck to get his rifle, shouting at the driver to move the truck behind the houses. Ri, Dan and I ran behind the truck. With shots that close, we assumed they were aimed at us. I found cover in the doorway of a house facing away from the river. Bullets ripped into the bamboo rooftops across the street and kicked up shreds of straw like puffs of sand. The driver parked the truck in the street where it was screened by the houses and got out with his rifle to find cover. The kitten sat on the roof of the cab of the truck, its nose sniffing the air, a climber on the summit.

Behind me, I heard the door of the house open. I panicked. *This is it,* I thought. *The house is full of VC and they're coming out to finish us off. I'm going to die.* I looked up on my hands and knees to see a barefoot man in his late thir-ties wearing an old-fashioned BVD undershirt and wrinkled boxer shorts standing in the doorway with sleep in his eyes. It was siesta time. First one, then another, and then a third child peeked out from around and between the man's legs to look at me. I was cowering on all fours with bullets buzzing into the rooftops across the street. Terrified, I said to the man, "I'm a jour-nalist, *'Bao-chi,'* not a soldier. See, no gun!" The man looked at me with bewilderment.

The children saw the kitten on the cab of the truck in front of the house and cried with delight. They pointed their fingers at it and shouted in shrill, high-pitched voices. None of them seemed frightened, as if the shooting were no more than traffic noise. The kitten looked down from the cab of the truck and measured the distance to the ground, leaning on its front legs, try-ing to find a way down. For a moment I felt proud of him.

The shooting slowed. I got up and ran away from the doorway along the line of houses to the corner of the spur leading to the river. The lieutenant was crouched down, M-16 in his hand, barrel up, waiting. He did not have a radio. 'The VC are on the other side of the river,' he said. 'They're shooting at something around the bend, maybe the supply boat, not us. A few rounds comin our way. Don't worry,' he said looking into my eyes.

After about ten minutes, the firing stopped. I asked the lieutenant if he would take us back to the aid station. 'Maybe there'll be a chopper,' I said, 'you never know.'

He listened politely and replied, 'I've got orders to wait for the supply boat.'

'The boat will never get through all that fire,' I said. 'Maybe it turned back. We could wait all night.' The late afternoon light was fading.

The lieutenant seemed sympathetic. He said something about "the Marine Corps way of doing things," but I sensed his ambivalence. At the Marine press center in Danang, where he was based, he was friendly, polite, helpful and good-natured—a true officer-gentleman. Ordinarily, he would have done anything possible to help us get a story, protecting our lives included. It was part of his job. But I knew him only as a public information officer, a PIO, and now he was acting as an infantry officer. If the boat arrived with casualties from the fight on the river and there was no truck to meet them, lives might be lost. The lieutenant waited for the boat. Another hour passed. The boat did not come.

Later, with the light almost gone, he decided to go back to the aid station. 'No chance of the boat coming up the river at night,' he said. 'They'd never find that landing in the dark.'

As the truck pulled up at the aid station, a big Marine helicopter was starting its engines. Wounded Marines were being carried on stretchers up the ramp and into the back of the fuselage, their fatigues and bandages blowing in the wind of the rotors. One of the Marines limped along with a leg wound. Navy corpsmen guided the three Marines with combat shock onto the helicopter with care, holding them by the arms like blind men. Ri ran forward to get a few shots. I shook hands with the lieutenant and thanked him for getting us back in time.

'You're really lucky to be getting a ride out this evening,' he shouted over the noise of the engines.

'Daily miracle!' I shouted back. 'Second one today.' There was more than enough room on the chopper for Ri, Dan, the kitten and me.

The pilots flew fast and low, skimming over the trees, banking sharply with the contours of the river, rising and descending and accelerating in swift undulating turns to confuse anti-aircraft gunners on the ground. Each time the CH-46 turned and dived, we gripped the aluminum seat supports, clenching our teeth, feeling the G force in the seats of our pants like dead-weight.

When the chopper reached the coast, the pilots pulled up through the clouds into the brighter light of early dusk and turned south toward Phu Bai. The sun hung in a fire-red sphere over the Annamite mountains to the west.

The air was clean and dry. I smiled at the three Marines from the aid station but their faces were vacant. One of them stared with dark hollow eyes out the window, looking out over the green-brown fields of rice below, beyond embattled Hué and the sand-white coastline, past the dark blue water of the South China Sea and the Pacific Ocean, focused on something infinitely farther away—truly a stare of a thousand miles.

The kitten scratched through the inside of my fatigue jacket and dug into my chest. I threw it on the floor of the helicopter and reached for my flask of cognac. The ritual drink. As usual, the first sip went down like acid. I passed it to Ri and Dan and the Marines and they passed it to the door gunner of the CH-46. The mood lightened a little.

"What the fuck is that?" one of the Marines shouted, pointing toward the floor near the front of the chopper.

We turned to look. In the middle of the aisle, dwarfed by rifles and field packs and combat boots, the kitten climbed slowly up the inclined plane of the helicopter floor, straining to keep its balance on the vibrating metal, heading toward the cockpit, the highest place it could find.

'Holy shit!' one of the Marines said.

'Man, will you look at that!'

'Hey! Who put that fuckin rat on board?'

The distraction brought some marginal relief to the Marines with the sad-eyed faces. The flask went around again. Two Marines looked at each other and shook their heads as if to say, Do you believe this? Their faces smiled a fraction.

The kitten disappeared. I was too tired to get up and look for it. Several minutes later, the door gunner came down the aisle, pointed his thumb at the cockpit and shouted, 'Pilot wants a word.'

I dragged myself up. The pilot and copilot were laughing. The kitten was sitting on the shoulder of the copilot, its claws in the heavy canvas straps of his seat belt. It sniffed the air, looking in all directions, trying to get a bearing.

The pilot shook his head. "What's this war coming to, anyway?" he said.

The copilot laughed.

When the helicopter landed at Phu Bai, I gave the kitten to Ri and Dan with instructions not to let it out of their sight. They promised. I hitched a ride to the Navy hospital to visit Al Webb, a United Press International reporter who had been wounded in Hué the day before. I did not know

Webb well but I respected him for his work and thought a visit might cheer him up. When I found his bed and called his name he looked up in surprise, then astonishment, as if at a ghost.

Webb said the Marines told him this morning that I was dead, shot in the same fight that wounded him in the Citadel. I said I was at the battalion CP at the time, waiting for Major Thompson. 'Well,' he said, 'it says something about the fucked-up reporting system, doesn't it?' I briefed him on what happened after he left Hué and promised to visit his office in Saigon and tell his colleagues how he was. Webb was brave. The only time he showed the pain was when he tried to move in the narrow bed.

Ri, Dan, Mèo and I rode an Air Force C-123 from Phu Bai to Danang. We introduced the kitten to the crew before takeoff and asked them to try not to step on it. In flight—a loud shuddering fiercely vibrating ride (a C-123 was a flying truck)—the kitten went toward the front of the plane, past the legs of the crew chief and up the steps to the cockpit. It climbed the back of the copilot's seat like a tree. To the amusement of the crew, Mèo remained on the copilot's shoulder for the rest of the flight.

At the Danang press center, Ri, Dan and I went to work immediately to write and record the narration, then ship the film cans to Saigon. By the time we finished, it was suppertime. We washed our hands and faces, left the kitten in the CBS barracks room, and went to the restaurant—a Third Marine Amphibious Force establishment that was furnished like a New Jersey roadhouse and catered American food for journalists, information officers and their guests.

The dining room was crowded and noisy. I went to the bar to buy a drink for the crew. Immediately, the room became silent. A reporter came up, eyes wide, and shook my hand, as if to confirm I was there.

'For Christsake, Laurence, you're supposed to be dead!' he said.

'Yeah, so I heard.'

'So, what happened?'

'I didn't get the message.'

A group gathered at the bar, shaking hands and slapping my back, exclamations flying.

'Headline,' a newspaper reporter shouted, *'Reporter Back from the Dead.'*

'Files Eyewitness Exclusive.'

'Hell Not So Bad,' he says.

'Hué's close enough,' I suggested.

'Hey, man,' another said, 'so what's it like in Forty-Two Corps?' (This was a mythical zone in the war, a fantastic place that had been invented by a few overly imaginative journalists, but no one had managed to find it yet.)

'Don't know,' I said, 'Never got there.'

'You better call your office. I think they told New York you're dead.'

'So when's the funeral?'

'The hell with the funeral, we'll just have the wake. Starting now.'

'Glad you guys didn't have to grieve very long.'

'Grieve, hell. We were just trying to figure out who was going to get your typewriter and stuff.'

I couldn't buy a drink all evening.

FEBRUARY 21, 1968

Mèo, Ri, Dan and I rested at the Marine Combat Information Bureau in Danang. We were greatly relieved to have got safely out of Hué and grateful to be enjoying the relative comforts of the press center. The combination softened my previous sense of purpose about going home immediately. The bureau chief in Saigon implored me to stay on in Danang to help CBS cover continuing developments in the Tet Offensive. A number of special programs were being planned. New York wanted me to stay on the story. 'Our whole operation is stretched thin,' he said. 'We don't have anybody to replace you. Stay up there for a few more days and then you can go home.' I agreed.

The CIB was a crowded compound of offices and living quarters occupying about two acres on the western shore of the Danang River, which led to the harbor that opened to the South China Sea. It was inhabited by military and civilian journalists who processed raw information about the war for relay to the world outside. The CIB was a ramshackle place: part military camp, part civilian motel, part news office. The compound was constructed of single-story buildings of plastered cinder block and wood with cheap metal roofing and spare furnishings: secondhand tables, chairs and metal frame beds with thin mattresses. For journalists, it was primitive but comfortable, without being luxurious. The walls of the rooms were covered with bare white plaster that gave off an unpleasant glare from the fluorescent lighting. Smells from the open sewers behind the buildings sometimes invaded the living quarters. The whole complex looked slightly seedy, as if it had once been kept clean and modern but had slowly deteriorated over the course of the war. One rumor said the press center had been a roadside motel for travelers between Saigon and Hanoi before the country was divided in the 1950s. Another said it had been a bordello for French officers in the first Indochina War. These days it was a major production center for news of the war in I Corps, sending out military as well as civilian dispatches. Its simple comforts—bars, restaurants, outdoor movies, basketball court—provided a modicum of basic American culture, but it was as distant from the Danang of the Vietnamese and their ways of life as America was from Vietnam. Similar U.S. military bases operated all over the country.

The kitten was confined at all times to the network barracks room to prevent it from wandering onto the main road nearby and being struck by one of the military convoys that rumbled over the primitive road in puffs of pale brown dust. The Vietnamese women who cleaned the rooms and washed journalists' clothes produced a scrap of old blanket for the kitten to sleep on and gave it leftover bits of food in plastic saucers. Mèo was uncomfortable in the strange new place. It had already expressed its aversion to Americans—a habit it picked up in Hué—and this place was swarming with them: mostly reporters, photographers and Marines, but also a few civilian aid workers, construction men, government officials, transient entertainers, and an occasional spy. On that first night in the barracks, Mèo paced up and down the linoleum floor in the grip of a great obsession. It prowled the edges of the narrow room, sniffed the legs of the chairs and tables, inspected each crack a dozen times. At the far corner of the room, it explored the toilet area, ran its nose along the drains and scratched the loose plaster where it joined the floor. It jumped up on one of the cots that lined both sides of the room and tried to climb the wall. Methodical, tireless, it stopped searching only to eat and rest—a prisoner of war planning an escape.

Outside the network room, the press center seethed with intrigue. Aggressive, competitive men and women tried to gather exclusive information about the war in I Corps and send it by phone to their offices in Saigon without revealing their stories to the rest of the press corps. The only means of communication out of the CIB were a few, inefficient military telephone lines whose signals were weak. Reporters had to shout each word or phrase of their stories over thick static as loud as they could in order to be heard at the other end by a colleague in Saigon. Sometimes the information got no farther than the courtyard outside and the ears of their competitors. At night, the compound was usually quiet. Reporters wrote feature stories in their rooms or drank beer and talked with their colleagues in one of the Marine bars or watched the evening movie on the terrace. Some played cards or wrote letters or read books. The more industrious took their civilian or military sources to dinner and talked about the fine details of the war. A few sat by the river smoking joints, dreamily watching the lights on the water. Others went into downtown Danang for more physical entertainment.

From time to time, a few journalists and Marines came to the CBS room to visit the kitten. All they'd heard was that it came out of Hué and had crazy eyes. It was true. Mèo's eyes were wild, untamed, furious at being captive. Visitors looked at it and asked how old it was and how it got out of Hué and what it was like in the Citadel and anything else we could tell them about the battle.

The only news most of the troops had heard was broadcast on the Armed Forces Radio Network. Announcers quoted U.S. officials in Saigon as saying the battle for Hué was no more than "a mopping-up operation" and would be over in a few days. The few days had become weeks. Officials had been making the same predictions since early February and the story was getting tired, as tired as the official claim a few months earlier that the VC and North Vietnamese were too badly hurt to launch a major offensive in the war. Marines had been mopping up in Hué for more than three weeks now, thousands of people were dead, and some of the stories making it back to Danang by word of mouth were as ghastly as anyone had ever heard in Vietnam. That information was not broadcast on AFRN. How could they talk about a cold-hearted killing of a prisoner? Or the torture of a civilian? Or the sad face of a young man with combat fatigue? Or the fading strength of Marines in the line? The true facts of what was going on in Hué or anywhere else were not broadcast on AFRN. In the bubble of unreality that surrounded the daily war news, the farther away you were from the front lines, the less you knew what was actually going on. Men like Lyndon Johnson and Robert McNamara and William Westmoreland, who were farthest from the front and consequently knew least about the reality of the war, were the very ones who were planning the strategy to fight it.

Ri, Dan and I locked Mèo in the room and drove across a causeway to the headquarters of 3d Marine Amphibious Force. The III MAF commander in Vietnam, Lieutenant General Robert E. Cushman, had agreed to be interviewed for a special broadcast on the Tet Offensive, particularly the battle of Hué. Producers in New York wanted Cushman's assessment of the military situation in I Corps, the northern provinces of South Vietnam under his command.

Ri and Dan set up the lights, camera and sound equipment in the general's small, neatly furnished office. When he arrived, Cushman shook hands with each of us and asked in a friendly voice what we had seen of the fighting. I told him we had been in the Citadel with 1/5 yesterday and that the troops were exhausted; they were being ground to nothing. It was a cruel price to pay, I said, for a few acres of territory. Listening, Cushman's eyes narrowed. The muscles tightened around his jaw and cheekbones. His face looked angry. I was afraid he might abort the interview, but I went ahead. Delta Company, I told him, had taken 75 percent casualties, and the other companies were almost as bad off. The understrength platoons were still two hundred meters from the southeast wall, going forward about fifty meters a day, at a cost of about ten to twenty Marines killed or wounded. There were several serious cases of combat fatigue, I said. Some of the Marines in the line were staring into space like zombies, waiting to lead the way into no-man's-land and be shot.

When I finished, Cushman said nothing. The room was quiet. Slowly, the features in his face changed. His expression went from anger to concern, then sympathy, as if he had not heard all of this firsthand before.

'General, it's bad up there,' I said, indicating the tone of our TV news report, now on its way to the States.

'I know,' General Cushman said, 'I know.' He nodded his head and sat down behind his desk and allowed Dan to attach the microphone to his uniform. Ri's camera rolled. Cushman said he knew the casualties in 1/5 were serious but that he was not involved in the hour-to-hour management of the battle.

"The gods of war are in their favor," he said. "Our firepower has been negated." He explained that because the flying weather was poor, Marine pilots could not bomb North Vietnamese positions and force them out of their bunkers where they could be attacked by ground troops.

"Still," he said, "we and the South Vietnamese have killed more than thirteen thousand enemy in I Corps since the start of the Tet Offensive. Militarily, they're not succeeding. I think they're playing for the world's press."

The Tet Offensive a publicity stunt? A way for the Communists to improve their image? That was a surprise. It was the first time anyone in authority suggested the attacks were calculated to affect public opinion. I wondered if it might be true.

It was an interesting idea. As it turned out, Cushman was right and wrong. The surprise attack and the record number of U.S. casualties helped turn American public opinion against the war, which led eventually to the U.S. withdrawal from Vietnam. But it was not the primary objective of these North Vietnamese attacks. By launching the Tet Offensive, the Communist high command in Hanoi wanted to inspire a general uprising of civilians all over South Vietnam to help them advance toward a final military victory. It was a grievous miscalculation. South Vietnamese civilians did not rise up, nor did they welcome the invading northern troops any more than they had welcomed the Japanese or French or Americans. Civilians were afraid of the Communists' violent power, just as they were afraid of anyone with guns, so they obeyed orders and tried to stay out of the way. But they did not embrace them as liberators. The Tet Offensive was a military catastrophe for the Communists, their most serious defeat of the war. Veteran battalions and companies of Viet Cong troops, fighting for the National Liberation Front of South Vietnam, were destroyed in open warfare by more heavily armed U.S. and South Vietnamese forces. Most of the VC units never recovered. Although North Vietnam's long-term strategy was to exhaust American public support for the war, it was not the purpose of the Tet Offensive. American and South Vietnamese armed forces inflicted enormous human losses on the Viet Cong and North Vietnamese, while suffering heavily themselves. However, by consistently lying to the American public in the period leading up to Tet, the U.S. government lost the support of a majority of its own people. At Tet, America was winning the war and losing it at the same time.

The battle for Hué was now in its twenty-second day and Cushman declared, "The troops are tired. Our Marines in there require relief. They've been fighting all this time. We want fresh troops rather than more troops." His candor was refreshing.

After the interview, one of the general's aides asked to speak to me privately. 'Don't worry,' the officer said, 'the Marines in Hué are being relieved. I can't say any more than that, but don't worry.' I learned later that a fresh company—Lima, 3/5—moved into the Citadel that afternoon and went straight into the lines. Bravo Company, which suffered heavy casualties, pulled out. The move spared the lives of the men who were most exhausted.

Ri and Dan carried their equipment to the outer office and packed it into cases. Hanging on the wall just outside the general's office, a picture frame caught my attention. It held a quotation that had been embroidered in colored thread on a piece of white linen.

The N.L.F. will entice the Americans close to the North Viet Nam border and will bleed them without mercy. In southern Viet Nam, the pacification program will be destroyed.

NGUYEN VAN MAI.

Nguyen Van Mai was a Communist official and the quotation appeared to have been taken from an enemy document captured some months earlier. It was a blueprint for the Tet Offensive, a condensed version of the overall Communist strategy, and it hung on the wall next to the door where General Cushman could see it each time he entered his office.

Back at the press center, I wrote a revised close for the story we had shipped the night before and recorded it on film and audiotape. The new close included the information that the Marines in Hué were being reinforced. It was shipped to Saigon in time to be fed on an audio circuit to New York and incorporated in the film story.

Mèo's reputation spread beyond the press center to the American bases around Danang—to the sprawling airfield at the edge of the city and the Navy boat docks along the coast. From time to time, visitors to the press center stopped by the room to look at the kitten, talk about it, and take pictures. It became known as the lucky little cat who survived the battle of Hué and made it out of the Citadel alive—the cat from Hué. Mèo took no notice of its celebrity. Detached and aloof, unwilling to behave like a pet, it was surly and arrogant. When visitors tried to get close and reached out their hands, it skittered away and hid under a bed or in the bathroom. Or else it tried to bite their hands. The visitors laughed. Only the Vietnamese women in baggy black pants who cleaned the room and washed clothes in the drainage canal behind the barracks got near it. It was fiercely anti-American, avoiding us at all times, biting and scratching when we managed to pick it up. I began to suspect that its sympathies might be with the other side.

★

With the battle of Hué near its end, Khe Sanh became the leading story of
the war. North Vietnamese regiments strengthened their encirclement of
the isolated base west of Hué near the Laotian border. They fired artillery at
it constantly. American losses went up. Some journalists made comparisons
with the military situation in 1954 before the final French defeat at Dien
Bien Phu.

I needed to find out more about what the Marines' high command was
thinking about Khe Sanh, what its strategies were. President Johnson was
reported to have demanded a guarantee from the Joint Chiefs of Staff that
Khe Sanh would not be lost. I asked for a background briefing from the senior intelligence officer at III MAF headquarters and drove to his office. The
J-2 was a rugged-looking man with rough skin, a small head and an abundance of energy who held the rank of colonel. His office was small and
cramped, large enough only for two people to sit comfortably. An air-conditioner built into the wall was turned off and the room was stuffy. Piles of
books, pamphlets and briefing papers were on his desk, dog-eared and
marked with red pencil. The literature included a collection of writing and
speeches of Vo Nguyen Giap, the North Vietnamese military commander;
Ho Chi Minh, the president; and other senior Communist officials. The
colonel was friendly. He recited statistical information about the situation
around Khe Sanh with comprehensive efficiency, giving an impression of
being educated, alert. As he finished the briefing, a curious intensity came
into his manner.

"Where do you think my counterpart is right now?" he said.

'Your counterpart?'

'Yeah, the People's Army J-2.'

"I don't know," I said, imagining an NVA corps staff officer in Laos or
Cambodia.

"You know where he is? In a *cave* somewhere. Out there." The colonel
waved his right hand at the wall, toward the west. "Probably in one of those
hills around Khe Sanh. Sleeping on a straw mat. Eating cold rice. *That's*
where he is."

His eyes glowed, little fireballs.

"And where the hell am I?" he said, shouting. "In an air-conditioned office
in a God damn headquarters!" He pointed his index finger sharply toward
the wall. "I should be out there! Sleeping on the ground! Like him!"

I smiled, embarrassed by his intensity, and got up to leave. We shook hands. On reflection, I understood what he meant. He was one of the many American colonels who were restless in their headquarters jobs. They wanted to be leading troops in battle. It often seemed as though every full colonel in Vietnam wanted a line infantry regiment or a brigade. Most saw their jobs as trivial compared with those in the field. They knew, of course, that colonels who commanded regiments or brigades in combat without making a mess of it usually got promoted to general, while most other colonels were forced to retire.

In the days that followed, Mèo wandered freely around the press center and returned to the barracks room only for meals and sleep. It was always on its guard, even with its eyes closed on the hot pavement outside the room, never deeply asleep. Its greatest danger was from reporters who drove their dilapidated jeeps into the compound at high speed, hurrying to file a story or make the start of the evening movie. Some drove recklessly out of habit. Mèo learned to recognize the sounds of grinding gears and revving engines and get out of the way before the old jeeps roared into the compound. Slowly, it began to grow bigger.

The war was close. Reporters could fly out to Khe Sanh on an Air Force or Marine cargo flight from Danang in one hour. Some journalists went up in the early morning, landed, ran for their lives across the tarmac, interviewed some of the officers and men while taking cover with them, waited out a barrage of incoming shells, took photographs and made notes, and then after a few hours caught an outgoing cargo flight and returned to the press center in late afternoon to file their stories and relax with a cold beer, shower and meal. It amazed and terrified and also delighted journalists that they could cover a war that way. Two- and three-man TV crews could go up and get enough dramatic action footage to have a story by early afternoon, ship it to Saigon by seven or eight o'clock, and retire to the press center restaurant in the evening to eat U.S. prime sirloin steaks and drink cold Budweiser, secure in the knowledge that their Saigon bureau chiefs would not force them to go back to Khe Sanh again for several days.

In the field, when Marines had been especially courteous, opening up and talking honestly, giving us a good story, I felt guilty about leaving them so soon to go back to the press center. Not because we were news vultures—most of us saw ourselves as messengers, not parasites—but because we hadn't stayed long enough to put our names down as truly having been there. Signing off a story with your name and "CBS News, Khe Sanh" gave the impression on the air that you were still there with the troops, taking it, when actually you were usually somewhere else, probably safe. By the time the story was shown on the network, we were back in Danang or Saigon, working on another story. We had it all—the war and comfort too. The Marines' *dis*comfort, taking all the risks without the rewards we had, made me fiercely sympathetic to the men on the line.

Gradually, over the next few days, my fear started to fade. For a while I leaped at loud noises, like Mèo. Then I got a hold on it, checking the impulse to jump or hit the deck, taking a deep breath instead, waiting for my heart to slow down again. The kitten, however, did not. A sharp sudden noise anywhere near and it went straight up on all four legs. A really close loud noise like a door slam and it got a full foot off the ground—legs stiff, fur bristling like a Halloween cat, eyes filled with fright. Then it ran off and hid in a safe place until its nerves settled down.

After a week of regular sleep, I began to feel lighter, able to breathe deeply, fully alive. Perceptions of time and reality changed. From the supercharged intensity of the Citadel, where every move had to be reckoned, my outlook shifted to the more relaxed routine of ordinary wartime. Just being able to sleep on a mattress with clean sheets and a pillowcase was a luxury. Coming out of Hué or Khe Sanh, Danang felt as refreshing as Hong Kong or Bangkok.

After work and on days off, journalists found amusement. Across the river, on the far side of the peninsula, China Beach provided a paradise of clean white sand, ocean swimming, bodysurfing, warm sunshine. Few others used the beach, least of all the Vietnamese, who hated the sun. For us, the atmosphere was idyllic. Sitting in the sand, leaning back on a blanket, smoking and drinking a little, staring across an ocean of pure blue water, you could imagine being on a beach in Hawaii or Tahiti, Florida or California. Closing your eyes, you might be anywhere. Perfect tranquillity. The lazy peaceful hours on China Beach were an antidote to the terror of the other places.

Amusements were simple. Late each afternoon, eight to ten Marine enlisted men who worked at the press center played basketball on an outdoor concrete court. The baskets and backboards were good quality, made in the States, and the concrete surface was reasonably smooth. In the games, physical contact was fundamental. Marines playing offense took the ball, dribbled it perfunctorily once or twice, and charged toward the basket in a straight line, head down, expecting to be hit. Most often they were. Marines on defense rarely gave ground. Collisions were common. It got so violent at times that reporters shouted from the sidelines, 'Hey! Why don't you wear your helmets?' and claimed the Marines kept score by the number of fractures they inflicted. They rarely bothered with a referee. When civilians got in the game, the Marines were exceptionally gentle, gave way for our modest drives and layups, did not steal the ball, did not try to block our shots. With us, it was as if they were playing officers. With one another, it was combat without weapons.

Downtown Danang was full of bars: rows of crude, bright-colored joints that catered to Americans from the military bases and construction gangs. Men got drunk and affectionate and imagined the Vietnamese bar girls actually cared for their company. It was only a charade, choreographed to the last move, but the women were convincing actors. 'Hey, man, you number one, you very handsome man,' they said in their limited repertoire of English compliments. And in the mellow, soft-focused reflection of an evening's drinking, far from the war, who could deny them?

At the big airbase south of town, Marine and Air Force pilots drank and sang and talked in the officers' clubs until two or three in the morning. Occasionally, they invited reporters to join them. The pilots were accomplished storytellers, raconteurs, and almost all the stories were about flying airplanes. They peeled off when it got late, one or two at a time, saying they had to catch a few hours before they got up and climbed into the cockpits of their F-4s and F-105s still charged with alcohol and took their million-dollar weapons systems into the naked air over North Vietnam. Laughing, the pilots said the world's greatest hangover cure was a lungful of pure oxygen from the tank in the cockpit. And nothing got you sober faster than discovering an inbound SAM on your radar screen.

Journalists drank too, some as long and hard as anybody, numbing themselves from the calamity they were covering. Coming in out of the field, drinking and smoking were what you did to shift the memory of what you'd seen to a place where it didn't keep you awake at night. Sometimes it worked. If you drank or smoked enough, you didn't dream. Certainly you didn't remember your dreams, which was just as important. But the sleep did not bring rest. You often awoke as tired as you were the night before. After a few days, the need for rest became so acute the effects were as frightening as what you were trying to forget. Sometimes you didn't get straightened out until you were back in the field.

Mèo's confidence was as unshakable as its appetite. It ate hamburger meat, leftover fish heads, canned tuna, warmed milk from the Marine kitchen. The kitten ate like a lion cub, attacking the food four or five times a day, as often as it was put on the floor, like it might be the last. Then it found a safe place and curled into a ball and slept. Sometimes, late in the evening when it was quiet, I was allowed to pick lice and fleas from its fur. Once or twice it slept on the blanket at the foot of the bed. If I moved my toes in the night, it bit them.

FEBRUARY 26, 1968

We heard the news at the press center. The battle of Hué was over. The last North Vietnamese soldiers in the Citadel had withdrawn during the night or were dead. The survivors walked into the hills west of the city with their wounded, their weapons, their prisoners, and their local Viet Cong cadre who had taken part in the failed attempt to promote a popular uprising and had revealed their identities to the local population. The NVA soldiers who were ordered to stay behind and fight to the end were buried in the rubble of bricks and stone where they died. Some were hunted down in narrow underground fighting positions (Americans called them spider holes) that became their graves. Both sides took few, if any, prisoners. An official news release said Marines were pushing into the suburbs of Hué to sweep for stragglers. Reporters coming back from the field said the grunts were edgy and exhausted but grateful it was over.

Late that afternoon, a few reporters and photographers sat on the stone patio of the press center along the river, staring across the water. They were dressed in shorts, sport shirts and sandals, wearing floppy hats in the fading sunlight, drinking beer and soda. One of them rolled a joint. They were more reflective than talkative. The news that it was over in Hué hung there, dominating thoughts, difficult to accept. Memories of the fight were alive in their dreams. They had been under fire with tired frightened Marines drawing on diminished reserves of energy and determination. Over the twenty-six days, they had seen the combatants become more alike, more akin to the most primitive warriors than to modern-day soldiers with different races and cultures, more savage than civilized, reduced finally to the mechanical actions of hunting, hiding and killing each other. At the end, all that really separated the two sides were their loyalties.

Sitting by the shore of the slow-moving river, the reporters tried to reconcile the severity of Hué with the serenity of Danang at this moment. The sun was behind them, its reddish light sparkling on the water, palm trees on the other side swaying in the soft ocean wind. The joint went around. Dana

Stone, the nonsmoker in the group, had stayed with the battle all the way through, from the fourth day to the end. Dana was not given to displays of emotion, so he joked about the absurdities he had seen, the poignancy. He had a good eye for it. Keith Kay, back from leave in Hong Kong, told the story of the Army captain at the MACV compound who invited Dana to take target practice and started a firefight. Everyone laughed. Mike Herr, a quiet, thoughtful writer, twenty-six years old, was working up a magazine article on the battle and made notes from time to time in a small notebook he carried in a shirt pocket. A few other journalists were there. Hué had been the longest, saddest battle any of them had covered, but it had also been the most thrilling, the one battle that had been like those in other wars. One of them shook his head.

'It was bad, man, really bad.'

'No shit, GI.'

'You're tellin me?'

'One of the Marines in there had "Hell Sucks" written on his helmet.'

'Hell sucks?'

'Yeah.'

'Far out . . .'

'I don't get it.'

'It was just an observation he was making.'

'Yeah, like, to hell and back.'

'Where's Audie Murphy when we need him?'

'Watching on TV, man, by the pool.'

The joint went around. The air was mild.

'I don't believe they did it.'

'Did what?'

'Got it all back.'

'Got what back?'

'You know, the city.'

'Yeah, for what?'

No one answered. The river moved slowly.

'Somebody said the Marines are gonna put David Greenway and Charlie Mohr in for medals, for carrying the wounded the other day.'

'Is that a fact?'

'It's what I heard.'

'Journalists aren't supposed to get medals, man.'

'What difference does it make?'

'Hell, they probably deserve it.'

'I don't know, doesn't seem right. Reporters running around playing soldier.'

'They didn't do what they did for a medal, man.'

'Of course not. But if they offer you a medal and you take it, you're playing the game. You're in it. Know what I mean? It's kind of a compromise. It makes you part of the story, in a way. We're supposed to be apart from what we cover. Observers, not participants.'

'Observer. That's a laugh.'

'So what do you do when you're in some horrendous shit and your unit is down to the last few guys and you're getting overrun? Stand up and say, "Excuse me, gentlemen, I'm an observer. I think I'll go home now?"'

No one spoke for long. Everyone was comfortable in the silence. Though they had been to Hué at different times and went in with different people, different companies, coming out of it they were attached to one another in ways they couldn't explain.

'What do you think they'll call it? Historians I mean?'

'Hey, that's right. This'll be one for the history books, won't it?'

'Battle of Hué, what else?'

'Battle of Hué City, man.'

'To distinguish it from what? Hué Province?'

'There is no Hué Province.'

'That's what I mean.'

'That's what the Marines call it, man, Hué City.'

'What the fuck do they know?'

'Well, they're not gonna call it the Battle of Danang, are they?'

'They could call it the Battle of Lost Illusions.'

'Or Lost Promises.'

'Yeah, Innocence Lost.'

'Paradise Lost, man.'

'Hué? A paradise? You shittin me?'

'They are never gonna put that city back together again.'

'Not the way it was.'

'You guys are fucking romantic. Hué is a shithole. Take my word for it. The Perfume River will always be filled with turds.'

'Always the cynic.'

'Realist, man.'

Another silence.

'One/Five really got their asses kicked.'

'Yeah, and kicked some too.'

'Nobody was taking prisoners.'

'Unless we were around.'

'I wonder how many people got killed. All told, I mean.'

'MACV will never tell.'

'MACV will never know.'

'Well, I heard the First Cav took as many casualties as the Marines. Got hit by all the NVA reinforcements coming down Route 1 tryin to get to Hué. Guy I met in Quang Tri said it was bad up there, really wicked, North Vietnamese had beaucoup rockets and shit.'

'Glad I don't have to go up there any more.'

'Yeah, man, Khe Sanh's bad enough.'

'Who're you kiddin? You love this shit. Couple a days you'll be dyin to get out there again.'

'Don't believe it.'

'Bored and restless . . . tired and scared. It's one or the other.'

'Name of the game.'

'Yin and yang, man.'

Some of us had been around long enough to have learned a little of the history of the war: from the centuries of conflict with the Chinese and Khmers, to the long occupation of the French and then the Japanese and then the French again, and now we Americans and our friends (the Koreans and Australians)—an unparalleled record of conflict and blood, resistance and repression. Reporters continued to read Vietnamese history even as they witnessed this version of it, contributing to contemporary perceptions in their daily work. Some of them saw this war, going on seven years now, as a continuation of all the others, as part of an unending Vietnamese war of independence. Finally, without being aware of it, they felt the history of Vietnam in their working bones, as if the war was in them, refracting through the prism of their reading and experience what they saw and photographed and wrote. Some of us visualized the war as a fog, a low malignant cloud that floated across the land, relentless, systematic, seeping into jungle forests, hamlets, villages, now invading the cities, infecting all who came in contact with it, Vietnamese and American, poisoning and corrupting everyone in its glooming mists.

'Well, man, Hué was worse than Ia Drang, you know. Went on so long. Had to be.'

'I don't know about that,' I said. 'Ia Drang was a real horror story. A hundred and fifty guys got it in one day. On one LZ. Like 90 percent casualties.'

'When was that?'

'Sixty-five. November.'

'Custer's outfit, Seventh Cav.'

'I know a guy was there, man. Print guy. Came back off LZ X-Ray and wasn't the same. A different guy, just shattered by it for a while.'

'It's hard to say which one was worse.'

'Who knows, man? I mean, really, who will ever know?'

'Doesn't matter. The last one you were in was the worst.'

'That's the truth.'

'Maybe they were the same, man. Hué and Ia Drang. Maybe they were exactly the same.'

The numbers came out later. Hué was the worst slaughter of the war—twenty-six days of violence and pain and more than ten thousand dead. When the wounded were added, the overall number of victims was much greater. The ten thousand dead included U.S. Marine and Army troops around Hué, South Vietnamese Army losses, VC and NVA dead, and all the civilians—like the family killed by the mortar in the house where I found the kitten. Far more civilians than combatants were killed. Marine officers said later the sight of so many civilian bodies—women and kids and old men—made them literally sick. Each time a platoon went forward they found another bunch, and threw up whatever was in their stomachs. No one kept count of the civilian dead.

Later, when mass graves were found, local authorities reported the organized slaughter of twenty-eight hundred people: South Vietnamese soldiers, police, civil servants, teachers, Catholics, foreigners (including the senior U.S. representative), diplomats, missionaries, priests and innocent bystanders who had seen too much—executed by NVA and VC troops. Some were found with their hands tied behind their backs with wire, beaten to death with clubs, buried outside the city along the routes the NVA and VC took when they withdrew. The actual number of people murdered was in dispute; the Communists claimed later that the dead were victims of American air strikes and artillery who had to be buried in a hurry in communal graves outside the city. But many of the dead were known enemies of the Communists, particularly the foreigners and civil servants. It seemed probable that at least hundreds had been singled out for liquidation.

More than half the city was damaged or destroyed; some estimates said 80 percent. Many of Hué's most precious treasures were looted, including ancient and priceless Cham sculpture that was hauled away from the Citadel palace in trucks by ARVN troops and criminals, the most ambitious of whom was a well-known Vietnamese journalist who transformed himself into a discerning and elegant antiques dealer with new shops in Saigon, Hong Kong and Singapore, claiming to his Western friends that he was preserving the treasures from the Communists, offering to sell you one at a good price.

In Hanoi, Saigon and Washington, the leading generals and politicians announced a great victory, each for its own side, as if the truth of what happened could be changed by formal proclamations of something as abstract as victory or defeat. For those who were there it was evident that nobody won, that the cost in lives and pain and fear and damage and grief and trauma overwhelmed everything, drowned it in blood, unless you counted your own survival as a small measure of achievement.

Overall, the scale of suffering and death in the Tet Offensive was staggering, not only in Hué. The North Vietnamese and Viet Cong had attacked with all the strength and cunning they could conceive. And even though they were forced to withdraw with terrible losses, they managed to inflict the heaviest toll of dead and wounded of the war on the United States and South Vietnam. In the week ending February 17, 1968, the number of American dead was reported as 543; the number of wounded 2,547. The implications for U.S. war policy were evident. The United States could not suffer losses at that rate, not in a war without end, not in a remote corner of Asia, the public would not accept it. By now, even the most traditionally patriotic, pro-military journalists were changing their minds about the war. They no longer saw it as a difficult but necessary undertaking in the struggle against communism, or even as a wasteful military deadlock, but as a lost cause, not worth American lives and treasure, ruinous to the Vietnamese. There were exceptions, but few.

When I heard it was over I thanked God. The last day of the battle was a Sunday. Bells rang in the Catholic churches of Danang. I wondered what

Thompson's battalion was doing, whether the sad-faced grunts who helped us get the story of Delta Company had made it through the week alive. In any case, I would probably never see them again. Part of me didn't care. It was too late to do anything anymore. For me the war was finished. My time to go was way overdue and I was anxious to get out. I had stayed in Danang to work on the latest network special and now I was ready to leave. I had been in so many bad places lately (another trip to Khe Sanh), my sleep had become an extension of my days in the field. Awake, I was tired much of the time.

My last night in Danang was spent drinking with Marine enlisted men and NCOs in their club at the press center. The outdoor restaurant was darker, quieter and more relaxed than the officers club, with checkered cloths on the tables and candles that flickered in the sheltered breeze. An officer sent word that reporters weren't allowed to fraternize with EMs and noncoms and that I would have to leave the club. The Marines said, 'Stay here. You're okay. The old man's got a bug up his ass. Don't worry about it.' They were combat photographers and reporters for *Leatherneck* and *Stars and Stripes* who had been at Hué and Khe Sanh and Con Thien. At one time or another over the past seven months we had been together in the field and shared information on getting the story. Anyone who spent time in the field developed a serious disregard for rear area rules and the staff officers who imposed them. We drank beer and talked about the war until we were drunk and stupid.

By now, Mèo was more comfortable with life at the network barracks room. It was allowed to roam freely around the press center. It had become one of the regulars. It behaved with an almost total absence of fear: darting in and out of doorways, poking its nose into strange corners, hanging out with the Vietnamese housekeepers, fishing with its paw in the canal behind the buildings, chasing everything smaller than itself, stalking small birds, lizards and crickets. It slept in a corner of the room and wailed at first light every morning that it was hungry and wanted everyone else awake. It grew bigger and began to clean itself seriously, though it still looked to me like a large white rat. Keith Kay and I wrapped it in a towel, held it down, turned it over and determined that it was male. Mèo never forgave us for the indignity of that inspection. Growing bigger and stronger, he became more aggressive and hostile, biting and scratching anyone who tried to pet him or pick him up. Most of the time we left him alone.

Marines came to the room to visit and look at him, bringing bits of food. Raw fish was his favorite.

'That's an outstanding cat you got there,' one of the enlisted men said. He was a farm boy from the Midwest and he said how much he missed his animals, especially his dog, back in the States.

'He's VC,' I said.

'How do you know?' he asked.

'He tried to kill me a couple of times.'

'No kidding.'

'Yeah,' I said, 'with his claws. He definitely doesn't like Americans.'

'VC, huh? What are you going to do with him?'

'Oh, I don't know,' I said, pretending not to care. 'Probably take him down to Saigon for interrogation.' We laughed.

'He'll never talk,' Kay said. 'He's hard-core.'

When it was time to go, I put Mèo in a cardboard box with his blanket and kitten toys and gathered my bags for the flight to Saigon. Standing in the courtyard of the press center, I said good-bye to Ri and Dan and the others from CBS and shook hands with friends in the press corps and the Marines. The Americans slapped me on the back and said they wished they were going home too and how lucky I was to be getting out of here alive. The Vietnamese held my arms and hands the way men embrace each other in Vietnam and said they wished me well back in the United States and that they hoped to come and visit someday. 'Maybe we come over and cover riots,' Dan said, his eyes twinkling. I knew I would miss them, their humor, the good times on China Beach, the camaraderie (friendships are what make war tolerable), but I knew I wouldn't miss the war. I was feeling a sense of relief that bordered on exhilaration. It was as if the accumulated fright of the past seven months was being lifted, retired once and for all, put to rest. I was going home where it was safe!

I piled my bags and Mèo in the back of the office jeep and headed toward the airport. Passing through the commerce of the streets, I studied the scene for the last time: men and women carrying heavy baskets balanced at the ends of bamboo poles across their necks and backs, bending under the weight, walking quickly. People on bicycles and scooters and in the backs of pedicabs. *Farewell, Danang*, I thought. *Fini, bibi*. I had no intention of coming back. For me, the war was over. I had volunteered to go in 1965 to cover the arrival of America's mighty war-making divisions and had gone into the field with American troops and reported some of the big early battles with the North Vietnamese. I had covered the new civil programs that were trying to win the elusive loyalty of the South Vietnamese. I had reported the suffering of civilians, the hardships of the troops, the corruption of the government, the sorrow and the pity. And now, having covered the Tet Offensive as well, I felt I had witnessed the beginning of the end.

I also suspected that my work was not finished. I needed to write something more substantial, more personal than the brief television news spots I had been sending home. I had kept notes for that purpose but didn't know what form they might take. That was for later. For now I had reported enough of the Vietnam War. It had been a great adventure: fascinating, frightening, fulfilling—more high drama than I expected for a lifetime. At my age, twenty-eight, I thought I was tough-minded enough to take it, absorb it, digest it, and send it home as hard news coverage without looking back. Later I was to discover how naive that was. I also thought I understood the war. In truth, I knew very little, understood less. All I knew was what I had seen and what I had been told, which wasn't necessarily the right information. In late February 1968, focused on the details of going home, I had no idea that my involvement with Vietnam was far from over, that I would be going back again and again, repeatedly, indefinitely.

In the years that followed, my ambivalence about the war deepened. I watched the news on television, read newspapers, magazines and books, watched movies and documentaries when they came out, kept in touch with friends coming home from the war to hear firsthand accounts. But I also wanted to forget about Vietnam, to put it out of my mind entirely, to leave the war behind. Talking about it to people who hadn't been there made me uncomfortable. How could they comprehend what it was really like? How could they appreciate what happened? They had never *felt* it. My problem was that I went on feeling it. After reading a book or watching a film about Vietnam, my own experiences from the war returned as nightmares—vivid, long-running visions of particular scenes, night after night, for weeks. In one, I am trapped in a cargo plane that is out of control and about to crash. Strapped into the seat, upside down, I watch out a window as the ground comes up fast. The land below is scattered with rice paddies. Always, the dream ends at the instant of impact. I wake up in panic. In another dream, I am lost at night in the streets of a familiar city. It is New York. I am trying to escape from gangs of armed, malevolent thugs who are approaching from several directions. Every time I turn a corner, another group of young men comes toward me. They carry guns and knives. At the moment of confrontation, unable to defend myself, I wake up terrified. They have got me again. Like many Americans who had been there, I had left Vietnam but it hadn't left me.

I tried to write about the war. It became an obsession. I decided to forgo everything else. In 1977, I left my job at CBS and started to write this book. I worked on it for a year. When money ran out, I went back to television news. A few years later, I took leave from my job at ABC News to try again. Something was compelling me to find meaning in America's violent engagement with Vietnam, to make sense of what I was coming to see as a terrible and ironic tragedy. Writing about it was painful (the memories kept coming back), but the writing helped me understand more deeply, more completely, what had happened. At the same time, I tried to unravel the colossal tangle of memories knotted in my mind. Old images of the war were floating like a thousand fragments of a puzzle that formed no coherent picture—confused, disconnected, nonsensical.

I began to feel my sanity might depend on being able to see my experiences in the context of what else had been happening in the war while I was there, and in the context of what had followed. I had to see the big picture. Maybe it would expel the demons that made my war go on and on.

It wasn't only that I needed to tell my story. I had to learn what the war had done to me. Something crucial to my understanding was missing from the books I had read, though many were excellent and helpful. The problem was I didn't know *what* was missing. There seemed to be a secret I had missed. But *what* secret? And what answer?

To find out, I had to explore the ground again, to retrace my route, to figure out what I had missed at the time, what I had repressed, what I failed to understand. Part of the process was to figure out what could not be understood while the war was being fought: the secret history of the war, the hidden agendas of the participants, the truth behind the lies and propaganda (and also behind the facts). I needed to unload the accumulated weight of what I had witnessed in those days in the field—so many battles, so much suffering, so much destruction. Was there a purpose for what I saw? For those who took part in it? For their victims? For me? What meaning did the violence and suffering have for each of us? Or was there no meaning? I wanted to uncover the secrets, understand the mysteries. Also, I needed to resolve years of doubts about some of my behavior during the war, feelings of guilt about what I had done and had left undone.

It was a long journey. At first, immediately after leaving Vietnam, I was unable to read anything but the most superficial accounts of what was happening there without the fear coming back. I could not watch TV news reports about Vietnam without becoming nervous, frightened, unable to concentrate. The big Hollywood movies about Vietnam were alarming, enraging in their dishonesty. All war movies, even the old ones on TV, became intolerable. I wanted to avoid violence, to find some peace of mind, some sanity.

But it was impossible. My work required me to cover wars and revolutions. I went to Northern Ireland and lived in Belfast for most of 1971, then to East Pakistan for the war between India and Pakistan for the independence of Bangladesh, then to Israel in 1973, Lebanon in 1975, and also to Ethiopia, Cyprus, Iceland (the amazing little "Cod War"), Angola and Rhodesia to cover wars for CBS. I was sent to Iran, Eritrea, Syria, Lebanon, China, Kuwait, Yugoslavia and other violent places for ABC News. I continued to believe that getting shot at and being scared was a part of the job that I could throw off when I got home.

By 1993, I felt ready to try writing about Vietnam again. ABC gave me another leave of absence. I assembled my notes, pictures and other research. Each morning at the same time, I got down to work. Writing the stories forced me to think about each moment of each event, scene by scene, conversation by conversation, word by word. I began to relive the episodes I had witnessed in the war. The old emotions came back. I tried to bring them into the open by describing them, putting them on the page in a way that would allow readers to feel some of the same reality, some of the magnitude, some of the true intensity. By thinking about each experience, feeling it again, reflecting on how it happened and what it meant, putting it into perspective as a reasonably mature adult, the scattered fragments of my time in Vietnam began to fall into place, to take shape, to become a coherent story.

And, one at a time, the individual pieces of the puzzle fit together. They illuminated some of the dark secrets of the war, some of the meaning of what happened there and, perhaps, some lessons about all wars. The completed puzzle also revealed some secrets of survival, ways of escape from the trauma of past experience. This I hoped would be true not only for myself, but also for some of the people I know, for my country, for the Vietnamese, and for veterans and survivors of the war who have struggled as I have with the ghosts of Vietnam. By writing about the war I have learned how to survive it.

So here is my story. Come, if you will. Come back, as I did, to the beginning, to the early days of the big American involvement, to the summer of 1965, when the U.S. presence was relatively small, when Marines, Army, Air Force, Navy and Coast Guard personnel were moving into position, when some of the best and brightest young men and women in U.S. government service were volunteering for duty in Southeast Asia, when reporters who wanted to make names for themselves (or build on reputations made in other wars) were moving to Saigon, when a few hippies wandering in Southeast Asia also decided to become journalists and photographers and drifted toward that wild tropical place to find work, and when Vietnam's destiny seemed undecided.

PART TWO

1965–1966

War knows no power. Safe shall be my going,
Secretly armed against all death's endeavour;
Safe though all safety's lost; safe where men fall;
And if these poor limbs die, safest of all.

RUPERT BROOKE
"Safety" (1914)

AUGUST 27, 1965

The beach at night at Nha Trang was at peace. Clean white sand curled along the length of the bay in a wide unbroken bend, embracing the sea, absorbing its strength. In the distance, black mountains shielded the harbor in silhouette. Waves rolled in from beyond the horizon and touched the shore with rhythmic splashes, the surf sparkling with phosphorescence, tiny lights dancing in the black water. The leaves of palm trees along the edge of the beach brushed together in the easy breeze and made a gentle shifting sound. Stars shone clear and bright. The air was warm and fresh and the strong smell of the sea was in it.

Sitting near the edge of the water in a dilapidated canvas deck chair, tilting slightly to one side in the fine sand, I was enchanted by the beauty around me. A woman's voice, singing in the upper registers of a strange musical scale, plaintive and frail, drifted down the beach. The music was made of melodies and instruments I had never heard before, fine and thin, sentimental and sweet, Oriental. An outdoor cafe on the beach was decorated with strings of lights: red, blue, yellow, green and white, like Christmas ornaments, suggesting late summer frivolity. *Idyllic*, I thought, feeling the warmth of a second gin and tonic. After a week in Vietnam, I was infatuated with the country and its people and the natural wonder of the place.

There was no war here. Nha Trang was a small fishing community on the South China Sea. Local residents were gentle people who charmed visitors with their modesty and good nature. There was none of the arrogance or hustle of Saigon, no hostile looks on the faces of people in the streets. If peace and harmony were characteristics of this ancient culture, they had found expression in Nha Trang. I looked eastward across the water and pictured a friend who was getting up in the States now, brushing her hair in the mirror, preparing to go to work, beginning her day as I ended mine. I felt my love for her as a physical sensation. From the beach at Nha Trang the world seemed a smaller place, closer than the distance between us.

"*Môt, hai, ba,*" said Le Sum, beside me.

"*Môt, hai, ba,*" I said, trying to memorize the words.

"*Un, deux, trois,*" said Le Sum, smiling.

"*Un, deux, trois,*" I said.

"*Bon,* good."

Le Quang Sum's lesson had begun in Saigon that morning soon after we boarded an Air Vietnam DC-3 that would take us to Nha Trang. On the plane, we discovered to our embarrassment that we were barely able to communicate. Le Sum spoke French, Vietnamese and maybe fifty words of English. My French was limited, studied in school and later forgotten. We spoke in short, broken sentences that mixed English and French, gesturing in makeshift sign language that was incomplete and frustrating. The Vietnamese passengers in front of us giggled.

We were going to be partners. Le Sum was a veteran cinematographer from the Saigon motion picture industry who now earned a living filming the war. CBS paid him far more than he could make in the movie business, and in dollars. He carried a silent camera in a padded box, a Bell and Howell filmo with three lenses that was driven by an internal spring he wound by hand. The bureau assigned him to work with me on the theory that his long experience as a photographer might make up for my total ignorance of television. I was a radio reporter, just arrived from the States, twenty-five years old. Le Sum, a veteran of the anticolonial war with the French, was twice my age.

'One, two, three,' I said, holding up one, two and then three fingers.

'One, two, three,' said Le Sum, smiling.

'Very good, *très bon,*' I said.

Whenever our eyes met, Le Sum smiled. Part of it, I supposed, was our new friendship. But it also seemed to be an expression of embarrassment at our inability to communicate clearly. We both wanted to express ourselves intelligently but we were as inarticulate as small children.

Le Sum was tall for a Vietnamese, broad and muscular in the shoulders and somewhat heavy around the middle. His face was round with soft curves instead of sharp angles, features that reflected his gentle nature. His hair was short and black and his skin was topaz, the color of golden wheat. His nose had no length to it, just a round stubby aperture for breathing. He sat beside me in a low squat—both feet flat on the sand, his torso upright, knees bent completely, the backs of his thighs touching the insides of his calves, all the leg muscles stretched, arms folded across his knees, his body resting—sitting and standing at the same time.

Our orders were succinct: "Get out there and find the war." They had been issued in Saigon the day before by the bureau chief, a gruff-mannered TV producer named Sam Zelman. He instructed Le Sum and me to cover the journey of a South Vietnamese army convoy from Nha Trang to Ban Me Thuot, about a hundred miles from east to west, along Route 21 in the Central Highlands of South Vietnam. Zelman said the convoy was scheduled to start in a day or two and the whole operation was top secret, whispered to him by a friend at MACV. The east–west road was an important line of communication across the highlands and was controlled by the Viet Cong. To open Route 21 to military traffic would be a significant victory for the Saigon government. Zelman said everyone was expecting an ambush.

Arriving in Nha Trang that afternoon, Le Sum and I hired a pedicab and went to find the U.S. Army public information officer, a lieutenant whose name we had been given in Saigon. He was not at his office so we went to his home, a two-story villa in a quiet residential street. A young woman answered the door. Le Sum asked her in Vietnamese if the PIO was home. She giggled, held her hands to her mouth, and closed the door. It was about four o'clock. After ten minutes, a young American with short hair wearing a white linen sarong and sandals came to the door. His eyes were just awake.

'Are you in charge of public information?' I asked.

'You got it,' he said, scowling. 'Who are you?'

'Jack Laurence from CBS. This is my cameraman, Le Sum.'

The lieutenant did not shake hands. Irritation showed on his face.

'We're sorry to bother you, but we need to know how we can get on the convoy that's going to Ban Me Thuot.'

'What convoy?'

'The one we heard about in Saigon.'

'There is no convoy,' the lieutenant said. 'Hasn't been a convoy to Ban Me Thuot in years.'

Le Sum and I looked at each other.

'Check back in the morning,' the lieutenant said and slammed the door.

'Convoy fini?' Le Sum asked as we walked away from the house.

'I don't know,' I said, puzzled. *Weird way to fight a war,* I thought.

Le Sum led the way to ARVN military headquarters for Nha Trang, a large complex of buildings with a maze of radio aerials strung across the rooftops. A sentry post stood outside the main gate, a covered wooden box painted in faded red and blue. It was only big enough for one soldier to stand in and the design might have dated from the Napoleonic Wars. The Vietnamese soldier standing inside was bored. Le Sum spoke to him and went into the headquarters. Time passed. The light faded and the sky darkened and filled with black clouds. After a time, Le Sum came out looking disappointed. The military had told him nothing about a convoy. Didn't seem to know about one. *Strange*, I thought.

We went to our motel by the beach, an old French building with individual bungalows for its guests. Just as we got inside, monsoon rains fell in torrents, heavy as a mountain waterfall. I understood then why everyone took siestas in the late afternoon.

'How say thank you?' I asked Le Sum.

He looked puzzled and shook his head, smiling.

'How say *merci*?'

'*Cám on,*' he said, his face brighter.

'*Cám on,*' I said, but the tones were wrong.

'*Cám on,*' he said, with music in his voice, high note, low note. '*Cám on.*' It was like trying to talk and sing simultaneously. I was not good at it.

'Your language is very difficult for me,' I said.

I tried to remember a word in French and in a minute it came. '*Très difficile.*' Le Sum smiled and said something in French I didn't understand.

It was late now and a fishing boat chugged into the harbor, a single running light on a forward pole marking its progress. Le Sum and I watched the boat and when it had docked he stood up.

'*Bon soir, monsieur,*' he said.

'Good night, Le Sum. *Cám on.*' I hit the notes.

He smiled like a happy schoolteacher and left the beach.

Nha Trang was virtually immune from the war. There were only a few military installations in the town and they were widely separated, standing behind long elegant palm and mahogany trees in pale yellow buildings with stucco walls and orange-tiled roofs that the French had abandoned eleven years earlier. The occasional sentry or policeman you saw seemed more drowsy than alert. The U.S. Special Forces had their headquarters in Nha Trang but they generally kept out of sight, staging military operations from Cheo Reo and other discreet bases farther inland. The Viet Cong rarely attacked targets in Nha Trang; no VC units were massed on the outskirts of the city; no ARVN troop convoys rolled through the streets in trucks; and there were no flares on the horizon after dark or the faraway rumbling of artillery. Nha Trang was less than two hundred miles northeast of Saigon but it seemed much farther away, as if the sleepy old resort town and its pristine beaches and sheltering mountains existed in another land, magically exempt from the fighting. The various parties to the war—VC, ARVN and Americans—were believed to allow Nha Trang to remain a rest and relaxation area for weary combatants from both sides, a neutral zone, off-limits from the war.

★

The next day, Le Sum and I were surprised by the arrival at the seaside motel of a CBS camera crew in full combat gear. Jim Wilson and Bob Funk made up a special freelance team that had been recruited in the United States to photograph the war for CBS. I had met them in Saigon but had not expected them in Nha Trang. They wore GI-issue combat fatigues, canvas rucksacks, canteens, combat boots, pistols and green Australian bush hats, turned up on one side. Their fatigues were bulging with batteries, connecting cables and other equipment for the camera and sound gear. Wilson had a scarf made from camouflaged parachute silk around his neck. They were both big men who had not shaved for several days and, seeing them in the field for the first time, I thought they had a dark and menacing look, like mercenaries.

'What are you guys doing here?' I said, shaking hands and introducing Le Sum.

'Came in on the convoy,' said Wilson. He explained in his slow western drawl that they had left Ban Me Thuot in the morning with an ARVN road convoy and crossed the country from west to east along Route 21 without stopping. Their bodies and clothes were dusty.

'It was a piece of cake,' Wilson said.

'Nice countryside,' said Funk, 'but boring.'

'Did you get a story?' I said, hoping we might salvage something for the effort.

'Nah,' said Wilson, 'hardly shot a frame.'

I was disappointed but tried not to show it.

Wilson and Funk were the network's ace combat camera team. They had shot daring close-up film of the revolution in Santo Domingo earlier in the year, followed by the urban rioting in Watts, Los Angeles, and had won reputations for being fearless, aggressive and professional. Their footage was sensational. Now they were in Vietnam.

Wilson, the photographer, was thirty years old, six feet one, about 210 pounds, none of it fat. The features of his face came together in a way that reminded you of Lee Marvin, the movie actor, and his dark narrow eyes sometimes gave him a sinister look. When he got excited, which was not often, his voice became shrill and didn't fit the size of him. At normal times it was pinched and nasal, not deep. He carried a Browning 9 millimeter pistol on his web belt that seemed to hang there naturally, as if he had always worn a gun. Friends called him Jimmy. He smoked Salem cigarettes that he bought in the PX and had an engaging smile that appeared when he was having fun and a tough, angry side that showed occasionally when he drank.

If Wilson was the Wild One, his sound technician, Robert Funk, was Bubba. Funk was thirty-five years old, six feet three, 230 pounds, not all of it muscle. He had a long kind-hearted face and a similar disposition. His nose was small, turned up at the tip, and his long dark hair was brushed on the sides in the slicked-back style of the 1950s. Everyone called him Bob. He wore glasses with metal frames. Growing up in rural Virginia outside Washington, he had the easy softness of the South in his voice. Funk got his first job with CBS as a motorcycle courier and moved over to sound recording, which paid more. He wore a Smith & Wesson .357 Magnum on his belt, which he said he hoped he would never have to shoot.

Both Wilson and Funk had beards they had started when they arrived in Vietnam and swore not to shave until they left. How long that would be was uncertain. They were being paid union overseas rates of about $1,000 a week plus bonuses (riding a helicopter earned them an extra $50 a day), and they wanted to make as much money as they could before they went home. They weren't afraid of getting shot at, but if they were shot, they wanted to be paid well for it. This was their first time in the field.

'They got any rooms in this place?' Funk asked.

Le Sum helped them register at the motel and when they had washed, changed into civilian clothes and eaten, the four of us set off on foot to explore Nha Trang. A few people in the streets rode bicycles or traveled in rickshaws that were driven by thin undernourished men who sat behind them on elevated bicycle seats, pedaling. The muscles of their thighs and calves were overdeveloped, like long-distance runners. Le Sum called the vehicles "cyclos." There were one or two automobiles but no one was walking, as we were, in the afternoon heat. A young woman pedaled past on a bicycle, her long silk dress trailing behind her in the breeze.

'Aó dài,' said Le Sum, pronouncing it aowd-zeye.

'I've gotta find out about the night life in this town,' Wilson said, leering.

Le Sum guided us along quiet unpaved streets. The sun was bright. An American soldier in floppy green fatigues came toward us. He was a young enlisted man with a round chubby face and none of the orderly spit-and-polish look of officers and GIs in Saigon. He had no patch on his shoulder to identify his division and did not carry a weapon. Being fellow Americans, we smiled as he passed. The top of his undershirt showed at the open neck of his fatigue shirt. It was dark green. That's not right, I thought. All the GIs we had seen so far wore white undershirts or none at all. The green T-shirt was out of place. As the soldier walked away, something clicked in my memory. A recent article in Stars and Stripes, the military newspaper, had reported that all fifteen thousand soldiers in an elite new army division in the States had been ordered to dye their underwear green, to camouflage it for jungle warfare. The division, as I recalled, was the 1st Cavalry (Airmobile) stationed at Fort Benning, Georgia. It was reported to be on its way to Vietnam by sea.

I turned and ran toward the GI.

'Wait a minute,' I called. He stopped and turned around. 'Excuse me,' I said, 'who are you with?'

'Sorry, I can't tell you,' he said politely. 'Who are you with?'

'CBS News,' I said. Wilson, Funk and Le Sum joined us on the street.

'This is Jim Wilson, our cameraman, Bob Funk, soundman, and Le Sum, who's also a cameraman. I'm Jack Laurence, the reporter.'

We shook hands.

'How long you all been in-country?' he said.

'About two weeks,' Wilson said.

'Just a week for me,' I said. 'Uh, Le Sum's been in-country all his life.'

The soldier laughed. Le Sum smiled.

'Are you guys really from CBS?' the GI said, 'the network?'

'Yeah, no shit,' Wilson said. He got his wallet and produced a Department of Defense press card with his photograph, fingerprint and simulated rank. All of us showed him our press cards. The soldier inspected the plastic laminated cards carefully.

NOTICE: THE BEARER OF THIS CARD
IS A CIVILIAN NONCOMBATANT SERVING
WITH THE ARMED FORCES OF THE UNITED STATES.

When he had seen them, the soldier relaxed. 'My name's Marv Wolf,' he said in a more friendly voice. 'I just came down here to get some stills developed.' He looked with envy at the new 35 millimeter Nikon still camera Wilson carried on a strap over his shoulder.

'You're with the 1st Cavalry Division, aren't you?' I said.

'What makes you think that?' he said.

'Your green T-shirt. Everybody else over here has got white ones.'

Wolf looked at his feet and pushed the toe of his boot in the dirt. He was sweating.

'Look,' he said, 'nobody's supposed to know where we are yet. I'm with the advance party. The rest of the division is on the way, in ships.' He looked at each of us and took a breath and let it out.

'If I trust you guys not to say anything about where we're going, do you want to come with me tomorrow and meet my boss?'

'Who's he?' said Wilson.

'Major Siler,' said Wolf. 'Charles Siler. He's in charge of the division PIO shop. Great guy. I'm his gofer.'

'Gopher?' said Funk.

'Yeah. What the major wants, I go-for.' We all laughed.

'Well, where is this major?' Wilson said.

'I can't tell you. Not until you meet the major. But if he gives the okay you'll get a helluva good story.'

'How far then?' said Wilson.

'About an hour by Caribou.'

'What's that?'

'A twin-engine prop,' said Wolf. 'Great little plane. We call 'em Caribous. We brought a bunch over. Got our own pilots and everything.'

Wilson, Funk and I exchanged looks.

'Well, we've got nothing better to do,' said Wilson. 'Might as well go along with you.'

Wolf said he would meet us at the airport in the morning and walked on. I liked him immediately. He was more like a civilian, cheerful and optimistic, much more helpful than the sleep-eyed PIO lieutenant. We were fortunate to have met him passing on the street. The convoy story was a bust but now we had a chance for another, perhaps an exclusive, if we were lucky. Better still, it would be with Americans.

'Let's ride back to the motel,' Wilson said.

With a wave of his hand, Le Sum organized four pedicab drivers who had been following at a distance. Climbing into one of the three-wheeled pedicabs and pulling away, Wilson told his driver to get ahead of the others and the driver pedaled harder. Seeing Wilson in front, Funk told his driver to go faster. The ride turned into a race. Le Sum followed a way behind, keeping us in sight.

"Come on!" Wilson shouted over his shoulder. "Last one back buys the drinks!" The driver of Funk's pedicab had difficulty pushing the weight with his pedals.

Wilson held the lead. He shouted at his driver, 'C'mon. Di-di! Di-di!' Looking behind him, he taunted the others in pursuit. 'Funk, you big lard-ass, you haven't got a chance.' The three pedicabs raced through the streets as fast as the drivers could pedal, careening around corners, Wilson, Funk and I leaning over the sides of the bamboo rickshaws to give them balance, like the crew on a racing sailboat. We laughed at the madness. The drivers laughed and called to one another in Vietnamese, pumping furiously on the pedals. Passersby stopped, staring at the three Caucasian men, two of them giants, racing down streets, driven by thin older Vietnamese men, all laughing and shouting in the heat. The race lasted several minutes. Wilson arrived at the motel first. Funk was third, ahead of Le Sum. The drivers looked exhausted, wiping sweat from their heads with their shirts.

'If you didn't have lead in your ass,' Wilson said to Funk, 'you might've had a chance.'

'Nah. I just didn't want my guy to have a heart attack,' Funk said.

A minute later, Le Sum rode up smiling. He tried to interpret for the drivers, who were out of breath. He said they wanted fifty piastres each, about twenty-five cents.

'Bullshit,' said Wilson, his anger quick. 'Tell 'em twenty.'

Wilson's driver refused to take the twenty-piastre note Wilson held out in offer, shaking his head no.

'What the hell,' said Funk, handing fifty to his driver. 'These little guys knocked themselves out.'

'It's the principle, God damn it,' Wilson shouted. He threw the note on the ground at the driver's feet and walked away.

In an instant, all the frivolity went out of the moment. It was replaced by something cold. I felt embarrassed. I handed Le Sum a hundred piastres to give to the other drivers. They smiled and put the palms of their hands together as if in prayer and bowed their heads and said, "*Cám on*" and turned to go away.

In the evening, Le Sum recommended a French restaurant just outside Nha Trang. Arriving, Wilson insisted that he and I sit at a table separate from the others, "to plan strategy." Funk and Le Sum sat on the other side of the room without speaking, unable to communicate. The owner of the restaurant, a well-dressed Frenchwoman named Françoise, came to the table and recommended the chateaubriand and a wine from Algeria. We ordered. Right away, Wilson started to talk business.

'So, how much television have you done,' he asked.

'None,' I said.

'How'd you get to CBS?'

'I worked in radio the last five years. New York, Washington, a couple of other places. I got hired by CBS Radio in January.'

'You been overseas before?'

'I was in Santo Domingo last spring. Did a radio documentary.'

'Yeah? We were there too. For TV. I don't remember seeing you there.'

'Well, I pretty much kept to myself.'

'You get shot at?'

'Yeah. A little. It wasn't much of a battle.'

After a few minutes, Wilson ordered a second bottle of wine. He drank faster than anyone I'd ever seen.

'I didn't want to be a TV reporter,' I said. 'I was happy doing radio.'

'What happened?'

I told him, before I left New York, Fred Friendly, the president of CBS News, had called me into his office to wish me luck. I'd never met him before. As I was leaving, he told me do an on-camera test. "Just in case," he'd said. The next day a cameraman took me behind the building on 56th Street and set up on a tripod to film me standing on the steps. I was really scared. I'd never been on-camera before. He told me to ad-lib something. All I could think to say was something about all the salt-of-the-earth newspeople who were hard at work inside the building reporting on the problems of poor people around the country while out here on West 56th Street I could see their expensive new cars and Friendly's long black limousine parked on the street outside. I described what was there for a couple of minutes until he told me to stop. I didn't know whether Friendly ever saw it.

'Well, they obviously want to see if you can do the job.' Wilson said. 'Zelman told me to stick with you for a few days, try to come up with something.'

'Looks like we're off to a start.'

'Yeah, this might be good.' Wilson seemed pleased. 'If you listen to me and do what I tell you. The most important part of a TV story is the pictures. If you've got good scenes, you'll get on the air. And we should be able to get some pretty good scenes if we ever find the war.'

He attacked the food and the wine.

'I'll let you in on a secret,' he said. 'I'm going all the way to the top in this game. I'm serious. It's not that hard. But I don't have a lot of time. I'll take you along if you want.'

'You'll have to teach me.'

'Nothing to worry about. Listen, I used to write for a newspaper in LA. It's simple. All you have to do is get the facts right. Let me worry about the pictures. Then I'll show you how to put 'em together and tell the story.' We drank a toast to the bargain.

Later, at the motel, I had difficulty falling asleep. The humidity was up. Mosquitoes buzzed. I had the sensation of floating adrift in a field of forces beyond my control, of being propelled by a power of great magnitude, as if I were a bit player stepping into a much larger drama without knowing my lines or moves. Since I had volunteered to come to Vietnam, each line of the script had been written by someone else: by Fred Friendly and the network; by Bob Little, the foreign editor; by Sam Zelman, the bureau chief; by military people I met; and now by Wilson. All were connected by the war. I had no idea where the forces were leading. At the same time, I had no fear, as if another part of the same force was assuring me it would be all right.

AUGUST 29, 1965

The Caribou took off in a single breathless leap, jumping off the runway like a giant grasshopper, springing into the air and then the clouds. The crew chief stood behind the seats of the two Army pilots and leaned forward to scan the sky for other planes and helicopters. He looked over his shoulder at Wolf, Wilson, Funk, Le Sum and me standing in the narrow spaces between the side of the cargo bay and the army jeep the plane was transporting, smiling at us with a mischievous sunburned grin that seemed to say, 'Some takeoff, huh?'

Marv Wolf, our new guide, smiled with unit pride. Le Sum held a strut on the side of the plane with all his strength, straining to see out one of the windows. Funk was bent over at the waist, too tall to stand up straight in the plane. Wilson sat down on the deck and closed his eyes. I was frightened. My usual fear of flying was compounded by being in a strange new airplane. It was all wings and tail with a short stubby fuselage fixed underneath and two powerful engines. In a few seconds the plane was enveloped by morning clouds. It flew blindly up toward the mountains, now invisible, guarding the beautiful town of Nha Trang.

Wolf leaned over and shouted above the roar of the engines, 'They just flew this bird all the way across the Pacific. Island hopping.' He gestured toward the cockpit with his free hand.

'Hawaii, Wake, Guam and the Philippines. The whole squadron flew over.' Wolf wanted us to be impressed, and we were, but I thought that pilots who flew across the ocean in such a small plane must be insane.

'Seventeenth Aviation Company,' Wolf shouted.

I wrote it in my notebook.

About an hour later the plane dipped through a hole in the clouds and banked sharply. Out the windows, a narrow river was visible. It wound through a brown-green valley covered with cultivated fields. The river crossed under a two-lane road that stretched away into a distant range of mountains. A cluster of trees was tucked inside a bend where the road crossed the river and a village was settled beside that. The rest of the land-scape was covered with farm fields filled with slate-colored water.

The Caribou hit the ground, bounced once and made a fierce rattling noise as the wheels hit rows and rows of metal sheets with holes in them that covered the surface of the airstrip.

'P-S-P,' said Wolf stepping off the plane.

The air was cooler than in Nha Trang and the sky was a wash of gray. Wilson spotted a round brick building near the airfield that looked like the turret of an old castle.

'That's the watchtower the French used to guard the airstrip with,' Wolf said. 'Nobody's been in here since they left.'

The watchtower was unoccupied, singularly alone in a field of mud, its faded red bricks crumbling slowly in the sun and rain, its Western military architecture out of place, a monument to France's misadventure.

Le Sum looked around, trying to figure out where he was. Taking off from Nha Trang, I tried to keep track of where the plane was flying, but without a compass I was lost.

Wolf apologized for the lack of transportation to meet us and helped carry the camera gear almost a mile along a slippery, muddy track to a large U.S. Army tent camp. Guiding the way through the camp, he went inside a large general-purpose field tent. Wilson put the camera gear on a poncho on the wet ground and looked around. The camp was set on a plateau that stretched across a wide flatland for several miles until it reached a range of mountains in the distance. A few short scrub trees were scattered around, but there was little grass or other vegetation, only acres of mud. Several dozen pup tents were pitched haphazardly, ringed with narrow drainage ditches and shallow pits filled with water and stacks of wet sandbags around them. The predominant colors were the mud-brown of the earth and the rain-soaked green of the tents. The camp appeared to be largely deserted. Everyone was out working.

Wolf came out of the tent with a portly officer whose loose-fitting fatigues were sweat stained and rumpled. He was thirty-five to forty years old and held a pipe in his hand. Wolf introduced him as Major Charles Siler, the division public information officer. He looked like a college teacher.

"Welcome to An Khe," he said with a smile. His face looked kind.

'You sure have landed in the middle of things,' Siler said. He explained that An Khe had been chosen as base camp for the Army's newest and most innovative infantry division, a fifteen thousand–member force that would move entirely by air. Airmobile assault on this scale was a concept that had never been fully implemented in war, Siler said. The 1st Cavalry had about 450 helicopters that would give it the ability to maneuver over a wide area on short notice. The helicopter was to replace the armored personnel carrier in fast-moving military operations as APCs and tanks had replaced mounted horse cavalry before it. The division called itself "The First Team."

Siler took us inside the tent and sent Wolf to get coffee. An Khe, he said, was located in the center of the country, about halfway between the Cambodian border and the South China Sea, about 250 miles north-northeast of Saigon. It was in the heart of the Central Highlands, an area of mountains and high valleys that began north of Saigon and ran up through Vietnam and Laos into China. He got out a large military map of the area and pointed out places of interest. The French called the mountain range Chaine Annamitique, and the larger mountains ranged from five thousand to ten thousand feet, he said. Most were covered with thick jungle foliage that made ideal sanctuaries for the mobile guerrilla warfare of the enemy.

Siler explained that fog and mists crept in below a blanket of clouds that seemed to shroud the mountains so much of the time that navigation around the peaks was a life-and-death calculation. An Khe sat on a plateau above thirteen hundred feet, astride Route 19, about halfway between the cities of Qui Nhon on the coast and Pleiku to the west. Part of the strategy in bringing the Army's newest division into the area was to block an anticipated attempt by the Viet Cong to seize the highlands and divide the country in two, isolating the northern part of South Vietnam from Saigon and the south. The First Cav was coming in to thwart that attempt. Its tactical area of operations would be everything within a fifty-mile radius of An Khe, covering a region that had been controlled by the Viet Cong since the French war. The area was considered to be hard-core VC territory.

Wolf brought a jug of coffee and poured some of it into our canteen cups. We sat on army cots as Siler continued his briefing. Only three days earlier, he said, a thousand men from the division had arrived in An Khe and begun building a base for the rest of the division. 'You're the first journalists to find us,' he said. 'Well done.'

'Can we film a story about what you're doing?' I asked.

'We'll see. Obviously, that's your job. And we'd like to see you do it. But there are other considerations. We don't want to tell the VC where we are and what we're doing. They'll probably figure it out soon enough, but we don't want to do 'em any favors.'

'What if we agree not to say where we are?'

'Well, that would have to be a necessary precondition. You'd have to sign off with something like "in a location that cannot be disclosed."'

'How about "Somewhere in Vietnam?"'

'That would be fine,' Siler said. 'The other problem is the terrain. We don't want to *show* them where we are, either.'

'How about if I shoot everything fairly close?' Wilson said. 'No identifiable features.'

'You couldn't use the French watchtower down by the air strip,' for example,' Wolf said.

'Definitely not the watchtower,' Siler said.

'That's a deal,' Wilson said.

'Well, I'll run it by the Old Man and let you know. Should be able to get a decision pretty quick.'

Within an hour, Siler had received permission to go ahead with the story. We agreed to shoot everything in close-ups and medium shots and instruct our editors in New York not to show identifiable terrain. Everyone seemed pleased.

For the next two days, Wilson filmed whatever he saw that looked interesting. The busiest soldier in the camp appeared to be Brigadier General James M. Wright Jr., commanding officer of the advance party. Wright had been a prisoner of war in a Japanese camp in World War II and was a survivor of the Bataan death march. On the first day he swung a machete to cut the first symbolic swathe of elephant grass from a 275-acre field that was to become the base for the division's helicopters. The general said he wanted the grass to be "as smooth as a golf course" to prevent soil erosion and dust clouds when choppers landed. From then on, the landing field was known as the "Golf Course."

Wilson and Le Sum took pictures of men cutting trees, filling sandbags, building bunkers for gun positions, bulldozing roads. Le Sum got a shot of two soldiers pulling out a tree stump that gave way so suddenly they both fell on their backsides. Wilson and Funk went up in a helicopter to get high-angle shots of the clearing of the Golf Course. Seventy bags of mail arrived, the first from the States. Many of the letters asked, "Where are you?" A soldier named Linwood Dixon set up a field barber station to cut other soldiers' hair, something he had never done before. When Wilson had enough footage of Dixon at work, he sat down in the chair and asked for a haircut. Dixon cut all but a few millimeters off and Wilson paid him thirty-five cents. Every few minutes there was something interesting to shoot or someone to interview. It was as new to us as it was to the soldiers. Wilson photographed a cook as he made a hot meal in the mess tent, singing "King of the Road." I interviewed line troops from 1st Battalion, 5th Cavalry, as they stood guard on the perimeter. Others laughed and joked while trying to clean their clothes in an old-fashioned hand-operated washing machine. A medic spoke while treating soldiers with blistered hands on the Golf Course. When they finished filming, Wilson and Funk put down the camera gear, picked up machetes and helped cut the grass.

As daylight was ending, it rained. The troops took off their clothes and stood naked in it. The medical surgeon for the advance party, Major Bailey, said he was worried about sanitation conditions in the camp. Everyone was working so hard, he said, there was no time to clean up. The river was too polluted to bathe in. "This rain," he said, "was a God-given bath." Wilson and Funk took off their fatigues and stood in the rain with the soldiers, laughing with them.

Lieutenant Colonel Edward Meyer of Springfield, Virginia, cleared brush with the others. In an interview, Meyer said there were indications that units of the People's Army of North Vietnam (PAVN) might be moving into the area to reinforce local Viet Cong. Today, he said, American fighter-bombers were fired on by .50-caliber anti-aircraft guns, a weapon the VC had not used in the area before. He said intelligence officers of the 101st Airborne Brigade who were providing security for the advance party of the Cav strongly suspected they might soon be fighting North Vietnamese regulars for the first time in the war.

Meyer appraised the situation with what appeared to be cool intelligence. His articulate speech, honest replies and confidence impressed me. No one in the advance party seemed worried about what might happen when the rest of the First Cav arrived and went into combat. The VC and the North Vietnamese, if they were around, were going to face a terrible force. With the Americans' air mobility, firepower, superior training, courage and confidence, the new division would secure the area quickly. No one expected anything else.

After chow, Major Siler and Marv Wolf talked late into the night about the First Cav. They explained how the division traced its military lineage to the mounted cavalry regiments of the U.S. Army a hundred years earlier, to the Indian Wars of the 1860s, to Custer and the Little Big Horn, through World Wars I and II, Korea, and, finally, to its designation as the 1st Air Cavalry this year. The order to deploy to Vietnam came only a month ago.

At the end of the second day, two jeeps arrived at the PIO tent with a young paratroop lieutenant from the 101st Airborne Brigade. Lieutenant Tower, the brigade PIO, said we were invited to cover a combat assault by a company of the 101st at dawn. Siler had arranged it. The 101st didn't want the First Cav to get the only TV coverage while the paratroopers were doing the fighting in the area. Lieutenant Tower explained that his unit was now being called the Phantom Brigade because no one outside the U.S. military knew where it was in Vietnam or what it was doing. Now, he said, we could show the men in combat, even if we couldn't say where they were fighting. We agreed to go.

Outside it was midnight dark and silent. The jeeps rode slowly out of the First Cav lines, the engines growling in first gear, advancing across a no-man's-land toward the 101st. It's very risky at night, Tower whispered, because the troops were new and jittery, quick to fire. The jeeps moved without lights at dead slow speed.

"Halt!" a low, guttural voice ahead cut the silence.

Tower stopped the lead jeep and flashed a brief beam of red light from his flashlight. Passwords were whispered across the line. The jeeps went on, crawling slow. It felt like a scene from an old war movie, back in time with Holley and Jarvess and the rest of the Hollywood cast at Bastogne. I felt safe with the paratroopers, but I was also scared. The soldiers moved with precision, cautiously, familiar with the drill of night movement, giving the impression they knew exactly what was going to happen next. I had the sensations of being frightened and calm at the same time.

At the 101st PIO tent, soldiers glanced at Le Sum with suspicion, as if he were not entirely welcome. Le Sum looked around and did not speak. I asked Tower to put my cot next to Le Sum's. Wilson and Funk stacked their camera and sound equipment, smoked cigarettes and went to bed. It was difficult to fall asleep.

AUGUST 31, 1965

At dawn we sat on the soft red soil by the edge of the runway waiting for heli-copters to take us on a combat assault. The air was fresh, rich with the organic odor of tropical vegetation and laterite earth. Beyond the runway, past the barbed wire and cleared fields of fire, the rainforest came awake, surging with life. Trees, vines and bamboo thickets warmed slowly in the light glowing behind a ridge of low hills. The jungle bush jumped with birds, insects and wildlife that sang and screeched and swooped through the tangled growth in the intricate dances of predator and prey.

Lieutenant Tower, the PIO, carried black coffee in steaming cups from the mess hall and gave them to Wilson, Funk, Le Sum and me. My mind was fogbound from lack of sleep. I had been awake much of the night worrying about what might happen my first time out covering combat in Vietnam. I had no idea what to expect or how I would behave.

More than a hundred paratroopers waited along the side of the airstrip bunched together in squads of ten to twelve men. A group standing near us gathered around one of the soldiers who was kneeling on the ground pour-ing aviation fuel from a used C ration can into a hole the size of a pencil in the bare red dirt. The soldiers leaned over watching the hole. Suddenly, a long thin scorpion as big as a human finger crawled out, dazed by the fumes, its legs wobbling. The soldiers shouted:

'Get 'im, boy!'

'Quick, now!'

'Don't miss him, buddy!'

'Aww, do it now, man!'

The soldier set the can of fuel on the ground, tore a match from a damp-proof pack, struck it and dropped the flame on the back of the scorpion. The insect caught fire with an audible *huwhup!* and began to twist in mad jerky movements, its body writhing in the flame. The scorpion had a long pointed tail with a stinger at the end and it swung the tail backward as if fighting off an attacker and stabbed itself in the back again and again. The troops cheered. After about ten seconds, the flame went out and the scorpion stopped moving. The soldiers stood up.

'At-*away!*'

'Air-*borne!*'

'Got you a VC scorpion!'

'*Toasted* that fucker.'

'Now that's one crispy critter!'

One of the paratroopers stabbed the charred remains of the scorpion with his bayonet and held it face high toward the others.

'Anybody want breakfast?'

'No thanks.'

For a hundred yards along the edge of the airstrip groups of soldiers burned scorpions, death images dancing like bright little fires in their eyes, until the helicopters came and took them away on the combat assault.

Wilson and Funk went with one of the lead choppers. A few minutes later Le Sum and I followed in the second wave. The crew chief said to sit on the nylon sling bench near the center of the helicopter facing forward. He fastened the heavy metal buckles of the seat belt around my waist. A half dozen paratroopers climbed in with rifles, machineguns and packs and sat on the seats and floor. The engine spun with a shrill whine and the turbine exhaust discharged hot sweet gases of burning kerosene. Engines roaring, rotor blades slapping the air, sixteen Army helicopters lifted off in swirling clouds of red dust. Ten feet off the ground, the choppers hovered in the air, dropped their noses low like bulls, charged forward slowly, then lifted up swiftly in gusts of power and joined formation in the air. The air rushing by the open sides of the ship filled the insides of my trousers. The troops were not bothered by the wind, their trouser legs tucked tightly into their boots. They held their rifles muzzle up between their knees and looked down at the landscape rushing below with the cold-eyed precision of hawks.

The assault group followed Route 19 east for several miles, maneuvered through the hills of An Khe Pass, then banked north and swooped down along the floor of a valley, skimming it at twenty to thirty feet, just above the treetops. The ridgelines of the nearby hills rushed by on both sides of the chopper. Looking forward between the pilots of the lead aircraft, I saw a line of trees at the top of the valley closing fast, on course for a collision. I held my breath. At the last second the pilot pulled the collective control and the helicopter jumped over the trees with the pull of two or three times the force of gravity and then dived down the other side, pushing me hard into the seat one moment and lifting me up the next. I blew out my breath. The formation snaked across the hills at over one hundred knots, racing a few feet above the surface of the ground, exaggerating the sense of speed. Everything looked exceptionally sharp. The flight gave a sensation of great power, the ultimate roller-coaster ride, totally reckless and exhilarating, as exciting as anything I'd ever done. Le Sum shut his eyes and lowered his head. The crew chief grinned beneath the black sun visor that covered his eyes inside the helmet, seemingly in a state of rapture. He came over and shouted in my ear above the roar of the engine, 'How d'ya like contour flying?'

A few seconds before landing, the door gunner pulled the trigger on his machinegun and sprayed .30-caliber bullets into the brush on a hill behind a small village in the valley, a hamlet. Columns of smoke appeared. More gunfire rattled on landing. Le Sum and I jumped into a dry field of rice shoots, looked around, and ran after the troops to the edge of the field and took cover behind a hedgerow. As soon as all the soldiers were on the ground, the helicopters took off and turned sharply away. Suddenly it was quiet. After the noise of the helicopters and the machineguns, the silence was powerful, as if one's hearing had been lost. There was no sign of Wilson and Funk.

A grenade exploded in the hamlet ahead, then gunfire, then a thunderous explosion that shook the ground and forced everyone down on their knees. I had not heard close artillery before and the sound made an extreme noise, a powerful blast of air bursting and metal splintering, the loudest *crraack* imaginable, loud as thunder. Several more explosions shook the ground. A machinegun rattled and rotor blades *whup-whupped* and a pair of gunships zoomed low overhead. The troops got up and followed a lieutenant single file to a dirt road that led into the hamlet. Le Sum and I got in line. The troops watched everything with great care, moving with caution, their forefingers on the trigger guards of their rifles.

'Hey, Jack! Over here!'

It was Funk, up ahead and off to the side of the road. Le Sum and I ran to him. Wilson came out of a clump of bushes cursing, his teeth clenched, angry.

'I've only got one roll of magstripe,' Wilson said, 'the one in the camera.'

He was using an Auricon 16 millimeter film camera that recorded natural sound along with the pictures. Each roll of film was four hundred feet long, running through the camera gate at twenty-four frames per second, lasting a total of about twelve minutes. Wilson was furious.

'Le Sum's gonna have to do most of the shooting,' he said. Funk listened and did not speak.

'We were taking incoming when we came in,' Wilson said, 'and I got so excited I shit in my pants. God *damn* it. I forgot the bag with the rest of the rawstock. Left it on the chopper.' He had gone into the bushes to clean himself and get rid of his soiled undershorts.

Two big airplanes swooped overhead, just off the deck, their piston-driven engines roaring. The face of one of the pilots was visible in the cockpit, smiling. Le Sum pointed toward the planes and shouted, "Vietnam! Vietnam!" Red and yellow markings of the Vietnamese Air Force were painted on the fuselage of the planes: VNAF. Le Sum was happy. The planes banked and disappeared, waggling their wings. We searched the sky waiting for them to come around.

'There they are!' Wilson said and pointed. The planes circled high.

'They're A-1Es,' Funk said, 'Skyraiders.'

Le Sum wound the crank on his silent camera, clicked the telephoto lens into position, and set the exposure. The first plane turned on its wing, rolled over on its side and began a wide-angled dive from about five thousand feet. I walked away from the others and switched on my tape recorder to describe the air strike. The planes were fixed wing fighter-bombers driven by a single propeller that was powered by a massive engine in front of the cockpit. They looked like oversized World War II fighter planes, Hellcats with bombs under their wings. The first plane charged down out of the sky and uncoupled a bomb at about a thousand feet. I saw that the pilot would not be able to pull the nose out of the dive in time, the angle was too steep. The plane was going to hit the ground.

"It's going in! It's going to crash!" I shouted into the microphone.

The plane swooped behind a line of trees just ahead of us and vanished. I winced, waiting for the sound of the crash and the concussion, but there was no fireball, no noise. A moment later the plane reappeared above the horizon farther away and climbed into the sky. I felt dizzy, disoriented.

Funk pointed to the edge of a plateau that connected the hillside with an escarpment that ran down to a deeper part of the valley where the plane disappeared. The edge of the valley was screened by a line of trees. The VNAF planes were bombing in the valley below, about three hundred meters away. I felt embarrassed. My description on the audiotape would seem hysterical when the radio producers listened to it in New York. I turned the recorder on again and apologized, saying the plane had dipped below the horizon for a few seconds and came up again safely. Then I continued the commentary, hoping the audio engineers in New York would edit out the mistake.

We moved on. Four soldiers with a light machinegun fired at a farmhouse across the river at the bottom of the valley. No one fired back. A person in a black shirt and pants ran out of the house, dashed across a field, and ducked behind a mound of dirt about three feet high. As he ran the soldiers tried to shoot him with the machinegun, shouting, 'Get 'im! Get 'im!' It wasn't clear whether the person running was a man or a woman, a soldier or a civilian. The machinegun stopped. Nothing moved. The soldier who fired the machine gun shouted in a southern accent, "Ah *killed* that gook muthafucker!"

An officer with two vertical strips of white tape on the back of his helmet appeared.

'Put a seventy-niner round behind that dirt pile and you've got him for sure,' the captain said.

One of the paratroopers aimed at the mound, angled his grenade launcher up a few inches and pulled the trigger. The M-79 jerked in his hands and made a distinctive *phoot*. The round exploded near the mound of dirt with a metallic *splaat*. An older sergeant said, 'You got him!'

The captain turned to the sergeant and said, 'Nice shot. Send your people over there and bring back the body.'

The sergeant looked confused. It was more than a hundred yards down the embankment, then across the open river to the house, and beyond that to the mound of dirt. The whole distance was over exposed terrain with no cover. The captain turned and walked away. The sergeant and the men in his machinegun team looked at one another in silence. They did nothing.

I caught up with the captain near the edge of the hamlet. He introduced himself as Williams Martin, commanding officer of C Company. He was in his mid-twenties. His hair was cut extremely short and he wore what looked like a military academy ring on his finger. He was alert without being nervous, giving the appearance of a bright efficient line infantry officer.

Martin and his command group walked into the hamlet single file: first the captain, followed by his radio operator, then the air liaison officer, his radioman, a Vietnamese army interpreter, a first lieutenant named Robert H. Vaughn who was acting as guide for the camera team, and the brigade sergeant major, Trinidad Prieto, a big kind-faced man with short black hair and brown skin who had been at Bastogne with the 101st Airborne and came along today to get away from the tedium of the camp.

Martin and his command group stopped walking. The radio operators kneeled on the ground and lit cigarettes.

'What's happening?' I asked.

'Well, the lead choppers in the first lift took some .50-caliber from near the village,' Martin said, 'so we know they're around.'

'Anybody hit?'

'No. None of ours. The pilots said they got three or four VC running away from the village.'

'What time was that?'

'06:30,' Martin said and looked at his military-issue wristwatch with its green cloth strap and tiny compass. 'We haven't had any serious contact on the ground, but we're not taking any chances. We're finding VC documents in several of these houses and there's no doubt in my mind that this is a VC village. The ARVN have probably never been in here before. But the VC don't want to stand and fight us, so they're bugging out.'

The hamlet was built on a plateau between the hillside and the valley and was organized in clusters of houses for the peasant families who farmed the fields around them. A narrow dirt road ran through the hamlet from north to south and led to Vinh Thanh, the main village in the valley. On the floor of the valley, near the river, small boats and fishing nets were stored near clusters of farmhouses. The valley was cultivated with rice, corn and other vegetables. Looking down at the tranquil setting on their helicopter reconnaissance missions, the Americans had nicknamed it "Happy Valley."

The houses in the hamlet were made of mud, brick and bamboo with thatched roofs that extended several feet over the front to provide shelter from the sun and rain. The walls of the houses were sturdy. Nearby were outbuildings for livestock, tools and food storage. Big earthen urns stood in the yards. Almost everything was made with materials that came from the immediate area. No cars or trucks or tractors were visible, and no electricity or telephone lines existed. The hamlet appeared to be entirely self-sufficient, its people living as their ancestors had lived for at least a thousand years, bound intimately to the land and the seasons by culture, tradition, family and philosophy. When a strong breeze blew across the fields, the deep green rice shoots rippled with the patterns of the wind like waves of water on the surface of the sea.

The soldiers walked through the hamlet and ordered people out of their houses. If the peasants did not obey on command, the soldiers pulled them out of the dwellings bodily. They searched inside the houses for weapons and military or political documents. When they found men of fighting age, they bound their wrists with pieces of rope and tied them behind their backs. The prisoners were forced to sit on the ground beside the dirt road in a group. The group grew larger as the morning went on.

Soldiers threw fragmentation grenades into underground bomb shelters in the houses and shouted, "Fire in the hole!" Some of them threw white phosphorous grenades in the holes and yelled, "Willie Pete!" (for WP). When they found documents they considered incriminating, they called on their radios to a team of Army engineers who put packages of plastic explosives in the houses and wired them to electrical detonators. Then, standing fifty yards away, the engineers shouted "Wetsu!" and fired the charges that demolished the buildings with thundering eruptions of mud and straw. Wilson and Le Sum filmed the houses disintegrating and Funk recorded the sounds. Funk asked a couple of engineers what "wetsu" meant, and they said, "Wetsu? We eat this shit up," and laughed.

Other soldiers went through the hamlet with five-gallon cans of gasoline and poured it over the debris of the houses and set it alight. Individual soldiers put flames from matches and cigarette lighters directly beneath the straw roofs of the houses and ignited them. Within the first hour of the sweep through the hamlet, more than a dozen clusters of houses and their contents were burning. Lieutenant Vaughn, the escort officer, explained that this was standard policy for the 101st Airborne in Vietnam. Whenever its troops were fired upon, the brigade retaliated by "leveling the village." It was happening every day or two, he said, up and down Happy Valley and all along Route Nineteen, from Qui Nhon to Pleiku. 'If we take fire,' Vaughn said, 'we level wherever it came from.' The brigade was carrying out in the most literal way the emerging American military strategy of "search and destroy," in this case the destruction of a hamlet whose defenders fired at the invading helicopters. One of the principal architects of the policy was a former commander of the 101st, General William Westmoreland, the senior officer of U.S. forces in Vietnam.

The peasants watched. They did not protest. Their faces appeared to be puzzled, as if in shock, unable to understand why this was happening to their hamlet, or what was in the minds of these strange men who looked like the French. The peasants stood out of the way and watched their houses burn. Children stood beside their mothers and older sisters. One man in a black shirt and shorts with his arms tied behind his back cried without shame.

A left-handed paratrooper tossed a hand grenade casually into a bomb shelter beneath one of the houses, stepped back and ducked his head. Seconds later, a muffled blast was heard. The soldier looked into the hole in a cursory way and left.

Later, when the smoke had risen out of the shelter, villagers pulled out the body of a woman and lifted her onto a metal plank of PSP and tied her to it with a strip of clean blue cloth. They carried her to the dirt road that ran through the middle of the hamlet and left her lying on her back across the road. She was young, not more than nineteen or twenty, with a soft round face. Her black hair was tied behind her head in a matted bun, dirty now. She wore a long-sleeved black cotton shirt. The front was torn open, exposing her chest and stomach. Her breasts were cut and spotted with dirt and dried blood. She was pregnant. Her bare feet were black with blood.

When I saw the body of the young woman, I felt distress. This wasn't part of the plan. American soldiers weren't supposed to kill innocent civilians, especially not women and children, most of all pregnant women. It didn't happen in the movies or in the war novels I had read and it wasn't supposed to happen in true life. My equilibrium was upset. Standing there, looking at the body of the woman, I tried to imagine what it was like in the hamlet when our helicopters had landed: the cracking of gunfire and artillery, panicked animals running in all directions, villagers dashing to the shelters, shouting to their children to take cover, trying to hide beneath the ground. I pictured the young woman crouched by herself in the dark hole in the earth, worrying, the seconds passing slowly, waiting for the noise to stop, hearing the footsteps of the soldiers approaching, the squawking of their radios, conversation in a language she did not understand, then the shouts: "Fire in the hole!" and feeling the bump of the strange metal object falling into the bunker with her, hearing the hiss of the fuse burning in the moments before the consciousness-shattering blast. *God, how terrifying that must have been,* I thought.

The young woman's body lay in the middle of the road. Some of the villagers came to look for a minute then turned and walked away. Their faces were blank, impassive. A small child with tousled black hair, two or three years old, wearing only a cotton top, stood by the body of the woman. Waiting, the child made no sound. An hour later, when everyone in the hamlet had seen what had been done, an older woman took the child up in her arms and balanced its weight on her hip and walked away.

Le Sum rolled film. An American soldier walked to the body and pulled a piece of the clean blue cloth over the woman's face. He looked at her for a minute, then walked away, his head down. Le Sum stared at the body and closed his eyes.

When Captain Martin heard about the killing of the woman, he called his platoon leaders together and told them to stop their men from throwing hand grenades into bomb shelters. "These bunkers," he said, "are like breezeways or garages back home. They're part of the house. Everybody's got one."

The platoon leaders nodded and went away and passed the word to stop throwing hand grenades into the bunkers. Instead, the soldiers started to throw smoke grenades in the bunkers. Smoke grenades were normally used to signal the location of a unit in the field and produced thick clouds of colored smoke that, in confined spaces, could suffocate a human.

The peasants were trapped. If they took shelter when their hamlet was attacked and hid in their bunkers, they were vulnerable to being killed by grenades. If they stayed above ground when the helicopters came in, they were in danger of being killed by artillery, air strikes or gunships.

Dozens of village men were forced to wait by the side of the road with their wrists tied. One of the prisoners told Le Sum that the heat from the sun was unbearable. I asked Captain Martin if it was necessary to keep the prisoners in the sun, that they were burning up. He said he hadn't thought about it and ordered them moved to the shade of a house. Le Sum and I poured water from our canteens into their open, upturned mouths and two soldiers did the same.

The Vietnamese army interpreter with the company spoke with each of the prisoners. Those who were not suspected of being VC were released. About a dozen men in their twenties and thirties were to be taken to brigade headquarters for interrogation. One of the men was identified by the interpreter as a VC platoon leader. When he was first taken prisoner, the suspect's face was hard, his eyes cold and angry, but as the day went on and he saw the hamlet being destroyed, he looked more and more fearful.

Wilson said he was out of film and sat down. He lit a Salem and took a deep drag. I was dizzy. I had given away most of my water and had not drunk enough myself. The heat was oppressive. I couldn't get the image of the pregnant woman on the road out of my mind. Wilson was pleased with the outcome of the story. By conserving his shots carefully, he had managed to get it all filmed in four hundred feet. There were no interviews or on-camera but Wilson said, 'We don't need any, we've got plenty of action.'

The troops finished searching the hamlet and broke out C rations to eat. Captain Martin said choppers were on the way to pick up the company and take it back to An Khe. Far down the road, a kilometer from the command group at the other end of the hamlet, a medical evacuation helicopter came in for a wounded soldier. Martin listened to his radio and said, 'Sergeant Major Prieto stepped on a punji stake and cut his foot. He should be okay. Get himself a purple heart for sure. Our only casualty.'

*

In Saigon the next day, I wrote the story of the operation and called it "Dawn Attack." I was not accustomed to writing for television news with its complicated combinations of visual, audio and narrative storytelling. I wrote at least one paragraph to accompany each of the scenes Wilson and Le Sum had shot. The process was difficult. I had to imagine the look of each scene, put it into some kind of order, reduce what happened to its simplest form, and write the voice-over narration. I was writing blind, trying to tell the story without seeing the pictures. I had witnessed the events as they happened, but I didn't know how they would appear on film. There was no film processing laboratory available in Saigon, so the exposed black-and-white footage had to be shipped to the United States for developing. There, editors would cut and match the film to the narration to produce the broadcast report. The process was complex, the finished product simple.

After finishing the script, I sat at the correspondents' desk in room 206/7 of the Caravelle Hotel, the CBS office, and showed the pages to Peter Kalischer. The veteran correspondent had black hair with a small patch of white on one side where he twirled it with his index finger when he was thinking hard.

'It's too long,' Kalischer said.

'Will you edit it?'

He gave me a long, serious look. 'You sure you want me to?'

I said I was.

Kalischer sat down at the desk with a marking pencil that was red on one end and blue on the other and started to read. Immediately he began to cut. The pencil flashed in his hand like a scalpel, cutting out sentences, phrases and individual words. Every adjective and adverb vanished under his pencil. He looked up to ask a few questions about the story and then crossed out several paragraphs. He did not change the facts or structure of the report, only the length. When he was finished, the pages were covered with red lines.

'Okay,' he said in a gruff rasp of a voice, 'now rewrite it, maybe in the present tense. You've got a helluva good story here.'

Wilson had suggested we start the story with the first wave of helicopters landing in a field, the troops jumping out and taking position. The final version of the narration began: *"We come in by helicopter, swooping down into a rice paddy at the first light of dawn. The time is six-thirty."*

Recording the voice-over, I spoke in a low flat voice, trying to sound like the recordings I had heard of CBS Radio correspondents broadcasting from Europe during World War II. As a child, I had listened with my mother and grandfather to the wartime broadcasts from London of Edward R. Murrow, chief CBS foreign correspondent, and his reports had made a permanent impression. Murrow was my idol. I tried to add dramatic inflection where it seemed appropriate but the reading was not very polished, nothing at all like Murrow.

When the film arrived in New York, a producer and film editor studied the narration and cut out more lines. They mixed others together to construct a modified account of what happened. The revised narration continued over pictures of the soldiers running into position: *"The objective of this mission is to trap a Viet Cong force and hammer it toward another unit of American troops advancing from other directions."* The producer then cut two lines and inserted a phrase to make it say: *"The paratroopers of the 101st Airborne must move into position quickly, for the choppers are vulnerable now and must get off the ground again."* Another line was cut, then: *"There's gunfire from ahead. And it's returned. The attack has begun."*

The producer in New York interrupted the voice-over narration to make room for about forty-five seconds of natural sound: gunfire, explosions and shouting. The pictures showed the troops running through the hamlet, taking cover, and shooting their rifles, machineguns and grenade launchers. One of them, left-handed, threw a grenade into a bunker.

The film editor opened the sound track for the angry voice of the Southern soldier saying, "I killed that . . . ." but covered the words "gook motherfucker."

The narration resumed: "*Now machine-guns and grenade launchers are brought to bear on the enemy position across the river. Nothing moves.*" A pause, then: "*It seems apparent now that the enemy is choosing to flee rather than stand and fight.*"

The pictures showed the body of the young woman in the road with the blue cloth being pulled over her face: "*This woman is killed in the attack. She was hit by a grenade thrown into a bunker.*" The narration ran for five seconds over the picture of the body of the woman.

"*The commander changes the order. Smoke, rather than fragment grenades, are to be thrown into suspected hideouts. The commander wants to make sure no more villagers are killed, and he tells his men to be careful with their grenades. 'These Vietnamese bunkers—or bomb shelters,' he explains, 'are as common as garages back in the States.'*"

Next, the rounding up of suspects: "*Some Vietnamese men are seized as Viet Cong suspects. This suspect is identified by a Vietnamese Army advisor as a Viet Cong platoon leader. VC documents or ammunition or supplies were found in these huts. The order is given to destroy them. The demolition experts do their job well.*"

Here, the pictures and sound showed an engineer setting off an explosion that demolished a big house, debris falling around him.

"*If the enemy return to the village tonight, they will have no homes.*" Another explosion.

"*The operation is almost over now. A few more artillery explosions are heard in the hills. But the enemy—what little was seen of him—has taken cover and is not coming out. The day's toll includes five Viet Cong killed and about five wounded. A number of prisoners were taken—a dozen perhaps—and a dozen homes were destroyed.*"

The signoff said, "*John Laurence, CBS News, with the 101st Airborne Brigade, somewhere in South Vietnam.*"

The story ran on the *CBS Evening News* of September 3, 1965, for three minutes and three seconds.

SEPTEMBER 2, 1965

Saigon was the most exotic city I had ever seen. Everything about it was unusual, unfamiliar, mostly alluring. Built on the side of a river that flowed down out of the Central Highlands and into the South China Sea, the city had handsome fine-boned people, blazing heat and monsoon rains, decaying French colonial architecture, a blend of European and Asian styles, and, because of the war, an edge of intrigue and mystery. The broad old boulevards that carried the city's commerce were lined with plane trees that stood tall and straight like sentries and cast cool shadows onto the streets, sidewalks and dull yellow buildings below. Graceful fawn-eyed women with long flowing hair glided by on bicycles as light as the wind. Thin black-haired men looked out from behind cold expressionless faces they wore like masks. Rough poverty infused the smell and feel and texture of the city with a rotting hothouse air. Behind everything, the resurgent guerrilla war and the increased American commitment to it charged each transaction between the two cultures with incalculable degrees of risk and reward. Nothing was immediately measurable. All you could do was feel it. Mysterious, strange, beautiful—Saigon was a wild tropical orchid.

In the early days, traffic was not yet anarchic. Drivers and cyclists still obeyed signal lights and the instructions of traffic police foreigners referred to as "white mice" because of their all-white uniforms. Living space was not yet inundated by hundreds of thousands of refugees fleeing the war. The economy hadn't been bloated by the flood of American dollars. Night life had not degenerated into drunken street corner trade in sex and drugs. Instead, in the late summer of '65, the tempo of life in Saigon was still relatively relaxed, the foreign influences on the outward face of society still seemed more French than American, and the visible evidence of the increasing U.S. presence more resembled an invasion of wide-eyed tourists than warriors.

The Vietnamese I met were exceptionally polite and modest in their manners, clean and attractive in appearance, friendly and engaging in conversation, and rigidly uncommunicative about their opinions. Revealing nothing personal seemed to be a game they played. Peter Kalischer warned me that the Vietnamese only told us what they thought we wanted to hear, mainly good news, as if *we* were the ones being patronized. But it was more than that. Government officials I visited in their dark paper-filled offices told me less than I already knew. Even then their comments were guarded. It was as if they saw no value in revealing information that might be helpful to an outsider. There was nothing to be gained by expressing a personal opinion or by criticizing anything. Public officials were cautious to the point of paranoia. It made them sound stupid. For a young American journalist who needed to know how the war effort was being managed, how decisions were being made, how the bureaucracy functioned, the process of finding out was frustrating, exhausting. Eventually I gave up. I was too new to know that pervasive secrecy in the civil service was necessary to protect the intricate networks of graft, bribery, nepotism, payoffs, kickbacks and other corruption that permeated official South Vietnamese institutions. Nor did I understand that most Vietnamese saw us as transients, another temporary army of occupation, like the French. Some with a knowledge of history saw themselves more like the Vichy-era French of 1941–1944, or their own ancestors under the Chinese. They knew, or at least suspected, that we would go home and leave them for the reckoning with their next masters. Anything they said now—anything that hinted of collaboration—could hurt them later.

Americans were more helpful, or at least appeared to be, even if they were not always honest. Most of the time I couldn't tell. In my first weeks in Saigon, I made the rounds of U.S. military and diplomatic offices and introduced myself to dozens of military and civilian officials. I met career diplomats with long experience in Asia and young embassy operatives on their first overseas posts; retired army officers called back to service and newly promoted captains and majors working for MACV; academic scholars from private sector think tanks and foreign aid workers from foundations and charities. Hundreds of American bureaucrats flooded into Saigon, too many to meet, more arriving every week. Their responsibilities included armed military operations, planning, intelligence, counterintelligence, psychological warfare, propaganda, public affairs, communications, construction, logistics, agriculture, health, education, refugee affairs, studying the Viet Cong, studying the Vietnamese, advising the Vietnamese, aid and pacification program management, police training and supervision, and other more sensitive programs including operations in Laos and North Vietnam. A fabulous bureaucracy was being created to conduct war-fighting ops on multiple fronts at the same time.

I met young hopeful foreign service officers who spoke of the urgent need for the American and Vietnamese governments to spearhead a social and economic revolution in the countryside, to redistribute land and resources, to win the allegiance of as many peasants as possible, and take the responsibility for radical change away from the Viet Cong. They talked patiently for hours, trying to make the case that only by implementing generous new programs to improve the living conditions of the common people could the initiative be seized and the war be won. This meant that the present U.S. strategy of trying to achieve victory primarily by military force would have to be modified. Instead, a genuine revolution was necessary. The narrow-minded attitudes of U.S. military leaders in Saigon, they said, would make that difficult.

In early September, a U.S. embassy official phoned me at the CBS bureau to say a friend in the States had seen my first work on the air and had recommended me to him. He invited me to join him for lunch at the open-air restaurant on the roof of the Rex Hotel in downtown Saigon. I accepted. The menu at the Rex was primarily American and the food was served by Vietnamese and Filipino waiters in uniforms. All the other patrons were Americans. The embassy official introduced himself (let's call him Bill Svenson) and sat down at a corner table with his back to a column where he could see everything that moved on the floor. Svenson was in his mid- to late forties, maybe fifty, with a solid build and a casual confident manner that seemed to match his intelligence and authority. Over hamburgers and iced tea, he spoke knowledgeably about political activities in Saigon and seemed well-informed about conspiracies within the Vietnamese officer corps. He was strongly opinionated, and he supported the views of the young American civil servants who wanted to make a revolution in the countryside. Svenson told me he was trying to find out more about U.S. military activity in the provinces, especially in places I had visited recently. He said he'd welcome anything I had observed. I told him about the 101st operation in Happy Valley in which the young woman was killed and the preparations for the arrival of the First Cav. It had surprised him that we found the division and had been able to do a story about it. I described the chance meeting in Nha Trang with Marv Wolf and his green T-shirt. I did not say where the Cav and the

101st were located but Svenson knew. He said the rest of the division was scheduled to land at Qui Nhon in about ten days. By now, we agreed, everybody around the new base at An Khe knew the division was coming, including the Viet Cong.

'What section of the embassy do you work in?' I asked. We had been talking for almost an hour.

'Political,' Svenson said, lighting a cigar.

'State Department?'

'I work closely with State,' he said, looking at my eyes.

'What do you do?'

He thought a moment. 'Well, what I do basically is gather, report and analyze information.' Again, the straight look. 'Like you.'

'Well, I try not to analyze. Just send our stories back and let our listeners figure them out.'

'Yeah, us too,' Svenson said. 'Problem is they don't always listen, and they don't always figure it out correctly.'

He got up and took the check to the cashier, saying, 'This is on me.' When I protested, he said, 'You can get the next one.'

'Okay. It's a deal.'

'Next time you get back from one of your trips, give me a call and we'll have lunch. I've enjoyed hearing your stories.'

We shook hands. I walked back to the bureau feeling satisfied, professionally proud. Svenson had given me some useful information, inside stuff that might be helpful later. To be in contact with a well-placed source inside the embassy was part of my job. It did not occur to me that trading information with an official in the U.S. government might be less than ethical. I knew that journalists were supposed to be impartial, even in war, but I did not suspect that Svenson might be gathering information for the Central Intelligence Agency. CIA reported directly to the White House, not to the American public, and its methods of extracting information were often immoral. Any doubts I had about the propriety of our exchange were overruled by my need as a journalist to know as much as possible about what was going on, to cover the story as thoroughly as I could, and also by my personal loyalty to the American cause.

I was living out of a shabby room at the southern end of Tu Do Street in a hotel called the Majestic. It was anything but majestic, a four-story mausoleum on the Saigon riverfront with dark ill-lighted rooms that defied the efforts of the Vietnamese staff to keep them clean, tidy and free of insects. The bureau had booked me there when I got off the plane from the United States and promised me a place at the Caravelle when one became available. I shared the room with an odd assortment of other guests: predominately mosquitoes but also ants, lizards, dragonflies, geckos, household flies, spiders, beetles, cockroaches and families of unidentified bugs that checked in and out under the door. Apart from providing an overly soft mattress and shelter from the rain, the hotel was not much of an advance on sleeping in the field. The food was barely edible. Hallways were dark and smelled of insecticide. The walls were decorated with framed tourist posters that had been printed in the 1940s and 1950s by Pan American Airways and offered tourist enticements like, "Fly Pan Am—Discover Viet-Nam." The rooms had simple wooden furniture that was more decorative than functional and appeared to have been built locally. The length of the bed and size of the chairs made them more suitable for children. After a while, I began to feel out of place. Saigon was losing its allure. I was more comfortable in the field.

I saw thousands of prosperous Saigonese riding comfortably through the city in pedicabs and cars, eating well in air-conditioned restaurants, and wearing clean tailored clothes, while woefully poor people in the countryside wore black work clothes and raised malnourished children who were naked much of the time. *Why should there be so much difference in people's lives?* I wondered.

At the bureau office in the Caravelle, a phone call came from Major Siler, the First Cav information officer in An Khe. His voice coming through the military telephone system was faint even though he was shouting. "We're having a party in a day or two," Siler cried. "Come up and join us." He was using a prearranged signal to alert us to an impending operation.

The next morning, Wilson, Funk and I flew to Qui Nhon on the coast north of Nha Trang, then hitched a ride west to An Khe. By the time we arrived the assault had already taken place and the Americans were in full battle. Paratroopers of the 101st Airborne were fighting for their lives. At brigade headquarters, an officer gave us a briefing. Two rifle companies of the 2d Battalion, 503d Infantry Regiment, he said, were heavily engaged with at least one battalion of main-force Viet Cong. The officer pointed to the location of the battle on a large field map covered with a clear plastic overlay with black and red markings drawn on it in grease pencil to designate the units involved. The fight was taking place around a landing zone in the Vinh

Thanh Valley about twenty miles northeast of An Khe. *Happy Valley again*, I thought. *Same place we went last month.* The paratroopers had returned to the valley and this time the VC stood and fought. The date was Saturday, September 18. The operation was code-named Gibraltar.

The briefing officer said the attack had begun at 0715. The first lift of helicopters had taken light enemy fire at the landing zone. By the time the second lift arrived a half hour later, the fire had become intense. Several choppers were shot down or seriously damaged by VC anti-aircraft batteries. The paratroopers quickly found themselves outnumbered. They were being killed and wounded by Vietnamese mortars, automatic weapons and small arms. One platoon was completely cut off from the rest of its company. A furious battle had been under way for six hours, so intense it was impossible to send in reinforcements or resupply. The ground fire was so heavy, helicopters could not get near the troops to help them.

A chopper landed at the command post with the brigade commander, Colonel James Timothy, who had been flying over the scene of the battle all morning, directing air and artillery strikes, trying to maneuver blocking forces into position, and reassuring his junior officers on the radio. I had met Timothy two and a half weeks earlier when we went out with his men.

'There's a helluva fight going on out there,' he said. 'Charlie is taking one Godawful beating. The pilots are reporting VC bodies all over the place. Our people are holding their own. Getting a lot of help from the Air Force. The Cav is giving us artillery support with their 105s. This is probably their first combat action in Vietnam.'

Timothy said that at least three helicopters had been shot down. Fifteen of the remaining twenty-one in the squadron had been damaged by ground fire. I asked if there was any way we could get to the scene of the fighting. 'No. Not yet. I can't get my *own* people in there,' he said. 'We'll get you in as soon as we can. Don't worry, you'll get a good story.'

The brigade had set up a field command post in a clearing on the crest of a small hill near An Khe. It was a neat clean circle of general-purpose tents, map stands, tables and chairs. It looked similar to field headquarters I had seen in old photographs of the Confederate Army in the Civil War. Inside the tents, soldiers listened to radios and charted the course of the battle on maps. From time to time a staff officer ran to a nearby landing zone, climbed into a helicopter and flew away. Few of the men sat. With the constant chatter on the radios coming out of the tents and the quick serious movements of the officers, NCOs and enlisted men, there was a sense of ordered urgency. A neat hand-painted sign in the area said,

H.Q. 101st Airborne Brigade–ALWAYS FIRST.

Frustrated at being so far removed from the story, I wandered away from the CP and sat nearby in an area of light brush to make notes. A slapping sound came from behind one of the larger bushes. Every five or ten seconds there was a loud *smack*. Quietly, I pushed my way through the brush and looked into a clearing on the other side. An officer from the 101st was standing next to a Vietnamese Army officer, the two of them looming over another Vietnamese who was sitting on a folding metal chair with his hands tied behind his back. Every few seconds the Vietnamese Army officer asked a question and, getting no reply, slapped the prisoner hard across the face.

I stepped out of the brush and took a photograph with my still camera. Hearing the shutter click, the two officers looked up. I recognized the American as the brigade intelligence officer, the S-2.

'Excuse me,' I said. 'What's going on?'

'We pulled this one out of the bush,' the American officer said. 'We're trying to make him give us the direction of the escape route. If we find out which way they head when they break contact we can clobber them with arty and air.' He seemed embarrassed by what I'd seen. The prisoner's face was flushed with red welts.

'Do you have to beat him up?'

'It's the only way he'll talk. This guy is hard-core. Won't say anything.' I excused myself again and walked back to the command post where Wilson and Funk were waiting.

A few minutes later, as if on signal, an officer announced that a helicopter was inbound to take us to the battle scene. We would be taken to an observation post overlooking the action from a kilometer or two away. 'Maybe you can work your way in to the LZ later,' he said. The fighting was still too heavy to get to the rifle companies in contact.

Wilson, Funk and I took off in the helicopter and flew out toward the battlefield. The chopper landed twenty minutes later in a clearing on top of a ridgeline where a squad of paratroopers had established an observation post. In the distance, about a mile and a half away, one could see explosions tearing at the heavy jungle terrain, loud *crummps* and *braaacks*, first from artillery and then from air strikes. Clouds of white smoke rose in the sky and mixed with black plumes from napalm dropped by the planes. The shrill high-pitched shrieks of jet engines tore the air. A young major wearing a military academy ring watched the bombardment through binoculars. From time to time he spoke on his field radio reporting what he saw. His hair was cropped extremely short and he wore a black, white and gold patch on his left shoulder bearing the profile of an eagle. Above the patch it said "Airborne."

An Associated Press correspondent had joined us on the helicopter. Robin Mannock was a thirty-five-year-old Englishman from near Oxford, six feet tall with a reddish beard and mustache and deep gray eyes. He was an experienced war correspondent who had covered the civil war in the Congo for the past three and a half years for Reuters and had served in the British Army in Suez and Jordan in the 1950s. Educated at Oxford University, he had the accent to match. He wore a floppy olive-green British army hat with no shape to it. With his height and beard and big-boned features, Mannock had the look of a large gnome.

There was no story at the OP. The battle was too far away and impossible to reach by foot. Wilson looked through the telephoto lens of his camera and said, 'I can't shoot a damn thing this far away.' He put the camera down.

'We're going to be stuck out here all bloody night,' Mannock said, 'and miss the story entirely.' It occurred to me that we might have been sent to this isolated place by the brigade staff to get us away from the command post and the interrogation of prisoners.

The day dragged on. The weather was overcast and damp. Every hour or so, Mannock asked the major to call in a chopper to take us out. The major said there was a small chance they might get a supply ship late in the day. Mannock badgered him. Finally, the major shouted, 'I've got better things to do than provide transportation for the press,' though he was not busy. From this distance, the major could see little of the battle. We were clearly on the periphery of the action.

It began to rain. Mannock and I snapped our ponchos together and made a shelter. Wilson and Funk did the same.

'God, I hate being stuck in the boonies all night with nothing to show for it,' he said.

'We're not going to be stuck here all night,' I said.

'Well, I must say I admire your confidence,' he said, 'but I don't share your optimism.'

'You'll see.'

'See what?'

'How lucky I am.'

'Well, I'm bloody well *not* lucky. Anything but. Nearly got killed last week and I've still got the stitches to prove it.'

Mannock had been flying back to An Khe after an operation when the helicopter he was riding in lost power, probably because of mechanical failure. With the existing momentum of the engine and rotor blades, the pilot was able to auto rotate down to a safe altitude and was heading for a small clearing in the bush when he misjudged the height of the trees and pulled pitch too early. The chopper hit the trees, crashed on its side and caught fire. Mannock got out but the pilot was pinned in the burning wreckage, critically injured. Despite the fire and danger of an explosion, two crew members disassembled the front control panel, tore it away and pulled the pilot out of the chopper. Less than a minute later the fuel tanks exploded.

Mannock bet me that we would not get off the ridge tonight.

'We're going to have to spend the night here. I can feel it in my bones,' he said.

'What's the bet?' I said.

'Bottle of whisky.'

'You're on.'

It was agreed. If we didn't get off the ridge, I would buy him a bottle of Black Label and if we did, he would owe me a bottle of Chivas. We shook on it. His hands were huge.

Just before dark the major told us to pack up, a chopper was inbound to drop off food and water for the squad on the OP and would take us back to An Khe. He seemed relieved.

'Laurence, my dear boy, I shall happily present you with a bottle of Scotch when we get back to Saigon,' Mannock said in his impeccable Oxbridge accent.

'I told you I was lucky.'

'Lucky? I'll say. This is a *miracle!*'

It was the first.

★

The next day we did on-camera interviews with some of the soldiers who had been in the battle.

"I was like a proud papa out there," an older sergeant said. "The privates led the charge. The privates went first."

"How did you feel yourself?" I asked.

"Scared," he said and smiled. Then he nodded his head. "Everyone was scared."

The battle was fought at close quarters, the soldiers said, at a range of five to ten feet at times. It lasted all day Saturday and into Sunday before reinforcements arrived.

"It was a nightmare," a private said. "Nobody slept all night."

"There were mortars all around us. Everybody got hit by shrapnel," another said.

A sergeant said, "I spent three years in Korea and never saw nothing like this."

"This is the best I've felt since I been in Vietnam," a soldier said, happy to have survived.

"How long you been here?" I asked.

"Three weeks."

The men said they ran out of food and water during the battle and ate corn from the fields where they were fighting. One soldier asked where I got my new jungle combat boots. I told him they came from the black market in Saigon. He said the leather jump boots the paratroopers were wearing fell apart during the battle. The thread in the stitching had rotted away in the jungle humidity and heat. It was a severe handicap, he said, trying to fight in bare feet.

"We can't get the new GI tropical boots for love nor money," he said in a bitter voice. "Just like the Army. Fightin men come last."

Later Colonel Timothy briefed. He said he was "real proud [that] we did not leave a missing man or body behind" when the troops withdrew from the battlefield. He said that his airborne troops, the First Cav artillery and the Air Force had killed at least 226 enemy troops. "The actual body count is fifty-five," he said, "but we know we got more." It was the first time I heard the expression "body count" used by an American officer.

A final figure had not been recorded yet but the 101st knew it had lost more than twenty men killed and over forty wounded. I was not allowed to report the actual numbers because of the MACV censorship rule. I had to say "light to moderate U.S. casualties" in order not to reveal to the Viet Cong how seriously the battalion had been damaged. The engagement was the first major battle between regular American Army forces and main-force Viet Cong. After the briefing by Colonel Timothy, the brigade intelligence officer asked to speak to me privately. He said the prisoner I had seen being beaten finally gave away the direction of the VC escape route.

'We hit the valley he told us about with air and arty,' he said. 'Later the pilots saw fifty to sixty bodies there. We just tore them to pieces.' I thanked the S-2 for telling me and said I was not going to report what I had seen of him and his Vietnamese translator beating the prisoner. 'That's the way it is in war,' he said.

I wondered whether the fierce resistance the Viet Cong put up in Happy Valley might have been related to the search-and-destroy operation there eighteen days earlier when the paratroopers killed the pregnant woman, burned dozens of houses, and tied all the men in the hamlet and forced them to sit for hours in the sun.

SEPTEMBER 3, 1965

Wilson, Funk and I arrived in Danang, South Vietnam's second largest city, headquarters of the U.S. Marines 3d Amphibious Force. It was the first time for all of us. We flew up from Saigon on an Air Force C-123, the big awkward cargo plane the size and shape of a whale. The plane landed at every major airfield from Saigon to Danang, dropping off troops and cargo, picking up more, shuddering back into the air, screaming and vibrating like a jackhammer. The flight took half a day. As we were climbing down the steps on the edge of the runway in Danang, our bodies felt numb. A Marine driver with a truck from the press center waited to help with the baggage.

'Welcome to Danang,' he said.

'Thank you,' I said, looking around. Jet fighter planes roared down the runway and screamed into the sky with the loudest noise I had ever heard, afterburners firing orange flames.

'How close is the war?'

'Oh, not far,' he said. 'A few clicks. You'll see.'

We loaded our equipment into the back of the truck, climbed in after them and set off for the press center.

Danang was a frontier town. American troops walked the streets with casual ease, loose-fitting fatigue hats on their heads, pistols in holsters on their hips. They sauntered in long loping strides past frail-looking Vietnamese with their light cotton clothes and delicate manners who looked up and saw warrior giants from another planet—tall, confident, fearless—an army of Martians. Fifteen thousand American Marines had arrived since March and more were arriving every day. The streets of Danang were crowded with convoys of jeeps, trucks and tanks—engines wheezing, air horns blaring—transporting men and equipment from the docks at the harbor to line infantry positions on the fringes of the city. Moving fast, the mammoth trucks forced Vietnamese on bicycles and scooters off the streets and onto the curb and dusted them with particles of fine brown dirt. The metal treads of the tracked vehicles chewed up the pavement and left ruts in the roads, their exhaust pipes belching oily gases of blue-black smoke that hung in the air behind them. Danang was dust-choking hot and loud and filling up fast with Americans and their energy.

The buildup was under way all over Vietnam—at Danang and Chu Lai, Qui Nhon and An Khe, Bien Hoa and Cu Chi, Cam Ranh Bay and Saigon, and at hundreds of smaller places spread across the lush green landscape. The U.S. military was moving in, some said invading, not just with soldiers, sailors, Marines, airmen and women, but also with diplomats, government officials, technicians, clerks, cryptographers, spies, military police, aid workers, architects, construction gangs, engineers, entrepreneurs, businesspeople, journalists, prostitutes, writers and entertainers—a representative sample of the commercial population of an American city. Vietnam got it all. Anyone in the States who wanted a piece of the action was welcome to come and try. An advanced Western culture was being superimposed on a mainly agrarian, conservative Asian society and it made an awkward fit. There was little that an ordinary Vietnamese could do to stop it except wait patiently for it to pass or join the resistance and fight.

Battalions of American troops walked off their airplanes and troopships after traveling halfway around the world (in less than twenty-four hours sometimes) and descended on a strange humid overheated place where the light was brighter than anywhere they'd ever been. Tens of thousands of loyal young men from California and Alabama and Nebraska and Massachusetts and almost everywhere else in the country were answering the call to arms of their commander in chief, Lyndon Baines Johnson. Elected president by a landslide the year before, now he was sending them on an undefined mission (officially, it wasn't a war) to fight for their country on the mainland of Asia, something one of his predecessors, Dwight Eisenhower, had warned against. A fair number of the new arrivals were too young to vote.

Confident of quick victory, some of the Americans swaggered. Straight-backed, self-assured, they walked the streets of Danang and other cities through a sea of smaller, self-effacing Vietnamese who stood aside for them with the outward appearance of deference. From the start, some Vietnamese hated the Americans; hated their smell, hated their wealth, hated their noisy habits and crude manners and quick tempers that seemed so uncivilized by their own standards. Some Vietnamese saw the Americans as English-speaking replacements for the French who had humbled and humiliated them for most of a century. They were afraid the Americans were coming as an army of occupation and conquest. They hated their attitude.

Many U.S. military officers were in a hurry to get to the war before it was over, punch their career tickets in time to advance: six months in command of a combat unit, maybe a medal or two, perhaps a promotion. For military careerists, the war in Vietnam was the fast track to success. Nobody believed it would last long enough for a second tour. The most optimistic thought the war would be over by Christmas; the pessimists said it might take a year. Even the remaining French, who had seen their pearl of a colony collapse in chaos at Dien Bien Phu eleven years earlier, thought the Americans would win it quickly.

"Oh, your helicopters!" one of them said to me. "Your helicopters will win this! The Viets cannot hide from your helicopters!"

The words were spoken over lunch in a cool sophisticated restaurant by a French settler, a veteran of the first Indochina War, who spoke with such conviction I thought he must be right. In those early days I believed everything I was told.

"Of course, *we* did not have so many helicopters," he said, as if all that had prevented the French from winning their war with the Vietnamese was more firepower and greater mobility.

It was the perceived wisdom of the period: the army with superior firepower and mobility would prevail. Officials took it for granted that U.S. troops were better motivated. It was what American generals had learned from two hundred years of collective military experience, from Bunker Hill to the Chosin Reservoir. American military superiority was a given. The country had never lost a war. Not much attention was paid to the historical fact that the Vietnamese were much more experienced in warfare than the Americans, that their ancestors had fought wars of independence against one foreign power or another, mainly Chinese, for most of their two-thousand-year history. No one seemed very concerned that the Vietnamese might be capable of absorbing thousands of foreign troops and their firepower and the punishment that fell on them with endless, torrential force — millions of tons of high-explosive fragmentation bombs and artillery shells and aerial rockets and napalm canisters and cluster-bomb units and land mines and claymores and chemical defoliants and grenades and small arms and every other nonnuclear instrument of destruction—without breaking their national will.

In August 1965, the U.S. military buildup announced by President Johnson in July was fully in motion. Already, 100,000 troops had arrived in Vietnam, a total of 200,000 would be in place by the end of the year, 300,000 by the end of the next year, a half million by the next. On the pretext of punishing North Vietnam for a mysterious nighttime incident involving U.S. and North Vietnamese ships in the Gulf of Tonkin the year before, the president and his cabinet sent the armed forces into South Vietnam in strength. (A limited number of military "advisers" had been in the country since the late 1950s.) The administration was given a blank check to wage war by a nearly unanimous majority of the U.S. Congress. There had been only two votes against the resolution in the Senate.

In the early days, the plan was simple. From their new bases and outposts along the coast and at strategic points inland, American troops and their Vietnamese allies, the Army of the Republic of Vietnam (ARVN), would secure the heavily populated areas. Then they would send out troops to search the surrounding countryside for indigenous South Vietnamese resistance fighters, the Viet Cong, and their North Vietnamese allies. They would hunt them by helicopter and foot patrol, flush them from their hiding places, engage them in combat and kill them with the combined arms of infantry, artillery, armor, naval gunfire and air forces. The plan would require the most sophisticated system of command and communications attempted in the history of warfare. For the Americans, ten to fifteen troops would be needed to support each infantryman in the field.

At the same time, an extensive program of civic action was created to try to gain the support of Vietnamese peasants and bring them under the control of the military government in Saigon. It was called the "pacification program." Roads and bridges would be built, wells dug, food and building materials distributed, medical care and hygienic instruction provided, classrooms constructed and staffed with teachers, educational and propaganda matter printed, loans and grants arranged, local and national elections held to teach political democracy, something ordinary Vietnamese citizens had not been allowed to practice before. In some cases, entire villages would be moved out of Viet Cong territory and the peasants relocated in government-controlled refugee camps. By the end of August 1965, there were approximately 620,000 refugees. About one-third of them were scattered among the camps, and the rest lived in slums around the cities. The pacification program became known by the slogan "winning the hearts and minds of the people."

The effort was to be managed in close collaboration with the military, paramilitary, police and civilian apparatus of the Saigon government, which, in turn, would provide administrators at every level. Money was not a serious problem. Saigon wrote up the requirements, and Washington wrote the checks. The bureaucracy allowed the central government to control billions of dollars of American funds, flooding the country with cash and commodities, creating an irresistible temptation for illegal personal gain.

Clandestine operations organized by the CIA, including counterterrorist assassination squads such as the Provincial Reconnaissance Units and the Special Operations Group of Army Special Forces, ran parallel to the public programs and were relatively secret. From time to time, reporters came in passing contact with "black operations" but were not allowed to cover them in any depth. Those who knew what was going on did not talk about it; those who did not know didn't ask.

With sincerity and hard work, ingenuity and armed might, the United States intended to preserve South Vietnam among the non-Communist nations of Southeast Asia and demonstrate to the Communist world, especially China and the Soviet Union, that subversion and armed aggression would be challenged, contested and defeated. No matter that the Geneva Convention (which had ended the last war in Vietnam) required free elections for a new national leadership by 1956. No matter that the most popular leader in Vietnam was Ho Chi Minh of the north. No matter that South Vietnam was now in violation of that Geneva Agreement. No matter that the rulers of South Vietnam were as ruthless and dictatorial and corrupt in their ways as the single-party leaders in the north. Communism was an evil the United States had to fight, even though its allies in the fight were corrupt.

Newly arrived, young, impressionable and idealistic, I thought it was an honorable cause and that success was certain. So did the great majority of Americans. The U.S. commitment to democracy was righteous. It had never entered a war it had not won. If the country followed the lessons of Western civilization and the principles of modern political and military science, the mission would be accomplished. A bright young secretary of defense, Robert S. McNamara, was in charge of the war-making program. He and the team of presidential advisers installed by the late President John F.

Kennedy seemed to be uniformly intelligent, articulate and hardworking. They were also exceedingly confident.

After all, history had taught us that courage, self-sacrifice and teamwork win wars. If our soldiers were as brave as our ancestors who had defeated the British in the War of Independence, who had civilized the great North American wilderness, who had cultivated the Great Plains and conquered the west, who had fought and won two world wars, surely we would prevail in Vietnam. The courage of Washington and Lafayette and Lee and Patton and so many others was in our blood and bones. Vietnam was to be a great adventure, another New Frontier, a modern extension of the civilizing drive to the west. If we Americans followed the fictional heroes of Melville and Clemens and London and Hemingway, how could a culture as primitive and small and insignificant as Vietnam defeat us? If we could act in the drama of real life as well as our heroes in the pictures—Cooper, Stewart, Tierney, Fonda, Flynn, Leigh, Gable, Hayworth, Bogart and Wayne—we would be invincible. There was no doubt. The idea of defeat, the very concept, was not part of a logical equation. With such a superior history, the country was an indestructible force. Americans had faith. Whatever happened to anyone else, we were not going to get hurt. The idea of being hit by a high-velocity lead slug the size of a fingertip spinning invisibly through the air or being struck by a sharp-edged piece of steel moving faster than the speed of sound and bleeding until the conscious world became as blank as the deepest sleep and the body died—the idea was too abstract, too unimaginable, too grotesque to be considered seriously. There would be casualties, yes, and that is what they would be called, "casualties," an expression as cold and impersonal and as easy to skip lightly across in a newspaper summary as the very word: war.

The ride to the press center was bumpy and slow. Danang is about 375 miles northeast of Saigon on the coast of the South China Sea, roughly the same distance and direction from Washington, D.C., to Boston. U.S. military intelligence had reported four enemy regiments of about a thousand soldiers each operating in I Corps, the Marines' area of responsibility in the northern quarter of South Vietnam. The Viet Cong had just fought the first major battle of the war with regular American forces, a brutal blood-washed encounter on the white sandy coast of the Batangan Peninsula, about seventy miles southeast of Danang—in the proximity of the new Marine combat base and airfield at Chu Lai. A battalion of Marines had gone ashore in a traditional amphibious landing the generals called Operation Starlite and, without realizing it, overran a main-force Viet Cong regiment. Observing the Marine landing and advance, the VC took cover in tunnels. When the Marines had passed over them, the VC came up out of the ground behind their lines and attacked from the rear. In savage, close-quarters fighting over several days in August, the VC lost over six hundred troops killed. Marine losses were fifty-one killed and over two hundred wounded. Both sides declared the battle a victory. The action was reported by journalists from the Danang press center, though one of the best accounts was written by a young Associated Press reporter who had hurried up from Saigon. Peter Arnett, a New Zealand citizen who had been working in Vietnam since 1962, got to the scene shortly after the battle ended and reconstructed the details in dramatic style.

Arriving at the Combat Information Bureau, Wilson, Funk and I were given a cool but formally polite greeting by Marine public information officers. They did not smile or shake hands. Unlike U.S. Army officers in An Khe who had been pleased to have us, the Marines were reserved. We had not expected a friendly welcome. At the time, CBS News was in poor favor with the Marines. A few weeks earlier, correspondent Morley Safer and his Vietnamese camera crew had gone on patrol with a Marine platoon and came back with a report Safer called "The Burning of Cam Ne." According to his narration, the Marines burned a Vietnamese farm hamlet in retaliation for being fired upon by a sniper. The film showed one of the Marines setting fire to the thatched roof of a peasant's hut with a Zippo lighter. "This is what the war is all about," Safer said on camera as an old man cried pathetically in front of his burning home. Safer's sardonic narration suggested the platoon had been unnecessarily severe with the peasants, punishing them for a sniper attack the peasants had been unable to prevent. The Marine Corps reacted with outrage at all levels. Safer was accused of fabricating the pictures, of providing the lighter used in the burning, of being a Communist sympathizer, of being an untrustworthy journalist, and of being an unpatriotic foreigner (Safer was born and raised in Canada and had not been imbued with loyalty to the American way of life). Other than his being Canadian, none of the accusations was true. In Washington, a large section of the American military and political establishment judged the report to be significantly harmful to U.S. interests. CBS News management was heavily criticized for allowing the report to be broadcast. The network defended its right to show an honest news story even though it was painful to watch. In time, the Marines presented a version of the incident that was at variance with Safer's but did not justify the severity of the platoon's reaction. After the incident, Marines were forbidden to burn villages.

Most journalists who managed to see Safer's piece judged it to be an accurate, hard-edged war report that continued the tradition of Vietnam coverage established earlier in the 1960s by pioneering reporters like David Halberstam of the *New York Times*, Neil Sheehan of UPI, Malcolm Browne of AP, Charles Mohr of TIME and later the *New York Times,* Francois Sully of *Newsweek* and several others. Safer's style of ad-libbing part of his narration on film as events took place in the background was widely copied by other television correspondents in Vietnam and then elsewhere. "The Burning of Cam Ne" carried American television's first serious warning that the introduction of large numbers of U.S. troops to Vietnam brought with it the danger of brutal wartime behavior, that Vietnamese civilians were at great risk, and that the unpredictable forces of military violence now being unsheathed would not go easily back into the American scabbard.

Wilson, Funk and I had been sent to Danang in part as peacemakers for CBS. The bureau chief in Saigon hoped that our work might balance Safer's critical reporting and reestablish good relations with the Marines. No one told us to moderate our coverage, but the purpose of our assignment was obvious: to cover the news and mend fences with the Marines. The TV networks needed the Marines' public information office for access to major combat stories when they happened, and also for human interest features in relatively quiet times. Viewers in the States wanted to know how their troops were doing in Vietnam, and it was in the interests of both the networks and the armed forces to tell them. No one from CBS suggested how to cover the story in Danang, but the delicacy of the visit was understood. I wanted to please my superiors. The day after we arrived, I discussed the Cam Ne incident with a Marine officer who ended the conversation by saying, "If that sonofabitch comes up here again he better not turn his back." I passed the warning to Morley in Saigon and he reacted by scheduling a visit to Danang to do another story as soon as possible, though this one was with the Air Force. Wilson, Funk and I settled in at the press center to wait for something to happen.

A few noncommissioned officers tried to make us welcome, especially the Marine photographers and reporters. They wanted to know how Wilson's sound camera worked, how the film wound through the shutter and was exposed to light, how the sound was recorded on the edge of the film. Most news film at the time was shot on silent cameras that were light and easy to carry. Wilson, who was big enough to hold a thirty-five-pound Auricon on his shoulder in the field, was happy to show them. Each evening, the three of us bought rounds of drinks for Marines at the press center bar, a simple platform of plywood and shellac, and asked them about the war. Drinks were cheap—ten or fifteen cents for a beer, twenty-five cents for spirits and mixed drinks—and they were served by young Vietnamese women hired for the purpose. Everyone drank together: reporters, officers, NCOs, enlisted men, civilian visitors. The atmosphere was convivial, relaxed—an island of newly arrived U.S. culture in an old Asian war zone. Wilson, Funk and I had not seen serious fighting in Vietnam yet and we wondered what it would be like, how we would behave.

A tall gunnery sergeant in his late thirties took me aside and told me what to do when shooting broke out.

"Look around for the senior NCO," the gunny said. "Do what he does. Okay? Never mind the officers, they got other things to worry about. Follow the sergeants, understand? They'll know what to do." He took my pen and notebook and made a list of all the enlisted and noncommissioned ranks in the Marine Corps, from private to sergeant major, drawing the insignia for each, so that I would be able to address Marines correctly by rank.

The press center provided permanent offices and sleeping quarters for about a dozen representatives of the American wire services, TV networks, major newspapers and newsmagazines. Reporters and photographers came up from Saigon for shifts of a few weeks to several months. Most were young men covering war for the first time, but there were also several women, including a few veterans of World War II and Korea, Dickey Chapelle among them. Freelance journalists rented more modest accommodations at the press center and used the same facilities as the others. Reporters for smaller newspapers who could not afford the cost of international cables sent their stories home by army post office letter. A few lived full-time in crowded dormitories within the press center and rarely ventured out of I Corps.

The competition was vigorous, at times cutthroat. Reporters and photographers tried to beat their rivals to the best stories of the day, get back to Danang with them faster and write them more accurately (in some cases more dramatically) than their competitors. The most professional reporters cultivated sources throughout Danang and the rest of I Corps who gave them information ahead of the others. Highest journalistic honors went to those who covered major combat action, especially if they were alone on the story. Reporters who missed stories or came in second received sharply worded calls from their bureau chiefs and picture editors in Saigon or, worse, cables from executives in New York, dictated word by painful word over the phone. For the American wire services, the competition was as tough as professional sports. Each day, someone in New York counted the number of AP and UPI stories and pictures on the front pages of the biggest U.S. newspapers and wired the results to their Saigon office. A major exclusive, especially in combat, could give one wire service a clean sweep of the papers, humiliating the competition. The most intense rivalries were waged between the two main television networks, NBC and CBS, and the three wire services, AP, UPI and Reuters. The networks competed by trying to get exclusive stories on the air, especially from combat zones, thereby excelling as journalists, and did not pay much attention to which got the most viewers. Executives at CBS News considered the ratings game unjournalistic, even vulgar. Most viewers at the time watched the *Huntley-Brinkley Report* and the *Today* program on NBC.

A few reporters made a specialty out of the sport of outwitting their rivals. Simon Dring of Reuters—a tall, thin, fair-haired Englishman—was the champion. Dring, who was twenty, cultivated a debonair, adventurous look by wearing tight-fitting camouflage fatigues and a 9 millimeter Browning. He drove the Reuters jeep at reckless speed all around Danang and the countryside. A notice posted at the press center said, "All Drivers and Simon Dring Go Carefully." His main competitor, George Esper of the AP, was shorter, dark-haired, stoop-shouldered and American. Esper wore a permanent expression of deep worry on his face that made him look perpetually as if he were getting beat on a breaking story. After dinner one evening, several journalists sat around a table in the dining room talking and drinking. Esper sat alone at another table eating a late supper. Unexpectedly, Dring drove into the courtyard at speed and jumped out of his jeep with a noisier than usual screech of brakes and skidding tires. He walked smartly into the dining room, sat down with the group at the table, and whispered to them conspiratorially. Then he walked out with affected calm, got back in the jeep and drove off in a hurry. One by one, trying not to appear obvious, each of the reporters at the table got up, went outside and drove away. When they were gone, Esper jumped up, got into his jeep and drove toward the airbase on the other side of town as fast as he could. Meanwhile, Dring and the others circled quietly back to the press center and gathered in the dining room to laugh and drink and wait for Esper to return. It was more than an hour before George got back, having checked the airbase, MACV, Marine headquarters and the center of town to learn that nothing worth reporting had happened in Danang. Sad-faced and gloomy, he came back believing he had been scooped on an out-of-town story the others knew about and he did not. He walked into the dining room to a long burst of abusive laughter from Dring and the others. Esper shook his head slowly and said, 'You guys . . . You guys . . . You guys oughtn't a done that.'

Reporters and photographers who were not in competition formed alliances. The Associated Press and NBC News often shared information, kept offices in the same Saigon building, and had the biggest networks of freelance stringers around the country. Occasionally, NBC broadcast exclusive pictures from a remote battle scene that had been shot by one of its Vietnamese photographers working alone. The stringer brought his film to Saigon and gave details of the story to one of the NBC News correspondents who then wrote a voice-over narration that sometimes gave the impression he had been present at the battle. At least one NBC correspondent filmed his on-camera appearances in a lush Saigon park so that the background would look more like the jungle and would match the stringer's footage from out of town. At CBS, such deception was considered unethical.

The press center had a social pecking order based on the length of time you had in-country, the quality of the work you did and how you behaved in combat. "Grace under pressure," Hemingway's definition of courage, was the behavior most admired. To some it was as important as being a good reporter. The dean of Danang combat journalists was Eddie Adams, an AP still photographer and former Marine who had proved himself steady under fire. Adams—short, broad-shouldered and friendly—had small blue eyes that smiled easily. The Marines at the press center treated him as one of their own and gave him exclusive access and information. Adams founded an elite fraternity of Danang journalists who called themselves TWAPs. They printed calling cards identifying themselves as members of the International Association of TWAPs, (Terrified Writers and Photographers). Members had a secret password: "Are you a TWAP and will you stick with me?" The countersign was: "Working . . . in a pig's ass I will." Incorrect responses cost the offender a round of drinks. Late at night in the bar, members who were too drunk to carry on a conversation shouted the password at one another trying to cadge free drinks. Television reporters were not accepted as members of TWAPs. TV journalists were generally regarded as "Saigon cowboys" or "news actors" by most print reporters who considered them to be lazy, overpaid, intellectually shallow egotists who wore hand-tailored bush jackets they called "TV suits" and rarely took risks. With the condensed, picture-intensive requirements of their medium, TV reporters had to compress details of their stories into fewer words than print reporters and, as a result, sometimes got the emphasis wrong or oversimplified the facts. Television news had little time for subtlety or nuance or detail. When Wilson and Funk appeared at the press center in their combat fatigues, Australian cowboy hats, scruffy new beards and pistol belts, veterans in the press corps looked at them and me with icy disdain.

Danang was too remote from the world outside Vietnam for editors in the United States to contact their reporters directly. This was a Godsend. Journalists were spared editorial suggestions from home about how to cover the story. On occasion, editors did have original ideas for stories that their reporters had overlooked, but they were sometimes ludicrous. One news executive in New York asked his Saigon office to explore the notion of the American command sending helicopters over the jungle during battles to spray everything below with indelible dye. After the battle, any Vietnamese peasants with dye on their skin could be identified as Viet Cong and arrested. The idea originally appeared in the *New York Times* and was put forward as a serious suggestion to help win the war. There were many others, equally far-fetched and impossible to implement.

The main communications link between Danang and Saigon was the telephone system, a device so antiquated and frustrating to use that reporters suspected it was there to paralyze the flow of news and punish them for being critical. A line at the press center was permanently connected to a military telephone exchange in Saigon. The Saigon exchange was staffed mainly with Vietnamese operators and was known as "Tiger." To reach one's office from Danang, it was necessary to ring the exchange in Saigon, tell the number to an operator and wait to be connected. The telephone instrument was equipped with a hand crank that, when it was rotated briskly, sent a ringing signal down the line. The Saigon operator answered, took your number and dialed it. Simple. But the system was so old and the connections so tenuous that it was extremely difficult to comprehend a voice speaking from one end to the other. Everyone had to shout. Lines got crossed regularly. Conversations were interrupted for military calls of higher priority. Operators pulled the plug, seemingly at random. It often took an hour to get a connection that might last a minute or two. Voices went hoarse. Tempers were lost. Deadlines missed. Late in the night, when everyone else had gone to bed, you could hear the cries of a print reporter trying to file a story, shouting at other voices to get off the line, begging operators at the Saigon exchange to put a call back through to his office, beseeching them, "Hello, Tiger? . . . Hello, Tiger? . . . Hello, Tiger? . . . Working, God damn it! . . . Get off the line! . . . Yeah, same to you, buddy! . . . Hello Tiger?" I never heard of anyone suffering a heart attack or nervous breakdown trying to make the phones work but I wouldn't have been surprised if I had.

The first Marine infantry units had landed at Danang in March and had prepared the ground for thirty-five thousand more who were now arriving. They had come ashore near the buildings that soon became the press center, and it was rumored that one of the Marines' first missions was to occupy and secure the place for the new Combat Information Bureau, as a top priority. The Marine Corps prided itself on its good relations with the press. Until Cam Ne, most stories about them in Vietnam had been positive, praiseworthy. The Marine high command took news coverage as seriously as battle.

The press center was also headquarters for the Marines' own public relations staff, a team of reporters, editors and photographers who gathered pictures and stories for military periodicals and films. They developed skills some hoped would qualify them for jobs in the civilian press when they finished their time in the Corps. A few were as good at their work as some of the professional journalists. These Marine reporters and photographers went all over I Corps, even to the most dangerous places, and were an excellent source of information about what was going on in the field.

The press center also provided escort officers who accompanied journalists to Marine units in the field and helped them get their stories. These junior and noncommissioned officers acted as go-betweens with Marine field commanders, arranging transportation and other logistical needs. In combat, they tried to keep us from getting hurt or getting in the way of military operations. The escort system also allowed the Marines to monitor informa-

tion being gathered about them before it was published or broadcast. They
did not normally censor or interfere with news gathering, except in a few
cases of military security, and were generally helpful. If you wanted to go in
the field with the Marines, an escort was mandatory. Only journalists who
were trusted to report favorably at all times about what they saw and heard
were allowed to travel alone.

Being in Danang that summer of 1965 gave me a sense of being part of a
team, one of the players in an important cause, part of a small but influential
group of network reporters. Wilson, Funk and I saw ourselves as a bridge, a
link between American troops in the field in this daring new adventure and
the millions of Americans at home who watched our stories for news of
their men abroad. Almost everyone wanted them to win. We took it for
granted (and assumed our viewers did as well) that the cause was honorable,
that the result would be successful. In our own way, Wilson, Funk and I
wanted to show the public how their fellow Americans were getting along in
this difficult, faraway place, where the people they were fighting were almost
always hidden. As professional journalists, we would try to be honest and
fair. We would report hardships and setbacks as well as good news. If the
effect of our coverage was to boost morale at home and contribute to the
overall success of the war, all the better, though we did not see ourselves as
propagandists. Our first loyalty was to the American public to be truthful,
then to the Marines we accompanied to be fair, then to CBS News to be
competitive and hardworking. Of course, we would be loyal to each other.
Everything fit neatly together. It was a comfortable, secure, protected feeling. We were on the starting team. An officer said, "Gentlemen, you are *with
the program.*" Wilson, Funk and I were definitely with the program.

SEPTEMBER 5, 1965

In the hour before dawn, a pale glow of gray-yellow light gathered at sea where the water met the sky and cast faint shadows from the palm trees across the river. The air was cool with the night, fresh and invigorating. The Marine duty watch banged his fist on the door of the network barracks room and shouted, 'Up and at 'em!' then walked on. Sleep-eyed, semiconscious, Wilson, Funk and I pulled on our fatigues and boots, loaded the jeep with camera gear and packs, and drank hurried cups of coffee in the dining room of the press center. No time to wash or shave. The Marines were ready to take us on our first trip to the field. It was a Sunday.

The escort officer was a clean-shaven, bright-eyed sergeant named Paxton who was in his early twenties and was so alert and energetic he must have been awake and getting ready for an hour. He wore immaculately clean pressed fatigues that were tucked neatly into the tops of his polished combat boots. He had on a spotless utility cap with the anchor and globe symbol at the front and carried himself confidently, proud to wear the uniform, naturally relaxed, nothing formal or officious about him. Next to him in our baggy fatigues, Wilson, Funk and I looked like vagabonds.

We had requested a visit to a frontline combat unit and it had been approved the night before. A Marine officer said we would be allowed to spend a working day with a rifle company on the perimeter, to film activity at the company base, and to interview the officers and men. Nothing more. No patrols. No spending the night. (No burning villages.) We had accepted the conditions without protest, happy to be allowed to work on a story.

Paxton said we would go in two jeeps, his and ours. 'That way,' he said, 'if one breaks down we won't be stuck out there.' I asked where we were going but he said only that we were heading south.

The rest of the press center was asleep as Paxton drove out of the compound. I rode with him as passenger. 'It's good to get away from the CIB,' he said on the road to the airport. 'All that desk stuff gets to you after a while.'

We drove through Danang, silent and still in the early light. There was no other traffic. Everyone seemed to have the day off. Our two jeeps—one military, one civilian—skirted the edge of the airfield and then rolled onto the flat coastal plain that ran along the South China Sea. It was a long jolting ride over bad roads, heading south and west.

'The mission is to spread out from these base areas like Danang,' Paxton said, 'and pacify the villages as we go. Root out the VC infrastructure. Win the allegiance of the locals. Give 'em schools and bridges and things. Then move on, further out, and pacify some more. Eventually, you get the whole country pacified.'

'Is it working?'

'Seems to be. Ask me again in six months.'

The route ahead was blocked by a small detail of Marine enlisted men. Two of them walked slowly down the road with minesweepers in their hands, passing them back and forth over the dirt surface of the two-lane road in slow even swings like a pendulum. Paxton stopped the jeep and got out. He explained that the VC buried land mines in the road during the night. 'They explode under the wheels of the first vehicles that drive over them in the morning,' he said. We waited by the side of the road with the rest of the men in the detail. The sun burst over the eastern sea with clear yellow light and climbed rapidly into the sky.

The men in the detail were amused by the appearance of a TV crew. They asked how long we had been in-country and when Wilson said just a few weeks, they laughed.

'You're still cherries,' one of them said, 'but you'll learn.'

The Marines told us where they came from in the States and how long they had been in country. All had arrived in March.

'What's the war like out here?' I asked.

'The VC are downright *evil*,' one of them said. The others joined in, speaking quickly one after the other so that their sentences overlapped, running together in a stream.

'They got a whole bag of tricks to hurt you.'

'No shit.'

'They hide in the treeline where you can't see 'em and open up when you're right on top of 'em.'

'Yeah, get the point man and maybe one or two others.'

'Then they break contact and run off before you can get the mortars and maybe an air strike on 'em.'

'Yeah, and they snipe at you from inside the villages.'

'It's like they know the officers won't let you put arty in usually 'cause of the civilians in there.'

Listening, I tried to appear casual, as if their story sounded as routine and matter-of-fact and unemotional as they were telling it. Privately, though, I began to feel a sense of danger, a wariness of what might be waiting ahead.

'An' they set booby traps on the trails with these thin, invisible wires like fishin lines that they got hooked up to Chicom grenades,' one of the Marines said.

'Or, even worse, one of our own 155 rounds that they dug up someplace or captured from the ARVN.'

'And the gooks dig these deep pits in the ground and put a real thin layer of sticks and leaves over the top of 'em so when you step on it you fall in the hole and get stuck.'

'*Impaled man!* On these fuckin punji stakes at the bottom which have poison on the tips of 'em.'

'Heard of one guy lost a foot 'cause of a punji stick.'

'Day and night, night and day, you worry all the time about what it's gonna be next.'

'Believe it, man. Charlie's got ways to hurt you that he ain't even *thought of* yet.'

When the minesweeping was finished, we got back in the jeeps and drove down the road into the clear morning air. Sergeant Paxton drove slowly to keep down the dust that puffed out in little clouds behind his wheels and into the path of Wilson and Funk in their open jeep. Paxton's eyes focused on the hard-packed dirt just ahead of the jeep's wheels. I looked out at the countryside. Farmhouses stood on the land away from the road in clusters—tidy bamboo and mud-brick homes with roofs of thatched straw and bamboo pens of chickens and pigs around them. The hamlets were surrounded by rectangular fields of rice paddies and vegetable gardens that covered the land for miles, from the white sands along the sea in the east to the mountains far inland to the west. The rice fields were bordered by irrigation canals, dikes, hedgerows and occasional clumps of trees and bamboo thickets—a broad, flat farming plain. Occasionally, a man or a woman farmer stood with hoe in hand. Most of the land was dry and baked hard. The primary colors were deep green and dust-brown. The long coastal plain was framed in the west by a chain of massive, jungle-covered mountains that rose toward the blue-gray haze of distant sky and into the clouds. The landscape looked peaceful, unthreatening. The only sounds from inside the jeep were the rolling whine of the engine and the squeaking of the springs. In the distance, dull hollow screams of jet bombers roared off the airfield at Danang.

Sergeant Paxton stopped the jeep next to a short rise in the ground just off the dirt road. A camp of Marine infantry was established around the high ground—a wide clearing of tents and radio aerials encircled by barbed wire and gun emplacements.

'Welcome to Alpha Company, 1st Battalion, 1st Marines,' Paxton said. 'We just call it Alpha 1/1.' The military camp seemed out of place on the broad, tranquil Asian farming plain. Everything in it was red-brown, the color of the dirt: tents, vehicles, sandbags, crates of ammunition and food, water tanks, weapons. Even the Marines in the camp were powdered with dull brown dust, blending with the earth. Most of them were not wearing shirts. Sergeant Paxton went to look for the company commander. The sun was up over the sea and heated the air like an oven warming.

The commanding officer of A Company walked up and introduced himself as Jack Maxwell. Twin silver bars on his shirt lapels identified him as a captain. Relaxed and friendly, Maxwell had the wholesome good looks you saw on Marine Corps recruiting posters. He appeared to be about twenty-five years old, the same age as me, though the resemblance stopped there. He was strong and fit and tanned and clear-eyed while I was thin and out of shape and sunburned and farsighted with glasses, the last face you would find on a recruiting poster. Trying not to embarrass myself, I kept my shoulders reasonably straight as we shook hands.

'We're the oldest company in the Marine Corps,' he said proudly. I wondered how he happened to know that, given all the rifle companies there were. *Four companies to a battalion. Three battalions to a regiment. Three regiments to a division. Must be hundreds,* I thought, *going all the way back to Tripoli.* Later I figured out that Alpha 1/1 was the oldest company in the Marine Corps simply because it had the first unit designation.

The company had been in the area for one week, Maxwell said, and had not made contact with the local Viet Cong. A platoon went out every night to reconnoiter and set ambushes while the rest of the men took turns standing watch on the perimeter.

"We've had to play their ballgame," Maxwell said. "We have to wait for the VC to probe our position before we can fight them, because they're so elusive." In the meantime, he explained, the company was trying to win the trust and respect of the local villagers.

"It's a public relations war," he said. "You have to play by those rules. You're dead if you don't."

Maxwell said the morale of his Marines was good. The men had everything they needed: mess tent, hot food, mail, even cold beer and Coke from time to time. "We really have it made," he said and smiled.

I looked around at the barren ground, the shallow fighting holes, the sandbags and barbed wire, the dust-covered water truck baking in the sun, the slow-moving troops. It was uncomfortably hot in the open sunlight. The camp was too far from the water for the offshore breeze to reach. Maybe a young captain in command of a Marine rifle company at war felt he had it made, but I wondered about everyone else.

Wilson set up his camera to film an interview and Maxwell repeated what he had just said off-camera. He was articulate, confident and sincere. After the interview, Wilson asked him if there was anything going on in the camp that we could film. Maxwell led the way to the perimeter where the company first sergeant was giving C rations to a group of Vietnamese women and children from the nearest village. Wilson rolled film as John Patrick Murray, whose family lived in Santa Ana, California, bent over with a tin can of C ration jam and offered it on a white plastic spoon to a young boy.

"You want to try some of this jam?" Murray said. He ate a mouthful to show it was safe. He put more jam on the spoon and handed it to the boy. The boy took it, put it in his mouth and, tasting the sugary goo, smiled. The villagers standing around the two of them nodded their heads and spoke in Vietnamese in approving tones. Murray and a few other Marines passed out C ration food and candy to the group. Everyone smiled warmly. Wilson recorded all of it on film—wide shots, close-up, reverse angles—while Funk recorded the natural sound. Watching, I thought the scene would be interesting to viewers in the States: generous Americans sharing their food with the poor grateful Vietnamese they had come to defend. *Good stuff*, I thought.

When Wilson finished shooting, Maxwell said we were welcome to film the 81 millimeter mortar section going through its drill. Wilson said that was exactly the kind of scene he needed to fill out the story with pictures. At the company mortar pit and fire coordination tent, Sergeant Julius Bethea, the section leader, and his gunner, Lance Corporal Robert Kelly, and the rest of the Marines in the unit put on a realistic demonstration of an engagement. Standing around the mortar, they shouted, "Fire mission! . . . Three-seven-zero-six! . . . Deflection! . . . Charge-four!" as loud as they could, really screaming, moving around the mortar pit as if they were loading and firing the shells in combat. I asked Maxwell why they were shouting when it wasn't necessary and he said it got very noisy in battle and that it was imperative to get the coordinates right or the shells might hit the wrong target. So they shouted in practice. Wilson worked quickly, shooting from several angles and getting close-ups of the men's faces as they shouted. Funk stood just out of camera range and pointed his microphone at the men to record the sound. Whenever Funk got his mike in the picture frame or failed to get out of the way fast enough, Wilson hissed and scowled, waving him away with his hand. Usually, Wilson changed his position without warning and two or three times Funk was caught in the frame. When Wilson snarled at him, Funk seemed hurt. Suddenly, Wilson stopped filming and put the camera on the ground. He was sweating hard. 'That's enough to make a scene,' he said. I thanked the mortar team and they stopped practicing immediately.

Nothing else was happening. The sun was high, the heat intense. We sat in the shade of the open command tent and drank water. Wilson and Funk took off their shirts. Captain Maxwell left to attend to other business. Sergeant Paxton relaxed. Time passed. After a rest, Wilson pointed to a group of young Marines standing outside their fighting holes on the perimeter, bare-chested in the heat, joking.

'Let's go,' Wilson said. He picked up his camera and walked toward the enlisted men. Funk and I followed.

'Don't pay any attention to me,' Wilson said to the Marines, focusing his lens on the group. 'Pretend I'm not here.'

The Marines grinned and shifted the weight on their feet. I introduced myself and asked them their names and wrote in my notebook: Lance Corporal Charles H. Peterson, 21, Montgomery, Alabama; Private First Class David Domingus, Grants, New Mexico; and others.

Wilson started to roll. Immediately Sergeant Paxton interrupted. He ordered the Marines to put on their T-shirts and helmets. 'The brass at the Pentagon'll blow a gasket if they see you without your covers in a war zone,' he said. 'You call this a war zone?' one of the men said and the others laughed. Grumbling, they put on their T-shirts and helmets. 'At least we don't have to wear our flak jackets,' one of them said. Wilson started again.

One of the Marines swatted a mosquito on his arm. I asked him how much trouble the bugs gave them.

"Lots," he said. "They've got mosquitoes as big as B-58 bombers around here. They've got bugs *you can ride*." The others laughed.

"Did they train you how to fight bugs back home?" I asked.

"Actually, there isn't too much you can do to combat bugs," he said, "cause you put the mosquito repellent on you, it'll burn you up." He laughed. "And if you *don't* put it on you, the bugs'll eat you up."

We all laughed. I turned to another Marine, "What do you think of this country?"

"Oh, it's hot, humid and lousy," he said, "nothing like the States."

"Are you thinking about home?"

He nodded. "All the time . . . All the time . . ."

"What do you think about most?"

"Oh, I guess being back in New Jersey, down on the beach, drinking beer . . ." The other Marines laughed. "American girls, what else?" He laughed.

"Well," I said, "you've got beer and beaches around Danang."

"Yeah, but (at home) you don't always have that constant fear that somebody might be in the bush with a rifle trained on you. . . ."

His words trailed away into silence and no one spoke. An awkward moment passed. Wilson switched the camera off and put it down. 'Man, *it is hot*,' he said, wiping his arm across his forehead.

I felt comfortable with the young Marines, kidding with them, exchanging quips, laughing together. Our rapport had been immediate. We were close to the same age, products of the same American culture of the 1950s and early 1960s. We had read many of the same books and comic books, learned the same lessons in school, played the same games and sports, listened to the same songs on the radio (the daring new music of Elvis Presley and Chuck Berry and the others), danced the same dances, watched the same movies and TV shows, identified with the same heroes. They reminded me of my buddies from high school—adventurous, happy-go-lucky, too young to be serious—a few years further along in their lives.

We thanked them for talking to us and shook their hands. Wilson told Sergeant Paxton we had enough for a story; it was time to go.

In the late afternoon, back in the barracks room at the press center, Wilson, Funk and I sat by the typewriter and tried to work out the voice-over narration for the story, our first with the Marines. It seemed like a fairly straightforward feature.

'When you're writing the words,' Wilson said, 'think of the pictures and sound. Make 'em go together.' I looked at him.

'Just remember the idea is to let the pictures tell as much of the story as possible,' he said. 'The narration should *complement* the pictures, not lead them.'

Wilson knew I was used to writing radio stories in which the first priority was to tell the news. If you had time, you added a little description, "word pictures" as we called it in radio, to describe how the scene of the news event looked. In TV news, no description was necessary. What I had to do was tell the basic facts of the story that were not obvious from the pictures—the who, what, where, when and how. I also had to learn to write much shorter sentences. Wilson was a patient teacher.

"Always lead with your best pictures," he said.

The half day with Alpha Company had not produced any dramatic pictures. Wilson suggested we start with the scene of the mortar-firing practice. 'That'll get their attention,' he said. I wrote it that way and followed with shots of the first sergeant giving jam to the Vietnamese boy. The heart of the story would be the interviews with the enlisted men. We called the story "Waiting for Charlie." I wrote a simple script about what Captain Maxwell and the men told us, counting on the pictures and interviews to carry it. Without combat, we figured it might have a fifty-fifty chance of getting on the air. We recorded the voice-over narration and Wilson and Funk shipped the film cans and narration to Saigon, where they were transshipped to New York. There the film was processed, screened and edited. Three days after we shot it, the story ran for four minutes on the *CBS Evening News*. The executive producer sent a cable to Wilson, Funk and me that said you are doing fine, really listening to the troops, keep up the good work. We smiled when we read the cable. It gave us a sense of accomplishment to know our work was appreciated.

The evening we finished "Waiting for Charlie" the press center was unusually active. Marine officers and enlisted men moved swiftly back and forth through the compound. They spoke to one another in whispers, checked lists written on pieces of paper they carried, lifted boxes of supplies and field gear and stacked them neatly in the courtyard. Other journalists huddled in groups of two and three and spoke conspiratorially. Eddie Adams, the Marines' favorite photographer, was gone. When we asked what was going on, the Marines said, 'Don't leave town' and turned away. The other journalists told us nothing. Wilson, Funk and I went to sleep worried.

SEPTEMBER 6, 1965

Everyone was up before dawn. A Marine NCO banged hard on the door of the network barracks room, shouted at us to wake up, and went down the line waking reporters. Wilson, Funk and I got up and dressed. In the thin yellow light of the courtyard, Marines were loading stacks of equipment and supplies onto a six-by truck with its tailgate down and checking their lists. The entire press center was awake and moving. Reporters and Marines ate breakfast in the dining room, packed bags, filled canteens, checked cameras, studied maps and talked. The Marines appeared to work always according to a plan, orderly and efficient, following orders from higher up. PFCs, corporals and junior NCOs did the heavy work of lifting and loading; senior sergeants gave the orders and did the paperwork. They packed cameras, film, processing and enlarging equipment, typewriters, paper, files and unit histories along with their personal effects and weapons. Everyone had an M-14 or a sidearm. An officer with an expression of foreboding on his face came to the breakfast table and told Wilson, Funk and me to pack enough gear for a week in the field: sleeping bag, poncho, extra canteens, toilet articles, change of clothes, the whole kit. None of us had a sleeping bag but we didn't say so. The officer said not to tell anyone we were leaving, not even our bureau chief in Saigon. If anyone called us, he said, they would be told we were on a story and were not available.

'What's happening?' I asked.

'We're going on an operation,' the officer said in a gruff flat voice that did not change expression. He moved to the next table and repeated his instructions to another group of journalists.

The Marines in the courtyard broke open cardboard cases of C rations and gave boxes of canned food to each reporter and photographer who was going—about twenty-five in all. Arms full, Wilson, Funk and I carried the C rations back to the barracks room and loaded our packs. There was not enough room for all the film, extra batteries, food and personal gear we wanted to take.

'Don't forget to bring extra plugs and cables,' Wilson barked at Funk.

'I'm taking *two* extra sets!' Funk shouted back.

I lifted my tape recorder—a Swiss-made Nagra Kudelski the size of a large dictionary. In its black leather case and shoulder strap, it was more than twenty pounds with the microphone. The machine was capable of recording sound on spools of quarter-inch audiotape spinning at fifteen inches per second. It produced the finest sound possible on a portable, battery-powered tape recorder. I had carried Nagras in the field for several years, often in difficult places—a revolution in the Dominican Republic, urban disorders in the States, marches and demonstrations in New York City, a major flood in Ohio —but never on a long march or in serious heat. I worried about how long I could carry it in the field.

'Bring it,' Wilson commanded. 'We can do sound on it if the camera breaks down.'

Adjusting the straps of our packs, Wilson, Funk and I wondered what was ahead. We were hoping for a good story, maybe a big one like Operation Starlite a few weeks earlier. Other reporters talked about Starlite as if it had been their own private battle with the VC, their personal rite of passage with the Marines. Because we had not been there, we were regarded as novices, outsiders, untested by combat. Wilson, Funk and I hoped we might have a chance to show we were not afraid, that we could do the work, that we were capable of covering a story under dangerous conditions.

By chance, neither NBC nor ABC had a team in Danang at the time. Their camera crews were out covering other stories. As a result, CBS would have exclusive television coverage of whatever happened. With no competition, all we had to worry about was covering the story. The Marines were taking care of everything else. I expected them to fight in the same way they did all their work—confidently, efficiently, according to a plan. With so many Marines involved and the operation so well organized, it seemed no harm could happen to us. We had protection; we felt secure. The Marines prepared themselves for combat with such meticulous care that we paid closer attention to our own. We checked every detail at least twice—camera, sound gear, tape recorder, spare equipment, clothing—even the hang of the packs on our backs to see how we looked. We wanted to appear as much like seasoned Marine infantrymen as possible, so as not to look awkward or out of place. Getting ready for what we expected to be a major battle had a peculiar allure. Facing danger and the fear that went with it was exciting, challenging.

Each step in the process of preparation added a degree of assurance that we were ready, that we had everything we needed, that we were in control of our fears, at least for the moment. My thoughts danced in a whirl of unknowns: boyhood fantasies of action and drama, possible tests of judgment and character, the chance of witnessing a big event, the risks of being hurt, the prospect of coming out with a good story. All the conditions of honor and shame would be on the line. The internal effect of so much high-risk uncertainty was a sensation of mild elation, a likable buzz, a heartlift that gave everything clarity and purpose that were not normally present. It was the most powerful attraction of being a reporter. From the scary uncertainty at the start of an assignment to the pleasant satisfaction of the finished work, this was why I did it—to witness a dramatic event and to report it to the public. Each experience added an extra dimension to my existence. Attaching the straps of my pack to the eyeholes of the web belt, I felt more alert, more responsible, more fully alive. Wilson and Funk cleaned the working mechanisms of their pistols with patches of gun oil and squeezed small cardboard boxes of copper-nosed bullets into their packs.

By eight o'clock everything was ready. Reporters, photographers and Marine escorts climbed into the backs of three flatbed trucks in the courtyard and rode out of the press center in noisy procession. Watching the convoy leave, a group of Vietnamese women who had started to clean the rooms waved and smiled and chattered to one another in words of worried exclamation, as if we might be going for good. The trucks turned left at the main road and headed for the airfield. In the open back of one of the trucks, journalists sat on their packs and joked with one another with the casual familiarity of old-timers who had done this before. One of the veterans of Starlite told the others how scared he had been when the shooting started, how heavy and accurate the incoming mortars had been, how clever the VC were at hiding in tunnels and crawling out fighting, how brave they were to stand up and die in the close assaults.

Wilson, Funk and I sat apart from the others. None of them spoke to us. If our eyes met theirs, they turned away quickly. They did not acknowledge our presence in any way, their indifference meant to make clear they didn't want to know us. As far as they were concerned, we were not in the truck. Feeling the snub, I thought something was wrong with me, as though I had worn the wrong clothes, though I looked and acted like everyone else. *What's the matter?* I wondered.

It was a mistake to take it personally. I didn't realize then, as I did later, that all newcomers were ignored equally, the same way these old-timers had been shunned when they arrived in Vietnam weeks or months or, in a few cases, years before. I figured out why later. One was competition. By ignoring new, inexperienced journalists, the veterans wouldn't have to share information with them, as they might do with their friends, especially in a combat zone. Another reason was that new arrivals had to prove themselves worthy. No use making friends with someone who might later turn out to be incompetent or embarrassing or extremely nervous under fire. Another important reason was that TV reporters, in general, were not much respected by print journalists for reasons of professional pride, snobbery, jealousy (TV people were paid more), social posturing, masculinity games, and, again, competition. TV news was a powerful new force in American society. It attracted millions of viewers and was seen to be taking away newspaper and magazine readers, despite the fact that TV news was perceived to be a less serious form of reporting, more visceral than factual, more sensational than realistic, ultimately misleading. Finally, and perhaps the most important reason for the coldness: old-timers had an aversion to making any new friends, given where they were and what they were doing and the high risks of losing their lives. Their attitude made Wilson, Funk and me feel like new kids in a schoolyard.

Everyone got out of the trucks and waited on the tarmac at the airport. The escort officers tried to track down a plane to provide transportation. Minutes passed. The sun came up and burned off the morning chill. Rising over the rooftops of the city and then high above, the sun scorched the ground, tempering all it touched with heat. The only relief came from passing clouds, temporary shields from the relentless light. Hours went by.

The escorts became more and more exasperated with Marine aviation. I began to wonder about the efficiency of the operation. *This is not the way it's supposed to happen. Why do we have to wait hours in the heat when the press center is only a couple of miles away?* Finally a plane arrived. The press group climbed aboard an aging propeller-driven C-47, which taxied out to the runway and took off at a low angle over the sea, turning right along the coast, heading south. About sixty miles out of Danang, the plane landed on a long new runway at Chu Lai airbase. Another long wait on the tarmac while the escorts tried again to locate transportation. All of our hurried preparations for the trip followed by two interminable delays reminded me of the expression, "Hurry up and wait," used by American GIs in World War II.

By now, the sun was arching toward the distant mountains. The press group moved to another part of the airfield and climbed aboard three helicopters—noisy old UH-34s the Marines had been flying since the Korean War. Shaking violently, the awkward machines struggled into the air and flew out over the sea. The air was surprisingly cool, a relief after the long wait in the heat. As the helicopters passed over the horizon, a small battle group of U.S. Navy ships came into view. The fleet was dominated by a large gray-hulled cruiser with long-barreled guns pointing out its sides and two fierce-looking destroyers with gray metal guns. The ships circled slowly, heaving in light swells of moving water. One at a time, the helicopters landed on the helipad of a troop carrier at the center of the battle group and the journalists and escorts disembarked.

Aboard ship, Marine infantry with their weapons and vehicles occupied all the available space. The Marines looked at the reporters and photographers coming aboard with alternating reactions of relief and dread. They laughed and called out questions ('Welcome to the cruise!'), and took snapshots as reporters adjusted their unsteady legs to the rolling deck.

One of the enlisted men said to another, 'Well, this here operation can't be that dangerous if all these people are coming along. I mean, the brass wouldn't risk so many civilians on it, would they? This one's gotta be easy.'

'Yeah, maybe,' the other Marine said. 'But what if that's what the brass wants? You know, a lot of publicity for what they're doin over here? Big Marine landing on the beaches? Like Tarawa. Blood up to the gunnels. Maybe that's just what they want. So what if they lose a few press?'

'Yeah,' the first one said. 'The pictures would be worth it.'

'So hard to figure the odds on one like this.'

Wilson, Funk and I were escorted to a small compartment below deck and told to stow our gear and come to a briefing in half an hour. None of us had been aboard a warship in combat before. We acted relaxed, as if we knew what we were doing. A sailor showed us where to go and said, 'You're only with us a few hours; make yourselves at home.' The compartment we were given for the night had been vacated by junior officers. It had four bunks, one for each of us and one for the camera and gear. The beds had blankets but no sheets or pillowcases. Immediately, Wilson got out a dry cotton cloth and cleaned salt spray from the camera lens. Funk organized his sound equipment into separate piles and cleaned the cables, microphones and amplifier. The quarters were cramped, especially for the two big men with their equipment, but they worked cheerfully, without complaint. The spectacle of a U.S. Navy battle group and a Marine battalion landing team aboard ship added to a sense of drama unfolding.

At the briefing, a senior Marine officer stood in front of a large map of the Vietnam coastline. An amphibious assault would take place at 0700 hours the next morning, he said. The beach under attack was part of the Batangan Peninsula, not far from where Operation Starlite was fought in August, three weeks ago. This one was called Operation Piranha. A small Marine reconnaissance team (accompanied by Eddie Adams, the AP photographer) was already ashore and reporting intelligence. Tomorrow, before dawn, the navy cruiser and destroyers would fire their heavy guns at the coast for thirty minutes. When the bombardment was finished, the Marine battalion aboard ship would go ashore in multiple waves of landing craft and assault the beach. Another Marine battalion and two South Vietnamese battalions moving by ground and air would take up blocking positions farther inland, trying to intercept any escape. The number of Viet Cong troops in the area was estimated by Marine and South Vietnamese intelligence as between fifteen hundred and two thousand. 'Main-force regulars,' the briefing officer said, 'hard-core, willing to fight.' He spoke the words without fear.

SEPTEMBER 7, 1965

Below decks on the U.S. Navy troopship early in the morning, the dawn was dark as night. Wilson, Funk and I stood with a platoon of Marines in a narrow passageway waiting for orders to go above and board the landing craft to take us to the beach. There had been no breakfast. The passage was jammed with Marines in full battle dress: helmets, M-60 machineguns, ammunition belts, radios, rockets, mortars, M-14 rifles, grenades, field packs. The only light came from a few red bulbs spaced along the bulkhead. A faint pale-red glow illuminated the dark outlines of helmets, packs, weapons and equipment, shadow figures without faces. There were no portholes in the corridor. The boom of nearby naval gunfire hit the ship with sharp shocks, some in a series of muffled rolling reports, one after another, like jabs from a fighter. No one spoke. The Marines seemed to know what to expect and contemplated it in private. The smell was of stale breath, sweat and gun oil.

The scene felt oddly familiar, as if I'd been there before, in a movie or a newsreel a long time ago: waiting in a crowded red-tinted passageway, submerged in steel, listening to gun thunder outside, standing with William Bendix and Lloyd Nolan and a line of nervous stone-faced kids smoking cigarettes, holding their BARs and carbines and boxlike walkie-talkies, about to go over the side and down the ropes into the landing craft floating on an Asian sea, and then through fire and smoke in water to their waists, all the way to the beach if they were lucky. The scene appeared as vivid as the moment fifteen years earlier when it flashed across my neighborhood movie screen and we wide-eyed kids held our breath and hung on every word, every frame. Alone now with my imagination, lost in it, the childhood tension that went with the old war movie came back in force, dramatic and exciting, exaggerating the effect of each new image as it appeared now, placing it in fresh perspective, focusing what was going on in terms I understood more clearly than the confusing, impersonal military operation around me, making it more real. The memory of having seen a Marine landing before, if only by actors, and the shared experience of having been through it with them in the visceral reality of the movie, made it less frightening to stand and do it now.

The orders came to move. Wilson, Funk and I followed in a line of Marines to the end of the passageway and climbed a ladder, the first of several, and then went through a series of hatches and eventually came out through a doorway into the soft yellow light of dawn. A warm breeze brushed our faces. The smell of salt saturated the air, clean and sharp, enhancing the other senses. The sun was behind the other side of the ship, just up on the horizon, laying long shadows of ships and boats on the gray water. The coast was a hazy line in the distance, white sand and palm trees. Gray smoke rose from the tree line. It was 0650, ten minutes to zero hour. Marines moved in every direction, pushing on the crowded deck, wrestling with their packs, shifting their feet, fastening the chin straps of their helmets. A sergeant called an order and five men with rifles and packs climbed onto the side of the ship and poised for an instant to set the weight on their backs before hurling themselves over the side, like paratroopers making a jump, and climbed down the rope netting alongside the ship. Line after line of Marines climbed over the metal side and went down the netting. When our turn came, Wilson threw himself over with reckless enthusiasm, as if unable to wait his turn. The weight of his camera shifted and pulled him off balance and in that instant the ship rolled sharply to the side and threw him out into space and a sideways fall. Wilson's legs flew into the air away from the ship and in the same moment as he was falling nearly upside down his left arm caught one of the ropes and took some of the weight and the rope slipped down to his wrist and his hand closed on it in a tight fist. The bulk of his body swung back into the ropes and crashed against the side of the ship. Wilson's feet found the nets and he took a breath and cried, 'Ooooo-eee!' in his high-pitched voice as if the fall had been no more than a minor slip. Then, looking over his shoulder, he started to climb down the ladder.

Funk, the bigger man, stepped over the side gingerly, found his footing on the first rung of the rope, and moved down slowly in short steps, one rung at a time. I was next. I climbed over the side and took one of the ropes in my hands and looked down to see where to put my feet. More than a hundred feet below, the landing boat looked impossibly small, just a slight open vessel like a barge with black numbers on the side bobbing wildly on the sea— heaving and pitching and yawing on the undulating surface of the water, moving four ways at once. *This is entirely unnatural,* I thought, *climbing into a little boat like this.* The metal side of the landing craft pressed hard against the much larger troop carrier and made a low creaking noise, like the door of a crypt opening. Then it pulled away again and the heavy ropes holding the boat and ship together groaned with the tension. I looked up, unable to move. Marines waited to climb down after me. One part of my mind said *it's okay, you can do it, you're strong enough, just get on with it*, but another voice said *you're not going to make it, don't take a chance, don't go any farther or you'll fall*. (I had heard once that Marines who fell from landing nets were usually crushed between the boat and the ship or knocked unconscious and drowned.) Looking down at me, the face of one of the Marines above showed sympathy, as if knowing how I felt. A sergeant's voice shouted, "Just hang on and keep moving! Don't let go and don't stop!" without addressing me specifically, not meaning to embarrass me, but giving me a clue how to do it. (Marines could be polite in the most unlikely situations.) But I was embarrassed, worried that I was holding everyone up. I moved one leg slowly to the rung below, then moved one of my hands, then the other leg, and finally the other hand. Each effort felt unbearably hard. My arms and legs were wooden, as if disconnected from the rest of me. The weight of the field pack and tape recorder made everything more awkward. Meanwhile, Marines moved down the ropes on both sides of me with smooth accomplished purpose. A quick look over my shoulder saw Wilson and Funk at the bottom of the ropes, navigating into the landing craft. At that moment the ship heaved over to one side again and the ladder swung away from the ship and into empty air. I seized the rope and held it with all my strength. *God help me*, I thought, *I'm going down.* The rope netting swung back to the side of the ship with me attached and steadied. Taking a breath, I tried again. Shifting all my weight onto one side and holding on with one arm, I swung the free arm and leg of the lighter side down a step. Then, taking a firm grip on that side and shifting the weight over, I swung the arms and leg of the other side down another rung and took hold. Repeating the movements, I moved down the ropes, faster with each sequence. It was like climbing down out of a tree for the first time, branch by branch. The fear floated off. At the bottom of the net, Navy and Marine hands reached up and guided me into the landing craft. Their faces were smiling.

On the beach, there was no resistance. It was a textbook-perfect landing. Ebb tide, fairly calm sea, no contact, no accidents, no victims. Only the pristine white sand of the beach was churned and blackened by the oily treads of the huge amphibious tracked vehicles—amtracs—that chugged smoking out of the sea like intergalactic battle wagons. A Marine colonel stood at the open back ramp of his command track and snapped orders over the radio, organizing companies into action. More Marines waded ashore. Wilson stood in the low surf and got pictures of the men coming ashore with the sun sparkling on the sea behind their backs. Light bounced off the water and the sand and magnified the heat. The beach was dazzlingly bright.

A platoon formed a line and set off along the shore, parallel to the waterline, moving south. The platoon leader, a young lieutenant, said they were going to search for any enemy who might be hiding along the coast. His men would cover the battalion's left flank along the water. I asked if we could accompany him and he said, 'Sure thing, you're welcome to join us.'

The column advanced to the end of the beach where it came to a low ridge of rock. Curving inland around the coast, the ridge led upward into a smoke-gray mountain that rose vertically from the sea, its seaward face lined with cliffs and outcroppings and pocked with caves, some of them hundreds of feet above the water. Birds nested in the cracks. Far below, waves rolled toward the coast in low even lines and broke gently against the stone-black boulders lining the shore. The water was azure blue, clear to the seabed. Walking along the shoreline at a slow even pace, the men in the patrol looked up at the caves. No one could scale those cliffs. If the VC were in there, the Marines would be like ducks on a pond.

A gentle wind blew in off the water. After the insufferable heat on the beach, the fine sea spray carried on the breeze felt refreshing. Stepping on the smooth rocks and then through shallow pools of water and then onto more rock, following the man in front, I became aware of a strange other presence around the platoon. The rock-faced mountain and its slate gray cliffs came down in jagged stone and shale and touched the gently rounded surfaces of the shoreline and the blue methodical sea in intimate embrace, as if the two had been touching forever. Plodding over the rocks and through the pools of water, thoughts adrift, I was becoming enchanted by the rough, unspoiled beauty of the place, privileged to be there. Surely, I thought, humans rarely came this way. I wondered if anyone had ever been here. Seabirds flew out of the caves and circled the edge of the water, ignoring the patrol but keeping a distance. The sea flapped gently, almost silently. Perfect peace, powerful but unthreatening. How permanent it is, I thought, unaffected by the hubbub of human purpose, our wars and our science, our philosophy and our art. Here is changeless, timeless. The smoke-gray mountain and the azure blue sea displayed the natural harmony of Vietnam, reminding me of my own inconsequence in a mighty, more durable world. I was filled with wonder and joy.

The platoon came to a deep break in the coastline that could be crossed only by wading through a larger body of seawater trapped in the rocks. The water was about fifteen yards across and four to five feet deep and disappeared into a cave at the base of the mountain. One at a time, Marines waded into the water and stepped carefully on the stony surface of the bottom of the pool, holding their rifles above their heads. The water went up to their chests. Wilson carried his camera over his head with his arms stretched above him and pushed through the water in the steps of the Marine ahead. Funk did the same with his sound gear. I started across after them, trying to balance the bulky tape recorder on my head. The water was warm, unmoving, heavy against the legs. The short, stocky Marine ahead of me went in up to his neck. Wading slowly across, he was near the middle of the pool when he took a step forward and disappeared under the water. In an instant, he was gone. He struggled under the surface to get his arms out of the straps of the heavy pack pulling him down. Instinctively, I stepped forward and reached out to grab him. My chest and then my head went under the water and I realized as my foot went into a deep hole there was nothing to step on. A flash of panic and I went down into the water next to the struggling Marine. All the air went out of my lungs. In the next moment I felt myself being jerked sharply backward by my collar and then my head was above the water and my feet were touching the firm bottom of the pool again. I stood up and looked around.

'Had a feeling you might need help.' It was our Marine escort officer, a smiling, soft-voiced lieutenant who had been walking behind. 'That tape thing on your head was heavy as an ammo can,' he said. I looked into the pool. The $600 Nagra was somewhere on the bottom.

'Forget it,' Funk shouted from the other side. 'It wouldn't be any good with all that saltwater in it anyway.' The Marine who went down ahead of me had managed to get out of his pack and swim to the other side.

After moving several hundred yards along the coastline, the patrol turned to go back to the beach. Wilson, Funk, the escort officer and I decided to go our own way. We found a pass through one side of the mountain and followed it inland. Our intention was to link up with one of the forward infantry companies. We had heard rifle shots in the far distance, but only infrequently and nothing to indicate a battle. Wilson said we needed action

to round out the story of the landing and the patrol. Turning right and walking parallel to the coast, we came upon a flat sandy plain that stretched
inland for several hundred yards, past the first line of palm trees and
hedgerows and up to a cluster of hamlets. The midday heat was blinding,
suffocating, overpowering the senses. Walking in the sand, each of us felt
dizziness, headache, disorientation, our brains roasting inside our heads. It
was impossible to think clearly. The lieutenant suggested we stop and sit
under a tree with low branches and green leaves. We drank water and rested
for a few minutes. Then we got up and went on.

We walked for more than an hour. Small patrols of Marines we met said
they hadn't seen or heard anything. It was apparent the Viet Cong were not
in the area or did not want to fight. Other than scattered sniper fire, the
Marines and South Vietnamese were not making contact anywhere in their
area of operations. It was a big AO—about 120,000 square meters. If the VC
were around, they were trying to hide or escape.

Wilson, Funk and I and the escort officer trudged across the sand until we
came upon a platoon of Marines who were taking a family of Vietnamese
civilians out of a small hole in the ground. There were five people—a husband
and wife in their late twenties, two young children and an older man with
white hair and wrinkled skin. As they came out of the hole, the adults knelt on
the ground and bent their heads and held their hands together as if in prayer
and rocked their bodies up and down. They cried in a low wail that sounded
like they were offering their gratitude to the Marines for not killing them. The
old man bowed on his knees until his head nearly touched the ground. All five
were covered with sand and dirt from inside the tunnel where they had been
hiding. The entrance to the tunnel was obscured by a big thorn bush that
formed part of a hedgerow. The Marines said the opening led to a long tunnel
that went beneath several rice paddies, deep underground. They suspected the
men were Viet Cong and tied their hands behind their backs and covered their
eyes with strips of black cloth. One of the Marines said they had taken fire
from the mouth of the tunnel before we arrived. A South Vietnamese Army
interpreter spoke to the villagers. Wilson rolled film as the people from the
tunnel spoke to the interpreter, who translated what they said for the Marines.

'They say they are farmers, not VC,' the interpreter said. 'They say many
more people from their village are in tunnel.'

'How many?' the platoon leader said. The interpreter translated the
question into Vietnamese and asked the villagers.

'They say maybe sixty or seventy people down there. Men, women, babies. They too frightened to come out.'

'Why?'

'They say VC come through village this morning and tell them not go near foreigners or they kill them.'

'Who? The VC?'

'No, *you* kill them.' The interpreter paused. 'That what they say.'

Time passed. No one seemed to have a clear idea what to do. The South Vietnamese Army interpreter said the area had been under VC control for many years.

'Saigon have no say over this place, not even army. Never have. These people fight against French. They Viet Minh long time ago. Now they fight us. If they are not VC, then they *help* VC,' he said.

The Marines kept watch at the two openings to the tunnel they could observe, one at either end. No one had forgotten what happened on Starlite.

After a long wait, the platoon leader announced that he was going to put charges of C-4 explosives at both ends of the tunnel and blow the damn thing. He called his company commander to get permission. The CO said, 'Negative. That doesn't sound like a good idea.'

'What about tear gas?' the lieutenant asked.

'Negative on the Charlie Sierra,' was the reply.

Everyone waited. The Marines had no way to confirm that there were people inside the tunnel, and, if so, whether they were Viet Cong troops or innocent villagers. Everyone waited. Hours passed. Nothing happened. The escort officer checked on the radio and said there was no action anywhere in the AO. Wilson, Funk and I looked at one another and wondered whether to go back to Danang. Even without a story, we were tired. The prospect of spending the night on the sand was not appealing.

'If you want to make it back to Danang tonight,' the escort officer said, 'we need to leave now. We have to find a chopper going to Chu Lai before dark.' It was late afternoon.

'What the hell,' Wilson said, 'we're not gonna get anything here.' We packed the gear and said good-bye to the Marines. As we left, the platoon leader sat by his radio waiting for a decision about the tunnel.

At the airfield in Chu Lai, we put our names down for a flight to Danang. Other reporters who had made the same decision were waiting by the runway. A group of veteran newspapermen talked among themselves. Basically, the operation was a failure, they agreed, because the VC got away. Simple as that. All that talk at the briefing about main-force regulars ready to fight was bullshit, they said. The reporters sounded cynical, blaming the Marines for bringing them all this way for no action.

The next day at the press center, the Combat Information Bureau issued a statement about the operation under the headline:

66 VC KILLED IN TUNNEL COMPLEX IN OPERATION PIRANHA

The press release said the tunnel was demolished with explosives after the people inside were warned repeatedly to come out. Reading the statement, I asked our escort officer to check the location and unit involved. He confirmed later that it was the same tunnel we had been watching much of the previous day.

'Too bad we left. Would've been interesting to see what they pulled out of there.'

'Never have happened,' Wilson said. 'That lieutenant wasn't going to do anything with us around.'

'What if those were civilians down there?' I said.

'You don't want to know,' Wilson said.

With the press of other stories to cover, I never made the time to go back to the Marine platoon that blew up the tunnel and killed the sixty-six Vietnamese to ask what happened. I did not find out whether the victims were soldiers or civilians.

The original Marine Corps news release reporting the deaths also included the following information: after the explosion, the lieutenant in charge of the platoon went by himself into the tunnel to count the bodies and assess the damage. He had to carry a lighted candle to illuminate the tunnel because all the platoon's flashlight batteries were dead. While in the tunnel, the lieutenant was overcome by fumes from the explosions and died of asphyxiation.

SEPTEMBER 9, 1965

The word at the press center was they had real American burgers at the USO in downtown Danang, so, at lunchtime, Wilson, Funk and I climbed in the rented bureau jeep and drove into town to find it. The jeep was a relic—an old, dilapidated Willys that had somehow survived the slow assaults of age, wear, climate and the mechanical ministrations of its Vietnamese owner who, because he could not get spare parts, fabricated and installed his own, some with old bits of wire, some with string, some with electrical tape. The jeep rode like a sled over the rutted tracks that passed for roads, bouncing on broken springs, rattling over potholes, grinding through transmission gears that had lost most of their teeth. The clutch engaged with the drive shaft intermittently. Riding in the open jeep through swarms of Vietnamese cyclists, their eyes on the three of us, we tried to give the impression we knew where we were going, but it was an act. We knew how to get to and from the airport and III MAF headquarters and the beach but that was all. For us, driving into downtown Danang was an adventure, like going into the field with the Marines, so unusual were the sights, so mysterious what might happen.

I had assumed that the USO had gone out with all the other cultural icons associated with World War II: tea dances and the jitterbug and Willie and Joe, but the Vietnam War had revived it. "USO" stood for United Services Organization. Its American volunteers had rented an old colonial house on a quiet street with shade trees and converted it into a clean orderly club. It was designed to give servicemen an alternative to the lowlife bars and brothels that sold alcohol and sex in other parts of town. Wilson parked the jeep under a tree in front of the building, got out, carried his camera with him.

'Nothin's safe in an open jeep,' he scowled.

A group of Vietnamese children—mainly boys of ten or eleven in shabby shorts and dirty shirts—stood outside the USO house watching. Wilson went over to the children and pointed his finger at them and then at his eyes and then at the jeep. He spoke as he pointed, 'You . . . watch . . . jeep. Okay?'

Immediately they smiled.

'Okay, GI!' one of them said, and they gathered around the jeep with proprietary hustle, touching the white-painted fenders with tender care. As we went inside it wasn't clear whether the children were being hired to guard the jeep or bribed to leave it alone.

The main room of the USO was bright and colorful. A makeshift cafeteria had been constructed with wooden tables and chairs and plastic tablecloths with salt and pepper shakers and ashtrays on them. Airline posters of American cities and landscapes were hung on the walls. The furnishings were clean and the room smelled lightly of paint, like a high school clubhouse patched together with a little money and a lot of work. The food was served by three American women in their twenties—USO volunteers who were good-looking in a wholesome, fresh-scrubbed, midwestern way. When we appeared in the line to order food, they asked, "Where are you guys from?" and, when we told them, they said, "How long have you been over here?" as if that was what they asked everyone. Conversation progressed from there. The women were attentive, prepared to talk as long as we wished, seeming to enjoy it. We told them we were a TV news team for CBS, that we had been in-country for less than a month and were still finding our way around. They asked what we had seen of the war, how it was going, what we thought. They seemed genuinely interested in what we said, though we didn't know much. Serving the food, one of the young women said, 'We don't get to see much of what's going on out there from here in Danang.' Her voice was wistful, her eyes lowered, as if she might wish to go out in the field and see some of the war zone if she could. I didn't offer to take her. It would have been easy enough to drive her around the perimeter on her time off, show her some of the military encampments, explain a little of what was going on, probably make the Marines we met happy too—she was that pretty. But I didn't suggest it. Being in the company of bright, cheerful, attractive American women my own age was both delightful and unnerving. Talking to them, enjoying the banter, I didn't dare try to get to know them better. The idea of achieving any kind of intimacy, even a casual friendship, was beyond my imagination, too unlikely to consider seriously. The USO women were symbols of life in another world—too clean and wholesome and healthy to be blighted by association with me and the war.

Sitting at a table with Wilson and Funk, eating the food, the taste of a cheeseburger made with American beef and fresh lettuce and tomato and an order of French fried potatoes with ketchup and salt and a vanilla milkshake made to American tastes was a treasure. We had eaten nothing like it for weeks. The familiar food and friendly surroundings separated us from the poverty outside and transported us back to the States for an hour or so, a clean break from the cauldron of I Corps. Eating his burger, Wilson grumbled, 'Too bad they don't have any onions.'

Wilson and Funk attracted attention. The oversized Auricon film camera resting on the table, the pistols on their belts, the Australian bush hats, the scruffy black beards and the CBS News name tags on their fatigues set them apart, like visiting celebrities. The other guests were mostly Marines and sailors and airmen from the enlisted ranks with leave from work. None appeared to be from a combat unit. No in-country R and R facilities had been established in Danang yet, so GIs had to find entertainment where they could. The ramshackle bars that called themselves "nightclubs" with garish neon lights and noisy recorded music and aggressive Vietnamese prostitutes with come-ons like circus pitchmen didn't get going until later in the day.

When we finished our meal, GIs came over to the table and asked Wilson and Funk why they chose to come to Vietnam and if they'd been shot at yet and other questions about their work. One asked what kind of movie film they were using and whether the bright sunlight was a problem with the exposure. Wilson sat at the center of attention and beamed like an actor in lights, answering the GIs' questions with politeness and modesty, as if the cowboy hat and beard and pistol were only a costume that went with his job. He asked them where they worked and what they were doing and if anything interesting was going on, trying to discover if they might have a story for him to film. They all did, of course, but their jobs kept them in the rear areas.

I left Wilson and Funk at the table and went to a reading room in another part of the building and sat in a big overstuffed armchair. I picked up an old copy of LIFE magazine and casually turned the pages. A full-page advertisement for a brand of gin caught my attention. The color photograph showed a man relaxing in a leather easy chair. He appeared to be a successful businessman, an advertising account executive perhaps, with his suit jacket off and tie loosened. He sat in the foreground of the picture with his legs on a leather hassock, slippers on his feet. An open book rested on the table beside him. The background showed a living room decorated with expensive furniture and fine fabrics, a fire burning in a large slate fireplace. It was a picture of perfect middle-class comfort, the successful man surrounded by his acquisitions, unwinding at the end of day. The man held a half-empty martini glass in his hand, savoring the gin and its effect between sips. A caption beneath the photograph captured his thoughts. "Ah, this is the life," it said.

I stared at the ad. The man's expression looked smug, self-satisfied, as if his brand of gin were the ideal accompaniment to his success, as if nothing could go wrong with his private world. Looking at the photograph, I thought it unfair. *Why should he have so much comfort when so many Americans were sweating out here in the sun? Living on the ground like animals? Risking their lives to preserve his freedom to drink dry martinis in that pristine, climate-controlled living room? What does he care what goes on in this wild otherworld of heat and blood?* To me, it was worse than selfish; it was obscene. Anger ignited in my heart and spread into my veins.

Two men walked into the room. They wore khaki trousers and short-sleeved white shirts with breast pockets and appeared to be in their mid- to late twenties. Both had short, neat haircuts and fit, erect postures, almost military in bearing. At first, I thought they were American soldiers in civilian dress, but they introduced themselves as field officers for the United States Operations Mission (USOM) and the United States Agency for International Development (USAID), which I knew to be State Department offices that administered foreign aid, training and self-help programs for the Vietnamese. They were part of the American government's "country team" in Vietnam.

We shook hands and started to talk. The men were bright, articulate. They seemed to know more of what was going on in the countryside than the military people I had met, and they spoke knowledgeably about Vietnamese culture. Their manner was relaxed, casual. They asked who I worked for and what stories we had covered. When they learned that I had been in-country only a few weeks, they started talking about the Vietcong. The VC, they said, used terror against the civilian population routinely as one of its tactics in guerrilla war. The VC buried mines in country roads that exploded under civilian cars and buses. Its agents assassinated local bureaucrats who cooperated with the Saigon government. They set off bombs in crowded city restaurants and killed innocent people, dozens at a time. The men spoke in low, angry voices. I thought they might be establishing their anti-Communist credentials with me, and, maybe at the same time, measuring my reactions. I was suitably shocked. I had read plenty of VC atrocity stories (the Saigon government propaganda machine was fueled by them), but none were as convincing as firsthand accounts from Americans in the field.

The two men got chairs and sat down and shared my pack of Camels. 'The first thing you've got to understand,' one said, 'is that the war is psychological as much as military. It's not like World War II and Korea, where the lines moved back and forth and the territory was ours or theirs. This is entirely different. It's about hearts and minds. No use killing a bunch of VC if the people in the countryside won't play ball with us. They're the key. If we want to win, we have to have their loyalty.'

'And you don't get loyalty by shelling their hamlets at night,' the other said. 'They hate us for that.'

'And they help the other side.'

The men were angry about H and I, which stood for "harassment and interdiction," they explained. American and South Vietnamese gunners fired long-range weapons with high-explosive shells far into the countryside to disrupt Vietcong activity. The artillery shells were fired from bases near Danang and exploded so far away you could barely hear the impact. Usually, they said, the shells were not aimed at specific targets but were fired at random at areas of the countryside controlled by the VC, supposedly unpopulated forests. In theory, they said, H and I fire exploded among the VC without warning, keeping them awake at night, wearing down their nerves. In fact, they said, the targets were chosen by local South Vietnamese officials who gave grid coordinates to American artillery officers who had only a vague idea what they were shooting at. Sometimes the targets were villages whose farmers had not paid taxes to local government bureaucrats or were suspected of being sympathetic to the VC. The shells, they said, were killing and injuring Vietnamese who had nothing to do with the war other than being caught in it. Most shelling took place at night, and it made the peasants crazy with fear. The men said H and I was inhuman, criminal.

'Go out there sometime,' one of the men said, 'and check it out. See for yourself.'

I believed them. But I was surprised to hear open criticism of U.S. government policy from two of its own employees. It sounded reckless, almost subversive. They knew I was a reporter and might make a story out of what they told me. But it didn't occur to me that they actually *wanted* me to report what was happening with H and I, that their concern for the Vietnamese was more important to them than blind obedience to unknown government bureaucrats far removed from the reality of the fighting. I didn't understand that their sense of duty *required* them to speak out. They were telling me what was going wrong in the war.

We talked and smoked cigarettes and drank coffee for about an hour. Mostly I listened. The two men made a case for giving more material aid to peasants who wanted to modernize their farming methods. Farmers did not have tractors to plow their fields. No wood or cement to build houses, barns and wells.

'The best way to win hearts and minds out there,' one of them said, 'is to improve the farmers' lives. Give them tools. Help them make a little money.'

'So they won't want to give it all up to the Communists,' the other said.

They said it was important to try to educate the Vietnamese about the dangers of Communism as a philosophy, teach them how it suppressed individual freedom and civil rights. At the same time, peasants should be taught the benefits of political democracy—concepts most Vietnamese did not understand. The men invited me to visit them in the districts where they worked. I promised to come and see them when I was free from covering the Marines every day. Listening to them talk—honest, sincere, intelligent men my own age—was refreshing, enlightening, the high point of my visit to Danang. Their passion for the well-being of ordinary Vietnamese peasants was infectious. In my notebook I wrote the names Jack Stockton and Phil Thomas.

That night, I wrote a letter to a friend in the States. The USOM and USAID men, I said, were the kind of Americans President Kennedy inspired with his inauguration address a few years ago. I admired them for their dedication, their willingness to work for the welfare of the less fortunate, their sacrifice of personal comforts, the risks they took. No comfortable easy chairs and dry martinis by the fire for them.

Outside the USO building, Wilson gave the Vietnamese children who had been guarding the jeep a few pennies worth of coins in the local currency. The children cried in protest, 'You gimme ten P!' 'You beaucoup cheap Charlie!' Wilson curled his hand into a fist and cocked his arm behind him and snarled. The children recoiled. Wilson climbed in the jeep, put the camera on the backseat and started the engine. At the same time, Funk took a small piastre note from his pocket and slipped it secretly to the children. They looked at it, smiled and shouted. 'Okay! You number one!' Pointing to Wilson in the jeep, they cried, 'He number ten. Cheap Charlie.' Funk and I waved good-bye as the jeep pulled out and drove down the street. 'Bunch of God damn thieves,' Wilson mumbled as he shifted gears.

A plume of smoke rose on the southwest horizon, above the shade trees lining the streets. Wilson turned the jeep sharply in the direction of the smoke and pushed hard on the accelerator. 'Let's find out what the hell that is,' he said. The jeep raced forward with a loud whine of the engine and grinding of gears. Funk and I held onto the sides of the jeep. Speeding through the afternoon traffic, Wilson steered around corners and roared down straightaways without caution, as if chasing a fire engine in Los Angeles, seeming to enjoy it. Vietnamese pedestrians jumped out of the jeep's way, staring after us with solemn faces.

The smell came first. About a mile outside of town, west of the airbase, a vast smoking wasteland spread across the landscape, acres of ripe garbage smoldering in the heat. The smell was of rotten meat and vegetables and human waste. An attempt had been made to burn it but had not succeeded. The dump appeared to be the main repository for all the garbage of the Marine division guarding Danang, perhaps twenty thousand men and women. It stood in individual ten-foot piles, neat orderly rows. Marine trucks backed up to the piles and dumped cargoes of fresh garbage over them.

Vietnamese women and children with tattered clothes and conical straw sun hats crawled over the mounds of refuse, picking up bits of rubbish and dropping them into straw baskets they carried by their sides. One woman found an empty dark brown beer bottle, its Asahi label intact, and put it in her basket with care.

Wilson parked the jeep, jumped out, and in one smooth series of motions took a meter from his breast pocket and read the light, checked the exposure on his camera, put it on his shoulder and started shooting. No time wasted. Funk plugged his sound amplifier into the back of the camera and undid the strings that held the cables in loops. It was after three o'clock in the afternoon and rain clouds were gathering. Marines drove up in jeeps and trucks and turned metal cans upside down onto the edges of the dump. As each truck dropped its load, the women and children swarmed over the fresh piles of garbage and picked at them with their hands. Their faces were dark with soot and dirt. The air was sharp with putrefying waste.

A broad-shouldered Marine sergeant ran after the Vietnamese, chasing them over the mounds of garbage, scampering like a giant crab. He shouted and cursed them in English and Vietnamese, '*Di-di! Di-di mau! You little sonso-bitches!*' The Vietnamese ran just ahead of the sergeant's reach and when he stopped they stopped and looked at him, pink-faced and sweaty in the heat. As soon as he turned to run after another group, the Vietnamese returned to the smoking piles, as if the chase were a ritual.

The sergeant stopped to talk. He said his name was Charles Reid from Youngstown, Ohio. He was the senior NCO in charge at the dump.

'It's a losing battle,' he said. 'The Vietnamese are so damn poor this garbage is valuable to them. All it is is mostly leftover food being thrown away.' Reid said the people practically live on the dump. 'They get food and firewood here and anything else they can sell in town at the market. Believe me, this garbage isn't fit for pigs.'

Reid stopped speaking at the sound of an explosion. Everyone at the dump heard it at the same time—a loud muffled pop, like a bottle bursting. Wilson, who was rolling, looked up from the viewfinder and said, 'What the hell was that?'

'Sounds like a grenade,' said Reid. He ran toward the explosion. Wilson, Funk and I followed. A hundred yards away, a boy of about nine lay on his side, his hands holding his stomach. A Marine enlisted man leaned over the boy and opened his shirt and felt inside for the wound. When he took his hand away the insides of his fingers were wet and red. Two older Vietnamese, a woman and a teenage boy cut by flying shrapnel, sat on the dirt, waiting to be treated. No one cried.

'Some joker left a live one in the garbage and it went off,' the enlisted man said. Another Marine drove up in a truck and the Marines carried the three injured Vietnamese onto the back of the truck and drove away. Wilson recorded the scene on film.

When we got back to the press center, Wilson said, 'Good story. Just write it the way it happened, in chronological order.' Funk checked on flights to Saigon. There was an Air Force C-130 leaving in an hour. I wrote the voice-over narration quickly, checked it, showed it to Wilson to read, and spoke into the microphone Funk held in front of me. "Garbage Dump at Danang," I said, "Laurence voice-over, take one."

"*These are the scavengers of war,*" the narration began. *The Vietnamese*, I said, *"come here because there is such a shortage of everything else—tin cans, wood and clothing—that the American refuse is reusable. They come here because they have nothing else—and the garbage gives them something."*

The narration ran about two minutes. Wilson and Funk put the exposed film into metal cans and sealed them with white adhesive tape and put the package in a black and yellow shipping bag addressed to the bureau in Saigon. They drove to the Air Force operations office at Danang airfield and gave the bag to the copilot to carry to Saigon. When they returned to the press center, we sat down around a table in the restaurant and drank a beer. Wilson smiled.

'That's the way to do 'em,' he said, 'short and sweet.'

'No, quick and dirty,' Funk said and we laughed. The garbage smoke was still on us. The story had been shot and shipped in about two hours. Two days later it got to New York where the film was processed, edited and broadcast on the *CBS Evening News*. In the days that followed, we did not check on the condition of the wounded boy. Events were moving too fast to do follow-ups on stories. We did not see Sergeant Reid again, though we heard at the press center he was reprimanded by his superiors for talking to us. The garbage dump story was seen in Washington as unfavorable to the image the Marine Corps brass wanted to project to the American public.

On the way back to the press center from the dump, our jeep had stopped on the road that ran past the far end of the runway while we waited for a flight of Air Force fighter-bombers to land at the airbase. The jets circled low and came in over the road. I looked out the side of the jeep and saw a Vietnamese farmer working in a field with a long-handled hoe. He looked at least sixty years old with long white hair and a stringy white goatee and large bones that pushed against his gold-brown skin. The farmer swung the hoe high in the air with his thin muscled arms and dug into the dry unplanted earth and pulled on the handle and the ground turned. He lifted the hoe and swung it a second time and pulled on the handle and the ground turned. Then he lifted the hoe again and swung and pulled and the ground turned. After three times the old man stopped and straightened his back and looked at the end of the runway with an expression that was so passive it was no expression at all. A few seconds passed. The farmer turned and spit in the palms of his old bony hands and rubbed them together and took the handle of the hoe and repeated the process of turning the land as it had been turned by all the farmers of Vietnam before him, smooth and practiced as a yoga exercise, timeless and simple and hard.

After sundown, Wilson, Funk and I drove to the airbase and checked in with the 513th Marine Attack Fighter Squadron. Wilson thought the pilots might make an interesting sidebar, a short film story about what some of the pilots did when they were not flying combat missions, a brief look behind the scenes of military life. When we arrived, the pilots were sitting at tables in a bar of the officers club, drinking and singing fight songs and telling war stories like college fraternity boys. Most of them were in their twenties with ultrashort hair and shaved faces except for a variety of mustaches that were in fashion with Marine aviators. The mustaches gave their faces a rakish, debonair look, casual and carefree. But their innocent, boyish faces were belied by their eyes. They had the eyes of birds of prey—ice calm, alert, all-seeing. Sitting around a cluster of tables, they told each other stories about their flying adventures in Vietnam and other places. Some of them were about pilots who were no longer alive. The stories were spoken quickly and with polished rhetoric, as though they had been told before. The pilots seemed to sing and drink with the same intensity that they brought to flying in combat.

One of the songs was repeated several times during the evening. It was sung to the melody of the "Battle Hymn of the Republic." Everyone sang the refrain especially loud:

> *Glory, glory what a hell of a way to die,*
> *Glory, glory what a hell of a way to die,*
> *Glory, glory what a hell of a way to die,*
> *And he'll never fly home again.*

Death was in the theme of almost every song: *surprise* death, *cruel* death, *ironic* death, *unfortunate* death, *swift* death, *foolish* death, *near* death. The songs were macabre, dark and humorous, without being especially morbid. They had a purpose. By focusing on the prospect of death casually in their songs and stories, the young men were preparing themselves to absorb the impact when the time came to face the fear of death in their work. '*Oh, well, it's only death,*' they seemed to sing. '*My death, your death, what the hell? This is war. Somebody's got to die.*' Laughing at death, mocking it, inviting it into the room with them, the pilots were diminishing the mystery that went with the danger. But there were no songs about the people their bombing missions struck.

Wilson and Funk set up the camera to do on-camera interviews. The pilots said it was frustrating to fly north every day without meeting Vietnamese pilots for air-to-air combat. 'That's what we were trained to do,' one of them said, 'but the North Vietnamese won't come up and engage.' Off-camera they said the United States was bombing the same targets—roads, bridges, railroads, ammo dumps—over and over again. It wasn't doing much to hurt the North Vietnamese, they said, because the Vietnamese rebuilt or repaired the things as fast as the Americans blew them up. 'No way to win a war,' one of them said.

When the filming was finished, the pilots invited us to join them for drinks. Funk, who did not drink, left. The alcohol was cheap, shipped from the States, and was served by Vietnamese waiters in starched white uniforms. One drink became two, two became three, then it was freefall. The storytelling continued long after midnight and the drinking, which was secondary to the stories and songs, evolved into a competition among the pilots to determine who would stop last. Olympian quantities of beer were consumed. Empty cans filled a large tin garbage pail against the wall. Wilson fell asleep. One by one, the pilots got up from the tables and excused themselves saying they had missions to fly in a few hours. After two o'clock, most of the remaining drinkers spoke in words slurred beyond comprehension. Sentences no longer made sense. Stories were told for a second time. Finally, the one officer left at the table said it was time to call it quits. 'You drink like a jarhead,' he said. It was true. Since my teens, I had drunk larger quantities of alcohol than other people but with less effect. We carried Wilson to the jeep with his arms over our shoulders and when he was securely inside I drove over the dark empty road back to the press center, mildly drunk and happy.

SEPTEMBER 15, 1965

Slowly, methodically, the Marines moved farther into the countryside around Danang. They set off in convoys of trucks and jeeps, one company at a time, two hundred men with weapons and equipment moving slowly along the soft dirt roads that radiated out from the city, clouding the roadsides with dust, showering children they passed with candy and C rations until they arrived on the flat green farmland of the outlands. The countryside was tranquil, baking in the sun. Along the route the Marines saw straw-roofed houses of mud and clay and thatched bamboo, slow-working farmers in silent rice fields, water buffalo grazing almost without motion, tall thickets of bamboo rustling softly in the wind. The Marines stopped and climbed down from their trucks in noisy confusions of heat, dust, sweat and war-fighting equipment. The NCOs directed them to stow their gear and begin to stake out circular cordons of barbed wire, bunkers, mortar pits and machineguns. Fences went up. In the evening, patrols went out. In a few hours, they had set up two-acre bases for their defense. Everything outside the perimeter was considered hostile or potentially hostile. The men dug holes in the ground and slept in them.

Observation posts were deployed to screen traffic that passed through their areas of operation. The Marines questioned villagers, searched for weapons, interrogated suspects. They began modest programs of medical aid to local civilians. At first the Marines were polite. Some of the villagers they met were friendly, some were wary, others were cold and distant. Making friends with the children was easiest. The Americans offered them food and the children took it gratefully. Winning hearts and minds, one at a time. The American high command planned to protect the Danang airbase and other installations by gradually pacifying areas around the city in a slowly widening arc, hoping to force the local Viet Cong off the heavily populated coastal plain and into the distant jungles and ultimately out of the war. The strategy was known as "expanding the oil slick."

Company C, 1st Battalion, 1st Marine Regiment—a sister to Alpha Company—had moved into its new area of operation on September 13, two days earlier. The command tent was located on a bare dirt knoll just off a road seven miles southwest of Danang. It was the farthest any Marine company had penetrated the countryside. The commanding officer, a young captain, greeted us with a warm smile and friendly handshake. He said his men had been shot at by snipers on their first full day in the area but none had been hit. After a quick briefing, he said he had to prepare for an important visitor the next day. I asked him who was coming but he would not say. The captain turned to his gunnery sergeant. 'Gunny,' he said, 'see that these gentlemen get a place to sleep for the night.' The sergeant was a veteran Marine warhorse in his mid-forties with broad shoulders and a thick chest and deep sweat lines in his sunburned neck. His eyes were alert but cold, as if they had seen more than they should. The gunny took us into the big open-sided command tent and pointed to a place to put down our packs.

Wilson and Funk had been replaced by another CBS team, this one from Tokyo. The photographer, named Alex Brauer, was French. He was twenty-eight years old with dark hair and sloping shoulders and a round, full face that matched the heavy stature of his body. His fatigues were bulky, unwilling to stay in place, sliding around the folds of his body. The sound technician was a Japanese named Kojiri Sakai. He was in his forties, short and strong with black hair, dark features, a polite disposition and a desire to please his American colleagues. Both Brauer and Sakai-san had been in Vietnam before, usually for a month or two on rotation from their base in Japan. The two men carried themselves with dignity, giving the appearance of an accomplished team who rarely needed to speak to each other. I had difficulty communicating with them. They spoke little English and I knew only a few words of French and no Japanese. Moreover, Brauer made it clear he was not entirely comfortable working in the field with me. He had been assigned to Danang against his wishes. He would rather be working with his regular correspondent, Peter Kalischer, the Tokyo bureau chief, a veteran of Vietnam and other wars. To Brauer, I was an inexperienced rookie, potentially dangerous.

In Saigon a few days before, Wilson had complained secretly to the CBS bureau chief that he was tired of working with "a tenderfoot," as he called me. No matter that most of our work had been broadcast on the *CBS Evening News*, some of it to accolades. The bureau chief told me later Wilson needed a change. He wanted to do something more special than routine news reporting, something sensational, and I wasn't experienced enough to write a memorable script. The bureau chief obliged by sending him and Funk on a military operation in the Central Highlands with the older, more experienced Kalischer.

Brauer refused to take direction from me. He insisted on being consulted about each decision, especially if it involved risk. At the press center the night before, he wanted to know exactly what the story was, where we were going, how dangerous it was going to be and how long we would be away from Danang. It took a long time to explain. Although he was friendly, Brauer's manner was also surly at times, uncompromising. *How different he is from Wilson,* I thought, *how stubborn and uncooperative, as if cares less about getting a good story than being absolutely safe. No spirit for the excitement of the work, no sense of adventure.* Uncomprehending and insensitive myself, I equated his caution with cowardice.

In France, Brauer had grown up with the history of French Indochina, France's century of intimacy with its faraway colony and its lost war. From what he had seen on his previous visits to Vietnam, Brauer had concluded that the zealous American campaign to pacify the place was doomed, as hopeless as the French one before it. Covering combat in this war, he believed, was not worth the risks that doing so demanded.

The gunnery sergeant's eyes followed Sakai around the tent, watching his moves, measuring them. His face was darkly malevolent with an expression of restrained violence, as if he were waiting for a chance to strike. It was uncomfortable to watch. Sakai was being observed as one of the enemy. The gunny seemed obsessed, as though he could not understand why this modest Japanese technician was allowed inside his company perimeter, as if the true purpose of Sakai's presence would be revealed to him only by constant, unremitting vigilance. Sakai paid no attention to the gunnery sergeant, or appeared to pay none, and organized his sound equipment in silence.

I dropped my gear on the dirt floor of the command tent and wandered alone along the perimeter to talk with the Marines on the line. By now it was late afternoon and the sun was falling behind the dark tree-covered ridgelines of the distant mountains. The air was cooling. Marines worked on the defense positions in sweaty green T-shirts or barebacked—securing barbed wire, filling sandbags, digging holes, cleaning their M-14s and machineguns. I walked up to a group of enlisted men who were resting and asked them how they liked being out here.

'Boring,' one of them said.

'We're just here to protect the airbase,' another said. 'Keeps Charlie from settin up to shoot rockets and mortars at the air force.'

'It's not very interesting.'

'Not much chance of catching the VC.'

'Rather be out in the boonies fightin the way they're doin down at Chu Lai.' *Starlite again*, I thought.

There was no aggression in their voices, no anger or self-pity. They spoke in the stoical manner of the infantry, accustomed to accepting the way things were, powerless to change anything. We talked a while and I moved on to another group and then another.

The sun was gone, the sky nearly dark when I got back to the headquarters tent. Under the canvas, a corporal sat with his elbows resting on a table with a pair of portable radio communications sets, bulky old PRCs, listening to the low hiss. The platoon RTOs checked in periodically with brief situation reports. A kerosene lamp burned. Outside the CP, a squad formed up to leave the perimeter and walk out into the surrounding rice paddies and set up a night ambush position.

Brauer and Sakai sat on the ground in front of a low wood fire eating chow with the gunnery sergeant. The gunny sat on a straw mat, his legs crossed. He was no longer angry. He dipped into a can of C ration peaches with a plastic spoon and lifted a slice into the air and across the low fire and gently fed it into the open mouth of Sakai. Sakai smiled and chewed briefly and swallowed the peach slice. The gunny's hands moved with delicate care, holding the can under Sakai's chin to catch any drops of juice that fell, feeding him like a child. I sat and watched. Brauer leaned over and whispered in his heavy French accent that Sakai-san and the sergeant had fought against each other in World War II. It had taken them a long time to figure out using words, place-names and sign language. Both had been in the infantry. Where didn't matter: maybe it was the Philippines, maybe Okinawa. They were not able to communicate to each other all the battles they had fought in, but there had been many. It was enough to have the war in common. Brauer looked up and smiled. The gunny's eyes glowed with friendship. Sakai sat on the other side of the fire with his legs crossed and his face engaged in a big child's grin, happy in himself. They had been drinking beer, one can after another, and their eyes were wet. The gunny got up slowly and went to his wooden footlocker at the corner of the tent and came back with several cans of food that he had kept for a special occasion. Bowing deeply at the waist, he showed each delicacy to Sakai and requested which one he would be pleased to eat next, offering the small treasures with the formality of a Japanese tea ceremony. Sakai refused nothing. They sat and smiled and looked at each other and talked in broken English and Japanese until the fire and the kerosene lamp had been extinguished. There was no pretense between them, no insincerity, no sign of mistrust. When it was time to sleep, the gunny offered Sakai his cot. At first, Sakai refused. The gunny insisted, politely. After three requests Sakai accepted. He got onto the cot, took off his boots and lay his head on the canvas. The gunny put a clean, folded towel under Sakai's head and draped a lightweight poncho liner over him and tucked it in. When he was sure that Sakai was comfortable, the gunny made a simple bed on the ground next to the cot and slept on it.

*

Second platoon went on patrol just after dawn. The Marines walked single file out of the camp and along the banks of a narrow brown river and onto the hard dirt embankments of rice fields and across open fields of unplanted farmland and finally under the shade trees of a hamlet where women and children held one another in the shadows of their straw houses and watched as the Marines passed by. The platoon leader was a tall dark-skinned lieutenant named Walter Levy who had a brush of a black mustache and thin serious eyes. He carried an M-14 on a canvas sling over his shoulder and walked near the front of his platoon. Brauer, Sakai and I followed behind Levy's radio operator. The gunnery sergeant came on the patrol even though his usual duties were at company headquarters. He walked behind Sakai and watched every step he made, instructing him to put his feet in the footsteps of the person in front and not to stray from the trail of the column. The gunny carried some of Sakai's equipment, pointed out dangers along the way, and guarded him like a member of his family. Sakai accepted the gunny's attentions with exaggerated gratitude.

The sun rose high and shone on the column, heating the hard earth and baking everything that grew in it. The patrol stopped every fifteen or twenty minutes. Brauer put down the film camera and wiped his face and neck with a handkerchief. The gunny smoked a cigarette. Sitting next to him, I asked if there had been a lot of humping like this in the Pacific in World War II. He thought for a few seconds and looked at me with his hard eyes, as if he hated to be reminded. 'Them islands was worse than *hell*,' he said. 'Fire and blood. All fire and blood. And bodies.' He looked around. 'This here is nothing. Just heat and bugs.'

The platoon passed a large bomb crater on the left of a trail that crossed an open field. The hole went down into the ground about fifteen feet. At the bottom, the crater was filled with oil-black water. In the middle of the water, an elaborate handmade decoration of woven bamboo floated on the surface, nearly filling the bottom. The decoration was in the shape of a five-pointed star surrounded by concentric circles and a radiant sunburst. The bamboo had been dyed red, yellow and blue but the colors were pale from long exposure to the sunlight. Passing it on the trail, Marines in the column looked at it over their shoulders. Their eyes were cold. I recognized the decoration as a symbol of the National Liberation Front, the formal name of the Viet Cong. It floated in the water like a defiant flag in the pastel-colored fields. I wanted to reach down and take it out and keep it as a trophy but I remembered the warnings about booby traps and left it.

Farther along, a huge black water buffalo bellowed from a dry field on the left as the patrol passed. The animal was frightened by the presence of so many strange figures. It jumped up and down on its front hooves and spun itself in circles in the dust. Its head shook and its eyes bulged. Bleating and snorting, it paid no attention to the entreaties of a boy of about ten who tried to make it behave. The patrol stopped. The water buffalo stomped and shook its head and kicked its hind legs out behind and then ran forward a few yards as if to charge the Marines but then stopped. The Marines watched, their fingers on the triggers of their rifles. One by one the safeties clicked off. Again the water buffalo started to charge. The lieutenant gave a signal and in a few seconds a half dozen M-14 rounds cracked sharply along the dike and echoed across the field. The water buffalo stopped snorting and looked rigidly at the patrol as if shocked by the sudden noise. Its shoulder muscles trembled. One of its legs wobbled. The animal tried to lift its feet but staggered in place. It did not move, nor did the Marines. Time passed: ten, fifteen, twenty seconds. Then all at once, like a great black boulder, the beast fell to the ground and rolled on its side. The boy ran to the animal and threw his arms around its head and touched its black skin with his cheek and held it without moving.

The patrol went on. With the weight of his camera and the heat and the

long walk, Brauer fell behind. The patrol stopped and he took out his handkerchief and wiped the sweat from his face and said in his French accent that
we were stupid to go with the Marines where the VC would not fight. I
offered to carry the camera for a while, as Wilson sometimes allowed, but
Brauer refused. The gunny gave his canteen to Sakai, who drank from it.
When he was finished, the gunny handed the water to Brauer and told him
to drink, it would make him feel better.

The patrol moved back along the banks of a river that meandered through
a shaded village. In one of the hamlets the Marines searched the thatched roof
houses and discovered the concealed entrance to a deep tunnel and a bunker
system below. Lieutenant Levy said the VC used tunnels as hiding places and
stored weapons and ammunition in them. He gave the order and a team of
demolition experts put explosive charges in the tunnels. As Brauer rolled film,
the Marines ran quickly out of the house. A few seconds later a loud explosion
shook the ground and the house disintegrated in a cloud of broken timber,
raining dirt and bamboo all around. Some of the Marines shouted, 'Hey!'

When they got back to the CP, the Marines in the patrol grumbled about
'another walk in the sun' and complained to friends in other platoons that
nothing had happened, killed a gook buffalo was all. They dropped their
packs and helmets and fell on the ground, Brauer, Sakai and I with them. An
officer appeared and said to get ready. Still exhausted, Brauer got up and put
the camera on his shoulder. I respected his determination not to quit.

A pair of H-34s circled over the camp once and landed quickly in clouds
of dirt. Out stepped Major General Lewis Walt, the Marine commander in
Vietnam, and a group of aides. Walt was a short, rugged-looking man who
strode confidently forward under the wash of the rotor blades, giving the
appearance of a prizefighter on his way to the ring. He wore dark green
combat fatigues and a helmet with two stars on it and a pistol belt with a holster and a .45 on his hip. He shook hands with the company commander and
his platoon leaders and went immediately to observe a U.S. Navy doctor
treating sick and injured Vietnamese from a nearby village. The peasants
were dressed in ragged clothing and stood in a line to receive vitamins, soap
and cigarettes from a group of navy corpsmen. One little boy was seriously
sick. The battalion doctor, Captain John Bocker, said, 'There's not much I
can do for him. He needs hospitalization.'

Brauer took pictures of the villagers being treated as the general
watched. Walt had hawk eyes with lines around the edges like bird's feet.

"You see the friendly people we've uncovered from VC control?" he said to the camera. "We're giving them medical support and they're real glad to have us here."

The expressions on the faces of the villagers were empty.

I told the general about the patrol that morning. "Will there be further pushes in the future?" I asked, meaning more military operations outside of Danang. I was trying to dig some hard news out of the story of his visit.

"I hope there will be," Walt said. "That's why we're here. Free as many people as we can."

Walt's remark seemed important. For the six months since they landed in Vietnam in February, most of the Marines in Vietnam had remained in defensive positions without pushing very far inland. The exceptions had been the two big Marine landings near Chu Lai. Walt's remark suggested the offensive phase of the American military strategy was now under way. He had given us news to report.

When he had seen enough of sick call, the general walked over to talk with his Marines. He found a young enlisted man sitting outside his tent writing a letter.

"Writing a letter?"

The Marine stood up.

"How you getting along? How are you today?" the general asked.

"Fine," said the Marine.

"Where's your home?"

"Pittsburgh, Pennsylvania, sir."

"How long does it take to get a letter from Pennsylvania?"

"It's averagin about four to six days."

"Pretty good, huh?"

The young Marine nodded his head in the affirmative and chewed gum.

Turning to another Marine, the general said, "Do you have enough stationery so that you can write on?"

"We can't get enough stationery, sir." The Marine looked down at his feet.

"Well, there's some coming along on a ship today," the general said as if he knew for a fact. "So you're gonna be all right."

"That's good," said the Marine.

The general walked along the line.

"You had any action recently at all?" he asked another Marine.

"Uh, about two nights ago, sir. Had about three grenades among us."

"Did you get 'em?"

"No, sir."

The general nodded his head, as if the answers were not coming as he might have wished.

"Well, you're out front here now where you'll have a chance to see a lot of 'em." His face bloomed in a smile.

A young, blue-eyed corporal stood at ease as the general approached. A jagged rubber strap held the camouflage cover in place on his helmet.

Walt asked him how often he'd been on patrol.

"I guess I've been out a few times," the corporal said.

"Two times?"

"A few, sir."

"At night?"

"Yes, sir."

"How long were you out at night?"

"Once we were out all night. Once for a few hours."

"Set up an ambush?"

"Yes, sir."

The general did not ask if the ambush was successful. "Find this pretty interesting work?"

"Yes, sir. Once you get away from a tactical area like this." The corporal looked over toward the camp tents, jeeps, the landing zone and mortar positions.

"What do you think of these VC?"

"I'd like to see some sometime." The corporal smiled. Without being impolite, he was matching wits with the commanding general in front of a TV film camera.

"Like to see some, huh?" Walt thought what to say next. "Uh . . . you'll probably have a lot of opportunity."

"I imagine so."

"Well, keep up the good work."

"Thank you, sir."

The general put out his hand and the corporal shook it.

A few minutes later, when the general and his entourage and the helicopters were gone, I asked the corporal what he thought of the visit. Other Marines gathered to listen.

"I didn't know he was the commanding general at first. You don't expect to see him on the front lines."

"What does a trip like this do for your morale?"

"Um, it kinda boosts it up, in a way . . ." He paused and thought for a moment. "I'd rather see some dancing girls."

Everyone, including the corporal, laughed. I asked him his name and hometown and he said he was David Stein from New York City.

When it came time to say good-bye to Charlie Company and return to the press center, the gunnery sergeant and Sakai took a long time to say farewell. They looked awkwardly at each other. Neither wanted to be first to turn away. They bowed stiffly and shook hands and wrote their home addresses on pieces of note paper and gave each other little gifts from their personal possessions. They posed together for other Marines to take still photographs of them, standing with their backs straight, the gunny much taller and looking melancholy in his starched Marine utility cap with a hand-rolled brim, Sakai-san smiling modestly in his loose-fitting American battle dress. The younger Marines in the camp looked at them with puzzled wonder, not knowing what to make of it. The few older Marines watched with awe and reverence, as if by witnessing the meeting and patrol of these two veterans of the Pacific island battles they too had been touched by the history of that haunted bloodletting, and relieved finally of the horrors that happened there.

SEPTEMBER 25, 1965

Wilson and Funk returned to Danang. They had gone on a long combat patrol with the 101st Airborne in the mountains around Thuy Hoa, a wild hostile place in the Central Highlands near the coast. As Wilson had wished, they were accompanied by Peter Kalischer, a veteran who knew how to get a story on the air. He had covered the Korean War in the early 1950s, Vietnam since the early 1960s, and he knew everyone in non-Communist Asia who was important. Kalischer, an American, was a French-speaking connoisseur of food, wine and all-night poker games played for high stakes. Partly as a result, he was not in peak physical condition. On patrol with the paratroopers, Kalischer dragged himself along behind Wilson and Funk up and down the sides of jungle mountains for three days in monsoon rain and heat. He slept on the ground at night in a light poncho, ate cold food out of cans, fought swarms of mosquitoes. The paratroops did not make contact with the VC and so there was no story. Kalischer returned to Saigon exhausted. Talking to me in the bureau, he confided that he had been tense the night before the operation, worrying what might happen, unable to sleep. Camping in the wet bush also made sleep impossible. He swore he would never go in the field with Wilson and Funk again. 'Those damn cowboys can go out and play soldier all they want,' he said. 'But not with me. I'm too old. That patrol nearly killed me.' Kalischer was in his forties.

I was happy to be working with Wilson and Funk again. They seemed pleased to be back in Danang. They did not mention the patrol.

At the press center, Marine commanders had seen our coverage of General Walt's visit to the front (the quality of Brauer's pictures was excellent) and rated it and other recent stories as fair to the Marines. An officer said the military brass in Washington was no longer angry at CBS, although they were still unhappy with Morley Safer. They saw his report on the burning of Cam Ne in August as a product of personal antimilitary bias and would not cooperate with him in the future. Other CBS News reporters such as Kalischer and I were judged to be more objective and would be welcome to cover Marine activities. News of their decision delighted us. They now seemed to trust us. We would be given regular access to their operations: cover them in combat, inspect their pacification efforts, interview the troops. The Marines made us feel welcome, like special guests, honorary members of the team.

In the same spirit, MACV made it possible to see our work soon after it appeared on television in the States. The Pentagon recorded film copies, called "kinescopes," of American TV news reports about the Vietnam War and shipped them to Saigon for showing at major bases around the country. After dark, Marines screened the film on a 16 millimeter projector set up on an outdoor table at the press center. Made of low-quality film with scratchy sound, the primitive kines were a weekly compilation of Vietnam news stories that had been introduced by Walter Cronkite on CBS, Chet Huntley and David Brinkley on NBC, and Howard K. Smith on ABC. Other journalists watched the black-and-white films with as much interest as the Marines, surprised at times to see stories they hadn't been aware of themselves.

Wilson, Funk and I watched broadcast copies of "Waiting for Charlie" and "Garbage Dump at Danang." The producers and film editors in New York had combined the pictures, soundtrack and narration into a smoothly flowing narrative, eliminating everything not essential to reporting the basic story. The voice-over was edited to make space for natural sound and quotes from the troops. For a few minutes everything in the two stories seemed to come alive again—the smell of the garbage dump, the heat and smoke, the wounded boy, then the Alpha Company camp, the mortar drill, the humor of the troops. Within a few minutes, my original memory of the experience was modified by this new condensed version on film. The two were different. In reality, the experiences had been hot, dusty, noisy and timelessly slow-moving except for the few moments of activity that made the event a news story. On the screen, however, all activity was compressed into its fundamental elements with no room for elaboration or nuance. Everything was fast, simple, cool.

I saw myself on television for the first time. Standing at the scene of the story in combat fatigues holding a microphone in front of me, I spoke into the camera for about fifteen seconds, addressing the viewer directly. The tone of voice was serious. The picture showed a young reporter wearing a floppy bush hat who was about the same age as the troops. At first, watching it was difficult. Seeing myself on film made me uncomfortable. The on-camera looked like I was reciting lines of a script. It did not appear as natural as the rest of the story. There was something artificial about it, out of place, popping up on the screen at the end of the story. Also, I looked unattractive. Since early childhood I had seen myself as awkward, skinny, plain-looking, a shy kid with bad eyesight. I had worn glasses since the age of two, vulnerable to teasing from other children in the tough working-class neighborhood of Bridgeport, Connecticut, where I grew up. Over the years my negative perception had developed into extreme sensitivity. Seeing myself on television at the press center that night, I felt the faint stirring of a sense of accomplishment. *Maybe it's all right*, I thought. With Wilson and Funk's help, I was proving able to report for CBS. Network producers in New York had judged my on-camera appearance acceptable, though they said later I looked too young to be a news reporter. Seeing myself on TV gave me a degree of self-assurance. Appearing on national television was providing an opportunity to create a new identity, a more positive sense of self, a reporter who covered the fighting without obvious fear—a *war correspondent*. For a few days, I was pleased with myself. But the idea was too seductive to entertain very long. Here I was, just a few weeks after arriving in Vietnam, and my outward image was being changed from that of an average radio journalist of no distinction to a network television reporter who was appearing regularly on the *Evening News*. The transformation brought recognition and status, at least within the immediate worlds of the network, the U.S. military, and my family and friends. I was making a name.

The stories were popular with the Marines. It pleased them to see what other Marines were doing in the field. After the screening, some of them came by to compliment Wilson, Funk and me for our work. Print journalists treated us with less disdain. Still photographers like Eddie Adams and Tim Page were openly friendly. The commanding officer of the press center asked for a copy of "General Walt Up Front" to present to the general as a gift.

I sat by the bank of the Danang River and stared out over the water. The day, like the river, was calm, nothing going on. I sipped a beer and savored the comfort of my new celebrity. *Life is good*, I thought, a feeling not unlike, "Ah . . . this is the life." All it needed was the gin and tonic. Then, for no apparent reason, I felt a chill. The image of myself in the on-camera standup came to mind. The feeling it brought was too comfortable, too euphoric, too self-assured. I recalled the myth of Narcissus, the ancient Greek who was so good-looking he fell in love with his reflection in a pool of water, and, trans-fixed, fell in and drowned. Looking out over the river, the idea of being bewitched by my own image and giving expression to an unchecked ego produced an annoying fear. *What happens if I like myself on-camera too much?* I wondered. In time I would become proud, arrogant, a spoiled shadow of my true self. The thought made me want to hide, to get out of television. Maybe I should go back to doing radio. That was what I knew best, where I belonged. No stand-ups, no camera crews, no hassles working with others. Then a solution suggested itself. I did not have to appear on-camera. It was as simple as that. I wouldn't do any more stand-ups unless ordered. *What the hell,* I thought, *television is visual. The pictures should be the story, not the story-teller. Who needs to see my face just because I happen to be reporting the story?* Wilson had taught me that dramatic action was what made the best television. Why did I have to be on-camera? The answer was *I didn't.* That settled it. I finished the beer and walked across the courtyard to the network hooch. The seductive glow that had accompanied my first reaction to seeing myself on TV was gone.

Wilson, Funk and I asked the Marines to take us as far into the field as possi-ble. We wanted to film a small group of troops in a distant dangerous place for a human interest feature that would supplement the network's daily war report. I wanted to ask Marines how they coped with the fear, loneliness and discomfort, the heat and rain, the isolation and strangeness of the place—frontline reporting like World War II and Korea where there were regular battle lines. Of course, Vietnam did not have battle lines, but sectors were controlled by one side or the other. In most cases, the Marines and South Vietnamese prevailed in the daylight, while the Viet Cong held most of the countryside at night. We wanted to find the most remote outpost the Marines had—deep inside VC territory—and do a story about it.

The problem was getting there. The press center had no helicopters under its operational control, only jeeps and trucks, and had to rely on the goodwill of field commanders for air transportation. An early-morning meeting was arranged with the commander of the First Marine Regiment in the hope he might fly us to one of his forward outposts. Waiting at his CP, the colonel greeted us warmly and delivered a briefing on his mission. Then he gave us his biographical details: medals for valor and leadership, distinguished service in World War II and Korea, a steady rise up the chain of command. When I had written it all down, I asked if he would take us to the regiment's most forward position. He agreed.

It was a Saturday. The sky was bright and blue and the heat was building rapidly. At midmorning, the colonel flew us to the peak of a mountain about ten miles southwest of Danang. It was called Dong Den and the observation post on it was twenty-eight hundred feet high. A small detachment of Marines held the top of the mountain and the VC controlled the slopes. As soon as the colonel's helicopter landed on the tiny LZ, Wilson went to work. He filmed supplies being unloaded, mail call and Marines watching to see what the regimental commander was doing in their area. The colonel stood in the clearing beside the LZ and looked around. He had nothing to do. Unlike General Walt, he did not greet his men. Wilson ignored him. After a few minutes, the colonel realized we were less interested in him than the enlisted men and NCOs at the outpost. He turned to leave. I thanked him for the ride up. 'Have them give us a call when you're done,' he said, 'and we'll send a bird up here to pick you up.' His face was hard.

Conditions at the OP were ideal for working—cool, clear and quiet in the shade of abundant trees. The top of the mountain was at the high end of a long ridge that rose from the valley floor and was covered by multiple layers of trees, vines and elephant grass woven into an impenetrable screen. The troops called it "triple canopy." Three sides of the mountain dropped to the valley in steep vertical precipices, but the remaining side ran down a long sloping ridgeline. Near the top it was cleared of trees and fortified with coils of barbed wire fencing and claymore mines. A small section of the mountaintop had been blown off by high explosives to expose the bare earth and leave a rough landing zone for helicopters to carry Marines to and from the position. From the OP, Danang airbase was visible—slate-gray shapes of jet bombers landing and taking off in distant silence—and beyond that the city and the harbor and most of the surrounding countryside for twenty to thirty miles. The view to the west was screened by trees and taller mountains, but from the helicopter coming in you could see the looming mountains of Laos dark in the distance, seventy-five miles away.

The sergeant in charge of the OP said he had seventeen men in his detachment, including a Navy corpsman and a naval gunfire coordinator.

The detachment rotated every eleven days. The mission was to watch for movements of the VC and to call artillery and offshore gunfire on them. The sergeant said the VC moved supplies along the rivers at night. Sometimes the Marines on the OP spotted them and directed fire at them, but most of the time they stayed out of sight. 'They know we're up here watchin 'em,' he said, 'so they stay low. We don't kill 'em too often but we mess up their mobility. Make 'em work harder.' He smiled and looked around. 'Sure is beautiful up here, ain't it?'

The sergeant led a fire team of four Marines along a worn trail through the foliage to the highest point on the mountaintop. They came to a massive tree with a wooden observation platform built among the branches. The Marines called it the "bird's nest." To reach the platform, they climbed a ladder made from wooden planks nailed to the tree and looked out over the trees on the mountaintop and across the river to the land below. The overall view was a panorama of rice paddies and canals and thin snaking rivers and patches of vegetation around scattered villages. From above, the land looked like a vast green and brown chessboard.

A Marine in a T-shirt sat under the camouflage cloth canopy over the platform and spoke on a portable radio set, a cigarette smoking in his fingers. Wilson climbed the ladder, waited for the heavy camera to be passed up to him, put it on his shoulder and made a high shot of the area under observation. Then he filmed the Marine in the OP in a sequence of angles and frames, climbing up to a higher branch, shooting back down on him, building a scene for the story. To get back to the ground, the Marines slid down a heavy rope tied to a tree limb. "Tarzan in Veet-Naam," someone called out. The others laughed. Wilson thought about it for a second but decided not to slide down the rope.

He worked his way through the camp shooting scenes and filming interviews. A team of surveyors with a tripod took measurements for the building of a more permanent installation. Another work party cleared rocks and tree stumps from the landing zone, digging into the earth with picks and shovels, hauling the rocks away by hand. They worked in the open sunlight, feeling the radiant heat on their bare backs.

When the work was finished, the sergeant radioed for a helicopter to take Wilson, Funk and me back down the mountain. We said good-bye to the Marines and thanked them for their help with the story. They asked when it was going to be on TV so they could write to their families and tell them to watch. A Marine from the OP with work to do in the rear also prepared to ride down the mountain, happy to be getting away.

A half hour later, an H-34 arrived in a rustle of wind and dirt. The Marine pilot tried to put the wheels on the ground of the small LZ but had trouble keeping the helicopter under control. The air was thin and the engine strained to hold the weight of the heavy chopper as it slowed, hovered and landed. It was old and worn, its paint peeling, a tired machine compared with the colonel's clean, well-serviced bird that had flown us up in the morning. I wondered how many hours this one had been in service since its last overhaul.

I made a note of the time: ten minutes past two o'clock. The pilots and crew prepared to take off with four passengers and the equipment aboard. The old gas reciprocating engine roared. The pilot pulled pitch and the H-34 rose slowly off the mountain and held in an unsteady hover at fifteen feet for a second or two. Suddenly the helicopter dropped to the ground in a violent shudder. My backside struck the metal deck and pain stabbed up from my tailbone. I looked around, worried. *What's going on?* The pilots sat in the cockpit high above, waving their hands in animated expression, their words lost in the noise of the screaming engine. A minute later they tried again. The engine roared and the body of the big machine vibrated furiously, metal joints rattling, rotor blades straining against the air. The pilots revved the engine beyond the tachometer redline and one of them pulled up hard on the collective and the rotors cut the thin mountain air and the trembling old machine shuddered up five, ten, fifteen, twenty, twenty-five feet and held for half a second then abruptly lost its grip on the fickle atmosphere and fell like four tons of metal scrap.

I was scared now. All the Marines from the OP stood on the fringes of the LZ and watched with worried looks, not moving, not speaking, expressions somber as morticians. The Marine passenger got up to get off and lighten the load but the crew chief grabbed his arm and shouted something into the roaring clatter, motioning him to stay. Funk and I looked in each other's faces and saw reflections of our fear. Overhead, the blades swirled faster and faster, spinning like manic scythes. I felt an urge to escape, to jump for safety, but the fear of being seen as a coward in the eyes of the others was stronger than my instinct for survival. I couldn't move. How many otherwise brave and sensible men have discovered their deaths like this, I wondered, caught in a moment of extreme danger, paralyzed into inaction by fear of failed honor, hesitating to take a brief opportunity to escape and being subjected therefore to a passive vainglorious end?

The pilot revved the engine to the maximum and the rotor blades turned faster and the fuselage shook hard and the helicopter screamed a wild wind-whipping cry and the metal bolts holding the joints in place rattled like loose teeth in a hollow skull. I held the support struts of the cargo bay with all my strength. Wilson and Funk squatted, their knees bent, gripping the sides. The helicopter lurched into the air, rising quickly, holding itself forty feet above the LZ. In the same instant the pilot pushed the stick forward and tried to drive over the edge of the precipice to gain forward speed and transla-tional lift in the heavier atmosphere of a lower altitude and take whatever mercy was offered by a twenty-eight-hundred foot fall of a loosely con-trolled dive. The nose of the chopper turned to face down the cliff and the tail swung around sharply. The end of it struck an outcrop of earth on the edge of the LZ the pilots couldn't see and the spinning tail rotor snapped off and flew haphazardly into space.

The helicopter went into a spin. With no tail rotor to stabilize the main body, the whole machine whirled out of control, turning with the reverse torque of the main rotor blades, spinning faster and faster until the sight of the sky and trees and Marines standing outside—pointing at us now and back-ing away from the LZ, their eyes focused with fierce scrutiny—became a blurry swirl of shapes and colors narrowing into a luminous spot of white light at the end of a black anoxic tunnel and dissolving into a rapid series of bright sharp images that I recognized at once from my childhood: long for-gotten memories of important moments flashing by faster than anything I'd ever experienced, twenty to thirty frames a second, each one of them origi-nal, like perfect photographic slides from the archives of my young life, every scene compressed into a complete story with sights and sounds and smells and feelings from the time. Each image was euphoric, rapturous. The smiling face of my beautiful young mother / a gentle touch from her hand on my face / absorbing her love / playing in the sand at the seashore with my father / waves washing up on the beach / feeling the strength and security of his presence / soothing, kind-hearted praise from a teacher at school / faces and voices of adoring aunts and uncles / steam trains coming in at the local rail-road station / hearing myself say "choo-choo" / the excitement of shared dis-covery with my brother on Christmas morning / running free through a familiar forest with a happy dog / hitting a baseball hard and hearing encouraging cries from my parents behind me in the bleachers / shooting baskets in a backyard court with a buddy from high school / a tender kiss from the soft warm lips of a lovely teenage girl / the encouraging thrust of her stomach and thighs against mine.

Dozens of images, sounds and sensations sped across the screen of conscious vision. Memorable moments of early life were reduced to small fractions of standard scientific time but perceived with perfect clarity and precision. The capacity of my mind to recognize so much sudden information expanded to meet the fast-moving conditions of the moment, propelling my consciousness into a world that transcended ordinary reality, producing a warm, blissful ecstasy, sensuous as a lover's embrace. The sensations overrode my fear of the spinning machine I was trapped in, as if the chemistry of my brain was preparing the rest of my body for the shock of what was about to happen next, flooding it with sedatives, anesthetizing it. Or, perhaps, the last moments of this life had begun a comforting transition to the mystery of the next.

The chopper hit the ground. The force of the crash drove the big rubber wheels two feet into the baked earth and buckled the mainframe. One wheel landed within a foot of the edge of the precipice. Bob Funk's strength ripped away the aluminum strut he was holding in the cargo bay and cut his right hand deeply between thumb and forefinger. My backside hit the floor of the chopper and, as X rays showed later, the impact squeezed the cartilaginous tissue from between two of the vertebrae and sent spasms of pain through my lower body. Wilson, the Marine passenger and the four crew members were cut and bruised. A few minutes later when everyone was out, the crew surveyed the damage. The copilot's hand trembled. 'Looks like it's totaled,' he said, shaking his head. The pilot said it was the combination of high altitude, heat and humidity. The chopper was too heavy for the altitude density of the mountain. 'We couldn't get enough lift,' he said. He lost control when the tail rotor broke off so he tried to crash land back on the LZ. 'That was real close,' he said. 'I just couldn't fly the thing.' Marines from the OP gathered around and tried to help, checking for injuries, calling a stretcher for me, radioing back to headquarters for another chopper to evacuate everyone. The Navy corpsman cleaned and dressed Funk's hand. The Marines said how lucky we were.

'That bird was right on the edge,' one of them said. 'We thought you guys were goners.'

SEPTEMBER 29, 1965

A volcano erupted in the Philippines. News bulletins from Manila said hundreds, possibly thousands of people were missing. Thousands of others were trying to escape. General panic was sweeping the region. American news agency reports based on early Filipino newspaper stories were vivid and dramatic. The volcano erupted without warning in the middle of the night. Terrified peasant families were trapped in their homes. Emergency rescue workers were trying urgently to reach the scene. Hospitals in the area were inundated with casualties. The wire service stories said the volcano was located about one hundred miles from Manila and was surrounded by a large lake known as Taal, where fourteen hundred people died during an eruption in 1911.

In New York, the CBS News foreign editor sent an urgent cable to Saigon instructing the bureau to cover the story. Since the network did not have an office in Manila, Saigon was the nearest news bureau, due west across the South China Sea. A new CBS bureau chief named Dan Bloom had replaced Sam Zelman. Bloom alerted Wilson and me to get ready to go. It was essential to get there fast, he said, while there was still time for dramatic pictures. We also had to get there ahead of NBC News. The problem was that there was no direct flight between Saigon and Manila. It would take two days to get there via Hong Kong.

Bloom got on the military telephone in his office and called a friend with the U.S. Air Force in Saigon. He explained the problem to Lieutenant Colonel Dave O'Hara, a senior information officer, and asked if the Air Force could fly Wilson and me to Clark Air Force Base outside Manila on a military flight. That would avoid the time-consuming civilian requirements of passports, visas, immigration and customs. Bloom was told to wait. O'Hara said the Air Force was not in the business of flying civilian journalists across international boundaries without observing local immigration laws. He did not say that he was in the business of getting good publicity for the air force in Vietnam, and that Bloom, who made story assignments for the network, was in a position to help. Bloom told Wilson and me to pack. Sometime later he got a call back. There was a medical evacuation plane flying to Clark in a few hours. We would be given two slots. Our names would not appear on the flight manifest. No questions were to be asked. No one was to talk about how we got to the Philippines. Once there, we would be on our own. If there was any fallout later, as far as the Air Force was concerned, the trip never happened. Bloom told us to cover the volcano story and keep quiet about how we got to it.

At Tan Son Nhut airport, Wilson and I walked up the open tail ramp of a C-130 Hercules and sat down. The cargo bay of the plane was rigged with vertical aluminum beams to hold racks of stretchers, one above the other, four high, row beside row. There were dozens of stretchers carrying wounded soldiers, all of them critical. Young men who had been healthy and fit a day earlier had been transformed into victims, weak and helpless, their camouflage battle dress, helmets and flak jackets replaced by yards and yards of white gauze bandages fixed with adhesive tape to their heads, eyes and across their chests. Some of them had lost entire arms and legs, some only fingers, hands, feet, eyes, ears, pieces of skull. Sedated with morphine, none of them spoke. Clear soft plastic containers hung on hooks above them and dripped fluids into their veins. The hospital plane was called a "mobile trauma ward."

The ramp went up and the C-130 took off. A blast of freezing air filled the cabin, ice-cold jets of white vapor puffing from air ducts in the fuselage. There were no windows in this part of the plane. Air Force nurses and doctors in clean green fatigues and aprons went from stretcher to stretcher checking the patients, examining their records, giving a gentle word of encouragement or a touch to those who were conscious. Some of the soldiers' faces were limp and gray.

A few hours later the plane landed at Clark airfield in a scream of brakes. Alarmed, one of the wounded men opened his eyes wide, stiffened his body, and tried abruptly to sit up. As soon as the plane stopped, the ramp went down and young stretcher bearers in Air Force uniforms carried the wounded men to ambulances, small trucks emblazoned with red crosses that sped away to the big hospital on the base with their warning lights flashing.

Wilson and I were greeted by an Air Force lieutenant who introduced himself as an information officer and was much more formal than officers in

Vietnam. He made a note of our passports and warned us to keep quiet about the arrangements.

'You guys are not here, understand?' he said.

We said that we did.

'If you get into trouble or are picked up by the police or whatever, we don't know anything about you. Got it?'

We said we did.

'And when you want to go back to Saigon, call me and I'll get you back the same way you came in. Okay?'

'Okay,' we said.

'Our people must have their heads up their asses sending you in here like this. What happens if you guys get buried by the volcano?'

'Then I guess you won't have to worry about getting us back,' Wilson said. The lieutenant did not laugh.

After a long wait, a truck appeared and took us to one of the base gates. We rode into town in a brightly colored Filipino taxi with a driver who insisted he knew all the best places: bars, restaurants, casinos, nightclubs, bordellos—whatever we wanted. Riding into the city, we could see that we were still in Asia. Manila, the capital, was surrounded by poverty. The decorations were bright and colorful, reminiscent of Mexico. At the hotel downtown, a big expensive place, it was too crowded to get separate rooms, so Wilson and I shared a double.

At dawn the next morning we set off. A taxi driver took us out of the capital and along narrow provincial roads that went through dusty villages separated by tropical jungle and verdant farm fields. It looked a lot like Vietnam without the war. Several hours later the taxi passed through the town of Banan, in Batangas Province, and from there drove to the edge of Lake Taal. The volcano rose from the middle of the lake, dominant and ugly, spewing clouds of white steam and occasional bursts of coal-black ash. The villagers at lakeside were relaxed. There were no signs of casualties or refugees. *What's going on?* I wondered.

An American jeep pulled up carrying a Filipino Army sergeant with square shoulders and thick sunglasses and an army-issue baseball cap. He was accompanied by a younger man, a private with short black hair. They got out of the jeep with the slow deliberate composure that characterizes men of authority. They inspected Wilson and me carefully, as if trying to measure our importance, smiling formally and shaking hands. Wilson and I were wearing khaki green military fatigues with no markings, so we could easily have been mistaken for American soldiers. The sergeant was small and thin and dressed in a Filipino military uniform similar to the U.S. Army one, with his unit patch and insignia sewn on the left shoulder. A ballpoint pen stuck from his shirt pocket. The sergeant did not understand English. Wilson explained to him in limited but forceful Spanish that we needed to go out to the volcano and take pictures. He pointed to his Auricon. The sergeant considered this carefully. He said it would be difficult to find someone with a boat because the villagers around the lake were frightened of the volcano. Wilson assured him he would pay them *muchos dineros* for a ride to the island. The sergeant thought about it slowly and said he would do what he could do.

A crowd of people including a pack of children gathered. When we asked if there was someone who would take us to the volcano, they shook their heads and said no, it was not safe. The sergeant shouted at a group of men by the pier at the side of the lake in a language I'd never heard before. He seemed to be ordering them to take us. The local radio had reported that an official American delegation was on its way from Japan to inspect the volcano and make recommendations to Washington for emergency aid. Wilson and I were probably the first Americans to reach the volcano and the sergeant may have assumed we were the official delegation—seismologists sent by the White House and therefore deserving of all the assistance he could give. We did not pretend to be seismologists but we did not admit we were not. Wilson held his light meter in the air above his head and took a reading.

Two men with long black hair and grease-stained shirts drove a motor launch around to the pier and waved us aboard. The men were older, around forty, with the hollow bony faces of poor fishermen. They looked sad, as if being punished. The sergeant and private got in the boat and stood aft, supervising the launch. Wilson took out a large folded wad of American money with a rubber band around it and gave the fishermen $200. They smiled.

The motor launch was long and narrow and made of wood, only slightly wider than a canoe. There were benches for seats and an inch of water in the bottom of the boat. A pole was fastened to the hull next to the steering wheel carrying a small running light with a flag at the top. We pushed away from the pier and set off at top speed toward the volcano in the middle of the lake. Two-thirds of the way across the lake the boat slowed. The fishermen put their hands in the water and shook their heads. Their faces were serious. They looked at the volcano.

Taal was not a great mountain of a volcano like Agung in Bali or Yake Dake in Japan. It was no more than a thousand feet at its highest point and its base was long and wide, a large round caldera that rose up out of the lava of past eruptions. Eroded by years of rain and wind, the caldera had collapsed in on itself to create the island in the middle of the lake. Spewing steam and ash from fissures at the base of the crater, it looked more menacing here in the lake than it had from the shore—an angry beast boiling up out of the hot shifting bowels of the planet.

I felt the water. It was hot.

'Let's go, let's go!' Wilson shouted, the camera on his shoulder.

The fishermen looked at him and then at the volcano. The sergeant and the private and the fishermen did not speak.

'C'mon you guys, it's not gonna hurt you,' Wilson said. He waved them on with the back of his left hand, urging them forward.

The driver of the launch circled the boat in the water slowly, the engine at near idle speed.

Wilson handed me the camera and moved back down the boat until he was next to the helmsman. He reached into his pocket with his big hands and withdrew the wad of dollars. He took a twenty-dollar bill and handed it to the sad-faced fisherman who held it in his hand and looked at Wilson without moving. Wilson got another twenty-dollar bill and gave it to him. The fisherman looked at Wilson with an expression of unremitting sorrow. Wilson gave him another twenty. And another. The fisherman took the money and put it in his pocket. Then he turned and pushed the throttle and pointed the boat toward the volcano.

A few minutes later the boat approached the shore of the volcano and again the fisherman slowed the engine. This time the sergeant shouted at him harshly and the fisherman brought the boat in and landed it on the island. It appeared to be deserted. The shoreline was covered with dark brown ash and debris, pieces of timber and trees, rocks, and the carcasses of several cows lying on their sides and bloating with gas in the sunlight. I looked carefully for human bodies but saw none. Wilson got out of the boat and began to shoot film. The sergeant did not get out. He shouted in Spanish at Wilson and me to hurry.

The landscape was barren, desolate. Blackened stumps of trees stuck out of the ash, giving the island the look of a wartime no-man's-land. There was no life. Wilson stepped through several inches of ash to get his pictures.

'C'mon, we're going up,' he said, climbing onto the steep side of the crater.

'Are you sure?' I asked.

'Yeah, this thing's not going to blow. I want to get a shot looking down into the crater.' He smiled.

Wilson seemed amused. He often tried to anticipate the reactions of producers and film editors in New York who would be screening his work. Coming across a shot looking down into the crater of an active volcano, they would be amazed. Wilson was instinctively reckless. Connected to him by the sound cable, I had to follow.

When Wilson finished shooting on the island, we returned to the shore and drove to the nearest hospital. The medical staff assured us that very few people had been hurt. Residents of the island had felt tremors caused by the volcano and had evacuated their homes days before the eruption.

We took the film to the airport in Manila and shipped it to the United States. The narration knocked down earlier press reports of a major disaster. I filed several radio spots over the telephone. When I was finished, I called Associated Press correspondent George McArthur and told him what we had seen and filmed. McArthur thanked me for the call.

At the hotel, there were several telegrams from New York instructing me, *ordering* me, to remain in Manila for another day. The CBS radio network was planning to broadcast a special report on the American buildup of forces in Vietnam. I was needed to provide technical assistance for Peter Kalischer who, it was hoped, would arrive in time for the broadcast but was having difficulty getting a flight to Manila. The broadcast was scheduled for midnight, local time, around noon in the States.

The phone in my room rang a few hours before the radio feed. It was Kalischer. 'I made it!' he said. 'Come on up to my room and have a drink.'

A few minutes later I knocked on the heavy mahogany door to Kalischer's suite. Silence. I knocked again. Still no answer. Finally I heard the high-pitched voices of what sounded like children inside. The door opened to reveal three Filipino girls wearing only the briefest of underclothes and standing in bare feet. They looked like they were sixteen or seventeen years old. They held their tiny hands to their faces and giggled at me, then ran away together into another room.

I went inside. Kalischer sat at a table in the bedroom twirling the patch of white hair on his head with a finger. He and two other men were studying a set of documents on the table closely. They barely acknowledged my arrival. One of the men was examining an American passport with a magnifying glass. On a chair next to the table was an open briefcase holding printer's tools, rubber stamps, brushes and inks, some of which were spread on the table. A bright desk light shined on the work at hand.

Kalischer stood up and introduced a Filipino man he described as an old friend named Feliciano Levista, the governor of Batangas Province. Governor Levista looked up and said hello, but his concentration was on the passport. His suit jacket was hanging on the back of a chair, and he had rolled up the sleeves of his immaculate white dress shirt. He held a tiny paintbrush in his fingers. The other man, a young light-haired American in short sleeves, was introduced as the governor's adviser from the U.S. embassy. He did not say his name. Kalischer explained that they were removing the date from an expired South Vietnamese visa in his passport and were going to put a valid date in its place. This would allow him to get back to Saigon without having to wait several days for a new visa. The three of them leaned over the table and worked on their forgery as routinely as if writing postcards.

Why not? I thought. *This is how the system works.* After a month and a half in Asia, I was becoming aware of a network of American correspondents, foreign service officers, military officials, intelligence agents, businesspeople and friendly authorities of local governments who worked alongside the formal official system in a parallel world of mutual favors and influence. Members of the network cooperated with one another by sharing information, secrets and other forms of assistance to satisfy the needs of each other's governments, companies or individuals. Their positions of authority allowed them to bypass ordinary boundaries of legal and ethical convention. It was, I realized, a secret network of special interests. All you had to do was be on the team and play by the rules. Friendly journalists who wrote news reports that reflected favorably on the work of government and military officials were rewarded with information, interviews and logistical support not easily available to others. They were trusted to support the status quo. Exclusive news stories, free rides, favorable publicity, forged papers, sex, operational tip-offs, enhanced reputations, black market profits, PX privileges, expensive gifts and entertainment of every kind—almost anything was possible as long as you were on the team and played by the rules. The rules, of course, were understood, not written. Wilson and I had just benefited by being allowed to

ride into the Philippines without visas. As a reporter for CBS, I was automatically entitled to join, but I would have to prove my eligibility for continued
membership by what I reported on the air. As a newcomer, I was flattered
that Kalischer took the trouble to introduce me.

After the midnight radio broadcast, Kalischer, his friends, Wilson and I
went in a group to a Manila casino. The place was ultraluxurious. Filipino
croupiers at the card and dice tables wore starched white shirts with oversized cuffs that nearly touched the knuckles on the backs of their hands. I
considered myself a serious gambler, but after losing a few hundred pesos I
realized I had no chance against the long-sleeved croupiers at the tables. I
excused myself and went back to the hotel. Wilson and Kalischer stayed.
Much later, after I was asleep, Wilson banged on the door of our hotel room.
It was four o'clock in the morning. He was drunk and angry.

'What's the matter?' I said.

'God damn whore stole my money. Took it right out of my pants while I
was in the saddle. Do you believe that? I'll kill that little bitch.'

He went to his suitcase, took out his Browning 9 millimeter, and loaded it
with shells from a cardboard box. It was his combat weapon.

'Jim, are you sure this is wise?'

'I know what I'm doing.'

'But we're in the country illegally. If you get picked up there'll be hell to
pay.'

'Let me worry about that when the time comes.'

He stormed out of the room and slammed the door. I tried to go to sleep.

At dawn the door opened and Wilson came into the room with his head
down. He looked tired, drunk, depressed. I said hello and asked him what
happened and he said, 'Don't ask.' He took off his clothes and climbed into
bed and went to sleep. The pistol was gone.

OCTOBER 9, 1965

A candle burned on top of the table, casting light and shadows across the cards. The flame from the candle flickered in the eyes of three men, painting their faces yellow with light. A bottle of bourbon, almost empty, stood off to the side, awaiting its turn. The men played and talked and drank and sweat. Perspiration rolled down the surface of their skin. At the end of the tent a soldier snored.

J. D. Coleman held the pinochle deck with the three good fingers and one shorter one of his left hand, and dealt the cards with his right. In an army of tall big-boned men—professional warriors—Coleman was bigger than most, about six feet six. His head was the size of a volleyball. His face was dark and creased with a crooked tree of a nose near the center of it. His voice came from the deep resonant caverns of a chest the size of a beer keg and his long ears hung loosely from the side of his head like a hound dog's. His eyes were hazel brown. His light brown hair was cut extremely short so that it was no more than fuzz on his skull. Short hair was the fashion among paratroopers like Coleman, who had forty-seven jumps. His appearance gave him more than a passing resemblance to John Wayne. Around the An Khe press area, where he was assistant information officer of the 1st Cavalry Division, the troops called him "Duke."

Coleman was an infantry captain but nothing he wore identified him by rank. He had on an oversized green T-shirt that was black with sweat, fatigue trousers rolled up at the ankles, and all-purpose rubber sandals, flip-flops, in place of his size fourteen boots. When senior officers were present, Coleman carried himself formally—even around Camp Radcliff, the First Cav base: straight-backed, square-shouldered, alert and respectful. His trousers were correctly bloused above his boots. He routinely wore the paraphernalia of a Ranger: helmet, web belt with braces, sidearm, rappelling rope, D-ring, K-bar knife, compass, combat flashlight, camouflage scarf. He strove to command an infantry company and presented himself in camp accordingly. Now, however, in the late informal hours of the night, a few hours before a major

combat operation, Coleman was at ease. His pleasant nature came out especially in the company of journalists and whisky.

'Jack, if we get shot at tomorrow,' Coleman said, 'I'm gonna get you a
CIB. I had a word with the old man and he wants to do it.'

I smiled with polite ignorance.

Coleman explained that a combat infantryman's badge, a long rifle with a
wreath around it, was an American soldier's badge of honor. It was his primary decoration, a record that he had fought for his country. All other
medals were secondary. Coleman wanted the commanding general to award
it to a few favored journalists who went on combat missions with the Cav,
even though as civilians they did not usually fight and were not entitled to
decorations.

'Already got mine,' said Charlie Black, laughing. 'In the Big One.'

Charlie Black laughed with a long rasping wheeze that launched itself
from the depths of his smoke-ravaged lungs, pushed up through the tar-cov-
ered lining of his trachea, and burst into a bright smile that spread across his
copper-colored face. Charlie Black's voice was vocal sandpaper. Part Ozark
Indian, part-time warrior, full-time journalist, he was military correspondent for the *Columbus Enquirer* of Columbus, Georgia, home of the First Cav
at Fort Benning. He was the best-informed journalist in the division. He
lived with the Cav, covered it, fought with it, bled with it, got drunk with it—
did everything but draw pay from it.

Black told me the basics of his story. As a teenager in the early 1940s, he
joined the U.S. Marine Corps and went on to fight with Carlson's Raiders at
Guadalcanal. At Tarawa, he got a bad wound and a silver star. Then he got
into journalism. His short black hair was turning gray but was often covered
by a red beret that had been the gift of a British paratrooper. The distinctive
beret and his World War II camouflage fatigues set Black apart. His green-
gray eyes lurked behind large black bushes disguised as eyebrows. His mouth
sparkled with gold crowns that glowed through the gap made by the
absence of front teeth. Five feet, seven inches tall, Black's body was gnarled
and weathered and shriveled like an old dwarf tree. He was forty-two years
old, though he could have passed for fifty or fifty-five. When the subject of
his accumulated war experience came up, he liked to say, laughing and
wheezing, "Avoid ever being born in 1923. You catch everything."

Charlie Black enjoyed telling a story. When he told one that amused him, his eyes brightened and his body became animated and he moved his arms and legs in exaggerated expression to make a point, giving him the look of a leprechaun letting you in on a secret. Black had read the classics, especially Xenophon and Herodotus, and sprinkled his more serious conversation with references to them. He was something of a scholarly redneck, a compulsive storyteller and entertainer. His repertoire ranged across the broadest of American landscapes, from war stories in the Pacific (he had also fought in Korea) to drinking stories (he drank heavily) to stories about women to his-torical and true-life tales of his native North Carolina and the American South that variously delighted, saddened and infuriated him. The props he needed to put on a show were a bottle of booze, preferably bourbon, a pack of unfiltered Camels, and an audience.

Now, in the mellow candlelight of the tent, playing pinochle with Charlie Black and J. D. Coleman, drinking the bourbon I had brought as a gift from Saigon, I was mildly flattered by the prospect of being awarded the CIB. But I was much more interested in what was going to happen at dawn. In a few hours the Cav would launch the largest U.S. military operation of the war. At least twenty journalists, including reporters from all three TV networks, had been invited to cover it. The division was sending a reinforced brigade of three full infantry battalions plus other units on an airmobile assault into an area that had been controlled for years by the Viet Cong. Four hundred heli-copters and more than forty-five hundred American troops were involved in an operation that would cover twenty square miles. For the first time, the U.S. Army would test airmobile warfare in combat conditions on a large scale. Although the concept was designed for battle on the plains of Central Europe and not the opaque wilds of Southeast Asia, American generals and their staffs were confident the Cav would succeed.

The military objective was a valley of rice fields and hamlets twenty-five miles northeast of An Khe, the next valley north of Happy Valley. The valley was called Suoi Ca after the narrow river that ran through it. The hamlets were Hoi Son One, Two and Three. U.S. Army intelligence believed a regi-ment of the People's Army of North Vietnam was operating in the Suoi Ca: resting, propagandizing, recruiting and training local units of Viet Cong. It was the 325th, the same regiment that fought the ferocious two-day battle with the 101st Airborne in Happy Valley three weeks earlier. If the surprise American attack worked, the 325th would be trapped and overwhelmed by the greater firepower of U.S. forces. Not only were the tactics of airmobility being tried on a massive scale for the first time, the American strategy of search and destroy was getting its biggest test.

Earlier that day in An Khe, in a tidy general-purpose tent with the side flaps rolled up, journalists had gathered for a tactical operations briefing by the brigade commanders. Waiting for the briefing to start, a senior officer came up to me, introduced himself, shook hands and complimented the stories Wilson, Funk and I had done about the Cav and the 101st in late August. He said that friends and relatives of the headquarters staff had seen our reports on the *Evening News* and had written to say the reporting was good, reassuring them the troops had arrived safely and were settling in. He had also heard that Funk and Wilson helped cut the elephant grass on the Golf Course the first day it was cleared, and he thought that was outstanding. The officer was respectful and friendly and his complimentary manner made me feel like I was being accepted as a guest at the gathering of an exclusive club. I noticed Major Siler, the division information officer, watching from a corner of the GP tent, puffing his pipe, smiling.

It was a special relationship. In keeping with my most-favored status in the division, Siler and Coleman gave me first choice of battalions to accompany in the attack. The decision was important. Each of the three infantry battalions going into the valley would take one network camera crew. The choice of battalion might determine which network got the best film for the evening news. If only one of the battalions got into a fight and the others did not, one network crew would get a dramatic war story. The others would fail. One correspondent's career would be enhanced and the others' would suffer. As a result, competition between the three networks was intense. On the eve of the operation, the reporter for NBC News walked past me in the camp with a cold angry look in his eyes.

Charlie Black suggested we go with 1st Battalion, 12th Cavalry, an all-paratroop, all-volunteer battalion. Its 650 men were being inserted by helicopter at the most northern end of the valley. It was Black's guess that 1/12 was more likely than the other Cav battalions to catch the retreating PAVN and VC. Black had been allowed to sit in on classified intelligence briefings by brigade and division officers while the operation was being planned and had figured out what he thought was most likely to happen.

Late in the afternoon before the attack, Black unfolded his map of the region, spread it on an outdoor wooden table and traced his fingers over the terrain of the Suoi Ca Valley, the mountains and ridgelines around it, and the string of hamlets along the valley floor. He explained how the operation was going to develop. It was a large, complicated maneuver involving blocking forces farther north, thousands of ARVN troops, other Cav units to be used as diversions, and teams of U.S. Special Forces as reconnaissance. Black had a more critical appraisal of the plan than some of the brigade officers who had briefed journalists and were promoting the idea that a great trap was about to be sprung on an unsuspecting enemy. By contrast, Black was skeptical. He didn't think there would be much of a fight.

'Charlie's too smart to take on a whole brigade of American killers,' he said. 'Not with all these God damn helicopters!'

His eyes were bright, his voice hissed like a blowtorch. 'They'd have to be fuckin crazy!' he said.

He smiled his sly leprechaun smile. 'They'll probably bug out and live to fight another day.' The quickest escape route was over the low ridge at the northwest corner of the valley where 1/12 was going.

'If we catch any of 'em,' Black said, 'it'll be there.'

OCTOBER 10, 1965

Operation Shiny Bayonet began at 0830. The helicopters took off from An Khe in swirling twisters of red dust, fifty ships at a time, wave after wave, howling and buzzing like swarms of bees. The soldiers sat inside, back to back, four across on canvas jump seats, rifles between their knees. The shimmering black forms of the fuselages lifted up in long columns and occupied the sky, the clatter of steel blades slapping the sweet morning air.

My photographer on this assignment was Tom McEnry, a sad-faced Oregonian in his mid-thirties who was short and stocky with thin fair hair balding at the forehead. He wore a blue baseball cap that increased his five-feet-six-inch height by another inch. The sound technician was Pham Boi Hoan, "P.B." for short, an enthusiastic young Vietnamese who had just joined the staff. Wilson and Funk were taking a break in Saigon.

Moving just above the trees at more than a hundred miles an hour, banking from left to right with the changing contours of the terrain, McEnry, Hoan and I held tightly to the aluminum struts of the helicopter seats. Hoan's eyes were wide with excitement, like a child on his first airplane ride. McEnry showed disinterest. Charlie Black looked out the open doors with small observant eyes, his face fixed in a smile.

The helicopters turned into the Suoi Ca Valley at the southern edge and raced across the valley floor to the northern end and pulled up abruptly to a shuddering, metal-wrenching stop and hovered above a field of knee-high rice shoots. The troops jumped out four at a time, two from each side. A machinegun rattled from a gunship strafing a ridgeline off to our left. I jumped from the chopper with the others and landed heavily in a foot of water and was pulled down immediately into the muck by the heavy weight in my pack (I was carrying an extra camera battery and two rolls of film). My center of gravity was up around my chest from the momentum of the fall and the weight of the pack. My boots stuck in the mud as my body pitched forward. Helpless, I fell over and hit the rice paddy face down. The water was warm in my face. For a few moments I couldn't move. McEnry said later he saw me go down and thought I had been shot. *Shit,* he said to himself, *now I have to carry that fucking film myself.*

The choppers flew away and it was quiet. Soldiers nearby breathed heavily. I struggled out of the water and got in line with a column of troops walking toward a cluster of bamboo houses at the edge of the fields. When they got near the houses, the soldiers spread out on line and took cover behind palm trees and rice paddy walls and hedgerows and watched the houses closely. Smoke came from one of the huts. No gunfire could be heard, only the occasional squawking of radios and the sergeants shouting commands.

Charlie Black moved quickly among the soldiers, crouching down on one knee beside them, asking each of them in a polite voice, "What's your name, son?" When they had spelled it for him and he had written it in his notebook, he asked, "Rank?" and they told him "Private" or "PFC" or "Spec-Four" and he wrote it down. Then he asked, "Where you from, son?" and, "How old are you?" He didn't ask them what they were doing or what they were thinking or anything other than name, rank, age and hometown. When he finished he got up and ran, crouched over, to the next young soldier he could find, one after another, and asked the same set of questions again. Watching him at work, writing down the details of each soldier, I thought: *that's how Ernie Pyle must have done it in the Big One.*

A group of villagers crawled out of bomb shelters in their houses. When they had dusted the powdered dirt off their clothes, they looked up at the tall American paratroops with their weapons. Then they started to walk away. The villagers moved slowly, with caution, as if they were not sure what was allowed and what was not. Their faces were worried but they were not nervous. They looked curiously at McEnry with his film camera and Hoan connected to him with the sound cable. The soldiers did not speak to them. The villagers walked in a file toward the edge of the hamlet and sat on their haunches in a shaded corner of a rice field, chattering softly in the discordant cadences of their language. They were all women and children.

An officer from C Company, 1/12, spoke into the handset of his radio, "Uh, Four-Six. I'm right here at this village. There's smoke right to my front. Uh, over."

"This is Six," came the reply. "Roger. Uh, marry up with the rest of your people."

Everyone waited. The radio squawked. "Charger Three, Pacer Six, over."

"This is Charger Three."

"This is Pacer Six. Situation negative at this time."

I signaled to McEnry and Hoan to follow and walked to the northern edge of the hamlet to a small clearing that was being used as a command post by the battalion commander of 1/12, Lieutenant Colonel Robert Shoemaker. He spoke on his radio. "We need something as soon as we can to get this rice out," he said.

Shoemaker was a thin cold-eyed officer regarded as one of the most promising in the division. He was forty-one years old, a graduate of West Point, a veteran of Korea and an earlier tour in Vietnam as an adviser. His helmet was off, exposing his bristle-short paratroop haircut. He spoke on the radio in the brisk but relaxed style of an experienced commander, organizing his rifle companies into position.

A group of soldiers moved into the hamlet to search the farmers' huts. Their heads turned from side to side as they walked, their rifles ready, lifting the tops of food baskets to look inside. The simple straw houses were empty, the tables cleared and the utensils stored neatly in the bamboo rafters high above the hard-packed dirt floors. I took a rice bowl from out of a rafter and examined it. It was perfectly made, forged from a piece of tin, beautiful to observe. I stood in the hut for a moment looking at it. Then I opened my pack and put the rice bowl inside. *Souvenir of the war*, I thought.

Outside, a Vietnamese army interpreter spoke excitedly with a GI who held a small stack of documents he had discovered.

"VC! VC!" the interpreter shouted. The soldier nodded his head.

Shooting started ahead and to the right—single shots, loud and sharp—about five hundred yards away on side of the ridge that ran up from the north end of the valley. The soldiers dropped to one knee and looked in the direction of the shooting.

"Let's go!" I said to McEnry and Hoan and then ran toward the sound of the gunfire in a shallow irrigation ditch that ran parallel to the edge of the hamlet, trying to keep my head below the level of the higher ground. I ran about eighty yards. Out of breath, I stopped to look back and saw McEnry and Hoan waiting where I had left them. Just above me, an officer stood on the higher ground casually observing the gunfire. Seeing him, I stood up and shouted to McEnry and Hoan, "Come on! It's safe!"

They ran along the bottom of the ditch, their heads hunched over their equipment. When they reached my position, we moved toward the hill and the noise of the shooting. A group of soldiers waited by the edge of a field in a deep ditch that protected them from the gunfire. McEnry and Hoan jumped into the ditch and squatted on the bare earth. I stood by the edge of the ditch trying to figure out what was going on. The shooting was sporadic from the hill ahead.

A sergeant noticed our arrival in the ditch and said, "Get low, men."

The troops held their fingers on the trigger guards of their M-16s and pointed them toward the trees on the hill.

"You people hold your fire in here," the sergeant said.

Another shot cracked across the fields.

"He's up in those trees somewhere," the sergeant said, nodding his head toward the tangle of jungle brush on the hill.

The next shot from the sniper came in at a downward angle across my chest, one to two feet away, kicking up the dirt on the far side of the ditch. The bullet hit the dirt before I heard the shot. I jumped into the ditch and ducked, then looked up, embarrassed by being caught in the open that way. One of the soldiers said, 'I'd keep my head down if I was you.' McEnry said, 'I thought I was going to have to carry that pack again.'

It was the first time I had been shot at in Vietnam and there was no fear because it was so fast. The danger passed before I was aware of it. I had jumped into the ditch as much because I thought it was expected of me as for my own safety. The truth was, I didn't know how to act. With no experience in combat, all I could do was try to imitate the officers. The sergeants were much more cautious. Most of the time the officers stood up, even when their troops were low to the ground. At times they spoke on their radios and told their sergeants to move the men from one location to another. The officers did not appear to be frightened or reckless or even daring, just doing their jobs. It looked natural.

A great shout of American voices was heard, a war cry of blood and fury from the trees on the side of the hill about fifty yards ahead. Cries of *Yaaar-rrggh!* and *Airborne!* went up as soldiers charged up the hill. It sounded like a scene from *Battle Cry!* taking an enemy bunker, or the break from the huddle of a high school football game. *Yaaarrrggh!* As the soldiers stumbled through the undergrowth up the hill, single shots from the snipers cracked through the trees. Then quiet. Then more shouting, now for help, 'Medic! Hey! Medic up here!'

McEnry, Hoan and I climbed out of the ditch and ran toward the sound of the shouting. Crossing a rice paddy, we saw Shoemaker, the battalion commander, calling into his radio, "Medevac! Medevac! This is Charger Six, over."

Farther forward, three wounded soldiers lay in the lee of a hedgerow. A medic put a dressing on one of the soldiers and spoke to him in a calm southern voice, 'Don't worry, y'all gonna make it out. Old Man's callin in a bird.'

"I just want to know if it's bad," the wounded soldier said.

'Don't look too bad to me. Get you back to the doc and he'll tell you for sure.'

A few feet away, another soldier lay on his back holding his leg with both hands. His eyes were full with tears. The medic glared at him while he worked on the other man.

"Give me a shot, Doc, please, give me a shot," the soldier with the bullet wound in his leg pleaded. The medic ignored him.

"Doc, *please*, it's hurtin bad. *Real* bad. I'm not foolin you, Doc. Give me a shot. Oh, *please*, Doc."

The medic said, 'The pain can't be that bad, you ain't hurt bad.' His voice was scornful.

He leaned over to me and whispered, 'He's fakin. He wants me to give him a shot 'cause he likes the stuff. I can't be givin out morphine every time somebody asks for it.'

The soldier continued to groan and cry. I wondered how the medic knew whether the pain was serious or not. I wondered if it had anything to do with their race and background. Although both were paratroopers from the same battalion, the wounded soldier was black, the medic was white. I had not seen a soldier cry before.

It was quiet for a few moments. Then on the other side of a hedgerow, out of sight, someone opened a soft drink can with a noisy *pop* and *fizz*. A voice drifted across the rice fields, a high musical southern boy's voice, singing, "*Coca-Cola refreshes you best . . . .*"

It was a good imitation of a popular TV jingle from back home, one that showed beautiful young people with blond hair and perfect teeth having fun at a beach party in Florida or California. Everyone behind the hedgerow laughed. Then the whole squad sang out, in harmony, "Coca Cola refreshes you best." Everyone laughed louder. Otherwise it was quiet.

A helicopter approached from the left, still far away, beating the air, the sound of it getting louder, *thudda, thudda, thudda,* an inbound medevac for the wounded. Then the close sharp *crack* of snipers' rifles from the trees on the ridge. The chopper swooped overhead low and fast—no power to hover and land, just a brief flare at the last moment—and hit the ground hard in the middle of a rice paddy. Tons of barely controlled machinery auto-rotated into the ground and sank on the skids in the muck of the farm field. More shooting. A man in fatigues threw himself out of the chopper and ran for cover, then another, and another, Wilson and Funk among them. *Wilson and Funk? What the hell are they doing here?* Seeing them, I felt confused, disoriented, as if waking from a dream.

Wilson and Funk ran to the corner of a hedgerow and disappeared in a clump of foliage. I went over to them. Parting the branches of a bush, I found them shooting an on-camera of their correspondent, Morley Safer, who was holding a microphone and describing what had just happened to them: "The chopper must have taken five or six hits," Safer said, his voice short of breath. "One went past my face, broke the plexiglas, and hit—or rather bruised—the arm of my soundman, Bob Funk."

Safer looked back and forth from the crippled helicopter to Wilson's camera, speaking his words in a serious voice, appearing to be worried and, at the same time, relieved to be alive. When he saw me, Safer smiled with surprise and waved for me to join him. Wilson continued to roll film.

"I feel something like Stanley and Livingstone," he said. "The first person I run into when we were shot down is another CBS News correspondent, Jack Laurence."

"Small jungle, huh, Morley?" It was the only thing I could think to say.

Wilson switched off the camera.

'I don't believe this,' I said.

'You better believe,' Funk said. 'That was the hairiest ride we'll ever have.'

I shook hands with each of them. 'Tom McEnry and P. B. Hoan are back there with the battalion CP.'

'What's going on?' Safer asked.

I gave him the basic facts of the operation, told him where the snipers were, described the assault up the ridge and the wounding of the soldiers. Sporadic gunfire continued to come from the hill. Safer looked frightened.

'It's safe where we are,' I said. 'The snipers are way up the hill and they aren't shooting at us.'

I asked how they got here and Wilson said Bloom, the bureau chief in Saigon, was worried that CBS didn't have enough people on the operation. So he sent them up to An Khe this morning, too late to catch the assault helicopters but in time to get aboard the first medevac going out to collect the wounded.

Safer asked me to move out of the shot so he could record another on-camera with more detail and accuracy. He did his stand-up again. When he finished, Wilson asked where the wounded were and I pointed to a clump of trees nearby. Safer, Wilson and Funk walked away. I went back to McEnry and Hoan and told them what had happened. Two camera teams on the same story! Virtually in the same rice paddy! It seemed to be incredibly good luck. With two crews, CBS could cover anything that happened and come out with the best stories.

A few minutes later, at the battalion CP, Safer asked Lieutenant Colonel Shoemaker to bring in a chopper to take him back to An Khe with the news film. Shoemaker said the area wasn't secure enough to bring in another chopper; he would have to get his wounded men out first. 'I'll do what I can when I get a chance,' he said. Safer paced back and forth in the shallow ditch of the command post, smoking one cigarette after another. He asked Shoemaker how long it would be before he could get out. Shoemaker said he didn't know. He asked if the colonel understood how important it was to get the film back to An Khe. Shoemaker said he did, but he was becoming exasperated. The rest of us looked at one another, wondering if we could do anything. I told Morley to take it easy. 'We've got a great story, don't worry. There's still plenty of time before sundown. We'll get out of here all right.'

An artillery round shrieked overhead and exploded at the foot of the hill with a *krrrack!* of splitting steel, shaking the soft earth. Then another, *krrrack!*

Shoemaker stood, talking on the radio to the commander of an artillery battery miles away. Together, they adjusted the range and direction of the fire, trying to walk the shells down the side of the hill where the snipers were dug in. The battalion had suffered several more wounded. Shoemaker was trying to suppress the snipers with the brigade's big guns.

Another round came in, much closer, only a rice field away.

Shoemaker's eyes were bright. He shouted over the noise into the radio, "That's great where it is! Drop fifty and fire for effect!"

Jesus, I said to myself, crouching for cover, *fifty yards closer and we're dead.* Hearing the colonel's order, Safer, Wilson, Funk, McEnry and Hoan got down. Shoemaker continued to stand.

An officer seized the radio from the colonel's hand and shouted, "That's right on top of us!" It was the battalion executive officer, a young major, and his alarm was visible. He squeezed the transmit bar on the radio handset and screamed, *"Check fire! Check fire!"*

Shoemaker did not move or speak, the cigar burning in his hand. The radio hissed in reply, "Uh, Roger that." The artillery fire stopped.

The major gave the handset back to Shoemaker and walked away. Shoemaker and the junior officers and NCOs on his staff stood for a moment without speaking, then walked off in different directions as if they had something important to do.

The helicopter that had been shot down by the snipers lay in the field, burning now, struck by the short round of artillery that landed a minute before. Wilson looked at me and said, 'Come on.' I followed him and Funk along the hedgerows to a place where he got a good angle on the burning chopper. 'Christ,' said Wilson, 'will you look at that.' The fuel tank was fully alight. Rich black smoke puffed into the air with hot fury. The flames burned through the metal skin of the helicopter and consumed everything inside, making a smoking black skeleton that looked like the hollow carcass of a grasshopper.

Returning to the shallow ditch of the CP, Wilson announced that we would do two stories: one of the operation and fighting with the snipers that I would report, the other of the helicopter crash and burning chopper by Safer. It would make a nice package: two reporters, two crews, two stories. Everyone, including Safer, agreed.

'Look, Morley,' Wilson said, 'you take all the film back to An Khe on the first bird that comes in and wait for the rest of us at the PIO shop. We'll divide up the film there. Call Saigon and tell 'em what we've got.' Wilson and McEnry wrapped their film in metal cans, put the separate stories in a CBS shipping bag, and gave it to Safer to hand-carry.

McEnry, Hoan and I went back up toward the sounds of shooting. We came to a small clearing in the brush where a wounded soldier lay on his back. He was barely conscious, in shock. An officer with small Christian crosses in the lapels of his fatigue jacket—the battalion chaplain—hunched over the wounded soldier and spoke to him in a low voice. A medic appeared on the run, out of breath. He knelt down beside the wounded soldier, cut away his undershirt with a knife and examined the wound. There was a small hole in his chest but there was no blood, just a thin black ring around the opening.

The medic worked quickly. He shouted over his shoulder for someone to bring him his bag.

Another soldier tossed a canteen to the medic, who caught it and poured a few drops of the water onto the face of the wounded man. His eyes were unfocused and cloudy, his neck limp, his right arm folded across his stomach. The color of the skin on his face and chest changed slowly from sallow brown to ash gray.

"C'mon, wake up! Wake up!" shouted a comrade who had helped carry the wounded man down the hill.

The chaplain put the side of his head on the chest of the soldier and listened. The medic stopped working and leaned back. There was a long silence. McEnry's camera whirred softly.

The chaplain lifted his head from the chest of the wounded soldier and looked up into the lens of the camera. His expression was a mixture of sadness and supplication. The chaplain shrugged his shoulders and turned the palms of his hands toward the sky. Then he dropped his hands and then his head and turned it slowly from side to side.

I checked the name, rank, age and hometown of the soldier who died. He was seventeen years old.

A short time later, soldiers brought two Vietnamese men down the side of the hill. The gunfire and artillery had stopped.

'We got 'em,' one of the soldiers said.

The prisoners were young, dressed in short pants and black cotton shirts with long sleeves and white buttons up the front to the neck. Their clothing and legs were smudged with dirt, as if they had been dragged out of holes. Their hair was thick and black and cut short on the sides but was long in the front and fell over their foreheads. Their faces were frightened.

Safer, the two camera crews and I gathered in a field to look at the prisoners. Wilson started to film. McEnry held Wilson's battery pack, which weighed almost half as much as the camera. Safer wanted to do an interview. P. B. Hoan would interpret. Hoan was a big strong young man whose black hair was neatly trimmed and parted on the side. He had white even teeth and an olive-brown complexion that he protected carefully from too much exposure to the sun. New to the CBS staff, he was still learning his craft.

Hoan asked the first prisoner a question in Vietnamese. The prisoner shook his head and pointed to his ears, suggesting his hearing was gone. It made sense. If the two men had been on the side of the hill when the artillery came in, they were likely to be deaf for some time.

Hoan asked the second prisoner a question about why he was on the hill. The first man, supposedly deaf, flinched when he heard it. Instantly, Hoan struck him hard across the face with his hand. The prisoner did not react. Hoan asked the question again, this time to the first prisoner. When he did not reply, Hoan slapped him again. The second prisoner suddenly answered. It is true, he said, we fired at the invaders.

I was shocked by what Hoan had done. It was unlawful to strike a prisoner of war, and it was especially wrong for a journalist, supposedly a noncombatant, to interfere forcibly in a story he was trying to cover. It was one thing for a soldier to mistreat prisoners in the heat of a battle as I had seen with the 101st Airborne the month before, but for a journalist to do so was even more abhorrent. I snapped a picture of the prisoners with my still camera. Safer told Hoan to stop hitting them.

With the snipers in custody, the shooting stopped. More helicopters came in to evacuate the wounded. Safer left, carrying Wilson and McEnry's exposed film. Wilson, McEnry, Funk, P. B. Hoan and I stayed with the story the rest of the day but there was no more fighting in the Suoi Ca Valley. None of the other battalions in the brigade made contact with the Viet Cong all day. Operation Shiny Bayonet had been a useful test of combat skills for a small number of American soldiers who fought the snipers, as a training exercise for a larger number of U.S. troops and their equipment, and as a demonstration to the Vietnamese of American power and mobility. Plenty of search but no destroy. Charlie Black stayed in the field for several days, moving from unit to unit, getting the full story. As he had predicted, the main force of PAVN and VC troops had slipped out the northwest end of the valley, leaving a small unit of snipers behind to cover its withdrawal.

Wilson, Funk, McEnry, Hoan and I came out of the field at last light and returned to An Khe. At the PIO shop, Safer announced that he was taking the two stories back to Saigon for shipment to the States. The bureau chief, he said, wanted the two crews and me to remain with the First Cav. Still in a hurry, Safer urged me to finish writing and recording my narration for the story of the combat assault, the fight with the snipers, the wounded, and the seventeen-year-old soldier who died. He was anxious to get away, but his pressure was distracting me from the work. When I told him to be patient and wait, he'd get it when I was finished, he became irritated. Standing over the table where I was working, Safer said, "How would you like a punch in the nose?" I stood up and faced him. Wilson and Funk intervened before it came to blows.

When he got to Saigon, Safer took my script and all the film McEnry and I had shot, added it to what he and Wilson had, and wrote a single narration incorporating elements of the two stories that both of our teams had shot that day. He called his piece "The Helicopter and the Dying Soldier." It was broadcast on the *CBS Evening News* and later won him many broadcast journalism awards for his skill and courage.

OCTOBER 17, 1965

Three days of introductions, briefings, medical checks, parachute fittings, emergency rescue instructions, interviews, drinks, bull sessions and we were ready to fly. Wilson, Funk and I had been invited to film a combat air strike with the U.S. Air Force. Preparations took place at Bien Hoa airbase, fifteen miles north of Saigon. Wilson filmed the air crews at work, rest and play. The pilots were a wild bunch—mischievous as small children, funny and egocentric, late adolescent boys in men's bodies who drove their fantastic machines like teenage kids racing souped-up cars in high school. The pilots' lives appeared to exist solely for planes and flight. When they weren't actually flying or getting ready to fly, they were talking about flying, thinking about flying, writing home about flying, dreaming about flying, or listening to one another tell stories about flying. Much of their time was spent waiting to take off on short notice in the operational ready room, the "ops shack," a cold prefabricated air-conditioned hut, sterile as a hospital waiting room.

The pilots were comfortable with our company—partly out of politeness, partly because of shared adventurous spirits, partly, I suspected, for our ability to get them on network television where their families and friends would see them. Waiting in the ops shack, Wilson and Funk told them about the helicopter crashes at Suoi Ca and Dong Den and our experiences with the Army and Marines. The pilots listened closely. They were interested to know what it was like on the ground: not only the fighting but also descriptions of the extreme heat, dust, rain, mud and biting insects—a war they did not experience themselves other than for the few seconds the ground flashed by on their bombing runs in a blur of flame and smoke. Their sympathy for soldiers and Marines fighting in the field was sincere.

'I'll do anything to help those ground doggies out of a jam,' a pilot said. 'I mean *anything!* Up to and including gettin my ass shot at.' He paused for emphasis. 'But I thank the good Lord every night of my life that they're down there' (pointing his finger down) 'and I'm up here' (pointing up in the air). All the pilots laughed.

To the crew and me, the prospect of military flying provided fresh expectation, a new thrill, as daring as anything we had ever done. To the pilots, combat aviation was routine. They were mostly casual about it, as if the danger of getting shot down was part of their job, what they did for a living.

No TV crew, we were told, had been allowed this much freedom to film a bombing mission in Vietnam before. The Air Force was giving us an inside look at its tactical operations in South Vietnam. From the big airfield at Bien Hoa, as well as from bases at Saigon, Pleiku, Qui Nhon, Danang, Chu Lai and from U.S. Navy aircraft carriers in the South China Sea, American pilots were flying scores of missions each day. They struck preplanned targets and provided tactical air support for American and South Vietnamese infantry forces through the country. For this story, the unit chosen for us to cover at Bien Hoa was the 602d Fighter Squadron. Its pilots flew Douglas A-1E attack bombers, "Skyraiders."

TV news coverage of the U.S. armed services in Vietnam focused primarily on the Army and Marines because ground troops did most of the fighting and were more easily accessible to camera crews. Now the Air Force wanted a larger share of public acknowledgment. Senior information officers in Saigon who approved our project trusted us to report what we saw in a favorable or at least objective light. We had asked for permission to fly on a bombing mission over North Vietnam, but our request was denied.

Wilson, Funk and I were back together as a team. Since the Suoi Ca Valley incident the week before, a new bond existed among us. We had more respect for one another, for our abilities under pressure, for being able to work calmly in danger. Wilson was furious with Morley Safer for taking all the film of the crashed helicopter and dying soldier and using it without crediting McEnry, Hoan or me. Wilson swore he would never work with him again. He promised to find an even more dramatic combat story with me. He was serious. The day after the helicopter crash, Wilson flew all day with First Cav medevac pilots hoping to get shot down again. He did not succeed. But he did get an interesting story about two wounded Cav soldiers who were rescued by helicopter and flown to a field hospital for treatment. We shipped it to the States for broadcast with my narration, but it was not as dramatic as Wilson wanted. The three of us were once again looking for a story and this time treating one another more as friends. We had formed a kind of brotherhood in adversity, like the allegiance between children in a troubled family.

The bombing mission was being carried out by a flight of four planes. I sat next to one of the pilots, Major Charles Vasiliadis, a dark, square-faced veteran who had flown over 350 missions, more than any American pilot in Vietnam. Starting up, the giant gas-reciprocating engine that filled the nose of the A-1E crackled, coughed, sputtered and roared with such ferocity I feared it was going to blow up. Just the sounds of the Wright R-3350 engine attested that enormous forces were engaged. One at a time, the big planes rolled down the mile-long runway at Bien Hoa before struggling slowly into the air, bombs and napalm canisters heavy under their wings.

Skyraiders had been in military service since 1946, when they were known as "Able Dogs" after their original designation as AD-1 (Attack Douglas). Standing fifteen and a half feet high and forty feet long, with wings of fifty feet and tall straight-up tail assemblies, they looked like the cartoon drawings schoolboys copied out of war comics, muzzle flashes spitting from the wings. These E models carried four 1,000-pound bombs, eight 500-pound bombs, canisters of napalm and hundreds of rounds of 20 millimeter cannon. The 8,000 pounds of ordnance and fuel made up more than a third of the planes' total weight and pulled hard on them as they lumbered off the runway and gained altitude foot by foot. The clouds ahead of us were washed in solemn shades of gray and white.

Wilson, Funk and I flew separately in each of three planes, sitting on parachutes in the passenger seats to the right of the pilots. We were strapped to the seats by shoulder harnesses and seat belts that were joined by metal fasteners at the chest. The copilot's control stick had been removed from its base between our legs although foot pedals for the flaps remained. The instrument panel was a screen of lights, dials, meters and switches, incomprehensible to me except for speed and altitude. Wilson had a small silent camera that gave him more maneuverability in the confined space of the cockpit. Funk recorded the natural sound of the planes, the rushing wind, and the radio conversations of the pilots.

Major Vasiliadis was thirty-seven years old but the softness of his face, the short curly black hair, his large straight nose and the mole on his left cheek made him look younger. Some of the pilots in the squadron tended to flamboyance, but Vasiliadis had a modest, unpretentious manner. A graduate of Harvard University, he had twice been decorated with the Distinguished Flying Cross. The other pilots called him "Vas," pronounced Vazz.

At about three thousand feet, the planes climbed into a black cloud. Except for the dim red lights on the instrument panel, the cockpit was dark. Rain splattered hard against the windshield. The aircraft bounced and yawed and pulled with sudden jerks, hurtling it forward as through dense fog. Vas held his eyes on the maze of instruments moving in front of him and tried to steady the gyrating plane with his gloved right hand on the control stick that twitched violently between his knees. The thirteen-ton machine bored through the clouds like a snowplow. Vasiliadis had an expression of calm concentration. I breathed slowly in and out and tried to force myself to relax.

Higher up, the plane broke through the tops of the clouds and skimmed over puffs of gentle white fluff. The plane emerged in bright sunshine and clear blue air that reached to infinity. After the dark confinement of the clouds, the brilliant sky felt refreshing, liberating. Elation hit me at the same time as the warm sunlight and I lowered the sun visor on the hard plastic helmet. Vas joined formation with the other pilots and the flight turned west and south on a heading toward the border of South Vietnam and Cambodia.

Speaking on the internal intercom before each maneuver of the aircraft, Vas announced what he was going to do next: 'Okay, turning left now. You'll hear a little more throttle,' taking me through it step by step so that I knew what to expect and wasn't alarmed by sudden movements of the plane. I was no longer afraid. Vasiliadis seemed confident with what he was doing, as fearless as the young army officers who stood up straight during the sniper fire in the Suoi Ca Valley. *If he isn't scared,* I thought to myself, *why should I be?* Not knowing what emotion to feel, I borrowed his. Total calm. It did not occur to me that Vas and the other pilots were concentrating so carefully on the dozens of details they had to remember to fly the mission correctly— the actual mechanics of flying, navigating, communicating, targeting, attacking—that there was no space left in their conscious minds for fear. They were too busy. Nor did I consider the possibility that any serious fear they felt could not be revealed: to the other pilots, to the CBS crew, perhaps to themselves. It had to be suppressed. Maybe the fear of something going wrong had become so familiar with them that it was part of the background by now, another detail in their long checklist of mechanical considerations, like the steady drone of the engines.

The flight leader was Jay Ledbetter, a thirty-six-year-old captain from Melbourne, Florida. The other pilots were Major Gale Kirkpatrick, 35, of

Selma, Alabama, and Captain Adrian (Jack) Geraghty, 36, of Amityville, New York. All were experienced fighter jet pilots who had been switched to A-1Es for duty in Vietnam. The Air Force considered the prop-driven planes more useful than jets for some of the work in the guerrilla war. A-1Es could carry twice as much bomb weight as a jet plane, and could stay airborne four to five hours a flight, waiting on station to provide tactical support to ground troops on short notice. What they gave up in speed, the A-1Es gained in destructive power and time on target.

Kirkpatrick was a large handsome man with a slow drawl, a quick sense of humor and a gregarious disposition that fit his big frame. Ledbetter and Geraghty were thinner, wisecracking, more like flying stuntmen. I had the impression that all four were pleased to be chosen by the Air Force to fly us, though they tried not to show it. They were exceptionally attentive to our needs in the air.

The flight to the border was long and slow. By the time the A-1Es arrived at the target, a forward air controller (FAC) was waiting. This was another Air Force pilot who circled over the countryside in a small single-engine spotter plane. His altitude was a few hundred feet. The A-1Es stayed above five thousand feet in tactical formation.

'Do you see the village just to the east of the river?' the FAC said on the radio. 'Just off my left wing?'

'Roger, the village east of the river,' Ledbetter answered.

'That's it. That's the VC village you're going to hit.'

'Ah, roger that.'

"On the west side of the village, you can consider that the border," the FAC said. "We don't want you to go past the buildings on the west side. So, if you make a left-hand pattern, it'll have to be tight into this village with a tight left break to stay a couple of clicks away from the border."

'That's affirmative, this side of the village.'

'Okay, it's all yours. I'll get out of the way. Happy hunting,' the FAC said.

The planes circled in a wide arc between scattered clumps of cotton-white clouds. Below, the countryside was a green-gray checkerboard: hundreds of square miles of flat farmland and long straight rows of rice fields and irrigation canals that reached to the horizon—part of the massive expanse of the Mekong River Delta. Rectangular pools of water, peaceful in the morning light, reflected the sun. Speaking on the radio, the pilots decided on the order of bombing. Vas would go third, after Kirkpatrick.

"If you have to throw up," Vas said, "try and do it in the helmet, okay?"

'Affirmative,' I said, pretending not to be worried. At Bien Hoa, Wilson, Funk and I had been warned that we would probably be unable to keep our food down after the first couple of passes. Then we'd be all right. I had chosen not to eat breakfast.

'Okay, hang on. Here we go.'

Vas flipped toggle switches on the controls to arm the bombs and jerked the control stick hard to the left and the plane rolled over on its side. The engine, wings and ailerons strained with the force. The horizon tilted suddenly to the right and then disappeared and all I could see was a great dark mass of earth rushing up toward us. The plane pointed almost straight down, turning from side to side on the axis of its nose. The engine roared with the added power of the dive and the air rushed past the canopy of the cockpit fast and loud. My body felt light, like a leaf, without weight.

I was off balance, disoriented, unable to tell up from down. The strongest sensation was one of rushing forward, complicated by the weightless twisting motion of the plane. I was frozen in the seat, too frightened to breathe or move or cry out. At the same time, I felt a strange exhilaration. My physical senses were warning of danger but my cognitive reason was saying it's all right, nothing is going to hurt you, this is thrilling.

Time stopped.

The straw roofs of a village appeared a thousand feet below, racing toward us fast. Sunlight flashed off a flooded rice field. Vas made sight adjustments and the wings came level for a second and the bombs fell away from under the wings with a metal *clank*. An instant later, he pulled the control stick all the way back and the aircraft shuddered with the competing forces of weight, drag, lift and thrust. The engine screamed and the nose came up and the plane strained into the sky. I felt the sudden pull of five times my weight sucking me into the seat. My chin was driven into my chest. All the strength went out of my arms and shoulders, making them heavy and lifeless, no longer part of me. I could not lift my head. Simultaneously, my vision went black around the edges and formed a tunnel around a circle of light that narrowed to a sharp solitary point and then went out. I was unconscious.

Time passed. As I came to my senses, Vas was talking on the intercom. I pulled my head out of my chest and turned to look. He was smiling.

'How did you like that?' he asked.

'Amazing,' I said, feeling the breath come back.

'You feel sick?'

'No.'

'Good. You're doing better than your buddies.'

Kirkpatrick and Geraghty were talking on the radio about Wilson and Funk.

'Damn. I'm gonna have to open the canopy,' one of them said.

'We got enough puke in here for a swim.'

'Shit, I forgot my snorkel.'

'He who barfs before lunch buys the drinks before supper.'

Wilson's voice came on the radio. 'At least the camera's still dry,' he said, a laugh in his voice.

A minute later, Vas said, 'Here we go,' and the plane rolled over and turned a perfect pirouette on the tip of its left wing. The wing came back to the right and the plane dived straight at the village. The straw roofs were on fire now. Flame and smoke reached up to touch the plane. Vas released more bombs and a few seconds later the cockpit shook with explosive shocks. The plane climbed out of the dive and raced through clouds of black smoke.

The periphery of my vision faded, a dark circle formed around the edges of light, but this time I did not black out. Vas turned his head and looked at me with an expression vaguely suggesting approval.

On the fourth or fifth pass, I saw individual farmers—women and men—standing in fields outside the village in round straw hats with hoes in their hands. They looked up at the diving plane. Vas squeezed the trigger on the control stick and the cannons in the wings of the Skyraider fired a long burst of 20 millimeter shells—explosive metal missiles almost an inch thick. The shells struck the ground among the farmers, chopping the earth and sending up spouts of brown dirt and also striking the men and women farmers and tearing through the delicate assemblies of their bodies. The plane zoomed over and past before they fell.

"Why do they just stand there?" I said on the intercom. "Why don't they run away?"

"Cause they don't know any better," Vas said. "Dumb bastards."

He said it with such authority I didn't doubt him. But I wondered, *If they're all VC as they're supposed to be, why don't they run for cover?*

When all of the bombs, napalm and cannon had been dropped and fired, the flight headed toward Bien Hoa. Vas slid the hard plastic canopy back to

let in the cooler air. He switched the radio to a special air force frequency
that was playing gentle instrumental music, mostly strings arranged in the
style of Mantovani, aerial muzak. *How different from the last few minutes.* The
tedium relieved the tension of the bombing strike. Vas and I did not talk
much. Warm sunlight bathed the cockpit. The ride back to base was as easy
as driving home from a Sunday afternoon ball game.

At Bien Hoa, the plane passed over the runway at 500 feet, flying level
with it, the control tower just to the left. Suddenly, the plane flipped over on
its right wing with such violent force I feared we had collided with another
plane. I panicked. My hands reached forward and seized the edge of the control panel. Heart pumping, body rigid, I thought we were going to crash. But
the plane only went around on its side in a hard right turn, 180 degrees, taking us back to the end of the runway for the final approach.

'What was that?' I said.

Vas turned his head to look at me. He was smiling—a wry, knowing
insider's smile that seemed to say, "Gotcha." It was the look of a warrior,
smug in victory, the only time I saw it. Maybe he had just forgotten to warn
me, but I didn't think so. He had been meticulous in describing every other
sharp movement of the plane in advance. Vas could have mentioned "the
pitchout," the hard turn combat aviators make over the runway after a mission, showing their empty bomb racks to the control tower just before landing. He had managed to scare me in the last moments of the flight and I had
shown my fear.

"That was the *break*," he said.

Later, in Saigon, Wilson and Funk described the scenes they had recorded
and I wrote a story on the anatomy of an air strike, focusing on the skills of
the pilots, the versatility of the vintage airplanes, the thoughts of the pilots
from interviews at Bien Hoa. I wrote nothing critical about them or the mission. I did not draw attention to the farmers they killed. Wilson said his pilot
had not strafed any farmers, so he had no pictures of it.

A day later a message arrived at the bureau from Russ Bensley, the pro-
ducer in New York who was responsible for film coverage of Vietnam on the
CBS Evening News. Bensley's message said that the UN representative from
Cambodia was claiming that American planes had bombed and strafed a
Cambodian village near the border with Vietnam. Bensley asked us to find
out whether the Cambodian protest had anything to do with the air strike

we had filmed and would soon be arriving in New York. It was only an off chance, he said, but we should check.

I called the Air Force public information office in Saigon and explained Bensley's query to the two officers who arranged our coverage of the air strike. Lieutenant Colonel Dave O'Hara and Lieutenant Colonel Dan Biondi were friendly acquaintances. We had lunch when I arrived in August and I was indebted to them for getting Wilson and me on the Air Force plane to the Philippines to cover the volcano eruption three weeks earlier. They said they were not aware of the official Cambodian protest but would find out what happened.

Biondi called back later in the day. His voice was strained. He asked to go off the record and I agreed.

'Ah, Jack,' he said, 'I've checked around about your request. I'd like to give you an answer, but I can't. I hope you'll understand, but we can't talk about this one. If you understand what I mean. We can't say anything.'

His voice was worried, vulnerable, no confidence in it. I asked him several questions but he resisted answering.

'Jack, it would be better all around if you'd just keep this one quiet,' he said. 'I'm asking for a favor here.'

I said I understood, thanked him and hung up the phone.

Biondi's honesty surprised me. He could have denied there was any connection between our mission and the Cambodian protest and that would have been the end of it. My superiors in New York probably would have accepted the word of the Air Force spokesman in Saigon and dropped the issue. Instead, Biondi chose to let me know something was wrong. But he had not confirmed that U.S. planes struck Cambodian territory. Nor could I quote him. He was enlisting my cooperation in covering up any trouble ("just keep this one quiet"). The truth, presumably, would have embarrassed the Air Force, the Pentagon and the U.S. government.

I thought about it all day and discussed it with the bureau chief. It was a tough call. On the one hand, it was a good story. U.S. planes bombing Cambodia would make headlines. I felt sympathy for the innocent farmers who had been killed. A big news story might help prevent it from happening again. But we didn't have confirmation. It would be impossible to prove where the planes had bombed without help from the Air Force. On the other hand, I didn't want to jeopardize our relationship with Biondi and O'Hara.

Reporting a bombing of Cambodia would cause a major rift between the Air Force and CBS News, and it might seriously affect future news coverage. The story could also be inaccurate. *What to do?*

The next morning I composed a short message to Bensley saying that the Air Force could not confirm that any of its planes had struck Cambodia. That *was* the end of it. The A-1E story went on the air in its original form. The pictures were dramatic but it was just another air strike in South Vietnam.

Without realizing it, I had become a player in the official Saigon information/propaganda game. I had demonstrated my willingness to accept favors from the U.S. mission and also to return them. By broadcasting uncritical stories about American military activity, I earned special access to other military stories in return. Because I believed what I was reporting was accurate, I felt no guilt. Reporting everything I saw or was told or believed to be true in a spirit of full disclosure seemed less important than maintaining my good military contacts, keeping the information officers happy, and moving ahead in my career. I saw the war as an honorable cause, fought in the national interests of the United States and South Vietnam. I was still, as they said, "with the program."

Later in the month, I had lunch at the Rex Hotel again with my contact at the embassy. By now I knew that he was a senior officer in the Central Intelligence Agency, the Saigon station chief. Svenson and I talked about the war. He knew about the air strike on the Cambodian border but we did not discuss it. After lunch, we rode down to the ground floor in the narrow hotel elevator. There was enough room for three, possibly four, people. The third person in the elevator, a young Air Force captain in uniform, stared at me with curiosity, as though trying to place where he had seen me before. On the sidewalk outside, I was saying good-bye to the CIA man when the Air Force officer approached.

'Excuse me,' the captain said. 'Do you work for CBS?'

I said I did.

'Are you the reporter who went on that A-1E mission over on the border?'

'Yes I am.'

He smiled, pleased with himself.

'I'm the FAC who was spotting for you on that one. Saw your report on TV. Thought I recognized you in the elevator.' We shook hands.

'Do you remember that village we hit? Where the dinks just stood there and took it?' His tone was serious now.

'Uh huh.'

'You know, it was driving me crazy that we might have got the wrong place. So, I went back on my own the other day to take a look. You know what? We hit the wrong target. I got the rivers mixed up. When I told you guys to bomb on the east side of the village we were already two clicks inside Cambodia. I read the map wrong.'

'Yes,' I said. 'I heard that might have been the case.' The CIA officer listened with interest but did not speak.

'Well, I just wanted you to know that,' the captain said. 'It's really been on my conscience.'

OCTOBER 23, 1965

The field was filled with helicopters and soldiers waiting. Two long rows of leaf-green Hueys stood on their skids, nose to tail, engines down, rotor blades bent and secured with cord, limp and lifeless in the languid noontime heat. Pilots and crews sat in the narrow band of shade beside the machines. Hundreds of Vietnamese soldiers were spread across the field in squads, eight or nine to a squad, standing or squatting or sleeping on the bare red dirt a safe distance away from the Hueys, killing time. Some of them cooked rice or noodle soup over small fires on the ground and ate. The men were thin and laconic with smooth hairless arms and brown skin. They wore tight-fitting olive green fatigues with bright red scarves around their necks that made them look like Boy Scouts. Their old American carbines were stacked neatly against one another with the muzzles pointed in the air. Bare metal helmets lay scattered across the ground upside down. The red scarves around their necks gave the soldiers a dashing carefree appearance but the primary expression on their faces was fear.

The usual duty of the 22d Ranger battalion of the Army of the Republic of Vietnam was to protect ARVN military installations in Pleiku, a remote mountain town on the western edge of the Central Highlands. Pleiku was not far from the Cambodian border, fifty miles west of An Khe, and was the western gateway to the Central Highlands. Any attempt by the North Vietnamese to strike across the highlands, capture the main roads and towns, and divide South Vietnam at its geographical center would have to begin around Pleiku. Such was the apparent intention of the Lao Dong (Communist) Party high command in Hanoi, and it was perceived by U.S. and South Vietnamese strategists as a serious threat.

Pleiku itself was not much of a prize: a dusty slow-moving backwoods town that the sudden infusion of U.S. military personnel at Camp Holloway was rapidly transforming into a dollar-rich boom town by Vietnamese standards. The young soldiers of the 22d Ranger battalion waited with their

American advisers for orders to take off in the helicopters, although none seemed anxious to go.

I stood talking with one of the American advisers. Jim Wilson, P. B. Hoan and I had just arrived in Pleiku and were trying to get a sense of what was going on, how dangerous it would be to go with the soldiers. The adviser said his name was Edward Brady, a U.S. Army first lieutenant from Port Richey, Florida, who was twenty-four years old. He was lightly built with short red hair and a camouflage-dyed cowboy hat with one side of the brim turned up. A thin cigar smoking from the side of his mouth gave him a jaunty look. Brady said he had graduated from the U.S. Naval Academy in 1963.

'Annapolis?' I said.

'Yeah,' he said. 'I transferred to the Army so I could get over here. It was the only way.'

All around the world—at U.S. military bases, NATO stations, war colleges, embassies, training posts, the Pentagon—American career officers were volunteering for duty in Vietnam, hoping to punch their service tickets with combat assignments before the war ended. "It's the only war we've got" became a cliché among ambitious officers anxious for the opportunity to distinguish themselves in battle and win promotion. "Fighting a war is the ultimate test of how well I do my job" was another explanation heard. Brady's decision to scuttle his Navy career for an uncertain future as an Army infantry adviser seemed as radical as it was ambitious. He told us he had been in-country for about three months.

It was a Saturday. Wilson, Hoan and I had flown to Pleiku that morning from An Khe, where we had been scouting for stories with the First Cav. Bob Funk was ill and Hoan was recording sound in his place. In An Khe, J. D. Coleman, the assistant public information officer, had come back from his morning visit to the division Tactical Operations Center and told us about "a hell of a fight" that was going on at a distant Special Forces camp. It was called Plei Me, pronounced *Play-may*. None of us had ever heard of it. Coleman was excited about the prospect of a set-piece battle between the Cav and the Viet Cong. He showed us Plei Me on the map—a dot in the wilderness about twenty-five miles south of Pleiku along an unpaved secondary road. Plei Me was just on the edge of the First Cav's tactical area of responsibility.

'It's pretty hairy in there,' Coleman said. 'The VC have been hitting the place with everything they've got since Tuesday night. Some of them even got up to the wire. A lot of people are getting zapped.' Wilson, Hoan and I looked at each other. 'If you want to cover it,' Coleman said, 'your best bet is to get with an ARVN relief column that's mounting up at Pleiku right now. They're going to press on down to Plei Me by road.'

It sounded like a good story. There would be Americans in the camp, so-called Green Berets, probably twelve or so, and the battle might make big news in the States, depending on how it developed. Special Forces were popular heroes at home, subjects of a best-selling novel by Robin Moore and a hit record by one of their medics, Sergeant Barry Sadler. Among journalists in Vietnam, however, there was ambivalence about the Special Forces. The secrecy of their operations, their connections with the CIA, their reputation within the Army itself (many saw them as elitists) and their abhorrence of publicity combined to relegate the Green Berets to a role as shadow figures in the war, hidden largely from the bright light of press coverage. About the only time we heard what they were doing was when one of their camps was in trouble. Occasionally, a camp was overrun. I had no idea what happened when a Special Forces camp was under attack. I imagined gray grim-faced Communist troops assaulting with AK-47s at their hips, wave after human wave, images of the Korean War. I felt an unfamiliar lightness at the center of my stomach. Wilson, Hoan and I were silent for a time.

'What the hell,' Wilson said. 'That's what we're here for.'

'Keep your heads down,' Coleman said as we left.

By the time we got to Pleiku, it was too late to accompany the armored relief column. A U.S. officer at province headquarters said the ARVN task force had set off down the dirt road on Friday, the day before. He said it consisted of a battalion of infantry, a company of M-41 tanks, several armored fighting vehicles, and a troop of armored personnel carriers and supply trucks—about eight hundred or nine hundred South Vietnamese troops in vehicles accompanied by about a dozen American advisers.

'Why did it take more than two days for the relief column to get on the road?' I asked, 'Especially if the camp is so desperate for reinforcements?'

'Vinh Loc is afraid it might be a diversion,' the officer said. 'He doesn't like leaving his headquarters undefended.' Major General Vinh Loc was the ARVN commander of the area and the task force was all he had to defend Pleiku.

Waiting in the field of helicopters with the 22d Rangers, Lieutenant

Brady explained that senior ARVN officers were pretty sure the armored relief column was going to be ambushed.

'The VC are using one of their favorite tricks,' he said. 'They do it all the time. First they attack a really remote Special Forces camp and keep the pressure on for a few days. Then, when the ARVN get their act together and send in a convoy to reinforce the camp, the VC ambush it with a larger force hidden along the way. It's happened again and again. The ARVN always take a hammering.'

'This time,' Brady said, 'it's going to be different.' He unfolded his map and explained that the 22d Rangers were going to make a helicopter landing near the road where the VC were most likely to ambush the relief column. The location was a narrow pass through the hills about five miles north of Plei Me. The rangers would occupy the pass and provide flank support for the relief column *before* the VC could ambush it.

'That's the plan,' Brady said, folding his map and putting it away. His expression was confident.

To me it looked like a game of chess. On both sides, the generals moved their battalions around like pieces on a board—an armored task force here, an infantry battalion there, an artillery battery in that space, a regiment in ambush there—maneuvering troops, tanks and helicopters in and out of various grid squares on their maps. Always with the intention of surprising and overpowering the other side, trying to find a winning combination of forces, moving swiftly for the kill. Like chess players sitting in padded armchairs, the generals made their moves far from the fields of battle.

"How good are these troops?" I asked Brady, recalling stories I had heard in Saigon about the dangers of going into battle with particular ARVN units. Since 1961, the history of the war was punctuated with accounts of ARVN soldiers panicking in battle, cowering under fire, lacking the ability to fight, throwing down their weapons and running away.

"I'd go anywhere with these little guys," Brady said. "They're great fighters."

"How do they compare with American GIs?"

"If the Rangers had as good small unit leaders—platoon sergeants and lieutenants—they'd be as good as Americans," he said.

That settled it. Wilson, Hoan and I decided to go along. It was the only way to get to Plei Me.

'Let's stick close to the lieutenant,' Wilson said.

The helicopters loaded the troops and took off to the south. From the air, the countryside looked benign. Vegetation lay in soft green shapes across gently sloping hills undulating away toward dark higher hills on the horizon, toward Kontum to the north and Cambodia to the west. The dense green foliage was broken in places by patches of brown-red volcanic earth and fields of charred black tree stumps, scars from the slash-and-burn subsistence of native tribes. On the high ground, scattered human settlements were surrounded by fields of maize, cut forest and pens for livestock. The tranquil-looking topography masked the violent environment beneath the foliage. The rainforest was a fierce unforgiving wilderness, a refuge of wild animals and lost tribes, a primordial jungle fastness as near as anyone could get in a land of deathly surprises to the end of the world.

Pleiku Province was carved out of the southwestern edge of the Annam Cordillera, the long uncharted mountain range that runs the length of Vietnam from China almost to Saigon. At Pleiku, the range flattens out to form a broad plateau covering thousands of square miles. In times of peace this was tiger and elephant country, a high sweeping savanna of tall grasses and thorny brush, where anthills stood four feet high and were defended by warrior insects with sharp biting fury. Most of the province was uninhabitable. The only people living there were mountain tribes and clans, the Jarai, natives descended from early settlers of Vietnam who were driven away from the fertile coastal plains centuries before by the stronger lowland cultures who came to be known as the "Vietnamese." Most Vietnamese considered the primitive societies of the Jarai and other mountain tribes to be uncivilized and treated them with contempt. The French called them "Montagnards," mountain people. The Americans who worked most closely with the Montagnards, the Special Forces, called them "'Yards."

The helicopters landed in a field of dead corn stalks near the top of a hill. A tribal village burned quietly from the gunship attack that preceded us and gray smoke drifted up through the trees. There was no resistance. The Rangers jumped out of the helicopters and walked to the edge of the field. When the villagers saw they were not going to attack, they came out of their hiding places and started to cry in front of the soldiers. They were extremely small people with dark brown skin and wild black hair held in place with colored headbands. A few wore cloth garments like sarongs and kebayas, but most had on nothing more than thin strips of cloth or string over their genitals. Men and women had simple decorative earrings and necklaces and their feet were bare. Their size and simple manners gave them the appearance of children.

A man with black teeth stood in front of Wilson and waved his arms, motioning to come toward the village, pleading in a strange singsong language. Wilson, Hoan, Brady and I followed the man to a long building that sat on log stilts, about five feet off the ground. The building was fifty to sixty feet long with a peaked roof and scrap-metal sheeting fastened to its sides. Inside, it was dark and musky and smelled of smoke.

A wounded man lay on his back on a straw mat on the floor. His jaw was closed and the muscles in his face were taut, as if fighting pain. The villagers lectured us with stern expressions as though we were responsible for the wounded man on the straw mat. Hoan tried to talk with them in Vietnamese but they turned their heads in puzzlement.

The man who had brought us to the longhouse described the attack with his hands, curling them above his head like a helicopter, pointing his fingers toward the ground. 'Tack-tack-tack-tack!' he said, hissing.

'I can't get a God damn exposure in here,' Wilson said, holding his light meter in front of him, shaking it.

Brady examined the wounded man and motioned to the villagers to carry him outside. Wilson, Hoan and I walked ahead into the late afternoon sun. Outside, Wilson took a quick light reading, put the camera on his shoulder and rolled film as seven village men carried the wounded man out the door and down the steps of the longhouse. I snapped a still picture of the litter bearers. Brady and the senior adviser to the Ranger battalion, a U.S. Army captain, got on the radio and called Camp Holloway in Pleiku for a medevac. Three more wounded people were carried to the edge of the field. Their families prepared to go with them, binding up parcels of food for the trip to the hospital. Vietnamese soldiers stood to the side and watched with amused smiles. They seemed surprised that the Americans were going to so much trouble to help a few wounded savages. The small village people looked up at Brady and the captain with gratitude in their eyes and smiled at them with their black teeth.

When the medevac had taken the wounded, we asked Brady to give us an on-camera description of the military situation. He agreed. Wilson lined up the shot with Brady standing beside a fence, looking down the side of the hill toward the road where the task force was due to pass. Brady lit a cigar and puffed on it with the assurance of a military academy graduate about to face a challenge, in this case an interview. He said, 'The battalion is going to walk a kilometer or two south, toward the camp at Plei Me, and secure the pass where the VC are probably going to try and ambush the task force. We should get there just before dark.'

As Brady spoke, gunshots came from the road at the bottom of the hill about 2,000 yards away. The long straight line of the road was obscured by thick brush on both sides. Brady continued to talk. Gradually there was more gunfire, then automatic weapons, then the *whump whump* of hand grenades and rocket-propelled grenades. It was apparent that the VC were springing their ambush early, a mile ahead of the pass, surprising everyone, especially the soldiers in the relief column. The exploding shells made so much noise that Brady's voice could not be heard clearly and the interview had to stop. We all turned to look. Down the hill along the road, bright orange tracers zipped back and forth through the foliage and ricocheted off the steel hulls of the tanks and APCs and shot into the air at strange obtuse angles. Bullets flew high over our heads, buzzing faintly. Standing close together in a group behind us, the nearly naked Montagnards winced at each loud noise and put their fingers in their ears. Some of them closed their eyes. It was nearly six o'clock. The sun was sliding behind pink-colored clouds floating over the hills to the west in a flourish of pastel light.

The Rangers fanned out and took up fighting positions in a broad clearing on the slope of the hill. Some of them started to dig holes. The rest sat or stood to watch the flashing lights from the battle less than a mile away. Their commander, a lieutenant colonel with a thin face and an expression of strained intensity, spoke into his radio. His name was Phuoc and he was arguing with someone on the radio. I asked Hoan what was going on. He said the colonel was telling higher headquarters that his battalion was not going anywhere.

Wilson found a mortar team and photographed three men as they set up the weapon to fire at the VC down the hill. First they fitted the bipod of the mortar to the baseplate and then attached the tube, which was about two and a half feet long, and adjusted the azimuth and deflection. Then one of the soldiers dropped a 60 millimeter shell down the muzzle of the tube. It made a hollow *clunk* and hung there at the bottom of the tube without firing. The soldiers became excited. All three shouted at one another and danced around the mortar as though it were a bad spirit refusing to cooperate. Nothing happened. The soldiers looked at the mortar. Two of them unfastened the tube from the baseplate and bipod and gently turned it on its side, slowly easing the shell back out of the tube, one of them shouting in a rapid hysterical voice to the others, shifting the weight of the missile with breathless delicacy so that it did not strike the ground and explode in their faces.

It was getting dark now and we heard the sound of planes circling overhead, their turbojet engines whining, alternately shrill and dull as they shifted speed, still out of sight. Far below near the road, 150 feet over the trees, a small spotter plane, a single-engine o1 Bird Dog, floated in and out above the battle like a lazy summer butterfly, turning in low easy arcs along the line of the road, ignoring the fiery trails of machinegun tracers weaving around it.

"There is enemy to the east, right along that ridgeline, over." The radio crackled with traffic, urgent American voices shouting over the noise of the battle raging around them, exchanging information.

Finally, the pilot fired a rocket into the brush by the side of the road and a cloud of white phosphorous drifted up through the high grass to mark the target. The FAC flew away and the first jet rolled in, a sleek silver-gray F-100, wing light blinking on and off, diving like an illuminated arrow into the glowing volley of orange and red tracer bullets racing up to meet it. The long slow lines of the anti-aircraft shells intersected with the fast-moving shape of the streamlined plane to form a furious pattern of crisscrossing colors, hot against the pale pink and blue of the evening sky. Bombs tumbled out from under the wings and the jet turned sharply away from the road and jinked out of range as its afterburners cut a white-hot trail in the twilight and the ground erupted in a convulsion of sparks and earth and flame.

After the F-100s made their bombing and strafing runs, the first A-1E rolled in, all the way from Bien Hoa. It dived nose down into the flaming torrent of machinegun tracers. The pilot fired long crimson bursts of 20 millimeter cannon straight into the gunners on the ground. The tracers crossed like swords. Then the pilot pulled out of his dive in a tight turn and struggled to escape the swift angry flashes of bullets chasing him low across the sky.

The battlefield shrieked with the lightning cracks of bomb bursts and the thunderous roar of airplane engines and the *cack-cack-cack-cack-cack* of anti-aircraft shells—hundreds of large and small explosions blasting the air simultaneously, the drumbeats of air strikes adding to the crescendo of ground battle, a crude cacophonous symphony of destruction playing for us in our open-air seats on the side of the hill.

We watched for more than an hour. I was spellbound by the spectacle of

American pilots in their vertical dives and Vietnamese gunners shooting up into the flight of bombs and bullets falling on them. Their courage was incomprehensible. I couldn't imagine how the pilots and gunners managed to aim and steer and push the buttons and pull the triggers in the flaming thundering terrifying fury of battle.

It was like a medieval duel, knights and archers in modern armor, fighting to the death, as cruel as combat ever was, each warrior trying to destroy the other, each aware of the danger of being destroyed. I couldn't understand why they did it, why they would want to do it, how they could allow themselves into it, why they didn't drop their weapons and run. Then the thought occurred that maybe it wasn't a conscious choice they had made to fight, but rather that they were obeying the ultimate truth for all men in war, the only option at the final unavoidable point of armed conflict, the fast instinctive reaction that is less choice than imperative, the need to fight or die.

I watched the duel in the night sky transfixed by the cruel beauty of it, the iridescent embrace of speeding jets and machinegun tracers dancing a deadly ballet. But I was not close enough to feel the physical intensity of it, the breathless noisy insane panic of it. That I could only imagine.

Wilson looked up at the fading light and cursed. 'They'll have to push this roll in the lab. Don't let me forget to mark it "Push One Stop," okay?'

He put the heavy metal film magazine in a black cotton changing bag, zipped his arms into its light-proof sleeves, and transferred the exposed film to a round metal can and sealed it with white adhesive tape around the edge.

'Twelve point seven millimeter,' the voice next to me said.

I looked around. It was Vo Huynh, a cameraman for NBC News. He was making sure I understood the type of antiaircraft weapon the VC were firing.

Huynh spoke in a low rough-edged voice that matched his fierce-looking physical appearance: tall, square-shouldered and muscled. His face was dominated by dark brown eyes and drooping black eyebrows that gave the impression of ferocity even when he was relaxed.

Huynh was working alone, without a correspondent, using a small silent film camera and a separate tape recorder, the way much of the war was being covered by the TV networks. With our Auricon sound camera, Wilson, Hoan and I had a big advantage. Everything Wilson photographed was also recorded in natural sound on the same strip of film, "single system sound-on-film," giving us the ability to shoot scenes with synchronized sound, including on-camera interviews and stand-ups.

Huynh explained that the ambush had taken place well ahead of the pass through the hills farther down the road. He borrowed Brady's map and showed me where the South Vietnamese had been expecting the ambush to take place, the location our battalion was supposed to secure ahead of time.

'VC very clever,' he said with his French accent. 'This was very big ambush. *Formidable.*'

Given the competition between the networks, it was surprising that Huynh bothered to talk with me, much less explain what was going on. For a civilian, he had an expert's understanding of military details. He seemed to need to share his knowledge with a reporter, *any* reporter, even the competition. I guessed that Huynh was so accustomed to explaining these situations to NBC reporters that he briefed me because I was the only American TV reporter around. Perhaps he was just being polite. Later I saw that Huynh was more courageous than some of the officers he covered on operations. He was one of the very best film photographers of the war.

It was difficult to understand why the Ranger battalion didn't move down the hill and attack the VC from behind in order to take the pressure off the armored column on the road. Brady said that's what he and his captain wanted to do, but the battalion commander, Colonel Phuoc, thought otherwise. Vo Huynh explained that Phuoc was afraid his men might be outnumbered by the larger force of enemy troops attacking the convoy. He feared the Communists might turn their heavy machineguns and recoilless rifles on his lightly armed battalion and destroy it. The colonel was also worried about exposing his troops to the line of fire coming from the relief column or getting too close to the strike zone of the American bombers. 'Too many chances,' said Huynh. In my naïveté, I judged Phuoc's behavior to be cautious to the point of cowardice.

The shooting slackened. Irregular bursts of automatic weapons fire sounded from the valley along the road. The U.S. bombers flew back to their bases. A propeller-driven cargo plane circled high overhead and dropped flares that illuminated the night. The battle appeared to be over. Brady announced that the battalion was going to spend the night on the hill. The commanders would reassess the situation in the morning. Wilson, Hoan and I rolled out our ponchos and made beds in an open space not far from the headquarters group. I set myself about fifteen yards away on a flat patch of ground near a small tree. Camped nearby were Vo Huynh and two other reporters who came in with the battalion. Charles Mohr of the *New York*

Times was a tall round-faced thoroughly pleasant Nebraskan, aged thirty-seven. Despite his impressive knowledge of military affairs, Mohr looked awkwardly civilian in his baggy army fatigues and fishing hat, more like a correspondent for *Field and Stream*. The other reporter was Robin Mannock of the Associated Press, my tall English friend from our rainy afternoon together on the ridgeline with the 101st Airborne. One by one we fell asleep with the occasional crack of gunfire and the eerie light from flares falling over the battlefield.

I was surprised at the arrival, in the middle of my sleep, of a tall fine-boned American woman. She and I were friends but I never expected to see her here. She crawled under the poncho liner beside me and held me close to her.

'What are you doing here?' I asked.

'Caught a chopper in Pleiku,' she said. 'I asked Vinh Loc to get me out here and he needed somebody to hand-carry a message to the Ranger colonel here. Something he didn't want to say on the radio.'

'What was the message?' I said.

'Who knows? It was in an envelope. It probably said, "don't forget who you're working for."'

'His name is Phuoc. He's very cautious.'

'Aren't they all?'

'What time is it?'

'About 2:30. Is it over?'

'Don't know, I've been asleep. Hey, it's lovely to see you.'

Flares were falling. Except for odd bursts of gunfire, the sounds of heavy battle had stopped. The light of the flares floated in her eyes, sparkling specks of white-yellow light swaying against the dark blue-green of her irises. Her skin smelled of rose petals. A soft unfocused glow seemed to radiate from around her head and shoulders. Though I had not bathed for days and my body was soiled with sweat and dust, I felt refreshed. Lying side by side, we kissed one another and gently pressed our bodies together. Beneath her combat fatigues she was wearing thin silk underwear that enhanced the smoothness of her skin and embraced the perfect softness of her breasts and the fine fluffy hair between her legs. Her breath tasted of honeysuckle.

She put a bold tongue in my ear, filling it with hollow wetness, and at the same time touched my stomach and slid her hand below my waist. Her long fingers skimmed delicately across the surface of my skin and then folded around me with strong hands and slowly stroked the muscles firm.

I moaned.

'Shhhhh,' she whispered next to my ear. 'We'll wake the others.'

Suddenly the noises of battle cracked again, slowly at first but then in all fury—machineguns, rockets, tank cannon, grenades, mortars, small arms—a new middle-of-the-night VC attack. A radio squawked on the hilltop. More planes arrived and made strikes. Heavy sustained shooting and explosions drifted up from the valley and resonated in the night air. Locked in each other's arms, we took little notice of the battle. We made love in a vacuum, secretly, holding our voices in close check, restraining our excitement, stealing immeasurable increments of passion, feeling the short sharp sensations of delight build toward a climax of physical pleasure and emotional joy to match the intensity of the bombardment of light and sound on the battlefield below. Time and space did not exist. Only the slowly soaring exhilaration of our senses.

Later I awoke while it was still dark and turned on one side to rest on an elbow and gaze across the valley below. The shooting had stopped. The air was cool and wet although there was no rain. I shivered in the bedroll. A brilliant white flare swung in an arc beneath its miniature silk parachute, illuminating the battleground and casting long dark images over the sleeping earth, shifting with the slow descent of the swinging flare. Everything was black or white. Trees danced with their shadows. Nothing else moved. Staring at the changing light, I saw the souls of the dead rise from the battlefield, dozens of ghostly gray wisps in forms of human figures, pale translucent phantoms that rose up off the valley floor and floated into the sky and merged in silence with the night air.

OCTOBER 24, 1965

At dawn she was gone. The scent of her was on the nylon poncho liner and in my nose. The ground was cold and my bones ached but the memory of her face and the lingering pleasure of our encounter suffused my senses, filled me with warmth. I shifted my weight on the poncho and felt an embarrassing wetness between my legs. *Oh, no. Was it only a dream? But she was so real, so alive, so loving.* The memory of her presence was still too vivid, too seductive for me to believe she was only a figure in a dream. I was deeply disappointed. I did not want to believe she was gone. I wanted her back. *Who was she? Who did she represent?* I tried to picture her face again and identify her by name but nothing came. All I could recall was the intense feeling that she was a special friend, the embodiment perhaps of the women I had loved—independent, adventurous, thoughtful, beautiful—or perhaps the archetype of a woman I would love. Afterward, for months, I tried to bring back the dream in my sleep, to recreate the experience by force of imagination and reclaim the pleasure of her company, but she did not return. Only her spirit remained as memory. Sometimes, in the field, the memory gave me strength. In times when I felt trapped, unable to escape the wretched jungle prison in this dark otherside of the world, when I wondered what I was doing there and why I endured the punishment, when I yearned for the comforts of home and friends, the memory of the tall fine-boned woman in the dream cut through the gloom and gave me hope. *Someday,* I thought, *I'll find her again.* The images of the battle had intensified my awareness, stimulated my imagination, sharpened my senses—even into my dream. After that night on the hill I never questioned the power of the connection between violence and sex.

At daybreak the planes came and dropped more bombs, but there was no anti-aircraft fire. The Rangers made breakfast and rolled up their ponchos. Wilson checked his camera and discovered that the inside of the lens was fogged with moisture. He cursed hard and held the end of the lens up to the sunlight for it to dry.

Some of the soldiers started to shout and point down the hill to the left.

Five hundred yards away in the valley below, groups of soldiers in mustard-brown combat uniforms moved across open fields, dozens of them, loping at an easy trot through the grass and then disappearing into the treeline ahead of them.

'Can we get any of that?' I said to Wilson.

'No, God damn it!' he said. 'It'll look like shit.' He was angry at the lens for fogging.

The enemy soldiers continued to move west, away from the road and the battlefield, escaping. Wilson swore. Vo Huynh tried a long lens shot with his silent camera, but when he took his eye away from the viewfinder he shook his head as if it was no good. The Rangers stood and watched, chattering to themselves. Lieutenant Brady paced back and forth. He went to the U.S. Army captain who was advising Lieutenant Colonel Phuoc and asked them to order the mortar to be fired at the retreating enemy. The captain said, 'No, we don't want to stir up a hornet's nest here,' supporting Phuoc. Brady stood nose to nose with the captain, arguing, but it was no use. About an hour later, an Air Force plane flew over and bombed and strafed the area where the enemy had been, but the bombs were way off target and it was too late anyway.

Late in the morning, with the sun up and strong and insects chanting at full pitch, the Ranger battalion set off down the hill toward the road, single file, one at a time. Lieutenant Colonel Phuoc seemed confident the battle was over and his men would meet no resistance. *These guys don't want to fight,* I thought. But I couldn't imagine why, with all the firepower they had on call, they did nothing. They seemed too cautious to be fighting a war. *How can they hope to win if they let the enemy get away so easily?*

The column moved down the hill. Wilson, Hoan, Huynh, Mohr, Mannock and I followed. The farther down into the valley the soldiers walked, the heavier the vegetation got. They moved slowly through a dense thicket of hostile foliage. Every yard had to be hacked through by machete. The stench of decaying undergrowth trapped in the dead jungle air rose out of the brush and made it hard to breathe. After two hours, everyone was bleeding from the bites and scratches of ants, mosquitoes, thorns, briars and elephant grass as high as our heads. Each blade of grass was sharp as a knife. The bad air made me dizzy, then nauseous.

At the bottom of the hill by a stream the column came upon the first of the bodies. Five enemy soldiers lay in a clearing around the tripod of an anti-aircraft gun—a long-barreled .51-caliber with its ammo case loaded and its muzzle pointing aimlessly at the sky. The ground around the gun was gouged by deep symmetrical craters and littered with ugly black chunks of sharp-edged steel. The dead were dressed in bloodstained brown uniforms with ammunition pouches strapped to their chests and rubber sandals cut out of old tires on their feet. One of them, a teenager with dense black hair that looked like it had been cut with a bowl over his head, lay on his back next to the anti-aircraft gun. His eyes were fixed in a blank blind stare of surprise. The uniform he wore was soiled with dry sweat and dirt. About a third of his skull had been sliced away at one side by a bomb fragment, neatly opened like a watermelon, exposing the blood-red interior of his brain to the sunlight and flies. He looked innocent. *How vulnerable*, I thought, *how fragile*. All it took was a flying piece of steel and it was over for this kid. *How brave he had been, how loyal, how disciplined*. I recalled the air-ground duel of the night before, the gunners and pilots locked in their death dance. And here on the ground was the final awful resolution of it. I looked away. It was too messy to look at for long. The soldier's eyes drew me back, challenging me to look again, warning me, mocking me with his condition, inviting me to bear witness to his violent wartime death, permanently etching the image of his final moment into my own brain.

"This one's for the guys in the cutting room," Wilson said with a snide half smile. He put his camera on the ground a few feet from the dead soldier, focused the lens, and, with the picture frame filled with the soldier's brains, rolled film for almost a minute. "They'll never use the shot," he said, "but it'll sure as hell fuck up their lunch." Wilson laughed. His eyes were narrow slits.

Vo Huynh filmed the bodies, rolling a few feet on each, then stood back and studied them. '*North Vietnam* soldier,' he said in a soft gruff voice just above a whisper. 'People's Army. This PAVN soldier.'

It was soon apparent to everyone—the Rangers, their American advisers, and the journalists—that the Vietnamese troops who launched the ambush were not the usual guerrilla fighters drawn from the local population and armed with captured ARVN weapons. Nor were they a unit of Viet Cong mixed with North Vietnamese trainers and support personnel like those who fought the 101st Airborne a few weeks earlier in Happy Valley. These were regular soldiers from the People's Army of Vietnam, part of a well-organized, thoroughly trained regiment commanded by veterans of the war of independence against France. It was one of the first times in the war, perhaps *the* first, that a regular infantry unit of the North Vietnamese Army was fully engaged in combat in the South. It was a big story, though none of us— journalists or military—understood the full implications. American forces were deploying in Vietnam expecting to fight a guerrilla war against units from the south, not North Vietnam. We had been using the terms "PAVN" and "VC" interchangeably, as if the difference was not important.

The Ranger column reached the road. Provincial Route 5 was a narrow strip of hard red dirt wide enough for a single vehicle, an unpaved backwoods track. It had not been used for months, maybe years, and was overgrown on both sides by aggressive jungle, now shredded, scorched and wilted by battle fire. The road was empty in both directions, no sign of the armored column.

A debate began over what to do. Lieutenant Brady suggested moving down the road and linking up with the ARVN task force to make a combined unit. Colonel Phuoc said his battalion was not moving anywhere; the task force could come to him if it wished. Wilson said, 'Fuck 'em. Why don't we just walk down the road till we find the tanks? They can't be that far.'

The six reporters started down the road. Vo Huynh and Robin Mannock took point, followed by Wilson and Hoan with the camera and sound gear, then Charlie Mohr and me in the rear. Each pair was spaced about ten yards apart. It was an odd patrol: half a squad of civilian journalists—three Americans, two Vietnamese and an Englishman—walking through an active war zone with barely any protection. Wilson was wearing a new pistol on his belt and Mohr had one in his pack for emergencies—no match for one soldier with an automatic weapon. A hundred yards down the road, surrounded by heavy brush and cut off from contact with friendly troops, I realized how wildly reckless this little patrol of ours actually was. Armed with a couple of pistols but without a radio or map or signal flare or even a first aid kit, we had put ourselves in a most dangerous place—in the midst of no-man's-land hours after a major battle. The possibility of meeting North Vietnamese stragglers from the fight was real. Mouths dry, sweating hard, we walked several hundred yards along the road, our eyes watching the sides. The constant buzz of insects was the only sound. Mannock turned and called in a stage whisper, 'I hope we don't need one of your bloody miracles, Laurence.'

Up ahead, Vo Huynh called out in Vietnamese. ARVN soldiers stood in the road. We had arrived at the point of the armored column. The Vietnamese soldiers stood in the road as relaxed as weekend campers. No security was out.

The armored troops had arranged the bodies of North Vietnamese killed in the battle in rows along both sides of the road. The lifeless forms wrapped in the bloody cloth of their uniforms looked like sacks of refuse awaiting collection. The South Vietnamese were in a jubilant mood, standing with pride around their tanks and armored cars, glancing at the fly-covered bodies stretched out in the sun. They laughed and smiled and chattered to one another, touching each other's arms and hands, joking, expressing the relief they felt after nearly losing their lives.

The commander of the armored task force was a jovial South Vietnamese lieutenant colonel named Nguyen Luat who welcomed the six reporters and introduced us to his U.S. advisers. I shook hands and wrote down the names of Paul Leckinger, 32, a captain from Rochester, New York; Lieutenant Brady Thompson, adviser to the tank troops; First Lieutenant Stewart Sherard, 26, of Marshall, Missouri; and Captain John Bates. There were others. Standing in a circle, they told us the story of what happened.

"They ran right over us," said Leckinger, who had been at the rear of the convoy with the supply trains.

'We got caught just before sundown. I looked real quick at my watch and it was 5:45. They were dug in close along the road, maybe twenty-five meters. Must have been two, three companies in our sector alone, maybe more. Brave little fuckers.'

'Did you see that guy on the antiaircraft gun? Shooting at our planes?' another of the advisers said. 'Now that sonofabitch had *balls.*'

The reporters gathered around the Americans and wrote down their words. The other advisers nodded in agreement and added their own comments.

'The VC had all kinds of heavy stuff, .50-cals and 57 mill.'

'The whole length of the column was covered, at least two clicks. I mean, that's one helluva long ambush.'

'The ARVN were riding on top of their tanks and APCs, just as exposed as they could be. I told them to keep buttoned up but they wouldn't listen. When the shit started they went down like ducks in a shooting gallery.'

'The PAVN cut the column in two places, had us surrounded for a while. They completely overran the trains. Blew away the two howitzers and most of the trucks. The Air Force saved our ass. God bless those pilots. I could feel the heat of the napalm going in on the other side of the road. Yeah, I heard on the radio they lost a couple of planes. Hope the pilots got out. Jesus, what a mess.'

The reporters asked what the casualties were and the advisers said they figured them at about thirty, maybe thirty-five ARVN killed, approximately 106 North Vietnamese killed.

'You can't tell for sure,' one said, 'because they carried most of their dead and all of the wounded away with them.'

'The ARVN fought well. Man, you don't beat off a whole North Vietnamese regiment every day. But a lot of our infantry back with the trains bugged out, just panicked when the shit got heavy and took off. Probably turn up in Pleiku in a few days.'

With the contact broken everyone was relaxed. Air Force cargo planes flew over the task force and dropped ammunition and other supplies by parachute. A helicopter landed with senior officers from Pleiku and several more journalists. Mohr of the *Times* got on it and went back to Pleiku to file his story. Wilson, Hoan and I decided to stay, along with Vo Huynh and Robin Mannock. Our objective had not changed. We were trying to get to the Special Forces camp at Plei Me. Wilson pointed out that we had been in the field for two days without getting combat footage. We'd been too far away from the action.

'I'm gonna run out of juice for the batteries pretty soon,' he warned.

A young clean-shaven reporter for an American newsmagazine came in on the helicopter from Pleiku and joined the group. New in-country, he wore a fresh pair of fatigues and was red-faced from the sun. This, he said, was his first time in the field. He was about my own age so I shook hands and filled him in on the details of the ambush. (I had not developed an antipathy to newcomers.) Lieutenant Colonel Luat announced that the task force would spend another night on the road before pushing on to Plei Me. He ordered his tanks and APCs to gather in a tight circle with their guns pointed out toward the darkening bush, like wagon trains in the Old West. Wilson, Hoan, the magazine reporter and I found a secure spot in a shallow dip in the ground behind an armored personnel carrier and made camp. The sun drifted behind the hill where we had watched the battle the night before.

Without warning, gunfire exploded everywhere, wild unrestrained shooting—tank cannons, machineguns, automatic rifles, grenade launchers, small arms—catching us completely off guard. We threw ourselves on the ground and tried to make ourselves small, burrowing in the dry dirt with our fingernails. The suddenness and intensity of the noise was terrifying. *How could the North Vietnamese sneak up on us so quietly?* Soldiers in the APC in front of us were firing the .50-caliber machinegun on top with wild abandon, blazing into the semidarkness, throwing hot empty shell casings down on the ground and across our necks and backs. There was no cover. The heavy iron door on the back of the APC swung shut with a loud *clank* and someone inside bolted it. Unable to shoot film in the dim light, Wilson was useless. Hoan tried to curl into a tiny ball in the dirt, his arms over his head. The gunfire created an ear-splitting eruption of sharp rapid-fire noises that broke the air all at the same time in continuous explosions. It was worse than a rifle range without ear protectors. The noise was suffocating. It was too loud to think.

The magazine reporter crawled to the back of the APC and pounded on the iron door with his fists. "Let me in! Please let me in!" he screamed. Nothing happened. He beat his hands against the locked steel, "Oh, God, will you please let me in!" Crying into the storm of noise from the guns, "Please, God, let me in!" his voice came from the depths of a broken spirit, pleading for admittance to the sanctuary of the APC and away from the assault on his senses. The door remained shut.

As suddenly as it started, the shooting stopped. Everything was silent. My hearing was gone. All I could hear was a shrill internal sound pitched higher than any musical note I had ever heard, a long continuous one-note echo of the gunfire *eeeeeeeeeeeeeeeeeeeeeeeeeeeeeee*. The magazine reporter fell back from the door of the APC and sobbed with his face in his hands. Wilson looked up and said, 'What the fuck was that?' and checked his camera for damage. Hoan held his head. Then a radio squawked. The back door of the APC swung open and a cheerful Vietnamese soldier poked out his head and looked at us smiling and said, "Mad minute!"

It had been make-believe, of no importance. All the gunfire had been outgoing. No one had warned us about a mad minute, a planned round of free-fire mayhem, shooting wildly into the brush around the armored laager to flush any PAVN who might be sneaking up to attack the task force. There had been no return fire. The North Vietnamese were long and far gone.

The magazine reporter trembled. His face was a mess of tears and snot and dirt. I felt sorry for him. He had changed from a confident rosy-faced young man working for an important American publication into a pale

whimpering boy, like a beaten child. I fumbled in my pack for the flask and
gave him a drink of cognac. It took him a long time to regain his composure.
After a while, still nervous, he said, 'This isn't my scene. I've got to get out of
here. I'm not cut out for this.'

'Don't worry,' I said. 'You'll be all right,' not knowing what else to say.
'We were all scared.' It was true. Even Wilson had shown his fear.

Wilson turned his back and ignored him.

The magazine reporter, whose name was Bill, didn't realize that he had as
much courage as any of us. Forcing himself to come into the field and face
combat with the degree of fear he was carrying was more than the rest of us
might have been able to do. Once he had been in it, though, he discovered
that his tolerance was lower than ours, that's all.

OCTOBER 25, 1965

The next day on the road to Plei Me, Wilson balanced on the bouncing hull of an armored personnel carrier and rolled film on the task force commander. Lieutenant Colonel Luat was a heavy square-faced man in his mid-forties with a thick neck and weathered skin that was worn and wrinkled as the leather of an old baseball glove. His command track was an open-top American M-113 armored personnel carrier fitted with a late-model radio communications package that squawked and hissed with the chatter of Vietnamese and American officers in the convoy. The cargo hold of the APC was stacked with crates of machinegun and rifle ammunition, grenades, C ration food, water, cases of beer, and a living room easy chair fixed to the floor of the hold for the colonel to sit in. Luat barked orders into his field radio one minute, then joked casually with his American advisers and journalists the next. Wilson filmed sparingly, trying to save his battery. Luat sat on the cushioned chair in the middle of the lurching APC and drank from a dusty bottle of Bierre Larue, a rancid honey-yellow liquid that came in large brown bottles and was known with some legitimacy by Western reporters as "the beer that kills." The colonel sipped continually from the one-liter bottle, and as the day went on, his eyes became cloudy and moist. Speaking English and Vietnamese in a loud voice from his makeshift throne in the hold of the APC, Lieutenant Colonel Luat bounced merrily along on the road to Plei Me like a potentate at the center of his realm.

In the afternoon, the sun bore down on the open track and made the exposed metal body of the machine too hot to touch. Luat reached up with his half-filled bottle of beer and offered it to me. I took a swig of the warm sudsy liquid, recognized the taste of formaldehyde, and swallowed hard. Luat watched my eyes lose focus and fill with fluid and my upper body shake for a second. He laughed hard from his stomach and reached to take the bottle back. Within a minute I felt a pleasant sense of relief from the tensions of the past two days and hoped for another drink, but the bottle was not offered again.

One of the American advisers said that Luat wanted to abandon the mission to relieve Plei Me and return to Pleiku but was ordered to keep going by General Vinh Loc. The camp was less than five miles away and the chance of a second ambush was unlikely. Luat sent his infantry ahead of the column and held his fighting armor in reserve near the rear. An American adviser pointed out that tanks should go closer to the front of an armored task force so they can absorb the punishment of an attack if one came, maneuver swiftly into fighting position, and spearhead a counterattack in force. Colonel Luat believed otherwise. His tanks went at the rear. Some of the American advisers wondered about the wisdom of such a deployment.

The column stopped while an air strike was called on a copse of trees ahead. When the bombing was done, a troop of APCs drove up the line to the front of the task force and opened fire on the woods with machineguns and M-79s, blasting the empty bush for fifteen minutes.

'What's going on?' I asked an American officer.

'Recon by fire,' he said and paused. 'Waste of good ammo if you ask me.' No fire was returned.

Near sundown, two full days after being ambushed on the road, the long armored column arrived outside the gates of Plei Me Special Forces Camp. The drivers gunned the powerful diesel engines of their tanks and APCs. The engines roared, transmission gears whined, and smoke belched from the exhausts. The drivers smiled proudly, showing off their prowess with the tracks like tough veteran fighters, wheeling the mighty armor into a defense line near the north point of the perimeter. Dust swirled off the road in big reddish brown clouds and rose high into the air, signaling for miles that the cavalry had arrived.

Inside the camp, battle-tired Montagnard and Vietnamese soldiers waved their green and black camouflage bush hats and yellow bandannas, shouting at the arriving troops in hoarse high-pitched cheers, their voices gone. After six days, they were saved. Jarai women and children stood with the men by the wire in ragged dirt-covered clothes and stared at the arriving column with looks of relief on their small dark faces.

The camp was built on several acres of dry iron-red dirt and scrub in the valley of a high plateau. Full green hills and ridges rose around it. A disused dirt airstrip lay outside the southern boundary of the camp. On the other side of the airstrip, fresh water flowed through a meandering rivulet. Beyond that were low hills where senior PAVN officers could survey the battlefield. The camp formed a large triangle, menacing in appearance, protected by a perimeter of wood and sandbagged bunkers, gun emplacements, and several rows of coiled, waist-high barbed wire. Strong points with heavy machine-guns were placed at each of the three corners of the triangle and were rein-forced with concentric rows of trenches, bunkers, sandbags and other fortifications. Inside, the camp was organized into sections for living quarters, mortar pits, an ammo dump, a first aid station, kitchen, mess hall, truck park and more bunkers. The American sector had a deep underground concrete shelter, stores, communications bunker and a barracks. All the surfaces of the camp were covered with fine layers of powdered red dirt and black dust. The smell in the air was of smoke, gunpowder, rotting garbage and decomposing bodies. Plei Me was a fortress, a lethal end-of-the-world killing station. After six days of siege, the little outpost on the frontier of the Southeast Asian wilderness was near the critical points of exhaustion and collapse.

Colonel Luat strode with purpose to the entrance of the camp, his stout chin was pushed forward, his shoulders squared, his back straight. He carried a leather swagger stick in the style of the French colonial army. Luat was met in the road outside the gate by the senior American officer, a scowling Special Forces major who wore camouflage black and green battle dress with a bush hat several sizes too small that made his head bigger and more intimidating. The major, whose name was Charlie A. Beckwith, shook hands with Colonel Luat and thanked him for coming to the camp's defense. What he was actually thinking at the time, Beckwith recalled later, was, *Where the hell have you all been? Should have been here a couple of days ago when we needed you.*

With polite formality, Luat said that he was going to bring his command staff and some of his infantry into the camp. He wanted a safe place to bivouac. The armor would remain outside.

'No,' Beckwith said, shaking his head. 'I'm afraid you can't bring your people inside.'

'What?' said Luat, incredulous. 'Of course we go into this camp! It is safer for us. We must to go into this camp!'

'Sorry, Colonel,' said Beckwith in his flat southern monotone. 'There's no God damn room. You and your people can camp here on the plain.'

Luat was furious. He began to shout, first in Vietnamese, then in French, then English. '*Merde! I* am senior officer here. *I* say who go in camp and who do not.'

Luat paused to catch his breath, staring into the American's face.

'If you do not obey order,' he said, 'I shoot you.'

Beckwith did not react. Behind him, three tall foul-smelling American soldiers stood in filthy tiger-stripe fatigues open down their chests with long hairy arms hanging slack by their sides and holding M-16s and an AK-47. In the same instant Luat said, 'I shoot you,' the eyes of the soldiers dilated to cold black marbles. Without looking down or moving more than their thumbs they slid the selector switches on their rifles off safe and onto automatic. Reporters who had been taking notes next to Beckwith and Luat looked up from their notebooks and stepped back out of the line of fire. Beckwith did not blink. The soldiers behind him did not move. No one spoke. Seconds passed. Colonel Luat turned without speaking and walked in a rolling waddle back to the armored column and his command track.

Beckwith took a breath. He noticed the group of journalists as if for the first time with an expression of contempt.

'I don't know what all *you* fucking people are doing here,' he said, 'cause I sure as hell didn't ask for you.' His voice growled in a low rasp that had the texture of sandpaper on stone. 'I need the God damn press in here as much as I need a dose of the clap.' A cold blue vein stood out on his hard-boned forehead.

'And I do *not* want you getting in the God damn way. As far as I'm concerned you're just tits on a bull.' He turned to walk away, reconsidered, and turned back.

'Now that you're here you better get one thing straight,' he barked. 'Every damn one of you is gonna help defend this camp. Is that clear? You're gonna stand watch like everybody else. Take your turn on the perimeter.' He turned again, halfway, as if speaking to himself. 'I'll use anybody I can get. God damn reporters or not.'

No one spoke. The three soldiers behind him stepped back for Beckwith to pass. His face was peppered with short black whiskers and his eyes were red burning coals throwing heat.

Beckwith turned to the group and spoke again, this time in a softer voice, almost politely, 'So you people might as well come inside and share what we have. It ain't much. Just keep your God damn heads down. I don't wanna lose *another* fucking reporter.' He turned and walked through the front gate into the camp and the journalists followed.

Charlie Beckwith was hard, hard as a woodpecker's teeth as they say in his native Georgia, a full-blooded professional warrior. Tall, broad-shoul-dered, strong, his physical appearance intimidated all but the most coura-geous or foolhardy. He was two hundred pounds and six feet two when he stood up straight, though that was not often. Usually he was hunched over at the shoulders like some large predator man-beast. It was his overwhelming intensity, his unshakable self-will that made his presence so dominating. His small red eyes sat far inside a long bony forehead that protruded above his nose and ended with a ridge of dense black eyebrows. The nose was long and sharp and peaked at the end where the nostrils flared. With Beckwith looking closely into your face, you had the impression of being watched by a hawk.

He was born in 1929 in Atlanta to hardworking Baptist parents who owned three trucks and made a living delivering gasoline for the Pure Oil Company. His father died when he was eleven years old and after that his mother raised him alone. He was an enthusiastic Boy Scout and entered the ROTC program at the University of Georgia where he studied physical edu-cation on a football scholarship. He played guard but not well enough for the first team. Much of his time at school, he admitted, was spent playing pool with his friends and trying to seduce women. When he was twenty-two years old, he joined the Army and was commissioned an officer. He com-manded a rifle company in Korea at the end of that war. In 1958, Beckwith joined the Special Forces and served fifteen months in Malaysia with the British Army's Special Air Service, which pioneered counterinsurgency war-fare. The jungles of northern Malaysia were so rugged, Beckwith said, they made the terrain in Vietnam seem like a piece of cake.

He was thirty-five years old and a major by the time he got to Vietnam in the summer of 1965. He took command of Detachment B-52, Project Delta, a long-range reconnaissance and reaction force that conducted clan-destine operations in Vietnam, Laos and Cambodia. Delta was designed to provide tactical military intelligence for the U.S. Army and CIA, and also to reinforce Special Forces A camps like Plei Me when they were attacked in strength.

On Wednesday, October 20, the morning after the attack on Plei Me began, Beckwith was ordered to organize a reaction force of American and South Vietnamese troops to relieve the camp. He arrived in Pleiku by air later that day with fourteen U.S. Special Forces soldiers and two companies of ARVN paratroopers, about two hundred men who were trained as Special Forces, the Vietnamese acronym being LLDB. Thursday morning, October 21, Beckwith's force landed by helicopter eight and a half miles north of Plei Me in difficult terrain.

"We came to a village about seven clicks en route and it was totally vacant," Beckwith told me later. "The smoke from the fires was still going and we all realized this whole village was abandoned. So what the hell's going on here? That sort of bothered the Vietnamese who were with me. They became very uneasy with this and we moved very slowly. We wanted to keep our presence unknown to anyone.

"Then all of a sudden two North Vietnamese soldiers . . . stumbled directly into our column. They were shot. One of them had an AK-47 and the other one had two 75 millimeter recoilless rifle rounds under his arm. One got away and one got killed there. This scared the hell out of the Vietnamese with me. These were Vietnamese Special Forces—LLDB. They went through all (the enemy) documentation and Major Thut—I was supposed to be his adviser—told me that this was the 88th NVA Regiment. These guys were from there, dressed in khakis, had on an NVA belt buckle. The Vietnamese said they weren't going to go any further, they were going to stop right there. They were scared. I said, 'Bullshit. We're going to press on.' And we had a bit of conflict and I said, 'I'm going to take these fourteen Americans and we're going to go ahead.' And so we did.

"We moved on until nine o'clock and stopped to make radio contact with the camp," Beckwith continued. "We were about a half mile from the camp itself. It was dark and I was very comfortable with that. I made radio contact with them and I was very discouraged when I got a radio message from the camp, 'Come on in and join the party.' That made me very uncomfortable because, based on what I was hearing and reports received, there'd been a lot of people hurt there and I didn't consider that to be a God damn 'party.' I was talking to the team sergeant. He really pissed me off when he said to come in and join the party. Made me very, very angry.

"About that time here comes the Vietnamese. They'd been following way behind, unbeknownst to us. Needless to say, I was glad they'd decided to come with us. The area we'd just covered with fourteen Americans—we'd taken a lot of risks and we knew what the risks were, and if something had happened we'd have been in serious trouble. We didn't have enough people. So I was glad to see the Vietnamese there.

"I could hear the firing from the camp. So I called back to the camp and said, 'We're not going to come in tonight because, number one, I'm afraid you'll shoot me up. And with the attitude you all got I'm not coming in there tonight. I'm going to wait and come in first thing in the morning.'

"As soon as first light came—I think it was 5:15, you could see—we began to move. We moved toward Plei Me until we came to the last little knoll where I could see the camp. So I said, 'Let's move over, get on this road, and let's run as fast as we can to get into the camp.'

"We took some fire going in and we had one photographer killed, shot right through the side of the face, killed him. I don't remember his name. He had long blond hair and my sergeant major kept telling him, 'If you don't keep your hat on you're going to get porked.' And, as fate would have it, he had his hat off and he was running down the road, and about halfway to the camp he got shot right through the face.

"When I got to the camp a number of Montagnards were still laying in the wires, laying out there and nobody'd gone out to pick them up. A lot of dead people laying around there. I immediately said to myself, *there's a lack of discipline in this camp*. So, the first thing I made clear when we'd got everybody in there, that I was the law and order of this here camp.

"When I met the commander, Captain [Harold H.] Moore, I asked him, 'What's the situation here?' And he didn't answer well. He said, 'Well you can see we're surrounded. Got everybody around us.' And I didn't like that. And I said, 'Shit, if that's the case then what are all these dead people laying up here in the wire? If you're going to run a camp like this then it would appear to me that you aren't prepared for an attack. If they do attack, they're going to wipe you out. So let's get this God damn thing sorted out!'

"I told him, 'I'm here now and I am in charge. I am the mayor of Plei Me. You and your guys are gonna fall in line and respond to what we have to say. *You will respond!*' Wasn't a word said. And we began to clean it up and make sure everything was proper, make it so the people on the perimeter had enough ammunition, that they would pull the trigger, that all the fields of fire were covered. Then I began to realize we could be hit pretty bad in there (and survive). I didn't worry about it."

Beckwith said the friction with Captain Moore continued. As commander of the American garrison at Plei Me when the attack began, Moore's courage was not in doubt. During the early fighting, he led a three-man patrol outside the perimeter to try and rescue the crew of an American helicopter that had been shot down nearby. First Sergeant Joseph Bailey of Lebanon, Tennessee, was shot and killed during the rescue attempt. Moore's valor was in vain. When he got to the chopper, all four American crew members were dead.

Leadership in the camp was the problem. "I had to get physical with the captain one time," Beckwith said. "I gave him one push and that was to get him down into a bunker during an air strike. Maybe I saved his life, I don't know. He wanted to take a picture of an air strike and I felt that was poor judgment. We were bringing air in at one hundred or two hundred yards. Eventually he did get hit with a piece of shrapnel from taking a picture of an air strike."

Moore was evacuated by helicopter. Of the original nine Americans at the camp, six were killed or wounded. Beckwith imposed his will on the remaining troops with fierce authority. On Saturday, just outside the camp, he was leading two platoons of camp defenders when a solitary North Vietnamese soldier holding a hand grenade charged directly into the middle of the group. The Vietnamese scattered immediately. 'Like scared chickens,' Beckwith said. Other American soldiers reported that Beckwith stood where he was and fired seven shots from his M-16 at the North Vietnamese, killing him. "Now that was a *real soldier*," Beckwith said, praising his victim.

The journalists from the armored relief column followed Beckwith through the gate and dropped their packs outside the American teamhouse —a long wooden building with an enclosed courtyard at one end and a four-foot-high log and sandbag palisade around it. The teamhouse was the Americans' living quarters and entrance to their underground command bunker. The courtyard at the end was about twenty feet wide and seemed safe from anything but a direct hit. A pile of brightly colored parachutes left over from aerial resupply drops lay on the ground.

'You can sleep here,' Beckwith said.

'Anywhere I can get some juice for my batteries?' Wilson said, looking around.

Beckwith thought for a moment. 'Yeah, maybe you can. Come take a look at our generator,' he said. Beckwith, Wilson and Hoan walked through the door of the teamhouse and disappeared.

Simon Dring knelt down and arranged his pack in a corner of the courtyard, propping it against the wall for safety, spreading several layers of nylon parachutes out for a bed. Dring—the tall, thin English reporter for Reuters—

wore his usual tailored combat fatigues, pistol belt and boots. He was one of a group of print journalists who had arrived on a medevac helicopter from Pleiku a few hours earlier. Charles Mohr of the *New York Times*, Martin Stuart-Fox, a young Australian reporter for UPI, Joseph Galloway of UPI and Robert Poos of the Associated Press had managed to get in on the same medevac. Seeing them in the camp when we arrived, the rest of us felt uncomfortably late. After three days and two nights in the field, we had lost the race to get to the camp by a few hours. Although we had the story of the ambush along the road, Dring, Mohr, Stuart-Fox, Galloway and Poos were ahead with firsthand details of the more important story, the siege of Plei Me. We were forced to play catch-up. Mohr had managed to file a brief story of the ambush when he was in Pleiku, the first eyewitness account of the battle by a journalist. Although they had been in the camp for only a short time, the other journalists saw us as outsiders trying to take over their territory.

Robin Mannock of the AP walked into the camp and was greeted by Dring, his fellow countryman and wire service rival. Dring wore an expression of smug superiority.

'Robin, old chap! What took you so long?' he exclaimed.

'Bloody convoy got ambushed down the road. Bit sticky. Good story though. One or two nice snaps.'

Dring frowned.

'Have you been here long?' Mannock said casually.

"Simply *ages*, my dear fellow. *Ages*."

I asked one of the Special Forces soldiers if there was somewhere I could go to sit and write for a few minutes. 'Yeah, follow me,' he said. He got up and led me down the corridor of the teamhouse, the single-story barracks built on a log frame with thatched bamboo walls and thin wire mesh screens for windows to let the air in.

'You can bunk here for now,' he said, opening the door to a room off the corridor. 'He ain't gonna need it.'

Inside the room was a narrow bed with a mattress covered by a poncho liner and enclosed by mosquito netting. The bed was unmade and dusty and had not been slept in for days. A gray military-issue table stood against one wall with letters, writing materials and a months-old magazine on it. Other furnishings were a folding garden chair with brightly colored webbing, a large faded green footlocker, an ashtray made from the empty brass casing

of a howitzer shell, and color photographs carefully cut from glossy magazines and fastened to the walls to display young American women in seductive poses revealing their large proud breasts and perfect pink buttocks. All
the furnishings, including the mosquito netting and pinup pictures, were
pocked or punctured by small holes from bullets and shrapnel that had
ripped through the room and shredded the thin bamboo walls. There was
one exception. The dress uniform of a U.S. Army sergeant E-7, green beret
and all, hung immaculately on the wall behind the door still wrapped in plastic from a dry cleaning shop somewhere far away. The clean well-tailored
symbol of Army pride and achievement looked totally out of place in the
damage and filth of Plei Me, like a museum costume from the dimly recalled
culture of an alien civilization. Fine red powder from dirt pulverized by
explosions and blown through the window screens lay like a veil over all the
objects in the dead sergeant's room.

I sat at the table and made notes for a radio report. (I had replaced the
expensive Nagra tape recorder lost in the sea with a lightweight Stellavox.)
When I finished, I walked down the corridor and out the door at the far end
of the teamhouse. The last of the daylight was fading. Some of the Special
Forces soldiers were gathered in an open area just outside the door of the
teamhouse. Most of them were big men who, like Beckwith, seemed to
resent the presence of journalists but were also fascinated by them. Their
cold hostile looks made me uncomfortable. A few of them sat on wooden
ammunition crates and hard cloth bags of dirt that littered the camp, smoking and talking among themselves in short clipped sentences that were
heavy with sarcasm and an attitude that went beyond anger or irony. Their
faces were streaked with powdered dirt and sweat that had dried into a rich
cake the color of copper. No one had washed or shaved for days. The black
and green tiger stripe fatigues they wore were torn and smudged with dirt
and their hands were black with grime that ran across the backs of their
hands and covered their fingernails so that only the worn palms showed the
pink flesh, like coal miners at the end of day.

I asked if any of them had been in the camp since the beginning of the
attack, six nights before, and one of them said, 'Yeah, there's three of us left.'

'Ask me where I'd rather have been,' another one said.

'Let me guess,' another said and they all laughed.

They were surprised at my interest in what had happened to them. I
asked them their names and wrote them in my notebook: Master Sergeant

Everett Hamby, 37, Fayetteville, North Carolina; Staff Sergeant Cornelius
Clark, 27, Akron, Ohio; Private First Class Eugene Tafoya, 29, Albuquerque,
New Mexico. Tafoya had a thin mustache and goatee that was growing into
a beard and paratroop wings sewn above the name tag on the right breast of
his fatigues, a combat infantryman's badge on the left. His round fleshy face
bunched up into a smile and he spoke in a soft voice.

The soldiers appeared to be at the edge of exhaustion.

'Since the first night,' one said, 'the VC hit us with every fucking thing
they had—mortars, machineguns, 57 mike-mikes, RPGs, small arms, Chicom
grenades, sniper fire, you name it.'

'It was a shitstorm, man, a nonstop storm of shit.'

'When the gooks got to the wire they set off bangalores, you know, to
blow holes in it. We just kept shooting the little bastards down off of it.'

'You wouldn't *believe* how fuckin crazy they was.'

"If they'd a' had air strikes they'd a' hit us with them, too," one said.

'Did you think you might not make it?' I asked.

'Hell, no. We was too fucking *busy* to think about makin it or not. Too
busy tryin to get these fucking Vietn'ese off their ass to fight. Little pissant
cowards.'

'No time to worry about makin it.'

'Once you *think* you're done for, you're done for, you know what I mean?
That's when you're finished. You think you're done for, might as well kiss
your sorry ass good-bye then and there.'

'Well, I don't know about y'all, but I ain't afraid to say I had my doubts
once or twice, 'specially that first night. No two ways about it. They come
mighty fucking close to gettin *in* here.'

'I never seen anybody take so much shit and keep comin at us.'

'The Air Force is what saved us.'

'Fuckin a.'

'You better believe.'

'They put that nape right in next to the wire. I mean right *on* it. You could
feel the heat. Give me a sunburn, I swear.'

'Yeah, gave the gooks more than that. *Fried* their fuckin rice.'

There had been no incoming for several hours. Listening to the soldiers
talk—as much to each other as to me—I got a sense of how fearsome it had
been, how physically punishing, what hard work it had been to hold the
camp. Now that the worst was over, they found some humor in it.

'They had a system, see, like a rotation,' one of the men said. 'First the flare ship comes over and lights us up. Then the VC range in and pop mortars on us. Then the FAC comes over and takes a look. Then the gooks get down in their holes. Then the pilots drop all kinds of bad shit on them and go back to Bien Hoa and have a cold beer. Then the Cav puts arty on 'em for a while. Then it's quiet for a minute or two. And then the whole thing starts all over again.'

'And we don't get no fuckin sleep, night or day.'

'Shit, man, enough to give ya a headache.'

They were angry and tired, exhausted by the uninterrupted emergency of combat alert and the physical strain of fighting to survive, running through the camp trenches as another NVA assault came at the wire, popping their heads up long enough to fire a clip and then take cover, moving on, wondering if the VC were inside, looking for targets, helping to bandage the wounded, leading by example, trying to get the Montagnards to shoot, screaming at them over the noise, *'Get your fucking head outta your ass and fight!'*

And when air strikes came in all they could do was get down and pray, *'Godalmighty don't let that shit fall on me,'* fight and stop, dry mouth and sweat, move on, fight and rest, out of breath, pop Dexedrine when the adrenaline ran down and wait for the speed hit that made everything so edgy and weird, their breath coming in short little bursts so they could barely breathe the cordite air, feel the alternating mix of heart-pounding fear, anger and fatigue until the day ran into the night and back into day again, brains so disoriented by lack of rest they could not think clearly, and everything they did operated by pure conditioned reflex the way it was supposed to.

Two haggard, bad-smelling soldiers sat quietly by themselves outside the teamhouse, their shoulders hunched, looking out of hollow unfocused eyes suggesting stages of combat fatigue and depression that made the prospect of a killing wound seem like no more than the next indignity.

'God, I don't know if I can hack it back there,' one of them said.

'Stateside?'

'Yeah.'

'Yeah, I know, be kinda boring.'

'Naw, not that. Won't be boring enough.'

Wilson came up the stairs out of the deep communications bunker next to the teamhouse, smiling. 'Got the batteries charging off the generator,' he said. 'Should have some juice by morning.' He and P. B. Hoan followed a

Special Forces major named A. J. (Bo) Baker to one of the corners of the camp to learn how to operate the heavy machinegun.

'Got me a couple of candidates for the heavy weapons squad,' Baker said, smiling at the others.

'Make sure they got plenty of bennies,' one of them said.

'Hey, TV man! Not this way, understand what I'm saying?'

Without his camera on his shoulder, Wilson was more like a soldier than a civilian. His imposing size, gun belt, beard, cowboy hat and cigar made him one of them in appearance as well as attitude. Unable to take pictures at night, he and Hoan had decided to become participants in the story they were covering. A few minutes later, several short bursts from the machinegun sounded. Then one long hissing rattle of fire after which Wilson cried, 'Eeeeeeeeee-haawwwww!' his voice echoing into the jungle. He and Hoan stood watch behind the .50-caliber all night.

It was dark now and a line of Montagnard soldiers walked past the teamhouse on their way to the main gate to go to a listening post outside the wire. Beckwith went by carrying a radio and said, 'I'll take the other end of the teamhouse for the night. Might get some sleep. If anything happens I'll know it. Give me a radio check in a minute.' His communications officer, Major Charles Thompson, sat on a stack of sandbags with the handsets of two radios hissing softly in his hands and nodded his head. Thompson, of Morristown, Tennessee, was a quiet dark-skinned man in his mid-thirties with a broad African nose. He was executive officer in Beckwith's command, the number two. His job was to monitor radio traffic in and around the camp so that he and Beckwith knew what was going on at all times. The arrival of the armored column with its several different units and American advisers with radios made Thompson's work of keeping in touch with them on their different frequencies complicated.

A mortar tube popped. A few seconds later a flare ignited in the sky.

Beckwith's voice called on the radio, 'How d'ya read me, Tommy?'

"Two-two-two," said Thompson.

"What?"

"Two-two-two."

"That bad, huh?"

"Yeah. Too *loud*, too *clear*, too *aw-ful*."

Everyone who heard it laughed, including Beckwith.

Thompson, Charlie Mohr and I sat with some of the men who drifted back and forth from their fighting positions to the teamhouse, talking softly in the light of the flares that fell over the camp and the surrounding plain.

'You wouldn't believe some of the shit that's been coming over the radio, I'm telling you,' said Thompson.

'Like what?'

Thompson was quiet for a few seconds, as if deciding whether to say any more.

'Like, well, last two days we've had dumb-ass requests from Pleiku to let Senator Edward Kennedy land here and take a look around. Do you believe that? A United States Senator wants to drop in on this shithole?'

'I heard he was in-country,' said Mohr.

'What's he doing, fuckin campaigning?' one of the men said.

'Can you imagine us trying to watch after his ass with all the shit flyin around here?' said Thompson. 'It'd be a nightmare.'

'Man, it's already a nightmare, my baddest fuckin dream ever.'

'Maybe he wants publicity.'

'Shit, man, he can have all the publicity he wants. All mister Teddy fuckin Kennedy has to do is take over the gun on the south wall a couple a nights.'

They all laughed. Someone lit a cigarette under his shirt and held the glowing end inside his cupped fist. A casual bottle of whisky was going around, no one drinking hard.

'I think they bugged out,' said Thompson. 'Now that we've got the armor. I don't think they want to mess with the tanks. They haven't thrown anything serious at us since this afternoon.'

Time passed.

A radio operator came up out of the bunker, looked around and said, 'You ain't gonna believe this.'

'What's that?' said Thompson.

'Nha Trang is up. Say the president's got a message for the old man.'

'Say again?'

'LBJ, man. He's got something to say to the fucking major. Oops. Sorry, major. I mean, Major Beckwith, sir.'

'Hold on,' said Thompson. 'The president of the United States wants the CO? To pass a message?'

'You got it, major. I think he wants a sit rep. Asap.'

Thompson sent the radioman down the corridor of the teamhouse to wake Beckwith, and a minute later the two of them appeared in the doorway.

'I don't fucking *believe* this,' said Beckwith, sleep-voiced.

'You'll believe in a minute,' said the radio operator.

'Hey, major, if LBJ wants a sit rep, tell him our ass is dragging,' one of the other men said. They laughed.

'I got better things to do than talk to that guy,' said Beckwith, growling.

Charlie Mohr, who had covered the White House and knew Lyndon Johnson personally, asked Beckwith to let him say hello. 'It'll really surprise him,' Mohr said, 'coming from out of nowhere.' He followed Beckwith down into the bunker. The rest of us waited. I envied Mohr for the story he was about to get, and his ability to write it without the need for film.

A half hour later they came out of the bunker. They had not spoken directly to the president, though Beckwith got a personal message from him.

'What it said was, something like, "We are all very concerned,"' said Beckwith. '"The American people are thinking about you and praying for you. God bless you. Hang on. Lyndon Baines Johnson." Ain't that something?'

'Jesus, who would've believed anybody cares about this place?' one of the soldiers said.

'It's a front page story,' said Mohr.

'Yeah, thanks to you guys.'

'Well, would you rather nobody knew what was happening?'

'That ain't what I meant.'

'Yeah, all them asshole civilians back home readin bout us gettin our asses shot at. Big fuckin deal. Smile and say, sorry bout that you guys. Keep your head down, you hear? And they's a crawlin into their nice warm bed with clean sheets and pillows and havin a nice ole piece of ass while they're at it. And us livin out here like fuckin animals. For what, man, I ask you? For a bunch of raggedy-ass slopes who won't even fight for their own country?'

'Shut your fucking mouth,' said Beckwith, growling. 'This is what we're getting paid for.' The words cut like shrapnel. Everyone was quiet.

Beckwith was impressed that the president of the United States went to the trouble to send him a message. When he thought about it, he suspected there was a more subtle message behind it. 'The real message,' he recalled later, 'was that the whole country is looking at us out here and we had better make sure we've got our act together.'

Hey boy, you got a big job! Beckwith thought. *When the president of the United States sends you a message, he's trying to tell you something. So don't screw up!*

I walked to the opposite end of the teamhouse and lay down on a parachute in the courtyard behind the palisade with the other reporters and went to sleep.

Late in the night, I woke up. The sky was clear. Flares fell every few minutes from a C-47 on station high above the camp. There was sporadic gunfire and the occasional crack of friendly artillery hitting the trees to the south and west. The noise of the shelling had become familiar. I heard scratching near my head and turned to see a large rat who gave me an evil look from a foot away. It was furry brown or black and fat around the waist, maybe seven or eight inches long, the size of a squirrel without a big tail. The rat twitched its nose and turned and scurried across the parachute beds of the sleeping journalists and disappeared.

Charlie Mohr was awake and smoking a Salem. He leaned over and whispered in his flat midwestern voice, 'Don't get bitten by one of them, Jack, or you'll get something awful.'

OCTOBER 26, 1965

Smoke floated over the camp and hung in the early morning mist rising out of the rainforest. The sun was above the tops of the trees and throwing heat, but there was no wind to move the wet white fog-smoke. Cooking fires flickered in dugouts along the perimeter where Vietnamese and Montagnard soldiers and their families heated soup for breakfast. A bonfire blazed up near the north wall where a soldier was burning empty shell canisters, garbage and human waste from the fragile wooden latrine that had taken a direct hit from a supply drop earlier in the fight and crushed one of the Montagnard soldiers to death. The ground of the camp was strewn with debris: bloody bandages, broken glass, empty ammo boxes, shell casings, odd M-16 rounds, metal stakes, smashed machinery, spools of wire, broken sandbags, splinters, parachute cord, C ration cans, cardboard, string, cigar butts. A layer of red grit covered everything in the camp. Except for distant irregular cracks of friendly artillery fire, it was quiet. The day was a Tuesday, the seventh day since the start of the attack.

There was no water to spare. Food was scarce. A huge metal cooking pot, big enough to stand in, rested on the floor of the teamhouse with a few inches of cold stale coffee at the bottom. American soldiers washed their feet in it. I took a can of C rations from my pack, opened it, and forced myself to chew the bland-tasting meat. After keeping watch with the machinegun all night, Wilson and Hoan slept late.

I walked through the camp. Montagnard families sat in sandbagged shelters along the perimeter. Men, women and children looked up and smiled as I walked past. Boys not yet in their teens wore makeshift battledress with yellow scarves around their necks and bush hats too big for their heads. Some had carbines they carried on shoulder straps muzzle down like their soldier-fathers. One of the boys, a slender kid with a rifle as big as he was, said he was eight years old, though his face looked older. Americans in the camp called him "John" and said he wasn't a bad soldier, that he had fired his weapon in the fight. Posing for pictures, the boys stood with their backs straight and stuck out their small chins with pride. Robin Mannock of the AP took a picture of a soldier and his wife sitting with their infant child in a fighting hole just behind the wire. The soldier held the sleeping baby in his arms and his wife held his rifle in her lap beside him.

Camp records showed that about 350 Montagnard troops along with about 100 of their family members had been stationed at Plei Me when the attack began. The soldiers were part of the Civilian Irregular Defense Group (CIDG), a paramilitary force created by the Saigon government to arm and train local people to resist VC control in areas where they lived. The Montagnards were commanded by a Vietnamese officer but he had no authority in the camp, partly because of antagonism between the races but also because the fighting soldiers did not respect him. The Vietnamese commander of Plei Me had not been seen since the battle began. Leadership of the camp had fallen to the nine U.S. Special Forces who were there when it started.

To American eyes, CIDG was not an organized fighting force. CIDG troops were motivated less by collective security than by individual self-interest. If that seemed to mean fighting, they fought. If it meant hiding, they hid. They did not ordinarily observe the discipline of organized team defense. Some were suspected of betrayal. When the assault on the camp began, a few of the CIDG troops were believed by the Americans to have opened fire on their own soldiers.

The stench coming from a low building in one sector of the camp was so strong everyone tried to avoid the area. Inside, more than thirty corpses were piled. The decomposing bodies were a health hazard. Major Beckwith growled, 'If it stays quiet, we'll get some choppers in here later today and haul them out to Pleiku where they can get a decent burial.'

When I got back to the teamhouse, Wilson and Hoan were awake. Wilson was proud they had stood watch all night with the machinegun. This morning, some of the American soldiers were more friendly to him and Hoan. Activity in the camp picked up. A work party was organized to go outside the wire and police the battlefield. Just over the knoll to the north, the ARVN armored column revved up to sweep the jungle south of the camp where the main North Vietnamese force had massed for the original attack. No one worried about meeting resistance.

★

'Let's go do a stand-up in front of the gate,' Wilson said. 'It'll make a nice shot with the tanks and stuff going by.'

By directive from New York, each story we did now required an on-camera open and close. Network producers said they wanted the option of using one or both of the stand-ups when they cut the film for broadcast. Sometimes they used none, a practice I favored. On-camera appearances still made me self-conscious and I had not given up my vow to avoid them when possible, but I obeyed this order. Wilson, Hoan and I walked outside the camp. Just beyond the main gate, a small orderly pile of stones supported a Vietnamese flag on a pole. It was a memorial to ARVN dead of the past week. The sign over the entrance to the camp read, TRAI PLEIME (CAMP PLEIME). The metal sign was punctured by small jagged holes. Another sign, just below it, was written in Vietnamese or Jarai. I asked Hoan what it said. He looked closely and said, 'It say, "Welcome to Visitors,"' but he wasn't sure. I tried to think of what to say in the stand-up that wouldn't be out of date in three or four days when the piece went on the air. Wilson showed me where to stand by the side of the road with the sign in the background. An APC rumbled toward us. Hoan handed me a microphone with the CBS logo, a black-and-white eye, clipped to it. Wilson balanced the camera on his shoulder, focused the lens and signaled me to start. I took a deep breath and looked at the camera lens.

"The sign says 'Welcome Visitors,' and the bullet holes are evidence of the six-day siege of Plei Me," I said. "Now, on the seventh day, the Special Forces camp is returning to normal. Reinforcements have arrived in strength."

As I finished speaking, an APC clattered through the frame. Wilson got shots of the armored task force rolling across the field and into the treeline to the south. The 22d Rangers, ordered into the forest by Colonel Luat, walked in loose formation with their carbines and BARs resting casually on their shoulders. A few of them looked at the camera and smiled.

'We're not gonna get any action,' Wilson said, 'so we might as well check out the perimeter and get some aftermath.' He set off in the lead looking for pictures with Hoan attached to the camera by the sound cable.

The battlefield along the north side of the camp was quiet. The ground was charred black and scarred with bomb craters, broken trees, barbed wire and collapsed trenches. Silent bodies lay in shell holes alongside abandoned weapons, ammunition cartridges, web belts, field packs, canteens, wallets with photographs inside of families and lovers, letters from home, long black socks filled with old sticky rice and cigarette packs from strange far-away places. All the arms and accoutrements of a living army lay on the bat-tlefield beside the soldiers who had carried them into the fight. Wicked-looking tail fins of unexploded mortar shells stuck half-buried out of the ground. Chunks of exploded shrapnel littered the landscape like dry autumn leaves.

A burial detail of CIDG soldiers picked up the bodies of the North Viet-namese dead from the trenches and carried them back to the camp in pon-chos. The bodies were burned black by the sun and napalm and were bloated with gas. A teenage boy with crow black hair lay on his back in an L-shaped trench. Canvas ammunition pouches for his rifle were strapped across his chest and an AK-47 with a shattered stock was on the ground beside him. His leather belt was punctured by holes the size of ten-penny nails where the bullets had gone into his stomach. His head and chest were not injured. It appeared he had not died immediately. One of his final physi-cal movements had been to cover his eyes with his left arm which lay folded over his face.

When Wilson finished the shot, I reached down and removed the brown leather belt from the soldier's waist. The buckle, a People's Army–issue brass fixture with a five-point star etched on it, was coveted by American sol-diers as a war trophy. Part of the clasp was broken off and the buckle was held in place with a piece of old string. I rolled it up and put it in my pack. The belt was two inches wide but the length of it was short enough to have belonged to a child.

The L-shaped trench was one of several firing positions dug in the open field less than fifty feet from the perimeter. It was visible from the north wall and was clearly covered by its field of fire. *How did the NVA get so close?* I won-dered. *How could they dig all these trenches without being seen from the camp?* Later, a Special Forces soldier explained that no one spotted the NVA before the attack because the fields were covered with scrub brush. During the siege, the Air Force bombed everything flat and then burned it to bare earth with napalm and white phosphorous.

ARVN soldiers in the burial detail covered their mouths and noses with the bandannas from around their necks. As they lifted the bodies by the arms and legs, some of the joints separated in their hands and the limbs came loose. The odor of decaying flesh hit their senses and caused them to retch and vomit on the ground. One of the bodies moved as though a gray blanket were being pulled over it. When I looked closer, I saw the body was being devoured by a dense swarm of maggots. *How efficient the jungle is at clearing up,* I thought. *Nothing survives on its own for long in this place.*

After all the bodies in the fields had been collected, an official figure was given as 164 North Vietnamese dead. Many more bodies were carried away when the surviving troops withdrew. The final American estimate, including those killed by air strikes and artillery, was over a thousand, the highest body count of the war.

Wilson, Hoan and I walked back to the camp. We went to a small clearing not far from the American quarter where Vo Huynh, the NBC cameraman, was talking with a captured North Vietnamese soldier. The prisoner was a thin frail-looking young man with tousled black hair. Fear showed on his olive brown face. His foot was injured and he said he had malaria. Huynh gave him a cigarette and the soldier took it gratefully. He sat on the bare ground with his legs crossed. His khaki-brown uniform was stained with sweat. The prisoner said his name was Cao Xuan Hai, that he was twenty-two years old and came from Phu To in North Vietnam. He said he was an assistant platoon sergeant in one of the assault companies of the 33d Regiment, which had left its base in North Vietnam in July and arrived in the area of Plei Me just over a week ago. His company had waited in position for four days and nights for the attack to start. He and his comrades had expected to die.

Major Beckwith and some of his soldiers came to the clearing to look at the prisoner. When Cao Xuan Hai had finished, Beckwith stood up and said in his rasping voice, "Let's put this guy on the north wall and get rid of these God damn ARVN. He could probably hold it by himself."

"Yeah," one of the soldiers said, "find another one and he can guard the south side. It'll be safer than the fucking ARVN." Everyone in the clearing laughed except Cao Xuan Hai, who did not understand English, and Hoan and Huynh, who did.

Wilson suggested we do an interview with the prisoner that Hoan would translate. He lined up a shot sitting on the ground in front of the prisoner and rolled film. Cao Xuan Hai started to answer the questions again but a minute into the interview the air above the camp exploded.

Machinegun fire raced overhead. A flaming sheet of crimson tracers flashed a few feet off the ground and tore into the sandbagged buildings around the camp. Everyone fell flat on the ground: Beckwith, his soldiers, reporters, the camera crew and the prisoner. Bullets streaked over like lightning flashes, fast and fierce, not the softly floating tracers of the ground-to-air duel two days before. The sounds of machineguns firing followed a second or two later from the treeline south of the camp. Rocket grenades and recoilless rifles exploded with the dull heavy cracks of AKs. The battle was just outside the camp, spilling inside. Beckwith and his men crawled on their knees and elbows toward the teamhouse, sliding fast across the flat ground like lizards, then got on their feet and ran with heads low and upper bodies parallel with the ground. They moved like wild animals, not at all like the First Cav officers in the Suoi Ca Valley who stood casually with bullets buzzing around them. In a second Beckwith and his men were gone.

The immediate ferocity of the attack surprised me. The sight of so many tracers coming over close and fast was a completely new experience, amazing and humbling. When the shooting started and everyone got down for cover, the prisoner fell over on his side and did not move. His eyes were alert. Vo Huynh ran in the direction of the firing. Wilson pointed his camera at me and shouted, 'Do an on-camera bridge!' I took the microphone from Hoan, leaned up off the ground, looked into the lens and said something about Plei Me being under attack again just when everyone thought the siege was over. Charlie Mohr, who had been taking notes during the interview with the prisoner, waited on his stomach until Wilson was finished rolling and then called over, "Hey, Jack! Is that what you call a stand-upper or a *sit-downer*?" He laughed and wrote in his notebook.

The fire slackened. Mortar shells struck the western end of the camp.

"Incoming!" a soldier shouted.

"No shit," said another. Everyone ran off to take their fighting positions.

Wilson, Hoan and I were left with the prisoner. I took him by one arm and we ran crouched over to a nearby shelter and ducked inside through a canvas flap that covered the entrance. Inside, the bunker was hot, airless, dark. Changing from the bright light outdoors to the subdued darkness was disorienting. When my eyes adjusted, I found myself in a strange candlelit room, like a French salon, with blankets, rugs and other decorations hanging from the walls and on the dirt floor. Shadows danced on the walls. Sounds of the shooting outside were subdued. In one corner, a uniformed Vietnamese officer lay on his side with his legs stretched in front of him. Several other men rested on their sides on cushions along the walls of the room. The officer was a big man with his uniform shirt unbuttoned and a large stomach hanging loosely over the belt of his neatly pressed trousers. The insignia on the shoulders of his uniform identified his rank as a colonel. He leaned on his elbow on a wide cushion draped with cotton cloth and a pastel-colored blanket. A long wooden pipe with an elaborately decorated bowl elevated near one end rested on a low wooden table with a burning candle beside it. Wax from the candle had formed a pool on the wooden surface of the table. As we burst into the room with our camera equipment and the North Vietnamese prisoner, the colonel stared in surprise for a few seconds but did not move. Then he laughed. He laughed again, louder, and again and again until his eyes watered and his heavy frame rocked on the cushions. The other men in the bunker joined the laughter, giggling in high-pitched voices, their eyes blurry and bloodshot. They seemed not to notice the war outside. The colonel motioned for us to sit down. Just behind me, Hoan whispered nervously, 'Jack, it's no good here. Let's go out from here. Right away, please!'

I apologized to the colonel for the intrusion, turned around and led the crew outside. In our haste to get away, we left the prisoner behind. Outside, Wilson looked at me, smiled a crooked half smile, and shook his head as if to say, 'What next?'

Mortar shells were falling in the camp with sharp menacing shrieks. Bright crimson tracers from machineguns outside the camp flashed overhead. Wilson jumped into a three-foot-deep communications trench and shouted, "Come on!" He began to run toward the western part of the camp where the sounds of incoming were heaviest. Hoan stopped where he stood, his body hunched over, looking around as if lost. Wilson cursed him and jerked hard on the camera cable. The movement pulled Hoan off balance and forced him to stumble along behind Wilson in the trench.

We came to a wide circular pit dug in the ground and protected by a low wall of sandbags. At the center of the pit, Montagnard soldiers fired an 81 millimeter mortar. They worked nonstop, sending off round after round, as fast as they could load, one shell every few seconds, aiming with almost true vertical elevation toward the forest to the south. They were practiced and efficient, loading the round, turning away, lowering their heads, covering their ears, *BANG!* One of the Montagnards looked up for a moment and smiled. Wilson rolled on one knee and changed position for separate angles. Somewhere in the south woods an acre of ground and everything on it was being blown apart by the three-inch wide shells the Montagnards were firing.

A big blond-haired Special Forces sergeant with a dirty fatigue cap ran up to the mortar pit and waved his arms, shouting at the Montagnards.

"Cease fire!" he screamed, "cease fire!" Cornelius Clark was the camp's mortar specialist and his face was contorted in fury. The Montagnards ignored him. Clark jumped into the mortar pit and seized a shell out of the hands of one of the Montagnards and pushed him out of the way. 'Number Ten!' he screamed. 'No fire! No fucking fire! Got it?' The Montagnards looked disappointed. They stepped back from the tube and dropped their arms. Clark climbed out of the pit and ran toward another mortar that was still firing from the camp.

Nothing else moved above ground. The heavy machineguns on the corners were quiet. All the soldiers in the camp had their heads down. Wilson, Hoan and I ran to the teamhouse to take cover with the other Americans. An air strike came in close to the perimeter and the first bombs exploded with a thundering *crack!*

The safest place in the teamhouse appeared to be behind the refrigerator, a massive old machine that hadn't worked for a week and was useful now only as a symbol of more civilized times in the camp. Beckwith was already there, crouching low. I laced up a spool of quarter-inch tape on my recorder, switched it on, and tried to ad-lib a description of the air strike. Bombs exploded near the wire and a few seconds later pieces of shrapnel clattered on the tin roof of the teamhouse like hailstones.

I asked Beckwith what happened. Speaking into the microphone, he said the armored column with the 22d Rangers ran into heavy resistance just outside the camp and they were taking a lot of casualties.

A bomb exploded close, shaking the ground beneath the teamhouse, releasing a cloud of red dust from the rafters that fell on our heads and shoulders.

Major Thompson looked over at Beckwith and laughed. "We like it!" he shouted, "We like it!"

As the planes circled overhead, Beckwith moved a few feet to the courtyard end of the teamhouse with the wood palisade around it and sat against a wall with his back to the south. One of the Special Forces men, a PFC with crazed eyes, popped his head above the palisade and fired an M-79 grenade round into the air over the south wall. A few seconds later it exploded with a hollow metal *splaat.*

"Don't fire in that area!" Beckwith said. "We've got friendlies out there."

The PFC looked at Beckwith with cold eyes. He turned his back on him and loaded another grenade in the launcher and locked the breech in place. He popped his head above the wall and fired again. *Phoooht . . . splaat!* In the same instant Beckwith moved to the wall and seized the PFC from behind with both hands at the shoulders and lifted him off the ground with rough force and hurled him against the sandbagged wall of the teamhouse. The PFC fell on his back in an awkward heap. Beckwith said nothing. The PFC got to his feet, picked up his M-79, replaced his fatigue hat and walked away. A blurred slow-moving shape whooshed just overhead and exploded with a loud bang in the camp. 'Recoilless rifle,' someone said. Single rifle shots went over, buzzing.

"Get down now," Beckwith shouted. "We got snipers!"

A few journalists sat in the courtyard listening to the sounds of the fight south of the camp. Beckwith was calm, as if unconcerned about the course of the battle. "Let's all just sit here and take it easy," he said. "It's nice and safe right here behind this palisade. It's not our problem anymore. We got friendlies in the north and the other people in the south," seeming to demonstrate that there are times in battle when it is wise to sit and wait.

A tall wild-eyed sergeant in a floppy bush hat stumbled into the courtyard and stood with his head above the wall looking south. His speech was slurred and his legs wobbled. He appeared to have been drinking alcohol.

'We gotta get some people out there right away!' he shouted. 'They're gettin their fuckin clocks cleaned! We gotta do something! Help 'm out.'

"Just sit down and shut up!" Beckwith said. "You're gonna get yourself waxed."

The sergeant looked bewildered, as if Beckwith was out of his mind. Then he shook his head and walked away, mumbling to himself, standing up straight while shrapnel from the air strikes flew overhead.

"Dumb sonofabitch," Beckwith said. "I hope he gets killed."

At the other end of the teamhouse, Major Thompson sat on a wooden box on the ground with his back to a wall of sandbags, radio handsets in each hand. He worked with deliberate concentration, talking in a steady voice to American advisers with the armored column fighting in the south and an Air Force FAC overhead who was guiding pilots on their air strikes.

'Tell those fucking 'Yards to cease firing!' Thompson called out to Sergeant Clark, the blond-haired mortar specialist. 'They're still dropping that shit on our people!'

Clark ran back across the camp to the mortar pit where he had been earlier and tried to stop the Montagnards from firing. A few minutes later, he ran back.

'This is fucking insane!' he yelled at Thompson. 'I make 'em stop, they stop. Then as soon as there's incoming, they start shooting again. Doesn't matter what I say. They can't stop. They're fucking *brainwashed!*'

An APC from the armored column raced into the camp churning up red dust and stopped near the teamhouse. The hydraulics whined and the rear gate went down to reveal more than a dozen ARVN soldiers huddled close together, holding one another, trembling. Some were without weapons.

'I don't believe this,' one of the Americans said. 'They ain't even bringing back the wounded.'

The driver of the APC climbed out of the track and announced in a loud voice that he was not going back to the battlefield. Jet bombers shrieked over the camp on strafing runs.

Thompson took the radio handset away from his ear and shouted, 'We've got *American* WIAs out there! The fucking ARVN won't bring them in!'

Beckwith quickly assembled three men who put on their ammunition belts and harnesses and rushed into the APC, surprising the driver. Beckwith put the flash suppresser of his M-16 against the face of the track commander and screamed, '*Take us to those American wounded or you fucking die! Right now, motherfucker! Di-di! Go!*' and pointed south with the muzzle of his rifle. In a few moments the APC roared out the gate.

Time passed.

Beckwith and his fireteam returned on foot carrying a wounded American adviser from one of the ARVN units, a red-headed lieutenant whom I had not met before. He was hit in the side but was no longer bleeding and appeared to be stable. Beckwith helped him down the stairs to the communications bunker deep below ground where the doctor, Captain Russell Hunter of Abeline, Texas, dressed his wound and called for a medevac. While he waited to be evacuated, I asked the lieutenant if he would give us a radio interview about the fight. He smiled, as if embarrassed to be wounded.

'They surprised us,' he said in a calm voice. 'Hit the point and the flank at the same time. They must have been waiting for us. Or maneuvered real well. The tanks turned around and bugged out. RPGs scared 'em right off. We didn't have much left to fight with. We killed a bunch of them though. Lot of mortars came in on us. I'm not sure whether I got hit by one of theirs or one of ours. Damnedest mess you ever saw. Total confusion.'

He was modest and honest, and I thanked him when the interview was finished.

A helicopter landed in the middle of the camp. Red tracers streaked above the spinning rotors. When the Vietnamese pilot saw the bullets, his eyes opened wide and he shouted at his crew to move fast. Several reporters jumped off the helicopter and ran for cover. Soldiers and journalists unloaded boxes of ammunition brought in by the chopper and carried them to the edge of the helipad. Everybody worked. The pilot kept so many revs in the engine the rotor blades whipped up specks of dirt that stung everyone in the face. Soldiers carried the wounded lieutenant up out of the bunker and got him aboard the chopper. It took off low over the northern ridgeline and disappeared in a hurry. Then it was quiet.

The wounded came into the camp in large numbers, some in the backs of APCs, some on foot, many limping with leg wounds. They sat on sandbags around the edge of the LZ waiting for helicopters to take them to the hospital in Pleiku. Uniformly, they looked at the ground. Some had blood-soaked bandages on their heads where they were struck in the scalp, jaw, eye, nose or ear by flying pieces of shrapnel. Others wore arm slings and field dressings. Their expressions were sad, as if they had been beaten up in a fistfight. Four of the wounded were American. One, a tall big-boned captain with streaks of dirt on his face and a bandage just below his right knee, sat alone on a crate of ammunition and stared in the distance. Later, APCs brought in twenty-seven ARVN soldiers dead. Eighty others had been wounded. The brief engagement south of the camp was a battle lost.

The shooting stopped. Medevacs came in one after another, kicking up clouds of tiny stones that whizzed through the air at speed. Around the LZ, everyone turned their backs and covered their heads until the helicopters cut power in their engines. The choppers were H-34s, vintage machines that stood high off the ground and were flown by brave Vietnamese crews who were anxious to get away. The wounded soldiers rushed at the first helicopter that landed and tried to get aboard all at once, climbing over each other's backs, clutching for the open hold of the cargo bay, every one for himself. A Vietnamese woman in a white blouse stood at the edge of the panic and tried to push her way forward against the backs of the men, but they stuck their elbows in her neck and forced her back. Two American soldiers pulled apart a swarm of smaller men and tried to put the most seriously wounded soldiers aboard first. An angry American sergeant grabbed one of the ARVN soldiers who had climbed aboard over the backs of the others and ripped away the field dressing from his arm to expose clean unmarked skin beneath the bandage. The sergeant seized the soldier by the front of his shirt and hurled him over the heads of the others and onto the ground.

The Vietnamese army colonel who had been entertaining his friends in the candlelit bunker a few hours earlier appeared at the edge of the LZ with his leg wrapped in bandages and limping on a bamboo cane. I went over and tried to talk with him but he turned away. His eyes were clear. A chopper landed and in the swirl of flying red dirt I saw the colonel drop the crutch and run in swift unhindered strides to the open door of the H-34 and force his way aboard, climbing over his wounded men. A Special Forces soldier saw this and pulled him out of the helicopter. A minute later the colonel tried again and made it into the cargo hold. Beckwith, Thompson and a few of the other Americans saw it happen and shook their heads in disgust.

"So this is supposed to be *their* war," one of them said.

When the last of the wounded soldiers had been taken away, the helicopters came back for the dead. Journalists helped carry greasy ponchos onto the chopper as gently as possible. But the bodies were loose unbalanced weight with no hard edges to grasp and were awkward to lift. At least one of the bodies slipped out and fell on the ground. Several soldiers and reporters threw up. Most of the bodies got out, including some of the decomposing week-old corpses from the earlier fighting, but some were left on the LZ as the sun went down and cold night embraced the camp.

The new arrivals included an NBC News correspondent named Ron Nessen, a dark-haired network veteran of about thirty who was a serious competitor. As soon as he linked up with Vo Huynh, his cameraman, Nessen must have realized that he was going to get beat on the story because he was four days behind and because he had only silent film and audiotape to work with while we had sound-on-film. Nessen acted excited, jittery. He asked Beckwith for permission to fly his film to Pleiku on one of the choppers but Beckwith said, 'No fucking way. You just got here. I got to get the rest of these bodies out.' Other reporters and photographers who had been in the camp for days suggested a sharing arrangement known as a "pool." A few would be allowed to leave with all the film and copy for everyone else. There were more than a dozen journalists in the camp and all wished to get their stories out fast. After listening to entreaties for several hours, Beckwith

assembled the press around the teamhouse and announced that there would
be space on a helicopter in the morning for three journalists to go out: one
of the photographers to take all the rolls of still pictures to Saigon, one print
reporter to carry copy to Pleiku for transmission, and one TV person to
deliver the two networks' film to Saigon. Nessen and I argued angrily about
which one of us would go. The print journalists decided that Mohr, who was
senior among them, could be trusted to deliver everyone else's copy before
he filed his own story. It was a matter of honor that a pool courier deliver his
competitors' film and copy to their offices before he filed his own because he
had a big competitive advantage by getting out first.

Wilson resolved the argument with Nessen. 'Let him go,' he said. 'We'll
get out of here in a day or two. Write your narration tonight and I'll record
it in the morning and we'll send it down to Saigon with the sonofabitch.'

A few hours later, when I had written the narration, I went outside and sat
with some of the American soldiers by the end of the teamhouse. Flares fell
over the forest outside the camp. The soldiers had taken a bottle of whisky
from a full case that had been airdropped during one of the resupply missions
earlier in the week. Several boxes of cigars had also been parachuted in. Beckwith had radioed for the extra supplies to be delivered but made it an order
that no one was allowed to touch them until the fight was over. The senior
army officer in Pleiku, a colonel, objected but Beckwith insisted. He thought it
would be good for morale if his men knew whisky and cigars were waiting as
a reward at the end of the siege. The soldiers sat on empty ammunition crates
in the dark and smoked their cigars and passed the whisky bottle slowly, each
of them holding it for a minute or two, as they talked.

They were no longer openly hostile toward the journalists. Wilson,
Hoan, Mohr, Dring, Galloway and Mannock had taken turns on the corner
machineguns, and most of the others had helped carry wounded and dead
onto the helicopters. But the Special Forces men were still not friendly. They
were a closed tribe: primitive, warlike, insular, suspicious of outsiders, even
other Americans. Beckwith was their chief.

Talking softly in the dark, Beckwith and his sergeant major, Bill DeSoto,
reminisced about quail hunting with dogs on fresh misty mornings in Georgia and North Carolina. They discussed the advantages of setters versus
pointers in a quiet wistful way, ignoring everyone else, close friends talking
privately. Beckwith was lyrical about the pleasures of hunting in Georgia.

'What I'd give to be back there right now,' the sergeant major said. 'Back in those woods on a fine October morning, good old dog with me, not this godawful place.'

"Good times, sergeant major," Beckwith said. "We had them before and we'll have them again."

A long silence followed. Flares popped in the sky.

'No more of this shit for me,' one of the soldiers said. 'When I get back to Bragg I'm gonna get myself retrained. No shit. As a clerk.' The others laughed. "You better believe. I'm gonna become the world's fastest typist."

The radio operator came up the stairs out of the communications bunker and whispered something to Beckwith. There was a long silence and then Beckwith said to the others, 'He didn't make it.' The words came out in a flat monotone, without emotion, as if everyone understood.

'Who?' one of the journalists asked.

'That Ranger lieutenant.'

'The one with red hair?'

'Yeah.'

Another silence.

'He was a good man,' someone said. 'I knew him at Bragg.'

I couldn't believe it. The young Army lieutenant had not appeared to be seriously wounded when I interviewed him in the commo bunker a few hours earlier. He had seemed so healthy, so alive.

'What happened?' I asked.

'Bled to death in the chopper,' Beckwith said in his most scourging voice. 'Altitude killed him on the way back to Pleiku. Fucking pilot took him up too high.'

OCTOBER 27, 1965

"Goooood morrrning, all you lucky people in Plei Me!" Leo Drake, a skinny, fast-talking Special Forces medic, appeared before a group of fellow soldiers sitting on ammo crates in the yard outside the teamhouse. Drake was in his twenties.

'I hear the First Cav's comin in this morning to take over,' he said.

'They can have it,' one of the other soldiers said.

'Yeah, we 'bout finished with this place,' another said.

'Talk about a fucked-up piece of territory. This place ain't worth shit.'

'Far as I'm concerned, the Cav can have the whole country.'

'Couldn't fuck it up any more than it already is,' Drake said.

A long-handled medic's scissors was tucked through the buttonhole of Drake's fatigue shirt, and the front visor of his utility cap was turned back over his forehead like a city street kid. He held a small bowl of hot coffee in his hands, the first fresh coffee anyone had seen in a week. Steam rose out of the bowl and dissolved in the cold morning mist enfolding the camp. Supplies of water had arrived, enough for fresh coffee and shaving. The night had passed in relative peace. Reporters and photographers had pulled shifts behind the machineguns on the corners of the camp so that many of the American soldiers were able to get their first good sleep in a week. The North Vietnamese had not assaulted and the mood was more relaxed. It was the eighth day since the start of the siege.

Major Beckwith agreed to do an on-camera interview with us on the condition that the background did not show any of the camp's interior defenses. Wilson set him against an isolated wall that had a round Confucian symbol painted on it. The major wore a bush hat that was several sizes too small for his head so that it perched on the top like a beanie. He was in his usual gruff mood, head down, scowling. The noise of a stationary helicopter engine hummed in the distance.

Beckwith gave an account of the siege in terse descriptions. He praised the courage of the Americans who defended the camp.

"What kind of fighters are the Viet Cong that you met here?" I asked, still blurring the distinction between VC from the south and People's Army troops from the north.

"I would give anything to have two hundred of 'em under my command," Beckwith said. "They're the finest soldiers I've ever seen."

"The Viet Cong."

"That's right. They are dedicated and they're good soldiers. They're the best I've ever seen." Beckwith spoke with his head pointed at the ground.

"What about the resistance your own men put up?" I asked. "The Americans here and your own troops?"

"The U.S.'s here, as far as I'm concerned, did an outstanding job. Uh, of course, in my opinion, they're a helluva lot better than the VC and that's the only reason we survived." Beckwith pronounced it suh-*vived*.

Looking up briefly, he added, "I do not want to make any comment regarding the Vietnamese that were here in the camp."

Later, I asked Beckwith what lessons were learned from Plei Me. "The biggest lesson I learned was that the Vietnamese had problems," he said. "If I got myself in a box, I wasn't sure they would bail me out. That was the biggest lesson I learned. I felt that the role of the Delta Project to advise the Vietnamese LLDB on long-range patrolling and so forth was a big bunch of bullshit. If you wanted it done, then you had to get yourself a bunch of Americans to do it, and you had to get yourself the *right* ones. That's what I learned out of that."

I thanked Beckwith and went to help prepare the story to give to the pool journalists who were going to Pleiku and Saigon. Wilson handed the cans of film to Nessen of NBC who promised to deliver them to the CBS bureau in Saigon. Part of me felt sorry for him. He was carrying five days of his competitors' work knowing it was more thorough than his own. In those circumstances, I wasn't sure I could trust him.

Later in the morning, a battalion of American troops from the First Cav landed on the scorched wasteland north of the camp. The stench of bodies on the LZ was so strong the soldiers threw up as they got off the helicopters.

The arrival of 2d Battalion, 8th Cavalry was the beginning of a long fateful American military offensive that pushed into the high rolling savanna south and west of Plei Me in pursuit of the North Vietnamese regiments that had attacked the camp and the armored task force. Eventually the operation would take thousands of American soldiers and pilots into the tall grasses of the Drang River Valley to fight the first and most ferocious American infantry battles of the war with the People's Army of North Vietnam.

The siege of Plei Me was over, though the camp was hit by sporadic mortar and small arms fire for several days. Beckwith and his men left Plei Me and flew to Pleiku to reorganize, then took off on long-range reconnaissance patrols for the First Cav. Most journalists from the camp flew to Pleiku and Saigon to file stories, clean up and rest. Fresh reporters and photographers arrived from Saigon. Of the original group at Plei Me, only Joe Galloway of UPI, Vo Huynh of NBC and Simon Dring of Reuters stayed with the story through all the violent phases that followed.

Returning to Saigon two days later, I was told in the bureau that our film from Plei Me had not been delivered immediately to CBS. A friend from the Associated Press who worked in the same office building as NBC News told me he had seen a CBS shipping bag with film in it from the field sitting on a desk at the NBC office all day after Nessen got back. The broadcast logs from New York showed that Nessen's report appeared on the *Huntley-Brinkley Report* twenty-four hours ahead of ours. When our story was finally shown on the air, CBS producers and executives in New York sent cables to Wilson, Hoan and me with praise for our work. TIME magazine, which had not had a reporter at the scene, printed excerpts from my radio reports.

At the end of the week, I wrote a radio commentary on the Plei Me battle entitled "Who Will Fight the War?" The report described the valor of the Special Forces, U.S. Army advisers, Air Force pilots, Army helicopter crews and the North Vietnamese at Plei Me. In contrast, I drew attention to the shameful behavior of some of the ARVN, CIDG and LLDB officers and men.

At the *New York Times*, Charles Mohr wrote a military analysis combining his firsthand observations at Plei Me with the comments of military and civilian members of the U.S. high command in Saigon. Mohr's piece concluded:

> In the use of American troops so far, no chances have been taken: no small units have been thrown into the battle against odds, and losses and gains have therefore been modest. With such caution, officers say, the American and South Vietnamese allies probably cannot be defeated but possibly cannot win. Military victory in Vietnam, they add, will go to the people who can longest bear the suffering, the cost and the uncertainty of guerrilla warfare.

There it was, at the beginning of the war, for anyone to read.

Soon after, American and North Vietnamese commanders threw caution to the dry autumn winds. On November 1, about seven miles west of Plei Me, the 1st Cavalry Division's Air Cavalry Squadron, 1st Squadron, 9th Cavalry, met a large force of North Vietnamese around an NVA field hospital. In a day of fighting, eleven Americans were killed and about fifty wounded. Ninety-nine North Vietnamese were reported dead, forty-four were taken prisoner, and another 163 were believed to have been killed. It was the first heavy infantry engagement between regular U.S. and People's Army troops in the war. Two days later, a smaller unit of 1/9 engaged a much larger force of PAVN soldiers close to the Cambodian border. In a fierce night fight that lasted several hours, the Americans narrowly escaped being annihilated. Charlie Black was present and took an active part in fighting to defend the perimeter, firing and maneuvering for his life. Afterward, Black said, wheezing and laughing, 'It was a close thing for a while there whether we were going to come out with our asses in one piece or not.'

The war escalated rapidly. A few days later, the Pentagon reported the highest single weekly toll of American casualties: 85 dead, 478 wounded, 2 missing. After four years of military involvement in Vietnam, the total of all U.S. casualties for the war jumped more than 10 percent in one week.

Through the month of November, a reinforced brigade of the First Cav— approximately four thousand troops—pursued the North Vietnamese in a series of battles that spread over four hundred square miles of wild scrub country southwest of Plei Me. One American battalion after another joined the hunt, setting up artillery and support bases, ranging through the sky in helicopters and spotter planes, peering at the opaque jungle below, crossing the difficult terrain on foot, searching kilometer after kilometer. The results were two major battles and several sharp skirmishes fought in an area that later became known as the Ia Drang Valley. Many men died there.

One First Cav battalion of about five hundred soldiers walked into an ambush in the Ia Drang and gave up 155 dead in one day. Second Battalion, 7th Cavalry (the same 7th Cavalry of Custer's command a century earlier) was overrun and destroyed as an effective fighting force around a landing zone code-named Albany. Fighting took place at point-blank range. Soldiers from the two sides fought and died a few feet apart, in some cases on top of each other. North Vietnamese soldiers climbed into trees and fired down at the Americans, shooting them where they lay in fields of elephant grass.

Many of the U.S. victims were executed in the night, shot by NVA soldiers who prowled the battlefield searching for wounded GIs. Hundreds of North Vietnamese were slaughtered.

Another ferocious battle had been fought in the same valley four days earlier at a landing zone named X-Ray. For three days, 1st Battalion, 7th Cavalry fought off repeated assaults by a North Vietnamese regiment near the foothills of the Chu Pong Mountains close to the Cambodian border. It was a historic battle.

A total of 305 Americans were killed in the two encounters. It was a record high death toll for a single American campaign in the war that stood for more than two years, until 1968, when the Tet Offensive changed everything.

As soon as we heard the reports in Saigon, Wilson, Funk and I went up to Pleiku and then into the field to try to find out what happened. We found the few healthy survivors of C Company, 2/7, sitting around a smoky campfire resting. The soldiers had just come out of Ia Drang and some were in shock. Charlie Company had suffered the greatest losses of any company at LZ Albany, forty-seven dead and all but a few of the rest wounded. The men who were killed represented half the company's field strength and almost a third of the entire battalion death toll of 155. One of the soldiers was trying to play a harmonica he had been sent from home. He hadn't had it long enough to learn how to play, so the few notes he had managed to teach himself came out slowly, five solemn tones in the lower register of the instrument. Played one after another, they sounded like a dirge.

A dark-haired GI sat on the ground apart from the others writing a letter. He was in his late teens or early twenties, a young-faced kid with uncombed hair and fuzz for a beard. Wilson filmed him writing the letter from one side, quietly, so that the soldier was not aware of the camera. Wilson waved his free hand at Funk, motioning him to give me the microphone. I approached the soldier.

"How was it?" I said.

He looked up from his letter, paused and stared down at it. "It was pretty bad." His voice was low but steady. "We kinda walked right into a ambush. And, uh, we hit the ground. Tried to look round for trees. There was elephant grass about three feet high. And, to look over that, snipers could pick you up real easily and let you have it." He paused.

"Does it frighten you now to think about it?"

"Yes, it does." He looked up, shook his head for a moment, and looked down at the letter. "Yeah, it was pretty bad to listen to your friends crying out for help, not being able to do a thing. We just couldn't do anything. We were all pinned down."

"Are you writing home about it, just now?"

"Yes, I'm writing my father right now."

"What are you saying?"

"Well, I'm just trying to give him the facts of what happened. Not much else you can do. It's over with. Guess you gotta forget it now."

"Do you think you'll ever be able to forget it?"

"No, I won't."

Wilson, listening to the words, panned down slowly from the soldier's face to the letter and the pencil he was holding. A thin column of cigarette smoke rose from his hand into the air. Wilson switched the camera off. We thanked the young soldier and moved on.

A sergeant with dirty fatigues and a dark unwashed face and a short hair-cut said in a southern drawl, "Well, I tell you, it's about as close, to put it in words, it was like *hell*. It's about as close to being in hell and comin out alive. That's about the only way I can put it." His voice was firm, authoritative.

"What would you say is the most hellish part of it?"

"Actually getting shot at and seeing the bullet hit and miss you. And seeing your buddy get it. And when you see somebody out there injured and you can't get to 'em and you know what they're going through and you can't do a thing to help 'em."

I told the sergeant the interview would be on CBS in a couple of days and thanked him for talking to us.

Moving among the troops one at a time, we found a soldier named Bob who was smoking a cigarette. He had a narrow face and was wearing an army fatigue hat with the visor curled like a baseball cap. His voice was sad.

"The hardest part is trying to forget the deaths of your buddies," he said. "One company lost our whole mortar platoon. Twenty-eight men. One was from Oswego, Illinois. He knew some friends of mine that went to the same university I went to."

"Is it hard for you to believe that they're dead, so quickly?"

Bob took a puff on his cigarette. "Well, when you look at 'em, it doesn't even resemble a human body. It looks just like a mannequin. You look at 'em and you say that couldn't happen to me." He paused.

"It *is* hard to realize it. But then you walk back to their area, back at base camp, they're just not there." He shook his head slowly from side to side. I thanked him for talking to us and we moved on.

The commander of Charlie Company, 2/7, was Captain John Fesmire. He had narrow eyes and a pleasant disposition and his nickname was "Skip." Fesmire's helmet, possibly a new replacement, did not fit his head.

"It's a funny thing," he said, "but some of these men I've known for a long time and some of them I didn't know too well. But the one thing about battle that I found strange—the death part seems to be unrealistic. I don't know. You know it's true but you just don't really bring yourself to believe it. This is just the way it is."

"Do you believe it now?"

"I believe it, but, uh, I still think there's something in my mind that tells me it wasn't real. So, I don't believe I've felt the shock of it yet."

To the world outside, the reality of what happened in the Ia Drang Valley became apparent only slowly. MACV in Saigon and the administration in Washington portrayed the campaign as a great military victory for the United States. The American press largely acquiesced in this interpretation, stressing the scale of the combat. Near the end of November, MACV reported American losses for the previous week as 240 dead and 470 wounded, reflecting only some of the casualties at Ia Drang. The number of North Vietnamese dead was put at more than fifteen hundred. Graphic firsthand battle reports by Galloway of UPI and Dring of Reuters described in detail the ferocity of the fighting, the narrowness of the American soldiers' survival. The Johnson administration vigorously denied dark suggestions of battles lost, describing the Ia Drang campaign as a series of "meeting engagements" in which the U.S. Army prevailed.

In Saigon, General William Westmoreland called attention to the large number of North Vietnamese dead and weapons captured. "I consider this an unprecedented victory," he declared. "At no time during the engagement were American troops forced to withdraw or move back from their positions except for tactical maneuvers. The enemy fled from the scene." As far as Westmoreland was concerned, that was the end of any debate about winners and losers. If the North Vietnamese left the battlefield first, they must have lost the battle. Westmoreland's argument avoided the fact that taking and holding territory like the uninhabited scrub brush where the battles were fought in the Ia Drang was no measure of success in this guerrilla war. Nor did his argument recognize that North Vietnamese commanders had decided that nothing was to be gained by keeping their troops in an area being saturated by B-52 bombing strikes. A few days later, the First Cav withdrew as well. Two of its best battalions had gone into the Ia Drang to meet the enemy and had been badly mauled. The three North Vietnamese regiments involved in the fighting from Plei Me to Ia Drang had also suffered gravely. Physical control of the valley and its giant anthills returned to the wild elephants, tigers and swarms of insects that were native to it.

Officials in Washington and Saigon held to the logic of past wars that the U.S. Army would win this one because its soldiers were killing more of the enemy than they were losing themselves. Far more, in fact. At least ten to one. It was an enormous ratio, one that had produced victory in almost all wars in history. No army could long withstand such heavy losses, it was believed. And so the military policy called "attrition" was invoked. The long-term destruction of North Vietnam's human and material resources was codified, justified, rationalized, and reinforced as an attainable goal of U.S. military strategy. With ten enemy dead for every one of ours, it was thought, American power would grind the North Vietnamese into weakness, submission and eventual defeat. The flaw in the logic, the weak link in the American analysis, was the failure to recognize that attrition works both ways. Even as the war was gathering terrible force, like a hurricane over the sea, Hanoi was preparing to sacrifice as many as ten or more of its own men and women for every American killed. The leaders said so in their speeches, that they would fight until the Americans, like the French, grew tired of the killing. Their speeches were broadcast on Hanoi Radio and published in the international press, though few outside their closed world believed them. They too were fighting a war for hearts and minds—the hearts and minds of the American public.

The early battles in the Central Highlands had traumatic consequences at home. The domestic U.S. Army bureaucracy was not prepared for the volume of next-of-kin notifications it had to make to families of First Cav soldiers who were killed in action. Instead of finding army officers, religious ministers or family friends to deliver death notices and console each family in person, the army sent out formally worded telegrams by Western Union to homes around the division's base at Fort Benning, Georgia. The telegrams informed wives, parents and children that their husbands, sons and fathers were dead in Vietnam. Cold black words printed on yellow pieces of paper. Many of the telegrams were delivered by taxi drivers who rang doorbells, handed over the envelopes and walked away, some in the middle of the night. At least one telegram was left in a mailbox. The terrible shocks of the Ia Drang were not confined to the battlefield.

Military lessons of that autumn campaign became apparent even more slowly. What was clear immediately was that the North Vietnamese Army had undertaken its most ambitious military adventure since assaulting and defeating the French at Dien Bien Phu eleven years earlier. Its troops had proved themselves to be committed warriors ("the best I've ever seen," as Beckwith said), prepared to fight and die even in the most adverse battlefield conditions, without air support or heavy armor or rapid medical evacuation or aerial resupply. Its troops did not have metal helmets, much less flak jackets. Individual courage and dedication to their cause was enforced by iron-fisted discipline imposed by an uncompromising political apparatus. As the prisoner at Plei Me said, 'we all thought we were going to die.'

On the South Vietnamese side, the majority of Saigon government troops, the ARVN, did not appear to be motivated politically. They were trying mainly to survive. In many cases they were led by officers who owed their allegiance to senior patrons who cared less about winning battles than the acquisition of personal wealth. They tried to avoid contact with the North Vietnamese when possible and fight only when it was unavoidable. When they did fight, the ARVN usually suffered heavy losses because they were outmaneuvered so aggressively by the other side. Americans asked one another the question so often that it became a refrain: "How come *their* Vietnamese are so much better than *our* Vietnamese?"

American soldiers, moving in companies of over a hundred men and battalions of six hundred and more, were able to call on air and artillery support that enabled them to survive the fanatic close-in assaults of the North Vietnamese, but at heavy cost. Along with the individual valor of its soldiers, the most decisive American asset was often the devastating destruction caused by U.S. Air Force bombing.

However they were reported, those early battles of October and November 1965 focused the eyes of the American public on Plei Me and Ia Drang. They were front-page news, lead stories on TV newscasts, cover stories in newsmagazines. They not only told the country what was going on in Vietnam, but they offered guidance for informed decisions about the rapidly escalating war. As Mohr put it in the *Times:* "Military victory in Vietnam . . . will go to the people who can longest bear the suffering, the cost and the uncertainty of guerrilla warfare." America's political and military leadership seemed to believe that the national interest required its people to bear the suffering, cost and uncertainty of a long war in Vietnam, longer than the stubborn dogmatic group of committed Marxist-Leninist revolutionaries who ruled North Vietnam, if that were possible. The U.S. leadership wanted to find ways to defeat its Communist enemies, not just in Vietnam but in China and the Soviet Union. Unfortunately, they may have been projecting their own beliefs onto their enemy. Simple Western logic held by those in the Johnson administration suggested that overpowering American military force combined with continuous armed aggression on the ground and in the air plus time would produce suffering and death on such a scale that the North Vietnamese would eventually be forced to capitulate. It would not be the last time American politicians would succumb to that subtle self-deception. All wars begin with the belief by those who lead their nations into them that they are going to win.

Plei Me and Ia Drang provided a perfect paradigm, and therefore a warning, of the struggle of arrogant wills to come that would transform Vietnam into a vast slaughterhouse for the next ten years. American leaders—political *and* military—did not see the lesson clearly. Later it would be necessary to ask the question, How was it possible that an advanced technological society with a sophisticated political system and a vigorous intelligentsia that had produced a warrior class capable of dropping hundreds of thousands of pounds of high-explosive bombs on the heads of its enemies in a war at the far edge of civilization on the opposite side of the world (and also a case of whisky and cigars to its beleaguered soldiers) was, at the same time, incapable of foretelling accurately what it might cost or how it would end?

I had an idea of the cost already from what the soldiers who had been in the Ia Drang had told me around their campfire. I had seen some of the cost in Happy Valley with the dead mother, and on the Cambodian border with the falling farmers and elsewhere with the Marines. Sitting in my hotel room in Saigon, I composed a letter home. For the first time I expressed doubt about U.S. policy in Vietnam. Until now I had accepted the prevailing opinion that with the correct strategy and tactics, the war could be won. Now I began to ask whether it was possible that the Vietnamese might not surrender their struggle, a struggle for national independence that had been hundreds of years and thousands of lives in its evolution. I had read how the Vietnamese had demonstrated their unwavering determination to resist foreign domination in the past, how fanatical they were in their ferocity and belligerence toward outsiders. If the public statements of Communist leaders in Hanoi were accurate, they would continue to resist for years and years. In time I began to wonder whether Johnson and Westmoreland and McNamara and the rest of America's leaders were no smarter than poker players who foolishly pay for another card, chasing a big win even with questionable cards because they have so much invested already they can't bear to lose quite yet, and so throw in good money after bad. I wondered whether they were so obsessed with their idea of victory in this faraway foreign war that they were propelled by perverse lust, a death wish perhaps, leading the rest of the country, especially those who had to fight and die for them, in a blind headfirst plunge into a maelstrom of pain and anguish.

Drinking whisky, smoking cigarettes, I thought about it as hard as I could. My sense of logic said something is wrong. Something is wrong. I remembered the red-headed American lieutenant who died in the ARVN medevac and the black-haired Vietnamese anti-aircraft gunner with his head torn open, and the nameless others who were lost at Plei Me and Ia Drang and my heart cried for them, and again later in my dreams.

DECEMBER, 1965

Something was wrong with Galloway's eyes. The rims were red and raw and wet with moisture that highlighted the freckled pink of his face. The whites were a web of ragged veins, bloody and broken. When he spoke, he looked away, avoiding eye contact, as though he were embarrassed or unsure about something. Sometimes his eyes were completely lost, blank unseeing spheres in the sockets, following the private focus of his mind to somewhere far away. The haunted eyes made his normally cheerful, optimistic face look sad.

Almost overnight, Galloway had become shy, his usual confidence missing. His broad Texan shoulders drooped, his jaw was slack, his head was down much of the time. This night he sat with his legs crossed on a straw mat on the floor of a room at Frankie's House, the home of a few foreign journalists in Saigon, and smoked one cigarette after another. Occasionally he looked up to suggest he was listening but his expression was timid, self-conscious, his mind disengaged. In a room full of friends, Galloway seemed a stranger. He was one of the young reporters and photographers who lived at Frankie's House and gathered to unwind after forays into the field, relieved to be alive and safe. Now, though, he behaved more like a casualty. It was a shame to see it happen to so nice a guy.

Before Ia Drang, Joe Galloway was a happy young reporter, one of the legion of Western journalists who moved to Saigon to cover the war. He was twenty-four. He had a round face with red hair and a large frame that had become solid with the physical demands of life in the field. He listened more than he talked and when he spoke it was in the slow deliberate drawl of his native South Texas. Galloway worked for United Press International. Like other young reporters, he enjoyed the responsibilities of being a war correspondent, the tests of battle, and the camaraderie of the others who lived and played at Frankie's House.

Then, on the frenzied, flare-lit night of November 14, with more than a thousand First Cav and Peoples Army soldiers fighting at close quarters, Galloway climbed aboard an emergency resupply helicopter at a forward support base and rode the fourteen miles west of Plei Me into the Ia Drang Valley and landed at LZ X-Ray. He found himself in a firestorm of smoke, noise and flying steel. Lieutenant Colonel Hal Moore and troops of his 1st Battalion, 7th Cavalry, were fighting to survive. After two days on that killing ground, Galloway got out with a dramatic eyewitness report for UPI and the world.

Sitting on the floor of the room at Frankie's House, listening to music from a record player and to the conversation of colleagues, Galloway had trouble keeping his concentration. Some of the terror seemed to continue, even now, though he was safe and among friends. He was quiet, drawn into himself. In between cigarettes, he took one joint after another as it was passed to him. Then he fell asleep on the floor of the room where his friends were gathered to welcome him back. He snored softly through his mouth.

Tim Page, the young English photographer, got up from his seat on the bed, walked quietly out of the room and returned a few seconds later holding a can of shaving cream.

'Don't do it Page,' a friend said.

'Quiet, mate, you'll wake him up,' said Page.

'How would *you* like it, Page?'

'I wouldn't! That's the bloody point!' he said, giggling, mischief in his eyes. He leaned over Galloway's sleeping body and sprayed shaving cream onto his face and neck, creating a fluffy white beard of foam that ran down over the buttons of his shirt onto the front of his chest. Galloway stopped snoring but did not wake up. Page sprayed short bursts of lather over his eyebrows and then stood back to study his creation. He turned to the others who were sprawled on the floor and bed of the room, his eyes sparkling with wicked delight.

'It's *Santa Joe!*' he declared. 'We'll do him up like this for the Christmas party. The birds will *adore* him!'

'Page, you're cruel.'

'Page is not cruel,' said Page. 'Page is having fun.'

'Cruel fun, Page.'

Still standing, Page shook the can of shaving cream in his hand, leaned over Galloway's body and sprayed white foam around his armpits and over his crotch.

'Oh, Page, you're unbelievable.'

'Don't you know when to stop?'

'When are you going to grow up, Page?'

'You don't *understaaannd,*' Page said, whining in mock protest that he put on whenever he knew he had gone too far. 'This is *gooood* for Galloway. It'll save him time in the morning. Dig it, he won't need to lather up. Just get up, shave and go to the office. Heh, heh. I'm *helping* him.'

'Page, you don't give a flying fuck about anybody but yourself.'

'Roger that,' someone added.

Galloway woke up, raised his head a few inches off the floor, felt his face with his hand, looked with red blurry eyes at the glop on his fingers, frowned and put his head on the rattan rug and went back to sleep. The foam melted and ran down the folds of his neck and formed a white blob on the floor. Page went to his camera bag, got out a Leica with a wide-angle lens and, snickering, took several close shots of Galloway asleep.

'What's that for, Page? Blackmail?'

'Everything is on the record, lads. No secrets in Frankie's House.' He kept the Leica near his side as he crawled back on the bed.

Frankie's House was where a few adventurous members of the Saigon press corps, along with an occasional soldier, foreign service officer or visiting writer, went to soothe their war-tired minds and exhausted bodies with marijuana, opium, music and the attentions of affectionate members of the opposite sex. The combination of sex, drugs and rock 'n' roll was not invented at Frankie's House, nor was it perfected there, but it was practiced almost every evening with consummate enthusiasm. When added to the powerful sense of relief at covering combat and then coming safely out of the field, the mix produced an emotional high as potent as anything anyone knew.

Frankie's House was what a small group of young English-speaking reporters and photographers invented as an alternative to the established Saigon social scene with its polite cocktail functions, ardent dinner party discussions and discreet romantic liaisons that took place in the tastefully appointed private living quarters of diplomats, journalists and senior military officers who composed the American community's more refined social set. Frankie's House was also an alternative to the boozy, argumentative bar and restaurant war talk of old Asia hands in the press corps, and the garish smoke-filled honkytonks where GIs, construction workers and other civilians went to drink beer and shout over the noise of throbbing music and talk in pidgin English with the pretty Vietnamese peasant girls who pretended to be interested in them and fondled the insides of their thighs trying to work up a sale.

Frankie's House was something else. At one time or another it enacted all the styles of wartime Saigon: sophisticated and crude, noble and banal, sober and insane. Its occupants and regular guests were young men and women who had left behind many of the more restrictive conventions of their middle-class backgrounds in America, England and Australia, and now followed less inhibited fashions of dress, language and behavior, at least when they were at Frankie's House. They shared an appreciation of the interesting new styles of thinking that were evolving in Europe, America and elsewhere in Asia, the idea that political and cultural changes there were not without influence here, that they might even be connected in some ways, interacting with each other, although it was hard to see how because much of Vietnam was as dark and distant as the far side of Mars.

Being in a war zone allowed much wider freedom of expression. This was, after all, exotic Saigon—far removed in space and consciousness from the usual authority of Western cities and their tight time-honored codes of acceptable social conduct, or the judgments of watchful families and employers. Saigon permitted a degree of social experimentation that might have been less attractive or possible at home. Young men who spent most of their time living rough with troops in the countryside allowed themselves, when they were in Saigon, the indulgence of living largely for the pleasure of the moment. At Frankie's House, immediate sensual pleasure was available in abundance, readily, on demand.

By late 1965, the Saigon press corps had divided itself between the straights and the crazies, the serious reporters and the cowboys, and those who lived at Frankie's House were counted among the crazies. Though not a truly accurate description, by comparison with the rest of the press corps, it was an easy judgment to make. The straights were defined by their behavior as more conventionally respectable. They were generally older and more serious, worked hard on the story all the time, usually obeyed the ground rules and curfews, played a few hands of poker with embassy staff once a week, wrote home regularly, got drunk or tipsy on Saturday night, occasionally slept with someone who was not their spouse, and spent more time in Saigon than in the field. They won prizes for their photography and reporting. The crazies were uniformly young and rebellious, smoked dope, broke rules whenever possible, slept with anyone who would get in bed with them, drank brandy in the morning, and spent most of their time in the field with the troops, the first day of which was often needed to work off their hangovers. Saigon was for R and R. Frankie's House was where some of the most alienated of them met to pass the time between assignments—swapping information, reading, entertaining, arguing, relaxing, goofing off, getting high, getting laid, having adolescent fun.

Some of the serious discussions that took place there were as perceptive as any in Saigon. A visitor could get insights into the avalanche of problems caused by the war: deteriorating conditions in the countryside (everyone was getting poorer except government officials and their cronies), corruption and graft, military atrocities (our Korean allies were getting away with murder)—and also possible solutions to the problems *(if the people making the decisions would get out to the field and learn for themselves)*. Given the wild insouciance of its members, the quality of conversation could be stimulating at times. Mostly, though, the talk was silly. Frankie's House was where you went for a spirited discussion about what was truly going on in the war and where you also went to forget about it. It was a clearing house of frontline lore, mostly firsthand, a forum for contrarian opinion (the MACV information office was seen as the enemy of truth), a fallout shelter of free ideas, a Greenwich Village of the mind, a circus for the soul.

After the battles of Plei Me and Ia Drang, conversations about the course of the war turned pessimistic.

'I just want to be here when the VC come rolling out of the Ho Bo Woods and take Saigon, man.'

'What a fight that's gonna be, can you imagine?'

'Scary, man.'

'Not me, brother. I'll be watching you all through long lenses from Bangkok. They won't be taking any Bao Chi prisoners.'

'Yeah, what do we do, hold up our press cards?'

'Nah, just learn how to speak French, fast.'

'Or Russian.'

'You know who they'll send in first, don't you? The 320-B, I bet.'

'Naw, it'll be the big VC units from the Delta.'

'Can you imagine them with *tanks*?'

'How about *airplanes*? VC jets.'

'Bombing the fucking Presidential Palace.'

'Man, the U.S. Air Force ought to do it for 'em.'

A few of the journalists were as angry, reckless and cynical as anyone in the alternative culture emerging in Europe or America. Others were more thoughtful, quietly philosophical in their appreciation of Vietnamese society, its wild and delicate countryside, its culture and history, the long national agony. Some loved or hated the Vietnamese more than others, some had become cynical from seeing so much indiscriminate violence, all were enchanted in one way or another by the rare elusive beauty of the place. As journalists, most of them worked with words and pictures to cover what they saw as honestly as possible, but at the same time they were trying to experience the larger adventure of their lives freely, uninhibitedly, with all of the attendant seductions, hazards and mysteries. Most of the members of the group at Frankie's House had been born between 1939 and 1945, during World War II, in environments of absent fathers, wartime rationing, somewhat strict discipline and sometimes violent punishment, making the rebels among the group part of a generation in transition, post-Beat and pre-hippie, crossing tentatively from the culture of cool masculine hip of the late 1950s and early 1960s, to the newer attractions of laid-back, mind-blown, spaced-out, drug-enlightened, free-spirited, war-heroic—rebels with a cause —the cause, of course, being the war.

Literary heroes included Ernest Hemingway, Evelyn Waugh, Norman Mailer, J. D. Salinger, Jack Kerouac, Graham Greene and others. *Catch 22* and *The Quiet American* were among their favorite novels. Elvis Presley, Chuck Berry, Bill Haley and the Comets, Carl Perkins, Little Richard, and the Supremes had been early pop music favorites, though not necessarily now. James Dean, Marlon Brando, Richard Burton and Anthony Perkins played movie characters they identified with. If their adolescent attitudes were forged in childhood by the strict, intolerant, sometimes oppressive behavior of parents and teachers, they were validated by the fiery, brooding, irreverent heroes of the film, music and literary anticulture. Most of the residents of Frankie's House were studying, if not already practicing, Buddhism. Although they came from different continents, they were surprisingly similar in personality, drawn together by language, work, age and a shared spirit of independence. In the 1950s, teenage boys in America said good-bye to their friends with expressions such as "Be cool" or "Stay cool, man" or "See you later," which, loosely translated, meant, Keep your chin up or Fear not

or Hang on to your dignity, man, the enemy is everywhere. Parents, teachers, coaches, neighbors, bosses, police, bus drivers—every adult they came in
contact with—seemed authoritarian, always treating them like dumb kids. In
Saigon they were addressed as adults. The usual parting remark among field
reporters, straight or crazy, was, "Keep your head down." In Vietnam they
were learning to hold their heads up.

The more reflective among them believed that living, working and growing up in wartime Vietnam was like being in a documentary film of your own
imagination; you didn't know what was going to happen next except that it
was possibly going to be dangerous. All you could do was wait for it to happen and try not to look foolish when it did. Usually, you did what the calmest
person around was doing and often that took no more imagination than taking cover. After a while, though, you knew from experience what to do, which
made it no less difficult or frightening but did provide the pleasure of making
the choice. Then it became possible to work: to observe, take pictures, make
notes, spot a good shot for the camera crew, stay alert. Or, in desperate circumstances for some, to fight. Once in a great while you got the opportunity
to do something brave, but only rarely and always without warning. Then the
choices were not hard to make. Staying cool was simple. We had been there
before. For those who had grown up in tough violent neighborhoods or families, Vietnam was no more frightening than coming home.

Our private war movies reeled themselves out, scene after scene, act after
act, an unending serial of adventures played against the hot graphic back-
drop of the war: men and machines maneuvering for position across the
landscape looking for a fight, drawing you into their violent drama from
time to time, churning your emotions, testing your sanity with extremes of
cruelty and compassion, fear and courage, mayhem and boredom. The routine presence of serious danger had the effect of sharpening your perceptions to a fine-edged blade that cut away the requirement for peacetime
conventions of manners and etiquette. Behaving gracefully in extreme danger was considered honorable, even heroic. Physical courage was common.
Even love was possible. Each of us played a character in an ever changing
newsreel of events, making it up as we went along, playing off whatever happened, trying to find in each situation the appropriate model of behavior
from the roles we admired from our cultural past. What the young men and
women at Frankie's House were actually doing was inventing themselves,
defining their characters as adults.

The house itself was nothing special—a modern three-story white concrete and stucco building of no architectural attraction at 47 Bui Thi Xuan, a dead-end side street on the unfashionable west side of Saigon several hundred yards beyond the Central Market. At one end of the street was a one-pump gas station facing a busy thoroughfare and at the other end was the imposing barbed wire and sandbagged fortress that housed a complex of the United States Operations Mission (USOM II), an official U.S. government enterprise that provided funding for various in-country projects and was rumored to be run by CIA.

At the center of activity at Frankie's House was Frankie, the Vietnamese houseboy hired by the five Western occupants of the place to provide domestic services: shopping, cooking, cleaning, laundry, security, and then some. Frankie could get you anything: a friendly young woman, a sandwich and soft drink, a few leaves of marijuana, the opium man and his pipe. You name it, Frankie got it. It was suggested that Frankie could even produce a tank, American or Russian, if you had the cash, the only variable being the time it would take him to deliver. Smaller, more portable weapons were no problem. Frankie was well connected to the black market economy of Saigon that was now expanding like a shipboard crap game to meet the ravenous American appetite for civilian services and supplies. He was obliging to a fault, exceedingly courteous to residents and guests alike, willing to be awakened at any hour of the afternoon or night to get on his motorbike and go on an errand, always willing to please, always for a price, almost always cheap.

Frankie was somewhere in his thirties. (It was hard to tell in Vietnam—after a certain age in adolescence, most people looked older than their years.) He had black hair, a thin build, narrow face and features, quiet manners. He wore shorts and flip-flops most of the time and put on a shirt if guests came by. As he prospered from the largesse of the regular residents and their friends, his family grew. Frankie and his young wife, who was pregnant more often than not, lived on the ground floor of the house with two small children. Her mother moved in to help with the children, then a man who said he was Frankie's brother, and then an uncle. Frankie performed the multiple functions of cook, cleaner, housekeeper, mechanic, pimp, drug dealer and news source. He knew so much about internal Saigon politics he was suspected of being a secret agent, although no one dared to guess which side he was on. Probably none. It was said that he really ought to be living in Southern California, where he would fit in fine; Saigon was too small for him. Whenever police or ARVN troops came to search the neighborhood for draft dodgers and deserters, Frankie disappeared. Usually he hid on the roof.

The founder of Frankie's house was a young Cuban businessman named Leonardo Michaelangelo Caparros, better known as "Cat." Len was tall, handsome and well-educated. He worked for the International Telephone and Telegraph company. ITT had a contract to install microwave communications for the U.S. military in Saigon, and Caparros, along with several other Cuban exiles, was part of the team. He was also an amateur photographer with ambitions to become a professional (his father had a studio in New York City) and spent much of his time with photojournalists, accompanying them into the field on operations, hanging around with them socially in Saigon. Although he was intelligent, well-read and friendly, he was also mysterious about details of his work. This, added to the fact that he belonged to a posse of Cuban exiles who occasionally cruised around Saigon openly brandishing weapons and styling themselves like swashbuckling warriors, gave some of his acquaintances in the press corps the impression that Cat might be working, at least part time, for CIA. There was no evidence, of course, other than the fact that he fit the profile. No one at Frankie's House appeared much to care.

The other founder of Frankie's House was Simon Dring, the twenty-year-old Reuters reporter from Fakenham, England. Having been one of only two Western journalists to witness the battles at both Plei Me and Ia Drang, Joe Galloway being the other (Vo Huynh was the only Vietnamese), Dring was known and respected in the Saigon press corps as a serious competitor, fearless in pursuit of a story, whatever the risks. Some of the older news hands, especially the Korean War veterans, privately disparaged his flamboyant style.

Dring arrived in Saigon early in 1965 from Vientiane, Laos, the last stop on a trans-European and Asian expedition that began when he was seventeen. In Vientiane he worked as a freelance journalist, learning as he went along, living with his new friends Tim Page and Martin Stuart-Fox, the tall gangly Australian reporter for UPI. Both of them followed Dring to Saigon and moved into Frankie's House with him and Caparros. The fifth member of the house was Steve Northup, a twenty-four-year-old still photographer from Santa Fe, New Mexico, who had distinguished himself in the street fighting at Santo Domingo, Dominican Republic, earlier in the year. He was considered one of UPI's best young combat photojournalists. Northup was six feet two with a black mustache and soft dark eyes and was as gentle and mild-mannered as Page and Dring were freewheeling and boisterous. Page, who had a nickname for everyone, called him "Northpup." Northup and I first met going down the nets with the Marines on Operation Piranha, and soon after that he invited me to visit Frankie's House.

Going out past the Central Market by taxi—a miniature blue and yellow Renault that was so cramped Northup had to tuck his knees under his chin —we arrived at Bui Thi Xuan and went up the scrubbed tile stairs to the first-floor landing and into one of the bedrooms that served as a meeting place. The room was big and cool and dry, the air conditioner being its main attraction, and was dominated by a low bed where Tim Page sat rolling a joint.

'Hey, GI! You beaucoup welcome my hou',' said Page, welcoming me with his imitation of a Saigon bar girl. 'You hab numbah one dinky dao ciga-rette,' he said, lighting the joint, filling his lungs and handing it to me. The cigarette was an oversized creation the size of a short cigar, as grandiose as Page himself. Bright green marijuana leaf fell from the open end of the joint onto the straw mat on the floor. When I reached down to pick up some of the loose bits of marijuana, the others stopped me.

'Leave it on the rug, man, there's plenty more.'

'There's enough grass in that old mat to get all of MACV stoned for a week.'

'Never happen, man, they're too tight-assed. Might fuck up their promo-tions.'

'Yeah, but they ought to. Might open their minds a little.'

'*Blow* their minds, more likely.'

'Dig it. I mean, can you imagine Westmoreland stoned?'

'Trying to hold a news conference?'

'Ah, er, um, ah . . . Ladies and gentlemen . . . and you too, Page . . . hee-hee-hee . . .'

'I have decided, in the interests of winning the war, to order B-52 strikes on Hanoi, effective immediately. The planes will drop marijuana until the enemy surrenders.'

'Stone 'em back to the Stone Age.'

'Operation *Rolling Stoned*!'

Everyone laughed a long time and then there were giggles.

'I bet Ho gets high.'

'Shit, man, anybody who smokes straight Camels by the carton has gotta be a head.'

'Yeah, but not Giap, though. Too anal. You can see it in his face.'

"I swear," said Page, "if we ever run out of dope I'm gonna roll up the mat and smoke it."

'Not much chance of that, Page. You'll never run out.'

'That rug wouldn't last you more than a couple of hours, Page.'

The white walls of the room were decorated with war trophies and souvenirs from the field: a faded blue and red NLF flag with a big gold star in the middle, a pale bamboo-yellow straw farmer's hat, an olive drab VC helmet, the empty casing of a U.S. Army rocket launcher, and a Saigon government psychological warfare poster depicting a triumphant multicolored horse trampling the body of a frightened VC soldier with blood on his face, announcing the Year of the Horse. "TET DAN-TOC QUYET-THANG," the poster proclaimed.

The door of a dark wooden clothes cupboard hung open in the corner of the room. In the shadows inside, the dull metal glint of weapons could be seen, a menacing collection of American, European and Asian firearms stacked haphazardly in a corner. Also inside were clips of ammunition for the rifles and foot-long slabs of C-4, plastic explosive wrapped in dark green cellophane. All those weapons made me uncomfortable; they gave the room the aura of an armed camp, but no one else seemed to care. It was not unusual for reporters to carry weapons in the field—Caparros, Dring, Page, Galloway and others went armed—but I was surprised to see such an arsenal on open display. It was probably illegal, though it was apparent that the local law was not an object of veneration in the house. Later I realized the weapons were props for other people's movies. On the table next to the bed where Page sat smoking a joint was a statue of Buddha.

The bed was low and wide enough for three or four long-legged young men and women to sit on. It was in a corner of the room near the window where the air conditioner blew cold air across it. Next to the bed, closer to the center of the room, was a waist-high cabinet containing a stereophonic record player, a tuner and two speakers, and an eclectic collection of books, most of them about Vietnam. Residents of the house and their guests were expected to be familiar with Vietnamese culture and history, especially the basics of Buddhist philosophy, and the thousand-year succession of wars in Vietnam. Previous efforts to conquer Vietnam by the Chinese and French were seen as historical clues to what America might expect. Although residents at Frankie's House did not pretend to be experts, they encouraged a modest amount of scholarly knowledge among themselves to enhance and enlighten what they learned in the field. The books of Bernard Fall, Jean Lacouture, Gerald Hickey, David Halberstam and Vo Nguyen Giap were worn with use, but everyone's favorite was *The Quiet American*, by Graham Greene. The book was loved not only for the quality of the writing and the moral irony of the story, but for the similarity between its hero's experiences and their own romantic fantasies. We were all Thomas Fowler, for a time. Seen through the imagery of Greene's masterful storytelling, Saigon seemed more exciting, more mysterious, more sensual to the innocent eyes of young war reporters. We imagined comparable dramas happening to us, and eventually they did, although they would not seem so romantic at the time.

There was also a collection of phonograph records in the cabinet: fairly recent LPs by Bob Dylan *(Highway 61 Revisited)*, the Rolling Stones *(12 x 5)*, the Beatles *(Help!)*, the Dave Clark Five *(Catch Us If You Can)*, the Byrds *(Mr. Tambourine Man)*, and older recordings by Peter Paul and Mary, the Animals, Buddy Holly, Joan Baez and a few classical music records of compositions by Vivaldi, Bartok and others. A set of headphones was frequently in use. Page took charge of the records and made it a rule that anyone leaving the country on R and R should return with a few recently released LPs for the common entertainment.

The records turned, the joint went around, and the mood changed from light to dark and back again according to the conversation.

'Just a little one,' said Page. 'A bit of shrapnel in the leg, maybe.'

'Nothing too terribly bloody,' said Dring.

'Just enough to get mentioned in despatches.'

'Nothing disfiguring.'

'God, no. I don't want my face messed up.'

'Page, your face is already messed up.'

'Nothing wrong with my face, mate. It's me *mind* that's messed up.'

'That's for sure,' Dring said and laughed.

'You guys are fucking *insane!*' Northup shouted.

It was not the first time Page and Dring had discussed the merits of getting themselves wounded during an air strike. Deliberately. They spoke with the broad a's of their English accents.

'The wound has to draw blood or it doesn't count,' said Dring.

'Of course. Like the one I got on Starlite.'

'Bullshit, Page. That wasn't a wound. That was a scratch. You scratched your bloody ass on a thorn.'

'How the fuck would you know?'

'Cause you already admitted it, you bleeding wanker. Here, in this very room, when you were stoned.'

'That's affirm, Page,' someone said.

Page and Dring did not openly acknowledge their rivalry but it was apparent to the others and was always close to the surface, intense and unyielding. Both were English, close to the same age, anxious to make names for themselves in the world of journalism and photography, although to have revealed their ambition would have been considered bad taste. Anything daring Dring had done, Page had done better, and vice versa. They considered it important to dress the part, "sporting the image," as they called it. They collected wardrobes of hard-core combat gear: British and Australian bush hats, tight-fitting Special Forces jungle fatigues, unit cap badges, sweat scarves, web belts and, most important, exotic sidearms and submachineguns. One of Dring's prize possessions was a Swedish K, a submachinegun he had been given ceremonially by his friends in Fifth Special Forces. When it disappeared during a bacchanalian house party, he accused Page of stealing it, though the gun was never returned. Page and Dring seemed to be competing for the distinction of bravest (or most foolhardy) journalist in Vietnam. One measure of this distinction seemed to be the number of times each had been wounded in combat. Page, by virtue of the splinter he caught with the Marines in August, was leading. To Dring, reflecting later, the overall experience of being a war correspondent in Vietnam felt like racing a motorcycle down a road toward an oncoming car at a hundred miles an hour. To Page, who never forgot how good it felt the first time he fell off a motorcycle and his teenage girlfriends showered him with sympathy, getting wounded was another way of getting attention, an extra mark of personal distinction. No one spoke about a death wish.

'Wouldn't mind a nice little piece of shrapnel from an air strike,' said Page.

'It's tempting, isn't it?' said Dring. 'I almost did it at Plei Me. I mean, there were so many bleeding air strikes, all I had to do was stand up.'

Everyone was high. Page announced that he was going to play the house anthem. No one objected. A worn, tired album by the Animals was produced, the jacket frayed from use, and the needle went into the groove. The introduction began with two ominous bars of a low bass guitar and, during this, the volume was turned up to a point just below a level that would bring the police. Everyone listened seriously. No one spoke.

> *In this dirty old part of the city*
> *Where the sun refuse to shine,*
> *People tell me there ain't no use in trying.*
> *Now my girl you're so young and pretty*
> *And one thing I know is true,*
> *You'll be dead before your time is due.*

At the refrain, everyone in the room erupted in song, shouting as loud as possible, drowning out the Animals.

> *We gotta get out of this place!*
> *If it's the last thing we ever do!*
> *We gotta get out of this place!*
> *Girl, there's a better life for me and you.*

As written, the song had nothing to do with Saigon or the war; it was about 1960s alienation. It would have been the anthem if Frankie's House had existed in London, New York, Santa Fe or Sydney. It was a road song for young men with the kind of wanderlust that got them to Saigon in the first place. Here, the song had special resonance, combining their common anti-social feelings with a sense of doom and the morbid self-pity that accompanies young men to hard places.

"Page, what do you want to bet you don't make it till your next birthday?"

It was Martin Stuart-Fox, the ascetic blond-haired Australian. He stood at the end of the Page's bed wearing a cotton sarong around his waist, sandals, and nothing else. His tall thin body was white-skinned except for his face and arms, which were brown-gold from the sun. Stuart-Fox, the most academic of those at Frankie's House and the most paternal, was determined to get Page out of the country before he was killed or critically wounded. Like the others, Stuart-Fox believed that Page, in his quest for acceptance and fame, was truly crazy, blindly self-destructive, headed down a path that would surely lead to an early death. All his friends saw it. For Page, however, taking risks was the only way he knew how to live.

'Tell you what, Page,' said Northup. 'If you make it to your twenty-second birthday, we'll all chip in and buy you a new hi-fi. How's that?'

'I'll buy the turntable,' said Stuart-Fox.

'I'll get the tuner and amp,' Dring offered.

'I'll pay for the speakers,' I volunteered, joining in the spirit of the challenge.

'What if I lose?' Page said.

'You'll be dead, Page; it won't make any difference.'

'Yeah, then we get to split up your stuff.'

'I'll take your motorcycle,' said Dring.

'And I'll get your cameras,' said Northup.

'Fuckin 'ell,' said Page, 'it ain't bloody fair.'

Everyone laughed.

'Life's not fair, Page.'

'Yeah, look at the Vietnamese.'

There was silence for a time.

'Right, Page, how about it? All you have to do is stay out of the field until your birthday and you can't lose. Get it?'

'I'll think about it,' said Page. He sat back on the bed and was silent, apparently trying to figure the angles, scheming ways of winning the wager, what kind of hi-fi he would get.

There was something vulnerable about Page that made friends want to protect him. His dark eyes had a distant, helpless look that appeared when he was contemplative. At the same time, he could be so cocky, so outrageously boastful, that it made even those who loved him wince at his unrestrained self-centeredness.

"On the one hand you love Page," one of his friends said, "and on the other you don't."

He signed his name on notes and postcards, "Vulmit," which he expected you to read backward, and wrote a slogan on a wall of his room, "Humming Clune," which was what he called anyone who was being silly. In rare moments when he was not high on drugs, Page could be thoughtful, intelligent and sincere, but he was almost always stoned and therefore silly and self-centered. "Dope is hope," he exclaimed with the honest conviction of an addict.

Page was a masterful entertainer who was happiest when he was amusing friends and acquaintances, usually while consuming drugs with them.

He welcomed you into his circle like a lost brother, making you comfortable at once, learning your ways to tease you about them when he knew you better. His flattery could make you feel like the most exalted person in the room. Page was also generous, especially with his dope, but not to a fault. He liked to trade possessions: camera equipment, field gear, records—usually to his advantage. Coming out of a swap with Page, you sometimes found a defect in what you received.

Life was a play for Page, a living performance with the war as his stage. He played the lead as the craziest, funniest, weirdest war photographer in the world, making up the script as he went along. Any idea, any shred of information (real or imagined), anything that could be used to promote his reputation as a fearless jungle-survivor-warrior-photographer was incorporated into his personal story. Some of the feats of daring he described were actually true, but you could never be sure. He heard other people tell interesting stories and worked them into his own repertoire, inserting himself as the hero. After a time, Page began to suffer from an affliction that went with the drug use: a state of mind that made it difficult for him to think more than superficially about anyone but himself.

A visit to the opium den was suggested. A couple of hours remained before the eleven o'clock curfew, so it was decided to go. The group, including Dring, Page, Northup, Stuart-Fox, Robin Mannock and me, got aboard the motorcycles that Frankie kept for them in the garage of the house and headed toward the airport, laughing, singing and shouting to one another. Dring led the way. I rode on the back of Page's bike. It was surprising how accomplished a motorcyclist he was when stoned. The bikers wove in and out among the smaller, more polite Vietnamese on their bicycles, motorbikes and tiny cars until they arrived at an impoverished, darkened neighborhood. They parked the bikes on a side street near the edge of a canal and paid a few men who were sitting nearby to watch them. The group walked single file through the back of a store and out over a bamboo footbridge that crossed the canal, then along a path through a residential section where families lived in narrow boats on the water. After waiting a while outside a small house for preparations to be made, we went into a backroom with a low dark ceiling and thin mats with cushions on the floor. A tired-eyed woman who appeared to be in her late forties or early fifties, dressed in a shabby cotton aó dài, welcomed us in Vietnamese and motioned for us to lie down. Veterans of the den, Page and Dring immediately took off their shoes and sat and stretched their long legs out on the cushions and prepared themselves with accomplished skill. The woman brought a long pipe with a darkened mahogany bowl and handed it to me. Page and Dring showed me how to puff hard and inhale deeply as the woman held the low flame of a taper to a tiny black ball of opium that bubbled on the end of a pin in her hand over the bowl of the pipe. Then I was to hold the smoke in my lungs for as long as I could. The taste of it was bitter. I coughed. The old woman took the pipe to each of the young men in a slow ritual that went around and around what seemed like a dozen times, although the others warned me to stop after six pipes because it was my first time.

'Ohhh, yesh,' said Page after the third or fourth pipe. 'I dooo believe. . . .'

Except for various groans of pleasure, the others were quiet.

I was not conscious of any change. I was less intoxicated by the opium than I was impressed by the elaborate circumstances of the ritual—the darkened room, the strange new smells, the lighting and inhaling of the pipe, the conspiratorial nature of it all. Objects seemed more sharply focused, clearer, especially the dim light and the colors and sound—the kaleidoscopic brilliance of everything. My perceptions were sharpened and, at the same time, I felt mildly more comfortable, as though floating on air. The others began to laugh and joke and Page teased them about any lack of skill with the pipe, all except Dring, who appeared to be expert.

Outside the air was fresh, the colors vivid. A soft buzzing sensation pulsed through my nervous system—my senses experienced the world in a new way. I was also slightly nauseous.

'Let me drive back,' I said to Page.

'Do you know how?'

'No.'

'Right then, mate,' Page said without hesitation, 'I'll teach you.'

He left nothing out of the instruction: kickstand, lights, ignition, starting crank, throttle, transmission, clutch, brakes, balance, turns, the lot. The others laughed and made bets about how far we were likely to get before crashing. Page got on back and held us in balance while I engaged the gears. The start was wobbly but once I got the feel of the throttle and clutch we were able to make reasonable progress. Dring led the way home again but went slowly. Northup and Stuart-Fox shielded us from the other cars on the street. Page showed no fear, even in traffic, giving me encouragement, chastising the others for their lack of faith. In fact, we went some distance in relatively good balance, my adrenaline overriding the opium, before Page offered to take over. I felt a sense of accomplishment, proving to the others that I could smoke with them and still function. Such acts helped to win acceptance, and it pleased me to be a visiting member of their crazy gang. I had apparently passed the first initiation in the pleasures, though not yet the perils, of opium smoking in Saigon.

Drugs were the great leveler. They could blot out ordinary distinctions of nationality, class, age, education, job status or looks. High on drugs, every-one was equal. Dope was what you took instead of alcohol or sleeping pills, effectively medicating the nightmares that plagued everyone. (The picture of the dead PAVN antiaircraft gunner with his head cracked open on the road to Plei Me had recently replaced the image in my dreams of the young Viet-namese mother lying in the road in Happy Valley with her child standing beside her, but some nights they switched.) With drugs like opium and mar-ijuana, memories of traumas in the field got filed away for later, though none of us knew how much, or how difficult, later would be. Not long after, the expression "whatever gets you through the night" became a popular say-ing in the States, though it was hard to say whether it reflected a real need or was just an excuse to get high. Sometimes drugs took away reality so com-pletely it was possible to forget the war for a while.

One of my favorite escapes was to listen on the headphones at Frankie's House to Mary Travers singing "Five Hundred Miles." In her voice of perfect haunting clarity, the song came close to the melancholy in the music of the Vietnamese:

> *If you miss the train I'm on*
> *You will know that I am gone*
> *You can hear the whistle blow a hundred miles . . . .*
> *A hundred miles, a hundred miles, a hundred miles, a hundred miles*
> *You can hear the whistle blow*
> *A hundred miles.*
>
> *Lord I'm one, Lord I'm two, Lord I'm three, Lord I'm four,*
> *Lord I'm five hundred miles from my home.*
> *Five hundred miles, five hundred miles,*
> *five hundred miles, five hundred miles,*
> *Lord I'm five hundred miles from my home.*

Homesick and sad, none of us would have stayed in Vietnam were it not for the excitement and challenge of the work. We stuck it out because our jobs required us to be there and it was the work we had chosen to do. Only the most seriously disturbed young men and women enjoyed it. Some stayed longer than others. Some came for only a few days or a week. A few came and left immediately. Most stayed for a few months or a year. Some stayed forever. About 150 journalists died covering the war. Being brave about being there did not preclude feeling lonely and sorry for ourselves from time to time.

The distance from Frankie's House to the hotel where I stayed was about a mile, and I often walked back alone through the abandoned streets in the nighttime dark. It was the coolest time of day and the air was still warm but not so humid. The Saigon police who stood in pairs at the big intersections did not bother me for a curfew pass. Feeling light-headed and happy from an evening of frivolity at Frankie's House, I crossed the wide plaza in front of a block-long building that included the Central Market, a great cavernous structure that was filled with people during the day but was abandoned and silent at night. As I walked along the sidewalk, out of the far left edge of my vision I saw something move on the ground inside one of the empty stalls. I stopped to look. A bare lightbulb hung from a wire strung from the rafters threw dim yellow light on the pavement. A small cat, possibly a half-grown kitten, stood alone on the concrete floor, crouching in panic. It had dark fur and a head too large for the rest of its body. Like most dogs and cats and many of the people in the city, it was undernourished. The cat's back was pressed against a stack of wooden crates that were piled on top of each other, blocking its way to the rear. On the other three sides, the cat was surrounded by a pack of large brown rats. I did not move. The rats were big and fat and low to the ground and formed a semicircle about four feet away from the cat. They advanced toward the cat, a few millimeters at a time, moving together as a pack. The cat looked terrified, all its fur on end, no way of escape. There were a dozen or so rats and they moved forward as one, close enough for their whiskers to touch. Without thinking, I reached into the gutter and picked up a chunk of broken paving stone the size of a baseball and threw it quickly into the center of the animals. The stone landed with a heavy crash among the rats. They scattered immediately in all directions. At the same time, the cat sprang over the moving rats with an Olympian jump and disappeared down an empty corridor into the darkness of the vast open market.

Aha! I said to myself, skipping a step along the sidewalk, reflecting on the amazing acrobatics of the cat, dancing a happy jig in my mind, *That's one for us!*

JANUARY 31, 1966

From the air, the land looked wild and angry. Bright flames from burning houses glowed red beneath clusters of shade trees scattered across the coastal plain. Smoke rose in narrow plumes straight up through the windless heat and dissolved in the high haze. Clouds of dust swirled among circular batteries of U.S. Army field guns firing salvos of artillery shells into the air, the rounds visible as fleeting shadows leaving the tubes, puffs of white smoke spurting from their muzzles. Far away, geysers of earth erupted where the shells exploded, *brraaaak! brraaaak! brraaaak!* booming loud along the length of the sandy plain. Helicopters swarmed over the land buzzing with rockets and machineguns, swooping down into drop zones, disgorging soldiers, kicking out supplies, collecting the wounded and sick, mock assaulting, charging away again, swirling back and forth across the burning land in restless urgent profusion, like furious steel wasps. In the distance, airplanes circled in slow arcs, rolled over on their wingtips and dived at the ground, darting down through the gray air, letting loose shining metal canisters from under their wings that tumbled toward the ground and burst in bright flame-yellow clouds of burning napalm and dense black oil-smoke that stuck to whatever it touched and consumed it in fire.

Looking down from a helicopter at thirty-five hundred feet, I saw the terrain twitch with the recoil of the guns and flicker in the light of the flames. As far as the eye could see the land was under assault, the full expression of the Army's war-fighting fury: all its resources deployed, all its violence unsheathed, as if waging war against the land itself.

Operation Masher was the biggest search-and-destroy mission of the war. It covered hundreds of square miles along the central coast of South Vietnam, from Quang Ngai to Qui Nhon, in villages and hamlets where Saigon's official presence had not been felt for many years. Twenty thousand American, South Vietnamese and Korean troops swept across the land with the ruthless authority of their firepower. American soldiers patrolled north across a broad front: searching villages, interrogating civilians, taking prisoners, seizing weapons, crushing anyone who confronted them. Farther north, hundreds of Marines climbed down the cargo nets of Navy ships in the South China Sea, landed on the beaches, moved inland across the sand and turned south to hammer the enemy on the Army's anvil. Two regiments of North Vietnamese and two of Viet Cong were reported to be operating in Binh Dinh and Quang Ngai Provinces, and the purpose of this expansive, complicated operation was to force them into the open by saturating the area with troops, chase them across a wide plain, engage them in combat again and again, and destroy them as fighting units. When he learned of the operation, President Johnson was reported to have ordered the code name changed from "Masher," which he found too brutal, to the less militant "White Wing." By the time I got there a week after the operation began, it was apparent that Masher was a mild term for what was going on.

The main responsibility for the success of the operation was given to the 1st Cavalry Division's 3d Brigade. Colonel Harold G. Moore, who had distinguished himself in the Ia Drang Valley battles of November, was the new commander. The division was pushing farther and farther away from its headquarters at An Khe in the Central Highlands. Having swept the Vinh Thanh and Soui Ca Valleys, it was now operating more than fifty miles northeast of its base camp, several miles beyond the theoretical limit of its tactical area of responsibility. Now Hal Moore briefed journalists at his new brigade headquarters at Bong Son, a provincial town about 295 miles northeast of Saigon, six miles inland from the South China Sea. Moore, an affable officer with bright eyes and a quick mind, made friends easily with the press. He enjoyed the company of reporters and made them welcome, none more than R. W. (Johnny) Apple, correspondent for the *New York Times*. Round-faced and friendly, Apple was a hardworking journalist who had joined the *Times* from NBC News and had just finished a biographical profile of Moore, a "Man in the News" feature, for the newspaper. As one of Moore's favorites, Apple walked briskly through the Bong Son camp wearing a helmet and had an M-16 rifle slung over his shoulder. The rifle and helmet made him look more like a member of Moore's brigade staff than a civilian noncombatant. This did not escape the scrutiny of his peers, who, in the manner of U.S. Special Forces, did not usually wear helmets in the field, nor were any carrying weapons.

'What's the helmet for Apple? Getting your picture taken?' a journalist called to him.

'Gonna kill a few gooks, huh John?'

'Hey, Johnny, you know something we don't?'

'Yeah, we about to be overrun?'

Apple took the needling gracefully. He explained that Moore had ordered him to carry the rifle as a condition for accompanying troops in the field. Later in the day, however, the M-16 was gone.

Shortly after three o'clock the camp buzzed with reports that one of the brigade's rifle companies was taking heavy fire from a farm village about six miles north of Bong Son. A number of Americans had been killed or wounded. Not much else was known. For those of us at the camp, it was the story of the day. The only way to get there and cover it would be with medical evacuation helicopters that would be going in to rescue the wounded. I walked through the camp until I found the medevac operations tent and went inside. I was given a friendly welcome from Captain Guy Kimsey, who had been the main subject of a report we made about First Cav medevac pilots the previous autumn. Kimsey's friends and relatives in the States had seen the story on television and had written to him. He was a hero in their eyes. Listening to the brigade radio net in his command tent, Kimsey heard there were so many wounded waiting for evacuation that all four of his helicopters would have to go. He agreed to transport us to the battle.

'How many can you take?' I asked.

'Eight,' he said. 'Look, Jack, you and your crew can come with us. And five of the others. You decide who goes. Just make sure they understand it's a one-way trip only. No matter what happens on the ground, they can't come back out with us. We're going to be full. Okay?'

'Okay. I'll make sure everybody understands,' I said.

Discreetly, I told four friends to find their way to the medevac chopper pad. One at a time they slipped away from the main group of journalists so that no one knew they were going to the battle.

The camera crew and I got aboard Kimsey's helicopter. It was the first time I was working with a Danish-born film photographer named Carl Sorensen. Jim Wilson and Bob Funk had finished their tour and returned to the States. Sorensen was in his mid-thirties with a soft Scandinavian accent and fine thin hair combed straight back over his head. He had a reputation for steady nerves, having covered the revolution in the Dominican Republic the previous year. The sound recordist was Vallop Radboon, a twenty-four-year-old Thai from Bangkok, a polite young man who was new in Vietnam and not yet experienced in combat. The others I invited were Johnny Apple, Martin Stuart-Fox of United Press International, Eddie Adams of the Associated Press, and Sean Flynn, another new arrival to Vietnam who was accredited to the French picture magazine *Paris-Match*. Flynn was a part-time actor and playboy who had not worked as a professional photographer before and was learning how to take pictures. He had come to Vietnam as much to experience the adventure of war as to cover it. Because he was the son of Errol Flynn, his appearance in Saigon was assumed by many to be a publicity move by an aspiring young actor with nothing better to do. When he got off the plane at Ton Son Nhut airport in Saigon, he was reported to be carrying a tennis racket. Flynn came to Frankie's House with Page one night and charmed the rest of us with his modesty and humor. He was exceptionally handsome: tall, fit, long naturally blond hair, soft brown eyes, perfect teeth. His good looks transcended even Hollywood notions of phys-ical attractiveness. Yet it was soon apparent that Flynn was neither self-important nor conceited. He seemed more interested in the people around him, especially Page, who was cool and crazy. From his first appearance at Frankie's House, Flynn showed that he would like to be accepted in the group. After he had been accredited and had collected his field gear, he asked me one evening if he could accompany me and a CBS camera team into the field. Page and the others at the house had told him to go on his first operation with a network camera team because the Army took such good care of us. Moreover, Flynn said he wanted to learn how to shoot news film so that he might someday work for CBS, an opportunity I had given once to Page.

With the journalists aboard, Kimsey and the other medevac pilots started the engines of their helicopters. A thin frail-looking Vietnamese who spoke no English appeared from behind a tent and approached the group. Standing next to the LZ with a silent camera at his side and a camera bag with the ABC logo on it, he looked forlorn. Clearly, he wanted to come. I didn't want him with us. His film would be competitive on ABC, giving him the possibil-ity of scooping us. But he looked so helpless, so vulnerable, that at the last moment I waved him onto the helicopter and gave a thumbs-up to the crew chief. Sorensen looked at me with scorn.

The four helicopters took off and flew north at over a hundred knots, heading for a cluster of black dots on the pilots' maps marking a hamlet near the village of An Thai.

Thirty-five hundred feet below, the landscape swirled with movement and fire. A radio call reported that most of an American platoon, twenty-three men, had been killed or wounded in three hours of fighting in the hamlet. Alpha Company, 2/12, was still receiving sniper fire. Captain Kimsey waited in the air for a signal that it was reasonably safe to land, spotted a cloud of colored smoke marking the LZ, then led the flight in as low and as fast as he could, flaring hard at the moment of landing. It was just after four o'clock and the shadows of the trees ahead were getting long. The helicopters touched the ground a hundred yards from the southern treeline of the hamlet on a barren patch of white sand covered with mounds of earth and gray stone slabs. We had landed in the middle of a cemetery.

Wounded soldiers staggered toward the helicopters in a storm of fine sand the rotor blades blew at them, stinging like needles, the loose ends of their bandages fluttering in the violent wind. Noise from the rotors and engines muffled the shouts and cries. Journalists ran to the wounded soldiers and helped carry them to the helicopters, handing them to the chopper crews, globs of blood smearing their fatigues. A red-haired GI with a field dressing around his wounded leg limped forward alone, his face frightened. Crouching low, Eddie Adams snapped a picture of a broad-chested soldier, his fatigue shirt off, a bandage on his upper left arm, struggling against the wind and sand, his dark-skinned head tilted to one side, eyes in a tight grimace of discomfort and fear.

The moment the helicopters were loaded, Kimsey led them up out of the swirling sand and into the air, banking west sharply away from the hamlet, then circled south and east on a course for the 85th Field Evacuation Hospital at Qui Nhon. Sixteen wounded went, four to a ship. The sound of the choppers faded slowly, purring away in the distance. Then silence. On the ground beside the LZ, seven soldiers wrapped in ponchos lay without moving.

"You guys better get your heads down," a soldier shouted. Single shots snapped through the trees of the hamlet to our front.

The eight reporters and photographers spread out and took cover behind small headstones and burial mounds covered with bleached white sand forming the shape of coffins. The headstones were about two feet high and a foot across, old gray stone with faded names and dates. Many had no markings. A few short scrub bushes and cacti grew around them. The fine sand got into our hair, clothing, eyes, ears, mouth, nostrils, and it stuck to the sweat on our skin. Within a few minutes I felt as if I'd been in the field for days. Late afternoon sunlight reflected off the sand and held the heat above a hundred degrees.

Soldiers who had carried the wounded out to the graveyard turned and ran back toward the treeline. Rifles cracked. Sorensen, Vallop and I ran across the sand toward the trees, heads down, juggling the camera equipment that connected us, our boots sliding in the sand. At the edge of the hamlet we jumped into a shallow trench, a dry irrigation ditch about two feet deep with several inches of sand at the bottom. Palm trees and scrub brush stood directly in front. Fifty feet farther ahead were one-story houses of mud and clay with thatched bamboo roofs. Nothing moved. Single shots came from inside the hamlet.

"Keep down, right?" I said to Sorensen.

"Whew," he said, out of breath.

"Okay."

I looked through the treeline. Flynn appeared to the left sprinting into the hamlet, holding his Leica to his chest, running low like a veteran, a tall yellow-haired shadow disappearing into the trees. Rifle shots cracked. Watching him I thought, *How crazy! Who knows what's in there?* My reaction was automatic in these situations. I judged degrees of danger partly to justify my own caution, partly to preserve a sense of security that came from being more careful than others. *Flynn's going to get hurt*, I thought, *going forward like that.* At the time, I didn't know the full story of Flynn's agenda, that he might be trying to follow in his father's image, acting out in real life the parts his father had played in the movies, competing with those fictional characters, trying to do them better. Who could tell? Flynn had more to prove than the rest of us, although we were all trying to prove the same thing, especially to ourselves. Given my own situation at the moment, head down in a ditch, making fine distinctions between what was safe and what was not could hardly be considered sane or rational either.

The shooting stopped. Sorensen, Vallop and I lay in the shallow trench. Three soldiers lay next to us. On the left was the commander of A Company, 2/12, Captain Eugene Fox of Washington, D.C., a sturdy officer in his late twenties with short red hair and muscular arms now powdered with white sand. He held two clips of M-16 ammunition in his right hand and another was tucked into the cover strap of his helmet. Fox lay back on his side in the ditch next to his radioman and his first sergeant, William Stanfield of Terre

Haute, Indiana. I asked him what was happening. Fox said his company had been on the move for three days and had been in contact every day. This was the worst. His lead platoon had been badly hurt.

Sorensen lined up a shot and rolled film on the captain. Fox said his company had moved into the hamlet at one o'clock, started taking light sniper fire within an hour, then intense fire, then mortars.

"How many casualties have you taken so far?" I asked.

"I couldn't approximate."

"Ten? Twenty?"

"About fifteen so far."

"Fifteen today."

"Roughly."

"Just from this one village?"

"Just this one, yes."

"Have you been able to take the village yet?"

"Uh, negative. The sniper fire became increasingly intense. We started getting a couple of mortar rounds in so we pulled back to our present positions right over here. . . ."

"Is it start and stop like this? Heavy fire and then . . ."

"Yes, it's just, it's just sporadic."

I turned the microphone to the radio operator. "How do you feel?"

"Oh I feel fine."

"You mean you like this?"

"No, not exactly. But, since I'm over here, I might as well do my job while I'm here."

"You might as well get in the thick of it?"

He laughed uncomfortably. "Might as well."

Artillery fell with loud *braaacks* a few hundred yards away.

Fox spoke. "It's just a bunch a yokels that we can't get at, that's all. We can't see 'em. In order to get a shot at 'em we have to find out where they are. By the time we find out where they are, we've taken a couple of casualties."

A helicopter flew over low and turned away. A machinegun banged in the distance.

With no warning, suddenly, bright flashing bullets began to whiz overhead, flaming orange phosphorus streaks two feet off the ground accompanied by a rolling thunderclap of noise, *crackacrackacrackacrackacrackacracka-*

crackacrackacrackacrackacrackacrackacrackacrackacrackacrackacracka, hundreds of bullets breaking the sound barrier at the same time, .50-caliber machineguns rattling death.

"*Get down!*" I scream. "*Get down, get down! Carl, get down!*"

Instantly out of breath. "*Stay down!*" Clawing at the sand in the ditch with our fingers, elbows, knees, digging into it, faces pressed against the sand, feeling the heat on our cheeks, tracers flashing like lightning, burning orange darts illuminating the air, *pop-pop-pop-pop-pop-pop*, heavy insistent fire a foot above our heads, mixed now with other automatic weapons, long bursts of .30-caliber along with the .50, bullets hissing close. *Chuhhtt!* an M-79 round exploding.

"Grenades," I say, breathless.

Broken leaves and twigs flutter onto our heads, lightly, as in a winter wind.

Time slows and stops. Each moment expands a hundredfold. Vision sharp, hearing acute, mouth dry, breath short. Everything moving in slow precise motion except the mind, which is hyperalert, working faster than ever in my life, heart beating in the temples, fast rhythmic thumps, audible in my ears. Steady and cool inside now, the initial panic gone.

This is it. The NVA have got us outgunned and are going to overrun us. No way out. Can't change a thing. I realize that I am trapped in the unchangeable procession of fate: totally powerless, out of options, detached, accepting. *Nothing to do but wait and see how you get it.* The only consolation is that I am steady enough to watch it happen.

I look up over the edge of the ditch expecting to see a line of North Vietnamese assault troops running out of the hamlet with AKs firing in front of them, shooting us in the ditch like helpless animals. Overhead, branches flutter in the stream of bullets and a few leaves fall. No one in the ditch is shooting back; just a row of unmoving helmets tucked in the sand.

So this is how it ends, I think. *So simple, so impersonal. How humiliating to die of a bullet in the back.*

I feel alone. In another world. A few seconds pass.

Abruptly, the shooting stops.

In a few seconds, Fox is on his radio, calm, businesslike.

"Please do that. I'll get in contact with you, over. Blackhat this is Club Six, over."

The radio squawks acknowledgment, "This is Redhat X-Ray, over." (Redhat, I learn later, is the call sign of an American adviser to a South Vietnamese paratroop battalion that is now moving toward us from the north, trying to link up with Fox's company. The paratroops and their advisers wear red berets.)

"This is Club Six," says Fox. "If you could come around where I can see you. I didn't even see you that time except for a few of your tracers coming overhead. We'll orient, over."

"This is Redhat X-Ray. Roger, I think we're headed towards that, ah, church right now in town. I'll get back, over."

"I don't know what church you're makin reference to, but if I see you I'll let you know, over."

"Club Six, this is Redhat X-Ray. When you get us in sight . . ." A grenade explodes, *chuhhtt*, not far away. "Or you hear us . . .."

At this moment the attack resumes with great fury. Light and heavy machineguns, automatic rifles, grenade launchers—all firing with the force of a cyclone, bullets spitting into the sand, grenades exploding close by. Our heads are down, faces tight with fear, deafening noise in our ears. I look across the graveyard and see lumps of bodies on the ground, flat motionless figures, noses in the sand, Eddie Adams and Johnny Apple among them, bullets kicking up beside them. *They're dead. No way to survive exposed like that.* I was too frightened to feel remorse.

In the trench, Sorensen and Vallop are on their stomachs, the camera resting on Sorensen's back. I see a line of infantry on our right, dozens of soldiers in dark uniforms, 150 yards away. They are firing straight at us, the muzzles of their rifles flashing. The angle of the heavy machinegun bullets shifts around to the right, coming in now on our flank, bright orange tracers getting bigger, closer, faster . . .

"*Carl, we've gotta get some of this!*" I say. Sorensen is on the ground next to me, unmoving. I pull the camera off his back, prop it up between us on its shoulder brace, point the lens toward the incoming fire. *I've gotta get some of this on film*, I think, *even if it kills us.* The Auricon is heavy, awkward. I don't know how to focus the lens. All I can do is turn it on and off. Sorensen shifts over on his side and looks up at me. His face is rigid, eyes wide. He regards me as if I'm out of my mind, pointing his camera at the incoming fire. I fumble to find the cable to the camera battery and switch on the power. The camera rolls.

"*There! There! Focus!*" I shout at Sorensen. He turns all the way over on his back and tries to adjust the exposure. Then he reaches for the focus, setting it on infinity. Finally, he adjusts the focal length to wide angle. I hold the camera unsteadily, pointing toward the soldiers shooting at us. My camera work is unprofessional and Sorensen is irritated.

"I have a lot of things," he complains, "diaphragm, focus . . ."

"I'm sorry . . ." I say.

"A lot of things. . . ."

"Can you get it?"

"Get what?"

"Those troops moving across there, they're firing . . ."

"You want to waste all my film?"

The camera has been rolling continuously.

"I can't turn it off," I say. Finding the switch, I turn the power off.

"Okay."

The volume of fire slackens. Sorensen leans up on his elbow and explains that the light reading changes when you point the camera in different directions.

"There's *one* exposure," he says, pointing to our left, "there's *another* exposure. It's not a matter of (just) turning around."

"Well, I saw, there's a whole bunch of troops moving by. See if you can get them on a long-range shot."

Just to our left, Captain Fox shouts, "Smoke? Got smoke? Somebody throw smoke in the. . . ."

Raging gunfire swallows the rest of his words. Deafening noise. Everyone gets down. Dark shadowy shapes the size of small tanks move along our right flank, less than two hundred yards away. *Jesus, APCs!* Armored personnel carriers fire into our lines across a field of low green vegetables. A plume of white smoke rises behind them on the horizon. Bullets and grenades fly. A hailstorm of gunfire rips into the ground, trees, brush. Sorensen is pointing the camera, trying to focus, his eye behind the viewfinder, working. I fumble for the switch and turn it on. "Okay! Now! You're rolling!" A helicopter flies in behind the line, turns sharply to the right, races away, clattering. Very heavy fire, everyone pinned to the ground. In the trench, First Sergeant Stanfield pulls the pin on a smoke grenade and tosses it just outside the trench. *Sssssssssssssssssssssssssssss*, rich purple smoke billowing out of the can, the smell of it sharp and bitter in our noses.

CHUHHTT! An explosion on the edge of the ditch. Heat and blast on the side of my face. Wild noise. Someone in the ditch groans, *"God damn!"*

"Stop-stop-stop shooting! Stop firing!" Fox screams on the radio . . . *"Stop-stop-stop!"* Pleading . . . *"Redhat stop! God damn it!"* Desperate . . . *"Stop it!*

God damn it!" Bang! A close explosion . . . *"You stop, stop firing, over!"* Beseeching. . . .

Vallop lies on his back holding both hands over his lower right side, blood on his fingers. "He's hit," I say softly. Then, turning, I shout down the trench, "We've got a wounded. . . ."

"Redhat stop firing, stop firing! Can you hear me, over?" Fox pleads on the radio. "Corpsman."

"Redhat, Redhat, this is Club Six, over."

"Need a corpsman!" I am shouting.

"Yeah, I know," Fox says. The radio squawks. Redhat asks Fox to pop smoke to mark his position. "I haven't got any God damn smoke! You just fired an M-79 into it!"

I notice the stone in the ring on Fox's finger holding the radio handset. *West Point*, I think.

"Faith preserve us," he says, angry, disgusted. Then, in a voice filled with despair, the young company commander cries out, to no one, *"What kind of fucking war is this?"*

And then the shooting stops. No one moves. It is quiet . . .

Silence.

Sweet, still, absolute silence. Single moments of perfect peace, one upon another, second after second, ticking off in my head like the pendulum of an old clock in an empty house. The realization that it's over comes slowly. I hear nothing, feel everything, as if for the first time. The air is cool to the surface of the skin and smells of life. Exquisite relief, like being reborn, joy to be alive.

The radio squawks. A call comes in from Joker Six, battalion commander of 2/12. Fox replies, "Let everybody know that I cannot make contact with them, over." He listens for a moment. "I believe that but, uh, we're gonna need some more medevacs here now." Looking over his shoulder at me he mutters, "What a fucked-up war this is."

Vallop moans, "I'm hurt. I'm hurt." He rests on his back, holding a white handkerchief to the lower right side of his abdomen. The handkerchief is red with blood. I pull it back to look. There is a small dark hole in the skin where a fragment of shrapnel from a grenade has gone in. External bleeding has stopped. Vallop turns his head and rests it against the sand, eyes half closed.

Sorensen says, "Are you all right, Jack?" His face is white. He points at the side of my face. There is blood there. I have no idea how it happened. There is no pain.

I get up and run along the edge of the hamlet calling for a medic. I find one —his name is White—and bring him back to treat Vallop. Fox is on the radio calling medevacs. His leg was wounded by grenade fragments. Sergeant Stanfield is also wounded. Of the six people in the ditch, five of us have been hit by the M-79 round. Only Sorensen is not wounded. He shows me his camera. The right side of the metal film magazine is pitted by shrapnel.

The medic snips away the front of Vallop's T-shirt with his scissors. Ribs show through his narrow chest. The skin on his stomach is lighter brown than his face.

'Where'd this guy come from?' the medic says.

'Thailand,' Sorensen says.

'You hit anywhere else?' he asks Vallop.

'No.'

The medic puts a field dressing over the wound and assures Vallop he is going to be okay; a medevac is inbound. Vallop rolls his head to the left. The expression on his face is sad.

Sorensen suggests we do an interview with him. He gets the camera focused, framed and rolling.

"How long have you been in Vietnam, Vallop?"

"Two weeks."

"Two weeks you've been working for CBS?"

"Yes."

"This is your first combat assignment?"

"No, second time. Yeah, second time in combat."

"And fifteen minutes after you landed on a medevac you're about to be medevac'd yourself. Okay. We'll take good care of you. You'll be all right."

Just out of the picture frame, Vallop has the fingers of his right hand on the volume control knob of the sound amplifier, riding gain on his own interview.

Fox is angry now. His helmet off, arm resting on his pack, he waits for the medevac. "Worst situation I've been in Vietnam," he says.

Sorensen is rolling. I ask Fox, "Those armored personnel carriers were only one, two hundred yards away. How could they make such a mistake?"

"I don't know. I think they were misdirected down from the north. And, as they came by on the flank, they, ah, received fire from the Victor Charlies who had been, ah, north of us all day. Ah, I think they felt they were attacking into the heart of the VC concentration."

The camera stops. Fox looks up. 'Anybody got a cigar?' Sorensen reaches into his pocket. 'Here, you can have my last one.' Fox takes it and lights up.

A soldier comes by, stops at the command group and says in a low voice, "I thought I'd had it for good."

Sergeant Stanfield says, "I've been in three wars now, including Ia Drang. This was the heaviest attack I've ever seen. It was awesome. None of us gonna come any closer than this."

The first sergeant had a good point. That ten-minute concentration of gunfire Alpha Company just took was as heavy as any soldiers had ever experienced. Each of the American-made .30- and .50-caliber machineguns on the troop carriers were firing at five hundred rounds per minute, eight shots a second. When added to the rate of fire of the small arms and grenade launchers and then multiplied by the total number of weapons in the armored squadron, all of them shooting simultaneously, the mass of incoming fire was as intense and sustained as any ten minutes at Waterloo or Shiloh or Mametz Wood or Kursk. Especially at that range. Now I understood what it had been like for the North Vietnamese who ambushed the ARVN relief column on the road to Plei Me, advancing on foot through that fire, and what the NVA prisoner at Plei Me truly meant when he said, *we all expected to die.*

When the medics had treated the wounded, they reported to Captain Fox that three more men were dead and five wounded, plus Vallop.

One of the ARVN APCs lurched over the graveyard and stopped at the edge of the ditch. The South Vietnamese troops on the track were surprised to see what had happened.

An American adviser called down, "Guess we shook you up a little." His name was Sergeant Carmine McClellan, from Mount Carmel, Illinois, and he was laughing.

Fox looked up and said, 'Yeah, you sure as hell shook us up. Killed three of my men.'

"Oh, no," McClellan said, putting his hands to his head. "Oh, no."

I noticed the tape turning on my recorder and switched it off. The takeup reel was full. Everything from the time we landed in the graveyard had been recorded.

Another rifle company from 2/12 moved in column across the graveyard to reinforce A Company's position. The soldiers were silent, serious. They had not been involved in the attack on A Company. They walked past Vallop

and looked at him as if he were one of the enemy. They concentrated on setting up a perimeter for the night. With one rifle company passing through
the lines of another, one without its commander, and in semidarkness, there
was more than the usual confusion. Three soldiers from Alpha Company—
Lieutenant Paul Mobely, Specialist Fourth Class Theotis Young and the
medic, Private First Class White—helped me lift Vallop into a poncho and
carry him slowly to the LZ. Within minutes, a helicopter landed. Captain
Fox, First Sergeant Stanfield and the other wounded were carried aboard.
When we tried to climb onto the chopper with Vallop, the crew chief turned
us away. "Another bird's on the way for you guys," he shouted over the roar
of the engine. He pointed to the bodies of the three dead men on the
ground, and the soldiers loaded them on the chopper, which took off swiftly.

We waited. The sun slipped behind the mountains. Twilight shadows settled over the graveyard. I asked a young sergeant who was crouched next to
a radio when the chopper was coming. 'They're all busy,' he said.

'Where's your CO?'

'Don't know. Somewhere in the ville, I think.' His attitude was indifferent.

'Will you get on the blower and tell him we need a medevac? We've got a
wounded man here.'

'I'll try,' he said, but his voice was unconcerned.

The sergeant called on the radio. No one responded. Time passed. Nothing happened.

'Jack, you've got to do something,' Sorensen said. 'Vallop's not going to
make it.' The thin Thai sound technician lay on the sand with his eyes closed.

I went back to the sergeant and told him to switch the frequency of his
radio to brigade net.

'I don't know if I should do that,' he said.

'Just do it!' I shouted. He seemed intimidated by my voice and set the frequency. I took the handset and squeezed the talk bar.

"Medevac, medevac," I called into the mouthpiece, sounding as authoritative as I could. "This is Charlie Bravo Sierra. Repeat, Charlie Bravo Sierra.
We're stuck on the LZ where you dropped us off this afternoon and we
can't get out. My soundman is wounded and needs help. Repeat. One WIA.
We need help urgently. Medevac, medevac, this is Charlie Bravo Sierra,
over."

Chatter and cross talk came back on the radio. I couldn't make it out. The sergeant took the handset, placed it on top of the radio and switched the frequency back again without speaking.

A few minutes later, a long dark green Huey circled and landed. The pilot of a supply ship on its way back to Bong Son had picked up our call. Gently, Sorensen and I carried Vallop up and onto the floor of the helicopter and climbed in. We sat down and buckled the seat belts. A powerful sense of relief passed into me. With the engine revving and the rotors gaining speed in the seconds before takeoff, Johnny Apple appeared at the edge of the graveyard running toward the chopper. He had one hand on his helmet and the other holding up his trousers. He waved at us to wait. As the helicopter lifted up, Apple threw himself aboard, standing on the skid while I pulled him in. The back of his fatigue trousers slipped down below his waist and exposed his buttocks.

'Thanks,' he shouted. 'Got hit in the pants! Must've broken the belt!' He grinned in embarrassment. Two of his front teeth were missing.

At the brigade medical tent in Bong Son camp, an Army doctor examined Vallop and said he needed surgery to remove a piece of shrapnel from his lower intestine. 'No vital organs appear to be damaged,' he said. 'He's a very fortunate young man.'

Sorensen and I took Vallop in a helicopter to the 85th Evacuation Hospital in Qui Nhon. As he was being carried in on a stretcher, some of the wounded soldiers waiting for treatment glared at him angrily, mistaking him for Vietnamese. The operation to remove the shrapnel took place immediately. Sorensen and I waited outside. Later the surgeon came out and said the operation was successful—he got the piece of shrapnel. Vallop was resting and should make a full recovery. 'The wound was deep but not dangerous,' he said. 'Don't worry.' When we went to see him in a field tent, Vallop was asleep on a bed in a long row of wounded soldiers. Almost all of them were First Cav. One of them sat up in a bed near Vallop with a furious look in his eyes. I went to each of the doctors and nurses in the tent and told them who Vallop was, that he worked for CBS News, that he was Thai, not Vietnamese, and that he might need to be protected from the GIs who didn't understand that. The doctors and nurses promised to watch Vallop closely. 'He's safe with us,' one of them said. 'Don't worry.'

Waiting outside the hospital, smoking a cigarette, a Catholic priest came over to say hello. He said he was serving in Vietnam as an Army chaplain but needed to talk to someone who was not military. His name was Reverend

George W. Seaver, aged forty-nine, and he seemed distraught. I told him what happened north of Bong Son and he shook his head. "It's horrible," he said. "I'm too old to be over here. It's time to go home." I said I felt the same way sometimes, though I was half his age.

Sorensen and I caught a late plane back to Saigon and got out at Tan Son Nhut at the same terminal where we had started the day nineteen hours earlier.

FEBRUARY 1, 1966

After the attack at the graveyard, I couldn't sleep. Nightmares kept waking me. I got no rest. I sat at the desk of my room in the Caravelle Hotel drinking, smoking cigarettes and writing letters. When I did fall asleep, horror crept in: dark violent dreams of terror and blood. I awoke in the frigid air-conditioned room in a sweating panic. It felt safer to stay awake. During the day I was nervous, ill at ease. Nothing seemed certain anymore. My sense of security was gone. Images of the incident appeared at unexpected moments, sudden compelling flashes, taking me back to the graveyard. As I walked along Tu Do Street in a crowd of people that first afternoon back in Saigon, tracers flashed overhead, a grenade exploded. A moment later I was on the sidewalk, arms over my head. Vietnamese passersby stepped politely around me, glancing out of the sides of their eyes, silent, as if nothing an American did anymore could surprise them. When I got up, embarrassed, a Frenchman frowned, looking at me as though I were a coward, something missing in my character. Two American civilians, burly construction types, laughed out loud, 'Hey, soldier, wrong rice paddy!' 'Yeah, this ain't the boondocks, ha-ha-hah.' Later, when I thought about it, I understood how strange it must have looked to anyone who hadn't been taken by a seizure like that. It must have seemed pathetic, and in a way it was. I had survived the graveyard but not the experience.

I drank more than usual: cognac and coffee in the morning, beer and wine at lunch, gin and tonic in the afternoon, whisky in the evening, brandy at night. I was never sober. I ate very little. My weight dropped to under 130 pounds. Alcohol became an all-purpose tranquilizer, an antidote for distress, though I didn't know how much it was stealing my rest. The all-powerful fear from the graveyard seemed branded on me, burned into my circuits, shorting the old connections. Even in the safe precincts of Saigon, the tension allowed no relief from the hyperalertness my brain was telling me I needed to survive. Survival was killing me.

In the morning, I couldn't think clearly. It was partly because of a hang-

over and lack of rest, but also because my normal thinking process was dis-
located, confused. My mood became more and more depressed, nerves
shakier. For the first couple of days I spent most of the time in my room
with the curtains drawn.

I wrote the narration for the story of what happened at the graveyard the
morning after we got back to Saigon. Part of the script was written in the
first person, a form I had not used before, but the writing was muddled, too
emotional for daily journalism. I was too shaken by the experience to write
about it clearly. Johnny Apple filed a long, first-person account for the *New
York Times* which his editors matched to one of Eddie Adam's still pictures
and put on the front page. When my film reached New York, it took Russ
Bensley and a film editor several days of extra work to make it into a coherent story. Some of what I had written did not make sense.

The incident at the graveyard affected my attitude about the war. My
confidence in the orderly efficiency of the American military dissolved. I
knew now that despite the appearance of being resolutely in control at all
times, the U.S. Army was as vulnerable to disasters as any large aggressive
organization, maybe more. Given the danger the soldiers faced in battle,
given their fear of death and injury, given the lethal instruments in their
hands, the chances of their shooting one another was great. Captain Fox
summarized it for everyone: "What a fucked-up war this is."

The CBS Bangkok correspondent, Murray Fromson, went to visit Vallop
Radboon, our wounded soundman, in the hospital at Qui Nhon. Vallop was
making a good recovery. He would be well enough to travel home to Thailand in another week or so. Fromson said Vallop was in good spirits. The
doctors and nurses were providing excellent treatment, and even the
wounded GIs in beds next to him had made him their friend. He said Vallop
had decided not to continue his career as a combat sound tech.

Fromson also told an extraordinary story about Major Charlie Beckwith
that he heard at the hospital. Beckwith, the Special Forces officer who led the
relief of Plei Me, gave me more details later. He was brought in to the hospital gravely wounded a day or two after Vallop. Beckwith had been in a helicopter on a reconnaissance mission near Bong Son when a .51-caliber bullet
came up through the floor and tore through his intestines, bowel and stomach. By the time he reached the hospital, Beckwith had lost much of his
blood and was nearly unconscious. Eyes closed, he lay on a stretcher outside

the emergency operating room while two doctors and a nurse stood over him. He heard them talking:

'No sense working on him.'

'Yeah, the artery's gone. Multiple internal wounds. Bleeding a lot.'

'I don't think he's going to make it.'

'Too bad.'

The doctors left Beckwith to die without treatment along with a few other no-hope cases. Other seriously wounded soldiers with a better chance of survival were waiting for operations. Surgery time would be better spent on them. Beckwith had been "triaged." Listening to the decision being made above his head, he felt his anger rise. He reached up and grasped the nurse by the wrist and with all his remaining strength pulled her down close to his dirty whiskered face and hot breath.

"Get on with it," he rasped. "Can't you see I'm dying?"

The nurse leaned away. Beckwith held her tighter.

"Let's go now!" he ordered.

'Okay, okay! Let me go! We'll get working on you right away.'

They rushed Beckwith into the operating room and inserted an IV with blood plasma into his vein, administered anesthesia, cleaned the skin, made a large incision in his stomach and started to repair the damage, stitching him together piece by piece. Beckwith was on the operating table for several hours. Eventually, the bleeding was stopped. The doctors told him later his internal organs looked like Swiss cheese when he came in. After evacuation to the United States and eight months of additional surgery, convalescence and rehabilitation, Beckwith returned to active duty. He was promoted to lieutenant colonel and went back to Vietnam as commander of a paratroop battalion.

A week later, Sean Flynn showed up at Frankie's House. After the attack in the graveyard, he had spent six days with Alpha Company. 'Really got to know the guys,' he said. On the day of the ARVN attack, Flynn said, an explosion went off in the trees over his head and killed the man next to him. Didn't get a scratch himself.

'You gotta be *charmed*, Flynn,' one of the others said.

'You really think so?' he replied, innocently.

Flynn became a regular at Frankie's House and was invited to move in. A month later he was seriously wounded in the knee. When he recovered, he spent most of his time with Special Forces operating out of Nha Trang. He became a welcome visitor there, one of a few civilians they took on patrol. Within months he was good enough at his job as a photographer to shoot a story for CBS. Filming in combat with Dana Stone, the UPI photographer who had become his friend, Flynn strapped the microphone of his tape recorder to his chest and ad-libbed a running commentary as he shot silent film of the fighting. The audio tape became a voice-over narration and got Flynn on the air as a freelance correspondent. CBS News producers in New York praised the quality of his work, admired his coolness under fire.

A day after the graveyard, I met Eddie Adams at the afternoon military briefing for the press. He said the bullets were inches over his head on the sand; he thought he was going to die out there. I told him about what the company commander had cried out during the shooting and Adams asked for a copy of the tape. He said he was finished with the war. He'd written a letter to his boss at the AP asking to go home. I told him I was thinking of doing the same. If a tough old veteran like Adams could admit there was a limit to how much combat he could take, I felt less ashamed to be so afraid myself.

At the briefing, the public information officer refused to confirm the South Vietnamese Army attack on American troops at the graveyard. Instead, he denied it. Several of us who had been at the scene, including Adams and Martin Stuart-Fox, argued that there had been a catastrophic mistake. The briefing officer would not accept our word.

'I have no information that such an incident took place,' he said.

Other journalists joined in: 'Well, isn't *this* information?'

'They're *giving* you the information.'

'Yeah, what difference does it make where it comes from?'

'I respect your position,' the officer said, 'but I cannot confirm that such an incident took place. I have no such information.'

What he meant, of course, was that if it hadn't been reported through the military information system, the incident hadn't officially happened. And if it hadn't officially happened, it couldn't be reported.

I began to understand what tough-minded journalists like David Halberstam, Neil Sheehan, Peter Arnett, Malcolm Browne, A. J. Langguth, Ward Just, Charles Mohr and others had been writing since the early 1960s: The first casualty of the Vietnam War was truth. The official remarks of American officers and diplomats who kept reporting progress in the war were often inaccurate or misleading. They had been seeing gains and denying failure for so many years that thoughtful reporters no longer believed what they said. Each new claim of progress was met now with suspicion.

The whole information system was deeply flawed, as I was beginning to learn. High-ranking American officials saw progress where their own field officers saw failure. Critical reports sent by subordinates in the countryside were rewritten to fit the official Washington–Saigon line or, in some cases, suppressed. Even the brightest State Department and CIA officers, who worked hard to gather information with a high degree of accuracy and insight, were divided about what was going on. Saigon-based senior officials dismissed reports of failure from the field because they did not reflect the prevailing analysis that the war was being won. Subordinates were accused of getting too close to the situation, overreacting, "going native."

Another reason for faulty reporting was that the Vietnamese routinely lied to their American counterparts. South Vietnamese officials usually told their allies what they thought they wanted to hear, and, since the Americans wanted to hear about progress being made, that's what they were told, true or not. It made life easier. Fewer questions needed to be answered. Meanwhile, corruption flourished. The illusion of success enabled the South Vietnamese to tap the fabulous flow of American dollars without interruption. Fortunes were stolen.

The biggest source of bad information was in the military reporting system itself. The fault was in the way it worked. Sergeants in charge of ten- to twelve-man squads reported to their platoon leaders, usually second lieutenants. Lieutenants reported information to their company's commanding officer, usually a captain. Company commanders of 100–150 man rifle companies reported results of ground operations to their battalion commanders, usually by radio. The lieutenant colonels who commanded battalions of 500–650 men reported to their brigade headquarters. Brigade reported to division. From there, information went to corps headquarters and then on to Saigon. Each stage of the reporting system was vulnerable to inaccuracy. At times, lies were deliberate. Body counts were exaggerated. Civilian dead, wounded and captured became enemy dead, wounded and captured. The numbers of weapons and supplies captured and destroyed were inflated. Territory swept was misreported. Details of combat were adjusted to look more favorable to the U.S. side. Successful enemy ambushes were not reported. Casualties from friendly fire were listed as combat dead and injured. Mistakes of all kinds went unreported. Cover-ups were commonplace.

The problem was human. The chief measure of individual success on the American side was making a contribution to progress in winning the war. (For many high-ranking Vietnamese and some Americans, the chief measure of success was how much money they managed to accumulate in the war.) Signs of progress enhanced the reputations of those who managed the war. Progress gave them confidence they were doing their jobs well. Progress made them look good in the eyes of others. Their attitude was biased profoundly toward seeing progress, justified or not, because progress served each of their own interests. When they spoke publicly about achieving success, generals and government leaders were, in effect, assessing the results of their own work. Most of them were not capable of admitting failure. Moreover, senior officials invented a rationale for their optimism. They justified their public statements, not only by their analysis of data (however faulty) but also by the effects their remarks had on the American people. They assumed that negative reporting, however honest, would erode public support for the war. Eventually, they believed, low morale would lead to defeat. They thought it would undermine U.S. policy if they were too candid about failures of policy. Of course, that made it impossible to change policy. The tragedy of this self-serving logic was that the cost of official delusion and deception was being counted every day in human pain, ruin and lives.

Journalists, for all their hard-nosed cynicism, tend to be as patriotic as anybody else. In Saigon, most reporters tried to cover the war honestly. They did not usually worry about the effect their reporting might have on public opinion in the United States. Trying to figure out what the public needed to be told or not told for morale reasons was outside the responsibility of a daily news reporter's job. It made everything too complicated. It was hard enough to gather accurate information without trying to censor it for patriotic content. Some of us withheld a story or some details of a story as a favor to friends in the military, or interpreted events from a U.S. military point of view, but those were exceptional cases. Unlike the American generals and diplomats, journalists' reputations did not rise or fall with progress in the war. Privately, we may have hoped for progress eventually, but, as a group, we held to the principle that it was more patriotic to report facts as we saw them, even when things went wrong, than to recycle public relations propaganda. It was an old lesson. Since Thomas Paine, American patriots had taught that all leaders, from kings to mayors, lose the ability to make sound judgments when their decisions go habitually without criticism. As most journalists saw it, Americans were better able to form opinions based on accurate information reported by a fair but critical press in Vietnam. Anything else was misleading, dishonest, and, in wartime, dangerous.

The first skirmish in the battle for truth in Vietnam was fought by reporters and officials in the early 1960s. Oozing optimism, Defense Secretary Robert McNamara predicted in 1963 that the few thousand American military advisers then in Vietnam could be withdrawn by the end of 1965. At the same time, Halberstam, Sheehan, Browne and others were reporting the collapse of the South Vietnamese army in fighting with the Viet Cong.

By the time of the American intervention in 1965, McNamara had become more cautious. "We have stopped losing the war," he said at the end of a visit to Vietnam in November. The implication was that it would now be possible to win. "The prospect of military collapse. . . . has disappeared," said McGeorge Bundy, presidential assistant for National Security Affairs. With almost 200,000 American troops then in Vietnam, this was a relatively safe assessment. "This struggle could go on for a long time," warned Alexis Johnson, deputy undersecretary of state, without suggesting how long. The North Vietnamese had been saying the same thing for months. In Hanoi, however, Ho Chi Minh, General Giap and the others were predicting a war of decades.

What may have been the most cautious remark made by any senior official at the time was heard in a radio interview in Saigon in November 1965:

> When the American people read the headlines about victories, there may be a tendency for them to magnify the magnitude of these actions. I do believe that there is a certain danger that we will be overwhelmed by a feeling of optimism and may lose sight of what I consider a true appraisal of the situation. . . . It involves a long conflict and we must be prepared to accept this.

The speaker was General William Westmoreland, commenting a few days after the Ia Drang Valley campaign ended. His immediate superior, Admiral U. S. Grant Sharp Jr., the commander of U.S. forces in the Pacific, was more optimistic. "There's no doubt," he said, "that we can stay in there

[Vietnam] until we've got it cleaned up." And *his* boss, General Earle Wheeler, chairman of the Joint Chiefs of Staff, told Congress in February 1966, "I myself have no doubt that, in the long term, we can achieve military victory." With such optimism being expressed publicly at the very top of the U.S. chain of command, it was read and repeated in other words by military officers all down the line.

After six months in country, I was becoming aware of a bewildering complexity in the war. I saw that it was fought on many fronts, not just battlefields. There was interplay between military activity, combat action, dislocation of peasants, civil affairs programs, the cost of living, support for the Viet Cong, terror, vengeance, greed and corruption, inflation, suspicion of the Saigon government, suspicion of Americans, ideology, Buddhist political activity, the student protest movements in both countries, international diplomacy, press coverage, rumors, cosmology (the locations of stars were important to many Vietnamese) and other factors. The war's progress could not be measured accurately by simply counting and reporting the number of operations launched, villages searched, combat air missions flown, bombs dropped, hills taken and abandoned, human beings killed and captured. The military handed out such information every day of the war and the press passed it on to the public at home, but it was a more accurate reflection of America's obsession with statistics than with who was winning the war.

I learned that mistakes were not aberrations in an otherwise flawless winning strategy, but parts of a whole wartime reality that included contradictions, failures, paradoxes, ambiguities, secrets, deceptions and many other unknowns. The war was more complicated than the most intricate game of chess; in chess at least you can see where your opponent's forces are. The game of war was being played with one side mostly blindfolded, the other with less firepower. Both were well motivated. The leaders saw the political stakes as more important than life and death.

The bureau kept Sorensen and me in Saigon for ten days to recover from our trauma at the graveyard. We did not object. The bureau chief gave us feature stories to do. The first assignment was to cover a demonstration by American servicemen protesting the price of drinks charged in Saigon bars. It was a mildly amusing story that seemed to have absolutely no relevance to the war, or so it seemed at first.

The GIs, mainly Air Force noncoms and enlisted men from Tan Son Nhut airbase, were staging sit-in demonstrations at bars all along Tu Do Street.

Moving in a group, the GIs targeted one bar at a time, occupied all the seats, and then ordered and nursed a single beer for hours. They refused to pay the dollar or so that young Vietnamese hostesses charged for their own drinks. It was cold tea in a whisky glass known as "Saigon tea," and it was actually the price the GIs were paying for the girls' company. The bar owners, mostly older Vietnamese men and women who had the dark forbidding appearance of gangsters and were reputed to have connections with the military, retaliated by closing early, forcing the GIs to leave. After Sorensen and I covered the story, I wrote a radio commentary. The report concluded: "The GIs expect the price of Saigon tea to drop sharply any day now, but the bar owners are adamant. What the Americans don't seem to have anticipated is the extreme patience of the Vietnamese—who are used to long struggles." As a parable for the war, the moral may have been overstated, but I was trying to pass on a lesson from Vietnamese history. As for the protest, the GIs gave up after a few weeks and sometime later the price of drinks went up even more.

Another radio story from that week in Saigon:

An American soldier, just back from the battlefield and spending his first day in Saigon, looked at the Vietnamese people crowding the streets. He could have been standing in any other oriental capital, and he asked, "Don't they know there's a war going on?" The war does not show on the streets of Saigon, and the people seem insensitive to Americans.

The story also quoted from a recent letter written by an elderly Vietnamese civil servant to his brother-in-law, a writer named Nguyen Van Tao. The civil servant had four sons. His wife died when the youngest was an infant. His first son was killed at the age of fifteen fighting with the Viet Minh against French occupation. His second son disappeared ten years ago, killed or kidnapped or recruited by the Viet Cong. His third son, an ARVN lieutenant, had been killed recently in battle, leaving a young widow and baby. The civil servant, an old man, said he could no longer cry, not even for the loss of his third son. The writer's last line was: "Death has become so familiar a face it can move about without much stirring."

The more I worked, the better I felt. My symptoms of fear and sleeplessness began to fade. I drank less and rested more. My final story that week was an investigation into the Saigon black market. Large quantities of tax-free American goods were being sold illegally—everything from razor blades to radios. All the items were marked "For Use Only of U.S. Military Forces." The goods were bought illegally or stolen from the U.S. post exchanges. Cigarettes, the largest-selling items, cost eleven cents a pack at the PX and were being sold on the streets of Saigon for twenty-five cents. "Fifteen miles away at Bien Hoa," the story said, "servicemen run short of their favorite brands. Most Marines go without new jungle boots, but anyone can get a pair on the Saigon black market." I quoted U.S. Senator Wayne Morse, who charged that one news correspondent in Saigon "was making $80,000 a month in black market activities."

The story was broadcast on the *CBS Evening News*. What I did not report was that virtually everyone in the country who could get U.S. dollars—soldiers, civilians, diplomats—exchanged them illegally on the black market for Vietnamese piastres. Foreign money changers who were buying dollars paid twice the official rate of exchange in piastres. The official rate at the banks was seventy-two piastres to the dollar; the black market rate, 150. It meant that people with foreign currency could buy most things with piastres for less than half the actual cost: meals, drinks, hotel rooms, taxi rides, entertainment, souvenirs. Of course, it was the government's rate of exchange that was artificial, giving the currency more value than it was worth.

Big money was being made on business expenses. People who worked for American companies charged their expenses in Vietnam at the official rate of exchange, seventy-two to the dollar. Since they obtained the piastres originally for 150 to the dollar but were reimbursed by their companies at the official rate, they made a 100 percent profit. Every dollar spent was a dollar made. The practice led to magnificent displays of greed. My hotel bill, for example, was paid for in piastres by an American in the CBS bureau. So were the salaries of the Vietnamese staff, the drivers and camera teams, the office rent, automobiles, shipping costs, radio and telephone bills, fuel, entertainment and the rest. When the bills and receipts were submitted to CBS in New York, those who had paid the bills were reimbursed at the official rate. It amounted to hundreds of thousands of dollars a year.

On one early trip to Danang, Jim Wilson collected the bureau bills, paid the room and jeep rental charges for several months in advance, and made a profit of several thousand dollars. Later, in Saigon, Wilson said he was confronted by the senior CBS News correspondent who normally had the privilege of paying the bills in Danang. Wilson had got there first. Furious about Wilson's skullduggery, the correspondent demanded that he hand over the

receipts. Wilson laughed at the correspondent's display of moral indignation, gave him his narrow-eyed Lee Marvin sneer, and told him in a low
voice to fuck himself.

One of the first Saigon bureau chiefs for CBS finished his tour of duty in
Saigon and flew to New York. He walked into the office of CBS News president Richard Salant and put a briefcase on his desk. The briefcase contained
about $70,000 in $100 bills. The bureau chief confessed that he got the money
paying business expenses in Saigon with black market piastres. His conscience was bothering him and he wanted to return the money to the company. Salant, a lawyer, told him to get out of his office and take the money
with him. For his next assignment, the bureau chief found himself managing a small CBS News office in Africa.

The black market story was a turning point. Five and a half months after
I arrived in Vietnam to cover the war, it was the first critical report I filed.
The beliefs I had held since childhood about men and war and government
were changing. A different outlook was taking their place.

FEBRUARY 12, 1966

Women and children sat huddled on the dry earth at the edge of the village and cried—long anguished cries of fear, loss and desperation, cries of the heart. Their faces were twisted in contortions of grief, their mouths open, long strands of saliva spilling on the soil. Their noses dripped. Tears ran down their cheeks and made rivulets through the dust on their amber skin. Straw hats hung askew from the strings around their necks. Nearby, artillery guns boomed in the hot afternoon air and cracked against the sound of the crying women and children like exclamations, renewing their fears, replenishing their tears. They shrieked and sobbed and wailed with choking throats and fluttering lungs, one after another. Their cries became a single collective *aaahoowwanhhgh! aaahooieeeeh!* over and over. They cried as though their lives were being taken.

An American officer stood in the shadow of a palm tree at the edge of the village and looked down at the crying peasants. There were over a hundred of them: children with skinny legs and bare feet, teenage girls holding naked babies, women of all ages in black blouses and baggy trousers that looked like pajamas, and a number of silent older men who squatted on the ground away from the main group and watched with no apparent emotion. The American officer was a lieutenant colonel who wore a dark green army cap with a visor in front to shade his face from the sun and a fatigue uniform with paratroop wings sewn on the front. The name "Craig" was printed in prominent black letters on his shirt. He wore an olive green web belt around his waist with a .45-caliber Colt automatic in its regulation army holster hooked to it. He appeared to be in his early forties.

"I know how to stop 'em from crying," Lieutenant Colonel Craig said. He opened a cardboard box of C rations, picked out a round bar of chocolate, unwrapped the tinfoil and offered it to one of the children on the edge of the group. A boy looked up at the colonel, then at the chocolate. He did not move his hands. Artillery boomed and cracked. The women cried.

I asked my colleague, Le Sum, to speak with the peasants, ask them what happened to make them so unhappy. Several of them told him the story: 'Yesterday morning,' they said, 'we were working in the fields when bombs exploded around the village. Artillery guns. We ran for the shelters. Then helicopters came over the houses and we heard machineguns and rockets. So much noise and smoke. The animals became wild and tried to run away. All of us were very frightened. Then there was the noise of many helicopters. American soldiers came into the hamlet running and shouting and shooting. There was a Vietnamese army soldier with them. He told us to come out of our shelters. He said we had to leave immediately. We argued with him.'

'Where can we go?' we said.

'To your families, in the other hamlets.'

'But our families are here.'

'Then go to your friends.'

'All our friends are here. Besides, they do not have room for us.'

'You cannot stay here.'

'Why?'

'The Americans are going to be here. There is no room for you.'

'But we have no where else to live. These are our homes.'

'I'm sorry.'

'Who will take in the harvest? Who will look after the tombs? Who will plant the next crop? The Americans?'

'You cannot stay.'

That is when the crying began, the villagers told Le Sum.

Le Sum knew that nothing was more important to their healthy existence than living on this land. Their parents and grandparents and generations before that, longer than anyone could remember, had lived and worked and raised families and grown old and died here. The spirits of their ancestors were entwined with this place, living breathing integral parts of it, embedded in the soil and the water and the air and the other elements. They nourished the rice paddies. The spirits gave the village its harmony or, if something was wrong, its discord. The promise of immortality was in the land. The continuity of family and generations gave the villagers hope for eternal tranquility in the next world. When they died, their children would care for their graves, would perform the appropriate rituals at household altars, celebrate the renewal of Tet. The cycle of birth, growth, work, marriage, family life, aging, death and spiritual rebirth was without end. Their

beliefs were rooted in more than two millennia of Buddhist, Taoist and Con-
fucianist philosophy. The concepts were more far-reaching than religion.
They embraced every aspect of their lives, their culture, their identities as
individuals, as members of a family, as a community, as part of a larger
world and universe. The villagers had been taught by their elders since they
were children that to abandon the land and the graves of their ancestors was
to invite doom. Their spirits would wander in perpetual grief, haunting the
living. To take them away from the land was to take away more than their
lives. It was to condemn their souls.

The villagers told Le Sum that when the ARVN soldier ordered them to
leave they obeyed: they gathered up some food and cooking pots and straw
mats and family possessions and left with what they could carry. The women
and children cried. 'Behind us,' they said, 'the Americans brought in big tents
and long-barreled guns and water trucks and cases of food and many, many
helicopters. We had never seen Americans before. They looked so big and
powerful. We walked along a trail about two kilometers to this place. It is
another hamlet in the village. The village is called Kim Son. Our neighbors
gave us shelter. Some of us had to sleep in the open. The night was terrible.
The guns were shooting and the shells landed very close. The explosions
hurt our ears. It terrified the children. No one was able to sleep. Even worse,
we don't know what we will do. Our neighbors are very kind but they cannot keep us. If the Americans do not let us go home, we will have to move
somewhere else. But there is nowhere to go. And the crops will die and we
will not be able to eat. Then we will die. And no one will look after our
graves. You know what that means. Tell us why we cannot go to our homes.'

Lieutenant Colonel Robert Craig was sympathetic. He was from
Maryville, Tennessee, and as the senior civil affairs officer for the 1st Cavalry
Division, was responsible for improving the welfare of Vietnamese civilians
in the Cav's tactical area of responsibility. It was not the most rewarding job
in the division but Craig took it seriously. We had met him at Bong Son that
morning and asked him to help us with our story on pacification, winning
the hearts and minds of Vietnamese civilians. Pacification had become a
timely subject because of the publicity it got the previous week at a summit
conference in Honolulu between President Johnson and Vietnamese Premier Nguyen Cao Ky. With considerable fanfare, Johnson and Ky had
declared a war on poverty in South Vietnam. Whatever it cost, the two governments were going to try to win the allegiance of as much of the rural

population as possible. It was to become an important part of the war effort. Network producers in New York cabled instructions to me to do a field report. In Saigon, I interviewed senior American officials responsible for pacification, read everything I could find on the subject, and wrote a radio commentary that allowed me to express a personal opinion. It concluded:

> An effective pacification program may take as many trained social workers as there are soldiers. Unlike the United States, where illiteracy and unemployment are the major problems, in Vietnam there is a human enemy with ingenious methods to wreck a pacification program. Without it, though, we will lose the war.

The idea that pacification was critical to the war effort had come from American civilian administrators of the program who believed the U.S. Army was giving less priority to winning the hearts and minds of the Vietnamese than killing them. A pacification joke made the rounds in military circles at the time: "Grab the God damn Vietnamese by the balls, squeeze 'em until they holler, pull hard enough and their hearts and minds will follow." It was not clear which policy was being observed: the official civilian one or the military variation.

Lieutenant Colonel Craig said Kim Son was going to be used as the field command post for Second Brigade. Its soldiers had just launched a search-and-destroy operation in the nearby An Lao Valley and this location was needed for an operations headquarters, communications center, field artillery base, landing zone and refueling point. The An Lao was a prosperous belt of farmland west of Bong Son between two mountain ridges leading to the coastal plain. Thousands of Vietnamese peasants lived and worked in the valley. Many of them would be displaced. It was believed to be an enemy stronghold. At a briefing earlier that morning, the commander, Colonel William Lynch, said Kim Son was "a very important VC base area for the past three or four years." Standing beside him, the division commander, Major General Harry W.O. Kinnard, added for emphasis, "The An Lao is a long-known VC stronghold, a major installation with troops, installations and depots, hanging like a thundercloud on the right flank of our base camp at An Khe." When the U.S. Army entered an area where the Saigon administration was not established, American officers assumed that its residents were sympathetic to the Viet Cong and treated them as hostile.

Now Lieutenant Colonel Craig tried to find a way to get the displaced villagers out of the area of active combat operations and into some kind of safe housing. He was accompanied by the chief of Hoai An district, an ARVN captain named Le Nam Hai. Captain Hai was a small older man with long straight black hair combed back over his head, glasses, and a dark face with deep lines in it. He wore a combat fatigue jacket with three pips on the shoulders marking his rank. Standing in front of the villagers, Hai asked them to go around the hamlet and tell everyone who was hiding to come out. He had something important to tell them.

Some of the peasants went into the hamlet. After a few minutes, several dozen people joined the main group. They had hidden in underground bomb shelters and in the nearby woods since the helicopters carrying the American and Vietnamese officers had arrived. When they were all gathered, Captain Hai made a speech. He said that they could not go back to their hamlet. Not for the time being. Perhaps when the Viet Cong had left the valley they would be allowed to go back. In the meantime, the only place for them to live was district headquarters in Hoai An, about ten miles away. 'There is food and shelter there,' he said. 'You will receive medical attention. It is not so bad. Certainly it is better than trying to live here in the open with the gunfire and the fighting.'

The villagers said nothing. They looked with impassive faces at Captain Hai and the camera crew and Lieutenant Colonel Craig, who was trying to give small containers of peanut butter and jelly to some of the children. Craig smiled. The children looked at the food. A spotted black and gray dog pressed its nose into a long narrow C ration can that was too small for its snout. One of the children tasted the peanut butter and smiled. Then the other children began to eat. They smiled. The old men squatted on their haunches and conferred in a circle. After a time one of the women joined them. Then another and another, until most of the women were in the group. There was a long discussion. Two Vietnamese Air Force pilots who had flown the district chief to the hamlet went to talk with the villagers. They spoke in polite voices, with respect. They said the Americans would take them to Hoai An in helicopters. It would be a short journey, just a few minutes. Some of the younger women said they had never been as far away as Hoai An before. The pilots told them they had nothing to fear. Shells exploded nearby. The villagers said they would go if the Americans took them in their helicopters.

Lieutenant Colonel Craig got in his chopper and flew away to arrange transportation. Another helicopter landed with a team of Army medics. Word went around that the *bac si* was here to treat the sick. The villagers formed a line in front of the medics and waited to be examined. Most of them were children or elderly men and women. Other villagers packed their belongings, scurrying through the hamlet to collect them. A ripple of excitement was felt. The crying stopped. Some of the women put betel leaves in their mouths and began to chew. The villagers were beginning to trust the Americans who were so powerful with their guns and helicopters. They seemed to care. One or two of the women and children smiled at the camera. The afternoon sun headed toward the horizon. With luck, the people would be in their new homes by nightfall. In an hour, they were ready.

Lieutenant Colonel Craig returned in his helicopter. He went straight to the Vietnamese Air Force pilots. "There's been a mistake," he said. "I can't get any transportation. All the brigade choppers are busy with the operation. They can't take the people to Hoai An."

The Vietnamese pilots translated what Craig said. The villagers looked dismayed.

'What's wrong? What are we going to do?' they asked.

'You will have to go by foot,' said Captain Hai.

'How can we go by foot? It's too far. It will be dark in an hour.'

'Then you will stay here.'

'But it is terrible here! Listen to the guns! Would you stay here tonight?'

Captain Hai turned and walked to the helicopter. The pilots followed. Soon the engines started and the rotors turned and they left.

I asked Lieutenant Colonel Craig to stand in front of the camera and talk to us. He explained that the brigade's resources were stretched beyond its capacity to fly the civilians to their new homes; the helicopters were needed for combat priorities. 'It's one of those things that happen in a war,' he said. "These people have been disappointed many times before."

Craig got in his helicopter and prepared to take off. Le Sum and I got aboard. The engine started and revved and the rotor blades spun and the bird lifted off the ground. Looking down, we saw the faces of the peasants of Kim Son looking up at us. They wore the expressions of people who have been betrayed.

FEBRUARY 19, 1966

A week later we went back. From Saigon to An Khe by C-123, An Khe to Bong Son by helicopter, Bong Son to Hoai An by truck and jeep. By the time we arrived, it was the middle of the afternoon and the heat had made the place a furnace. Sunlight bounced off the bleached white sand and baked everything in its hot glare. The villagers of Kim Son had been squeezed into a refugee camp on the fringes of Hoai An district town. They were sitting in hot airless barrack rooms with no windows. The camp appeared to date from the French Indochina War almost fifteen years earlier when villagers were systematically driven off their land for the same reasons. In this camp, about thirty people shared each room. The insides of the buildings smelled of stale food and urine and wood smoke from cooking fires burning indoors in the heat. Many of the people were sick. Some had wounds from shrapnel and bullets. The sickest and most seriously injured lay on their backs on straw mats on the dirt floor looking with weak laconic eyes at the ceiling as if waiting to die. Children cried. There were no toilets. The stench was so strong it stayed in our noses when we left the building. Outside, on an arid piece of sand-covered soil, small individual piles of human excrement were arranged on the ground in neat even rows decomposing in the sun, fertilizer for some future crop. There was not enough food. The Vietnamese Red Cross handed out blankets and condensed milk that had been donated by the U.S. government. The refugees took what was given, though it was too hot for blankets and the milk was over a year old. An American relief worker, Steve Cummings, said the milk had been sitting on the shelves of the black market in Saigon so long it was worthless. No one would buy milk that old. It was not fit for babies to drink. Since there was no profit to be made from the milk, the Saigon government dumped it on the refugees. 'Several people die here every day,' Cummings said.

The hundred or so villagers from Kim Son were only part of the population. Six thousand refugees were crowded into the Hoai An camp. All had been driven away from their homes in the An Lao Valley in the past week.

Virtually overnight their lives had been transformed from well-ordered tranquillity to confusion and terror. They had lost their land, homes, crops, ancestral graves and personal possessions. They had no idea what was going to happen to them. The only improvement in their condition was that they were away from the worst of the violence.

The people of Kim Son were surprised to see us. They hoped we might help. They said they had spent one more night in the village where we left them the week before. With the guns firing all night, it was impossible to sleep. Everyone was frightened. 'The next day,' one of them said, 'we decided to leave. To walk to Hoai An. The road was full of trucks and jeeps. We had to walk slowly because of the old people. One old man is blind. And the children are slow. Also, many other people were walking on the road. It was like what happens in a flood. A catastrophe. Worse than a catastrophe. We could hear the American guns and we were afraid they would shoot at us. They shoot at anything. It took us two days to make the journey. When we got here to Hoai An, there was no food or water or wood for a fire. No one prepared for us. We were left to take care of ourselves. And now there are so many. More people arrive every day. It is all so terrible. What have we done to deserve this?'

I told them the Americans soldiers believe the valley is controlled by the Viet Cong, that the villagers support the VC.

'We are not Viet Cong!' a man said. 'Sometimes the liberation soldiers came to our village. They took some of our rice but otherwise they left us alone. The night before the Americans came, one of the men of our village went away with them. His wife says he was kidnapped.'

'Are you afraid of the VC?'

'No. They don't bother us. We are afraid of the Americans. With their soldiers and helicopters and guns.'

An American doctor arrived to treat the sick and wounded. There was no hospital for the refugees, only first aid. The doctor examined an injured child. 'Part of these people's problem,' he said, 'is hygiene. They don't know how to wash themselves with soap. So their injuries and sores get infected and don't heal.' The doctor had the impression that Vietnamese peasants didn't care about keeping clean, but I had observed more peaceful villages where the Vietnamese bathed two or three times a day, usually after work. They were meticulously clean. But they did not have money to buy soap.

We interviewed everyone involved with the refugees: the village chief, whose name was Tuong; the district chief, Captain Hai; his American adviser, U.S. Army Captain William Buchly of Myrtle Beach, South Carolina; Lieutenant Colonel Craig; Roy Eidem, the USAID liaison officer to the First Cav; Arthur Elmore, the regional refugee officer for the United States Operations Mission; and Steve Cummings, who was the assistant provincial representative for USOM. The officials explained that there was no pacification program for these people. It would be too expensive to hire the necessary aid workers and too dangerous to keep them in the villages. They gave the peasants shelter from the battle zone, first aid, and a few handouts. The governments of the United States and South Vietnam were unable to provide more than rudimentary relief to the six thousand people it drove out of their homes in the An Lao Valley. Officials argued that it was unfortunate but necessary to generate refugees while making war on an enemy who hid among the rural population. The VC had to be denied food, shelter and recruits one way or another. Others, especially journalists and some civilian agencies, questioned the logic of search-and-destroy operations that uprooted large numbers of peasants whose loyalty and trust the Saigon regime was supposedly trying to enlist.

We called the Kim Son stories "A Pacification Debacle." Part of the narration said: "For all their hardships, the Kim Son refugees would rather be here than home. Here they can escape from the frightening sound of the fighting. In a few weeks or months, when the shooting stops, they may be able to return to their village. They will be alone again, for the Americans will have left. There are not enough soldiers or civic action workers, and so, there is no pacification program planned for the village of Kim Son."

The report concluded with Lieutenant Colonel Craig saying, "This is not the end for these people." To which I added: "This must be the end of our report on the villagers of Kim Son. Their misery, their sickness, their fear— all are shared by other villagers all over Vietnam. It happens every time there's a battle. And until pacification *really* begins, these people and their children will suffer the same wartime fate as their parents and grandparents." I rewrote the close several times to make it more emphatic. As soon as the film arrived in the States, network producers put it on the air. In response, a number of viewers wrote to ask how they could help. Some wrote to me directly. One letter accused me of being a "Commie lover." I laughed at that.

At the end of August 1965, the official number of refugees in Vietnam was reported to be 620,000. About one-third of them lived in the 194 camps around the country. The rest had to fend for themselves. Most moved to shanty towns in the cities. Officially, each refugee was supposed to get seven piastres a day, free rice and shelter. Given wartime shortages and the culture of corruption, however, there was no guarantee they would get anything. The government budget for refugee assistance through August was $220,000, or about thirty-five cents for each refugee. The U.S. contribution to refugee relief consisted of a staff of fifteen people led by a retired Air Force colonel. The major reason the refugees gave for leaving their villages was incoming artillery fire and air strikes near their homes. That was the general situation at the end of the summer, before the big American search-and-destroy offensives began.

I was not alone in my concern for the refugees. Some U.S. government officials worried what the war was doing to innocent Vietnamese civilians. Charles Mohr of the *New York Times* reported a secret government study by American civilian officials in Saigon that expressed "increasing anxiety over the growing intensity of warfare and the effects on civilians. The study said the population resents undirected harassing and interdictory artillery fire even more than air strikes because the shells seem to come from nowhere with no warning. Officials said there is evidence that a good many churches, homes and public buildings have been destroyed in rural areas. The attitude of the population was summarized as being mainly passive, fatalistic and somewhat confused."

One year later, Tom Corpora of United Press International spent a night in a rural Vietnamese village north of Kim Son. He was concerned about the indiscriminate use of American artillery fire at night. He risked his life in the unprotected village to get the story from the peasants' point of view. When he came out, he was more worried than when he had gone in. Corpora was a regular at Frankie's House and he showed us his copy. It told the story of Ngo Thi Thi, a Vietnamese farmer of forty-five who lived alone with her teenage daughter. Her husband and five other children were dead. One child had been killed by a U.S. artillery shell that landed on her village.

"It's sad," she said. "Just the noise all the time. Every time it goes off we don't know whether it will come in here or not. When we go to bed we do not know whether we will wake up in the morning."

Corpora's story quoted another member of the village, a farmer and hamlet elder named Nguyen Van Khe.

"Vietnam is such a small and poor country," he said. "Why does your country come over here and fight?"

Corpora told the old man that the South Vietnamese government asked for help to fight the Communists.

"But there are no Communists here," he said. "I've never seen any. Tell the ambassador the Vietnamese want peace. They want to plant rice and be left alone. They want the Americans to go home."

"Then," Corpora wrote, "as an artillery round cracks the night nearby, Nguyen Van Khe grimaces and sighs: 'One night of peaceful sleep.'"

"Unless the graves are taken care of," said the old man, "the spirits wander around homeless. That's what makes it so sad, what makes things go so badly."

FEBRUARY 20, 1966

The next evening the residents of Frankie's House gave a party. A menu was planned, invitations were printed, and food, drink and flowers were purchased. The tiled floor of the living room was washed and polished. The hi-fi was moved from Page's room to the downstairs living room and a stack of records put on to play. Guests arrived wearing their best clothes: lightweight tropical suits, clean white sports shirts, pressed trousers, and bright summer dresses that showed bare brown shoulders, open necks, and a fashionable degree of décolletage. The men had washed and combed their hair. The women were cool and lovely. The smell of burning joss sticks mingled with the aroma of French perfume. Candles lit the long table. Conversation scintillated, infused with the irony and cynicism of the guests' youth. No one was over thirty. Everyone wanted to be happy, to have fun. Tonight they were trying to escape the drumbeat of daily misery that pounded everyone's senses, as if this were the way we would be living if it weren't for the war.

My transition had been total. In less than twenty-four hours I was transported from Hoai An refugee camp in Binh Dinh Province, a place of squalor, indignity and despair, to a Saigon dinner party held in an aura of refinement, gentility and taste. The mood was fraternal, as if Frankie's House were a club, an escape from the reality of what was going on out there, young journalists and their friends trying to forget the story. Conversation focused around the war anyway. Guests spoke with earnest compassion of the suffering of the Vietnamese between sips of imported French, Australian and Algerian wines.

Most of the regulars were there: Martin and David Stuart-Fox (who were chief organizers of the party), Simon Dring, Tim Page, Steve Northup, Joe Galloway, Robin Mannock—all on their best behavior. Sean Flynn was in the field. Several women attended, gracing the villa with their charm and intelligence, lending dignity to the ordinary decadence of the place. One was a freelance American reporter who had the bright personality, flawless complexion and natural beauty of a magazine cover girl. Blond-haired, blue-eyed, in her early twenties, she was among the most attractive women in Saigon, one of the few whose charm and good looks could compete with Vietnamese women. Secretly, all the men loved her.

Everyone was showing off a little, even Frankie. He and his family cooked a lavish Chinese meal of eleven courses. After dinner, Page rolled an extravagant joint and passed it around the table. Considerable silliness followed, mostly unprovoked giggling. The rooms vibrated with music and laughter. No one misbehaved. The party ended just before curfew with everyone full of food, wine, pot smoke, beer and bonhomie. Frankie organized taxis, tiny blue and yellow chariots, to take the guests home. For the next few days, whenever guests of that party met, they remarked to one another what a wonderful occasion it had been, how civilized and elegant, how much it reminded them of life in the real world. 'Oh, let's do it again soon,' they said. Actually, the party was more of a reminder of how rough our working lives had become, slogging around the country in the shadows of the guns, numbing emotions, hardening hearts. Bit by bit, the war was changing us, stealing our civility as it was ravaging the dignity of the Vietnamese. Polite dinner parties were an exception, symbols of what we had left behind. From time to time we needed to be reminded.

Sam Castan was a frequent visitor to Frankie's House at the time. He was a LOOK magazine reporter who came to Saigon every few months to collect notes for feature stories he wrote. A senior editor of LOOK, Castan lived in Hong Kong with his wife, Fran, and baby daughter, Jane. He had covered the war for about four years and went into the field often. At thirty, he was a few years older than the rest of us, with a round pleasant face that smiled easily. He was five feet nine inches tall, alert, funny, introspective and kind. When he learned about our bet to buy Page a new hi-fi if he survived until his twenty-second birthday, Castan offered an additional $500 if Page lived to be twenty-five. No strings. All he had to do was live. Castan worried more about Page's survival than his own.

Page owed him $28.50 for something Castan bought for him in Hong Kong. It had not been a gift. Page had avoided paying the debt for months.

'When are you going to settle up?' said Castan, gently.

'Bloody hell, I'm skint, mate!' said Page in mock alarm. No mention of the $10,000 LIFE had paid him a few months earlier.

'What'll you take in trade?' asked Page.

Castan looked around the room. He could see little more than cameras, guns and war trophies.

'How about your stash box?' he said, pointing to the foot-long wooden box with the printed inscription, "TWO SECONDS YOU'RE LOADED."

'Not on your bleeding life, mate,' Page said. That's going to the grave with me when I die, next to me Buddha.'

'Which may be sooner rather than later, Page,' someone said.

'How about your hat?' said Castan. Page had an Australian bush hat, a large green cover with a wide floppy brim that was decorated with metal badges from the military units he visited. He wore it everywhere outside of Saigon.

'That's me *lucky* hat! Can't give away me luck.'

'Page, with your kind of luck I wouldn't call that hat lucky.'

'Well, I don't know.' Page held the hat gently, feeling the worn crumpled weight of it, figuring how long it would take to find a replacement. He handed it to Castan. 'It's yours,' he said.

'Thanks Page,' he said, putting it on his head. 'Hey! It fits.'

'If the hat fits . . .' someone said.

'Trade it,' said another.

Page got up and took back the hat. 'Gotta do this properly. Kneel down, Sam.' Castan looked at him, curious. 'Go on, mate. Just do it,' said Page.

Castan kneeled on the floor.

'Right. Bow your head, then.' Page stood in front of him with exaggerated solemnity, trying to imitate the plummy accent of an English aristocrat.

"With this hat," he said, intoning the words, "I do knight thee, Sir Sam." Page put the bush hat on his head. Everyone cheered, 'Hip-hip, hooray!'

Castan smiled brightly, his perfect white teeth shining.

Later in the month, Steve Northup and I planned a trip to Hong Kong for two weeks of R and R. The bureau chief had encouraged me to go. Friends at Frankie's House gave us lists of things to buy and bring back for them: newly released records, photo gear, film, books, magazines, medicine, culinary delicacies—making themselves, in effect, part of the trip. The night before leaving, a farewell party was held and everyone sang "We Gotta Get Out of This Place" along with the Animals at full volume. Our friends' faces showed happiness and envy that we were getting out, if only for a short time.

At Tan Son Nhut airport, moving slowly through the check-in process (an exercise of maddening frustration), the usual excitement of going to an exotic new city was enhanced by the anticipation of getting away from this one. Who knew what adventures Hong Kong might hold? What new mysteries awaited? What interesting women we might meet? Whatever happened, we wouldn't have to worry about getting shot at, a factor of such significance it made the prospect of flying to Hong Kong seem like a journey to paradise.

Inside the Cathay Pacific jet, the cabin was cool and clean, more civilized than anywhere we'd been in months. There was no dust. The air was refreshingly dry, almost chilly. The seats were comfortable. Hot towels and cold drinks were offered. The young Asian women on the cabin staff were pretty and polite. Just being in the same plane with them gave me a sense of validation as a normal human being, though it felt out of place to be in such comfort.

In Hong Kong, Northup and I checked in to the Repulse Bay Hotel, a venerable institution of decaying colonial splendor that sat on a hill. The hotel looked over the water at ferry boats and fishermen and, in late afternoon, the last of the day's sunlight glinting off the waves. We got rooms with a view. Drank gin and tonic with pieces of lime. Were pampered by the hotel staff with the courteous efficiency reserved for the rich. After two days, we had walked everywhere, gone to the Foreign Press Club, met a few friends, got drunk, done the shopping, taken tourist pictures and explored the beach. We had done it all, almost.

At lunch in the coffee shop of a shopping arcade, Northup noticed a young woman sitting alone. She was quite tall, thin, blond and extremely pretty. As she finished her lunch, Northup kept looking at her over my shoulder.

"She looks so sad," he said. He glanced at her every few seconds. "I wonder why she's so unhappy," he said. Our conversation stopped.

Paying the bill, an unusual expression appeared on Northup's face. His eyes narrowed. His jaw clenched. Furrows gathered in his forehead. With a look of absolute determination, he got up from his seat and crossed to the young woman. Speaking in a soft, concerned voice, he said, "Why are you so sad?"

They started a conversation. Her name was Dodi Lucas and she was on holiday from her home in Australia. She was sad, she said, because she was engaged to be married when she went back and was not sure it was the right thing to do. She appeared to be well-educated, cultured and slightly shy. She

joined us for shopping. When it was apparent that she and Northup were
fully enjoying each other's company, I made my apologies and left. I saw little more of them for the rest of the trip. Before long they were making marriage plans of their own.

I hunkered down in my rooms at the hotel. They had high ceilings and
soft furniture and were darkly lit. The living room had a tired old sofa that
was ideal for lying on my back and reading. Wide French windows opened
out to the sea air and gave a splendid view across the bay. I felt comfortable,
protected, safe. No sound of artillery in the distance, no noise of helicopters.
I ordered three meals a day from room service and stayed indoors for a
week. It was the best way to pass the time: lazy, relaxed, totally self-indul-
gent. I drank but not to excess. Time passed easily. Whenever I got bored I
looked out the window or took a nap.

My sole entertainment was a book, *Catch-22*, by Joseph Heller. It was
enough. I lost myself in the bizarre world of Yossarian, Dunbar, McWatt,
Doc Daneeka, Nurse Duckett, Milo Minderbinder, the chaplain, Hungry
Joe, Orr, Colonel Cathcart, Major Major, Snowden and the others. My fantasy merged with their reality. I had read the book when it came out in 1961
and laughed at its zany humor and twists of plot. All my friends were reading it too. This time I understood the book. It was more thoughtful than I
first realized. After half a year in Vietnam, I saw that Heller had written
something wise and honest about war.

One of his themes was courage. Reading *Catch-22*, I saw that my concept
of courage was too simple. Since I was a teenager, I had believed that
courage was "grace under pressure," as Hemingway had defined it. How
someone behaved in danger was the true measure of his worth as a man. For
me, thinking about courage triggered associations with all kinds of heroic
figures: leaders, soldiers, writers, martyrs, athletes, saints, patriots, explorers,
philosophers. I believed in the value of having courage but didn't know if I
had any myself.

Courage, as defined by Hemingway, is the ability to control fear in situations of great danger and take heroic action. To be courageous, the paralysis
of fear has to be overcome. That covers combat. The sign of a brave soldier
is his ability to stand and fight instead of hiding in fear or running away,
which is the natural inclination. That much I understood. But what if the
danger that causes the fear comes from an act of insanity? Or irrationality?
unreason?

In *Catch-22,* Yossarian is forced to fly more than fifty combat missions against his will. He knows that his chances of survival are practically zero. The war has already been won but is not yet over. His death will not be for the benefit of his country, but for the illogical whims of his superior officers. They, the story argues, are the ones who are crazy, not Yossarian. "He had decided to live forever or die in the attempt, and his only mission each time he went up was to come down alive." I wondered which was more courageous of Yossarian: to survive even though he appeared to be cowardly, or to go obediently to his death without showing fear.

Sitting in the darkened hotel room, I asked myself whether those young second lieutenants I had seen standing up under sniper fire in the Soui Ca Valley had *true* courage. Were they really fearless? Were they concentrating so hard on leading their platoons that they weren't concerned for their own safety? That would have been courageous, surely, but I wondered whether they stood up to direct their men because it would have appeared less than heroic to command from a safer place. Was it bravery or bravado? Were they acting a role? Would that be 'grace under pressure' at *any* cost? Or is it necessary to be truly fearless? Selfless? I wondered whether the *appearance* of courage is as necessary as the action that accompanies it.

It was all getting complicated. I went back to Heller's book and read more. Time passed. I tried to concentrate. Grace under pressure, it seemed, may be true of *some* who show courage, but not all. What about murderers, armed robbers, criminal psychotics? Surely some of them show 'grace under pressure' when committing pathological acts of violence, but they aren't courageous. True courage must depend on the *kind* of behavior that takes place. I had to think harder. The hours drifted by in the hotel room without my being aware of it.

To fight for your country, to risk your life for the future well-being of your fellow citizens, is surely an act of courage. But what if your country's cause is questionable, or one you don't understand or don't trust? The Third Reich came to mind. Wouldn't it be more courageous to *resist* a bad cause than to fight for it? Wouldn't it be better to follow your conscience and do what you think is right? Even at the risk of appearing to be a coward? At the risk of imprisonment? Even death? I wondered whether physical danger was the only necessity for courage to take place.

I needed a better definition. I got out a pad of paper and made a list of things that would be necessary for courage to happen.

First, there has to be risk: some kind of physical, social, economic or other danger. The courageous person has to be threatened with loss of some kind, even if it's only face. Second, fear, at least in passing, has to be present, otherwise courage would be easy. Third, there has to be action because acts, not appearances, demonstrate courage. And, fourth, the action has to be correct, at least in the conscience of the individual. Differences of opinion about what is right are inevitable, but it's individual belief that counts. Fifth, another factor would be selflessness, doing something good for others. Finally, fearlessness might go with courage, but it isn't necessary. Courage can be present in someone who is trembling with fright.

I studied the list. It all seemed to be there: risk, fear, action, conscience, self-lessness and, perhaps, fearlessness. It added up to what might be called *honor*.

A better definition that seemed to cover most situations was emerging. Courage, I thought, involved taking a risk to do something good. Either directly for others or, indirectly, by being a good example.

The definition went through so many variations and refinements my head hurt. In the end, this came out:

> Courage is doing good in danger.
> The greater the danger, the greater the good, the greater the courage.

I slept on the definition and came back to it the next day. Vietnam was a world away. Hong Kong was an island of tranquillity, my refuge from the war.

I thought of another aspect to courage: Acting sane and taking the right action in danger, whatever madness may be spinning in your mind, earns the respect of others. That acceptance, especially when it has been withheld until then, creates self-respect, a healthy feeling of goodwill, security among friends. It was certainly true with TV correspondents and their camera crews. I guessed it might be the same with soldiers.

Later I learned that courage produces its own reward. Facing fear, accepting it, challenging it, fighting it, taking charge of it long enough to act with honor, gives back a sense of fulfillment that is among the most precious gifts in life. It doesn't matter that no one sees or knows what you have done.

MARCH 10, 1966

Something was happening and everyone knew. The word went around Saigon early Thursday. Reporters showed up at their desks, checked with MACV, got the word, sent cables to their home offices, passed it to friends, discussed it at lunch with their contacts. A major battle was under way. A Special Forces "A" camp was in trouble in I Corps. Not much else was known. In the late afternoon at the daily military briefing, the ground floor of the JUSPAO building was crowded with reporters, photographers, bureau chiefs, stringers, MACV staff, embassy officers and assorted scholars, writers and intelligence agents. The spooks stood at the back of the room, watching and listening, trying to look casual—as if they belonged to the fast competitive world of daily journalism and had already filed their stories. Urgent chatter buzzed through the corridors as journalists arrived, groups of two and three heading for the auditorium. Along the way they passed a five-foot-high map of Vietnam standing on an easel in a corner of the main corridor. The map was covered with a transparent plastic overlay and the words "Pucker Factor" written on it in red grease pencil. Below that the numbers zero through ten were drawn in a vertical line to indicate degrees of danger at various locations around the country. The higher the pucker factor, the greater the danger. Ten was the worst. "Pucker" was insider talk, a military colloquialism for the peculiar experience of losing control of one's anal sphincter in combat, feeling the muscle contract and expand in rapid involuntary movement, *puckering*. It was related to more graphic expressions like "getting the shit scared out of you" and "scared shitless," and was usually spoken with a smile that said it was okay to laugh about it now but it wasn't so funny at the time. The faded condition of the map and overlay suggested it had probably been drawn up in the early 1960s, when the war was more limited, to tell journalists planning a trip to the field which areas of the country were secure or not. But the overlay had been blank for months now; no one had time to keep it current, too much like charting hot spots on the sun. Journalists walked past the map without looking at it.

All the seats in the briefing room were filled. Thin clouds of cigarette smoke swirled in the cool conditioned air that gave the inside of the building its imported American smell. Breathing hard, a MACV sergeant hurried into the room carrying a stack of mimeographed sheets and passed them out. The one-page summary outlined the day's action at a remote Special Forces camp on the border with Laos. The camp was named A Shau for the valley in which it was located. Everyone read the briefing paper closely.

BACKGROUND ONLY—Not For Attribution

0050—All quiet at Ashau.

0136—(10th)—Friendly forces report they can hear VC digging in a hundred meters from the perimeter and that they expect a heavy assault. They are under heavy mortar attack at this time.

0335—Ashau reports it is under full scale attack but that the perimeter is holding.

0400—The camp reports it is badly cut up.

0425—Radio operator at Ashau reports he believes he is only one left alive. Reports that the camp wall is destroyed.

0435—Flare ship overhead reports it appears camp has been overrun however some people may be alive in the communication bunker.

0505—Communication still exists with a man on the ground at Ashau. The man says that everything he sees is destroyed or burning. Immediate air strikes on the camp are requested.

0530—Radio operator at Ashau says he hears a friendly mortar firing from somewhere.

0615—Radio operator at Ashau is still adjusting rocket fire from aircraft overhead.

0730—Bombing of the camp area continues through cloud cover although the camp can't be seen. Ceiling is two hundred feet scattered clouds. Two hundred to seven thousand feet solid cloud layers.

0807—FAC over the area reports he still has radio contact with Ashau.

0840—FAC says north section of camp is still intact.

0930—Communication continues with Ashau.

The briefing officer stood behind a lectern at the front of the room and said in matter-of-fact tones that the fighting was still going on. Heavy cloud cover was hampering air support and resupply. Some tac-air had gone in.

Other than that, he said, there was nothing more to report. His manner was all military, no emotion.

Reporters wanted details. Insistent voices called out: 'Are the attacking troops PAVN?' 'Which units?' 'Was there any warning?' 'Were reinforcements sent in?' 'What's the situation now?' 'How many friendly casualties?' 'Where are the survivors?' 'How about getting some of them down here to talk to us?'

To each question the briefing officer said he didn't know. 'I've given you all the information I can,' he said, again and again.

Joseph Fried took him on. 'What d'ya mean you don't know?' he shouted. 'Are you telling us you guys don't know what's going on up there? *Come on!*'

As Saigon correspondent for the *New York Daily News,* Joe Fried had clout. With more than a million daily readers, his tabloid tended to reinforce the promilitary opinions of its blue-collar readers. Fried was considered to be "with the program" and was kept well-informed by U.S. military staff. Short, slender and curly-haired, Fried was one of the more sarcastic members of the press corps, a cynical, abrasive New Yorker, though his tough questioning at the daily briefings in Saigon was not always reflected in the stories that appeared under his byline in New York.

'You mean to say Westmoreland doesn't know what's going on?' Fried said.

'Well, Joe, the situation is, ah, fluid, at the moment,' the briefing officer said.

'Are the Americans *in* the camp or outside it?'

'I'm not sure at this moment whether the team is inside the camp or not.'

'Well, is the camp under American control or PAVN?'

'I don't think anyone knows that answer, Joe.'

'Isn't it a fact the camp's been overrun? That our guys are outside the wire?' Fried usually knew more than what was announced at the briefing.

The officer stepped away from the podium and held a whispered conversation with a more senior officer. After a minute he said, 'On background, I would have to say that is correct. Our people have evacuated from the camp.'

A chorus of exclamations went through the room.

The senior officer, a lieutenant colonel, walked to the lectern. 'May I remind you gentlemen and ladies of the press that lives are at stake here and that you are bound not to reveal specific details of friendly casualties or operations in progress. On background I can tell you that an intensive search-and-rescue mission is under way at this time and it could be compromised by press reports. Please keep that in mind when you are writing your stories this afternoon.'

A senior bureau chief stood up.

'Colonel, don't you think the North Vietnamese have a pretty good idea of what's going on up there? I mean, they've overrun the camp. Presumably they've had time to search the place by now. Isn't it likely they know our people are not around anymore? That they're trying to escape and evade?'

'Who knows what the enemy knows or doesn't know?' The colonel's tone was hard, as if debating an adversary. 'As you were told, the situation is fluid. We don't want to take any chances. In a situation like this you can't be too careful.'

Sitting in the briefing room, listening to the exchange, I wondered whether the officers were being ultracautious because of the search-and-rescue operation or were trying to play down the dimensions of the defeat. Only two Special Forces camps had been lost before this one. A Shau, which everyone pronounced Ah-Shaow, was located in one of the wildest, most inaccessible parts of South Vietnam, a lone valley in the middle of a mountain range, more remote and vulnerable than Plei Me. It was on the western edge of I Corps, just east of the border with Laos. The center of the valley was only about thirty miles southwest of Hué by air (trying to get there by road was suicide), but it was much farther away from modern civilization, trapped somewhere back in the Dark Ages, truly a lost valley. The A Shau existed in a world of its own: of seven-thousand-foot mountains and ten-foot elephant grass, of haunting morning mists and suffocating rainforest, of darkness and demons and death traps as lethal as anything nature and the North Vietnamese could invent. In time, just mention of the name "A Shau" momentarily tightened the chests of those who had fought there.

A Shau was a major terminus of the Ho Chi Minh Trail. Thousands of North Vietnamese troops and supplies made the two-month journey down from the north through Laos and crossed the border into South Vietnam through the A Shau Valley. From there they continued eastward, toward the coast, where the main battles were taking place. Control of the A Shau was a military necessity for the PAVN. The small, vulnerable Special Forces camp at the bottom of the valley was in the way.

Before dawn the next morning, a camera crew and I got on an air force C-130 and flew to Danang. Checking in at the Combat Information Bureau, we met other reporters who had been trying to get to the battle area for two days without success. Marines and Special Forces at Danang were not being helpful. Little information, no transportation. A blackout on details of the story was in effect. Waiting all day around the press center with other journalists, we got nowhere on the story. In the evening, a Marine friend from the CIB took me aside and said, 'Get to the airfield at Phu Bai. That's where it's happening.' Nothing else.

Next morning the crew and I slipped out of the press center and caught a flight to Phu Bai. A veteran newspaper reporter, Jim Lucas, was also aboard. Lucas had covered the war in Korea and was much in favor with the Marines. He too had been tipped off. Arriving at the air strip in Phu Bai, we were surprised to find Sean Flynn standing by. He said he had been trying for three days to get out to the A Shau to take pictures but no one would take him. 'It's way too hairy,' he said. 'They don't want any extra baggage.' Now the battle was just about over and the main body of survivors had been rescued by Marine helicopter pilots. At the time of the attack, Flynn said, there were about four hundred people in the camp, including seventeen U.S. Special Forces soldiers. A relief force of Americans and ethnic Chinese mercenaries called Nungs had been flown in a few days before the attack. Five of the seventeen Americans had been killed and ten wounded. Marine pilots rescued most of the 220 Vietnamese troops known as CIDG, civilian irregulars who were stationed at the camp, and another 135 Nungs. During the battle, Flynn said, a bunch of CIDG strikers opened fire on their own troops and deserted to the other side. All the information had come from his friends in Special Forces.

It was good to see Flynn again. He was rarely in Saigon anymore, almost always in the field. He led us to a small wooden hut at the side of the airstrip and introduced us to the Special Forces commander of the A Shau camp, Captain John Blair, of Atlanta. Blair was twenty-five years old and wore a green T-shirt and fatigue trousers. He was the last American to come out of the jungle outside the camp, one of only two Americans who were not killed or wounded. Blair sat behind a metal office desk across from another Special Forces captain, Sam Carter. Three days before the battle started, Carter led in the company of Nungs to reinforce the camp. Flynn, Lucas and I took notes as Carter and Blair told the story in turns:

"A red star cluster went up and that signaled the start of the attack," Carter said. "They charged the wall one company at a time. Our guys were blowing the wire with claymores and stuff. We called in tac-air and the fighter pilots bombed and strafed the VC trenches. Didn't do much good. The VC came up and hit us again. They hit us a lot harder then we expected."

"I'm sure they were PAVN," Blair said. "They had uniforms, heavy weapons, plenty of ammo, good communications. Their mortars were coming in on us from three directions: 81s, 82s, 60s. Great mortar fire. They put it in on us right where they wanted to. Three to five hundred rounds at the start."

Carter was dressed in a green T-shirt, fatigue trousers and sandals. Both of them had just taken their first shower in almost a week. Their eyes were bloodshot tired.

Carter said, "A mortar hit the wall three feet away and blew the wall right in on me. I was completely buried. They thought I was dead. I did too." He laughed. "Later, I kinda wished I was."

"By noon we knew the camp was lost," Blair said. "The southeast wall was gone. The Nungs counterattacked the east wall and took it, but they had to pull back after an hour. Air destroyed the wall but we couldn't get the VC out."

"Three of us knew we killed fifty of 'em in a tiny area. I laid in one hole in the wall and killed twelve. Just in that one hole."

"At one point we looked at each other and said, 'Looks like this is the end.'"

A sergeant came into the hut. Blair and Carter greeted him. He said his name was Bernie Adkins, that he was thirty-two years old and came from Waurika, Oklahoma. He listened to Blair and Carter talk for a while and said, "The most heroic action was by the chopper pilots." The others agreed.

Blair explained that after they got out of the camp and tried to escape in the jungle, the Marines sent rescue helicopters looking for them. Anti-air-craft fire was everywhere.

"If I'd been flying those choppers, I wouldn't have gone in," Carter said. "The ground-to-air was unbelievable."

Flynn, Lucas and I finished writing the quotes in our notebooks. Blair and Carter said, "C'mon, we want you to meet the skipper." They took us out-side and introduced us to the leader of the Marine rescue force that got them out of the A Shau. Lieutenant Colonel Charles House was a strong, friendly man of forty-four who said he was from Burlington, Iowa. As commanding officer of helicopter squadron HMM 163 ("Ridgerunners"), House led the first flight into the A Shau.

"It was a suicide mission," he said. "There were tracer bullets going through our flight up, down and sideways—just a blizzard of incoming fire. I don't know how we got through all that alive. On the first day, we went in with eight choppers and got about eighty Vietnamese and seven U.S. out."

On the second day, House and his crew were shot down. The Marine lieutenant colonel found himself in the jungle with Army captains Blair and Carter and about seventy men: American, Vietnamese and Nung. As the senior officer on the ground, House took command of the survival group.

"I'm really sold on the Nungs," he said. "They came outta there with no ammunition. Some of those Vietnamese strikers went over the south wall, turned and fired at the backs of their own people on the north wall."

On the fourth day, House led the group to a clearing in the jungle where pilots from his squadron could pick them up. But the moment the helicopters landed, House said, the South Vietnamese in the group panicked.

"One of their officers, a Lieutenant Dang, was the first to run for the choppers. Then they all went berserk, running after him, piling in there, arguing. There were fifty of 'em hanging on one of the birds, holding onto the sides, grabbing on the wheels. We tried to drag 'em off, beat 'em off, kick 'em off—but they just came back. It was mass panic. Finally, we had to shoot 'em off. Boom! Boom! Boom! To make 'em obey."

House explained that the door gunners on the H-34s first fired their machineguns into the ground. Still, the South Vietnamese troops would not get off. The choppers were overloaded, unable to lift off. Finally, House said, he ordered his men to fire at the Vietnamese who would not obey. The shooting lasted a few seconds. Bodies fell to the ground around the helicopters. The other Vietnamese moved back. The choppers took off.

"We hated to do that," House said, "but no one would have gotten out if we didn't."

As House spoke, I recalled the panic at Plei Me when the first helicopters arrived to evacuate the wounded. Led by their senior officer, the South Vietnamese soldiers swarmed over the choppers as the Americans fought them off with their fists. I pictured the panic and confusion in the A Shau: Americans screaming at the hysterical Vietnamese, punching and kicking, pulling them off the bird, then, when nothing worked, blasting them point-blank with their machineguns, gunning them down, watching them fall on the ground, shouting in rage at the others, terrorizing them into submission. Madness.

Colonel House was giving us a big story. For Americans to shoot their South Vietnamese allies deliberately, for whatever reason, was extraordinary news. But I doubted he would say it on film. Officers' careers had been ruined by public admissions far less controversial than this. Military promotion boards were merciless: one black mark on an officer's record at his level was often the end. I asked House if he would repeat what he said on-camera. He was silent for several seconds.

"Yeah, what the hell," he said. "I've been passed over for promotion twice. So I'm on my way out anyway."

Standing in front of his helicopter with the camera rolling, House told us the story again. He held nothing back. His expression was somber, his manner modest, unapologetic.

When the interview was finished, House instructed one of the younger pilots, First Lieutenant Norm Urban, to fly us over A Shau to get aerial pictures of the abandoned Special Forces camp. When we got there, air strikes were still going in. The airstrip next to the camp was cratered by mortar shells. As the helicopter circled the camp, the crew chief pointed to the airstrip and shouted over the engines. He explained that an Air Force A-1E pilot was shot down during the early stages of the battle. His plane was barely in control when he managed to crash-land on the airstrip. He was in radio contact with his wingman circling overhead in another A-1E. The wingman bombed and strafed the edge of the airstrip, keeping the North Vietnamese away, then came around and landed on the runway itself through a blizzard of fire. The downed pilot jumped into his partner's cockpit—boots and legs hanging out the sides—as the A-1E turned and raced down the damaged runway with machinegun tracers flashing around it. They both got away safely. The plane was full of holes. 'That Air Force pilot who went down and picked him up oughta get a medal,' the Marine crew chief shouted. Later I learned he did. It was the Medal of Honor.

Word came over the radio that another A-1E had just been shot down in the valley. Lieutenant Urban flew back to Phu Bai fast, dropped us off to lighten his load, and returned to the A Shau. It took about an hour to establish radio communications, locate and rescue the pilot, Major Monroe (Buzz) Blaylock, out of the jungle. When they returned to the airfield at Phu Bai, the flight of Marine H-34s and Blaylock's A-1E wingman flew in tight aerial formation over the runway, wingtips to rotor blades, then made their pitchouts and landed one by one. From the ground, it made an emotional picture.

Several other survivors of the battle described their ordeal on-camera. Writing the narration, I got in as much detail of the battle as possible but without any pictures of the fighting. For the close, I tried to pull together the threads of the story into a simple concluding summary:

> The A Shau Special Forces camp is closed. But the story of what happened there—the overwhelming attack, the evacuation and dramatic rescue, the panic and confusion, and especially the shooting of South Vietnamese soldiers—will be debated for months to come. It has been said that this is a strange and ugly war. It has never been worse than at A Shau.

The story was shipped to Saigon slugged, "A Shau: Miracles and Madness." When it was shown in the States, it provoked alarm about the conduct of the war. In phone calls and letters, viewers expressed concern about America's wisdom in fighting a war for an ally whose soldiers behaved so disgracefully.

A few months later, the Marine Corps nominated Lieutenant Colonel Charles House for the Navy Cross, its second highest decoration, for "conspicuous gallantry" while leading the survivors to safety. The citation said in part, "His determination to survive contributed in a large measure to saving the members of his crew and many of the Special Forces and Vietnamese from capture or death." House was also awarded the Cross of Gallantry by the South Vietnamese military government.

Later in the year, the Marines completed their official investigation into the incident and reprimanded their hero. Led by Brigadier General Marion Carl, a board of inquiry criticized House, not for giving the order to shoot the panicked Vietnamese but for giving the story to the press. The board said he showed poor judgment. I was criticized for broadcasting the story. The board said I didn't realize the propaganda value to the enemy and should have kept the whole affair secret.

MARCH 27, 1966

They're . . . gonna put me in the movies . . .

The voice was clear and pure and right on the notes, a singer's voice that rang with the rich country twang of the American South, piercing the hot jungle gloom like an arrow.

They're gonna make a big star out of me . . .

Everyone in the column laughed, including the officers.

We'll make a film about a man that's sad and lonely,
And all I gotta do is act naturally . . .

Line troops loved that Beatles song. They listened to it on Armed Forces Radio and sang along with it on their tape recorders and savored it until the tune belonged to them. It was more poignant this time because a TV film crew was on patrol with them. The soldier who sang it was well forward in the column so I didn't get to meet him, but after that I sometimes told GIs who we were about to film, "Try not to look at the camera, just be yourself, act naturally," and they laughed, getting the joke, though they rarely allowed themselves to look as sad or lonely as they felt.

We were out with Bravo Company, 1st Battalion, 8th Cavalry, on patrol. The rifle company was part of Operation Lincoln, a sweep just north of the Ia Drang Valley, where the 7th Cavalry fought and bled so hard in November. The company had covered almost thirty miles in three days with no contact. The soldiers, who were paratroopers, were at the edge of exhaustion. The jungle was triple canopy, dark and wet, swarming with insects, strange little birds and snakes, heat like a sauna. The jungle was as much the enemy as the North

Vietnamese. Every fifteen minutes or so the troops took a break. On one of
the stops I asked a fire team leader, Specialist Fourth Class Carl Stark, if the
jungle ever got to be familiar. "No," he said, "I could walk through a place and
ten minutes later I wouldn't recognize it again. I never get used to all the walking. You sit down every chance you get." Stark, who was twenty-one years old
and from Fort Worth, Texas, had been in Vietnam since the First Cav arrived
six months earlier. "Going home couldn't come soon enough," he said.

By March 1966, the number of American troops in Vietnam had reached
200,000. They came across the Pacific in airplanes and troop ships and
marched or were moved by trucks to base camps where they were assigned
sleeping quarters they rarely slept in. They dug holes in the ground for
latrines and shelters and constructed small military cities made out of canvas, plywood, wire and cement. For one year, when they weren't in the bush,
it was their home, but most of the time they were in the bush.

The war was settling into a routine. Each day, all around the country,
infantry battalions set out in search of the enemy. Ground troops covered
miles of terrain: valleys, streams, woodland, coastline, lowlands, highlands,
tropical savanna, swamps, rainforest, rice paddies, rubber plantations, rivers,
ridgelines and mountains—most of it hostile. The soldiers went into villages, took away prisoners and weapons, destroyed food supplies, tunnels,
bunkers—anything that might be useful to the other side, never mind that
they were essential to the peasants who owned them. Sometimes the soldiers burned houses, especially when they were fired on from them, and
scattered the livestock, thereby making farm families into refugees. At times
they succumbed to their anger or lust and abused the villagers physically. In
some cases they shot them.

On patrol, American troops engaged the enemy in combat probably less
than 2 percent of the time. The North Vietnamese and Viet Cong tried to
avoid firefights whenever they were at a disadvantage. They withdrew rather
than engage, leaving snipers and booby traps behind to cover their exit.
Often they hid underground. The Western press called them "wily, elusive
guerrillas," disrespectfully at first because they did not fight like conventional soldiers. As the war went on, the VC and NVA tactics were recognized
as part of a war strategy that gave them a chance of winning if they could
keep fighting the foreign presence on their land long enough.

Their sanctuaries were the forest and the earth. The same wild jungle
that gave cover to the guerrillas swallowed whole battalions of American sol-

diers in their impenetrable midsts and attacked them without mercy. It gave them heatstroke, malaria, jungle rot, insect bites, heat rash, blisters, dysentery, foot sores, sprains, broken bones, fatigue and all manner of bacterial infections until the troops were dead on their feet. Month after month GIs trudged over the terrain in long looping sweeps, clover leafs, hammer and anvil patterns, pincer movements, combat assaults, ambushes, feints, usually without success. They thrashed through the black-green murk with no more visibility than the few feet ahead. Finally the rainforest became a giant quagmire for them, the embodiment of their country's deep entanglement in the Vietnam affair, a symbol of their government's limited vision and lost direction. The U.S. government followed a policy as incremental as the forward slog of soldiers on long patrol: slow, endless, step by step, going nowhere. The land, like the Vietnamese, was wilder, more enduring, more fiercely independent than the mighty American effort to tame it.

The grunts came to hate the war and, by association, the Vietnamese. Anger was a fire in them. They counted each day until they could go home. On the occasions when they made contact with the VC or North Vietnamese, they fought as hard as they could, in many cases bravely, at times with fanatical abandon. They called in helicopter gunships, artillery and air strikes and counted the bodies when it was over. Body counts were the chief measure of success. Capturing territory meant nothing, killing Vietnamese everything. The land of Vietnam became a vast blood-covered killing ground.

Bravo Company stopped at a stream of fast-running black water that was too deep and wide to wade across. The company commander ordered the men to blow up an inflatable rubber raft that had been delivered by helicopter that morning, the same chopper the crew and I came in on. The mood of the soldiers went sour. They grumbled about the extra work, not at their officers, but at the crew and me, glaring at us with mean looks that said, 'If it weren't for you we wouldn't have to hump this shit.' They were right. It appeared to be another useless exercise in modern technology versus nature, probably dreamed up in the Pentagon and designed as much to get on television as to work. There were so many gimmicks. American newspaper photographs at the time showed an army helicopter dropping a huge steel net onto the tops of jungle trees in an experiment to create an instant landing zone above the forest. Of course it didn't work. The troops struggled with the raft but it was too bulky and they were too tired to get it inflated properly. Finally, they ditched it in the brush and moved on.

It was now more than seven months since my first patrol. Flying out from Saigon, An Khe or Danang, I adjusted to the field within a few hours. I started each patrol full of energy—enthusiastic, my senses alert, looking forward to finding a story. Walking in the column of soldiers, my eyes scanned the trees and brush ahead and on the sides, looking for places to take cover in case of ambush. The soldiers looked less concerned about being attacked, more relaxed, more accustomed to the monotony of the march, although at the forward point of the column, where the danger was greatest, the soldiers were more alert. Behind the point men, everyone in the line slogged ahead, one foot after another, meter after meter. Within a few minutes of the march, I began to feel the heat rise up from my chest, tingling at first around the back of my head and neck. It was a familiar sensation; it only happened on patrol. The heat spread to the rest of my body until I felt hot all over. Sweat ran down my forehead and off my nose and stung my eyes with salt. Breath came in short dry gasps. My mouth hung open unless I remembered to close it. A dull ache set in between my lower back and shoulders and moved down into my legs. My feet were heavy and sluggish. Then the heat pushed up through my neck and into my head until my hot expanding brain felt as if it were going to burst against the inside of my skull. The skin on my forehead burned. Each step forward was a struggle. Haphazardly, my thoughts drifted to other times, other places, any distraction from the difficulty of the march. As the patrol went on, I began to think less about getting a story and more about how much longer I'd be able to carry on.

The physical requirement to keep moving in that heat affected your mental equilibrium. Your thinking became less complicated, more primitive, descending slowly in stages to a state better suited to the demands of the jungle. The heat assaulted your mind and body until you became so hardened you were able to take it, or you passed out and had to be evacuated. At the same time, just behind your conscious awareness, a subtle tension reminded you of the danger. Combat, and the madness that went with it, might start at any moment. After a while, the physical and psychological stresses of the forced march—pain, depression, fatigue, exhaustion—altered the way you looked: jaw slack, eyes vaguely focused, thoughts distracted, senses dulled, scared, lonely, mean—you were just another beast prowling the wilderness. The rainforest was always wearing you down, making you suffer, trying to take you.

Even the rain conspired to kill you. I went out with a unit of the First

Infantry Division in War Zone D, north of Ben Cat, to report the hardships of army life in the field. The story was to be called "Dog Faces of Vietnam." The date was November 17, 1965, still early in the war. The terrain was difficult. It took the company all day to cover less than three miles. The soldiers carried heavy long-barreled M-14 rifles, large packs, bottles of insect repellent tucked in their helmet cover bands. Soon they were tired. In the afternoon, they came to a small hamlet with houses of mud and bamboo. The troops searched the houses, found nothing incriminating, and moved on. As we were leaving, my sound technician, P. B. Hoan, took a blanket from one of the houses—a clean, thick, powder blue blanket—and stuffed it in his rucksack. *Same as the ARVN,* I thought, *stealing the peasants' stuff. Nobody respects anything in this war.* I considered asking him to return the blanket but did not. *It's his country,* I thought.

In the evening, after the troops had set up their night perimeter and eaten chow, rain began to fall. A monsoon wind came up and blew hard through the trees. In a few minutes the troops were drenched. Darkness came. The rain did not stop.

'I wish we could film in the dark,' I said to Tom McEnry, the photographer. 'It would give us great pictures of miserable GIs.'

He scowled at me. 'I don't know what the hell we're doing here,' he said. 'We can't work.'

The three of us sat in the dark with our backs resting against a stack of C ration crates that gave some protection from the wind. Huddled together, arms and legs touching, we tried to sleep sitting up. My poncho was a thin lightweight camper's type not designed to withstand a tropical monsoon. Soon the water soaked through to my skin. The night air turned cold. In the darkest hours I started to shake, lightly at first, shivering in the cold rain. Then the shaking stopped. A few minutes later it started again and did not stop. My teeth began to rattle. Then my bones. I couldn't stop it. I felt weak, helpless, no strength or will to save myself.

What a way to go, I thought. *You survive combat and near misses and die of hypothermia.* Then another thought, a new one: *What the hell am I doing here? Really. You don't have to be in this godforsaken place. You could be covering stories somewhere else. Back in the States. Anywhere. This place is hell.*

Then I heard a voice from beyond the night.

'Relax, Jack,' the voice said. 'It's almost over. Nothing to worry about. Get some rest and you'll be warm and peaceful. Always.'

I said a prayer for help and started to fall asleep, shaking, comforted by
the gentle voice. On my left, Hoan reached into his pack and pulled out the
powder blue blanket he had stolen from the house in the hamlet. Pulling
away my soggy poncho, he wrapped the blanket around my back and shoulders and then covered the blanket with the poncho. I was too grateful to
speak. After some time I stopped shivering. After an hour I felt a trace of
warmth in my bones. In the morning the sun dried everything.

All through February, the coastal plain around Bong Son seethed with violence. Masher/White Wing became the largest military operation of the
war. Ten thousand First Cav troops swept the fields searching and destroying. More refugees were created. Thousands of U.S. Marines pressed down
from the north, ARVN armor and infantry from the east. B-52s flew thousands of miles from Guam in the Pacific Ocean and blasted the jungle mountains west of Bong Son with thousands of bombs, each of them weighing
750 pounds. The sound of so much high explosive detonating at the same
time thundered through the sandy plain and rumbled in the earth.

Mistakes were made. A South Vietnamese target coordinator misread a
map reference by one digit and sent a flight of U.S. Air Force A-1Es into an
attack on the friendly village of Beduc, west of Qui Nhon. The peasants
were loyal to the South Vietnamese government in Saigon and did not
believe they would be attacked, so they did not take cover. Forty-eight of
them died and fifty-five were wounded. A MACV officer later described it as
"an inadvertent bombing."

American battle losses rose sharply in the first two months of 1966, a rate
almost four times higher than all of 1965. The 85th Evacuation Hospital at
Qui Nhon became so crowded that wounded soldiers had to be flown
directly to Clark Air Force Base in the Philippines for emergency treatment.
At Bong Son, Colonel Hal Moore told a group of reporters on February 11
that "everything has gone as planned." Moore claimed that his brigade was
running the legs off the North Vietnamese and VC battalions in Binh Dinh
Province, stretching them to the limits of their endurance, forcing them to
keep moving, hiding, fighting when they could not escape. Moore was running the legs off his own troops as well.

On a visit to the hospital in Qui Nhon, I saw some First Cav soldiers who
looked as though they had lost touch with reality. They stared into space
with dull unconscious expressions, unfeeling, out of this world. They did not

speak, though they were not physically wounded. The medical staff at the hospital said the soldiers were suffering from battle fatigue. It was the first time I'd heard that term used in Vietnam and it sounded like a story.

C Company, 1st Battalion, 5th Cavalry, was resting at Bong Son after nearly a month in the field. For the last ten days the company had been in almost constant combat. The soldiers had not had clean clothes or decent rest since the start of Operation Masher twenty-seven days earlier. Some of them had been evacuated with battle fatigue. The leader of 2d Platoon, Second Lieutenant William Farmer, was sitting near his tent when I met him.

"For the past three or four weeks we have been marching through hill after hill,' Farmer said. 'We haven't met too much action until the last week and a half when we were still walkin up and down hills." Farmer said he came from Wickliffe, Kentucky. He spoke with the slow drawl of the region.

"We finally met the enemy on one big hill. We had to climb this hill four times in three days, twice in one day. We met heavy fire on both occasions. During all of this walkin from hill to hill, the men were having to carry everything they needed to survive with, which meant they were carrying in the neighborhood of seventy-five pounds apiece on their backs." He stopped what he was saying and lit a cigarette.

"When a man gets physically tired," Farmer said, "he doesn't think well on his feet. He's not as alert as he should be, which will be very dangerous."

Following Farmer's lead, I went to the brigade field hospital at Bong Son to pursue the story. I found the Army doctor who dealt with battle fatigue cases and asked for an interview. Major Phillip Warner of San Francisco was youthful-looking with brown hair receding at the temples. He wore a green T-shirt and fatigue trousers in the heat.

"The men who suffer this term, 'battle fatigue,'" he said, "have usually been out for a long period of time, fighting or being under very, very adverse conditions of rain and rice paddies. And, although they may function very well for a period of time, for some reason they reach a point where they can no longer tolerate their situation. A man has no physical ailments. He's perfectly well in terms of his body condition. But certainly his mental condition is what is gone wrong."

I asked the Army doctor to describe it in medical terms. Farmer answered slowly, choosing the words with precision.

"Battle fatigue is simply a series of events which are characterized by a man being under tremendous pressure for a period of time due to the course of the battle, so that his psychological manifestations are very prolonged under this stress. He then, at some time or other during the course of his being in battle, presents with the symptoms of what we then call battle fatigue. These can be many and varied and we see all sorts of patients coming in with many symptoms. But usually the man is very, very fatigued, tired in the true sense of the word. He's been under tremendous stress and he loses contact with his own surroundings and his friends and what he knows in his own environment. These men usually cannot be talked to. They will not answer you. They will not respond to any type of your questions. And, uh, basically they have a psychological block."

"How do you treat it?"

"Basically, we treat this type of individual with sedation, give him one or another type of drug. Rest, which is most important because he's been out for a prolonged period of time. And the most important thing is, after he has rested, he must return back to his unit and return back to duty."

When the interviews were finished, I found a quiet place to sit and began to write the story. The voice-over narration started:

There is a new kind of casualty for Vietnam. It is battle fatigue. It has been as common to the fighting men in other wars as the sound of gunfire in this one. Now, for the first time, First Cavalry soldiers are suffering from battle fatigue in Vietnam.

The story told of 2d Platoon's ordeal of the past month and then introduced the interviews with Major Warner, Lieutenant Farmer and some of the line troops. The narration concluded:

So far there have been only a few cases of battle fatigue and most of the men have returned to their units. But the beginning of battle fatigue casualties is another indication of the mounting intensity of the war.

I signed off at Bong Son. The film and narration were shipped to New York where they were screened and edited for broadcast, but network logs said the story was not shown. I was not told why. I didn't realize it then, but I was beginning to develop some of the same symptoms as the soldiers.

NOVEMBER 1965–DECEMBER 1967

The war was strange and ugly, stranger and uglier than anyone knew, strange and ugly and fantastic and emotionally moving at times because of the compassion it drew out of people. In the crucible of combat, incredible things happened: tough guys cracked, reluctant draftees turned into leaders, officers lost their minds, pacifists became heroes. Ordinary enlisted men with no wish to be in the war performed in the superhuman stresses of close combat with amazing self-assurance. They fought and suffered with the modest everyday dignity of workers doing their jobs. Mostly, they obeyed. Grumbling, they went along. Everyone was in the same predicament. Usual measures of personal worth like family background, education, job status, looks, material wealth and social standing that meant so much in the United States were not important in the field. Courage, steady nerves, humor, strength, reliability, comradeship, generosity and teamwork were. In the madness of war fighting, insanity could be an asset. The demands were so extreme, so intense, they produced behavior that went beyond the usual definitions of right and wrong or good and bad. People behaved as well or as poorly as their capabilities for either. Routinely, they made decisions that determined whether they lived or died, and also whether those around them survived or perished. Decisions had to be made in an instant. And in that instant, in that fierce fusion of conflicting impulses and emotions—fear and duty among them—the testament of their true character was revealed. Wartime behavior not only defined character, it created new dimensions of it, new opportunities for its expression. Coming through a battle, soldiers were surprised to discover that they had outperformed their expectations. Young men fulfilled their wildest fantasies. Others died trying. A few failed altogether: froze up, broke down, ran away, faked wounds, killed their own, shot civilians. The worst punishment was the memory. The war magnified everything, even perceptions of itself, creating images of compassion and cruelty as gallant or grotesque as the imagination allows. Each battle brought its own apocalypse. The incredible was routine.

The airstrip at Duc Co Special Forces camp was unusually busy one November afternoon. Helicopters came in flurries of movement, lifting men and supplies from fire bases in the rear to landing zones in the field, churning up red-brown dust around the airstrip and blowing it around like billows of smoke. Officers moved briskly. Field radios crackled. Artillery roared. Second Brigade of the 1st Cavalry Division was beginning a new offensive into the Ia Drang Valley, where, five miles away, two of the most savage battles of the war had been fought the week before. The Duc Co camp was the brigade's temporary command post in the Central Highlands. The date was November 23, 1965.

One company was in contact. Machinegun fire rattled in the distance. Tom McEnry took pictures of artillery firing support for soldiers in the field. Just after eleven o'clock in the morning, McEnry complained about his light meter. "I can't get a reading," he said, shaking the small black instrument in front of him, banging it against his hand. At the same time, field commanders called in on their radios that something strange was happening.

'I don't know what it is,' one officer called, 'but it's weird. It's really gettin, uh, kinda *eerie* out here.'

The air became still. Insects went quiet. The artillery stopped firing. Radios were silent. The temperature, which had been about eighty-five degrees, dropped to around seventy or seventy-five. The light dimmed, though there were no clouds. The North Vietnamese broke contact. The war stopped.

Someone said, 'Look at the sun!' Everyone looked up. A thin black disc appeared at the side of the white-yellow sun, obscuring part of it, blocking the light.

'Far fucking out,' a soldier said.

'Would you believe it?' said another. 'A fucking ee-clipse? In fucking Veetnam?'

'I bet the VC think we done it,' a GI said. 'That's why they took off.'

'Shee-it.'

Several minutes passed in near silence. The hand of an unseen presence seemed to move across the tropical savanna. No one spoke. Then the light brightened. The temperature warmed. Insects screeched. A few gunshots cracked. Field radios came alive with chatter and hiss. Artillery boomed.

Helicopter blades whacked the air. The war, having skipped a beat, resumed as if nothing had happened.

A helicopter came into the Duc Co camp the next day carrying a wounded soldier. The GI had just been lifted out of Ia Drang and was exhausted. His face was dirty, his fatigues torn and filthy, his bloody left hand infested with flies. He had an expression on his face like an injured animal.

Word spread through the camp quickly.

'Hey, they just brought in a guy who's been lost for a week!' Soldiers and journalists gathered in front of the first aid station to look at the last survivor to be found from the battle of LZ Albany. The week before, 155 Americans had been killed in the area around Albany in one day.

The brigade doctor examined the soldier's wounds, cleaned them and ordered him to Pleiku for further treatment. Waiting for a medevac, the soldier told us his story.

His name was Toby Braveboy, he said, he was twenty-four years old and had been drafted from his hometown of Coward, South Carolina. 'Yeah, really, that's the name of the town I come from.' A private first class, he came over to Vietnam with the rest of the 1st Cavalry Division two months ago. Braveboy said he was point man for the lead platoon of Alpha Company, 2/7, when the North Vietnamese attacked on November 17. He was wounded immediately, his rifle shattered by incoming bullets.

"I was with three other guys when the shooting started," he said. "We were all hit. I crawled off through the grass to find a medic. I couldn't walk. Bullets were flying everywhere. I could hear the guys behind me calling, 'Medic!' When I got back they were all dead. The VC just shot them on the ground. One guy was almost sawed in two." Braveboy had large ears and sad dark eyes.

"I went off on my own in the bushes," he said, "just crawlin around, tryin to find help."

He said he had done a lot of hunting and fishing in his school days and that must have helped him survive. One of his ancestors was Creek, Native American. "I know how to take care of myself," he said.

Braveboy found a stream and filled his canteens with water. There was no food. He hid in the bushes. The bugs tried to eat him alive, he said. "The ants and mosquitoes were really terrible. Wouldn't leave me alone for a minute. All night long. Took turns chewin on me."

Whenever a helicopter flew nearby he waved his T-shirt at it, but no one saw him. "I didn't think I was ever going to get out," he said. "I was about to give up."

"What kept you going?" I asked.

"I prayed every night. Asked the Lord to help me get back. That kept me going."

Most of the time Braveboy hid in the bushes beside the stream. On one of the days, he said, "I saw a couple of VC pass four steps away from me. One of them saw me. He was real young, only a kid. He aimed his rifle right at me. My heart was about to jump out. I held my wounded hand up for him to see and shook my head back and forth, like to say no. He looked at me and put the gun down. Just walked on by. Didn't say nothin."

On the seventh day, a scout helicopter spotted Braveboy in the bush and called a Huey to pick him up.

"How do you feel now," someone asked.

"I don't hardly believe I'm back in civilization," he said. "I don't know how to feel." He was silent a few seconds. Then he spoke softly, as if to himself. "I'm nothin but an old farm boy."

Occasionally, someone in the field decided to have fun at our expense, to test us, measure our mettle. Journalists were seen as fair game. Routinely, we were invited to go on physically difficult or dangerous missions. The invitation almost always came from an officer, rarely a grunt. I got the impression it amused them to see if we could take it. *We* take it, their logic seemed to be, why not *them*? Sometimes they were showing off their skills for the camera and thus the audience at home, like the Air Force pilots at Bien Hoa who cut the angle of their bombing runs more acutely when we were aboard, who dived lower over the treetops, who pulled up a little tighter. Some of the invitations we got turned out to be sadistic.

Waiting with Tom McEnry at the airstrip at Plei Me in late November, a First Cav helicopter pilot came up and offered to take us for a ride in his gunship. They had a target in the jungle, the pilot said, and we were welcome to come along. McEnry and I had nothing better to do so we agreed. We didn't realize our mistake until we were in the air.

The aerial rocket artillery unit was called "Red Scorpions" and some of them were wild men. The crew chief and door gunner moved with the slow shuffle of normal soldiers, but the pilot, a captain, was excited, almost manic. The UH-1B he commanded was a flying gun platform: two rocket launchers, two flexguns, two M-60 machineguns, and a rapid-fire multiple grenade launcher—an aerial killing machine. We had seen gunships firing on the flanks of rifle companies enough times to know what they did but had never been inside one of them until now.

In the air, the Huey flew over a stretch of triple canopy forest, circled twice, and made an attack approach a few feet above the trees. Wind rushed through the open doors. Nothing was visible below except dense leaf-green foliage. Without warning, the sides of the helicopter exploded in flashing light and sound. Bright flames burst out the tails of 2.75-inch rockets whooshing toward the ground. Red-orange light sparkled from the muzzles of the M-60 machineguns. The noise was incredible, louder than battle, louder than a case of fireworks exploding in a room. The gun bursts merged into an ear-stinging shriek of high-decibel sound, a continuous roar of unmodulated noise. First my ears and then my head whistled with pain. The gunship crew wore hard plastic helmets and earphones that muffled the noise, though they hadn't offered us the same protection.

The jungle blossomed with flames and smoke. Trees exploded. Giant sparks shot into the air. In the midst of this mayhem, the captain leaned out the window of the left front door and fired his .45-caliber pistol straight down into the bush, the whole clip. His movements were jerky and abrupt, as if in a great hurry. *This guy's trying to kill the North Vietnamese army all by himself.* There was no return fire, no tracers, no sign of enemy troops.

Back at Plei Me, the pilot and copilot took off their helmets and got out of their seats. The captain's face was smiling, eyes wide, brightly charged. He walked around the outside of the chopper and found a bullet hole on the top of the left side landing skid, just below his door.

'Hey, guys, look at this!' he called. 'Must've taken a round on one of our passes.'

McEnry made a shot of the bullet hole. He was angry. Neither of us had recovered from the noise. The captain got out a still camera and had his crew chief take a picture of him pointing to the bullet hole in the skid. Later I examined the skid and saw that the broken metal from the bullet splayed away from the chopper, toward the ground. I didn't say anything. We boarded another helicopter heading to Pleiku and along the way McEnry took the exposed film out of his camera and threw it out the side.

Pilots sometimes gave business cards to visitors who flew with them. The printed white cards usually included the pilot's name, unit, base and sometimes an APO number. A Special Forces card I saw read:

> Join the U.S. Army.
> See the World.
> Meet Interesting People.
> And Kill Them.

Another, from a helicopter pilot, said

MY CARD

and nothing else.

A Marine pilot at Phu Bai gave out cards that said:

EXPERIENCED WORLD TRAVELER, PART TIME LOVER, ADVENTURER, CASUAL HERO

Soldier of Fortune Specializing in Civil Wars

Far Eastern Indochina Jungle Fighter's and Combat Pilot's Assn., Ltd.

Lieutenant Ed Ressler

Early in the war, Marine NCOs at Danang produced eight-by-ten-inch glossy prints of a drawing of a Marine infantryman on patrol. The top half of the cartoon Marine's face was obscured by an oversized steel helmet covered with camouflage cloth and decorated with leaf branches, a plastic bottle of insect repellent and an extra magazine of rifle ammunition. A stubby cigar stuck out of his stubble-covered jaw. The Marine carried an M-14 rifle with fixed bayonet, a walkie-talkie, a belt of machinegun ammo, an entrenching tool, grenades, web belt, canteens, ammo pouches and field pack. The visual suggestion of the character was deadly menace. It could have been the original grunt. The caption said:

YEA, THOUGH I WALK THROUGH THE VALLEY
OF THE SHADOW OF DEATH,
I WILL FEAR NO EVIL—
CUZ, I'M THE MEANEST MUTHA IN THE VALLEY!

A CV-2 Caribou circled over Bong Son in preparation for landing. The dirt airstrip below was exceptionally short. The Army cargo plane was designed for short takeoffs and landings, but this one was going to be a challenge. The runway had been bulldozed out of the jungle that morning. No planes had put down on it yet. The pilots had warned us earlier that it was going to be a difficult landing. But I was in a hurry to get to the First Cav operation around Bong Son to work on a story. The camera crew and I were the only passengers. We buckled up just behind the firewall as tightly as we could and held on. The plane circled the airstrip again and again. Finally, it dropped over the treetops with its flaps full down, hit the ground hard, shuddered for a second, and bounced high in the air. The two engines roared with reverse thrust. With the landing gear off the ground, the wheels were unable to brake the plane. The Caribou bounced several times, skidded off the end of the runway and crashed into the jungle with a grinding crunch of tree trunks, branches, wood and metal. Our bodies jerked against the aluminum struts of the seating gear and flopped back. The panels of the interior fuselage broke apart and fell open, flapping down from the ceiling. Dust and debris fell on top of us. There were several seconds of silence. The tentative voice of the crew chief shouted, 'Anybody hurt?' Shaken and bruised but otherwise uninjured, the camera crew and I unbuckled ourselves and stood up. The pilots climbed stiffly from their seats and down onto the ground. They examined the crushed nose and twisted propellers. Everything was tangled together: bits of airplane, jungle vines, landing gear, pieces of trees, nose assembly, fuselage.

'Looks like a write-off,' one of the pilots said. He was embarrassed, apologizing for the crash landing.

'No, don't worry about it,' I said. 'You got us here, didn't you?' Laughing.

'Hell of a way to extend the runway.'

We wished them luck and left to look for a ride the rest of the way by jeep or truck.

Fear of flying was a primary emotion. Every takeoff, every landing, every helicopter assault was a serious struggle in fear control. To my inexpert eye, the military contraptions that transported us around the country seemed to be designed more with the needs of war-making in mind than the safety of their passengers. With frightening abandon, helicopters challenged a fundamental law of the physical universe—that heavier-than-air objects without wings do not fly. Cargo planes lifted more than their own weight into the thin air like eyepopping weight lifters, groaning with the effort, sounding as if they were about to come apart at their bolted seams. The cargo they carried inside their holds was often inflammable fuel, ammunition or other explosive ordnance, ready to detonate with a single spark. Jet fighter-bombers flew faster and more acrobatically than wild hawks. Flying in-country, you were aware at all times that the machine around you could crash and disintegrate in a heartbeat, giant metal birds with the power to end your life in one quick helpless spiraling crush of smoke and steel.

It felt far safer on the ground, even in a firefight, where you had some kind of protection, if only the earth beneath you. The ground gave you a choice of where to go next instead of being at the mercy of a pilot whose competence was unknown to you. *What if this guy was up all night at the officers' club drinking,* I'd wonder. Still, the only way to cover the war was by flying in and out of it, and the only alternative to that was *not* to cover the war, an idea that became more attractive the longer I stayed. All I could do was strap myself in for each new takeoff or landing, breathe deeply, close my eyes and pray.

The airfield at An Khe was a small dusty strip plated with sheets of metal PSP that could take one cargo plane at a time. Coming out of the field with the First Cav, my crew and I were dropped at the airfield hoping to catch a lift to Saigon. It was late afternoon. The traffic controller said all the flights had gone for the day, nothing scheduled in until tomorrow. We decided to wait until dark, just in case. Tired and hungry, we had been in the field for days. We had a story and were anxious to get back, not only to ship the film but also to get a hot meal, a shower and clean clothes. The airfield was deserted. An hour before dark, an unscheduled Air Force C-123 came in and flopped down on the runway like a loaded pelican. What a beautiful bird! I hated riding in C-123s because of all the noise and vibration, but I had a sense this might be our daily miracle.

While the cargo was being unloaded, I asked the crew chief where they were headed next. "Tan Son Nhut," he said. My heart rejoiced. They were going back empty, he said, and we'd have to ask the pilot for permission to come along. I walked around to the front of the plane and introduced myself to the pilot, a tall Air Force captain wearing a regulation gray flying suit and blue cap. As we spoke, the copilot stared at me with fixed deliberation, as if trying to figure out a puzzle. He was short and slender, wearing lieutenant's bars. His name tag, black lettering on a white cloth strip over his pocket, said, "Crake."

'Excuse me, sir,' he said after a minute, 'Did you go to Fairfield . . . ?'

'Aren't you . . . ?' I said.

'Jack!'

'Roger!'

We spent the next several minutes talking quickly about the most important events in our lives since we had last seen each other at our high school graduation almost ten years earlier. Roger Crake and I had been in the same small homeroom class at Fairfield Prep, an all-male high school in southern Connecticut most notable for its rigorous education, corporal punishment, and winning the state football championship. It was run by Jesuits. Our homeroom teacher had been a fighter pilot in the Korean War, reputedly an ace, though he never talked about it. Fairfield was a school for jocks, a few future scholars, and other teenagers needing a good Catholic education. Although we had not been buddies, Roger and I were friendly with each other.

'So how do you like the Air Force?'

'It's not bad. I can think of better places to be stationed.'

'Do you keep in touch with any of the guys from school?'

'One or two.'

'Whatever happened to Bob Valus?'

'He went to college, I think, but that's the last I heard.'

'He was a good athlete, a great guy . . .'

The crew chief signaled that the plane was ready to continue. The pilot clapped Crake on the shoulder and said, 'Well, Rog, since you know these gentlemen, why don't you take the old bucket back to Saigon yourself.' Roger agreed. We exchanged APO addresses and shook hands.

On the flight south, the C-123 entered an enormous tropical thunderstorm. There was no way to fly around it. The plane twisted in powerful monsoon winds that tried to pull it apart. Lightning cracked over the howl of the engines. The sky outside was black, flashing with thunderbolts. The plane flew on the edge of no control. Memories of our days at Fairfield Prep added to my unease. I recalled that Roger had not been academically gifted. As a student, subjects like physics and math were especially difficult for him. He did not grasp the lessons quickly. Some of his grades were poor, even failing. In the demands of the final year, Roger worried about being able to graduate. He had no plans for college. A few of us helped him with his homework. Roger tried hard. With help from his friends, family and, perhaps, some divine intervention, the benevolent priests of the Society of Jesus decided to let Roger graduate. Now, however, rattling in the back of his shuddering C-123, with the image of my former classmate up front fighting the controls, instruments spinning wildly, the plane trying to drive itself into the ground, my nervous system bordered on a state of panic. Each time the plane hit a downdraft, my heart dived with it. I seized the struts of the seat. I imagined we were upside down. There was no way to tell. The plane bored a hole through the storm, flailing on the outside edge of a stable flight envelope, jerking and bucking like a wild horse. As usual, I prayed. Fear propelled me into a perfect act of contrition, not for the first time in Vietnam.

For the record, Lieutenant Roger Crake, United States Air Force, pilot, Fairfield College Preparatory School Class of '57, landed his C-123 in a thunderstorm at Tan Son Nhut airport on this day with a precise, hands-on, three-point landing as smooth as any by a flying drill team leader. We didn't feel the wheels touch.

In addition to the military action, another conflict was being fought—a parallel war between the MACV Office of Information and the press corps, a struggle for access to accurate information, a precious commodity when the war did not conform to the wishes of the U.S. high command. Skirmishes between reporters and army information officers occurred every day.

For example, on October 17, 1967, a battalion of the U.S. 1st Infantry Division, about five hundred line troops, got into a ferocious fight with a main-force regiment of Viet Cong. The soldiers were engaged in a foot patrol in Operation Shenandoah II near Lai Khe, northwest of Saigon. The first con-

tact quickly developed into an intense close-quarters battle that lasted about
two hours before the VC withdrew. Second Battalion, 28th Infantry counted
eighty of its men killed and sixty-six wounded, unusually high for the brief
duration of the fight. Estimated losses to the NLF's 271st Regiment were
over a hundred. The fighting was fearsome. Clearly, several platoons in the
U.S. battalion had been overrun. The Americans were not able to recover the
bodies of twenty-two soldiers who were missing. That, combined with the
disproportionate ratio of dead to wounded (80–66), indicated that Viet Cong
troops controlled part of the battlefield long enough to kill many of the
American wounded. No prisoners were reported taken by either side.

No journalists had been with the U.S. troops. Immediately after the battle, about ten reporters went to Lai Khe to gather details of what happened.
Army information officers refused to allow them to get near the scene. The
surviving soldiers were said to be in "a state of shock," unable to talk. Transportation to their area was denied. The Army did not want a detailed, factual
account of the battle to be reported. Instead, General Westmoreland flew to
the First Division headquarters and briefed us himself. With cameras and
tape recorders rolling, he declared: "This was not an ambush. It was a meeting engagement. The enemy stood and fought more than usual." Though
most journalists present were skeptical, Westmoreland's statement and the
Army's official account were all they had to report. They had no independent sources of information.

The other reporters flew back to Saigon. I sensed that there was more to
the story than what we had been told, so I stayed at Lai Khe and pressed division PIOs to provide witnesses. After a long argument, they produced three
soldiers to be interviewed. Sergeant First Class Jose Valdez was thirty-five
years old and came from Velarde, New Mexico. He was a fifteen-year career
NCO in the U.S. Army and appeared to be a good soldier, relaxed and confident, a combat veteran. He showed no signs of fatigue. He had not heard
what Westmoreland said. When I asked him what happened, Valdez said,
"They [the Viet Cong] were waiting for us. They were set up and waiting for
us. It was an L-shaped ambush." The two other men confirmed the ambush
in detail.

Exceptional men died in that battle. One was Lieutenant Colonel Terry
Allen Jr., whose father commanded the same division in World War II. With
Allen dead, Major Don Hollander, the brigade operations officer, flew to the
ambush site to take command. Hollander was a famous pass receiver for the

West Point football team in 1954. Standing outside the team huddle near the sideline while signals were called, he was known as "The Lonesome End." Hollander landed in a helicopter during the worst of the fighting, exposed himself to hostile fire by running alone toward the command group, was hit and killed.

A year and a half earlier, that same NLF regiment—the 271st—was reported to have been destroyed in an American operation called Silver City. The regiment was attacked by the 173d Airborne Brigade in March 1966, along the Song Be River. The reported losses were 338 VC killed, 21 U.S. soldiers killed, 73 wounded. After the battle, Americans said they found the body of an enemy soldier who had been firing his .50-caliber machinegun at them all day. "He had a metal collar around his neck, bolted and chained to the machinegun," one of the paratroops said. The commander of the 173d, Brigadier General Paul F. Smith, called the engagement "a very significant victory. I think we neutralized a VC regiment, riddled that regiment." If so, the 271st had reconstituted itself in the eighteen months since and returned to action with a vengeance.

When the interviews with the three soldiers from the First Division were over, First Sergeant Valdez showed me a piece of paper. 'The VC left a bunch of them behind,' he said. 'They were scattered all around the bodies of our guys.'

The paper was thin and grayish, slightly larger than a business envelope, just a cheap flyer. Printed on it was a black-and-white photograph of the body of an American soldier lying on a battlefield. The picture had been taken in some other place, at some other time. The print quality was poor, like that of English-language publications in Eastern Europe. Above the picture, two lines of English were printed in the delicate hand-drawn style of the Vietnamese:

YOUR X-RAYS HAVE COME BACK FROM THE LAB,
AND I THINK I KNOW WHAT YOUR PROBLEM IS.

Apparently it had been printed by the Viet Cong.

Looking over our shoulders, one of the PIO officers said, 'What do you make of that?'

'The gooks got a weird sense of humor,' Valdez said, shaking his head.

"Looks like Charlie's got his own psy-war program," I said.

For my television report, "Anatomy of an Ambush," I used maps and descriptions from the three soldiers to try to recreate the story of what happened. I thought the public should know that the Viet Cong, in some circumstances, were capable of ambushing and crippling American units as large as battalions. But my story lacked film of the actual fighting and was not broadcast. On CBS News at least, the censors won.

By its nature, war produces behavior to match the madness in which it is fought. Months before the Tet Offensive in early 1968, North Vietnam unleashed large-scale military offensives along the borders to draw the Americans away from the coast and into remote areas close to Cambodia, Laos and North Vietnam. Long serious engagements were fought, resulting in heavy loss of life on both sides. The North Vietnamese first attacked U.S. Marines near the DMZ at Con Thien in September 1967 and later at Khe Sanh, Gio Linh and an artillery base called the Rockpile. Farther south, in the area around Loc Ninh and Song Be north of Saigon, heavy battles took place. In the Central Highlands, near the conjunction of the borders of South Vietnam, Cambodia and Laos, there was fierce combat in the mountains north of Pleiku. North Vietnamese and Americans fought in heavy rainforest on the sides of some of the tallest mountains in Southeast Asia. One series of engagements around the valley of Dak To lasted twenty-two days in November 1967.

I was assigned to report on fighting around Dak To. One of the battalions of the 173d Airborne Brigade was trapped in combat on a hill designated by its height in meters: 875. Several reporters covered the fighting during the five days it was in progress. The North Vietnamese assaulted the Americans as they moved up Hill 875, cut them off from the rear, and attacked them day and night with mortars and machineguns. At a critical point in the fight, a U.S. Marine pilot flying a close-support mission at night released a bomb that landed on the battalion's command post, killing many of the officers and staff and those wounded by earlier fighting on the hill.

The commander of B Company, Captain James Muldoon, spoke to Tom Cheatham of UPI during the battle, "I don't care anymore if I get back to the world," he said bitterly, "a world too stupid to stay out of war, too stupid to know how to fight it, too stupid to know how to end it."

I arrived in Dak To too late to witness the fighting firsthand. But some of the stories I heard about what happened on the hill fascinated me. A GI confided that one of the American soldiers, a sergeant, had shot and killed another for his water. I decided to follow the story further, if I could, and called the CBS bureau chief in Saigon to ask if I could take some overdue R and R time. He agreed. I went to work for myself, intending to write a long story about Hill 875 for a book or magazine.

Wounded soldiers at the field hospital described how the five hundred men had gone up the mountainside with three companies in assault formation. They told me what they did when they were attacked, how they became surrounded by the North Vietnamese. Almost everyone fought bravely, they said, including the NVA. For three days I recorded their comments on tape and then flew out to the field to interview some of the soldiers who had not been wounded.

The battalion was camped on a gently sloping draw between two small hills with light brush around it and higher hills in the distance. A few mobile artillery pieces were stationed at the bottom of the rise. The men had been taken off Hill 875 a few days earlier and were standing down in light duty, resting, writing home, waiting for replacements. Nearly three hundred U.S. Army men had been killed in the Dak To battles and could not all be replaced at once.

It was late afternoon. As I talked with a GI under the flap of an open tent, a loud shrieking noise came overhead and a moment later a rocket artillery shell exploded. It fell outside the camp a few hundred yards away. 'Uh, oh,' the GI said, falling flat on the ground. Other soldiers ran for cover. I looked around. There was no shelter nearby. I felt exposed and vulnerable. I had to find somewhere to get my head below ground. Another rocket flew over and fell, closer.

I ran uphill toward the command post about two hundred yards away. The CP had been dug into the side of the hill by a bulldozer and was enclosed with a large green canvas roof and sides. I went in. The cave was about thirty feet deep with the operations area at the back screened by two tent halves hanging from the ceiling. I sat down in the dark anteroom where there were a few chairs and crates of supplies but no other people. Inside the operations section I could hear staff officers at work with maps and radios. A loud angry voice was shouting at them.

'What's the *matter* with you God damn people?' The voice screamed in a high register. 'I want it stopped! Now, God damnit!' He sounded out of control. 'Stop that fucking shit this minute! You incompetent turds. Hear me?'

Another rocket fell and exploded. Then another. Closer. I thought, *The NVA have the range and direction, now they'll be firing for effect.*

'Stop it! Stop it! Stop it!' The voice was shrill, insistent, hysterical.

'Find out where the fuck it's coming from! Get on the Goddamn horn and tell them to find it and fix it! Do you understand? 'Stop it! Stop it! Stop it!'

Rockets exploded inside the battalion camp.

A young officer hurried out of the operations area, parting the tent halves. Inside, a burly man about forty years old with a bright red face and crewcut and no cover on his head paced the ground, his arms waving at the other men in the room.

'Who's that?' he screamed, seeing me outside. No one spoke. I had not checked in with the command staff when I arrived a few hours earlier, not wanting to draw attention. The man came out of the ops area, bent his head forward and stared at me. His eyes bulged, unblinking, red around the rims. The insignia on the epaulets of his uniform identified him as a lieutenant colonel. It was the new battalion commander.

'I'm a reporter,' I said, seated, too frightened to stand up. Another shell exploded.

'What are you doing here?' he said.

'I'm doing interviews for a story about 875,' I said.

'875? . . . 875? . . . Oh, *Hill* 875.'

'I came in here for cover.'

'How long you been here?'

'Only a minute or two.' Silence. He knew I had heard him screaming.

'Well, try and stay out of the way,' he said finally, politely. He turned and walked back into the ops room and the tent flaps closed behind him. There was no more shouting. After a while another officer came out of the area and smiled as he walked past.

When the shelling stopped, I went outside as soon as I could and walked far away from the CP. I had not seen a senior officer hysterical under fire before.

At the bottom of the hill, a few of the enlisted men took me aside and showed me the remains of a track driver who had been inside one of the armored vehicles when it took a direct hit. The track had caught fire and exploded. They pointed to a knee joint, just a small bone-white knuckle, on the red dirt.

'That's all there is left of him,' they said.

On my way back to Saigon a few days later, I hitched a ride in an army truck to the airfield in Pleiku. I had a dozen audio tapes of interviews with survivors of Hill 875, as much as I would need for an article. The flatbed cargo truck stopped to pick up three soldiers who climbed into the back. Then the truck drove on, bouncing slowly over the rutted roads. The men were in their late teens and early twenties, PFCs and a Spec–4. They did not have unit patches on the shoulders of their unmarked green fatigues.

'Who are you with?' one of them asked.

'CBS News,' I said.

'No shit?'

I nodded my head.

'Really?'

'Yeah, really.'

'What are you doing here?'

'I was trying to get a story up at Dak To. With the 173d.'

There was a pause, then the specialist fourth class said, 'Oh, we know about *them*.' He looked at the others briefly and then back at me. 'They were *beautiful*, those guys. Really beautiful. We saw a lot of 'em before they went home.'

He paused as if deciding whether to go on. 'You ought to do a story about *us*. We've seen it all. Haven't we?' Looking at the others, nodding his head.

'What do you do?' I asked. Their faces were pale under the green fatigue caps, without suntans, milky. *These guys are definitely not infantry,* I thought.

'We take care of them after they're in the shit. You know, get 'em ready to go home. Fix 'em up nice, so they look good. You ought to come over and see what we do. It's good, really. The Army needs us. Especially right now. We work hard. Sometimes, like the last few weeks, we're working all night long.'

'Night *and* day,' one of the PFCs said.

I felt peculiar. 'What outfit are you with?' I asked.

'Graves,' the Spec-4 said proudly. *Graves Registration*, I thought. His eyes held mine. 'You should come over and see what we're doing. It's really interesting. Some of them come in and they're messed up, you know, pretty bad. We clean 'em up and, well, there's all kind of things we do for 'em. Cosmetics and stuff. Bathe them. Get 'em into clean uniforms.' He moved his hands and arms as if he were holding someone. 'We take really good care of 'em. You should see how beautiful they are when we're finished, some of them, so peaceful and like. Like they were sleeping.' His eyes were smoky. The others smiled in agreement.

'We've had so many come in the last few weeks we haven't hardly had time to rest. They had to send us extra help from Saigon.' He looked at his hands, nodded his head slowly. 'Really, you wouldn't believe how beautiful those guys are when we're done with 'em. I love 'em, I really do. They're just so *beautiful*. Lyin' there, asleep and all.'

MAY 19, 1966

A birthday celebration was under way in the spacious but crowded dining room of the Arc-en-Ciel, a popular restaurant in Saigon. Coming out of the hot dusty streets, you arrived in an oasis of cool elegance. Air conditioners took the edge off the humid evening heat. Slowly spinning overhead fans circulated clouds of cigarette smoke. The tables were wide and round, covered with white linen and set with polished silverware, cloth napkins and wine glasses. Candles glowed. All the places were filled. The waiters were slow and arrogant, crudely imitating the dismissive hauteur of the French, but the food made it worthwhile: rare chateaubriand, pommes frites and salade Dalat. After a few glasses, the Algerian wine was not bad.

Sam Castan, the LOOK magazine correspondent, had reached his thirty-first birthday a week ago and now he sat at the table flushed with wine and the attention of friends. Most of the members from Frankie's House were there: Steve Northup, Simon Dring, Tim Page, Martin and David Stuart-Fox, Joe Galloway, Robin Mannock, Tom Corpora, Sean Flynn. They had done a day's work and were winding down for the evening: telling stories over drinks, laughing, enjoying the food and company. Like this, life was good, bonhomie at its best.

The subject of death wandered through the conversation all evening—repeatedly, persistently, as if it had a seat at the table. Nothing morbid about it, nothing maudlin either, the subject wasn't even melodramatic. Self-conscious perhaps, but then who wouldn't think of his own mortality from time to time? Death was in the air; it was part of the atmosphere, giving the war its own special climate. Outside the restaurant, along the streets, men in steel helmets with M-16s and shotguns and killer eyes looked out from behind sandbagged bunkers with silent coiled insouciance, like loaded traps. Overhead, jet planes screamed through the clouds with a shrill afterburner whine that warned of ordnance on the way, death on delivery. Distant shells burst with dull hollow *crumps*. Helicopters *whup-whupped* over the roads outside the cities, winding into the wilderness toward the end of the line. It was death all around. You could go about your daily business pretending it didn't affect you, you could get your work done and go home and fall asleep (not always simple), but at some level the undertow of fear, anger and suspicion pulled at your sanity. The atmosphere was infused with it, magnifying the suffocating effects of the heat and rain, charging you with the war's fever and draining you at the same time. No way to avoid it. Unless, like some people, you accepted death—including your own—as an unfortunate but necessary consequence of the mission, the nation's purpose in making war. If you accepted the mission (military officers were required to accept it), you also had to accept the consequences, cruel as they were. You acknowledged the deaths, allowed them to register, filed them away in some unconscious sector of your brain and tried to forget about them. After a while, it was apparent that the mission *was* death, cold stinging death, an end in itself, the racking up of bodies—an NVA platoon here, a VC sniper there, a hostile village here, a few civilians there—like points on a scoreboard, adding to the illusion of a mission being accomplished. By the spring of 1966, a quarter of a million American troops ranged across the densely populated land like locust clouds, darkening the sky with helicopters and fighter-bombers, assaulting the countryside and its people with destruction and terror, slaughtering them like livestock. (That the North Vietnamese and Viet Cong also practiced murder and terror made it no less mortifying.) The U.S. government, the military, and by passive consent, most of the American population had embarked on a mission of large-scale violence against Vietnam. But by embracing destruction as its strategy, America was destroying itself. Waging war taught the lesson that more and more violence was the right thing for the Vietnamese, at least for those who survived, that winning was more important than any other consideration—*morality*, not truth, is the first casualty of war—and that the means, however loathsome, would be justified ultimately by the end, as long as the end brought victory. The war was undermining the nation's sense of propriety, the integrity of its culture, its political cohesion. The war corrupted everything it touched. Television images of the slaughter touched the eyes of millions of viewers, bringing the horror home. The effect of that transference, night after night for over ten years, was more apocalyptic than anyone knew. By the end, after all the violence radiating out from the American heart had come back home again to haunt it, the mission could be seen as suicide. Death all around. Like the crazed burning scorpion beside the airstrip at An Khe, America's dark orgy of destruction in Vietnam turned and stung itself in the back, poisoning its own body.

I arrived at Sam Castan's birthday party late. A three-day battle near An Khe had ended the day before and I had gone up to report what happened. One of the First Cav's brigades was engaged in hit-and-run combat with a regiment of North Vietnamese in the Vinh Thanh ("Happy") Valley, ten miles northeast of An Khe, a valley the Cav had supposedly cleared of enemy troops months before. Both sides had suffered heavy losses. On May 16, one of the brigade's rifle companies—Bravo, 2/8—was attacked by a much larger force of NVA. Nearly a hundred Americans were killed or wounded. The commanding officer of Bravo Company was Captain J. D. Coleman, the former assistant information officer who had just been given the command he campaigned so hard to get. He had held it only two weeks. Coleman led his 125 men through three long days and nights of intense combat. I flew back to Saigon to attend the birthday party and told the others what had happened. Most of us were Coleman's friends.

'J.D. tries for a year to get his own company and as soon as he gets it, it nearly gets wiped out.'

'J.D. knew what he was doing out there.'

'I heard they're gonna put him in for a silver star.'

'Wish I'd been with him,' Sam said.

'Yeah, J.D. could edit your story.'

'He's good at that.'

'Man, I thought they pacified Happy Valley a long time ago.'

'They did,' I said. 'I mean they *thought* they did. Listen to this.' The others were quiet. A bottle of wine was passed around.

'Last November, J.D. sets up a parade for us to cover in Happy Valley,' I said. 'A *parade!* Big exclusive for us. They flew the entire division *band* into the valley.'

'Oh, come on,' one of the others said.

'I don't believe it.'

'It's true, I swear. And all these guys, you know, twenty or twenty-five of them, march around the main street of the district town with their tubas and bass drum, playing tunes like "Yellow Ribbon" and "Colonel Bogey" and stuff like that.'

'Are you kiddin' me?' Some of the men at the table giggled.

'No, honest. It was a big show. The kids loved it. They marched along next to the GIs. The Air Force even ran an air strike in the mountains to impress the locals. For background effect.'

The others were laughing out loud, picturing the scene.

'Like, the purpose of the whole thing was to celebrate the end of VC control of the valley. You know, Charlie is out and the Cav is in. The district chief made a speech. Also the G-5.'

I took a sip of wine. The others laughed in disbelief.

'*Unbelievably* corny,' I said, 'but it made good pictures. Of course, the Vietnamese didn't understand what the hell was going on. You know, they see these Americans putting on a parade with a big brass band and it's all totally alien to them, completely outside their experience. The villagers didn't know what to make of it. You should have seen their faces. Like they're thinking, 'Are these guys *serious,* or what?''

'Of course they were serious,' Northup laughed, 'seriously insane.'

'And six months later Charlie comes back and tries to fix J.D.'s ass.'

'Oh, Jesus, did they ever.'

'Man, is that *ironic,* or what?'

'I bet the VC were waiting for J.D. to get his company.'

'Right, so they could stick it to him, personally.'

'That's not irony, man.'

'Coincidence.'

'Not that either. It's *payback,* man. Charlie knows all about payback.'

'Yeah, so does J.D.'

The food arrived and more bottles of wine were ordered. Cigarettes were smoked between courses.

'So what do you do if you're with J.D.'s company when it's getting hit?' Castan asked.

'Run like a motherfuck!' Northup shouted.

'No, I'm serious. Suppose J.D. and the officers are all wounded?'

'Depends how bad it is.'

'I know what I'd do,' Page said. 'I'd bloody well make sure somebody got on the horn and called in gunships.'

'And air strikes.'

'I mean, it depends on whether the lieutenants and platoon sergeants have got their shit together,' Page said. 'If they don't, you have to take over.'

'*You* Page?'

'Bloody right, mate,' Page said. 'Somebody's got to organize the defense.'

It was a regular topic of discussion among the members of Frankie's House. What do you do in combat if all the officers of a unit you're covering are dead and wounded and the troops need a leader? Most of the journalists at the table had seen more combat than the majority of soldiers they accompanied in the field. A few in the group, particularly Page and Dring, looked forward to an opportunity to lead a platoon in battle. In my own case, I remembered the nervous excitement of calling in an Army chopper on the radio when Vallop was wounded at the graveyard. It had given me a sense of participation, of being part of the team.

Castan listened with close interest. He had been covering the war longer and had reported more battles (though they were usually over by the time he got to them) than any of the others at the table.

'Who knows what you'd do?' he said. 'You size up the situation when you're in it. And you do what you have to do.'

Castan had a story in mind that he wanted to write for LOOK. He had observed the U.S. military's swift deployment around the country and its aggressive pursuit of the VC. At the same time, he saw the increasing reluctance of most South Vietnamese Army units to engage the enemy in combat. Castan detected an important change in the war. His story would be titled, "Are We Fighting Alone?" All he had to decide now was where to go in the field to get it.

"Come up to Danang with me and Flynn," Page said. "That's where all the action is, mate." Page was leaving in the morning to photograph the big civilian antigovernment uprising in I Corps. The so-called Struggle Movement was a coalition of students, workers and Buddhist monks who were bringing political pressure on the Saigon government with strikes, public speeches and demonstrations. It had been a running story with violent confrontations between government troops and demonstrators. The fundamental issues were corruption—the widespread theft of public funds by generals and their families—and the American involvement itself. Many of the protesters saw the U.S. presence as foreign interference in Vietnam's affairs. The government was taking a repressive stance against the movement, but no one knew what the outcome was going to be. A military coup was possible.

'It's been covered already,' Castan said. 'I've got to get out in the boonies. Maybe I'll go with the First Cav. It'll be over by the time I get there, but I might get some quotes.' Part of the lore at Frankie's House was that when Sam went in the field the war stopped. He rarely got shot at.

Someone said a helicopter pilot we all knew, a natural survivor, had been wounded recently and was lucky to be alive.

"Some guys are never gonna get killed," Sam said. "You can tell by their faces."

"It's true."

The group at the table agreed. A man's face could have the look on it. Or not.

"Now Hal Moore will never get killed."

"Nor Major Labrozzi."

"No, and neither will Steve Van Meter," I said. Van Meter was a skinny light-haired boyish ex-soldier who finished his army duty in Vietnam and signed on as a freelance photographer for UPI. He had a fresh, alert happy-go-lucky personality, no sign of death on him.

"And I know any one of us could easily get killed," Castan said.

There was nervous laughter. Eyes darted around the table. No one replied. Everyone knew. The work took us to the heart of the killing, the violent core of combat action, the show. We went out to look for it, needing it and dreading it. It wasn't enough to cover the war with words, we had to get it down on film. Again and again. Talk about our chances of getting killed was rare, but privately each of us knew the risks.

Sometimes, Castan's dark round face had the look: blank, preoccupied, eyes lost in an interior world. Usually, he was witty and relaxed, but at times he slipped into sullen moods. His movements became nervous, jerky, as if he were frightened by something he couldn't identify, something beyond his comprehension. At other times he laughed like a lunatic, manic with giddiness. Sam had the haunted presence of one who had been around death so much it had become part of him, a mark of the war.

After the meal, the group moved to Frankie's House to talk and smoke and listen to music. The air conditioner was running and the room was cool. The young men sat on the rattan rug on the floor or on Page's bed and stretched their legs. A large joint was rolled, English-style. Castan chose the records, a delicate task that required him at times to act as negotiator, bringing out his skills as a diplomat, since members of the group had different tastes in music and sometimes raised strong objections to his selections.

'Screw you,' he said. 'Tonight it's my party.'

He put on a Pete Seeger record and then he played one by Bob Dylan. Conversation stopped. The title song of the album had a fast driving tempo and a slide whistle in the opening bars before the lyrics:

> *Aw, God said to Abraham, 'Kill me a son,'*
> *Abe said, 'Man, you must be puttin me on,'*
> *God said, 'No,' Abe said, 'What?'*
> *God said, 'You can do what you want, Abe, but . . .*
> *'Next time you see me comin you better run.'*
> *'Well', Abe said, 'Where you want this killin done?'*
> *God said, 'Out on Highway Sixty-One.'*

"When Bob Dylan was writing that tune I was working on a story," Castan said, "but LOOK fucked it all up and I didn't like it."

'Hmmm. . . .'

'Yeah, and I was getting a round-the-world job by a beautiful bird in London,' Page said.

'Page, you haven't been to London in years.'

'Well, Vientiane, then.'

'More like a boom-boom girl in Cholon, Page.'

'What you *say?*' said Page with fake indignation. 'Birds *luuvvv* Page, specially young pretty ones. Little schoolgirls be best. Page numbah one bird catcher. Never pay for boom-boom.'

'Yeah, just ask the Trumpet.' Everyone laughed. 'Remember the time she gave you a marathon blow job and you wouldn't pay? Frankie hounded you for months.'

'She didn't finish.'

'Page, you were in there for two hours. She was exhausted.'

'Yeah but she couldn't hum "Satisfaction."'

Later, Sam played the song by Peter, Paul and Mary that made us melancholy.

> *Lord I'm one, Lord I'm two, Lord I'm three, Lord I'm four,*
> *Lord I'm five hundred miles from my home. . . .*

Castan was one of the more thoughtful, introspective, personable members of the press corps. Although some of the other New York City journalists could be brash and insensitive, Castan was consistently sincere and considerate. He took the work seriously. He worried about how the war was being reported, how honest it was or not. Earlier that week, he had invited me to dinner in Saigon. Both of us worked for large New York–based news organizations and we had much in common. Among other subjects, we talked about truth in war reporting.

'Everything's distorted,' he said. 'We're not reporting things the way they really are. The PIOs distort things because they're trying to cover up the Army's mistakes. They make it sound like we win every battle. And we don't. It's the old *cover-your-ass* syndrome. Who do they think they're kidding?'

I agreed. 'It isn't just that they put on a show for us. They pass the same stuff up the line to the Pentagon. I think some of these guys actually believe their own propaganda.'

'But we're as bad as they are,' Sam said. 'We exaggerate the violence as much as they play it down. Cause it sells copy. Whenever there's a conflict between making money and real honesty, money wins. It doesn't matter whether you saw something firsthand or whether you're rewriting somebody else's stuff. You exaggerate. Make it more dramatic.'

'True,' I said. 'But part of that is because we have to condense everything into a nice neat little story. Radio and TV especially. But also the wires and the papers. It's easy to use phrases like "waves of B-52 bombers" and "struck dozens of enemy targets" because they're shorter, simpler.'

'They're clichés, that's what they are. The stuff the wires and papers and networks send out is riddled with clichés. "Winning hearts and minds," I mean, really, man. The whole war is becoming a cliché.'

We ate the food and drank wine. And then we lit cigarettes. Sam had a metal Zippo lighter with LOOK Magazine engraved on the side.

'Everything's too cozy between the PIOs and the press,' he said, 'like we're all part of the same organization. A year or two ago it was different. American honor wasn't at stake. It was more adversarial, but honest. Now there's a tendency to conceal mistakes, to deny that we ever lose a battle. It saves face. We're as bad as they are. Really. None of us are being responsible in our reporting.'

I admired Castan's integrity. His idealism was contagious. It gave greater purpose to our work. We had only been acquainted a few weeks but, as happens in wartime, were becoming friends quickly.

'I've got to get this book written,' he said. He was writing his observations about the war based on events he had covered, like David Halberstam's *The Making of a Quagmire*. He had written an outline and a forward and had interested a publisher. One theme of the book was the lack of fighting spirit in the South Vietnamese army. In December 1964, Castan had reported a battle between government soldiers and the Viet Cong in the rubber plantations at Binh Gia, about thirty-five miles east of Saigon. Two of the ARVN's best battalions had suffered severe losses in traps Viet Cong forces set for them, two massive ambushes over several kilometers. The ARVN units, including a battalion of South Vietnamese Marines, were annihilated. A day or two after the battle, Castan watched as the bodies of the government dead were piled into mass graves and buried without funerals, no Buddhist rites. To the Vietnamese, the victims' souls were thus condemned to wander—lost and forgotten—around the battlefield. Sam believed that when word of this dishonor spread around the country, few young men would be willing to risk their lives for an army that would not give them a proper burial.

'People have got to know what's really going on over here,' Sam said. 'We owe them the *truth*. We owe it to the Vietnamese. And the GIs. Hell, we owe it to ourselves.'

The true war rarely got reported. A multitude of facts were reported instead. Every day, scores of journalists based in Saigon wrote news stories about any aspect of the war they could find to cover: battles, body counts, bomb strikes, bomb damage, pacification projects, progress reports, the rhetoric of generals and diplomats, details of the daily lives of American soldiers, some of the daily agonies of the Vietnamese. A mighty flood of facts flowed out from Saigon and across the Pacific each day and washed over the American public in waves: wire service bulletins, radio reports, newspaper stories, magazine articles, television pieces, still photographs, hard news, features, mailers, hometowners, sidebars, people stories, news analyses, editorials, commentaries, think pieces, radio and television documentaries—even books of history, policy and reflection. The stories described in an endless flow of detail how Americans and Vietnamese lived, how they coped, what they thought, what they did and said in the war. Mainly, though, the reports described how people fought, suffered and died. The facts were reasonably accurate, double-checked, attributed to the proper sources—most often MACV—but they were not necessarily true. They weren't altogether false, just less than the truth.

You could spend a few hours or a few days in the field with an American infantry unit, interview the officers and men, write down the most interesting quotes, make close observations, note the poignancy, and write it up in a neat story with a beginning, middle and end. Then send it off on the evening tide. But it was only a news story, your *impression* of what was going on, a condensed version of what you saw and what you were told, a description of what seemed important to you, a visitor. Your knowledge was always limited by your lack of access to what was going on when you weren't there (secrecy being a weapon in war), and by your ignorance of the complex cultures involved, Vietnamese and American. You rarely heard what was said in private. All kinds of agendas were hidden. So, what you wrote was a *version* of what was happening, what you believed was going on. It was not the same as truth.

Even on television, which relayed more graphic images of the violence and its consequences than press coverage of previous wars, it wasn't reality. Realistic and dramatic at times, but not real. What viewers saw on TV was a tightly edited version of a few particular moments taken out of twenty or thirty minutes of exposed news film that had, in turn, been recorded selectively. Extracts of an event. All the selections were made by two people, occasionally three: the reporter, the photographer, and sometimes the sound tech. They tried to be objective, but all through the process of gathering information and pictures for the story, often under deadline pressure, they had to make *subjective* decisions. They decided where to go, what to observe, what to film, what *not* to film, what questions to ask, and how to describe what they saw and were told. They decided how long to stay with a story and when to get out of the field. Even though they might be experienced journalists, they often disagreed. Once the film got to the States, a producer and an editor decided which extracts from the pictures and narration would be used on the air, and their selections were judged and edited by others. Though everyone tried earnestly to write and edit honest representations of what was going on, what came out was only a limited version of the truth. It was called "objective journalism" because what it reported was factually correct most of the time, but it was still highly subjective, more of a failed truth.

What readers and viewers in the United States could not know from daily

journalism, what they could not comprehend, was the wild rage of men trying to kill one another at close range, shooting and shouting and reloading
their weapons, the roar of gunfire like a long continuous explosion in their
ears, the frustration of a jammed rifle, the panic, confusion and fear, the
reckless valor, the anger and desperation, the shock of a gunshot wound and
then the slow burning pain, the sensation of one's own blood flowing away,
the uncertainty of survival, the acrid smell of burnt gunpowder, the stench
of the dead. Readers and viewers at home could not experience a soldier's
grief at the loss of a friend, or the intimacy and love between men, their loyalty to one another and their sense of honor even to the point of self-sacrifice, the loneliness, sorrow, frustration and despair that soldiers feel at times
in war, and also their obsessive hatreds, especially of the Vietnamese, as if
they were responsible for the misery of being there. We could not report
these things in truth because we were not soldiers ourselves, we weren't *living* it. We shared the risks and discomforts from time to time, but we were
always outside the disciplined authority and therefore the true experience of
wartime military life. We could leave the field when we wished. We did not
have to fight. Although we risked being killed, we did not kill others. Our
independence made us less perceptive of the actual lives and feelings of soldiers. Our stories never captured, for example, the mindless tedium of a year
in the bush or a year at a military desk job. (Boredom is the antithesis of
news.) How could a journalist express the cynicism of "the battalion commander's package," a collection of medals, including a Silver Star, routinely
awarded to lieutenant colonels for serving six months of command time,
whether they had earned it or not? In one division, award nominations for
battalion commanders were written up by members of the Public Information Office in standard language likely to pass the army's decorations review
board. Word got around. How could a journalist know or describe the effect
of such dishonesty on the minds of young soldiers who were being ordered
by the same ambitious commanders to sacrifice their lives for duty, honor
and country?

The U.S. military information system tried to be helpful but failed.
Although the armed services were more open to press coverage in Vietnam
than they had been before, they also manipulated, influenced and censored
coverage. They used a variety of measures. Like a large American business
organization, they tried to disguise their setbacks, mistakes and failures. Public information officers, the army's career public relations staff, shaped real-

ity to fit their version of events. An enemy ambush became "a meeting engagement." A rifle company that had been outmaneuvered and overrun "fought a running battle in hand-to-hand combat." When the enemy finished fighting and withdrew with its dead and wounded, it was said to have "fled the battlefield." These military versions of events were reported by the press without judgment. Truth and falsehood got equal weight. Editors called it "balanced reporting," believing it fair to report both sides of a controversial issue, no matter how much the facts might be in contradiction, no matter how certain the reporter was of the truth. In the name of balance, all kinds of lies and distortions were reported.

We wrote our news stories in a relative hurry for quick consumption at home, superficial sketches of what we saw on the surface of events, honest without being true. Even when we thought we *knew* what was going on—that the war, for example, had evolved from a limited program of military and political support for the South Vietnamese government into an uncontrolled campaign of violence and pain, a runaway rampage of murder and mayhem—there was no way to say it to the public. No one would print it or put it on the air. The language of our daily journalism was insufficient. For all the facts we poured out of Vietnam, we might better have served the truth by broadcasting some of the letters the GIs wrote to their families.

Of all media, perhaps still photography came closest to showing the truth. The best photographs captured a precise moment, holding it there for inspection, offering each image as a fragmentary symbol of someone's reality. By the nature of their ambiguity, those pictures gave viewers the privilege of using their imaginations to interpret the reality. The very best pictures needed no captions.

Sam Castan left the birthday party at about 11:30 p.m., shortly before the curfew, and went back to his hotel room. Sitting alone, he wrote in a small, ring-bound notebook:

Here you are, and aware for a change.

Now you know exactly what you have to do for *Look*:

(1) A combat picture story, to back up

(2) A text piece on "The State of the War Now," under the title "Are We Fighting Alone in Viet-Nam."

You gotta GO OUT INTO THE FIELD . . .
USE YOUR NOODLE !
And back from the field,
you work on the other
things, and go home
with a mass of
NOTES !!!!!

He left Saigon for An Khe the next day.

MAY 20, 1966

Inspired, happy, full of life, Sam Castan rode out to Tan Son Nhut airport in a taxi, checked in at the Air Force passenger terminal, and got aboard Flight 650 to An Khe. Late in the afternoon he arrived at the 1st Cavalry Division's public information compound, a semipermanent complex of offices, sleeping quarters and sandbagged shelters. He was briefed on the military situation in the division's tactical area of responsibility by Major Charles Siler, the senior information officer. In the evening, with the sky in twilight and the air still heavy with the day's heat, Castan watched as Siler and his staff worked with shovels in the trenches near their tents. Fatigue shirts off, sweating hard, they dug out months of accumulated mud and dirt and replaced sandbags broken by the corrosion of sun and rain. The struggle with the weather never ceased. The tropical climate attacked anything that tried to claim a place on the land: baked it, soaked it, cooled it, heated it, rotted it until it was reduced finally to fundamental elements of minerals and dust, making way for more forest to grow in its place. Nothing escaped the climate's relentless attrition.

The camp was on alert. The senior command staff wanted the division base to be prepared for a ground attack by North Vietnamese forces maneuvering nearby. One of the division's three brigades was engaged in a continuous series of sharp battles with a large enemy force about ten miles away in the hills around the Vinh Thanh Valley. Code-named Crazy Horse, the swift-moving airmobile operation had caused significant death and injury to both sides. The Cav was not always victorious. Around the press camp, no one called the Vinh Thanh Valley "Happy" anymore.

"Don't worry about an attack tonight," Castan said. "Not with me around. I'm the luckiest guy in Vietnam."

Siler and his men laughed. They knew Castan was an experienced war reporter who had studied Vietnamese history and culture and was not reluctant to take his chances in the field with the troops. As a senior editor at

LOOK, he had their respect. But Siler, a career Army infantry officer, was skeptical about Castan's proposed story.

"I want to know what soldiers think about when they're facing death," Castan said to him.

Smoking his pipe, Siler considered the idea. His eyes were kind, soft. "I don't think soldiers know what they think about death until they're about to die," he said. Death was not the best subject for troops in an active combat zone to be talking about, bad for morale.

Castan persisted. He asked Siler to get him out to one of the Cav rifle companies likely to make contact.

"There's a big hill not far from here where a lot of men have died in the last few days," Siler said.

"Then I want to get up there first thing in the morning," Castan said.

Siler stopped working on the trenches and left to check arrangements to get Castan into the field. That night the North Vietnamese did not attack An Khe.

At six o'clock the next morning, the division was awake and on its feet. Thousands of men moved slowly in the mist. Castan ate breakfast, filled his canteens with water, packed his gear into a backpack, and rode the PIO truck to the Golf Course, the heliport that was the hub of the airmobile division's activity. The field of helicopters was busy. Jeeps and trucks moved up and down the flight lines. Supplies were loaded into waiting choppers by young men in T-shirts. Crews climbed aboard, engines whined, rotor blades turned —slowly at first, struggling against weight and inertia, then faster and faster, whipping the air until they were visible only as blurs of dark light. The sweet high-octane smell of burning aviation fuel mixed with the wet morning mist. Castan wore an old familiar Australian bush hat, leaving behind the lucky hat Tim Page had given him.

The chopper crew was waiting when Castan arrived, their ship loaded with food, water, ammunition and mail to be delivered to the field. Castan introduced himself, shook hands and climbed aboard the dark green Huey slick for the flight into the Vinh Thanh. The chopper took off and came down about ten minutes later in the hills east of the valley at landing zone Hereford, a rough clearing cut out of a long ridgeline the troops called a razorback. The LZ was on a high ridge near the top of a hill that formed part of a range rising up to thirty two hundred feet, covered with trees, brush and tall grasses. Alpha Company, 1st Battalion, 12th Cavalry occupied the LZ, and as the Huey settled to its landing, Castan took several still pictures of soldiers looking up at him. The weather was cloudy and bright and was warming quickly. A faint breeze barely shifted the rising smoke from camp fires.

LZ Hereford was an ugly scar on the side of the hill. Tree trunks, stumps, branches, trampled earth, burned grass and debris covered the clearing. During the month that Operation Crazy Horse had been under way, other infantry units had camped at the LZ and moved on, leaving their waste behind. Ferocious fighting had taken place on nearby hills, but no battle had been fought at Hereford and none seemed likely. The soldiers were at ease. Security was minimal. Fighting holes formed a circle around the perimeter but most were not occupied. Though they were in the middle of hostile territory and the North Vietnamese had shown their willingness to fight, military alertness on the LZ was slack.

Castan moved easily around the camp, talking with troops, taking photographs, doing interviews. The men enjoyed his quick friendly humor, the relaxed way he went about his work.

At noon, another company from the same battalion arrived on foot at the LZ after a patrol through part of the surrounding area. Alpha Company was lifted out in stages by helicopters. Charlie Company, 1/12, took its place. After a short rest, the company commander ordered his mortar platoon to remain on the LZ while he took the three rifle platoons eastward to patrol the lower ridge. Castan decided to stay at the LZ with the twenty-two men of mortar platoon.

"You guys are the most likely to get hit," he said to Sergeant Robert Kirby, a twenty-nine-year-old regular army veteran from Los Angeles. Although Kirby and Castan had grown up in different parts of the country and were of different races, they were comfortable in each other's company.

"If you think you're going to get a story out of this platoon," Kirby said, "you're wrong. Nothing's going to happen here."

Some of the soldiers sat in foxholes facing downhill in the direction the rest of the company had taken. The upper part of the LZ was left unguarded. Twenty-two men were not enough to go all the way around the perimeter. No scouts were out. No listening posts were in place. The platoon had no observation of the forest farther up the hill. A few soldiers walked back and forth across the clearing collecting water cans and equipment. The sun appeared from behind the clouds and drove the temperature over 100 degrees. There was little shade on the LZ. Everyone moved slowly in the heat.

Sergeant Kirby received an order on his radio to fire the 81 millimeter mortar in support of the rest of the company on patrol. The rifle platoons were now far downhill, out of earshot. Kirby obeyed. The mortar fired seventeen times, part practice, part recon by fire. Soon all but one of the rounds for the mortar were gone.

The company commander called Kirby to say that helicopters were on the way, due to arrive within thirty minutes, to lift the mortar platoon off the LZ. Word went around the lines. The men were happy to be getting out of the field. None was more eager to leave than the senior platoon sergeant, Edward Shepherd, who was due to appear before a promotions board at An Khe. Shepherd was packed and ready to go. He had given Sergeant Kirby the radio and command of the men and sat now near a foxhole talking with Castan. Sunlight baked the LZ, the most brutal time of day.

On the way to Hereford, the commander of the lift ships that were to take the platoon off the hill decided to land at brigade field headquarters for a few minutes, delaying the extraction.

At 2:30 in the afternoon, two GIs on the perimeter spotted a small group of soldiers in the tall grass just in front of their position, about fifteen feet away. Three North Vietnamese, small thin figures in helmets and camouflage, crouched over as they sneaked through the brush. The GIs raised their M-16s and fired. Instantly, the LZ was struck by incoming fire. A storm of machinegun shells, rifle bullets, rocket-propelled grenades, mortar rounds and hand grenades ripped into the American lines, *buzzing . . . cracking . . . zipping . . . whizzing . . . whooshing* into them with fierce killing fury that pinned the Americans into the ground. Bullets, shells and shrapnel flew everywhere. No one could move more than a few inches. Each man tried to find cover where he could, crawling in the dirt behind tree stumps and fallen logs, burrowing into his hole. The sound was stupefying. A heavy caliber machinegun fired nonstop into the mortar pit with expert precision, wrecking the gun, pinning down the gun crew. From the flank, North Vietnamese soldiers moved through the brush at close range: crawling, standing, crouching, walking, running, firing as they advanced. The U.S. position was overwhelmed.

No organized resistance was possible. Soldiers held their M-16s over their heads and fired blindly back into the bush. Others froze, incapacitated by fear and shock. One veteran soldier went berserk, jumped to his feet when the shooting started, ran into the jungle and disappeared. The senior NCO, Sergeant Shepherd, looked up over the lip of his foxhole and was struck in the head by a bullet. He fell back into the hole and the life ran out of him. Low on the ground next to Shepherd, Castan felt a bullet strike his left arm. Then a mortar shell exploded near him and threw a white-hot cluster of shell fragments into his back. The others saw him bleeding, but Castan did not cry out or call for help.

It was apparent that the North Vietnamese had been waiting for some time in the ambush position. They were concealed when Alpha Company was lifted out by helicopter and the three rifle platoons of Charlie Company moved off the LZ and down the ridgeline. The attack was launched only when GIs on the perimeter spotted the NVA skirmishers and opened fire. At least two hundred North Vietnamese in mustard-brown uniforms and bush helmets, most of a battalion, were making a frontal assault against the twenty-two U.S. soldiers and one reporter. Within the first ten minutes almost every man in the American platoon was dead, dying or wounded.

Sergeant Kirby ordered his radio operator to call for help. Specialist Fourth Class John Spianza Jr. of Shelby, North Carolina, called the company commander and cried, "Come back, we're being hit!" Far down the hill, one and a half hour's march away, Captain Don F. Warren heard the anguish in Spianza's voice and realized at once how serious the situation was. He radioed his platoons to turn around and move back toward the LZ. "Get your ass back up that hill," he ordered the leader of First Platoon, Lieutenant Robert McClellan. The soldiers turned and raced back toward the LZ as fast as they could move, crawling at times on their hands and knees, clutching at jungle vines. But they were now moving uphill along the steep ridge and the men were already tired from the day's long march.

Sergeant Kirby was pinned in his fighting hole with two men: Specialist Fourth Class Austin Drummond and Specialist Fourth Class David Crocker. A rocket-propelled grenade came directly at them, whooshing through the smoke and dust thrown up by the battle. Kirby saw it coming, a slow, black, out-of-focus object shaped like a small football. "Watch out!" Kirby cried. The RPG exploded on them. Steel fragments ripped into Crocker's head, fracturing his skull and piercing his brain, killing him in an instant. Burning shrapnel hit Drummond in his arm and leg, and blood spurted out of the holes in his body and poured onto the ground in throbbing gushes. Four fragments struck Kirby in the head but he remained conscious. Drummond's blood ran into the jungle dirt. "I'm hurting, I'm hurting," he said in the minute before his life expired.

"Please, please hurry," radio operator Spianza called. "You must hurry." Downhill, the rifle platoons struggled, near exhaustion, to make it back to the LZ. They had covered about half the distance.

Circling in a helicopter above the hill, the battalion commander, Lieutenant Colonel Rutland Beard Jr., saw mortar shells exploding on the LZ. Higher up the hill, toward the crest, Beard saw a column of soldiers, most of a company, moving toward the battlefield. All were North Vietnamese. There was no sign of the American platoon.

Wounded in the arm and back, Castan picked up his camera, climbed out of the hole he had been sharing with the body of Sergeant Shepherd, sprinted the short distance to Sergeant Kirby's position and jumped in next to him.

"When are we going to get the hell out of here?" Castan said. His voice was high-pitched, forceful.

Kirby was annoyed. The civilian was giving him advice. But it made sense. The fight was lost. Outnumbered by at least ten to one, the platoon was nearly out of ammunition. Outgoing fire was sporadic. Further resistance would only signal the location of the survivors and draw the enemy to them. Already, NVA squads were inside the perimeter, moving from hole to hole, killing wounded GIs and looting their possessions. Downhill in front of him, Kirby could see a group of NVA soldiers about fifteen yards away gathering in the trees and tall grass for an assault against him. The situation was truly desperate. If the Americans were going to survive, they had to escape the LZ and evade in the bush.

"You're hit," Kirby said, looking at the blood on Castan's fatigues.

"It's my arm," Castan said. "I'm okay." Then, "I've gotta have a weapon."

Kirby unfastened the holster on his belt, took out his .357 Magnum, grabbed a handful of bullets from a pouch and handed them to Castan, who switched off the safety.

Turning downhill, Kirby picked up a fragmentation grenade, pulled the pin out of it, and threw the grenade at the enemy group down the hill. He ducked at the explosion. Then he threw another. And another. The incoming fire diminished.

"Let's make it!" he shouted.

Castan climbed out of the hole and ran ahead, leading the way. He ran down the hill with the pistol in his hand, his back straight and his head up. Kirby called after him, "You're leaving your camera."

"I'll worry about that later," Castan shouted back.

Two GIs saw the breakout by Kirby and Castan and dashed past them. Private First Class Wade Taste and Specialist Fourth Class Av Spikes ran, fell and rolled over the ground as fast as they could move. Then another soldier joined the rush downhill. Sergeant Isaac Johnson, his face covered with blood, ran past Kirby in the wild scramble for safety. Out of ammunition, Johnson dived down the hill—running, falling, rolling, crashing against the rocks and brush. When he had covered about 150 yards and could not run any more, he crawled about twenty yards to the bed of a tiny stream and collapsed face down in the water.

Castan took the lead for the main body of survivors and moved down the hill. Spianza, Taste, Spikes and Kirby followed. They gathered in a clump of elephant grass about eight feet high. Out of breath, with few weapons and very little ammunition, they were close to the main trail through the grass that led to a steep precipice covered with rocks. If they could get far enough downhill, Kirby figured, they might link up with the rest of the company, now racing up the ridgeline toward them. A squad of NVA soldiers maneuvered in the brush nearby. Bursts of AK-47 fire cracked in the air. Spianza, the radio operator, screamed, "I'm hit," and fell wounded in the head and legs.

"Hell, everybody's hit," Castan shouted back. Spianza struggled to his feet. Spikes felt a bullet pierce his right arm and cried out.

Walking upright, Castan led the group about twenty feet farther downhill. Spianza shouted, "Hold it up! They're in front of us!"

Kirby and the others halted. Castan pointed the Magnum in front of him and strode forward. A North Vietnamese soldier stood on the trail. Castan fired. At the same time, the soldier aimed his AK-47 and pulled the trigger. Kirby, his head down, heard a scream and then the thump as Castan's body hit the ground.

"I'm hit," Castan called out.

"Don't move," Kirby said, ten yards away.

"Stay away, I'm okay," Castan warned them.

Kirby obeyed. More North Vietnamese soldiers moved uphill toward Spianza, Taste, Spikes and Kirby. The four GIs tried to hide in the tall grass. Taste, wounded in the neck and back and losing blood, asked for water. No one had any to give. A close bunched enemy squad appeared ten feet away, searching the brush. Kirby and Spikes fired M-79 grenades at the center of the group. Five men fell. The others moved away. The fight continued. A North Vietnamese came upon Kirby and raised his rifle to fire. Kirby lay on his back out of ammunition and grenades. All he had was a flare pistol. He fired at the NVA soldier and saw the shell tear his head open. Downhill, a machinegun fired. A burst hit Spikes in the head, killing him.

Alone in the brush by the side of the trail, Sam Castan died. In his last moments he made no sound. The precise cause of his death could not be determined. It may have been loss of blood from the wounds in his head, arm and back. Or from a burst of fire from the machinegun down the hill. He may have been executed by a North Vietnamese soldier as he lay wounded. His body was found later. The borrowed pistol, some money and other valuables had been taken. Left behind in his pockets were half of a broken ballpoint pen, his LOOK cigarette lighter, a stainless steel money clip, a roll of unexposed film, and a small notebook, purchased in Saigon. Inside, a few words were written. "What is a Vietnamese?" The rest of the page was blotted by his dark red blood.

News of Sam's death reached Saigon by military telephone from An Khe. The connection was poor. I sat at the desk in my room at the Caravelle Hotel and took notes while Major Siler described what happened. The battle, or massacre, had lasted thirty minutes. By the time the rest of Charlie Company got back to the LZ, the North Vietnamese were gone. Out of the original platoon of twenty-two men, four American soldiers survived: Sergeant Kirby, Sergeant Isaac Johnson, who hid in the stream, Specialist Fourth Class Spianza, who played dead when the NVA searched his body, and Specialist Fourth Class Charles Stuckey, one of the two GIs who fired the first shots and who escaped from the LZ by himself. All four were wounded. Eighteen soldiers and Sam Castan died. Listening to Siler explain what happened on the telephone, my mind slipped in and out of disbelief. Sam dead? The information would not fit with my strong memories of his living presence: his bright humor, laughter, intelligence, his passionate concern about the course of the war. I refused to believe he was gone. The reality was too hard to accept. Although I did not know them, I thought of Sam's wife, Fran, and baby daughter, Jane, and how devastated they would be. Poor Sam, I thought, poor, poor Sam. Such a full happy life, so much to look forward to. His friends at Frankie's House loved him as a brother. How much we would miss his friendly presence. Poor, dear Sam. Sitting at my desk in the room, thinking of Sam and his wife and daughter and his many friends, I cried for all of us.

In September, a careful reconstruction of the battle (some of which I have used here) was printed in *Harper's* magazine. "Men Facing Death: the Destruction of an American Platoon," was prepared from interviews with survivors by the military historian S. L. A. Marshall, a retired army brigadier general. Marshall praised Castan. "In his last moments," he wrote, "the correspondent had the courage of a lion."

Sam had more than courage. With the platoon under fire at the LZ and facing destruction, Sam had come up with the plan to save himself and the others. Though he was not a soldier, he behaved like one at his best. Keeping calm, he stood up with bullets spinning around him and led four of the surviving members of the platoon down the hill and into the cover of the brush. He did not die because he ran out of luck—he was lucky to survive the initial assault—but because he chose to lead the others toward safety. Working closely with Sergeant Kirby, he had helped to command.

In the minutes before he died, he got the answer to the question he was asking for his story: the thoughts of men facing death. Siler was right. Soldiers learn what they think about death as they are about to die.

On the afternoon of May 24, 1966, friends of Sam Castan gathered for a memorial service in the third-floor chapel of the Rex Hotel in Saigon. Most Western journalists who had served any length of time in-country attended. Everybody knew Sam. The chapel was crowded, all the seats taken. Chaplain Alan Greenspan led the service. Several of Sam's friends gave brief eulogies. My own concluded:

Sam was concerned about the conduct of his colleagues, their relationship with the military office of information, and their responsibility to the public. The true facts, he felt, were often being distorted by both the military and the press. There is a tendency to exaggerate combat or violence, whether you were there as a witness or rewriting the reports of others. It sells copy. There is a tendency to conceal error or defeat, whether you witnessed it or not. It saves face. Neither makes for responsible reporting. It was on Sam's conscience. God bless him. We might do well to examine our own.

MAY 25, 1966

Sam Castan was carried home in a military casket on a military plane with the bodies of the American soldiers he died with. The silver and blue air force C-141 flew across the Pacific from Vietnam to Hawaii where Sam's body was claimed by his wife and transferred to the cargo hold of a commercial flight to New York. Fran Castan and her daughter, Jane, were joined by Sam's other relatives, friends and colleagues for the service.

Some weeks later, during one of his visits to the United States, General William Westmoreland, commander of U.S. military forces in Vietnam, attended a ceremony at the LOOK magazine offices in New York. He presented Fran with the U.S. Army's Outstanding Civilian Service medal, which had been awarded to her husband posthumously. The citation said:

> Mr. Sam Castan distinguished himself by bravery in action. Voluntarily taking up arms against a numerically superior enemy force, he fired his pistol at point blank range against an enemy machinegun crew. Thrice wounded, he gave his life in defense of his fellow Americans.

Fran did not want to take the medal. She was angry at Westmoreland and the Army for prosecuting a war that she opposed. To accept the medal, she felt, was a kind of complicity, an acceptance of the Army's ritual, but she thought it best not to make an incident at the ceremony and took the medal from Westmoreland and put it away.

I had sent two telegrams to her from Saigon with some details of Sam's death and the reactions of his friends there, but they were not answered. Fran did not know me, Sam had not mentioned me to her, and she was in shock. I wished to attend the funeral on behalf of Sam's friends in Saigon.

I asked CBS News for permission to come home. My assignment to Vietnam had not specified any length of time—just as long as I could take it. It had been nine and a half months. I had now served in Vietnam longer than anyone from CBS News. A cable from the foreign editor said, 'Come home, Tiger. Go to the funeral. Take some time off. See how you like working for the national desk.'

I packed to leave. My possessions fit into two suitcases, a duffel bag and a portable typewriter case. Some of Sam's personal effects went in the duffel bag. I carried home a few of my souvenirs: the tin rice bowl I had taken from the farmhouse in the Suoi Ca Valley; a Montagnard crossbow, quiver and arrows I had bought on R and R in Dalat; the brass buckle and narrow leather belt with bullet holes in it from the NVA soldier at Plei Me; a box of photographs, scripts and letters. I gave away the military gear—fatigues, field pack, web belt, canteens, poncho, liner, boots, socks, green T-shirts to other correspondents. I kept a small floppy bush hat. I had not acquired a helmet.

Sam's death left me with no motivation to cover the war. The original challenge I felt working on the story had diminished to the daily task of doing a job. I was out of ambition. Fear played a part. On the surface I was normal, but inside I was tired, nervous, depressed. It must have showed. Charlie Mohr of the *Times* asked me to lunch and listened sympathetically to my description of how I was feeling. He told me not to worry, the problem was all in my mind. 'There's nothing wrong with you that a good rest won't cure,' he said. 'If you ever get fed up working for CBS,' he said, 'there'll be a job at the *Times*.' Just talking with Charlie—a thoughtful, kind-hearted man —brought relief from the abiding dread. The only other times I felt safe were with friends at Frankie's House.

My normal sense of order in the world was confused. When the thought of what happened to Sam came to mind, the muscles tightened in the back of my throat. Tears formed in the ducts of my eyes. Part of me wanted to cry long and hard, but after the first day, I couldn't. Another part of me wanted to shut out all thought of Sam's death and think about anything else. I still couldn't accept that he was gone. It wasn't real. I imagined Sam's round happy face appearing out of the Saigon crowd and stopping to talk, telling me what he was doing, asking how it was going with me. It wasn't right that he was no longer around. On another level, Sam's death had caused some-thing inside me to snap, to make me feel empty. At times I felt unworthy to be alive, able to go on with my life when he was not. Life, I discovered, can be unbearably painful when a friend loses his. It seemed unjust for Sam to die while so many others survived: those corrupt ARVN generals and their rich wives, the black market bandits, the pimps and brothel keepers, the murderers and killers of every kind out there. The war rewarded evil by taking away the good. Sad, angry, guilty, I sat in my hotel room and wrote a long account of Sam's last days and cabled it to LOOK so the editors would have the story of his death.

On the morning after Sam's memorial service, I went to Room 207 of the Caravelle and said good-bye. The bureau chief, correspondents, camera crews and Vietnamese members of the office staff shook hands and gave me hugs.

'We will see you again, Jack,' one of the Vietnamese women who worked in the office said.

'Not me,' I said, smiling. 'I love your country but I'm not coming back.'

'You will see,' she said. 'You will see.'

'When the war's over,' I said.

'Then I hope we see you soon.'

I shook hands and kissed the Vietnamese women on both cheeks the French way. They had worked hard and had been helpful to me, meticulously polite and friendly, but I did not know them well. The formality of their manners and my own shyness precluded that. It did not matter. In my heart I knew I was not coming back. I was anxious to get away from Saigon and reminders of the wretched war.

Later that morning, friends gathered at Frankie's House for a farewell party. I was booked on an afternoon Air France flight to Paris that would connect with a plane to New York just in time for me to make it to Sam's funeral. My bags were packed and waiting downstairs. Everyone upstairs was high. Tim Page sat on the rattan carpet on the floor cleaning a pile of bright green marijuana leaves he had acquired from the Central Market earlier in the morning. He and Sean Flynn seemed to be engaged in a competition to consume the largest quantity of marijuana ever smoked by one person in one day. The next day they were going to Danang to cover the student–Buddhist demonstrations and had nothing else to do. As soon as one joint was finished, a new one was rolled. Page and Flynn tried to appear normal, but their eyes were glazed marble and their limbs moved in slow motion.

'Is Page zonked?' Page asked rhetorically, his voice giddy, his thumbs and forefingers fumbling with another joint.

'Yes, Page, you are *definitely* zonked,' Flynn said in a patronizing tone. 'Wasted, stoned out of your mind. Oh man, just think what this shit is doing to your brains.'

'Page is too stoned to think,' someone said.

'Page is stoned so he doesn't *have* to think,' another said.

'Page didn't have any brains to begin with.' Everyone laughed, including Page.

'Look at you, Flynn!' he said, standing up, pointing a bony finger, waving his hands. 'Just *look* at you! Lying there wasted. Bare feet. Red eyes. You can't keep them open. You're *lounging* Flynn. You're a disgrace to young American manhood. No virtue whatsoever. Totally wrecked. Doing nothing. Look at you Flynn. You should be out covering the war.'

'Oh, Page, I'll cover the war tomorrow.'

'It'll still be there.'

'That's for sure.'

'Jack sure as hell won't,' someone said.

'Laurence, you're the only one with any fucking sense. Getting the hell out of here.'

'I'll miss you guys,' I said.

'Yeah, we'll miss you.'

'Just don't come back.'

They all wished me well in the States. Despite my protests, Martin Stuart-Fox and Steve Northup insisted on driving me to the airport. Stuart-Fox had commandeered the UPI office mini-Moke for the purpose. Stoned, none of them had any sense of time. Whenever I suggested it was time to leave for the airport, one of them said, 'Don't worry. We'll be there by 12:00. Plane doesn't leave until 1:30. No sweat, man.' I accepted their judgment reluctantly.

As a good-bye gift, they presented me with a jacket made of green and black camouflage silk. Sewn on the front and sleeves were colorful cloth unit badges from a dozen different U.S. Army and ARVN outfits: Rangers, Airborne, Marines. One of them said, "War Dogs." On the back, a hand-embroidered map of Vietnam was stitched in bright-colored thread with the words,

> When I Die I'll Go To Heaven,
> Cause I've Already Done My Time In Hell
> Vietnam 1965–66

The effect was ridiculous, a parody of war emblems. But it touched my heart that they had it made up. I accepted the jacket with thanks but could not wear it outside the house. Page put it on and wore it proudly. The luggage was loaded into the back of the mini-Moke and the group set off toward the airport in a blast of noise and smoke, laughing and teasing, legs spilling out the sides of the small open vehicle. Riding their motorcycles, Page and Flynn gave directions, not always in harmony, trying to lead the way while Stuart-Fox drove the mini-Moke. Lunchtime traffic was dense. Vietnamese watched the silly, long-legged foreigners mingling with them in traffic with amusement. When I caught their eyes, they turned away as if what we were doing was too embarrassing to watch. Progress was slow. My sense of timing and punctuality was in alarm. No one else in the group cared that it was close to departure time. 'Don't worry, mate,' Page said with authority. 'Air Chance is always late. Here, have another toke,' handing me a joint. He and Flynn exchanged mischievous looks.

By the time we arrived at Tan Son Nhut, the Air France plane was nearly loaded and the ground crew was making final preparations for departure. Check-in, customs, emigration and police formalities would take at least an hour. I pleaded with the airline staff. I told them my friend had been killed in the war and I was going home for his funeral. The Vietnamese looked at me with mild sympathy but not as a special case. They seemed to have experienced wartime funerals themselves. 'Sorry,' one of them said firmly, 'we are not going to cancel our schedule just because you are late.' I felt panic. *How am I going to get to New York in time?* Flynn and Page giggled. 'Just have to stay another day, then, won't you, mate?' Page sniggered. Northup pointed to the departures board showing a Pan Am flight to Tokyo and then on to San Francisco in two hours. Perhaps it would connect with a flight to New York in time to make the funeral. Quickly, I bought a ticket and checked in. Relief. A newspaper reporter who was on the same flight arranged for us to sit together. The gang from Frankie's House said goodbye with brotherly hugs and handshakes and left the terminal, Page and Flynn giggling without interruption.

In Danang the next day, Page and Flynn went out in the streets to take pictures of students and Buddhists demonstrating against the government. South Vietnamese troops attacked the crowd of protesters. They fired an M-79 grenade and fragments hit Page in the face and hand. Flynn ran through the line of fire, lifted Page in his arms and carried him out of danger. Then he commandeered a jeep and drove him to a Navy field hospital. An operation to remove the fragments was successful and Page began his recovery. A few weeks later, he was invited to rest aboard a U.S. Coast Guard ship cruising in the South China Sea. The ship was attacked by U.S. Air Force planes whose pilots mistook it for a North Vietnamese vessel. F-4 Phantoms bombed and strafed the ship in nine separate passes, killing three American sailors aboard and wounding nine. Page was hit by dozens of pieces of shrapnel and critically injured. Other survivors said it was a miracle he lived.

My flight to New York arrived an hour after Sam's funeral had finished. Frustrated, tired, I got in a taxi and rode toward Manhattan. Cruising along the Van Wyck Expressway and over the Triborough Bridge, I noticed how the steel and glass skyscrapers gleamed in the summer light. I felt out of place, disoriented, as if entering a strange otherworld. By comparison with Vietnam, America moved at a much faster tempo, more purposeful and precise. Telephones worked. Cars, trucks and busses sped along well-paved highways. Drivers, even the most aggressive, paid at least passing attention to traffic laws. There was no comparison with chaotic Saigon. The climate was temperate. No oppressive heat, no monsoon rains. The air, even with exhaust fumes, was fresher. Streets looked cleaner. The ordered efficiency of the airport—planes and passengers taking off, landing, making connections—was startling to me, surreal. It was as if I had left America in the early 1950s and returned to a futuristic society on another planet. Everything was newer. Everyone had more energy. The fashions of dress were more attractive. The one thing about New York that was the same as Saigon was the incessant noise.

I stayed at the Plaza Hotel on Central Park South, a luxury I had promised myself. I was given a small dark room on the top floor just under the eves of the roof. It was smaller than a general-purpose tent. I called Len Caparros, the founder of Frankie's House who had moved home to New York, the one we all knew as "Cat." We agreed to meet for dinner at a bistro on Madison Avenue. Later, walking to our rendezvous, I looked in the windows and open doorways of bars and restaurants along the way. Young people who had just finished work were standing in couples and groups, chatting to one another—carefree, animated, drinking and laughing. Popular music played. Glasses clinked. The men looked cheerful and well-groomed, some with mustaches, wearing bright clothes with wide collars. Men were beginning to wear their hair long. The young women looked attractive in lightweight skirts and blouses. Short skirts were in style. Everyone laughed a lot. Other couples strolled along the sidewalks with their arms entwined, out for the evening, having fun. The country was at peace. There were no signs of the war.

I felt troubled by what I saw. The sight of so many healthy happy young people enjoying themselves in New York while so many others were living rough on the ground in danger and discomfort in Vietnam seemed obscene. *How can they be so happy?* I thought. *Don't they know there's a war on? Haven't they got any idea of what it's like over there?* They didn't deserve their happiness.

Cat arrived in an ebullient mood. We hugged each other, sat at a table and ordered drinks. When I told him how I felt, he said, 'These hotshots don't give a shit about the war. Couldn't care less. Nobody does. The only thing anybody in this town cares about is making money and getting laid.'

'It makes me sick to look at them,' I said.

'Yeah, it bothered me a lot when I first got back. I wanted to chuck a few frags around, wake some of these jokers up, teach 'em a lesson. I'm getting used to it now, though.' He turned to an anonymous group of people at the bar, made a fist with his middle finger stuck in the air, and raised it at them. 'I say, fuck 'em,' he said, laughing.

We drank and ate and talked but I was distracted by the noise at the bar, people talking in loud voices with nasal New York accents. They were from the same generation as Cat and me.

'I can't believe they aren't in the Army, or at least in one of the aid organizations,' I said.

'Draft calls are up to forty-five, fifty thousand a month,' Cat said, waving his hand. 'All these assholes have got deferments—National Guard, reserves, 4-Fs. All it costs is a couple a hundred bucks in the right hands. It's a big scam. Nobody goes to Vietnam. Just spades from the ghettos mostly and poor whites from the South.'

'What about Hispanics?' I said.

'Them too,' he laughed. 'But no Cubans. We're exempt. 'Cause we're too crazy.'

'You? Crazy? Nahhh. . . .'

'Yeah, really. The government's afraid we might get our act together and try another invasion.'

'What? Bay of Pigs again?'

We laughed. It was reassuring to have a friend in New York from Frankie's House. We were cheerful and trusting, as if we'd known each other all our lives. I would have at least one friend in the city with shared experiences from Vietnam. Cat and I split the bill and got up to leave. We agreed to meet again soon. In the weeks that followed, we saw each other a few times, but the pressure of my new job in the States kept us out of touch much of the time. Sometime later, I heard the news from a friend: Leonardo Caparros died in the crash of a small plane in the Caribbean. No one from Frankie's House ever got more than the sketchiest details of his death. Heaven knows what Cat was doing down there.

In those first few weeks back in the States my stomach churned when I saw young people behaving frivolously. It offended me. How important could the war be if people weren't paying attention? I didn't expect the country to be in constant mourning for its war dead, but I had expected more acknowledgment of the sacrifices being made. The news media covered the war dutifully, although incompletely, but always respectfully. Significant amounts of airtime, newsprint and public discussion were devoted to what editors regarded as important war news. But it seemed to have no effect on government policy. Few readers, viewers or listeners appeared to take serious notice. The antiwar movement was small and relatively powerless, organized mainly around university campuses. Antiwar demonstrations by as many as 10,000 people took place from time to time, touching off angry and sometimes violent confrontations with supporters of the war. Draft cards were burned. But the great mass of the adult population—what was coming to be known as "Middle America"—did not show much concern about Vietnam. The prevailing attitude appeared to be indifference, or possibly powerlessness. I was reminded of a description of New York City in the months that followed December 1941: *"a civilian society far removed from the war and safe at night in its beds, driven primarily by short attention spans, supreme selfishness and uninhibited sex."* It didn't occur to me that New York might be that way all the time.

I was invited to cocktail parties in fashionable apartments and suburban homes. Other guests wearing expensive clothes smiled politely and asked, "Tell me, Jack, what's it *really* like over there?" Or, more somberly, "How are we doing, really?" leaning in close to my face to listen over the noise of the party, expecting perhaps to hear something they hadn't read in the paper, ice cubes clicking comfortably in their cocktail glasses. I said what I thought: *It's not going well at all over there. It's much worse than the government and Army are*

telling you. The stories they're putting out are mostly propaganda. We're not win-
ning all the battles. The North Vietnamese are brave, better fighters than most of the
South Vietnamese, willing to die for their cause. Really.

If the person who asked the question was still listening, I said, 'We're
killing thousands of Vietnamese every week, an awful lot of women and
children and old men. Yeah, really. And we're destroying the countryside,
making peasant farmers into refugees, hundreds of thousands of people
with nowhere to live. A lot of them are sick, and hungry. We're driving them
off the land into camps. It's cruel because the Vietnamese are wedded to
their land. It's in their souls.'

I tried to speak without emotion or bombast, giving them an honest
briefing, but it was hard to keep the passion out of my voice. If they seemed
interested, I told them about the Air Force bombing of the Cambodian village, shooting the farmers in their fields, or Marines blowing up the sixty-six
Vietnamese in a tunnel under their rice fields, or the killing of the ARVN soldiers in the A Shau Valley. In most cases, their eyes slipped out of focus at
some point while I was speaking. They looked over my shoulder at the rest
of the party as if they had lost interest. Some looked ill, or shocked. Occasionally someone asked a follow-up question, but usually they thanked me
and walked away. What I was saying was unexpected, harsh for them to
absorb, brutal. Maybe they thought I was exaggerating, or that I was too
intense, or that the experience had made me a little crazy. After a while, I
stopped talking about the war to casual acquaintances. When I was introduced as someone recently back from Vietnam and people asked what's it
really like over there? I just said, '*Really, really* hot, *unbelievably* hot and miserable,' and changed the subject. Or made a joke. 'The Army thinks the best
way to win the war is to take all the women and children in Vietnam out to
sea and leave them on barges. Then go across the country and kill every living thing. Waste everything.' They'd smile at that. And I'd say, 'And then sink
the barges.'

A few people I met were genuinely interested, asked intelligent questions, wondered what could be done. Friends and family listened more carefully. 'You need time off, Jack,' they said more than once.

In the newspapers, the war was fought each day in editorial pages. James
Reston, an icon of moderation, attacked antiwar demonstrators in the *New
York Times*: "The trouble is they are inadvertently working against all the
things they want and creating all the things they fear most. They are not pro-

moting peace but postponing it. They are not persuading the President or the Congress to end the war, but deceiving Ho Chi Minh and General Giap into prolonging it."

A professor of physics from Syracuse University fired back: "With an arrogance that has no parallel, we have taken it upon ourselves to decide for a certain small Asian nation that its people are better dead than red. We are now helping them to achieve that goal."

In Britain, Nobel Prize–winning philosopher Bertrand Russell, aged ninety-three, resigned from the Labour Party after fifty-one years of membership to protest the British government's "complacency over the Vietnam atrocities" and tore up his party card at an antiwar demonstration in London.

Every day, the war news was carried to the American public in print. Tons of newspapers, magazines, pamphlets, periodicals, press releases, government publications, speeches and books were published, a weight that appeared equal to all the bombs being dropped on North and South Vietnam. And with about as much effect. Nothing changed.

Outside of New York and Saigon, I knew no one from CBS News. It was an organization of over eight hundred journalists, technicians, managers and office staff. I had joined the company in New York in January 1965 as a radio reporter and was sent to Vietnam in August. All my television experience was in the war. Now management decided to send me around the country to visit CBS News bureaus and work with the domestic staff. I would spend two weeks in each of three bureaus: Chicago, Los Angeles and Atlanta, replacing staff correspondents who were on vacation. It would also give me an opportunity to get to know my country.

America was experiencing one of its longest periods of sustained economic growth, fifty-six months of continuous expansion, largely because of the war. Four to eight billion dollars had been pumped into the economy by increased defense spending. Ten times as much was going into the space program. "Times are good and getting better" said one of President Johnson's chief economic advisers. The gross national product was up 6 percent over the year before. Arthur Rosenbaum, chief economist for Sears, Roebuck and Company, declared, "We *can* have our guns and butter." In October 1965, Wall Street recorded the heaviest volume of trading in its 173-year history with more than 44 million shares bought and sold in one week. Most companies reported record profits for 1965. The *New York Times* declared, "Never before have so many made so much."

Some of America's cultural entertainment was war related. Newspapers appeared with full-page pictures of giant battle tanks, guns blazing, to promote the Christmas opening of Warner Bros.' new Cinerama production, *Battle of the Bulge*.

UNLIKE ANYTHING YOU'VE EVER SEEN BEFORE!

said the headlines, as if what America needed now was the kind of patriotic, well-rehearsed courage acted by Henry Fonda, Robert Shaw, Dana Andrews, Robert Ryan, Charles Bronson and Telly Savalas, a celluloid curtain call for World War II to keep Americans in step with the current one.

Abercrombie & Fitch, the Madison Avenue hunting, fishing and camping store, held a ten-day Gun Fair offering weapons priced from $22.95 to $3,940. A quarter-page newspaper ad declared:

> My wife says I'm daydreaming ever since I saw that Remington
> 600 Magnum at their Gun Fair.

For $144.95, Abercrombie & Fitch offered a "remarkable bolt-action 4-shot carbine" guaranteed to "drop any big game in North America."

Arriving in Chicago, I was assigned to cover urban disorders. An incident involving the police had sparked a rampage of looting, burning and anarchy in the streets of the city's South Side. Chicago police tried to restore order and make arrests, using their weapons, but were attacked whenever they appeared vulnerable. The rioters were predominantly black, the police predominately white. Newspapers called the disorders "race riots." This was not the first time I had witnessed urban violence in the United States. Two years earlier I had covered street fighting between police and local residents in New York City's Harlem. Coming from Vietnam to the violence of American inner cities was not, I discovered, a difficult transition for a reporter.

Leaving the bureau the first night, I was appointed to drive the station wagon carrying the camera, sound and light crew—three men who needed to be able to jump out of the car on short notice. The wide boulevards of downtown Chicago were virtually empty. Almost nothing moved. All the street and traffic lights were on. Residents of the city were staying indoors. Only an occasional police car, fire engine, journalist or lost driver was out. Driving through a large metropolitan city deserted at night was eerie. The dispatcher on the police radio in the crew car called out one disturbance after another. Suddenly, an excited policeman shouted, "Shots fired at . . ." and gave the location.

'Drive fast,' the cameraman called from the backseat. His name was Isadore Bleckman and we had just met. Everyone called him "Izzy."

I put my foot on the accelerator hard and the car took off down one of the avenues. At the first large intersection, I hit the brakes and slowed to stop at a red light.

'Nobody's gonna give you a ticket if you jump the light,' the sound technician said.

I edged the car into the intersection and looked carefully both ways. The radio reported a patrolman down with gunshot wounds.

"Jack!" Bleckman said in a firm voice, "drive like you own the road!" From then on, I did.

Two weeks later, I moved to Los Angeles. A CBS documentary producer in New York assigned me to visit Big Sur and do an assessment of the Esalen Institute, a new California center devoted to alternative methods of exploring human consciousness and potential. Esalen was reported to be attracting psychologists, philosophers, educators and others trying to develop insights into human potentiality, perceptions, therapy, religion and physical relaxation. Its location on a cliff overlooking the Pacific Ocean and its natural hot spring baths made it physically as well as intellectually stimulating. I welcomed the assignment as a brief vacation from breaking news.

On the plane to San Francisco, a young man in the seat next to me was interested in what was going on in Vietnam. He was perceptive and bright and made a few sympathetic observations. We talked all the way. Near the end of the flight, he said I might like to meet his sister, a student who was just finishing her education at Berkeley, and gave me her phone number.

Reda met me on the doorstep of the house where she was living across the Bay. I was impressed by how tall and graceful she was, moving smoothly, comfortable with herself. Her hair was long and black and her skin was tanned golden brown. The curves of her face were accentuated by large cheek bones that gave her eyes a deep, thoughtful look, absorbing all that went on around her with easygoing confidence. She seemed to enjoy being with me. At dinner the first night, she listened carefully to what I said about Vietnam and suggested gently that I had a responsibility to inform as many

Americans as I could about what was going on there. For herself, Reda was
going to Africa to teach. She had learned to speak Hausa to improve the lives
of people in Nigeria. She would be going in a month.

I invited her to accompany me to Esalen the next day and she accepted.
We drove down the coast to Big Sur and arrived in the late afternoon. Our
unannounced appearance surprised the staff. At first they said we would
have to come back another day; no one had prepared for us, and there was
nowhere for us to stay. Reda and I felt awkward and considered going back.
Then the director of the institute, Michael Murphy, appeared. After asking a
few questions, he invited us to spend the night. A staff member called local
motels but there were no vacancies. Murphy, who had the polite manners of
Buddhist monks I had met, took us to a small room and gave Reda his plain
single bed. I was given a couch. We were not accustomed to such generosity.
In a few hours, we felt a spirit of friendliness that seemed to inhabit the
place. That night and the next day, Murphy and his counselors explained
what they were trying to accomplish at Esalen. Their idea was to create an
atmosphere of spiritual enlightenment where visitors could explore their
emotional and creative selves in surroundings of absolute tranquillity. The
grounds of the institute provided a spectacular view of the Pacific Ocean.
Hot springs ran underground and filled the outdoor baths. Esalen offered
sublime sensual pleasure. It was trying to be a place of peace. On the second
day, Reda and I were encouraged to take off our clothes and get in a hot
spring bath with some of the other guests. Being from California, she was
more comfortable with the idea. I had a soldier's tan and was self-conscious
about showing my body to strangers. Once in the water, though, the effect
was soothing and restorative.

When we left, I wrote a report on Esalen, the conversations we had with
the staff and guests, and mailed it to the CBS producer in New York. Later, I
suspected that the assignment had been arranged as much for my personal
benefit as documentary research. Esalen was enlightening. On the surface,
the idea may have seemed to outsiders like another self-absorbed California
fad, zany and indulgent, but being there put it in a different light. Interesting
ideas were being tested. People's perceptions were changing. All the time I
was at Esalen, I didn't think about the war.

Friends now, Reda and I agreed to see each other as much as we could.
Back in Los Angeles, where her mother lived, she came to my hotel in Bev-
erly Hills in the afternoon. It was a sunny day, as usual. We had lunch from

room service. Later, she took off her clothes and lay on her back on the bed, smiling, offering to share herself with me. Her long dark body was proportioned perfectly. *Aphrodite*, I thought. She had the beauty of a goddess. Sunlight pushed through louvered shutters on the windows and cast dappled shadows across the bed and her body. Her beauty amazed me. I could not comprehend the cause of my good fortune. With Reda, I felt alive and whole and healthy again.

We traveled together through the American South, riding with veteran camera crews like Lawrence Pierce and Bernard Noto in Mississippi and Alabama to cover civil rights sit-ins and marches. The crews were cordial. They asked Reda about her career plans and listened with interest, especially about her planned trip to Africa. They included her in the group and made her feel welcome.

Being journalists from outside the state, we faced the possibility of violence from local segregationists. Mississippi's recent history was a catalogue of racial violence: death on the campus of the University of Mississippi during the integration of James Meredith; the murder of the NAACP's Medgar Evers; the violent deaths of three civil rights workers in Philadelphia, Mississippi. Although local segregationists saw us as "outside agitators," which put us at risk, I was not frightened. No one here was shooting RPG-7s. Being with cool-headed camera crews and with Reda, who was utterly unflappable, gave me an added sense of assurance, a feeling of being safe among friends.

In Atlanta, the bureau chief made a hurried, last-minute assignment. In Grenada, Mississippi, the next morning, a school desegregation attempt was scheduled. Black high school students, mostly girls, were going to try to integrate an all-white school, and local whites threatened to stop them by force. It was too late to get us from Atlanta to Grenada by scheduled airline, so a small plane and pilot were chartered. Flying over Alabama, the twin-engined plane came upon a thundercloud reaching thousands of feet above our flight path.

'Can't go around this one,' the pilot said. 'Have to try and go through it. Hang on!'

The plane shuddered when it hit the hard winds and began to buck in the furious air. The pilot had a thick red sunburned neck and it was perspiring heavily. Beads of sweat fell into the deep folds of his skin.

'Haven't been in one like this in a long time,' he said in a pinched Georgia drawl, struggling with the controls.

The plane pitched and yawed and rolled with sharp sudden jerks, as if it might be pulled apart by the swirling forces. No one in the plane spoke. My internal warning system was in full alarm.

Sitting next to the pilot, I asked if we should turn back.

'Sir, that's entirely up to you,' he said, his eyes fixed on the blackness ahead, searching for a hole to steer through. I turned to the camera crew and asked what we should do. Their faces were pale. Reda was calm. No one wanted to be first to suggest we turn back. I wondered what to do. Having just come from Vietnam, it was no loss of face for me to order us back to Atlanta.

"Let's take a vote," I said finally. The crew nodded their heads. "I say we go back," I said. No one disagreed. The plane turned in a steep bank. Everyone, including the pilot, seemed relieved to get out of the storm.

We took off again the next morning but it was a long flight. In Grenada, meanwhile, local white adults attacked black children and their parents on their way to school. Teenage girls were beaten bloody with wooden pickax handles swung by angry, shouting whites. We heard about it when we got there. The plane had arrived too late for us to film the attack. Injured and crying, the black people retreated to a church in another part of town. Along the way, our car was stopped by a line of police blocking the road. A large uniformed officer with a bulging neck came up to the back left window of the car and stuck the end of his nightstick through the window. The braid on his uniform suggested he was the local chief of police.

'Roll film,' I whispered as loud as I could to the camera crew. The police chief smiled and looked at us with contempt.

'Where you boys from?' he asked, tapping the heavy wooden stick on the window.

'CBS News, Atlanta,' the photographer said in his pronounced southern accent. The film magazine turned slowly, just louder than the noise of my heart, the lens pointing casually at the police chief.

'Well, if y'all know what's good for you,' he said in a low voice on the edge of anger, 'you'll just get yourselves right out of our town. Hear? No need to come in here and stir up trouble.' He tapped the nightstick on the window harder, touching all four sides of the frame.

With the camera rolling, I asked a few polite questions until enough film had been exposed to cover the scene for the story. My heart pounded wildly. Driving away, I asked the crew if they got it on film. They assured me they did. 'Sound, too?' I asked. The sound tech nodded. He was an older man with a balding head.

'He'd of beaten us silly as soon as look at us,' the photographer said. 'Or let some of his boys take care of us.' He took out a handkerchief and wiped some of the sweat from his face and neck. 'We'll have to watch it from here on in.'

It's everywhere, I thought, *Grenada, Chicago, Vietnam.*

We drove to the church. The crew rolled film as the Reverend Andrew Young, an assistant to Dr. Martin Luther King and member of the Southern Christian Leadership Conference, spoke to the assembled parents and children from a pulpit. Many of them were still sobbing. At first, Young talked in low somber tones about the events of the morning. Slowly, he recited what information was known about the attack. He praised the children and their parents for their self-restraint, for abiding by the movement's vision of nonviolence. He consoled them for their injuries. Slowly, Young's voice rose in power and authority, preaching the passion he felt for the cause of nonviolent integration across the South, the tide flowing toward racial equality in America. His words stirred the audience. By the end, some two hours later, children and parents who had been crying were singing and clapping hands and shouting, 'Hallelujah!'

It was the most articulate, emotive speech I had ever heard, on a par with Dr. King's oratory. The crew drove me to the airport. I took the film and flew with it in the chartered plane to Memphis, Tennessee, the nearest city where the film could be developed, edited and fed to the network for the *Evening News*. I called the executive producer to tell him what we had. He knew what had happened from the wire services. I said we missed the violence because of the bad weather but had filmed a scene with the police chief threatening us, and also the church service with Andrew Young. The executive producer said to put the piece together and feed it in. When the film editor looked at the footage showing the confrontation with the police chief, he said, 'There's no sound here. The whole thing is silent. Look!' The police chief's lips moved but no words came from them. The film editor asked who the sound person was. When I told him, he said, 'That guy's stone fucking deaf! Don't you know that?' I recalled that my instructions to roll film in the car had been whispered. Either the sound tech had not heard me or he was intimidated by the police chief and didn't switch his equipment on. An essential part of the story was in the sound and we didn't have it. The edited spot would be less dramatic.

We fed the story to New York anyway. After the broadcast, the executive producer phoned. He was in a fury. He called me "stupid" and "incompetent." I tried to explain what had happened but he wasn't interested. "Do you realize how much that stupid piece just cost?" he yelled. His anger hurt. Soon after I returned to New York, I resigned my job at CBS News. I told friends at the network that I couldn't work for a bully like that. They assured me that the executive producer treated everyone the same way, that he had an uncontrollable temper, not to take it personally. I thought about it for a day or two and decided to quit anyway. I thought it was important to take a stand against that kind of tyranny.

A year passed. I went to work as an investigative reporter for radio station WNEW in New York, the newsroom where I had learned to write and report before joining CBS. The news director, Jack Pluntze, was a gifted journalist, tough-minded and often critical but rarely insulting and never extreme. His newsroom produced several outstanding journalists who went on to work at the networks: Steve Bell, Reid Collins, Christopher Glenn, Ike Pappas and Marlene Sanders among them.

Reda and I lived together in an apartment on Riverside Drive on the upper West Side of Manhattan. We were happy. We shopped and cooked and saw friends and attended many of the cultural attractions and entertainment events in the city. After several months, however, I became moody and difficult. Images from the war were appearing in my dreams, mutilated bodies of soldiers and civilians, some of the scenes I'd seen. I felt foreboding in the night that carried over into the day. Walking around Manhattan, sharp sudden noises made me jump or drop to the pavement. I felt safest in the solitude of the apartment, untroubled by the busy society outside. Most evenings, I drank. I got in the habit of taking one or two stiff drinks before I could manage my anxieties well enough to go outside, even to buy groceries. In that condition, it was impossible for me to have a normal, loving relationship with Reda, who was more stable emotionally. She had sacrificed her plans to work in Africa in order to be with me. Sadly, she returned to California.

I decided to get help. Each weekday morning at eight o'clock, before I went to work, I lay on the couch of a Manhattan psychiatrist and put whatever thoughts came to mind into words. I talked about images from Vietnam. I explored memories from childhood. I expressed my fears about everyday existence, about people and places and other things. The couch was comfortable. The room felt safe. The psychiatrist, a soft-spoken man in his forties, listened politely. He was sympathetic but rarely spoke. After a few months, the violent images from Vietnam appeared less often in my dreams and fantasies. My fear of death began to fade. In the cacophonous noise of New York, I no longer jumped at sharp sounds. Most mornings as I left the psychiatrist's office, I had the light-hearted feeling of being freed, liberated from another part of my past. I went to parties and began to go on dates. I fell in love with a delightful, intelligent young woman from Scotland. After almost a year in which every aspect of the past that I was capable of remembering had been recalled, relived and expressed, the psychiatrist said it was time to stop. We had done as much as we could for now. He gave me a prescription for a widely praised new tranquilizer named Valium and told me to take five milligrams four times a day to help me cut down on my drinking. A short time later, walking down Madison Avenue after taking Valium for the first time, I was lifted into a state of positive well-being, a feeling of calm self-confidence, as if I had been released from anxiety and delivered into a world of feelings that were normal, the way they should be, sane.

It was the summer of 1967. The news from Vietnam was grim. Also, the *way* the news was being reported worried me. Some of it was sensitive and true, especially some thoughtful reporting by R. W. Apple, who had become the *New York Times* bureau chief in Saigon. But so much else in the news, particularly on television, seemed to reinforce propaganda being promulgated by U.S. government and military leaders—that the war was being won, slowly, and that the North Vietnamese were gradually being defeated. Most people in the country wanted to believe that we were winning, so they believed it, but those of us who had been there and knew how dishonest our leaders could be, didn't. Apple wrote a long analysis that summer called "The Making of a Stalemate" in which he suggested that the United States might *not* be winning the war, that winning might not be possible. It was a long, well-researched article that dared to take an original position on the war. It reminded me of *Catch-22,* and the lesson that it was insane to fight and die for a war that has already been decided. I felt a need to find out what was really going on in Vietnam and tell the story on television. I thought of the courage that Edward R. Murrow demonstrated in World War II, staying

with the story in London through the Blitz and then for year after year, right
to the end, refusing to give up and go home. I felt a similar sense of responsibility to report this war.

That summer, I was invited to share a cottage on Long Island with David
Halberstam and John Sack, two gifted authors of books about Vietnam. In
East Hampton I swam, sunbathed, gave and attended parties, and was introduced to some of the most interesting people I had met outside of my profession. One of them was Michael J. Arlen, the *New Yorker* television critic
who was writing more and more critically about the quality of television
coverage from Vietnam. That summer the magazine published an essay by
Arlen called "Television's War," which impressed me as perceptive and true.
It praised the brave work of network camera crews, including Kurt Volkert
of CBS and Vo Huynh of NBC, and went on:

> Vietnam is often referred to as "television's war," in the sense that this is the
> first war that has been brought to the people preponderantly by television.
> People indeed look at television. They really look at it. They look at Dick
> Van Dyke and become his friend. They look at a new Pontiac in a commer-
> cial and go out and buy it. They look at thoughtful Chet Huntley and find
> him thoughtful, and at witty David Brinkley and find him witty. They look at
> Vietnam. They look at Vietnam, it seems, as a child kneeling in the corridor,
> his eye to the keyhole, looks at two grownups arguing in a locked room—
> the aperture of the keyhole small; the figures shadowy, mostly out of sight;
> the voices indistinct, isolated threats without meaning; isolated glimpses,
> part of an elbow, a man's jacket (who is the man?), part of a face, a woman's
> face. Ah, she is crying. One sees the tears. Two tears. Three tears. Two
> bombing raids. Four seek-and-destroy missions. Six administration pro-
> nouncements. Such a fine-looking woman. One searches in vain for the
> other grownup, but, ah, the keyhole is so small, he is somehow never in the
> line of sight. Look! There is General Ky. Look! There are some planes
> returning safely to the *Ticonderoga*. I wonder (sometimes) what it is that the
> people who run television think about the war, because they have given us
> this keyhole view; we have given them the airwaves, and now, at this critical
> time, they have given back to us this keyhole view—and I wonder if they
> truly think that those isolated glimpses of elbow, face, a swirl of dress (who
> is that other person, anyway?) are all we children can really stand to see of
> what is going on inside that room.

Arlen, it seemed to me, was doing more than compose an intelligent chronicle of television in New York in the shadow of the Vietnam War. His clear voice of reason and logic for anyone who was concerned about the conduct of the war and how it was being seen on television made him a keeper of the public conscience. His insights caught our attention, compelling us to act on them.

That same essay, "Television's War," concluded:

It is summertime now, or nearly. My kids were squabbling over bathing suits this morning, and who will learn to sail and who to ride. In summertime we cook outdoors a lot, play coronary tennis, drink, watch pretty sunsets out across the water. This summer, I will almost certainly perfect my backhand, write something beautiful (or very nearly), read *Finnegans Wake*, or something like it. This summer—already the streets outside seem quieter, more humane. A car rolls softly over a manhole cover—a small clank. All those quiet streets, all those brave middle-class apartments—and what lies beneath those manhole covers? Wires? Cables? Dying soldiers? Dying children? Sounds of gunfire? Screaming? Madness? My television set plays on, talking to itself—another baseball game, in fact. Juan Marichal is pitching to Ron Hunt. Hunt shifts his stance. Marichal winds up. The count is three and two.

I called the manager of news at CBS, Ralph Paskman, and asked if he would be interested in hiring me to go back to Vietnam. I told him I had been following the coverage in the newspapers, newsmagazines and on TV and wanted to go back and cover the war. A new executive producer was in charge of the *CBS Evening News* so there wouldn't be problems working with him. Paskman called back and said, 'How soon can you be ready?'

PART THREE

1967–1968

The air is loud with death,
The dark air spurts with fire
The explosions ceaseless are.
Timelessly now, some minutes past,
These dead strode time with vigorous life,
Till the shrapnel called 'an end!'
But not to all. In bleeding pangs
Some borne on stretchers dreamed of home,
Dear things, war-blotted from their hearts.

ISAAC ROSENBERG
"Dead Man's Dump" (1917)

SEPTEMBER 7, 1967

Artillery rounds crashed down on Con Thien like thunderbolts. North Vietnamese shells flew out of the long guns hidden in the mountains on the other side of the DMZ and swept across the sky in long looping parabolas, whooshing . . . whistling . . . screaming . . . shrieking . . . hurtling onto the Marine camp and cracking open in bursts of fire and steel. Long-range artillery, self-propelled rockets, recoilless rifles and mortars were fired at Con Thien, one angry shell after another, until the Marines in the camp counted them by the hundred, then by the thousand. The shelling became a siege. Life for the Marines at Con Thien existed largely underground. Visitors made comparisons with Verdun. It was not Verdun—fewer troops were involved and the lines were not as static—but there was a front and a rear on both sides, a no-man's-land between, and snipers, dugouts, trench lines, barbed wire, minefields, mass attacks, merciless shelling, and casualties—including shell shock—in near proportion to those at Verdun and the Somme in that earlier war. Among themselves, Marines had a name for the place. They called Con Thien "the graveyard."

Most of them had been wounded at least once, many twice, and even third and fourth wounds were not unusual that summer. Now, though, a third wound meant a mandatory ride to Dong Ha and the rear. Three wounds put you out of the show. Marines called their Purple Hearts "mistake medals." If you were out of your hole when the incoming landed, you were going to get hurt. Direct hits on bunkers didn't leave many wounded. There were no special medals for getting killed.

To look at, Con Thien was only a hump—three small hills about five hundred feet above sea level sitting alone on a wide flat stretch of scattered shrub and stunted trees a mile south of the DMZ. Its only value was its location. From the observation tower at the top of the hill, you could see everything that moved in all directions, ten to fifteen miles into North Vietnam. Otherwise it was worthless. Mud and dust. Sandbags and bunkers. Almost nothing grew on it. The only thing that thrived there were the rats.

The 3d Marine Division put an artillery base around the hill and held it with battalions from the 1st, 4th, 9th and 26th regiments, rotating them in and out every month or two, or until they suffered too many losses. In May, on the anniversary of their victory over the French at Dien Bien Phu, the North Vietnamese launched a human-wave attack against the Marines and got enough soldiers through the wire to kill forty-four Americans. They suffered horrific losses themselves, many more than the Marines, but the NVA high command was not concerned with body counts. In July, a direct hit from a 152 millimeter shell struck the battalion command post, and eleven men died in a terrible flash of fire. First Battalion, 9th Marines, was pulled out of the line. One/Nine suffered so many killed and wounded along the DMZ that summer its men called themselves "the walking dead." Death was part of daily life at Con Thien.

During the worst of the shelling, North Vietnamese gunners fired an average of 200–300 rounds a day from their bases west and north of the camp: 152 and 130 millimeter artillery (designations determined by the diameter of the shells), 140 and 122 millimeter rockets, 82 and 60 millimeter mortars. At first, senior American officers were surprised by the deadly shooting; they hadn't expected such sophisticated concentration and accuracy. Then, one day that summer, the NVA put two hundred rounds on the camp in less than fifteen minutes. Marine strategists got out their books on the People's Army siege of Dien Bien Phu and studied them more closely. French soldiers had come out of their lost war in Indochina saying the Vietnamese were the most deadly gunners in the world, and the Americans were beginning to believe it.

The Marines fought back fiercely. Artillery, mortars, tactical aircraft and B-52s blasted the mountains and coastal plain along the DMZ with the most frightful bombardment of the war, one lethal mission after another, a firestorm of bombs and shells so heavy they were counted in tons. But it was hard to measure what was accomplished. Often the targets were only guesses at where the enemy might be. The North Vietnamese were largely invisible, hidden below the jungle canopy and dug into the back sides of mountains. Their gun teams moved frequently, shifting location soon after firing, ducking into their bunkers, hiding from return fire. By the time Marines got targets spotted, organized their guns and fired counterbattery salvos, the North Vietnamese were often gone. It was like shooting into a black hole. Harassment and interdiction. The NVA absorbed everything the

Marines fired at them and kept coming back. Like the long middle years of World War I, no one was winning. Both sides were sacrificing their best young men.

Some days were worse than others. One afternoon in late September, an Associated Press reporter came out of Con Thien and stopped in Dong Ha on his way back to Danang to file his story. Ed White was an older man, a veteran of the war with a good reputation who ran the Associated Press office in Saigon. When he met me on my way to Con Thien, he took my arm in a tight hold.

'Jack, it's bad up there,' he said. 'I mean, really terrible.' His eyes were full of concern. 'Listen, don't go. I'm telling you, don't go. It's not worth it.' White's intensity surprised me. Keith Kay and I had already been in Con Thien and we knew about the danger, but it was still possible to work there. Kay and I had been the first journalists to report the siege and were committed to staying with the story. A follow-up was due.

But the biggest reason for going back to Con Thien was that Kay and I wanted to show Americans how costly the war had become, how brutal and wasteful it was, what it was doing to the individual young men who were trapped in it. For the past year in the United States I had been watching TV news coverage of the war with concern. Much of it was routine—straight, everyday reportage without the poignancy, irony or tragedy we believed was there. Television colleagues were risking their lives to go out in the field on dangerous operations and were coming back at times with powerful footage, but only occasionally. Kay and I were young, confident and arrogant enough to think our work would tell a more dramatic story more often. We knew that the majority of American TV correspondents in Vietnam were on short assignments of three to six months and were reluctant to challenge the slick upbeat propaganda of the American political and military establishment. Just as the correspondents began to understand some of the war's bewildering complexity, they went home, taking their insights with them.

The war between America and North Vietnam was in its third year. There was no end in sight; a stalemate seemed more likely. Yet, day after day, TV news reports told a familiar story: allied troops were engaging enemy forces everywhere they could find them, were grinding them down relentlessly, bombing them senseless in the North, killing them by the thousands in the South—*just look at that body count!*—measuring progress, like the establishment, by the number of people killed. The official organs of the U.S.

government claimed that the allied war effort was rooting out the VC infrastructure, pacifying more and more villages, helping to train more aggressive South Vietnamese fighting forces, and building more democratic institutions of government. Kay and I didn't believe it. We thought what was happening on the battlefields of Vietnam was more urgent, more dramatic, more terrible than the news reports being broadcast on American television. We wanted to capture on film and sound the *horror* of the war.

Our motivation was not high-minded or noble; there was nothing moral about it, not even political. Part of it was our empathy with the American troops. It seemed senseless for them to give up their lives for a war strategy that wasn't working. The more the United States escalated the war, the more the North Vietnamese increased their involvement. They had no shortage of soldiers or weapons. They controlled the time and place of most battles, even small skirmishes. They avoided combat unless they held an advantage. American patrols went out every day in search of the enemy and came back with their own dead and wounded from snipers and booby traps. Big battles got the main attention in the press, but most of the war was fought in brief small-unit engagements that the VC and NVA usually won. 'What's search and destroy?' a soldiers' joke went. 'We search, they destroy.' Of all the words American troops used to describe death in Vietnam—aced, blown away, bought it, croaked, dinged, fucked up, greased, massaged, porked, stitched, sanitized, smoked, snuffed, terminated, waxed, wiped out, zapped—the one I heard most was "wasted."

Over the course of the war, a bond was formed between some American journalists and the line infantry troops they covered. It was mutually supportive. Most soldiers and field reporters communicated well with each other, as well as the situation allowed. Although most of us were middle-class and civilian, and most troops were working-class and military, we had much in common, especially by being together in an alien land. We were about the same age, we came from the same culture, we had tough jobs to do, we endured danger and physical difficulties, we mistrusted many of the decisions of the high command. Most of us came to believe the war was an absolute failure of logic, a tragic waste of life. Being there, living it, thinking about it all the time, reporters and line soldiers were able to interpret events with special clarity. Out of our shared experiences came an understanding, an informal contract that was honored without being defined, a trade-off. When we visited them in the field, the troops made us welcome, shared their food and shelter, tried to see that we didn't get hurt, told us as much as they could about what was going on in their small sector of the war. In return, reporters told a part of the soldiers' story to the people at home. Even when there was no combat, the stories reflected the soldiers' courage, or at least their fortitude, by describing the hardships they suffered. Whether Americans who watched them on TV were proud of them, felt sorry for them or were outraged (sometimes you could feel all three), they had a pretty good picture of what it was like out there. After a while, the pictures became so familiar they were interchangeable from one war zone to another: young men in helmets with rifles and field packs walking single file through dark solid brush, knocking down elephant grass, hiking across rice fields and paddy dikes, jumping on and off helicopters, huddling under monsoon rains, stuck in mud to their ankles, fighting off mosquitoes, leeches, fire ants, flies, pressing on against the heat. Endless patrols, exhausted eyes, firefights, noise, confusion, pain, panic, wounded men, crying civilians. Medevac choppers flying over the trees. Tired faces. Homesick eyes hinting at lonely souls. And bodies, more bodies than anyone had ever seen: American bodies, Vietnamese bodies, bodies of soldiers, bodies of civilians, bodies of children, bodies in nylon bags, bodies on stretchers, bodies in ponchos, bodies piled on choppers, bodies in aluminum caskets—uniformly pale still bodies lying on the ground somewhere with ash-gray skin turning to dust.

Viewers could watch fragments of the war on television every morning and evening of every day, not on sixty or seventy channels but on the three network news programs. Usually it was a condensed version of military action from the previous twenty-four hours, any political or diplomatic news about the war, and a two- to four-minute film report from one of the network correspondents, usually a feature. Along with what they were presented by newspapers, magazines, books, speeches, films, or what they heard by word of mouth, Americans had the opportunity as never before in the nation's history to develop an informed position about a war, even if that position was *not* to think about it. Whatever confusion existed about America's cause in Vietnam, whatever argument it incited, whatever protest about its presence, one vision was unmistakably clear from the television coverage: American men, ordinary line troops, were in a strange inhospitable land being subjected to brutally hostile conditions, living and dying, enduring and hating it. Because of television and the written press, the troops got some measure of recognition for their ordeal. They knew how their story was being played in the press by letters they got from home. '*Saw a news report on the television last night from a place called Con Thien. It looked bad, Jim. I hope your company is not there. Our prayers are with you.*'

Another reason Kay and I were not worried about going back to Con Thien was that the Marines there were so casual about the shelling, so resigned to it, so outwardly loose and easy about the danger. They made it hard to take our own fears seriously. I never saw anyone play hero for the camera (their buddies would have laughed at them), but they did act relaxed in an incredibly unrelaxed situation. They were almost always cool-headed. Funny at times. Invariably sincere. There was no other way to behave.

Running into AP reporter Ed White at Dong Ha, I thought he might be exaggerating somewhat, that the fear had got to him, that he was warning us away for his own reasons. But later that day when we arrived at Con Thien, the Marines said that while White was with them that morning they took nine hundred rounds inside the perimeter in two hours.

'Six, seven, eight rounds a minute,' one Marine said. 'It didn't let up at all.'

'Charlie didn't even let us finish breakfast,' another said, laughing.

That day, September 25, Con Thien was struck by twelve hundred rounds of incoming. There had been nothing like it in the war. It *was* like Verdun.

The Marines adjusted to the shelling as best they could. Those who could not take it were evacuated to the rear with nervous breakdowns: gibbering, hysterical, or staring blindly into space, silent and immobile. Hospital reports called the cases "acute environmental reaction," as if by any other name—*shell shock, battle fatigue, traumatic shock, combat neurosis*—the diagnosis would have seemed insufficiently dispassionate. Everybody understood that battle fatigue was common to all wars and that after a few days of rest most people recovered, or appeared to recover. But knowing the history didn't make it easier to watch otherwise physically healthy young men shuffling along like half-dead zombies, dark eyes vacant, shoulders slack, the living embodiment of lost minds.

At the same time, Marines who survived at Con Thien developed senses as acute as wild animals'. They had extraordinary sensitivity to sound; their hearing warned them, like deer, when an NVA shell was closing in. New guys and journalists didn't have it. We'd hear the scream of the shell and the explosion almost simultaneously. Veterans at Con Thien picked up the faint *pop* of a round leaving its tube many miles away, tracked it moving through the air, and knew before it crashed roughly how close it was going to hit. Sometimes they got the warning from a slight compression of air in their ears, a tiny change in atmospheric pressure, a signal on the wind. They had contrived extranatural senses, a form of human sonar, superhuman perceptions of danger powered by their most primitive instincts to survive.

On one visit I was in the open when the first round came in and everyone scattered for cover. I ducked behind a low wall of sandbags on the slope of a hill, south of the CP. It was the end of the dry season and the red dirt was soft from the early rains. The earth shook every time a shell exploded. The cameraman was a French veteran of Dien Bien Phu named Gerard Py, a kind brave man with a serious limp, but I didn't know where he was at the moment and it made me feel alone and useless. No one else was in sight. The rounds cracked and the ground trembled. Then it was quiet. The first few seconds ticked off in my head. I heard sobbing. Out in the open, ten or fifteen yards away, a Marine lay on his side, his eyes closed. I went over and knelt next to him. He was young and seemed to be wounded but I couldn't see where. I shouted for a corpsman.

'Don't cry, you're gonna be okay,' I said, not knowing what else to say. The Marine looked up at me for a moment and turned his head away. He continued to cry without shame, soft low sobs from the chest.

'C'mon, man, you're gettin out of here,' I said, trying to be cheerful. His crying made me feel awkward. *Marines aren't supposed to cry,* I thought. A Navy corpsman and another Marine ran up and the corpsman quickly found the wound, a fragment in the leg. He put a compress on it. The young Marine sobbed.

"Hey, man, don't cry," I said, surprised at the words coming out of my mouth. "You're a Marine!" The wounded kid stopped crying and looked at me with an expression of genuine pity that anyone, even this strange dude in the area, could say something so ridiculously lame. He may have thought I was a new officer, a replacement fresh from the States.

'He's not scared,' the other Marine said. 'He's cryin 'cause it's his third wound. He's gotta go back to the rear. And he can't come back, not with three wounds. He's cryin 'cause he's got to leave all his buddies here.'

The first time I went to Con Thien, it wasn't my idea. In August, shortly after the start of this new tour, I was introduced to Keith Kay, a twenty-five-year-old freelance film photographer who was looking for work. None of the staff cameramen at the CBS bureau in Saigon wanted to work with me thanks to my reputation from the first tour. Kay and I met for a drink on the terrace of the Continental Hotel in Saigon. He had a low-key manner and a warped sense of humor. He said he had come to Vietnam in 1964 as a still photographer and had done some filming for ABC News. In 1965 he got his draft notice from the Army. He flew from Saigon to the States, did basic training at Fort Polk, and spent the rest of his two-year enlistment at a photo lab in New York City. He worried that the war would be over before he got out of the Army. The week he was discharged he flew back to Saigon. Kay laughed. He had a voice as deep as Basil Rathbone's. Drinking gin and tonic, smoking Camel cigarettes, we talked about covering the war. Most network correspondents and camera crews still tried to avoid nights in the field because they couldn't film in the dark and also because it was so uncomfortable. Kay said he didn't mind sleeping on the ground if it would help get a good story. He knew the wilderness, had studied forestry at college in northern California, and felt more comfortable outdoors than in. Kay was modest and relaxed about himself. I liked him immediately. We agreed to try to work together. I Corps seemed the best place to start.

At the Combat Information Bureau in Danang, we requested permission to visit Gio Linh, another combat base near Con Thien that was under heavy fire. Harry Reasoner, the veteran CBS News correspondent, had been there recently and wrote that Gio Linh seemed similar to what Verdun must have been like in World War I. The day after his visit, Reasoner flew to Saigon and sat in his room at the Caravelle. He could not stop his hands from shaking. Nothing in his life had been as terrifying, he said, as the few hours he and Kurt Volkert, the photographer, spent in Gio Linh. The shelling had been ferocious. He didn't understand how the Marines there could take it day after day. It was incredible. Coming from someone normally given to understatement, his words were believable. A waiter arrived in the room with a large gin and tonic, the first of several, and Reasoner's hands steadied. 'Be very careful if you go up there, Jack,' he said. 'You have no idea what it's like.'

A Marine NCO at the press center suggested we go to Con Thien instead. 'It's a helluva lot worse,' he said. 'Nobody from down here's been up there for months.' The main body of reporters and photographers who were based at Danang were in the field at the time, trying to cover a major battle in the Que Son Valley, southwest of Danang. Kay and I decided to go to Con

Thien. The Marines put together a multinational group to go with us. Our sound technician, Pham Tan Dan, was Vietnamese. A Marine sergeant assigned to escort us was a British citizen named Ray Wilkinson who had previously been an officer in the Australian Army and was trying to win a commission with the Marines. Wilkenson's appearance was immaculate: clean-shaven, crisply pressed utilities, polished boots, relaxed attitude. The fifth member of our group was Catherine Leroy, the diminutive photographer for *Paris-Match,* who was French. All of us were traveling and working together for the first time.

On September 7, we flew north to Quang Tri, hitched a ride farther north to Dong Ha, then drove to Cam Lo, where a convoy of trucks was getting ready to make the daily supply run to Con Thien. Seven flatbed cargo trucks were filled with ammunition, C rations, water, ice, beer and about a dozen Marines who were returning to their units at the front. One of them was Captain Ned LeRoy, 28, of Simsbury, Connecticut, a friendly, relaxed officer from 3d Battalion, 4th Marine Regiment, who was going back after a break. Three/Four was currently defending Con Thien, and Captain LeRoy said the battalion had been stationed there since July 14, a week short of two months. He was going up now to take command of Kilo Company. Security for the convoy consisted of two tanks and a couple of Ontos. The officer in charge of security was Second Lieutenant Brian K. Lile, 29, of Los Angeles. Lile, who was with India Company, said the fall monsoon was starting and when it was fully under way the road would be too muddy to travel by truck. Con Thien would be isolated. Resupply and medical evacuation would have to be by helicopter and that would be difficult in bad weather. Nobody knew what would happen. 'We'll just have to stick it out and see what happens,' he said. 'Like always.'

Kay, Dan, Cathy Leroy, Sergeant Wilkinson and I climbed on one of the trucks and introduced ourselves to the five enlisted men waiting there. They showed immediate interest in Leroy with her long blond braid poking out from the back of her helmet. I asked each of them his name, age and hometown. Lance Corporal Robert McCabe, 20, of Honolulu, had been at Con Thien for two months. PFC Robert Cassaday, 19, of Fort Wayne, Indiana, was reading a comic book. PFC William Olson, 20, of Chicago, wore a faded green utility cap with the brim turned up. PFC Norman Benton, 20, of Philadelphia, said he worked in an 81 millimeter mortar crew for Headquarters and Support Company. One Marine seemed more introspective than the others, possibly because his thirteen-month tour of duty in Vietnam was almost over. Corporal Edward Broderick, 20, of Alton, Illinois, said he was scheduled to go home in fifteen days, on the twenty-second. He had been at Con Thien for nearly two months and in that time he had carefully printed a poem in blue and red ink on the back of his flak jacket. The cloth cover was torn and stained and the words of the poem were not very clear. I asked him if he would read it for us on camera.

"I don't know that I can remember it right off," he said. "It's been a while." His manner was shy, self-conscious.

"Well, try it once on your own," I said.

Broderick took off the flak jacket, read the poem to himself, and put it back on again. "Okay," he said, more confidently. With the camera rolling, Kay signaled that he was ready. Broderick recited in a flat, even voice:

> When youth was a soldier
> And we fought across the sea,
> We were young and cold hearts,
> Of bloody savagery.
>
> Born of Indignation
> Children of our time
> We were orphans of creation
> And dying in our prime.

No one spoke. Other Marines in the truck shifted their weight. Flies buzzed.

"What made you write that poem?" I said.

"Well, just the way things are," he said.

I asked him about life on the DMZ, the morale of the troops, the NVA, the weather, going home. Broderick said he preferred to be at the front with his friends rather than back in the rear at Dong Ha or Danang. He was looking forward to getting out, he said, but he would miss his friends. Best bunch of guys he ever knew. I asked him what he thought about the war. It was a difficult question because most troops didn't talk about it often. It was hard to put into words. Even when they did, it was impossible to give a short honest answer without getting in trouble with the higher-ups. Broderick thought about it. He said he didn't think it made sense to sit in one place and let the North Vietnamese keep hitting them. Better to get out and go after them in the hills. As for the war, he said, "I guess we're better off fighting the Communists here than fighting them back in San Diego."

The convoy started off, rumbling up the narrow dirt road. The immediate terrain was fairly flat, a few undulations in the ground, not much more. The road was mainly straight. Kay took pictures of the Marines on the truck as they inserted clips into their M-16s, slapped them in tight with the palms of their hands, pulled back the bolts to slide rounds in the chambers, and checked they were safe. They looked out the sides of the truck and searched the scrub brush and low trees on the sides of the road with their eyes. The convoy rolled past the hulk of a tank, hollow and black from fire. One of the Marines came over to us and talked about the ambush ten days earlier in which the tank was hit. His voice was tense, eyes bright with the memory of the fight. He described what a furious battle it had been and how lucky they were to break through. Other Marines in the truck put on their helmets and watched the brush along the road.

The convoy arrived at Con Thien around noon and came to a halt at the end of the road. The camp was quiet. Artillery pieces were dug into the ground in deep gun pits, the barrels of the guns sticking just above circular walls of sandbags, red and white aiming stakes pointed to the north. The landscape had the appearance of a derelict field, an abandoned dump. Bunkers, barbed wire, trenches, sandbags, firing holes, wooden ammo crates, stacks of shells, C ration cases, water trucks, barrels, latrines, canvas tarps, stretchers, garbage, empty shell casings, commo wire, shovels, field packs and debris lay across the surface of the camp, all covered in ruddy red-brown dirt and drying mud. Very little moved. Life existed below ground, in holes. It reminded me of the Special Forces camp at Plei Me two years before. A few Marines moved above the surface, some of them bare to the waist, working in the bright ninety-degree air.

The driver of the truck, Staff Sergeant Joseph Wright, debated whether or not to go the rest of the way into the camp. It meant driving across several hundred yards of ground, the primary impact zone, and up a shallow grade to the base of the main hill where the CP was located. Wright, from Vista, California, was the convoy sergeant and could make the call. "Hell, let's take 'em right up," he said, and gunned the engine up the hill with us in the back. When the truck stopped, everyone jumped out and helped unload ammunition and supplies. We worked quickly. Wright took a deep breath and lit a cigar, pointing the way to the battalion command post near the top of the hill. I thanked him, shook hands and started up with Kay, Dan and the others. We walked through the lines of Echo Battery, 2d Battalion, 12th Marines, and their 105 millimeter guns. A few men worked in the pits. They stopped to watch us pass, especially Cathy, whose helmet, flak jacket, rucksack, camera bag and cameras weighed almost as much as she did. Walking up the hill, I heard their voices behind us.

'Did you see *that*?'

'Yessir, that was a *woman, a* living, breathing *female*, the real thing.'

'I don't believe it.'

'You forgot what they looked like.'

'She's jes' a bitty little thing.'

'Wonder what's up.'

'Them's photographers, that's all, don't mean nothin.'

'Aw, man, she can come and take pictures of me in my hootch, *anytime*.'

'You wish.'

Farther up the hill was a heavily fortified bunker built into the south side of the hill, near the top. The battalion executive officer, a major in his mid-thirties, waited outside the entrance. He did not seem to be expecting visitors.

"Hi," I said, introducing myself and the others. "We've come to take pictures of you winning the war up here." Sergeant Wilkenson saluted him briskly.

The major shook hands with each of us. He seemed slightly tense. "How long are you planning to stay?"

"Oh, as long as we need to get some action," I said. "A day, a week." Kay, Dan and I had agreed before we set out that we would stay as long as it took to get a good story.

The major shook his head. "You really want to spend the night up *here*?" he said. "We haven't had any press around in weeks."

'All the better for us,' Kay said, looking around the camp.

The major said to leave the equipment outside and follow him. He walked into the command bunker. Inside, the ceiling was high enough for us to stand. The bunker was constructed of foot-square wood beams, metal sheeting and sandbags. Hundreds of sandbags. Communications wire ran around the edges of the room. Kerosene lanterns provided light. A small group worked quietly at portable tables, studying charts and maps. Radio operators listened to traffic from the field. Standing upright near the center of the bunker was a large map of the surrounding terrain divided into three sections and marked with black and red grease pencil to indicate the positions of friendly and enemy troops.

"Come on, I'll give you a briefing," the major said. Pointing to the map, he showed us where the battalion's rifle companies were operating outside the camp and where the North Vietnamese held the mountains. A young Marine ran into the bunker and handed the major a message. He looked at it and said, "Kilo Company has contact with snipers." He pointed to a place of level ground on the map about fifteen hundred meters west of the camp and said, 'That's where Kilo Company is at this time.' I thought of Captain LeRoy, the Kilo Company commander whom we met on the convoy, and wondered whether he had linked up yet with his men.

Marines in the bunker looked at Dan, our soundman, with suspicion. There were no other Vietnamese in the camp. Dan looked around the command bunker without meeting their eyes. The major led everyone outside. He said the battalion commander was busy now but would be available later and introduced us to a staff officer.

"Captain Jansen will look after you," the major said, and went inside. Jansen was thin and fair with red hair and a mustache. He wore a green T-shirt with no flak jacket. Jansen's eyes glowed with intensity, as if the concentration required to survive at Con Thien had given him a greater appreciation of each moment he was alive. Gathering the group around him, he explained what to do when the incoming started.

"Above all, don't follow me when I take off down the hill," he said. "I like to be off by myself when the shells come in. I have this feeling that the round that has your number on it shouldn't kill anyone else. And I certainly don't want to get someone else's round."

Kay, Dan, Cathy and I looked around for a safe place to hide. There were holes in the ground everywhere.

"Actually," Jansen said, "the best thing for you to do is watch the guys. When they start running, you run after them."

The battalion sergeant major arrived. Kay asked if they had any food. He hadn't had much breakfast and he was hungry. 'Let's go see what we can find,' the sergeant major said and they went to look. Cathy Leroy wandered off to take still pictures. I walked alone to the top of the hill above the command bunker, passing the ruins of the colonel's shower that had taken a direct hit sometime earlier in the siege and had left broken two-by-fours, torn canvas and bits of pipe in a tangled heap. At the top of the hill, I checked my compass and looked out. To the north, I could see across the DMZ into North Vietnam. The Ben Hai River, which marked part of the border, was visible to the right. Then rolling green lowland, gentle hills and valleys, late summer haze. The air was quiet. A few miles to the west the edge of the long Annamite Cordillera began in hills and ridges that rose into a dark wall of mountains up to a mile high in the far distance. The hills were covered with unbroken thickets of jungle-green trees. To the east was Gio Linh, the Marine outpost a few miles away, and beyond that was the coastal plain, a flat expanse of shimmering white sand that threw up a wavy mirage in the heat. Finally, about twelve miles to the east lay the tranquil, gray-blue water of the South China Sea, a world away.

Nothing moved on top of the hill. The air was hot and still. I heard a young man's voice in a nearby hole talking to another Marine. "I swear," he said, excited, "I got the actual word. We're going in four days. Colonel's orders." The word passed from hole to hole, bunker to bunker. More voices. "Hey! We're getting out! We're getting out of here!"

A corporal appeared and introduced himself. He asked in a polite, welcoming way if I wanted to see the new infrared radar machine nearby. I went along. The radar device was mounted on the back of a jeep and resembled a large searchlight painted olive green. The corporal explained that the machine could shine an invisible beam of infrared light on the surrounding countryside at night. If you wore special goggles, he said, you could see the North Vietnamese moving around in the dark and bring fire down on them. Suddenly, the corporal stopped speaking and turned his head toward the DMZ. Then, in the same motion, he dropped to the ground and stared at it for a moment. "Hell," he said, getting to his feet, "no sense staying out here. Let's get in the bunker." We ran across the hilltop. A great whooshing sound like a large truck passing roared overhead, a few feet above. "Recoilless rifle," the corporal said over his shoulder, hurrying down some steps into a large underground room. The dugout was supported by big solid beams of wood a foot square and illuminated by oil lanterns and candles.

Ten or twelve men sat on their cots, reading and talking, their helmets and flak jackets off, at ease. Most were shirtless.

"Hi, I'm Jack Laurence from CBS News," I said.

"Have a beer," one of them said.

"Have a joint," someone else said. They all laughed.

"Thanks," I said, "not while I'm working." More laughter. I got out a tape recorder and switched it on. The Marines made space for me to sit on an ammo crate and gathered around, sitting and standing. I asked them what life was like in the camp. They explained that each of them had a job but mainly they were there to protect the perimeter in case of a ground attack. They hated being on the defensive, they said, it's not what they were trained to do. It made them angry to sit around all day and take all the stuff Charlie threw at them. They did not complain about the danger. They did not seem sorry for themselves. No one mentioned the fear.

"What makes you crazy enough to come up to Con Thien?" one of them said.

"Because you're here," I said. "Might as well tell the people back home how well you're doing."

That surprised them. They hadn't seen a reporter at Con Thien before and found it hard to believe anyone would take the risk to be with them just to tell the story. It didn't make sense.

Several of them judged my decision to be insane and swore to one another that nothing, no amount of money, *nothing in the world* could force them to go to Con Thien if they didn't have to. They were quite rational about it. *I* was the one who was crazy. They were pleased to have me as a visitor.

We talked about the war. I asked what they thought of the North Vietnamese. A big corporal with a southern accent replied, "When we first came up here, we used to call the enemy Victor Charlie," he said. "But now we call him Charles. *Mister* Charles."

"*Lord* Charles," another Marine said and everyone in the bunker laughed.

We talked for about twenty minutes. When the shelling stopped, the corporal suggested taking a look at the observation post. Outside, the sky was bright. An elevated tower about thirty feet high stood at the highest point of the hill. At the top of the tower was an observation post with sandbags about three feet high all around it. The corporal led the way up the ladder. Two young Marines sat inside the observation post with a field radio and a telescope next to them. Their backs were against the sandbags on the side of the tower with the top edge above their heads. Outside, someone cried, "Incoming!" and Marines on the ground ran for their holes. An explosion sounded in the distance. The field radio came alive in the watchtower.

"Do you see where those rounds are coming from?" an officer's voice said on the radio.

"No, sir, don't see a thing," one of the Marines in the tower said in reply. He smiled at the suggestion that he put his head above the sandbags and look. More explosions hit the camp. "Every time we get incoming," the Marine said, confidentially, "that lieutenant calls and asks if we see where it's coming from and every time we say, 'No, sir, don't see a thing.' Fact is, those damned guns of theirs are firing from the back slopes in the DMZ. We can't do much about them."

I wondered about the logic of having an observation post that didn't observe. The Marines had built a combat base around a hill whose main function was observation, but they didn't appear to be observing. Why provide a fixed target for the enemy to shell and sacrifice men every day to defend a position that wasn't working? The two young Marines in the OP sat back against the sandbags and lit cigarettes, the radio squawking intermittently.

When the incoming stopped, I thanked the corporal and the men in the OP, wished them luck and walked back to the command post. Lieutenant Colonel Lee R. Bendell, commanding officer of 3d Battalion, 4th Regiment, was waiting. He shook hands and welcomed me. He said they were busy now because Kilo Company was still in contact about fifteen hundred meters west of the base, on the plain between us and the mountains. Bendell was a tall, robust, pleasant-faced man in his late thirties with dark hair and the controlled manner of so many Marine officers, alert and relaxed at the same time. He offered to point out Kilo Company's position from a better vantage point around the side of the hill. Leaving the bunker, he led the way along a shelf of disused ground cut into the side of the hill. About fifty feet from the CP he came to a cleared piece of earth with five rectangular foxholes neatly dug in a line, each about five feet long, four feet wide and three feet deep. The holes looked as if they had not been used since the last war, in the early 1950s. The position faced west, toward the mountains.

Bendell looked through his binoculars toward the scattered trees and scrub on the low ground about a mile west. "You can see Kilo Company moving down there," he said, pointing to a large tree in the foreground. "Look. Three fingers to the right of this tree. See them?"

A platoon of Marines, forty to fifty men, were moving north (from left to right as we looked) spread out in a skirmish line across an open field. Suddenly, dark puffs of smoke and flame burst among them and the Marines dropped to the ground. A second or two later we heard the sharp *brraaak* . . .

brraaak . . . brraaak. . . . of the mortar rounds exploding, one after another. When the explosions stopped, the line of men got up and moved forward in a run. Some did not get up.

Bendell was joined by men from his command staff.

"Are you sure those are *our* troops?" I said. "Aren't *we* shelling *them?*"

Bendell said nothing. Captain Jansen arrived beside him with a PRC-25 field radio on his back. Another string of mortar shells exploded in the field.

Kay tried to hold his camera steady to take pictures of the action below. He cursed under his breath.

"How much of that can we get?" I asked.

"Just the smoke," he said. "The damned lens isn't long enough."

"Well, get a little of the smoke. Maybe we can use it."

"Okay, but it's not going to be very clear."

Bendell watched the movement of his Marines in the field through binoculars and listened to the radio traffic between the platoon leaders and the officer commanding Kilo Company. Bendell took the handset and called the company commander.

"Every time we move," the officer said, "we take heavy fire."

"Okay," Bendell said. "It looks like we've got the grid on the one that's getting—that you're getting the incoming from. Hold your present positions. I hope you're in holes there as best you can."

One of the platoon leaders shouted on the radio, "We're in very heavy contact here." His voice was excited.

Two jet bombers came in directly overhead, screaming at high speed, circled several times, then dived toward the ground, one at a time. The first Marine F-4 released a bomb from under its wings and pulled up out of the dive. Nothing happened.

"A dud," said Jansen.

The second F-4 dropped a pair of gleaming metal canisters along the far edge of the field where the Marines were pinned down and the canisters exploded in a brilliant flash of orange flame and oil-black smoke. The trees where they struck burst into a high wall of fire.

An officer shouted on the radio, "Tell him to make his strafing runs one hundred meters in *another* direction," great urgency in his voice.

Lieutenant Colonel Bendell spoke to him in a calm, fatherly way, asking where his platoons were located and which way he was facing.

"We're still in very heavy contact," another officer called on the radio.

"Okay, Bill," Bendell said in an even voice. "Just try to pull your people together and get them linked up to Mike Company. This is still your show."

The radio was quiet for a few seconds. Then a desperate voice, "I think we may have to have help. We might get overrun."

"All right, Bill," Bendell said. "I'm going to try to bring Mike Company up to you. I'm positioning tanks to fire in your support. But I *have* to have your coordinates—your position."

Kay and Dan stood a few feet away from Bendell, filming him as he spoke on the radio. I knelt on the ground to keep out of the picture and held the microphone up to record natural sound. A voice cried, *"Incoming,"* and everyone dived for cover. Bendell and the staff dropped to the ground. Kay, Dan and I jumped in a foxhole and ducked our heads just as a huge explosion burst on the other side of the hill. I looked up. Bendell and his men were flat on the ground, their heads pressed against the dirt. Only the olive-green backs of their flak jackets and helmets showed. The radio chattered. No one moved.

"We've *got* to get some of this," I whispered to Kay. He got the camera up on his shoulder and focused on the backs of the Marines on the ground. The noise of the camera alerted Jansen, who turned, saw us filming and told everyone in the command group to get up. Bendell got in a foxhole and put one foot on the edge, leaned forward, and studied the battlefield through his binoculars. Explosions came closer. Jansen tried to get the people in the command group organized into foxholes, assigning them here and there. Seeing a space, I moved into the hole with Bendell and Jansen. Taking the microphone, I told Kay and Dan to get ready for a quick on-camera. Several shells landed with loud, cracking explosions.

With Bendell and Jansen behind me, I looked into the lens and said: "You don't spend long in Con Thien before the action starts. Some time ago, two companies from the battalion defending this outpost ran into enemy contact, and it has become increasingly heavy. Colonel Bendell is watching the action less than a mile away and moving his troops into position."

A lieutenant came out of the command bunker and ran up. It was the air liaison officer, First Lieutenant Joe Conlon. He was trying to figure out where to adjust the position of the air strikes.

"Okay, look," Bendell said, pointing. "Do you see where that smoke is?"

"Yes, sir," said Conlon.

"That far, where the shells landed, is about three hundred meters," Bendell said. "Right where that big tree is out there, three hundred to four hundred meters southeast."

Conlon said he understood and ran back into the bunker to radio the pilots.

Shells fell on the camp with great cracking *karrummps*, one after another. Fighting continued on the plain below. Jet airplanes streaked overhead, blasting the battlefield. Near the top of the hill, odd buzzing noises zipped by. Bendell seemed distracted by them, as if they were flies or mosquitoes.

"Bullets," Jansen said. "Don't worry about them. They're almost spent."

The executive officer, the major, appeared at a run. "I've got to have those coordinates!" he shouted. "I can't fire if I don't have coordinates!"

Bendell called the company commander on the radio and asked again for his position. After a moment, the officer replied, "I didn't have my map, but I have it now. I'm trying to figure where we are."

As the major ran back toward the command bunker, his foot caught on the sound cable between the microphone and the sound amplifier. The mike went flying. "God damn wire," he grumbled, untangling his boot.

"Look, some of you people just move on back," Bendell said.

Jansen turned to me. "You're all right where you are," he said.

Kay stopped shooting and opened the side of his camera, pulling at bits of film stuck in the gears. He cursed, ran to the command bunker and returned with his black changing bag. He got down in the foxhole and removed the exposed film from the magazine and replaced it with rawstock. It took several minutes. Incoming shells landed directly in the camp. When he was finished, I asked him to shoot another on-camera bridge. Kay nodded his head, framed and focused the shot, and started to roll. Holding the microphone, I said, "That whistling sound you hear is incoming artillery fire. You may actually be able to see it landing."

Kay heard what I said and panned the camera to the left, widening the frame and changing focus. Just then, several shells exploded inside the perimeter of the camp, one after another, the last one closest to us.

"That one landed about 150 yards away," I said.

Bendell looked around. "Let's make sure we're spread out here," he said.

Kay ducked into the foxhole and began tearing at his equipment again.

"God damn camera won't work," he said while trying to fix it. "Got knocked around too much on the truck coming up." Then he had it going again.

Bendell stood in his foxhole talking calmly on the radio, trying to get his two companies linked up. A pair of helicopters landed on the edge of the camp and waited with their rotors spinning while wounded Marines were loaded aboard on stretchers. There were more than twenty. Kay put down his camera again. It wouldn't work.

"What is it?" I said.

"Battery pack," Dan said. "It's out of power." They went to work on it.

A shell exploded and the ground shook with terrific force. With a broken camera and nothing to do, I felt nervous. "It's okay," Jansen said. "It's not close enough to hurt you, and the next one won't be on top."

Kay looked up and said the camera was dead.

"Are you sure?" I said.

"I'm sure."

Jansen heard us. "If you want to get out of here, you can go back with the convoy," he said.

I thought for a moment. We had been at Con Thien for only a few hours and did not have enough film for a complete story. I had plenty of information but not enough film. We had the scenes of the convoy, the poet-corporal Broderick reading his poem, some incoming, Colonel Bendell directing his troops in battle and a couple of on-camera bridges. We needed more elements to make a beginning, a middle and an end. But there was no sense staying if we couldn't film. "Okay, I guess we will," I said to Jansen. I was relieved to be getting out.

The incoming stopped for a few minutes. Marine artillery opened fire in support of Kilo and Mike Companies. Cathy Leroy, who had been shooting still pictures from another foxhole, said she was ready to go back to Dong Ha; she had had enough. Her long Gallic nose was sweating. The group said good-bye to Lieutenant Colonel Bendell. I promised to return soon. Captain Jansen formed us into a line, saying to keep ten feet apart and follow him. He walked at a brisk pace down the side of the hill. Kay, Dan, Cathy, Sergeant Wilkinson and I followed. About halfway down, the colonel called out, "That's a real fine squad you got there, Jansen." The red-haired captain turned, smiled as if embarrassed, and waved.

At the bottom of the hill, a shell came over with a whooshing-ripping noise, tearing the humid air. We dived into a mortar gun pit, falling on top of one another, knees and elbows in each other's necks. Getting up a minute later, Sergeant Wilkinson brushed the dirt from his utility uniform, tucked the trouser legs into his boots and pulled the crease straight with his fingers.

Jansen sat on the wall of sandbags at the edge of the mortar pit. He had not taken cover. "I'll know when it's going to hit us," he said.

Another shell exploded, much closer, and all of us ducked except Jansen. The blast started a fire in a stack of wooden crates about thirty to forty yards away. The crates contained 105 millimeter shells. Marines ran away from the fire in all directions.

One of them rushed past yelling, "If that stuff blows, we're dead!" It was Joe Wright, the convoy sergeant.

An artillery lieutenant hurried by, shouting. "Get back! Get back! It's going to blow!" He jumped in a hole.

Marines climbed out of their bunkers and ran for safer cover. A thin young man dashed up to the flames with a fire extinguisher, hopped up and down on his feet trying to make it work, then gave up and dashed away.

Kay and Dan had got the camera working again and were taking pictures.

"Everybody in the hole," an officer yelled. Cathy Leroy and Sergeant Wilkinson ran a few yards and disappeared into a small bunker. Jansen sat on some sandbags, watching. I waited next to him. No one went near the fire.

"For Christ's sake, *somebody's* got to put it out!" Sergeant Wright yelled.

"*Incoming*," a distant voice shouted.

"Now," said Jansen. He sprinted toward the bunker and jumped in. I followed close behind. A mighty explosion shook the ground, then another. Inside, dirt fell out of the sandbags overhead and trickled onto our helmets and shoulders. Then, for a few seconds, it was still. The bunker was small, built for two or three people, with a low ceiling that forced everyone to sit on the ground. At one end of the bunker a few feet away, the young artillery lieutenant struck a match and lit a kerosene lantern. Next to him Sergeant Wilkinson cleaned the dirt from his clothes and straightened his creases. Jansen sat beside them looking weary, as though he had been through the procedure so often he found it boring. Cathy sat near the entrance facing me. Kay and Dan were outside. I looked out the hole at the landscape. Nothing moved, no sign of anyone, the fire still burning in the ammunition crates.

Suddenly the air screamed. Incoming shells crashed on the camp. Every few seconds something exploded. The artillery shrieked and whistled. The rockets rumbled over with noise like a freight train rushing through a tunnel. Then thundercracks: *Brraaack! Brraaack! Brraaack!* The earth danced.

Sitting in the bunker, feeling the ground tremble, listening to the storm of exploding steel, it seemed like the end of the world, the end of all conscious thought. The seconds between explosions stretched into an infinity, holding, suspended, beyond measure of time. No one spoke. Jansen's face was unsmiling, drawn and serious for the first time, almost grave. My fear focused on whether the next shell was going to land on top of us. I sat with the palms of my hands pressed against my ears and looked across at Cathy. One of her cheeks was smudged with dirt and her forehead was sweating. Her fingers twirled the loose hair at the end of her long blond braid. After one close explosion, she put the braid in her mouth and bit it. She was usually fearless, as tough as a Marine some said, but now her large brown eyes were wide, white, defenseless. She stared at me as if to ask for assurance and I smiled at her for a second. Our connected sight held us like a lifeline, our faces reflecting each other's fear, binding us in the intimacy of the doomed. The one comfort was the knowledge that we were not alone. All of us were going to come through this or all of us were not. If we were going to die, we would die at once, together. Sharing a common fate made the fear more bearable.

The barrage went on. The tension inside the bunker was tight as a gallows knot. My nerves vibrated wildly, my heart thumped, breathing was hard. My tongue tasted tiny grains of dirt from the sandbags. The bunker smelled of kerosene and sweat. Nothing before had been so frightening. At the graveyard I had expected to die; here I still had a chance. The Marines in the hole tried not to show fear. When one heavy explosion shook the bunker, I saw a shadow cross Jansen's face, a faint hint of frailty, a look in his eyes that suggested uncertainty, but only for an instant. Then he looked grave again. It was as if each close shell chipped a fragment from the foundation of his Marine Corps spirit, attacking his will to endure, challenging his private inner resolve at the place where his warrior self coexisted with his temporal vulnerable self. Each time his Marine officer identity slipped, Jansen pulled it back. He saw me watching and smiled.

Scared, uncertain, helpless, I closed my eyes and said a prayer.

Whenever I was in a jam like this, wherever my life was on the line, I reached inside for my boyhood faith, for the will of God to get me out of it, and made promises to be good, to be honest, to be kind to others, to be free of sin. Later, though, the memory of the fear and the memory of the prayer got separated from one another, so that when the danger was over I was not conscious of the deals I had made and the promises I was meant to keep.

Eventually, the shelling stopped. It had lasted about fifteen minutes but it felt longer. One at a time, we climbed out of the hole. Sergeant Wright walked toward us, away from the fire. He carried a five-gallon water can in his hand.

"Fire's out," he said matter-of-fact, discarding the can.

Kay and Dan appeared, smiling. Their fatigues were spattered with dirt.

'I think I've got a great shot,' Kay said. His eyes were happy. 'We were over there with a couple of grunts. I was rolling when a shell went off. A big one. I got most of it in the frame. Then I panned to this guy on the ground taking cover. As I zoom in on his face, you can see he's trying to whistle. Like he's not afraid. But he can't do it. His mouth is too dry.' Kay laughed and pursed his lips and made a dry blowing sound. 'Man, it was funny. I hope it comes out on film okay.'

Sergeant Wright said, "If you're all coming with me, let's get the hell out of here." He ran toward a jeep about fifty yards away. Kay, Dan, Cathy and Sergeant Wilkinson ran after him. I shook hands with Captain Jansen and thanked him for helping us.

'When's it going to be on TV?' he said.

'In three or four days,' I said, 'if we've got enough for a story.'

'Well, good luck to you. Thanks for coming.'

'See you next time,' I said, turned and ran after the others.

The jeep was already moving, Kay in the front with his camera, Dan and the others crowded in the back. I dived in the back as Wright pulled away and bumped my helmet on the crossbar holding the canvas top. My legs stuck out the tailgate.

"Everybody in?" Wright shouted. He spun the wheels in the soft ground.

"Incoming," a faraway voice cried.

Wright gunned the engine and turned the jeep sharply, twisting the steering wheel hard to the left, skidding in a four-wheel slide. Two shells fell close by. "Don't worry," Wright shouted, "We're going to make it." No one else spoke. Looking out the back, we saw the horizon whirl as the jeep hit a bump and all four wheels left the ground. More explosions. Concussions rocked the jeep. "God damn it, they're trying to get us," Wright yelled, "but they're gonna have to catch us!" He put his foot all the way down on the accelerator and sped through the camp. "Hey, kid," he said over his shoulder. He reached into the back of the jeep with one hand and picked up a Thompson submachinegun. "Know how to use this?" he said, handing it to me. I took the weapon, looked at it for a moment, and passed it to Sergeant Wilkinson who

made it safe and put it on the floor. A shell landed not far behind. The jeep
raced through the camp and came to the perimeter where the road south to
Cam Lo began. The seven trucks from the morning convoy were waiting,
Marines standing beside them. Wright brought the jeep to a fast stop and
shouted, "Everybody onto the trucks! Let's get the hell outta here!"

Kay, Dan, Cathy LeRoy, Sergeant Wilkinson and I climbed onto a truck
near the front of the convoy. Marines helped us up. The truck moved off
before everyone was aboard, and we pulled in Marines who were hanging off
the sides and tailgate. They armed their rifles and sat down on the metal bed
and looked out the sides. The trucks followed Sergeant Wright's jeep at the
front of the convoy, hurtling along the road at high speed. About halfway,
gunfire cracked from the bush on the right side of the road, a few single
shots at first and then automatic weapons—heavy, persistent. Muzzle flashes
from the rifles were visible about 250 yards away. Marines on the truck fired
back into the brush on full automatic. One of the trucks behind was hit and
crashed at the side of the road. The cab caught fire. Another truck stopped
beside it. Marines swarmed over the burning truck and pulled two wounded
men out of it. Then they sped away. No one was left behind.

The convoy came to an artillery post between Con Thien and Cam Lo
called C-2 and stopped. Sergeant Wright got out of his jeep and came over.
His right hand was bleeding, his face flushed. "I've had enough today," he
said. "I'm not goin any farther." He waved the rest of the convoy on toward
Cam Lo. Cathy Leroy went with it. "Come on and stay with us tonight,"
Wright said. "I'll buy you boys a beer." It was six o'clock. The sun was falling
behind the mountains.

Wright led us to a large half-empty tent where we dropped our packs and
gear. Kay and Dan left to find a generator to charge their camera batteries.
Wright went to get a beer. I sat on the edge of a cot, opened my notebook
and began to write the voice-over narration for the film. Thinking of the pictures Kay shot at the start of the convoy earlier in the day, I tried to write a
simple narrative that would complement the film.

"The convoy to Con Thien goes once a day and it does not stay long," I
wrote. "It is the only source of supply for the Marine outpost on the Demil-
itarized Zone, and it rides the only road that goes there. The convoy carries
food, water and ammunition, and returns the few men who have been lucky
enough to get away for a few days. The Marines say the worst part of a pass
from Con Thien is coming back."

At this point, I thought, the editor could insert the scene of Corporal Broderick reading his poem and the interview with him. Sergeant Wright came into the tent with a can of cold beer and gave it to me. I thanked him, took a sip and continued writing: "The enemy is one hazard, nature another. Two days of rain have nearly washed out the soft dirt road. It will be impassable within a month, with the coming of the fall monsoon."

Another break here, I thought, for film of the convoy's arrival at the camp to be used. Then: "The convoy arrives safely, unloads quickly, and turns around, because the camp is continually under artillery attack." I left a space for the on-camera bridge from the hill with Lieutenant Colonel Bendell directing the battle and the shells falling in the camp. How to describe the incoming? An image came to mind of a wooden coffin being made. "Every few minutes, and sometimes every few seconds, the guns go off, their guns and our guns, whistling and pounding with the incessant, methodical efficiency of a carpenter hammering nails. In the battle outside the camp, at least twenty men are killed on both sides, perhaps a hundred wounded, as each recovers its casualties quickly and prepares for the night of shelling, and the following day of fighting."

When the narration was finished, Sergeant Wright gave us another beer and we ate supper. I was too restless to sleep, so I wandered through the camp. C-2 was a small base with one or two artillery batteries and a few tents. Its guns supported Con Thien and the rifle companies that maneuvered in the field to the west and north. Coming upon the fire control center —a large, well-fortified bunker—I went inside. A young artillery officer stood in the middle of the room talking on the radio to a Marine officer in the field who was senior to him. The field officer was commanding a unit that was under attack by a larger force of North Vietnamese. There was tension on the radio between the two officers. The senior officer did not know the coordinates for his location. The artillery officer refused to fire the battery's guns in support until he had a map reference. He was a cool efficient young man, alert but not nervous. A map of the area with grid lines and coordinates was spread across a table in the center of the room. Kerosene lanterns hissed. Two tired-looking operators sat in front of their radios listening to squawk and hiss between calls. It was apparent that the night battle was not going well. The air in the bunker was charged.

The field officer shouted on the radio, angry, the noise of gunfire and incoming mortars blasting in the background.

'Give us your location and we'll shoot,' the artillery officer said evenly.

'I'm sittin here in a shit sandwich and you're back there sleepin in your nice cozy bunker!' the field officer shouted.

'We fire twenty-four hours a day,' the artillery officer said, his voice calm. 'Around the clock.' Weary looks of the radio operators confirmed it. 'You give us your coordinates and we'll give you all the support we've got.'

'Ah, lemme see,' the field officer said. 'Got my God damn map upside down.' A minute later he came back with the grid reference for his position. He no longer shouted. Explosions sounded in the background. The artillery officer wrote down the coordinates, repeated them on the radio to confirm, and calculated the distance and direction to the target with a slide rule. He worked quickly. Then he called the orders for a fire mission. 'Elevation . . . deflection . . . charge . . .' The eyes of the radio operators turned up in faint smiles. In a minute or two all the battery's guns outside the bunker were firing.

The next morning at Charlie-2, a tall suntanned Marine saw me standing alone by the road and asked if I was a reporter. He was about twenty years old and was exceptionally cheerful. 'I've got a great story for you,' he said in the intense happy manner of someone who had been in danger so long that just being alive made him naturally high. He said he was in the crew of an amtrack. Every night, he said, his crew drove the track into no-man's-land up near the DMZ to resupply engineer units working on the McNamara Line, a defensive barrier that was supposed to impede North Vietnamese infiltration and was named for Defense Secretary Robert McNamara, who had ordered it. Its actual code name was Practice Nine.

'Oh, you really ought to come out with us one of these nights,' the Marine said. 'It's really scary. I mean when Charlie starts shootin at us and the rounds are pingin off the hull, my asshole gets to puckerin like a goldfish's mouth, you know?' He smiled. 'We got plenty of room in the track if you want to come.'

I said we needed lights to film at night. He thought about it and said it wouldn't be a good idea to have any kind of illumination on the Z.

'Charlie ain't never gonna let us build that thing,' he said. 'Every time the guys get a bulldozer or somethin into position, Charlie brings a shitstorm down on them. Rockets, mortars, snipers, the whole nine yards. Can't work like that. Too much shit. Two, three guys gettin it every day. Don't care what anybody in Washington says. All they're doin is gettin a lot of good Marines and Seabees killed. It's a fuckin *meat grinder* up there.'

As I was walking away he said, 'You be sure an tell the people back home what's goin on, ya hear?' I promised him I would.

The guns at C-2 were screened by a low ridge. To the west, mountains rose above five thousand feet, cool dark green in the early light. Kay and Dan came up and said the camera was working; they had charged the battery overnight. We walked to the top of the ridge and looked up the road at a company of Marines with tanks and amtracks who were moving off the road from right to left into an open field of scattered brush about a hundred yards away. The company was fresh, from 3d Battalion, 26th Regiment, about two hundred men. The armored force was moving northwest of C-2, away from the road. Advancing toward the mountains, the Marines had gone a few hundred yards when an explosion burst in the middle of the formation, then another. Everyone ran for cover. Kay, Dan and I found a shallow trench along the ridge and ducked into it. Looking north past the Marines in the field below us, I could see flashes of light sparkling from the side of a mountain several miles away.

'Keith, look!' I said. 'You can see the muzzle flashes of the rockets! Right there, look!'

Kay aimed his camera at the mountain and looked through the viewfinder. Shells shrieked through the air. Explosions shook the ground. The guns at C-2 were silent. I wondered why there was no counterbattery fire. *Isn't anybody watching?* I thought.

'It's no good,' Kay said. 'All we can get is some of the smoke from the explosions. I need a longer lens.' The three of us were crowded into the small trench, shoulder to shoulder. I felt frustrated that we couldn't get any more of the shelling than the smoke. Rockets kept falling.

'Let's go down there with the Marines,' I said.

'Are you crazy?' Kay said. 'They're getting slaughtered.'

'Best stay here,' Dan said. Another shell landed among the Marines. A tank was hit and began to burn.

After several minutes of incoming rockets, Marine drivers gunned the engines of their tanks and amtracks, turned around and raced across the field back toward the road. The shelling subsided. Kay, Dan and I got out of the trench and ran up the road to meet the tracks coming back toward C-2.

Between twenty and thirty wounded Marines lay on top of the armor. Navy corpsmen attended them, cutting away clothing, applying field dressings, giving injections, inserting IV needles. Kay rolled film on a corpsman who was working with intense concentration on a wounded Marine on top of an amtrack. The corpsman looked up for a moment and saw another medic a few feet away who must have been an old friend. He shouted the other man's name, reached over, smiled and shook hands. Then both of them turned back to the wounded Marines in their care and continued their work. The rifle company pulled back to the road. The shelling stopped. The tops of the tanks and amtracks were covered with wounded Marines and their blood.

We got back to Danang before dark. I sat at the small desk in the CBS News barracks room at the press center and set up a portable typewriter. Kay brought me a beer. "The next day on the road to Con Thien," I wrote, "another American company is shelled in an open field a hundred yards ahead, again with amazing accuracy, this time with rockets. One tank is hit, a tread knocked apart, and the rest of the tanks, vulnerable to rockets, pull back out of range. They carry some of the casualties from the rocket attack —some of the young men Corporal Broderick wrote his poem about." I figured the editors could insert a reprise of the poem "When youth was a soldier . . ." if they wished. When the narration was written, Kay loaded the camera and, with Dan monitoring the sound level, recorded the voice-over track on film. A few days later, on September 11, 1967, it arrived in New York. Four minutes of film were shown on the *CBS Evening News*. Afterward, we received a cable from Walter Cronkite complimenting us on our work.

WINTER 1967

The war went on and on. All through the autumn and winter, from the Delta to the DMZ, Americans and Vietnamese fought each other. They fought mercilessly in ambushes, sniper attacks, bombings, firefights, brief encounters, night engagements, sieges, set-piece battles—in every possible way they could conceive of killing one another. They used minefields, booby traps, assassination, shelling, carpet bombing, torture, terrorism and execution among other methods. Thousands died, thousands more were wounded, many for life. Millions were made homeless. The destruction was devastating. And yet, for all of the effort, for all of the courage and energy and cunning that went into the fighting, nothing was gained. No one was winning, though both sides claimed victory. Only the losses were real. Military, political and government officials in Washington, Saigon and Hanoi talked about winning the war in terms that seemed to ignore reality. In truth, the war was a death machine. Though some in the press corps saw through the official deception, others did not. I found myself more and more estranged from these colleagues, unable to accept their point of view. I was seeing more of the horror than they were, which was affecting *my* point of view.

Khe Sanh was surrounded and put to siege. The pressure on Con Thien lifted. The mountains around Dak To turned into terrible battlefields. Loc Ninh became a bloodbath. Kay, Dan and I went to the worst places we could find and did stories about them. We also visited the 1st Cavalry Division, whose battalions were pushing farther and farther north from An Khe, taking over territory that was once the responsibility of the Marines who were now tied down defending their border outposts. We were being shot at or shelled an average of once a week, sending home a steady flow of combat stories for the *Evening News*. Between times we rested, at our hotel in Saigon or at the press center in Danang.

The Combat Information Bureau at Danang had expanded in size, importance and comfort in the year that I was home in the States. More offices had been built for the growing staff of Marine Corps information personnel, the bar and restaurant had been refurbished and expanded, a larger basketball court constructed, and a boat dock built for the colonel's launch. Colonel Fraser, the commander of the CIB, used a motorboat to travel back and forth across the Danang River to the headquarters of the 3d Marine Amphibious Force and did not have to negotiate the perilous Danang traffic. Some in the press corps felt sorry for Colonel Fraser. He was not happy with his assignment supervising the civilian and military press, and he said so frequently. He was one of many American colonels across Vietnam who were restless in their headquarters jobs. They wanted to be leading troops in battle. Colonel Fraser longed to lead an infantry regiment, to get out into the field, to wage war. In Danang his private quarters were furnished as comfortably as at a base in the United States: private telephone line, air conditioner, American fixtures and lighting, solid mattress—many of the comforts of home. But Fraser told journalists that he hated running the CIB, would give it up in a minute for a field command. Like other senior officers with desk jobs, he condemned the luxuries of civilian life in wartime (though he availed himself of their comforts) and aspired to the responsibilities and challenges of combat.

Kay, Dan and I became semipermanent fixtures in Danang through the months of September, October, November and December. When we heard that the First Cav was fighting daily small-unit battles with the Viet Cong south of Danang, we rode an Army medevac that was going in to pick up wounded from one of the fights near Hoi An, not far from the coast. As soon as we landed, Kay started rolling film. The platoon commander, Lieutenant Jamie Bass, was surprised when he saw that the medevac had dropped off an American camera team. Caught in the middle of directing the fight, he cried over the noise of battle, "You guys are on your fucking own!" Kay managed to get his warning on film. Bass ignored us and got on with his work. Viet Cong snipers had killed a young, red-headed soldier who was new to the platoon, so new that no one seemed to know his name. Kay shot close-up film of the American soldiers firing and maneuvering, running over hedgerows from rice paddy to rice paddy, and helicopter gunships blasting the hamlet with rockets and machinegun fire. Later, the body of the dead soldier was dragged through a rice paddy to be evacuated. Back in Danang, I wrote the narration for the story, ending it over that long closing shot. "There are a hundred small battles like this one that are fought every day in Vietnam," I said. "They are called firefights, and they have little meaning for anyone, except the red-headed kid who was killed here."

Kay and I spent Christmas in Con Thien. We had teamed up with a new sound technician named Chanh, a tall, skinny cheerful young man who was apparently fearless. If we weren't afraid to go to Con Thien, he seemed to believe, then he wasn't going to be. A new battalion had taken up the positions left by the old one. Everything seemed more worn and battered than it had been before. The commander gave us a small sandbagged bunker for the duration of our stay, which turned out to be four days, but nothing dramatic was happening at the base. No incoming rounds fell while we were there. The Marines were grateful that the North Vietnamese seemed to be observing a Christmas truce. The biggest drama was our nighttime fight with a platoon of rats, permanent residents of the old bunker, who clambered over us at will and kept us awake trying to get in our food rations.

On New Year's Eve, Colonel Fraser and some of his staff went around the press compound at Danang visiting the newspaper, wire service and TV network billets to wish each of the journalists who were there a happy New Year. It was a thoughtful gesture. Fraser rarely socialized with journalists because he didn't trust us. There had been no warning that he was coming. When he got to the CBS hootch near the center of the compound, a party was under way. It was in a late stage, having started in the afternoon. Six or seven reporters and photographers lolled on the beds, their boots off, listening to music tapes. The air in the room was saturated with pot smoke, layers of blue-gray smoke hanging in the diminished light. A couple of wire clothes hangers decorated with colored lights in the shape of a Christmas tree were hanging from one of the walls. Otherwise, except for a calendar and a poster or two, the room was bare. The colonel, a lean slender man with gray hair and a brusque military temperament, opened the door and walked inside. He wore an immaculately clean pressed uniform with silver eagles shining on the shoulders. In the same moment he began his greeting, all his senses were assaulted by a blast of sweet-smelling pot smoke, the noise of rock music blaring from the tape deck, and the sight of a half dozen long-haired journalists reclining on the beds, most of them zonked out of their minds on marijuana.

He gasped.

'Gentlemen . . .' he said, trying to clear his throat, his lungs trying to find clean air instead of pot smoke.

'God, what is that *smell?*' he said.

'Grass, sir,' one of the photographers said, his voice innocent. Everyone sat up.

'*Grass?*' the colonel said.

'Yes sir, grass, you know, weed.' Someone near the back of the room giggled.

The colonel said nothing. His jaw hung open. His eyes swept the room.

Someone switched off the music. An awkward silence followed. Some of the young men got on their feet. The colonel's deputy—a large, unpredictable major we all knew as "Mad Mike"—said something in a low voice.

'I don't believe it,' the colonel said, turning to face the major. The major nodded his head, affirmative.

'What does it do?'

'I think it makes them silly,' the major said, 'like children.'

Someone giggled.

The colonel stood in silence, his arms at his sides. Looking around the room, he appeared to consider the information, turning it over, memorizing faces, filing them away. Then he pulled up to his full five feet eight or nine inches and pushed his shoulders square.

'Well, gentlemen, as I was saying,' he said, 'I came here to wish you good luck and God's blessings in 1968.'

'Thank you, sir,' the reporters said, practically in unison, their eyes blood-red, their faces blank. 'Same to you.' We meant it.

The colonel looked at the group with an expression between disgust and pity, as though he felt sympathy for this pathetic group of drug-addict hippies who called themselves journalists. *What a sorry-looking bunch of young men,* he seemed to say to himself. He turned briskly and left with the others. The door closed behind them.

The young men bounced back on the beds laughing.

'Oh, did you see the *look* on his face when he walked in?' one of them said.

'He freaked, he positively freaked!' another said.

'Man, he looked like he'd been *gassed.*'

'Now he knows what it's like.'

'Hey,' someone said from the back. 'Do you think we've invented a new weapon?'

'Yeah. Pot gas.'

'I've got the headline: Colonel Gassed by Enemy Press!'
'What a gas!'
'Oh, no.'
The music started to play again.
'He was afraid to *breathe*.'
'Maybe he got a contact high.'
'Oh, I hope so. He could use it.'
'Yeah, the colonel could definitely use a little mind expansion.'
'You kidding? He's out there now doing deep breathing exercises.'
'Fifty on the floor.'
'I bet he can do 'em.'
'Hope the major didn't get a hit.'
'Yeah, you're right. Can you see it? Mad Mike stoned? On the rampage again?'
'Remember the night he got drunk and shot up the restaurant?'
'The ceiling's still got the holes in it.'
A noise came from outside. 'Hey, better lock the door.'
One of the reporters got up and turned the key.
'What do you think they're gonna do?'
'Kick us out?'
'Oh, I hope so.'
'Really, man, what d'ya think the Old Man'll do?'
'Probably write up a report. Put our names down.'
'Oh, God, there goes my career in government.'
'Never get in the VFW now.'
'Better hide the dope.'
'It's almost all gone.'
'Well, let's finish it then.'

One month later, on January 30, a much larger, more sustained party took place at the press center. It was the eve of the Tet holidays and a truce in the war had been declared for a few days, or so we believed. With the tension off, almost everyone, including many of the Marines who worked at the CIB, got mildly drunk or high or both. The celebration continued until dawn. No one imagined the VC and North Vietnamese were entering the city under cover of dark and were about to launch the largest, boldest attack of the war.

Very late in the night, a group of young Americans—reporters, photographers, Marines—got together on the boat dock alongside the river to sing folk songs and play makeshift musical instruments. These included a guitar, a harmonica, and several partially filled bottles that produced random notes not necessarily in key. One of the Marines found a washboard used by the housekeepers and played percussion. Someone wrapped a piece of tissue around a comb and made a mouth harp out of it. A kazoo appeared. The group created a collection of sounds in loose imitation of a jug band, stronger on volume and tempo than harmony, and played enthusiastically into the night. Overhead, flashing lights fired the sky.

The music attracted the attention of a young American woman who walked over to the group and asked politely if she could join in. She was thin-figured in civilian clothes with brown hair and fine skin, somewhere in her mid-twenties, and she seemed good-natured and happy. She said she worked for one of the U.S. government agencies and was having a night away from her usual crowd. None of us had met her before and we were surprised that she knew the words of every folk song any of us had ever heard and could sing them in a voice as pure and sweet as a nightingale's.

> Michael, row the boat ashore,
> Hallelujah!
> Michael, row the boat ashore,
> Hallelujah.

In the background, just above the city, white flares hissed over the rooftops. Flaming red-orange tracers raced into the sky. Rapid gunfire cracked in the distance.

"Those ARVN guys really know how to celebrate Tet, don't they?" someone said. The others agreed. It was the first time most of them had experienced a Vietnamese New Year and they assumed the gunfire coming from Army headquarters in downtown Danang was part of the festivities and not the beginning of a surprise attack and a long desperate gunfight that went on through the night.

> Jump down, spin around, pick a bale of cotton,
> Jump down, spin around, pick a bale of hay.

Oh, Lordy! Pick a bale of cotton.
Oh, Lordy! Pick a bale of hay.

The pretty young woman's eyes sparkled in the spectacular light. Her face radiated warmth. As she sang—sometimes the lead, sometimes in harmony—she smiled and looked into the eyes of the men around her, one at a time, holding each gaze as long as a minute, beguiling us with her musician's voice and her luminous eyes. There was no pretension in her eyes as she gently flirted with us, enjoying the moment. Relaxed and at peace, she led the singing with effortless modesty. It was apparent she had not been brutalized by the war. She was unspoiled, innocent. Her nature seemed to suggest that simple grace and beauty were not entirely lost in this violent place, that even amid the barbarity it was possible to be reasonable, humane, honest, warm. Watching the bright colors flash overhead, feeling the reflection of her charm, trying to sing harmony with her perfectly pitched musical voice, I felt enchanted. She made each of us feel worthy of her attention, valuing our company, delighting us. She was an angel. At dawn—tired, groggy, slightly inebriated—she left.

The Tet Offensive was under way. Kay and I went to Quang Tri for a night, got no story, and went to Hué, where we got the story and, eventually, I got the cat.

MARCH 1, 1968

Howling in protest, Mèo flew from Danang to Saigon imprisoned in a cardboard box. He was not a polite passenger. The kitten tried ceaselessly to escape, poking a foot through one of the air holes, twirling it in space, trying to catch something with his claws. Each time he put his paw outside the box, Ri or Dan slapped it with their fingers, laughing when it withdrew. Mèo pressed one of his eyes to the hole to see what was menacing him. The blue unblinking eye was wild with rage.

Ri and Dan had accepted the kitten as part of our entourage. They regarded him as an amusement, a plaything, not to be taken seriously, no matter how much he howled. He was not allowed to roam the plane. I worried that he might make his way to the cockpit and distract the pilots, cause them to make a mistake and force us to crash. No matter that they had probably flown through ground-to-air fire at least once during the Tet Offensive and had survived *those* distractions without a crash. Logic wasn't working for me anymore. I was too short, too paranoid about any imaginable danger to take chances. We were flying in a C-130, and the throbbing noise almost overrode the howling of the kitten.

Tan Son Nhut airport was hot, hectic and seriously at war. Fighter-bombers, cargo planes, reconnaissance aircraft, courier flights and helicopters took off and landed every thirty to forty seconds, one after another, sometimes simultaneously, coming and going on the twin runways with regular efficient purpose. Tan Son Nhut was the busiest airport in the world.

At last Saigon appeared to be taking the war to heart. For years the capital had held itself aloof from the fighting. Occasionally it had suffered the shock and carnage of bombings and other acts of terrorism but had reverted to its usual inscrutability within a day or two. Personal losses and family grief were swallowed in the general struggle to survive. Until now, the city had not been subjected to the artillery shelling, firefights and aerial attacks that had ravaged Vietnam's countryside. With the Tet Offensive, Saigon—like Hué—was at the heart of the war, an urban battlefield.

I carried the cardboard box with Mèo inside under my arm through the airport terminal. Ri and Dan organized a team of porters to transport their equipment from the plane to the arrival hall. The enormous room was dense with people trying to find their bags in the sticky heat—sweating, irritable, arguing with customs agents. Slow overhead fans did little to alleviate the discomfort. Other passengers heard the distressing noises coming out of the box and frowned at me. For a small animal, Mèo made fierce noises, wailing as if being tortured.

An American soldier in green fatigues came up and looked at the box. He stood a moment without speaking, then bent over and looked through one of the holes.

'Be careful.' I said, 'He's got claws.'

The soldier stood straight and smiled. 'What you got in there?' he asked, 'a wildcat?'

'I'm not sure,' I replied. 'I'm waiting to see when it grows up.'

The soldier smiled. 'Watch out,' he said, 'you might have a bigger one than you think.'

'And meaner,' I said.

Ba, the bureau driver, was waiting at the airport gate with a wide smile and his beloved Dodge, a four-door sedan that had been made in America in the 1950s and had been slowly disintegrating since. Under the hood, many of the parts were held together with pieces of wire and TV camera tape. On the road, the Dodge slouched through the turns like a sailing ship, Ba at the helm, listing with the car. He was young and thin with dark deep-set eyes and an expression of almost permanent melancholy. Ba tried hard to please his American employers. CBS had made him prosperous by Vietnamese standards, but he appeared to fear the largesse might run out any time. Greeting me, Ba looked curiously at the box. When he saw the kitten inside he turned away in distaste, as if my decision to bring a useless creature to the overcrowded city was unforgivably banal. After the long plane ride, the bottom of the cardboard box was damp and soggy and smelled of feline waste.

Saigon was tight with fear, more nervous than regular visitors had seen it since the early 1960s. Citizens were stunned by the scale and boldness of the Tet Offensive: the ground assault on the U.S. embassy, the attack on the presidential palace, the long fight for Cholon and the Phu Tho racetrack, other encounters. The magnitude of the offensive was beyond most people's imagination and still held them, weeks later, in stunned disbelief. No one knew what to expect. Prospects were scary. Every family had a story about being caught in a firefight, or losing a relative, friend or coworker, or seeing NLF troops in the streets of their neighborhood with rifles and RPGs and dusty brown uniforms and simple country haircuts. *How young and bold they are. How out of place they look here.* It was hard for the city's bourgeoisie to believe the war had come to Saigon. And Saigon, being an amalgam of many close-bunched neighborhoods, spun a daily web of gossip, rumors and fabrications with reckless speed. One of the stories, sworn to be true, said the North Vietnamese and Americans were working in collusion at Tet in order to get rid of the South Vietnamese government (which they hated), an alleged conspiracy many Saigonese took seriously. Long-time residents, newly arrived refugees, visitors and foreigners who lived and worked in Saigon worried about what the VC and NVA were going to do next. To the cosseted jittery Vietnamese, the ferocious determination of the invading soldiers and the mystery of how they had organized the surprise attack gave them an aura of invincibility. Even though the NLF and North Vietnamese were slowly retreating from Saigon—U.S. and South Vietnamese forces had fought running skirmishes with them through the city and suburbs—they were seen to be far superior to most of the ARVN. They were better motivated than the South Vietnamese, more aggressive in their tactical maneuvers, more daring in attack. This sense of military inferiority added to the general apprehension and dread.

On the surface, Saigon was overcrowded, noisy and noxious. Its wide, tree-shaded boulevards buzzed with motion and energy—a dazzling, bright-colored kaleidoscope of competing vehicles and passengers who appeared to bump and jostle and flow through one another without actually touching. The streets were jammed with vehicles in movement: bicycles, pedicabs, motor scooters, motorcycles, official limousines, tiny blue and yellow Renault taxis, sleek old American sedans, low-slung black French touring cars and motorized rickshaws known as *motorcyclos* that were driven by grim dark-eyed men whose long exposure to the poisoned air of the streets gave them a uniform look of derangement and menace.

Into this choking chaotic mess rode multivehicle convoys of U.S. Army transport trucks with gigantic engines that wheezed like battle tanks, their temperamental drivers sitting high in the cabs and driving as if licensed by their size and power. Sometimes the American drivers shouted down at lowly Vietnamese who got in their way and gave them the finger. Some of the Vietnamese returned the insult.

The noise and heat and smell of garbage and exhaust swirled among the slow-moving travelers, assaulting them with chemicals, carrying them around in a dizzying, claustrophobic spin of squalor, pollution, decay, luxury, confusion, frustration, anger and an occasional flash of beauty. The graceful young women whose flowing silk dresses billowed behind their bicycles revealed no more of themselves than expressions of disinterest, attitudes of life as usual, aloof and untroubled by the tribulations of war and the city. Nowadays in the streets, when a Vietnamese looked at you directly and stayed with your eyes long enough to react, what you often saw there was contempt, as if you personally were responsible for the whole ugly mix of their misfortunes, the maker of the misery at hand. They had a point, of course—we Americans were responsible for much of it—but the unrelenting volume of uncensored belligerence made me uncomfortable. Sometimes I resented them in return, just for looking so angry. Few Vietnamese had genuinely liked us when we arrived in large numbers in 1965; fewer liked us now that the war was going badly. I had the feeling it would not have made much difference if we were winning. We came to save the Vietnamese from their enemies and we had become the enemy ourselves.

Mèo and I arrived at my hotel. I didn't check him in at the desk, just carried him howling up the carpeted stairs, past the puzzled looks on the faces of the Vietnamese at reception. Members of the hotel staff had become accustomed to the return of guests like me at unusual hours, saturated with dust and mud and insect bites, smelling of sweat and cordite, asking humbly for our key and a bowl of ice, inexpressibly grateful to have simple comforts again. I had a room on the second floor near the corner of the building but did not sleep there often. Saigon was a place for rest and recovery, for reestablishing a sense of civility, and it was always a pleasure to get back for a few days, though the pleasure didn't last much longer than that.

The hotel was called the Continental Palace. A long three-story building along Tu Do Street that faced a big open plaza, the Continental looked like it dated from the 1920s and was built in French colonial style with high ceilings, shuttered windows and rooms that formed a quadrangle around a cool shaded courtyard at the center. It was a mystical place, nourishing the ghosts of mysterious guests who had slept there, men and women who had strange secrets to keep—princes and princesses, exiles, eloping lovers, adventurers, arms dealers, agents and spies of every loyalty (including none), gangsters, opium addicts, smugglers, drunks, warriors, filmmakers, writers and journalists from all over the world. The spirits of those former guests' intrigues, deceptions, decadence, suicides, romances, triumphs and private personal tragedies inhabited the rooms with the furniture. Graham Greene had lived there in the lush interior courtyard in the early 1950s and wrote parts of *The Quiet American,* a fabulous novel that all who studied the war had read at least once. The spirit of that book, if not the author, was still alive a decade and a half later, and some believed *The Quiet American* was the perfect augury of what was to follow. Though the pale outward face of the Continental was cracked and fading, sentimental as an aging movie star, the hotel retained enough of its air of grace and gentility to keep it attractive, more gracious than some of its current guests.

Room C-2 had tall white plaster walls and twin beds, a wooden desk and chair, two stuffed easy chairs with padded armrests, and a low polished wood table that stood between them. The room was spartan. No effort had been made to redecorate it for at least twenty years. A low bookcase stood against one wall and contained a phonograph turntable, an amplifier, and a collection of worn and scratched records that had survived from Frankie's House. Two music speakers stood next to the bookcase. A tired fan suspended from the ceiling created a slow breeze that shifted the hot heavy air from one part of the room to another. At one end, a door with a low handle led to a bathroom with a tiled floor and an enameled iron bathtub, a shower head, bidet, toilet, wash basin and water taps. At the other end of the room, facing the street, a high double window with wooden shutters opened onto the plaza below. Like the rest of the hotel, the room was shabby and comfortable.

I closed the door to the hallway and let Mèo out of the box. Within minutes he had attacked the fringe on the edge of the bedcovers. He sniffed the floors and moldings at the bottom of the walls. Finding no scent of another animal, he prepared to make the room his home. I put his Danang blanket in the box and pushed it into a corner. There was no problem about Mèo staying with me. The hotel staff was accustomed to more bizarre behavior than the presence of a pet. Since the previous summer, room C-2 had become a rendezvous for a group of reporters and photographers and their friends. They used it as a club, stopping by when they felt like company, crashing there when they needed a place to sleep, ordering meals and drinks from room service and charging them to my account (paid for at a profit by someone at CBS), sitting, talking, laughing, smoking cigarettes and sometimes grass, listening to music, winding down from the tensions of the field. At night, it could become raucous. The manager of the hotel, a quiet Frenchman in his mid-thirties, lived next door. One night at about four in the morning, during an especially noisy gathering, he knocked on the door and, in his most polite English, said in a soft voice, "Please, monsieur, please," his face an expression of abiding regret.

From the start, Mèo had the run of the hotel. I opened the windows and the painted shutters that led to an outer ledge that ran all the way around the building and invited him to have a look. The noise of the city joined us. Mèo jumped on the windowsill and stared at the swirl of shapes below. Logic suggested to me that if he was going to survive, he would have to fend for himself out there. Other than providing food and shelter, I wasn't going to care for him. I knew it was a gamble, but it made sense. Mèo needed to figure out how to survive without being closely protected by me. I figured he had already used up three or four of his nine lives. Whether he turned out to be a long-term survivor or not, he was a regular nuisance. He scratched or chewed anything he pleased, he howled in the night, he urinated in the bathtub, he attacked me and my guests without warning.

On our first day back from Hué and Danang and the battle of the Citadel, I ate a meal from room service, washed, changed clothes, said good-bye to Mèo and walked across the square to the Caravelle. It was the most expensive hotel in Saigon, owned in part by Air France and built in the late 1950s to resemble something that looked like the bridge of an ocean liner. The outside was white stucco. Inside it was equipped with an overactive air-conditioning system that kept the temperature at about fifty-five degrees at all times and made it the coldest place in Saigon outside of the morgue. Vietnamese staff wore sweaters and jackets and foreigners regularly caught colds, even pneumonia, crossing from the heat of the streets to the arctic chill of the rooms. I thought the temperature was a cruel joke or at least a sorry mistake, until I learned the designers meant it to complement the cold lines of postcolonial French modernism.

I walked up the wide spiral staircase to the second floor. CBS News rented a suite of offices in and around room 207 and occupied most of the rooms on the floor. The Vietnamese staff of CBS—a reporter named Mister Khat, a secretary named Miss An and several others—came up and smiled and touched my arms or kissed me on both cheeks.

'We thought you were killed in Hué, Jack,' one of them said.

'It was just a rumor,' I replied. 'Thank God it wasn't true.'

'I'm so happy you are alive,' another said, smiling.

'It must be a miracle, no?' Laughter.

'Yes,' I said, 'daily miracle.'

'They told us you have a cat, is it true?'

'Yes,' I said. 'His name is Mèo.' More laughter.

I answered questions and shook hands with other employees who were in the office. It was agreed that I was exceptionally lucky to have these life-saving daily miracles but also that I had not been in grave danger except for the moment with the bullet that sounded like a bumblebee. Dan, the sound recordist, told the story in Vietnamese and Miss An put her hands over her mouth as she listened.

The bureau chief, Dan Bloom, was a cheerful heavy man in his late thirties and a veteran network producer. He took me aside and said he had good news. CBS News executives in New York wanted me home, he said, to work on a documentary they were producing about a recent battle near Dak To in the Central Highlands. The film had been shot by a freelance European crew and CBS had bought the broadcast rights. The film was going to be a one-hour special and they needed me to look at the footage, write the narration, come back to Vietnam to do some on-camera parts, and see the project through to completion. As usual, they wanted me to travel as soon as possible. I was delighted.

I walked out of the Caravelle and into the Saigon heat, past orphan kids hawking packs of stale French and American cigarettes and little pink bags of peanuts, past money changers who leaned over and touched my arm and hissed in my ear with hot breath, "You buy money?" past clean-shaven GIs wearing starched fatigues and PX cameras taking in-country R and R, past tired hookers leaning against walls with their thighs exposed, past long-haired pimps with greasy clothes who spat casually just in front of my foot-steps, past the whole ugly ballet of Vietnamese hustlers and their American marks, the GIs holding the dollars and therefore the upper hand, commerce reduced to its lowest wartime denominator.

I walked across Tu Do Street and two blocks along Le Loi Boulevard to the JUSPAO building to pick up my mail and attend the daily military brief-ing. The Joint U.S. Public Affairs Office was the official voice of MACV, the public relations apparatus of the giant war-fighting institution of the U.S. government. Since the most fundamental mission of MACV was to kill Viet-namese, the key job at JUSPAO was to present details of the killing in as san-itary a version as possible:

A unit of the 196th Infantry brigade made contact with a suspected enemy force of unknown size at 02:18 yesterday morning in an area 12 kilometers southwest of Chu Lai. An unknown number of enemy were believed to be killed or wounded. U.S. casualties were light.

Journalists called the military briefing the "Five O'clock Follies." Actually, it was more of a charade, a kind of public relations theater of the absurd masquerading as a news conference. Briefing officers from the various branches of the armed services pretended to report timely military information from the field and reporters pretended to take them seriously. In reality, the news disseminated by briefing officers was a mixed collection of facts, half-truths, misinformation, distortions, lies and deceits—the daily exercise of war propaganda. The event was held in an American-style auditorium with a stage, a podium, briefing props and comfortable seats for the audience. Each afternoon at 4:30, the Follies were the best free theater in town.

The auditorium was jammed with reporters from all over the world, many of whom had flown in to cover the Tet Offensive. There were more than six hundred journalists in the country, a record for the war. Most of them wanted to know how severely the NLF and PAVN attacks had affected the war effort, where there was fighting still going on, what the casualties were, and what the generals had to say about it. Overcrowding in the auditorium created its own tension, charging the room with nervous anticipation, like a cage of big cats before feeding.

A loud voice, virtually shouting, sang out from a crowd of reporters behind me. "Where have all the flowers gone?" the voice sang, seriously off-key. I turned and saw the smiling face of Peter Braestrup, a *Washington Post* reporter who enjoyed teasing me with the first line of that antiwar song whenever we met. Braestrup had seen a TV story I had done at Khe Sanh a few weeks earlier in which a squad of Marines sang "Where Have All The Flowers Gone?" while incoming artillery shells exploded near their position in the center of the base. Braestrup, a former Marine officer, thought the piece was self-pitying and corny, and he enjoyed embarrassing me about it in public. This was the third or fourth time recently.

The gathering of journalists at the military briefing was also a social event where you could find out which friends were in town. I sat with colleagues who had come down from I Corps for a rest after Hué and Khe Sanh and said hello to others who had been covering the fighting in Saigon and Cholon. I told them I was going home to the States soon, and we agreed to meet for drinks and dinner after work.

At the briefing, U.S. public affairs officers announced the recorded numbers of air strikes, bombing missions, enemy contacts, dead and wounded, and various other military statistics and stories from the past twenty-four hours. The information came into Saigon from the field via the military reporting system, and the briefers tried to process and distribute it to the press in the best possible light, as if the simple accumulation and reporting of numbers made it obvious that steady progress in the war was being made. Except in very rare cases, the officers did *not* report such events as successful enemy ambushes, lost battles, lost outposts, casualties from friendly fire, battle fatigue, accidents, nervous breakdowns, atrocities by our side, mutiny, looting, rape, courts martial, rebellion, bombs dropped on our own troops, the shooting of ARVN allies, torture, theft, corruption, murder, fragging, suicide or anything that might reflect negatively on the public image of the U.S. armed services. All that other activity was happening, of course, but the facts were not made readily available to the press. Sometimes information officers withheld information. Sometimes they twisted the truth. Sometimes they played dumb. Sometimes they lied. It was done in the name of positive public relations and to encourage public support at home for the war effort. No matter that most of the television networks and major newspapers were reporting a different war, military briefers stuck to the story as their superior officers saw it. Insulated in their air-conditioned Saigon offices, limited in their ability to see beyond statistics, worried always about their chances for promotion, they did not appear to see much else besides the stats, the slick features, and the public relations rhetoric they composed for the press. Or, if they did know something horribly wrong was happening out there, that the war was *not* being won, they could not (or chose not to) report it at the briefing. Those reporters and their readers who still paid attention to the war-winning statistics from JUSPAO remained victims of the propaganda war, enabling the real war to go on.

APRIL, 1968

The cat looked out the open window of the hotel room and watched the slow evening procession along Tu Do Street. The sidewalks were less crowded now. During the day they overflowed with the ragged dirty poor of Saigon's streets—laborers, beggars, lunatics, orphans, AWOL soldiers, war casualties, widows, vendors and hustlers of every kind. In the evening, more fashionably dressed men and women appeared in clean well-tailored clothing of silk, cotton and polyester, no sign of sweat or unpleasant odors on their perfumed bodies, walking with proud easy paces past the old French opera house and the Caravelle Hotel to supper and other amusements. Darkness cast a silken veil over the city, covering its less attractive features, softening the sharp edges of its poverty and wealth. The air was cooler now —not the liquid suffocating daytime heat but still ripe with the fragrance of rotting garbage and exhaust gas. U.S. military police jeeps patrolled at a crawl, radios hissing, hard burly men inside wrapped in oversize helmets and flak jackets staring out at off-duty American soldiers wandering through the maze of ground floor bars and upstairs brothels. A journalist for one of the big daily newspapers walked out of the hotel with copy in his hand and hurried up the street toward the cable office to file. The procession along Tu Do Street was a regular nighttime parade, the wartime Saigon version of an evening stroll on the Champs Elysées. By day, savage street battles were being fought a mile or two away, but by evening the war might have been in Paris.

Even the night could not hide the giant black statue dominating the plaza across from the opera house where Le Loi Boulevard met Tu Do. Two stone soldiers—one Vietnamese, one American—stood twenty feet high on a pedestal the size of a truck. The soldiers leaned forward in fighting poses: heads and shoulders bent, knees cocked, granite-hard determination on their faces, as if advancing into fire. The GI stood behind the ARVN soldier as if pushing him forward into battle. The pose was melodramatic, too crude to be taken seriously. Most people I knew saw it as a joke, more sym-

bolic of the sculptor's imagination than the reality of the war. Only out-of-
town visitors paid attention to it. No one needed a statue to be reminded of
the war; no one was untouched by it. To the west, flares fell over Cholon.
Farther away, artillery shells cracked in the countryside with muffled
whumps. A swirl of blue-black smoke rose above the vehicles moving slowly
along the streets and lingered in the toxic air.

The ledge at the window was Mèo's observation post, his favorite station.
He watched all that moved below, fascinated by the perpetual motion of so
many people, machines, lights and colors, as if trying to comprehend the
practical meaning of so much random disconnected movement. He sat for
hours without shifting more than his eyes, fully attentive yet motionless,
blending into the bland indecorous background of the room, a statue himself.

He was healthy now, lithe and strong, with clean fur, whiskers, eyes and
ears. He had recovered physically from his adventures in Hué and was growing fast. His appetite was ravenous, his teeth tiny daggers. He ate four or five
times a day, a basic diet of leftover fish heads and rice from the hotel kitchen,
provided by the room boys. Three months earlier, the kitten's appearance
had surprised them. The kindly old men laughed when they came in the
room, pointing at him and then at me, jabbering to one another in rapid
musical Vietnamese, amused that anyone would want a scrawny animal like
him for a pet. In time, however, their amusement was tempered by regular
excessive payments of piastres to them to feed the cat, courtesy of occupants
and visitors to the room. Since the turnover in the room was constant, usually no one knew how long it had been since the room boys had last been
paid, so someone usually paid them every day. It wasn't worth much, a dollar or two, but it supported the room boys' families in times of shortages and
inflation, which was almost always. Feeding Mèo became a part of their routine. They treated him as a paying guest.

He looked like a crossbreed, red point Siamese. His eyes were azure blue,
his hair short and smooth. Apricot-orange stripes ran along the top of his
head, back and tail. His head was round and full like an ordinary housecat's
rather than long and narrow like that of a Siamese. He wore his lineage with
pride anyway, grooming himself regularly, sitting with the grace and style of
a purebred. Shortly after arriving in Saigon, he got his first and only bath,
much against his will, a scrub and shampoo with strong soap and disinfec-
tant. Fur flew. Claws slashed. Jaws and teeth bit. Tongue hissed. He had surprisingly strong legs and shoulders for a small animal and he growled like a

tiger. When it was over, the bath revealed a cat of two colors, not three. Mèo turned out to be almost all white, a few traces of orange but nothing else. His black fur disappeared during the bath, exposed as nothing darker than a full coat of fleas, oil and dirt, a mass of hungry parasites and soil that vanished down the bathtub drain and took his blackness with them. Mèo was less than the lucky black, white and orange kitten I first observed in Hué. He was an impostor.

In time, he recovered from the trauma of the bath and became more confident. He slept on the floor inside a fresh box he had converted into his war bunker. The box, an old shipping carton of thick corrugated cardboard, had been left upside down in a corner of the room. It took him a week to chew a hole in it just big enough to squeeze through. During the hottest part of the day he slept in cool dark comfort on the tile floor, safe inside his shelter. When he was not eating, doing observation duty at the window, or hunting outside the room, he kept to himself. He was not interested in people who came to the room. Unless it was to fight, Mèo ignored them. He appeared to have a grudge against humanity. Although he tolerated the Vietnamese room boys who fed him, he attacked all other humans, especially Americans, usually without provocation. He was easily spooked. Withdrawn and isolated, hostile toward all but the Vietnamese, he was a wild malevolent animal, a singularly deep and inscrutable cat.

The room where Mèo and I lived had become the social gathering place for a new set of reporters and photographers with shared interests—mainly the war, music, alcohol and bright green leaves of Laotian marijuana. Three years after Frankie's House, the scene at Tim Page's air-conditioned room on Bui Thi Xuan had transmuted to room C-2 at the Continental. Frankie and his family and the weapons were gone, but the same old hi-fi and speakers remained, along with the tireless collection of records. The rock 'n' roll that blared from the phonograph was updated now to include more recent albums, particularly by the Beatles, Rolling Stones, Jimi Hendrix and the Doors. Popular music seemed to be evolving into newer forms, becoming as unrestrained as the war, running parallel with it, connecting with its energy and violence, its performers driving headlong into new dimensions of heartbreak and destruction.

When they came back from the field (these days the field was Saigon and its suburbs), friends met in C-2 for a drink, a smoke perhaps, and conversation that included the latest war news from wherever they'd been. Close

friends addressed one another as "brother" and "sister." Most of the old faces
from 1965 were gone—Steve Northup, Joe Galloway, Simon Dring, Martin
Stuart-Fox and his brother David, Robin Mannock, Tom Corpora, Sean
Flynn. All had left, at least for a time, though Dana Stone was still in-country.
Some of the newer arrivals had already become old hands at the war: Arthur
Greenspon, my true brother and a freelance photographer for AP who had
taken a memorable photograph in the A Shau Valley; Keith Kay, my CBS
partner who lived around the corner in room 11; Mike Herr, who kept a
room upstairs while he worked on his first article for *Esquire* and also took
notes for his book; Hughes and Anne Rudd, a mature couple who had been
through World War II (Hughes with a Silver Star for his army flying over
Italy); Perry Deane Young, a gifted reporter for UPI from North Carolina
who hoped to succeed as a writer; David Greenway of TIME magazine;
Natalie (Pooh) Kuhn, a tall, thin freelance reporter who was visiting from
Rome; Bernie Weinraub of the *New York Times*; Jerry Liles of the International Volunteer Service; Peter Kann of the *Wall Street Journal*; Jeff Gralnick
of CBS; Kevin Buckley of *Newsweek,* and others. Friends dropped by after
work for a drink, coming and going through the winter and spring of
1967–1968. The conversation was convivial, anecdotal, sometimes outrageous. Occasionally, a more temperate member of the press corps walked
into the room to join us, caught the sweet herbal scent of marijuana, turned
around and left without a word. One or two of the original members of
Frankie's House had come back for another tour, Tim Page among them,
but most had moved on with their lives. Personalities changed with the war.
Some had outgrown it.

What had once seemed like the glory of war was gone, along with our
innocence and a lot of boyish adventure fantasies as well. We were still interested in the intricacies of combat action and the destructive power of America's war-making machine, but our earlier belief in the invincibility of the
U.S. military was gone, along with any lingering respect for the moral right-
eousness of the cause. The only causes left were personal: work, friendship,
survival. We were tougher now, more experienced, quicker to criticize, less
tolerant of the MACV mission of pacifying the country by pulverizing it.
Somewhere in Vietnam, every two minutes, someone died. We were numb
from watching the daily revealed tragedy of a war being lost by good intentions turned inside out. We talked about how the American government, in
the cause of anti-Communism, had unleashed the cruelest, most violent

impulses in our own society. A modern superarmy designed to be deployed on the vast open plains of central Europe had launched itself against a small densely populated backland in Southeast Asia and saturated it with violence —an unrestrained, mechanized destruction, killing not only enemy troops but also thousands of men, women, children, animals, allied soldiers and its own young men. Vietnam was being beaten to death. Some of us saw it as ironic tragedy, continuously evolving in new and repetitive forms of self-destruction. American leaders had sent many of the society's best young men and women to crush an evil system they saw in ascendance in Vietnam, trying to stop the gathering influence of Communism in Southeast Asia and grind it to dust. But in doing so they had created a monster that inflicted so much random violence and death it produced an entire new body of evil, a catalogue of cruelty that overshadowed any possible virtue that might have come from defeating the Communists. Moreover, the strategy was a failure. The country and its people were being wasted for nothing. America came to Vietnam to save it from evil and ended up sacrificing its own soul.

The war enclosed us in a hard shell of cynicism. We went out day after day to find what we could in one small corner of the war hoping to get in and out quickly and bring back a good story. Usually we did. But after a while the endless shocking succession of ruined lives became so emotionally shattering there was no room left for grief. Senior MACV officers argued politely that we were so absorbed with day-to-day details of the misery that we couldn't see what they saw, "the big picture," a picture that showed American and Vietnamese forces pacifying hamlets as never before, crippling the VC, killing them in larger and larger numbers and, therefore, by any objective evaluation, winning the war.

Of course, everything depended on your point of view. I was still amazed by individual valor. An act of courage, military or civilian, was a wonder to witness. To see someone risk his life for the well-being of another, or for the group, instilled faith in the human condition. But I was coming to see the war as inexpressibly sad, ruinous, wasteful in every way. Something close to truth was being revealed. If you stayed around long enough and went into the field often enough, what you saw was the best and worst of human behavior: heroic selflessness and selfish vulgarity, acts of gentleness and generosity, and acts of cowardice and criminality. Some of the behavior was so evil that few outside the experience of covering the war could understand it. The story about the police general, Nguyen Ngoc Loan, firing a pistol bullet into the head of a Viet Cong prisoner on the streets of Saigon (flashed around the world by Eddie Adams's wirephoto) was not so much that Loan was a drunken killer (American MPs who rode with him carried a fresh case of beer for him every morning), but that it was the first close-up photograph of an individual murder in the war. People outside Vietnam were shocked at what appeared to be such a cruel act, but those who were there knew that murder was common in the war. Corroding, decadent, corrupting, suicidal —the big picture revealed the darkest side of our collective American culture, a government-sponsored death machine careening out of control, little morality or restraint left in it. What some of us who watched and reported the war felt inside ourselves was empty and cold: dark humor, anger, irony, absence of hope, cynicism. At one stage the prevailing attitude was so nihilistic no one bothered to notice whether the war was achieving anything anymore. It no longer mattered whether it was being won or lost.

Not long after the Tet Offensive started, a man stood at the bar on the eighth floor of the Caravelle Hotel, late at night, few people left in the corner room. His heavy torso hunched on top of the bar, alone on his elbows. His face was flaccid, his words slurred. I was waiting at the bar for a round of drinks to take to a friend sitting at a table.

'What d'ya think about the war?' the man said.

'Tragic,' I said. 'We never should have come here.' That was my standard answer by now.

He measured me with his eyes. In Saigon these days, especially after Tet, it was not wise to tell strangers you hated the war. No telling what reaction you'd get. It could be unpleasant. But I was so far gone I didn't care.

'What're ya doin over here? Peace Corps or somethin?'

'No, I'm a journalist.'

He looked at me with relief, suspicion gone. 'Journalish, huh? Okay, listen, pal. Tell me whatcha think about somethin. Jus' came to me tonight.'

'What's that?' I said, ready to be bored.

"We have met the enemy and he ish ush," he said. "Wha d'ya think uh that?"

'Pretty good,' I said, recalling the famous military expression, "We have met the enemy and he is ours."

'Yesh, I thought so. I'm gonna use it.'

I assumed he was a reporter from a small-town newspaper or TV station in the States (Saigon was full of them now) and wished him well. The drinks arrived and I carried them back to the table. My friend asked if I knew the guy.

'No,' I said. 'He's drunk as a skunk.'

'Yeah, I can see. Know who he is?' I shook my head no.

'It's Walt Kelly,' he said, 'the cartoonist. You know, the guy who does *Pogo*.'

'Really?' I looked back at Kelly, slumped over the bar, his back to the room. 'He's got a good line,' I said: "We have met the enemy and he is us."'

My friend laughed. 'Not bad. He'll be too hung over tomorrow to remember it.'

Mèo saw enemies everywhere. All humans who entered the room were at risk. Lurking in his bunker, creeping in silence across the floor, pouncing on whatever dared enter his domain, Mèo was the small white hunter, a natural-born killer, an ambush waiting to happen. He sat facing the plaster wall on the east side of the room for hours waiting for a gecko that regularly appeared there. The gecko, in turn, waited to catch an occasional mosquito that arrived on an evening breeze through the wide open window. Mèo stalked, caught and consumed the lizard that ate the insects that ate us, another of the ways he made us suffer.

His concentration was total. Sitting by the window, he taught himself to make the sound of a bird, a deep guttural cat yodel that was a weak imitation of a true pigeon gurgle. He sat at the window ledge—motionless, silent, patient as a monk—waiting for a bird to come within range and then, "oodle-oodle-oodle." The noise was so unlike a cat it always drew the attention of everyone in the room. But not the pigeons. Even with their tiny brains, no birds came to the window to join him, at least none that we saw.

Out of the room, Mèo hunted all creatures great and small. Size was no factor. Lizards, snakes, birds, insects, even other cats—he chased and fought them all with fierce aggression. From time to time he disappeared on hunting expeditions that lasted several days. Sometimes he could be seen from the street, his half-grown white form gliding along the narrow cornice that ran outside the second floor of the hotel, sniffing the air ahead of him, out

on a mission to explore the other rooms, corridors and grounds of the building. He had no fear. Friends who saw him on the ledge were alarmed that I
let him prowl at such height. 'Aren't you afraid he's going to fall?' they said. I
told them that he knew how to keep his footing, he was a veteran traveler
(jeep, truck, helicopter, fixed-wing) and was steady under fire. I wasn't going
to worry about him. He seemed capable of surviving on his own. If not, it
would be his misfortune, *xin loi*. I had to be unemotional even at the risk of
seeming coldhearted.

Late at night, Mèo crept through the open windows of other hotel guests
while they slept, searching out their secret treasures (especially food), sniffing
objects, marking fresh territory with his scent, digging into the dirt around
their potted palms and making them his private toilet, surprising those innocent sleeping visitors to Saigon with his slinking unexpected catness. Sometimes you heard screams in the night and knew it was Mèo up to no good. He
seemed never to get caught. He escaped to the safety of the night and covered his trail. No one doubted that he was Viet Cong. Mike Herr called him
"the dreaded Cong," saying the words with deep exaggerated gravity, like the
line in *King Kong*. Other friends called him "the cat from hell."

Keith Kay woke up in room 11 in an early hour of the night, his head
heavy with drug sleep. Slowly, he became aware of two cat's eyes glowing
with evil light from the table beside the bed. Mèo was about to pounce on his
face. Kay did not dare move. The cat was more alert and faster, and he already
had the range. It was the most painful irony, Kay said later, to wake up from
an agonizing nightmare, feel the relief of conscious awareness, and realize in
one tortured breath that you were now faced with the living nightmare of the
cat. For Kay, who had seen the worst of the war, it was a form of pure horror,
the work of a merciless terrorist. Mèo made him into a serious cat hater.

My own encounters with Mèo were no less dramatic than Kay's. One
morning that spring, shortly before sunrise, with the room silent and dark, I
rolled out of bed and staggered half-asleep toward the bathroom. I had been
reading Sun Tzu's *The Art of War*, written twenty-four hundred years earlier,
trying to get another perspective on Vietnamese military thinking. *("Good
warriors cause others to come to them, and do not go to others.")* My chemical consumption the night before had been overindulgent and now I paid for it in
hangover pain. *("Strike the slumping and receding.")* I was not aware of anything more than the need to relieve my bladder and the general direction of
the bathroom. *("Victory is gained by surprise.")* The bathroom door was

closed. It had a low handle about three feet off the floor designed for shorter Asian guests. *("Attack when they are unprepared, make your move when they do not expect it.")* As I touched the porcelain knob to open the door, my hand was struck by a jolt of electricity, an astonishing pain that ran through the whole arm. *("So it is with skillful warriors—their force is swift, their precision is close.")* I came awake at once. My hand and wrist were in the powerful grip of the cat, nerves shrieking with pain. His whole body was deployed in attack, every erg of energy committed: his legs locked around my hand and wrist, his claws embedded in my skin, his jaws biting through the soft pink flesh between my thumb and forefinger, dagger teeth piercing the skin. *("Invincibility is in oneself, vulnerability is in the opponent.")* Screaming, I swung my arm across my chest and through the air, cat attached. As he let go, Mèo tore away small pieces of my skin, then spun in midflight to turn himself right side up and come down in a light-footed, four-point landing. He looked up at me for one instant with red glowing eyes and dashed out the window. *("To advance irresistibly, push through their gaps. To retreat elusively, outspeed them.")*

Not long after, I realized that he had been waiting in ambush for a long time, perhaps hours. He was ready to leap from the floor as soon as he saw my hand touch the doorknob. He knew where and when to strike, how much force to use, how to escape. Like a wise commander, he had measured the terrain and found it favorable, assessed the doorknob as the correct point of contact and my hand as the most vulnerable target, calculated that the right time to strike was before dawn when I was weak, compared these observations with all other possibilities and executed the ambush with perfect timing, concentration, speed and force. Then he escaped. As Sun Tzu had taught, *"The rules of the military are five: measurement, assessment, calculation, comparison, and victory."* That was it! He was the reincarnation of Sun Tzu. Intelligent, daring, cunning, ferocious. Who else? Mèo was a VietCong version of the Chinese warrior-philosopher in the body of a cat. Even on a small scale, Mèo's ambush was a flawless work of tactics and strength. My hand, wrist and arm hurt for a week. I couldn't figure out why he would do it unless it was political.

The feral cats that scratched a lean existence from the table scraps of hotel guests avoided Mèo. When they saw him coming, they backed away as if they had fought him once and were not ready for a rematch. Before he was full-grown, Mèo dominated the dozen or so hotel cats, defending his territory in the grounds, always trying to extend it, tiger in his veins. I watched him one morning after breakfast in the garden at the center of the Continental. The garden was insulated from the noise of the city by the walls and roof of the hotel and planted with small palm trees and shrubs. Mèo crept along a low-hanging gutter of the roof about eight feet above the ground and waited, body flat and low, head below his bony shoulders like a vulture. A peacock approached, one of the two ill-tempered creatures that lived on the grounds of the hotel. They were big haughty birds of beautiful color that were also mean. Just as the peacock passed below, Mèo threw himself onto its back and bit it hard on the neck, digging his claws into its feathers, twisting his body into the bite. It must have been his first attack on a peacock because the bird quickly turned its long, curved neck around and bit him back. Equally hard. After several sharp pecks, Mèo let go of the peacock, jumped to the ground and dashed away. *("Retreat in the face of superior force.")* It was the only fight I saw him lose. Some days later, one of the peacocks disappeared. What happened to it was a mystery, no one knew, but after that Mèo's command of the garden was complete.

At times he seemed to adopt the characteristics of other creatures. Crouching close to the ground in the garden, stalking some unfortunate game, he could look less like a cat than a reptile. Ears flat against the back of his head, whiskers in, tail straight, slithering with silent ease through the low grass, he looked like a fat white snake. In the room one night, when he didn't know I was watching, he scurried across the tiled floor standing high on his paws, prancing in an even rapid gait with the tiptoe trot of a rat. "Are you a cat or a rat?" I called out. He turned away with the embarrassed look of someone caught acting a private fantasy. He was probably practicing one of his imitations.

Mèo met Tim Page in room C-2 in the spring of 1968. It was as if two totally wacky cartoon characters had come together: Krazy Kat and Daffy Duck. It was love-hate at first sight, an instant game of chase and attack, an ultimate real-life loony tune. Both were already crazed: Page from the three wounds he had suffered in combat and Mèo from the trauma of Hué, so that mixing their psychoses in the same room initiated instant bedlam. Page went into offensive action as soon as he saw the cat. He curled the long bony fingers of his right hand into a bird's claw and reached toward the cat, scratching the air, threatening him with the claw. Seeing the gnarled, grotesque hand coming for him, Mèo assumed his fighting posture: legs stiff, muscles tense, head drawn deep into his neck and tilted to one side, ears flat, eyes narrow, fur raised straight off his back—armed and alert. When they came together, the battle was over in less than a minute. Mèo bit and scratched Page's claw-hand in a series of lightening strikes until it was bloody and raw. Page ended the fight by flinging the cat across the room hard against the wall. Mèo struck the wall and landed on his legs, licked his fur a few times and disappeared. It was a battle they fought again and again and they both lost every time, like combatants in the war.

Page had been living in the United States, out of funds and wired on acid in California when news of the Tet Offensive reached him. Seeing the war on TV and the front pages of newspapers, he tried to find a way back to Vietnam. He felt it was where he belonged. It might get him out of debt, clean him up a little, at least put him back with a few old friends. None of the photo magazines would send him; Page was considered too unpredictable. When the first of his cables arrived, the rest of us prayed he wouldn't come, for his own sake, though we knew that he would. When Page finally arrived back in Saigon, he was in a serious state of dementia: crazed by dope, alcohol, sleeplessness and speed. He had no visa. Immigration officials confined him to a police detention room at Tan Son Nhut. When his friends went to the airport to bail him out, Page waved his arms like a lunatic and shouted an incoherent stream of French, English and GI-Vietnamese babble that made no sense. 'Tres beaucoup miserable bloody mind fuck asshole Viets bon amis dinky-dao, oh, so sorry,' Page rambled, fumbling for a cigarette. 'If you please, Hendrix tune. Is this any way to treat a famous photographer? I ask you. Got a light, mate? Dope-is-hope, nest-pa?' His portable tape recorder blared acid rock so loud the speaker distorted. His eyes were shot with blood, lids draped at half-staff. Through the noise and babble and arm waving, Page grinned a silly smile that seemed to suggest it was all an act. After a day and night of phone calls, negotiations, blandishments and threats, weary Vietnamese authorities released Page into the custody of the bureau chief of TIME-LIFE. A temporary visa was produced. Officials smiled as everyone left, obviously grateful to be finished with the long-haired Englishman who held his hands in prayer and bowed like a Buddhist monk as he backed out of the detention room, grinning.

Page moved into C-2 and began at once to terrorize the cat. He blew clouds of marijuana smoke in his face. He fed him brandy, which Mèo enjoyed, licking it a drop at a time from the tip of Page's finger. Drunk and stoned, unable to navigate his way through the hole to his bunker (a cat

wrecked on booze and grass behaves no differently than a human), Mèo
passed out on the floor. Later Page sneaked up behind him and seized him
with the giant bird's claw, screeching like a hawk, '*Eeeek! Eeeek! Eeeek!*' lifting
him high into the air and laughing, 'Gotcha, mate!' Mèo went into a frenzy,
too terrified to fight back, struggling like a hooked barracuda. Whenever he
was bored, Page terrorized the cat, which made Mèo more and more paranoid. Everyone seemed to think it was hilarious except the cat. Both of them
had bad cases of PTSD long before it was identified as a medical condition.

The cat looked out the open window at the procession on Tu Do Street.
From the square below, passersby could hear loud raucous sounds coming
from the room: primitive chants, grunts, screams, groans, babies' voices, cat-
calls, ghoulish moaning, jungle animal shrieks, ape and monkey howls,
whining, panting, orgasmic sex cries—all of it in rough syncopated rhythm
punctuated by riffs of contemporary jazz from a saxophone. When they
looked up, they could see a haze of blue smoke drifting out the window and
the motionless form of the white cat staring back at them.

"Whooooo could imagine," an American voice sang, "that they would
freak out in Kansas somewhere . . . Kansas."

The noises on the hi-fi coming out the window of room C-2 were made
by Frank Zappa and the Mothers of Invention, a group as unlikely to be
played in the polite downtown precincts of wartime Saigon as Jane Fonda
singing "The Star-Spangled Banner." Zappa was one of the enemy. To people passing below, it must have sounded like the most aberrant American
perversion, an orgy at least. ('God damn weirdos up there screwin themselves silly I bet.'). But their imaginations were more prurient than the reality: half a dozen young men and one or two women slouched in chairs and
on the bed, fully clothed, laughing, a little embarrassed by the audacity of
the loud irreverent music, especially with the window open, wondering if
the people on the street were offended, feeling comfortable with it anyway.

Among regulars at C-2, "Help I'm a Rock" by the Mothers became as
important a theme as "We've Gotta Get Out of This Place" was to the earlier
group. "Brown Shoes Don't Make It" was another hit. My own favorite was
written in 1964 after civil disorders in Los Angeles but seemed just as timely in
Saigon four years later. The words came out in a rapid angry-cynical voice:

Well you can cool it, you can heat it
'Cause Baby I don't need it
Take your TV tube and eat it
'N all that phony stuff on sports
'N all the unconfirmed reports
You know I watch that rotten box until my head begin to hurt
From checkin' out the way the newsmen say they get the dirt
Before all the guys on channel so-and-so and further they assert
That any shows they'll interrupt
To bring you news if it comes up
They say that if the place blows up
They will be the first to tell,
because the boys they got downtown
Are workin' hard and doin' swell
And if anybody gets the news before it hits the street
They say that no one blabs it faster and their coverage can't be beat
And if another woman driver gets machine-gunned from her seat
They'll send some joker with a Brownie and you'll see it all complete
So I'm watchin' and I'm waitin',
Hopin' for the best.
Even think I'll go to prayin'
Every time I hear 'em sayin'
That there's no way to delay that trouble comin' every day,
No way to delay that trouble comin' every day.

"Trouble Every Day" made more sense to those of us who worked in television. To know that we were being satirized, even on the remote fringes of popular culture, helped us take ourselves less seriously. Outside of your work, there wasn't much you could take seriously for long. Friendships, perhaps, but not much else. The war worked its way into your consciousness whether you wanted it there or not, taking over your conscience, worrying you, demanding attention to its misery and pain. The war made you think about what was going on in places you couldn't see, creating the unbearable combination of imagination and memory. It *was* possible to care too much. Psychedelic reality, at least during off hours, put

psychic distance between us and the war. After a joint or two, everything in
the room seemed safer, more secure. That was our escape. For a few hours,
the war could wait.

It came back later. Nightmares haunted us. The number and severity
came in proportion to the frequency and intensity of fighting we were in.
No one had to go far to get shot at anymore, just down the road. The street
fights some journalists called "mini-Tet" weren't as frightening as Hué had
been (no mortars or artillery were being used on Saigon), but they were
more dangerous for reporters because there were no regular battle lines to
judge where you were. Viet Cong guerrilla squads and snipers took cover in
the warren of side streets, alleyways, windows and rooftops, and ambushed
ARVN and Americans who wandered into range. Saigon was a treeless jungle. A dozen journalists were killed or wounded driving down the wrong
streets or walking into the wrong neighborhoods. Some were friends. When
a reporter who was known to be cautious about taking combat risks got hit,
you realized your own chances of survival were that much shorter. Nightmares became a serious problem. The only way to make them stop was to
get out of Vietnam, take a long leave somewhere and try to think about
something else. Friends went home, they'd had enough. It wasn't a permanent cure, the war went with them, but it gave them a break. For those who
stayed in Saigon, one escape was to drop by C-2 in the evenings and get high,
have a few laughs, tell a story or two, knowing it was only temporary. Since
most of us weren't quite finished with the war (the war wasn't finished with
us either, but we didn't know that), we drank and smoked and talked and
passed out late at night too drugged and tired to care that the war also takes
its due when you sleep, though the nightmares were less frightening when
you couldn't remember them in the morning.

The cat, on the other hand, seemed aware of its reality all the time
(except when *he* was stoned, which was not often). Art Greenspon saw a blue
fire in Mèo's eyes, a burning spirit that embodied a wider view—transcen-
dent, spiritual, beyond the war. Art thought it had something to do with the
East. It wasn't that Mèo was Vietnamese or Viet Cong or simply a cat, he
appeared to understand what was going on better than any of us from the
outside. Mèo *knew*, Art believed. And that gave him his freedom, even in cap-
tivity. As he sat by the open window watching the evening procession on Tu
Do, enveloped in a fine haze of cigarette smoke, Mèo's eyes were as deep
and blue and numinous as the South China Sea.

MAY, 1968

It was time to go. Nine more months of covering the war and I was worn out again. Big news stories had been flowing from the battlefields all late summer and fall of 1967, and then through the winter and spring of 1968. Khe Sanh and Hué had been the biggest, and the hardest to cover. The resulting tensions of daily physical effort, concentration, competition and fear had accumulated over the months to give me another case of acute exhaustion. Call it fatigue, trauma, shock, whatever—it was too much to take any longer. You'd think I'd have learned my lesson after the first tour, but I hadn't. Again, it was time to get out.

The war had reached a critical point. General Westmoreland was asking for more troops to add to the half million already under his command, but the American public and its commander in chief were saying "enough." President Johnson turned down Westmoreland's latest request. The Tet Offensive was still not over. My colleagues went out each day to record the fighting and filed their stories while I was packing and getting ready to go home. A flight was reserved, a ticket purchased, books and records given away, parties attended, farewells exchanged. The old hi-fi system from Frankie's House and C-2 were bequeathed to the brothers. Other than attending the daily briefing and writing radio spots, I did not cover the war. The staff in the bureau mostly ignored me. My remaining time was short. I carried a three-foot long mahogany walking stick with a carved head at the top everywhere I went, even in Saigon, my personal short-timer's stick. Friends were amused. Acquaintances, sometimes even strangers, stopped and asked how long I had to go. When I said five days or four days or whatever it was, they smiled and nodded appreciatively, got off a short-timer's joke or two ('I knew a guy who was so short his ear lobes dragged on the deck.'), playing out the polite ritual for one who had made it through, a sign of respect. I had earned something in their estimation, if only the right to go home. Already, I felt distanced from friends and colleagues who were staying to cover the war, separated from them by my future. I was happy and sad at the same time.

The only problem was what to do with the cat. Mèo was more than four months old and growing like a lion. Fearless as ever, he devoted part of each day to sharpening his skills at guerrilla warfare. He waited hidden in shadows to ambush visitors to room C-2, pounced on their wrist or ankle when they weren't looking, bit hard into their flesh with hot-blooded fury. Veterans of fights with Mèo wore long bloody scratches on the backs of their hands like battle scars.

At other times he patrolled the grounds of the hotel—hunting, fighting, terrorizing anything in his way, guests included. Some avoided him at all costs. When they saw him ahead in the hotel corridor they turned and went the other way. His reputation became notorious. 'Le chat terrible,' that frightful cat, they called him. He was difficult to catch, impossible to tame. Keith Kay entered room C-2 only in a crouch, advancing slowly, one step at a time, his eyes scanning the furniture and floor for signs of the cat, ready for a fight. He saw Mèo, like the rest of us, as an NLF warrior who had infiltrated our camp—uncompromising, implacable, revolutionary. In the three months since I met him in Hué, Mèo had maintained a continuous campaign of violent resistance: fierce, unyielding, ready to die. And that, of course, made him free.

'Did you see the cat last night?' Kay said.

'No,' I said.

'You should have seen him in the garden, man. He had a French lady terrified. She was leaning all the way back in her chair with her hands up in front of her face. Scared as hell. And the cat was standing on the table eating her dinner. Right off the plate!'

'He's a pig.'

'He's a *terrorist*, man.'

'What was she having for dinner?'

'You mean what was *he* having.'

'Yeah, what was it?'

'It looked like pheasant, some kind of game bird. Maybe just chicken.'

'No wonder. Mèo really likes pheasant. It's one of his favorites. Only thing he likes better is peacock.'

Kay laughed. 'I thought he was redistributing the wealth or something.'

'Absolutely. As long as it got redistributed to him first.'

By providing food and shelter for the cat, I was affirming a life, however small and insignificant, in the midst of the slaughter. It wasn't conscious. Being young, I didn't dwell on my motives for doing things. It seemed right at the time. Though Mèo and I regarded each other as enemies, in a curious way we had come to depend on each other, just by being around, a kind of security in adversity. When I came back to the room after a trip to the field and heard him moving in his bunker or drinking water out of the tap in the bathroom or knocking something off the desk, it felt like coming home, belonging, feeling safe. Unprovoked attacks on me became less frequent, less ferocious, more of a ritual. Making it through Hué together must have formed a bond. Taking care of him gave me one small purpose other than reporting misery all the time.

As a half-grown cat, he was tough, independent, irascible. Soldierly and serene. A Zen warrior in white fur. Like some of the young men he hung around with in C-2, recklessness was part of his charm. He needed no initiation to the group. Walking along the outside ledge of the hotel, attacking larger animals, setting traps with wicked guile, he risked his life with the casual abandon of those who think they're invincible. Or fight for a cause. He was never nervous and never wasted energy. His moves were fluid, unfathomable. In time he came to be seen by all who knew him as a symbol of endurance and cunning, an authentic Vietnamese hero.

The problem of what to do with Mèo when I left Vietnam took some consideration. Friends and I discussed the possibilities. If we left him at the hotel, he might survive to become another feral cat living in the garden. Being leader of the tribe would give him first pick of the guests' scraps. Eventually, he would be completely wild. But it seemed heartless to abandon him there. Life in Saigon was too tenuous at the moment, too unpredictable. If the VC launched another big offensive, food would be scarce again. Mèo might get caught by one of the room boys and taken home for supper (not as a guest). Someone else might look after him for a time. Scrawny and malevolent though he was, he was an attractive kitten with white fur and orange-brown rings that could pass himself off as Siamese. But his temperament would be his doom. Sooner or later that ferocious disposition would get him in grave trouble, be the end of him perhaps, especially in a society indifferent to cats.

Other possibilities were considered. Taking him back to Hué was too much trouble; residents had enough to worry about repairing their homes.

Turning him loose outside Saigon—in the Viet Cong–controlled Ho Bo Woods—seemed like a good idea for a time, but on reflection was judged too dangerous for any of us to try. He might make it but we would not. Besides, if we let him loose in the jungle, how were the VC to know he was one of them? They would cook first and ask questions later. No chance of turning him in to the ARVN as a *chieu hoi;* he was too hard-core to change sides, amnesty or not. We considered all the options. Page suggested we ship him with no return address to the White House, into the central nervous system of the war-making authority, see what damage he might do there. Finally a decision was made. Since no one wanted take care of him in Vietnam, Mèo would have to come and live with me in the United States, deep in the heart of the enemy homeland.

He went, howling and scratching, head first into a bamboo cage, and then by car to the Saigon Zoo for inoculation. The zoo was a quiet park with hot dusty pathways and tamarind shade trees. It was virtually empty: no animals, no visitors. In the early days of the Tet Offensive, when Saigon shut its doors and stayed low, no one had come to feed the animals and some of them starved in their cages. Others, including many birds, were released into the open air and fluttered in the trees around the city, giving it a brush of exotic color.

We found the director, a sad-faced veterinarian named Vu Ngoc Tuyen, in his office. He did not smile. His mood seemed inexpressibly mournful, as if he had been responsible for the misfortunes of the zoo population.

'Why do you take it out?' Dr. Tuyen asked, regarding the cat.

'There's nobody to look after him here. He's an orphan,' I said.

'Lot of trouble for one cat.'

'Well, we've become attached, sort of.'

Dr. Tuyen held Mèo by the shoulders and examined him, looking inside his mouth and ears. The cat did not resist. The vet gave him a distemper shot. After a time he spoke again.

'Do you know how many animals are killed from this war?'

'No.'

I waited for the answer but the vet did not speak. A long silence followed.

Thousands and thousands, I thought: *birds, monkeys, water buffalo, elephants, tigers, snakes, lizards, dogs, cats—anything that got in the way. Who counts animals slaughtered in war?*

I understood his melancholy.

On our second visit, the vet gave Mèo another injection, examined him again, and signed a certificate pronouncing the cat "to be health and suitable for shipment, to have originated from an area free from contagious diseases of the specie and from rabies for more than six months, and at a distance of at least twenty kilometers from any rabies affected area, to have been vaccinated. . . ."

'*Bon chance,*' he said to the cat.

Mèo had a better chance of surviving than most animals caught by the war. Bombed, burned, shot at, starved, uprooted, displaced—animals suffered the whole vicious frenzy of violence that fate gave to living creatures in Vietnam. Sometimes, though, the animals held their own.

A Marine told me a story once about a big cat. His rifle company had just moved to a new position in bad country, close to Laos, late in the day. He was asleep in his tent on the edge of the perimeter. The weather was cold and raining. He woke up in the night. Something was chewing his boot.

'I put my hand down there,' the Marine said, 'and you know what I felt?'

'No,' I said.

'*Fur,* man. Fucking fur! All *kinds* of fur.'

I smiled.

'I start screamin and hollerin and tryin to get my weapon, and this, this fuckin *tiger* is all over me. I mean it's big as I am. Bitin and scratchin me to hell. The other guys said they couldn't shoot the fucker 'cause me 'n the tiger's wrestlin around in the tent tryin to kill each other, see?'

I nodded, writing in my notebook.

'So, finally, this fuckin tiger jes' ups and runs away, figures he's got enough of my ass, and I end up in Charlie Med with sixty-three stitches. No shit, man. I ain't never goin back out there again. Ever.'

He asked if I wanted to see the scars but I said no, I believed him.

On the morning of my departure from Saigon, not too early, friends gathered on the sidewalk outside the hotel. We had been up most of the night for a final farewell party and no one had had much sleep. We loaded the luggage into a jeep and Skip Brown, a CBS film photographer from San Francisco who had become a regular at C-2, volunteered to drive to the airport. Mèo, who was to remain behind for a few weeks, did not attend.

'It's good to see you getting out of here, pardner,' Keith Kay said. We shook hands.

'We're gonna miss you,' Mike Herr said.

'Don't forget to write, brother,' my brother Art said.

'I'll be thinking about you,' I said. 'Keep your heads down.'

'You keep *yours* down in New York, man.'

Keith, Art, Mike, Tim and the Rudds waved me into the swirl of Saigon traffic. I looked back at them without envy, though I knew I would miss their friendship and humor.

At Tan Son Nhut, the commercial airliner raced down the runway and lifted into the heavy air, strained with full power to put distance between it and the war, rose up out of the heat and filth and bounced lightly through cool white clouds. Inside the plane, a feeling of exquisite pleasure swept my senses, a sudden perfect freedom, as if a beast was off my back. The relaxation of the first gin and tonic made it sublime. Many hours later, flying over Alaska at night, passengers in the plane witnessed the aurora borealis, changing shapes of splendid light, haunting beauty. Drunk and sentimental by now, I thought, *Thank God the rest of the world isn't at war.*

A few days later, Mèo made the trip from Saigon to New York in the cargo section of a Pan American 707. No comfort for him. (A known terrorist, he was banned from the passenger cabin.) With transfers and delays, the journey took more than thirty-six hours. Immigration and customs formalities in New York took several more hours. When I heard he was waiting, I drove to a remote baggage depot at John F. Kennedy airport to collect him. The room was the size of an airplane hangar and filled with crates and packages awaiting collection. The faces of the two uniformed baggage officials were not friendly.

'I've come for the cat from Saigon,' I said.

A man in a short-sleeved white shirt looked at the health certificate.

'About time,' he said. 'That cat's a pain in the ass.'

Another clerk, younger, went to the back of the cargo shed and returned carrying the bamboo cage with the cat. I heard Mèo before I saw him. The howl came from some part of his most primitive being.

'We tried to give him some water but he bit hell out of us,' the first clerk said.

'This is a fucking *wildcat*,' the other said. Mèo tried to scratch his hand through the bars of the cage. He smelled of days-old feces and urine, the stench of Saigon still with him. His fur was a tangle, his eyes in a rage.

'He's Viet Cong,' I said.

'Yeah, well I been over there,' the younger man said, 'and I didn't see no VC cats. Not like this fucker. Would'a shot his ass.'

'He doesn't like Americans.'

'No shit.'

'There oughta be a law,' the older man said, 'an immigration law, against bringing Veetnese cats over here. They're a *menace*.'

They went through the paperwork in a hurry, handing me documents to sign, keeping their distance from the cage. Mèo growled.

I let him out of the cage when we were in the car on the road to Connecticut. Silent at once, he climbed onto the top of the dashboard, looked out at the passing traffic, sniffed the window, turned back and jumped to the top of the front seat, crawled onto my shoulder, then to the rear seat and the space under the back window, constantly sniffing, looking, moving.

'Well, cat, welcome to America,' I said. Mèo ignored me. 'You're going to stay with Nana for a while. I think you'll be happy there. Nana *likes* cats.' Nana was my mother, Doris, a great lover of animals. She had agreed at once to take care of Mèo until I found a place to live in New York, probably a month or two. Driving toward the Whitestone Bridge, I spoke to the cat for several minutes, asking him about his trip, commenting on the passing scenery, teasing him about the state of his fur, keeping my voice gentle. After a while, Mèo started to relax, though he remained vigilant. He appeared to recognize me, if only by smell and tone of voice. He was relieved to be out of the cage, though he soon discovered the car was a larger one.

Nana lived in a comfortable two-story red house near North Pasture Road in Westport, Connecticut, with her youngest son, Jeff, who was twelve years old and a junior high school student. The house was also the home of a six-year-old cat named Clem, a big lazy yellow and white tomcat who did little more in his tranquil life than eat and sleep.

As soon as he arrived, Mèo explored the interior of the house, climbing on top of the refrigerator, then the piano, on to the living room chairs, feeling their soft fabric, and finally up and down the curtains, clawing his way to the top like a rock climber, sniffing everywhere. When he finished his reconnaissance, he sat down and cleaned his fur.

'What does he eat?' Nana asked.

'He prefers fish heads and rice,' I said. 'At least that's what he's used to.'

'Oh, goodness! I hope that's not *all* he eats.' She had visions of cold gray fish eyes staring at her from the shelves of the refrigerator every time she opened it. She put a can of Nine Lives tuna fish on the floor. Mèo ate it enthusiastically, much to her relief. When he was finished, she picked him up and held him close to her. 'Nana's boy,' she said with a human purr, nuzzling him on the nose. It became her favorite phrase for the cat, "Nana's boy." I saw that he was in good hands and left to drive back to New York.

Nana sat in a chair to rest. There was silence for a time. Suddenly, a terrible noise filled the house: cat cries of pain and rage, objects falling to the floor. Combat! Nana ran upstairs. Clem, her housecat, was on the bed, eyes alight, body arched, fur up full, legs stiff, tail like an arrow—the image of a terrified Halloween cat. High above him, Mèo perched on the curtain rod above one of the windows, nimble as a squirrel, looking down at Clem with an expression of rage and contempt. Clem was not a warrior. Tufts of his fur were scattered on the bedcover. When Nana appeared in the doorway, Clem ran out of the room like a rifle shot and out of the house. He did not appear again for three days and nights. Nana, who recognized allegory when she saw it, thought there might be a lesson in the meeting of Mèo and Clem.

That summer I worked in New York and Saigon on a documentary about the hill battles around Dak To. Mèo lived in relative freedom at Nana's house in Connecticut. A few times a month I went to visit. He pretended not to know me. Sitting indoors one day, reading, I heard the shrieks of an animal crying for its life, noise like a violin screeching, *eeeek! eeeek!* I ran outdoors. Mèo was walking calmly across the lawn with a rabbit in his mouth. The animal was kicking and shrieking, powerless to escape. It was almost as big as the cat. I chased Mèo away and put the frightened rabbit under a briar patch. In the weeks that followed, Nana found other creatures that had been less fortunate.

Mèo spent most of those hot summer days sleeping in the sun on the rooftop of Jeff's treehouse in the woods. The place met the four conditions of Mèo's ideal sanctuary: it was isolated, warm, high and dry. For his indoor bunker, he chose the bottom drawer of a clothes chest that had been left open in Nana's bedroom. He curled up among her underclothes and slept. From then on, whenever the drawer was closed, he howled until it was opened again, whether he was in it or not.

A woman who came once a week to help Nana with her housework closed the drawer with the cat inside. He screamed feline insults until she opened it again, and it gave her a serious fright. The first time Mèo heard a vacuum cleaner he leaped fully four feet in the air—straight up, hairs on end—and ran upstairs to the safety of his bureau bunker. After that Nana made it a rule that the vacuum cleaner could not be used when Mèo was in the house. It must have sounded like the engine of a tank because it made him crazy. The housekeeper—a hardworking, friendly woman named Bessie Mae—found it difficult to adjust to all the new rules: no using the vacuum cleaner with Mèo around, no closing the bottom drawer of the dresser, no chasing the cat off the piano, no scolding him for climbing up and down the drapes, no stopping him from sharpening his claws on the Queen Anne wingback chair even though he was ruining the fabric. Patiently, Bessie Mae made the adjustments to her routine. One day as she worked quietly, lost in private thought, bent over, Mèo appeared out of the shadows and pounced on her back, hanging on to her skin with his claws. Terrified, she screamed. Then he was gone. She hardly had a look at him, he was away so fast. At the end of that work day, Bessie Mae quit.

'That cat is *spooked!*' she said to Nana. 'And you must be crazy to let him tear things to pieces like he does in this nice house you have.' Bessie Mae was the best housekeeper Nana had ever employed. (Also, perhaps, the wisest.) Nana was sorry to lose her but was more attached to the cat. "Poor baby," she said. "He's a war orphan. He can do anything he wants."

At night, sometimes, Mèo slept with Jeff. He curled up at the foot of the bed under the covers next to his feet. If, in his sleep, Jeff moved his legs and disturbed the cat, Mèo seized the offending foot with his paws, wrapped his body around it, and bit sharply into the ankle. Occasionally he closed his powerful jaws upon a toe. Once, in the middle of the night, Jeff cried out when the cat bit him, "Aaoow! Mèo! You oriental monster!" got out of his bed, stumbled into the guest bedroom and slammed the door.

"We never knew what to expect next," Nana said later, "but always he was the master and we were his slaves."

In time, Mèo became a favorite with the children in the neighborhood. They came to visit him and stroke his fur and ask questions about his homeland, which must have seemed to their young imaginations as far away as the moon. Usually he ignored them; tolerated them at most. But sometimes he played in the yard with the smaller ones, scurrying across the lawn like a big wildcat while the children watched, darting in and out of the bushes and around the house, showing off his speed, then racing directly at them as they screamed with wonder and fear, pouncing for an instant on their heads, patting their cheeks with the pads of his paws. Then he was gone. He did not bite or scratch them. He was the mighty neighborhood tiger, magnanimous in his power, all play with little children, a terror to all others.

Then he disappeared. For the first time he failed to appear for his supper. Nana worried. As the night grew late, she and Jeff walked along neighborhood streets looking for him.

"Here, Mèo. Come on, Nana's boy," she called.

The next morning, after Jeff went to school, she drove around a large part of Westport, along the main roads and up and down the side streets. She walked in and out of the woodlands. He was nowhere. She remembered that I had told her not to worry, that he might disappear for a few days but always came back. She was afraid of an accident. There were so many busy roads. He was truly missing.

The second day he was gone Nana put a picture of Mèo in the lost-and-found section of the local paper. She went into town and put handmade notices and photographs of him in public places. By the third day it seemed as if all Westport was looking for a missing white Vietnamese cat. Strangers appeared at the house with stray cats, two of them white. Nana stopped going out because her eyes filled with tears and her voice choked when she called his name, "Nana's boy." Jeff walked miles, up and down every road, checking the grassy sides for signs of the cat. Nothing was found.

On the morning of the fourth day the weather was wet and cool. Jeff was still so upset about he loss of the cat he did not eat his breakfast. Because of the rain, he went through the cellar and the downstairs garage on his way to school. Nana cleaned the breakfast plates. She heard a cry from the garage.

"He's home! Mom, he's home!" Jeff called. He ran up the stairs two at a time and rushed into the kitchen, his eyes bright with excitement. "Mèo's home! Come see! He's in a box and he's hurt real bad." In the garage, the cat lay on its side in an old cardboard carton on the floor. He did not move. His eyes were dull, dispirited, lifeless. His mouth was open, panting in short breaths. Nana ran upstairs, grabbed a blanket and brought it down to cover him. She was in tears.

'Don't worry, Mom, he's a tough cat,' Jeff said. 'You'll see. He'll make it.'

She called the local animal hospital. 'Bring him in as soon as possible,' the nurse said. Nana started her car. Jeff carried the box, blanket and cat on his lap, rubbing Mèo's head with his fingers, talking to him.

The veterinarian at the animal hospital, Dr. Shulhof, gave the cat an injection to ease the pain. Mèo did not resist.

'He's in shock,' the vet said. 'This shoulder is shattered. Feels like it's broken in two or three places. It's going to need a pin if we operate on it. The paw is broken too. Little fella looks like he's been hit by a Mack truck.'

'You've got to help him live,' Nana said. 'He's come all the way from Vietnam and he already used up most of his lives over there. My son's heart will break if he dies. So will ours.'

'I can't guarantee he'll make it,' the vet said. 'Cats are strange creatures. They're inclined to give up when they're injured this badly. He'll need a strong fighting spirit.'

'Oh, but he's got one. He's incredibly brave.'

'Fights like a tiger,' said Jeff.

'We'll do everything we can. Can't make any promises though. It's going to be very expensive, whether he makes it or not.'

Nana called me in New York. I told her to do whatever was necessary, the bill would be paid. I was delighted to hear he was still alive. For the first time since we had met in Hué, I was worried about his survival.

Mèo lived. The next day he underwent surgery for his broken shoulder and paw. An anesthetic was administered. It may have been the only time in his life he wasn't prepared for a fight. A lot of his fur was shaved away. The bones were set and a steel pin inserted to hold them in place. When the skin was stitched together, his fractured limbs were put in casts and the long operation was declared a success.

Six weeks in the animal hospital, he recovered slowly. Nana and Jeff visited three times a week, smuggling treats to him through the bars of his cage. Hearing his story, young people who worked at the hospital made him one of their favorites, giving him extra attention and affection. When one of the attendants cleaned the cage below Mèo's, she felt a paw poking her shoulder. He didn't stop until she reached into his cage and rubbed his head. 'What a clever cat,' she said.

The vet said Mèo had made a strong recovery, that he was impressed by the cat's will to live. The bones were mending properly. Later, he presented a bill for $1,500. The thought occurred that Mèo might be trying to terrorize me financially.

'You'll have to keep him indoors as much as possible,' the vet said, 'and quiet.'

Keeping Mèo quiet was like trying to restrain a two-year-old. The moment he got into the house he leaped to the floor, limped across the

kitchen, launched himself onto the top of the refrigerator and licked the
stubble where some of his fur had been.

For the next several days, Mèo howled at the kitchen door, demanding
freedom. Like a full-blooded Siamese, he made the most irritating noise, a
cry of frustration that could cause actual physical harm to human ears. It
was a weapon and he knew how to use it. Whenever Nana was within range,
he howled. Finally, to keep her sanity, she relented. Out he went, limp and
all. Mèo hopped around the yard inspecting his favorite haunts: the woods,
the treehouse, the stone wall at the edge of the property, and the garage. He
appeared happy to be home. With his injured paw and shoulder, he was no
danger to the birds and animals. But he could be seen at times in the woods,
climbing up and down the smaller trees, over and over, scurrying in short
bursts across open ground, doing wind sprints, teaching himself how to run
and climb again, working his private program of rehabilitation like a guerrilla warrior in training.

Two weeks later he began to sneeze. Repeatedly. *Sssnoot! Sssnoot!* His
whole head shook. Mucus came out of his nose. He could not stop. Sometimes the combination of head shaking and mucus secretion sent streams of
yellow phlegm flying around him. The lower walls around the house
became streaked with dried mucus. He stopped eating. He did not go outside. His eyes became dull and empty. Nana took him to the vet. Mèo was
not happy to be back in the hospital. When the vet tried to examine him, he
bit and scratched. The vet injected him with a sedative. Then he took his
temperature.

'Pneumonia,' the vet said. 'It doesn't look good. Cats don't have the best
immune system to fight it.'

'After all he's been through,' Nana said, 'it doesn't seem fair to lose him
now.'

'He'll make it, Mom,' Jeff said. 'You'll see.'

The vet prescribed a course of antibiotics and recommended confinement in the hospital. The routine was repeated: visits three times a week, cat
treats smuggled through the bars, the staff making a fuss over him. This time
Mèo's hospitalization lasted three weeks. In the end, he made a good recovery. Though the sneezing came less often, it stayed with him after that, a
mark of the pneumonia on him.

'He's indestructible, Mom,' Jeff said. 'I told you.'

JUNE, 1968

Something was wrong. I saw it in Ben Silver's face as soon as I got to the airport operations room while hurrying to make a flight. Silver, a young reporter from the New York assignment desk, wore an expression drawn with gloom—a sad, anxious look that said, *Bad news, Jack, you're not going to like this.* I had just covered a story in Atlantic City and was rushing to get to New York. The producers of the *Evening News* wanted the film as soon as possible for their newscast in a few hours. A pilot and helicopter were standing by to fly the film and me to New York, about 125 miles north. A motorcycle courier would be waiting at the other end. Time was short. The deadline pressure was intense. It was now after three o'clock in the afternoon—too late to drive to New York, develop, screen, and edit the film, and get it on the air by 6:30. The helicopter was the only way. Outside the operations shack, the weather was heavy: low clouds, wind, rain.

'The pilot won't go,' Silver said. 'He says it's too hairy to fly in this soup.' His voice was tentative, nervous, as if he might be blamed.

'When's it going to clear?' I said.

'They don't know. It's a big storm. All over the Northeast. It doesn't look good.' It didn't look good for Ben, either. There was fear in his face. Assignment desk reporters associated with too many missed stories didn't get promoted to correspondent.

Damn, I thought. *We've got a good one that needs to get on the air.* The National Association for the Advancement of Colored People had just opened its annual convention in Atlantic City and there had been a vigorous, sometimes angry debate in the main hall. Delegates from the African American community were divided between militants who wanted to use more aggressive tactics in the fight for racial equality and conservatives who wished to maintain traditional policies of passive, nonviolent action. The issues were more complicated than that, of course, but were important for the whole country, for people of all colors. The leader of the civil rights movement, Dr. Martin Luther King Jr., had been murdered in April and the future of the movement appeared to be at stake. Other organizations, such as the Congress of Racial Equality, the Student Nonviolent Coordinating Committee and the Black Panthers, were talking openly about more aggressive, confrontational strategies and tactics. The threat of armed conflict, even revolution, was in the wind.

The pilot stood behind the counter of the one-room office with a cup of coffee in his hand, looking at a teletyped weather report. He appeared indifferent, relaxed, almost laconic—a man in his late twenties with short hair and a windbreaker over his flying clothes. He lifted his head and looked at me. His eyes squinted. His face seemed curious, then puzzled. I walked to the counter.

'How bad is it?' I said.

'Getting worse all the time,' he said. 'Moving down from the north. We got in just ahead of it.'

I looked out the window. Dark light, some rain, dense gray clouds rolling away to the horizon. The cloud ceiling was below a thousand feet. Too dangerous to fly in a small chopper.

No one spoke. I felt disappointed about missing the show but was resigned to it. No way to beat the weather.

The pilot looked at me for a minute. 'I know you from somewhere, don't I?' he said. 'I'm trying to remember where.' I looked at him carefully. His eyes were clear, his face tanned and fit, a muscular neck on strong shoulders, broad back. Nothing registered. His appearance was indistinguishable from many other pilots I had met.

'You ever been in Vietnam?' he said.

'Yes, two times.'

'Were you in Hué? During Tet?'

'Yes.'

'With a kitten?'

I smiled. 'You mean Mèo, the VC cat?'

The pilot laughed. 'You don't remember, do you?' He studied my face. 'I flew you out of Hué near the end. In a CH-46. With the wounded and that Vietnamese camera jockey and another little guy. You were a pretty unforgettable crew.' He reached across the counter and offered his hand. I shook it firmly.

'I'm sorry I never got to thank you,' I said. 'You guys were pretty busy at the time.'

'Yeah. Guess you never met me with my helmet off.'

'When did you get out?' I said.

'Oh, pretty soon after that. Out of the Corps. What happened to the kitten?' He smiled.

'He's up in Connecticut, raising hell.'

'I remember him on my shoulder. I could feel a weight there but I didn't have time to look around. When I saw the kitten, well, it was mighty strange, I'll tell you. Thought I'd seen everything in that war. But that kitten was something else. Weirdest thing I ever saw. I must've told the story a hundred times.'

We laughed. Silver listened to the exchange, eyes wide.

After a time the pilot asked, 'How important is it for you to get to New York?'

'Very,' I said. 'We've got a good story.' I told him what it was about. 'We need to get it on the air tonight, otherwise it'll be old news. But there's no way if we can't fly.'

The pilot looked out the window. He was silent for a few moments.

"Oh, what the hell," he said, straightening his back, a decisive note in his voice, a Marine officer again. "It can't be half as bad as flying into Hué." He reached down, picked up his briefcase and walked toward the door at the back of the office. "Come on, let's give it a try," he called. I grabbed the bag of news film and said good-bye to Silver.

'Tell New York we're on the way,' I said. 'Have 'em meet us at the West Side helipad. I'll try and get back here tonight.' Silver nodded his head but said nothing. The expression on his dark round boyish face had changed to astonishment.

The helicopter was not much more than a plastic bubble with engine, seats, instruments and rotor blades. The pilot strapped in on the right side, went through a fast instrument check, started the engine and got on the radio. Turning his head to me, he said, "You're gonna have to help watch for power lines. That's the main thing I'm worried about." He looked out both sides and above. Visibility was still under a thousand feet. 'We'll follow the Garden State up to Perth Amboy,' he said, 'then the Turnpike to Manhattan.' Revving the engine, slowly at first, then faster, then above the green line. 'You all right? Hang on.' He took off to the west, above Albany Avenue and the Bay, the chopper wobbling in the hard wind. The pilot held the machine steady with the strength and agility of his hands and feet. He flew at about five hundred feet, just above the power lines, pylons and telephone poles, nose down slightly, as fast as it would go. The wind tossed the helicopter every way at once: up, down, sideways—rolling, yawing and pitching like a small boat in a storm. The landscape was a dull wash of gray and black: indistinct, foggy, the colors blurred. Heavy drops of rain pelted the cockpit with a *tat-tat-tat-tat-tat* sound. I gripped the sides of the seat with both hands, muscles tight, breath short, looking for power lines. They seemed to be everywhere, ranging across the flat Jersey landscape in an intricate web, lurking below us. My faith in the pilot, the one thought holding fast against the fear, wavered once or twice.

He landed on a pier at the edge of the Hudson River near 36th Street in a strong wind. I gave the news film to the motorcycle courier and watched him drive away to the lab. My hands hurt. Inside the little ops cabin, I lit a cigarette. The pilot smiled. He seemed pleased and exhausted.

'Not as bad as Hué,' I said, pouring a cup of coffee.

'Roger that. Helps me keep my eye in, though.' He laughed.

'Gets the adrenaline going.'

'Yeah, I'll say. Haven't had one of those since I got back.'

'Where next?'

'I'll try to get in to LaGuardia and call it quits. Enough excitement for one day.'

'Thanks for the ride. I really appreciate it.'

'No sweat. All in the cause. Hope you get your story on the air.'

'Thanks. See you again sometime.'

'You bet.'

I took a taxi to the CBS News offices on West 57th Street. There were two hours to airtime. A desk assistant met me at the door. Producers and editors were waiting. The film was being developed. I worried. *How was it possible to get the story ready in time?* In the States, everything happened faster. More transportation was available, schedules were met, people showed up on time. The whole system was quicker and more reliable than the slow, ponderous military procedures that I was accustomed to in Vietnam. In civilian life, I was learning, you got the efficiency you paid for.

I had been home less than a month and the CBS News operation in New York was unfamiliar. I didn't know most of the people, though they knew me from my work on the air. Walking across the newsroom, I caught some of their eyes following me—curious looks that seemed to say, *There's that kid who was in Vietnam. Look how young he is.* The recognition was reassuring but the effect didn't last. In the headquarters of the most competitive television news organization, it was often said, "You're only as good as your last story."

Sanford Socolow, an energetic producer with a quick mind whom everyone called 'Sandy' or 'Soc,' said the piece would be put together by Stanhope Gould, an associate producer, and Len Raff, a film editor. Socolow told me what aspects of the story were newsworthy, something he had already discussed with the *Evening News* staff. He knew that my knowledge of civil rights was outdated because of my long tour in Vietnam, so he passed along the consensus of the producers' expertise. Stories at CBS News were always written by individuals, but the editorial content was often decided by a group.

The film came out of the lab with an hour to air. As it was being screened, Socolow and Gould explained how the scenes would fit together. They would start with picture and natural sound at the top for a second or two, then would come about twenty seconds of voice-over narration covered by pictures of the convention, followed by natural sound of the debate for ten to fifteen seconds, then more narration, an interview, more narration, another interview, and finally the closing paragraph and sign-off. There was no stand-up. I wrote down their instructions and went to work on the script. Raff took the film into his editing room and closed the door. He wound the narrow roll of film through sprocketed loops on his editing console and spun through the pictures at speed, causing a high-pitched whirring noise. When he saw a shot he could use, he marked it quickly with a black grease pencil. Then he cut the length of film with a heated instrument and spliced it with clear adhesive to the next section in the sequence. Each shot lasted about three to five seconds, although some were longer. Stories like this usually had thirty or forty edits, maybe more, creating a physical chain of pictures on film. Raff's white-gloved hands twirled and spun like a magician, conjuring a visual story of the day's event from disparate bits of film.

I wrote the voice-over on a borrowed typewriter in Socolow's office, trying to tell the basic facts of the story (who-what-where-when-why) in the scenes between the interviews. It was impossible to know the exact length of each scene because Raff was still editing the film and the timings were uncertain. He cut the length necessary to make the scenes visually coherent. I was working blind. I finished about half an hour to airtime and gave the script to Gould. He said there wasn't enough time to record my narration and match it to pictures in the usual way. I would have to read the script live, he said, while the show was on the air. Suddenly the stakes involved in broadcasting the story were much higher. Reading a voice-over narration to a cut spot live into the show was harder to do than anything else. It was complicated enough to write a script to unedited film and give it to an editor to cut to your words, but to read a voice-over live to moving pictures was fraught with hazards. I had done it only once before, not in New York. My concentration would have to be total, the timing flawless, coordination precise. Moreover, terrified as I was of making a mistake, my voice could not sound nervous on the air. The possibility of embarrassment was great. A missed cue, bad timing, unsteady nerves or a weak voice and I would sound like an amateur on national television. It was a prescription for career death.

'Are you all right with that?' Gould said.

'Oh, sure, Stan,' I said. Inside, my stomach burned.

'Don't worry, man,' he said. 'I'll talk you through it.'

In the final minutes before airtime, the Cronkite studio swirled with people holding clipboards and stopwatches—producers, directors, writers, editors, assistants, secretaries—walking briskly in and out of offices, calling out last-minute details to one another, into telephones, over intercoms. Everyone was in a hurry. Serious faces, tense voices. 'One minute to air!' an assistant director shouted into the hubbub. At the center of activity sat the executive producer, Leslie Midgley, a tall, gentle, white-haired man whose eyelashes fluttered like a shy child's and who spoke with a voice so soft that much of what he said was inaudible. A former newspaper reporter, he sat behind a large gray desk covered with scripts and program lineups in an office with one glass wall known as "the fishbowl." A few feet away, in the studio, Walter Cronkite sat at the anchor desk surrounded by writers, technicians and a makeup artist getting him ready to go on. Cronkite was cool, unruffled, totally absorbed in his work. Reading pages of his script, making notes, changing a word or phrase occasionally, he was the emblem of an experienced news editor at deadline. Midgley reached into a cabinet in his office, carefully withdrew a bottle of Scotch whisky, poured a large measure into a glass of ice that had been placed there by his secretary, and left it to chill.

A minute or two before air, control of the broadcast passed from the executive producer to the director. Working down the hall from the newsroom, Fred Stollmack sat at a long desk in a darkened room facing a wall of flashing TV monitors. The control room was the cockpit from where he called out instructions to dozens of technicians, camera operators and assistants spread around the unit. Stollmack, known by his colleagues as "Freddie," was a man of fast timing and peripatetic attention. As the moment of air approached, exactly 6:30, eastern daylight time, the level of last-minute stress in the Cronkite area heightened exponentially. Producers ran. Secretaries shouted. Someone cursed and slammed down a phone. The pressure among people trying to put the broadcast on the air reached a point of tension so sharp it seemed to a visitor like barely controlled hysteria. The confusion and fear were not unlike the first minute of combat—totally chaotic.

'How long is Laurence?' someone shouted. 'Two-oh-five,' Gould called back. 'Get him in the booth!' Socolow ordered. I was taken to a small soundproof announcer's booth near the control room and given a seat at a felt-covered table. The air was heavy with dust. I put on a pair of headsets, wound and zeroed my stopwatch. Gould sat in the control room and said over an intercom that we had time for one rehearsal. He was calm. The edited film rolled. I watched the pictures on a six-inch monitor and listened to the soundtrack on the earphones. In one ear came natural sound of the cut spot and in the other the voice of Gould in the control room. In the background, Stollmack's urgent instructions could be heard getting the broadcast ready for air. As the film rolled, I read the narration into the microphone, trying to glance at the monitor and the stopwatch at the same time, following the pictures and the moving second hand as I spoke the words on the script. It was difficult, like juggling three balls with one hand. The scenes on the monitor changed faster than I could follow them. I tried to keep track of the elapsed times on the script but my sentences were too long or too short. All the timings were off. Raff had cut the scenes to irregular lengths. When the rehearsal was finished, Gould told me to take out several words to make the sentences shorter in some sections of the script, to add words in other places to make them longer. Everything was moving quickly. 'Okay, man,' Gould said, 'here are the timings I've got.' He read a list of numbers and elapsed times and I wrote them on the margins of the script. I could hear Raff's voice speaking to him in the background. Gould's voice was confident, reassuring. 'Don't worry,' he said. 'I'll cue you on the air.' I reset my stopwatch and took a deep breath. A reading on the air like the rehearsal we had just done would be a disaster.

An associate director counted down the seconds to the start of the broadcast, "Five, four, three, two . . ." The show went on the air with the recorded sound of a clacking teletype and then the deep voice of the announcer:

"Direct from our newsroom in New York, this is the *CBS Evening News with Walter Cronkite* . . ." And the fine sharp edge came off the frenzy.

Cronkite began to introduce the Atlantic City piece.

"Standby Laurence," a voice said. "Ready in the booth."

Film leader numbers rolled on the monitor, 5, 4, 3, 2, and the screen went black. Cronkite's voice said, ". . . our correspondent is John Laurence." Pictures of the convention flashed on the monitor. Natural sound burst abruptly in my ear. An assistant director screamed, "*Aannnnnd, announce!*" I took a quick breath and spoke the first sentence of the narration. In the earphones, my voice played back in one ear and the director's voice shouted in the other. I was concentrating too hard to be frightened. When the first paragraph was finished, I stopped. The debate came up, sound full. Right on time, thank God. Another breath. But I didn't know when this section was going to end. 'Okay, Jack, five seconds now.' Gould's voice in the earphones, composed. I took another breath. 'And, *cue.*' I read the next paragraph and stopped. On time. Again, the sound came up full. Amazing. I continued to announce, stop, announce, stop on Gould's instructions. My heart beat like a piston. Seconds ticked away on the stopwatch but I had lost all sense of time. I relied completely on Gould to take me through. Two minutes and five seconds later it was over. It had seemed like a few short breaths. After the sign-off, a commercial came on. My palms were wet. I took a big breath of stale air in the announcer's booth and tried to swallow. There was no moisture there. In the earphones, Stollmack's voice said, 'Thanks, Jack, nice job,' and went immediately to preparations for the next piece. A young woman with long blond hair and sparkling eyes looked into the booth as she hurried past and smiled at me for a second, sharing the moment of elation. I was too surprised, too flattered to smile back.

After the broadcast, Walter Cronkite stood at the bar of the saloon across the street on West 57th, his tie loose and jacket off, talking to the pretty young woman with blond hair from the office. The broadcast had gone well and Cronkite was in good spirits, unwinding from the pressures of the day. No one disturbed their conversation. Stan Gould invited me over for a quick drink before I flew back to Atlantic City. Outside, the storm was still blowing.

The Slate bar and restaurant was a popular hangout for employees of CBS News. The place was small, cheerful and informal with low ceilings and sawdust on wooden floors. It served simple, undistinguished food and fair-sized drinks. You could run a tab at the Slate. The owner, Seymour Rand, was a gregarious, sociable man in his mid-thirties with a broad, heavy frame who had padding in the shoulders of his suits and also on the soles of his shoes. When he saw you were about to leave his place after a drink or two, Seymour gave you one on the house, so that you often stayed for the rest of the evening. He played host to an unlikely assortment of New York and New Jersey characters, not all of them straight with the law: journalists, mobsters, secretaries, gamblers, union stewards, the odd celebrity—all found comfort and entertainment at the Slate. Sooner or later, everybody got to know everybody else. It was the kind of joint Damon Runyon might have liked.

Stanhope Gould was no dull character himself. His appearance was shocking, outrageous, beyond avant-garde. It struck your senses like a loud noise. Even by the permissive standards of dress and style in 1968, Stanhope's look was bizarre. Cynical New Yorkers, who were rarely surprised by what they saw on the streets of the city, turned their heads when Gould walked past to look again.

He was from Chicago, a veteran of City News Service, where he had served his journalistic apprenticeship. Six feet tall, large-boned and dark, his long black curly hair draped uncombed around his pale sick-looking white face like a theater curtain. A fierce mustache emblazoned his mouth; a black mole decorated his cheek. His eyes were small and dark, sinister at times, a look he cultivated. On his substantial head, he wore a large black hat with an eight-inch brim that gave him the look of a turn-of-the-century European anarchist. His politics were no less radical. His voice was deep and strong. He delighted in being provocative, especially toward authority.

Although his personal behavior might be Bohemian, Gould was a serious professional journalist—an imaginative field producer with an original mind and a strong sense of honesty. I never heard him lie. The *Evening News* valued his shrewd assessment of contemporary culture and politics, and his original ways of presenting stories on the air. He was bright, creative, open-minded and, working on deadline, as fast as anyone in the shop. His arguments on politics, social justice, economics and ethics were delivered with the unwavering conviction of a university debating captain. But louder. Much louder. People either loved and respected Stanhope or despised him. There were few in-betweens. He was always interesting.

'What'll you have?' he asked when we got to the bar.

'Dewars,' I said. 'No ice.'

'You ever tried Black Label?'

'No.'

'Try it, man. It's a better Scotch.' He ordered for both of us.

'You guys wouldn't know good whisky if it bit you in the ass,' a sharp voice cried from the end of the bar. It was Jimmy Clevenger, the assistant director of the Cronkite broadcast—a slight, mustached figure with reddish-brown hair that he mussed with his hand when making a point. Clevenger was another of the larger-than-life characters who drank at the Slate, a wildly argumentative whisky drinker and bibliophile. He had read as much serious nineteenth- and twentieth-century literature as anyone in the neighborhood and could carry on an intelligent conversation about authors and their works for as long as it took him to get to his fifth or sixth drink. His literary specialty was the history of war. Almost every night after work, Clevenger went to the Slate, got drunk, went home and read a book.

'If you want good whisky, drink malt,' he said in his high, pinched voice. 'Trouble is, Seymour doesn't stock the really good stuff. Nobody around here appreciates it.' He pointed to a green and black bottle on a shelf behind the bar that was labeled Glenfiddich. 'Try that sometime.'

'What are you drinking, Jimmy?' Gould said.

'Johnny Walker Black,' he said dismissively. 'Everyday shit.'

We drank and talked. Since 1966, Gould had been teaching me the basics of broadcast journalism. We had done several stories around the country, some breaking news and a few longer features for the *Evening News*. Now that I was back from Vietnam, we were working together again. Gould was one of the most interesting, original people I knew at CBS. He was also a fine poker player, a game at which he rarely lost money.

The mood in the Slate was buoyant, happy. Heat and smoke circulated with the chatter of conversation. Most of the customers in the hour after 7:30 worked for the Cronkite show: secretaries, associate producers, assistant directors, writers, technicians. It was the end of their workday. Mine was still not over. I had to be back to cover the convention the next morning. I drank in a hurry. A chartered plane was waiting at LaGuardia to take me to Atlantic City and I didn't want to be late. Gould volunteered to call the assignment desk to tell them I would be leaving soon. The desk told him I had to wait; the storm was holding up the flight. Better to wait at the Slate than in an ops shack at LaGuardia.

We ordered another drink. The young woman with long blond hair who had smiled at me earlier was still talking with Cronkite. She was more attractive in the relaxed setting of the bar. Her complexion was fair, slightly tanned, soft looking. Her whole body seemed to be soft, alluring, sculpted in gentle curves, no sharp edges anywhere. Her nose had a slight crook in the bone near the middle, a childhood break perhaps, a singular distinction on a long lovely face. Talking with Cronkite, laughing, she seemed radiantly happy. Our eyes met across the room. This time I smiled back.

'Stanhope,' I said, 'who's that good-looking girl with Cronkite?'

He looked around. 'Who, Joy?' he said.

'Yes. What's her name?'

'Joy Baker. Isn't she sexy? Man, I've been trying to get her in the sack for months. No luck. I think I scare her or something.'

'Is she going with anybody?'

'No, I don't think so.'

By the time the assignment desk called to say the plane was ready to take off, it was after nine o'clock. Most of the Cronkite staff had gone. Gould and I walked toward the door. Joy Baker saw us leaving and came over.

"What are you doing?" she said.

"Going to dinner with you," I said.

"Okay." She smiled. Her dark blue eyes danced with mischievousness.

"There's only one catch," I said.

"What's that?"

"It's in Atlantic City."

"Okay," she said, matter-of-fact. Then, after another look, "Are you *serious*?"

I told her a charter was waiting at LaGuardia. 'We could fly down tonight, have dinner and hold the plane until you're ready to go back.'

She laughed. 'You *are* serious.' Her pale yellow hair bounced on her shoulders. 'Let me find out,' she said. 'Can you wait a minute?' She turned to walk back to the bar. Her body moved with calm purpose inside a short close-fitting summer skirt and blouse, her long slender legs rising up into a flare of hips that narrowed again to a thin waist held close by a brown leather belt with a large brass buckle and then up to round small shoulders more like a young girl than an adult woman and the suggestion of soft full breasts inside the blouse. The smooth, graceful movement of her walk took her appearance into the realm of erotic beauty.

She spoke to her boss, Hinda Glasser, who sat at the end of the bar with her back to a wall. Hinda was tough—a short, older woman with a New York City attitude. She looked at me over Joy Baker's shoulder with an expression that said, *Wait a minute, pal, where do you think you're going with my girl?* Her job put her in charge of four or five young women who worked in the Cronkite unit. Then she laughed and I knew it was all right. Hinda would do anything for one of her girls. She said there was a condition: Joy had to get back in time for work in the morning at 9:30. We had a date.

I asked Stan Gould if he wanted to come. 'Yeah, why not?' he said. 'We'll have fun.' He asked a friend of his who was sitting at the bar, Christine Huneke, a researcher for CBS News, to join us and she agreed. Now we were four.

The idea of a spontaneous flying party to Atlantic City brought out some of Gould's most creative talents as a producer. First he phoned a nearby delicatessen, the Four-Hundred, and ordered chopped chicken liver, a house specialty, bagels, cheesecake and other delicacies to go. Then he called a liquor store and told them to chill several bottles of their best champagne. 'We'll eat on the plane,' he said, pleased with his production. Outside, the storm appeared to be easing. Stanhope called the assignment desk. The pilot, he was told, was flying to Newark Airport to be closer and would meet us there. Stanhope did not tell the desk that four would be on the flight.

We got into a taxi and started toward the airport in light rain. Sitting between Joy and Chris in the backseat was an intimate fit. Stanhope sat in front with the driver, directing the route and tending bar. We drank champagne from plastic cups, toasting one and other, Walter Cronkite, the NAACP, Ben Silver, CBS News, the Marine helicopter pilot and nature for bringing us together. We told stories. We sang. We joked. Leaving the Lincoln Tunnel toll booth, Stanhope held an empty champagne bottle out the window for an instant and dropped it on the pavement, shattering glass over the road. Thirty minutes later, when we got to the airport, a police officer was waiting at the terminal. He gave the taxi driver a summons for allowing passengers to drink in his cab. 'It's our fault,' Joy said immediately. 'The driver told us not to drink, but we did anyway.' The rest of us joined in: 'Honest, officer, we accept responsibility.' 'Give us the ticket.' 'Yeah, we'll pay for it.' The police officer listened politely while he wrote the summons, then drove away. The driver looked crushed.

'How much is the fine?' Stanhope asked.

'Fifty bucks,' the driver said, already in mourning. Getting out of the cab, Stanhope paid the fare in cash from his pocket and added a $50 tip.

The airport was deserted. It was nearly eleven o'clock and most of the scheduled flights had been canceled because of the storm. Gould handed me his flight bag with the champagne and food, and went away to find the pilot. Joy and Chris went to the ladies room. A few minutes later, Gould returned to say the plane would be ready in ten minutes.

'Where are they?' he said.

'In the ladies room,' I said.

'What are we waiting for?'

He led the way.

'Stanhope, you know they can lock you up for this?' I said.

'Don't worry, man. We can say it was an emergency. I'll think of something.'

The ladies room was brightly lit, with a row of wash basins and mirrors against the wall and a tiled floor, immaculately clean. The women were touching up the makeup on their faces, talking. No one else in sight.

'Stanhope, you crazy man,' Chris said in her deep voice, laughing. 'What if someone comes in here?'

'We'll give them a drink,' he said. He took another bottle from the flight bag, opened it with a loud pop, and carefully poured champagne for each of us. Like me, Gould had the capacity for consuming large quantities of alcohol without appearing drunk. As we stood in front of the mirrors talking, the door to the rest room opened and a middle-aged woman walked toward the toilets. When she saw a wild-looking man with a Zapata mustache and black anarchists' hat holding a champagne bottle, staring at her, she froze. Her jaw dropped and her eyes opened wide. No words came out of her mouth.

'Welcome to the party,' Stanhope said.

'Would you like some champagne?' Chris asked politely.

Quickly, the woman turned and hurried out.

'Is this how you guys behave on the road *all* the time?' Joy said.

'Only when we're not working,' I said.

The weather was still rough as the twin-engine Beechcraft took off. It was nearly midnight. The pilot did not object when he saw the extra passengers. Everyone was merry. We had consumed three bottles of champagne and were not bothered by the bouncing flight. I sat facing Joy Baker across a small flight table, our knees nearly touching. Gould, beside me, faced Chris Huneke. By now, the chicken liver was soggy.

'Hey, man, try some of this,' Stanhope said, passing it to Joy. 'It's the best in New York.'

'I've never had it before,' she said, looking with apprehension at the dark mass of chopped liver and onion spread on a cracker. She took a bite, chewed it for a second. She put her hand to her mouth, as if she were going to throw up, and put the food down.

'It's an acquired taste,' Gould said. 'It helps to be Jewish.'

'I don't like airplane food anyway,' Joy said.

We laughed. We talked. It felt increasingly pleasant to be with her. We seemed to enjoy each other's company equally. Her calm, cheerful nature blended well with her appearance. I found the combination of beauty and friendliness captivating. Even with the heavy drinking, the lack of nourishment, the late hour and the rough flight, her soft blue eyes flashed with merriment. When she laughed, her hair danced in the light.

'I'm a country girl,' she said, 'from Crystal City, Missouri.' She pronounced it *Missourah*. 'It's about fifty miles south of St. Louis, right on the Mississippi.' Her voice had the same softness as the rest of her—deep, resonant, gentle. There was no shyness about her, no lack of confidence, yet no conceit. Her manner was direct. She seemed to say what she thought whether it agreed with the rest of us or not. She said she was new to New York and was intimidated by the big city.

'Crystal City is Bill Bradley's hometown.'

'The Knicks player?'

'Yes. He used to help me with my homework. He was a year ahead of me at school.'

'Did you play basketball with him?'

'No,' laughing, 'I wasn't tall enough.'

Joy said she had worked in the newsroom of the local CBS television station in St. Louis, KMOX-TV. During a NASA space shot the previous summer, she had been on a live remote for the network's Special Events unit. The producer in charge, Jack Kelly, was impressed by her hard work and ability, and recommended her to the network. She was offered a job on the Cronkite show and moved to New York. Twenty-six years old, independent, honest, gorgeous, good-natured, I found out later that everyone who knew her loved her.

The plane hit a powerful gust of wind and lurched hard. Joy touched my calf with the instep of her foot and moved it slowly, lightly up the inside of my leg. When I looked at her eyes, she smiled across the table, mischievously. I felt physically excited.

'Listen, Joy,' Gould said. 'Say the name of the restaurant, La Poulialier, for me.'

She laughed.

'Come on, I bet you can't say it.'

'No, Stanhope, it's embarrassing,' she said.

'She asked me how to spell it a few weeks ago,' he said. 'When she had to make a reservation for Midgley.'

'Well, I don't speak French.'

'That's okay. You know how to say it. Come on, Joy, just once. Show Jack.'

'All right, Stanhope,' she said, 'but this is absolutely the last time.'

'You gotta see this, man,' he said to me, conspiratorially.

She took a breath, pushed her small shoulders back, and said, *"Lah Pool-ya-lee-ay,"* slowly, syllable by syllable. As she spoke, her lips came forward on her face into the shape of a circle and part of the pink insides turned out, like a kiss. Making the *lah* sound, her tongue flicked between her bright white teeth for an instant. With each syllable, her mouth and face formed a different shape, sensual, sexy. She had the same mouth as Marilyn Monroe.

'Oh, man! Isn't that sensational?' Gould said, bouncing on the seat. We all laughed. Joy too.

'Stanhope, you're a *lecher*,' she said, embarrassed and delighted.

'I admit it!' he shouted. 'I admit it!'

The next morning, I drove Joy, Stanhope and Chris to the airport in a rented car. The pilot had decided not to make the return trip the night before in the dangerous wind and had spent the night in the same motel, though he got more sleep. The four of us went dancing on the beach, playing in the fine halting rain, singing, skipping over the sand in our bare feet, falling finally into each other's arms in long loving embraces and exhausted sleep. Now, at eight in the morning, the night's frivolity had been replaced by the serious business of the journey back. Joy worried about being late for work. The wind was blowing hard. It would not be a gentle flight. Watching her step up into the plane, take her seat, wave out the window and then taxi out and take off, I felt a surprisingly strong longing for her in my heart, an acute sense of separation, a deep bearable ache.

A few months later, Joy Baker and I moved into a one-bedroom apartment in an old brownstone on the east side of Manhattan. Mèo, having recovered from his injuries and pneumonia in Connecticut, joined us. We were three. Most days when I wasn't on the road, Joy and I traveled to and from work together.

PART FOUR

TAY NINH
1970

Something made us bolt upright,
all zombie eyes, all ears and nerves.
Something out there in the dark
came breathing, stalking, waiting.

    ★   ★   ★

All night we hunched in what we wore
like turtles, like the frightened kids
we were and were not anymore,
silent, lost, half-crazed, and deadly.

W. D. EHRHART
"In the Valley of the Shadow"

MARCH 14, 1970

The light from the lamps above the seats illuminated the passenger cabin in pockets of yellow, gray and white—glowing beams of bright, high-intensity light suffused by wisps of cigarette smoke swirling in the air. Otherwise it was dark. Nothing moved but the smoke. Outside the plane, thirty-five thousand feet above the Pacific, the air was frozen dark. Stars displayed distant fire. The constant hum of jet turbines and the whoosh of rushing air pressed against the cabin, droning on and on and on through the minutes and miles of the night.

Keith Kay, Jim Clevenger and I sat in the first-class section of the Pan American 707 and shifted in our seats, wrestling with the tedium of the steady invariable vibration. This was the fastest flight to Vietnam, eighteen hours in the air, stopping at Honolulu, Guam and Manila, chasing one interminable night around the world. The plane took off from the United States on Saturday and arrived in Saigon on Monday. Sunday got lost along the way. No matter. Days of the week had no meaning in a place where all time was relative, speeding up or slowing down according to the circumstances. A few seconds could be more meaningful than whole days. The war went on in one place or another with the same violent intensity seven days a week. The plane passed through twelve time zones and the international date line, circling against the spin of the earth, moving with the darkness.

Kay, Clevenger and I were leaving behind our lives of familiar routine, civilian comfort and predictable order and heading into a world of remorseless melancholy and surprise fate. We sat back in our seats smoking cigarettes and sipping cognac from glass snifters provided by the cabin staff. The flight attendants were talkative and polite, fascinated by us and our work. They asked about the war and the country and what life was like in Vietnam. We told them it was frightening and hot and poor and the United States didn't belong there. The younger crew members nodded their heads in agreement but the older ones seemed skeptical, as if by suggesting such a thing we were less than patriotic, that we'd got it wrong. All of them worked hard to anticipate our wishes. The service made me feel special. One of them said she was amazed we could drink so much without passing out. 'You've finished all the Scotch and now we're almost out of brandy,' she said. 'How do you guys do it?' We laughed. No one answered. To say it might have something to do with where we were going would have sounded portentous.

Clevenger was reading a book, as usual. This one, *The Defector*, was a novel about intrigue and subterfuge in Vietnam written by Charles Collingwood, chief foreign correspondent for CBS. Turning the pages, Clevenger declared it to be not bad. He was happy to be going back to Vietnam. For ten years he had labored in the colorless labyrinth of CBS News headquarters in New York, starting as a clerk in the mailroom and working his way up to assistant director of the Cronkite News. He had been successful in everything he did at the network. Plotting to get into the field to cover stories, his true love, he was not beyond intrigue and subterfuge himself. For each of the past several years he had waited for a big story to break in Vietnam. He would then announce that he was taking his vacation and would fly immediately to Hong Kong. There he would cable or call Saigon and offer his services to the bureau chief, who would be short of staff with a big story breaking. 'Just happen to be out here in Asia and thought you might be able to use an extra hand,' he'd say. 'Help out around the bureau.' It worked every time. The bureau chief consented and Clevenger caught the next plane to Saigon, working happily as a producer, the job he wanted, until the story went quiet or executives in New York uncovered his plot and ordered him out. At that point he took his vacation elsewhere in Asia. When he got home, he submitted expense accounts that covered most of the trip, Saigon and the vacation included. This time he was going with approval. To those who knew him, Clevenger was wild and untamed, a colossal drinker, but good at his work.

Kay sat in another row of seats talking with a beautiful young cabin attendant. They laughed together, telling stories, making fun, flirting. Everywhere he went Kay was unable to resist the affections of young women who were attracted by his dark movie-star features, his canyon-deep voice, his relaxed wit. Being a network film photographer who risked his life for the pictures he took did not detract from his appeal. At the same time, he was genuinely modest and self-effacing. It was not an act. Kay loved women naturally, spontaneously, whether they were beautiful to look at or not, and they loved him in return.

I sat back in the seat and listened to a tape of a concert Johnny Cash had given at Folsom Prison. It was a new release of a recent live performance, and the recording captured the raw heat, energy and repressed violence in the prison yard audience. In one of the songs, Cash sang in his cold flat monotone, "I shot a man in Reno just to watch him die . . ." The convicts erupted in a wild outburst of cheers and applause, wicked noise, fired with evil intent. Hearing the song for the first time, I felt strangely amused, as if listening to something I shouldn't hear. *What a weird idea*, I thought, *getting off at the sight of another man dying—even your enemy—watching his face as he bled to death, talking to him, making it more painful. The guy who wrote that song was bad, really bad*, I thought, *a hard-core sadist, even if the song wasn't true, even if it didn't put the idea into one of those vengeful minds in the prison yard.* The song was repulsive and attractive at the same time, titillating and shameful. The idea of absolute evil touched a part of me I didn't want to know. Random anger and violence made me uncomfortable, driving me away and drawing me close, offering clues to an unknown self. The thoughts it brought up were too confusing, too frightening, too close to a deeper mystery to want to know more. Of course, what Cash was singing about was crime and punishment, pleasure and pain, rebellion and retribution—the oldest song in the book. The plane pushed on through the glooming dark toward Vietnam.

A newspaper lay open on the seat tray in front of me. A headline read, "Troublesome Troops Sent to Front Lines." The story said the U.S. Army was punishing GIs who opposed the war by putting them in line infantry units. *Might make a good story*, I thought, *if we run into any of them*. I wondered if we would. *Will we see insubordination in the field? Fragging?* Press reports said the army had morale problems trying to wage war and withdraw from Vietnam at the same time. Soon 150,000 troops were going home. The overall strategy, conceived in Washington, was to transfer the burden of ground combat gradually to the South Vietnamese and then get out completely. Say we'd won the war and go home. But no one knew when that might be or how it was going to play out. The army's problem was that its soldiers knew what was happening and none of them was willing to die for a lost cause. It was the story of *Catch-22*.

One by one, I opened the jars of tablets I had bought before leaving and filled each of the five narrow glass tubes of my new portable pill case: vitamins in one tube, aspirin in another, Darvon for serious pain, Lomotil for diarrhea, Valium for everything else. This time I was better equipped to go into the field: compass, first aid kit, Swiss Army knife, tape recorder, micro-phone, music tapes, portable typewriter, extra notebooks, waterproof plas-tic bags, pewter flask, flashlight, rose-tinted sunglasses, photographs of loved ones, still camera, old combat boots, green T-shirts and my venerable lucky hat and charms. I had everything the soldiers had and more, but no weapon. Everything I wasn't wearing would fit in a new state-of-the-art backpack with a lightweight aluminum frame and padded belt to hold the weight on my hips. No matter that the outfit made me look more like a Boy Scout than a grunt. I was determined on this, my third tour, to get it right.

Kay, Clevenger and I were going back to Vietnam as a team. We wanted to make a film about the daily lives of American soldiers in the field. Our plan was simple. We would find a squad of twelve men or perhaps a platoon of thirty who were willing to let us live with them, patrol with them for a month or two, and see how they got along. We would record everything they did that looked interesting and make a film documentary for CBS News. The only condition was that the soldiers had to be in an area where there was serious combat, where the war was still being fought. We believed that our film had to have spontaneous dramatic action, sequences that were completely unplanned. The danger of fighting and death, even on routine patrol, would cause viewers to want to know what was going to happen next. The risk was not a major concern. Getting a good story out of a dan-gerous place was part of the challenge, part of the attraction of doing it. Along with the GIs, we would take our chances.

The idea for the film came out of a conversation at the Slate. Stanhope Gould, Keith Kay, Jim Clevenger and I had been watching TV news coverage of the war for the past eighteen months and thought something was being missed. After five years of covering the war, the television networks were now giving it less attention. They didn't ignore it, but they didn't cover it with the same intensity. Since the Tet Offensive in 1968, followed by Presi-dent Johnson's decision not to run again, then the violence at the Democra-tic Party convention in Chicago, and finally the election of Richard Nixon, the country appeared to be less concerned about Vietnam. Some troops were being withdrawn but many more remained. Peace talks, fruitless so far, were taking place in Paris. In the United States, life went on normally. The economy was struggling through a recession. Other than the families of the troops, the antiwar activists, the military and the press, not many Americans seemed to worry much about what happened in Vietnam. It was harder to tell the country was at war. Fewer pictures of war casualties appeared. The television networks, the press, the government and the general public had become so accustomed to the weekly toll of dead and wounded that violence no longer surprised them. The war was like a chronic long-term illness; people wanted to forget about it, wished it would go away. The issues were too complicated and too contradictory, the bloodshed too painful to contemplate, the possibility of defeat too distasteful. At times the war seemed to be happening on another planet, outside the limits of ordinary comprehension, so far away and so far from sight that any urgency to stop the slaughter was diminished by the distance and the endless repetition of its horror. Nothing could shock anymore. Finally, the American public had been exhausted by the war. After being alarmed by it, then sickened and numbed by it, they were driven beyond ordinary compassion into a collective form of combat fatigue.

Throughout 1968 and 1969, I had covered stories and developments on the home front. Some of the big stories of that year and a half were street fighting at the Democratic Convention in Chicago, the ensuing trial of the Chicago Eight, the brutal reaction of police forces to political disturbances in their cities, the Black Panther movement and its war with the police, student rebellions at university campuses, the wave of urban ghetto violence, the Woodstock festival and the counterculture in general. One of my continuing assignments was the antiwar protest movement. Large and small, peaceful and violent, from Chicago to Washington, D.C., to New York to Boston, I tried to report the stories accurately and fairly, though my private sympathies were usually with the demonstrators. Trying to stop the war was a burning issue with me. But no matter how much media coverage they got or how violent they were (the two often went together), the demonstrations had no real impact on U.S. government policy. Nothing seemed to change. Or, if it did, the change was incremental, too slow to save lives. The antiwar movement until then had been seen by many in the United States as an anti-American campaign led by leftists, radicals, revolutionaries and pacifists. Most of its members were college students.

President Nixon had promised in his election campaign to find a way out of the Vietnam puzzle, but in office he pressed the armed forces for victories on the battlefield. He was more of a military hawk than his predecessors, more even than President Eisenhower, under whom he had served as vice president. The North Vietnamese, intransigent in their determination to prevail in their struggle for independence, showed no inclination to make compromises for peace. The war seemed endless. By now, it had lasted longer than World War II. The stalemate was as deeply entrenched as that of World War I. The U.S. generals' strategy of attrition, like the British General Haig's in 1916, was a failure. More than a million soldiers and civilians had been killed. The U.S. Air Force, Navy and Marine Corps had bombed North Vietnam virtually back to the Stone Age, at least by modern standards, yet Hanoi produced soldiers faster than the United States and ARVN could kill them. North and South, people were dying and suffering in huge numbers without much apparent notice in the United States. Kay, Gould, Clevenger and I wanted to report the story of the war in an original way, to get more people to pay attention.

'You can't do it, Jack,' another CBS News correspondent said at the Slate. Jed Duvall was scheduled to leave soon on his first tour in Saigon. He had been standing at the bar listening to a conversation between Gould, Kay and me. 'You can't go over there and try and stop the war. It isn't right. You can't cover the war if you're trying to subvert it.'

'Why not?' I said, turning to face him. Duvall had been drinking a little but was not drunk.

'Because it's wrong,' he said. 'Morally and professionally it's just all wrong. It's not our job to take sides. Besides, they won't let you get away with it. The front office, I mean. You're asking for trouble.'

'You mean it's okay to cover the war as long as you support it,' I said.

'It's okay to cover the war as long as you're *objective*. It's *not* okay to go over with the intention of condemning it. That's not reporting, it's editorializing.'

'How can you be objective about this war?' I moved down the bar to get closer. On this subject, my patience was short. 'Tell me. How *can* you? I mean, we've been killing people for five years for no reason other than to prop up a bunch of thieving Vietnamese generals who've made themselves rich on our money. That's all we've *really* done. Communist menace, my ass. The whole system is rotten.' I caught my breath and sipped my drink. 'We're in so deep we can't get out because it would look like we've lost. It's madness. We're not going to win, everybody knows that. But we won't admit it and go home. So we go on killing people, thousands and thousands of people, including our own. And for what? For pride! For the egos and vanity of a bunch of old farts in Washington! How can you be objective about that?'

'Hey, Jack, take it easy,' Duvall said. 'Just remember it's not our job to judge the war, which is what you're doing. We just report what happens. In an honest way. That's all. Let other people make the judgments about whether it's right or wrong.'

'Fine, Jed. If you want to live with that logic, fine. I can't. My conscience won't let me. If I don't do something to try to change things, I'll go crazy.'

'Laurence, you're already crazy,' Gould said.

'It's immoral to go over there and report antiwar propaganda,' Duvall said. 'Who gave you the right to play God?'

'He's not playing God,' Gould shouted, pushing his forefinger in Duvall's chest. '*Nixon's* the one playing God! And those assholes in the White House!' Duvall tried to hold his place but Gould, slightly larger, leaned into him.

'Tell me, man,' Gould shouted, 'what's more immoral? To sit around and pretend that Vietnam isn't a monstrous fucking war crime? That shouldn't be stopped immediately? Or pretend it's not happening? That all those women and kids and old men aren't dead? Or that it's a just cause? And do nothing. Or is it more immoral to go over and try to show how senseless, how totally fucking insane it is? Tell me, man, what's more immoral?' He was shouting at the top of his voice. Other patrons at the bar were silent, watching.

'Just calm down and I'll tell you, Stanhope,' Duvall said. 'Morality is relative. What you and Jack think is moral and what I think is moral are different. My responsibility as a reporter is to tell the truth. To report the facts as I find them. Now that's morally right and you know it. I am *not* responsible for the Vietnam War or the government's foreign policy or anything else they decide. I do not think it's morally correct to tell people what's right and what's wrong in Vietnam or anyplace else.' Gould started to interrupt but Duvall leaned forward. 'Understand? It's not our business to make judgments about things. Otherwise, we'd be going around telling people what to think all the time. What's good and what's bad. The next thing we'd be telling them who to vote for. Then where would we be?'

'But this is a special case, don't you see?' I said. 'The jury has been out on Vietnam for five years! Ten years, if you think about it. Don't you think it's time for a verdict?'

'Look,' Duvall said, 'I don't like the damn war any more than you do. Really, I don't. But I'm not going to compromise my values as a reporter by trying to change it.'

'See what you think when you've been there,' I said and turned away. I was angry at him. Duvall turned back to his drink.

'It doesn't make any difference anyway, man,' Gould said. 'TV news has no effect on the war. Absolutely none whatsoever.'

'This is where you and I disagree,' I said. We had debated the issue a dozen times, working together on stories all over the country.

'Well, you're wrong,' Gould said. 'Look at what Cronkite did. [Shortly after Tet, Walter Cronkite went to Vietnam; returning home, he finished his report with an appeal to the American government to make an honorable withdrawal from the war.] Do you think his little sermon had any effect on the war? Hell no. Other than getting Johnson to quit, nothing. Two years and nothing has changed. We're still at it, killing gooks. One more news story about the war or one more documentary isn't going to change one fucking thing, man. The truth is nobody cares. And it wouldn't make any difference if they did. Because they don't have any power to change it anyway.'

'Stanhope, you're a nihilist.'

'No, man, I'm a *realist*. Nihilists don't give a shit.' We all laughed, including Duvall.

Our project had been accepted by CBS News, though management seemed less enthusiastic about giving us an hour of airtime to show our proposed documentary than having us cover the war for the regularly scheduled news broadcasts. They expected us to get more film like the footage we had produced in 1967 and 1968, dramatic war stories for the *Evening News*. But they did like our idea of living in the field with the troops, telling the story from their perspective, taking our time instead of rushing to meet competitive deadlines. Our hopes for an hour broadcast rested mainly with the executive producer of a special reports unit, Ernest Leiser, who promised to consider anything we came up with. 'If it's good enough for an hour,' he said, 'we'll do it. But no promises. Don't get your hopes up.'

'Who's gonna be your soundman?' Clevenger asked.

'Don't know,' I said. 'But it's gotta be a round-eye.'

GIs were more relaxed around all-American camera teams than they were with crews that included Vietnamese, Japanese or other Asians or Europeans. Most GIs didn't trust the Vietnamese, no matter how pro-American or anti-Communist they were. In addition, they had become symbols of the American misfortune and were held responsible for the soldiers' year of misery in their hostile land.

'I'll do sound if you want me to,' Clevenger said.

'You?' Gould said, surprised. 'Jimmy you're a *director*, not a *soundman*.' He had no technical experience as a sound recordist.

"Hell, I can learn that stuff," he said. "Just don't ask me to fix the camera."

In the weeks that followed, Clevenger read and absorbed everything he could find on the subject of sound recording, enlisted friends in the camera department to teach him some of the fine points, learned how to adjust the bias on an MA-11 sound amplifier.

For us, Clevenger's biggest asset was his nationality. Amateur soundperson though he was, he would give the team homogeneity: young, male, American. Jimmy was also fun to be around, full of interesting stories and offbeat ideas, intelligent and crazy, willing to try anything.

Stanhope Gould was on the team until the final days. Two weeks before we were due to leave, his presence on the trip was vetoed by the manager of news, Ralph Paskman, who was worried about the cost of sending four people to Vietnam when the job could be done by three. CBS News was under pressure to cut its costs of covering the war, said to be over a million dollars a year. Our expedition, which would cost tens of thousands of dollars, was being funded as an extraordinary item in addition to the normal Vietnam war budget. Gould, an *Evening News* producer, made it too expensive.

We had all seen and admired a documentary made in Vietnam five years earlier by a French filmmaker, Pierre Schoendoerffer—a thoughtful, literate man who had served with the French army and had been at Dien Bien Phu at the end in 1954. His film, *The Anderson Platoon,* had been broadcast on CBS in 1966 to high critical praise. Schoendoerffer and his crew had spent several weeks with a platoon of the First Cavalry Division during the Bong Son campaign. They filmed combat including the crash of a helicopter and the wounding of a soldier in a firefight, and achieved a strong level of visual realism. Kay, Clevenger and I wanted to improve on Schoendoerffer's work. We would shoot color film instead of black-and-white. We would make it an hour long instead of thirty minutes. Most important, we would try to learn about the personalities and private thoughts of the GIs we followed—their backgrounds, their attitudes about the war, their fears, hopes, dreams. If we spent enough time with one small unit, a squad perhaps, the soldiers might trust us enough to talk honestly about the war. We wanted to know each one as an individual so that viewers would care about his well-being and worry about his survival. Inevitably, there would be combat. Some of the soldiers in the squad might be wounded or killed. And that, we believed, would give viewers a measure of individual human loss in the war. It had to be visceral. People had to feel some of the pain. If enough viewers had strong reactions to what they saw in the documentary, they might be motivated to bring stronger pressure on their representatives in Congress and on the government to get out of Vietnam. Our personal motives were more humanitarian than political, but in trying to stop the war for humane reasons, we knew we were also pursuing political objectives.

On February 8, the *New York Times* magazine ran a lengthy article about the lives of American soldiers serving in the front lines in Vietnam. It was titled "The Hours of Boredom, The Seconds of Terror," and it was a thoughtful, sensitively written piece by James P. Sterba, one of the best reporters to cover the war. Seeing that story convinced Walter Cronkite and the management of CBS News to send us to Vietnam.

Halfway across the Pacific, the Pan Am plane landed at Guam to refuel. The long night was nearly over. Kay, Clevenger and I walked past a row of empty customs and immigration desks in the arrival hall to a parking lot outside the terminal. A few overhead lamps lit the sandy pavement. Palm trees ruffled in the warm breeze. The air was soft and fresh. The airport was a sleepy place at the busiest of times, but at five o'clock in the morning it was almost totally deserted and still. A few refueling trucks and service vehicles hummed on the tarmac. We wandered away from the passenger terminal and lit a joint. Kay kicked a loose coconut on the ground at me. I kicked it back.

'Come on, Jimmy, time to start getting into shape,' Kay called.

'Okay,' Clevenger said, 'Jack and me against you.'

'Consider this basic training,' Kay shouted.

'For what?' Clevenger said.

'For your legs.' Kay, who wore leather cowboy boots, kicked the coconut straight at him, high and hard. Clevenger jumped aside.

What followed might be called a game of coconut hockey. Goals were marked out with palm fronds at opposite ends of the parking lot. Kay stood at one end facing Clevenger and me at the other. The match was notable for the unusual ball in play (it was as hard as a boulder though not as heavy), and the level of violence. Whenever Clevenger came close to scoring a goal, Kay blocked his way with a flurry of kicks and body checks. Elbows flew. Ankles were struck. The coconut smashed into soft body parts, inflicting bruises. Cries of "foul" got no response. Clevenger, fearless and reckless in equal measure, got his shins and ankles kicked ferociously. Anesthetized by the booze he had drunk on the plane, he suffered no pain. The game ended after about ten minutes in a bloody draw. We were ready for Vietnam.

MARCH 16, 1970

Saigon

The city had changed. The mood was more relaxed, more secure, less urgent about the war—more like the summer of 1965. Twenty months earlier the war was as close as the next corner; driving down the wrong street could get you killed. Now there were fewer American troops in the streets, fewer convoys, fewer MPs. The big tamarind trees that had given Tu Do Street its shady elegance were gone, chopped down to make room for the wide cargo trucks moving the continuous flow of American supplies away from the docks on the Saigon River and into government warehouses in the countryside. The removal of the trees had taken away much of the shade on the street so that the bars and brothels and shops were bathed in bright sunlight. By night it was neon.

There was no change in the suffocating heat and humidity or the pervasive corruption. American aid poured into Saigon for the purpose of improving the lives of Vietnamese who needed it: food, medicine, clothing, timber, tools, machinery, television sets, dollars—only to be stolen and sold by the wealthy gangs who controlled the country. Stealing from the United States was the national sport, and even the VC were in the game. Those who couldn't play had to feed off the fringes or beg. The sidewalks were occupied by homeless children, hungry poor, widows with babies, half-American half-Vietnamese orphans and Vietnamese Army veterans with missing arms and legs who held up their open hands to you in desperation as you walked by. Young men with greasy hair and wasted faces spat on the sidewalk in front of your steps, just to remind you that you weren't welcome, so that you could walk from one end of Tu Do to the other on a film of saliva. In the streets, slick-haired young men with the money and influence to avoid conscription tooled around on new Japanese motorcycles, snatching wristwatches from the long arms of Westerners. Others like them sat in the bars drinking brandy, gossiping, inventing rumors. Some of the evidence of official larceny could be seen in the lazy ostentation of the Saigon bourgeoisie, lounging in tennis whites or bikinis and sandals at the Cercle Sportif, wearing their arrogance like expensive frocks. There was no justice, no fair play, no apparent morality in the wartime streets. The winners flaunted their wealth with pride and the losers displayed the poverty of their expectations, few hopes beyond the next meal. In that sense, Saigon was the same as it was when I left in 1968: cruel, unequal, oozing decadence and decay, rotten at its poisoned heart.

I moved into my old room, C-2, at the Continental Hotel. It was like coming home again. Nothing was out of place, nothing had been altered in twenty months. It looked as if someone had decided that the room had been furnished adequately twenty or thirty or forty years ago; there was no need to modernize. The room boys, old enough to have been with the original staff, came in at once. They smiled and put their palms together and bowed their heads politely and asked, "Où est le chat?" I told them Mèo was with my girlfriend in New York and showed them pictures of Joy and Mèo together. 'Oh,' the room boys said, 'très belle.' They moved briskly around the room, unpacked my suitcase and hung up the clothes, opened the typewriter case and dusted the keys, set out fresh towels, tidied up. They put a pitcher of potable water in the bathroom, cleaned the surfaces of the furniture, turned on the air conditioner, and offered to get me 'un gin tonic.' They treated me as if I had been away for only a few weeks.

Keith Kay checked into his favorite room around the corner, C-11, and asked to be excused for a few days. Clevenger and I were surprised. We had expected him to make the rounds of military, political and diplomatic briefings with us in Saigon as we planned the documentary. With unusual deference, Kay said he would leave it to us to decide where to go for the story. 'If you need me I'll be in my room,' he said. He disappeared inside it with the young flight attendant from the airline who was laying over in Saigon. A layover it was. Neither of them appeared for three days. All their meals were taken in the room. They emerged, disheveled and exhausted but with bright happy smiles on their faces, a few hours before her flight to the United States. After he had driven her to the airport and said good-bye, Kay appeared in public again, smiling modestly, singing, 'Yes, it's me and I'm in love again.'

'You're incorrigible, man.'

'Can't help it,' shaking his head. 'She was a tiger.'

'You'll probably never see her again.'

'Yeah, probably, but I'll have the memory.'

I shook my head.

"You know," he said, "it's still the best way to get over jet lag."

Clevenger knew his way around Saigon well enough to explore the camera stores, book stalls, libraries and black market, outfitting himself for the field. Each day produced a new book. He stocked up on Scotch and Camels at the PX. One thing he needed but could not find was a good Swiss Army knife. 'Don't worry,' I said, 'I know where to get one.'

At the CBS News offices at the Caravelle, I introduced myself to the bureau chief, David Miller, a man of formidable size and energy. Miller said the bureau was at our service; anything he could do to be of assistance, all we had to do was ask. He had orders from New York not to intrude on our work, to let us get on with preliminary plans. My first call was to the First Cav. Since I had spent so much time with the division on previous tours, it was the logical place to start. When the senior public information officer came on the line, the deep gruff voice sounded familiar. It was J. D. Coleman, my friend from An Khe in 1965–1966. A major now, Coleman was based at the new division headquarters in Phuoc Vinh, about thirty miles northwest of Saigon, just a helicopter flight away. I told him we didn't know yet what we were going to do, but that we'd come up and see him in a few days. 'Bring a deck of pinochle cards,' he said, 'I'll get the table ready.'

At lunch, Dave Miller gave us a briefing. The war was winding down, he said, though sharp battles were being fought in a few places. 'The NVA look like they've got their heads down,' he said, 'but nobody really knows if they're pulling back for good. Or for how long.' In the competitive war between the networks, the struggle with NBC News was as intense as ever. CBS was winning, Miller said, with Dick Threlkeld, Skip Brown, George Syvertsen and a team of talented correspondents and camera crews. Competition to get on the air was sharp. 'This is a very strong bureau now,' he said. 'We've got contacts at the embassy, MACV and with the Vietnamese. We usually know what's going on.' Miller seemed to know how to play the public relations game without being intimidated or compromised by MACV. At the same time, he said he was trying to balance the demands of network executives in New York with the needs of his camera teams in the field. Keeping New York happy was hard, he said. 'They never seem to get enough bang-bang,' he said. 'And they're always second-guessing our coverage.'

The main subject of the lunch was Dana Stone, the red-headed still photographer who had become our friend on earlier tours. Recently, Stone had joined CBS News as a freelance film photographer. I wanted him to work with us on the documentary. Though he had little experience with film, he had an excellent eye for pictures and was steady and alert in combat. He was one of the best photographers of the war and one of the most amusing to be around. I told Miller the story of how Stone started a firefight at the MACV compound in Hué during target practice in 1968. Miller laughed. He hadn't seen that side of Stone's personality.

'When we get in combat,' I said, 'we want to shoot it from several angles. At least two, maybe three cameras. We're going for the most in-depth coverage of battle possible. I mean, beyond anything that's been done on film before.' Miller smiled. 'If we can,' I added.

'Stone's in Laos at the moment,' Miller said. 'I'll bring him back to Saigon to work with you.'

After lunch, I walked to the MACV office of information in the JUSPAO building and applied for a military press card, the third in five years. An Air Force sergeant took my photograph and fingerprints and gave me a form to fill out. When it was issued, a laminated plastic document the size of a credit card declared that I held the assimilated rank of major in the U.S. Army. The noncombatant's certificate of identity was designed to ensure my safety and treatment in the event of capture. If I was taken prisoner by the North Vietnamese, the card was supposed to guarantee I would be given the same treatment as a captured U.S. military officer of the same rank under the Geneva Conventions on prisoners of war. That was a joke. In the hot fury of battle, an NVA soldier was less likely to check my ID and escort me to a prisoner of war camp than shoot me in the head. The real value of the card was admission to the PX.

The next day I wrote a cable to the CBS News foreign editor in New York. Robert Little was a wild spirit, alternately grim and manic, a few years older than most of his correspondents. Thin and balding, he tried to run the foreign desk like a military operation, barking orders, sending rockets, often unable to control his sharp tongue, a trace of dementia in his manner. Like Clevenger and a few others at CBS, Little was a maverick. Lightheaded after my first day back in Saigon, I wrote to him:

LITTLE FYI KAY, CLEVENGER, EYE ARRIVED SAIGON BATTERED FROM
GUAM HOCKEY MATCH KICKING COCONUTS AND EACH OTHER STOP FIND
BUREAU FANTASTICALLY EFFICIENT STOP REQUEST MISTER MIDGLEYS

SECRETARY RUSH CLEVENGER ONE LARGE SWISS ARMY KNIFE FROM
HOFRITZ STOP JOY (SIGNED) LAURENCE

Les Midgley was still the executive producer of the *CBS Evening News,* and
his secretary was Joy Baker. Sitting at her desk in New York later in the day,
she watched as Sandy Socolow read a copy of my cable.

Socolow launched a tantrum. 'What the hell do those guys think they're
doing over there?' he shouted to the room. 'They act like they're on a fucking picnic.' No one in the office spoke. Joy held her breath. 'What's the front
office going to think when they see this?' Socolow yelled. 'Doesn't Laurence
know he's on a serious assignment? Or does he think we sent him over there
to have fun?'

At home that night, Joy wrote a letter describing Socolow's outburst and
sent it to Saigon the next morning in the daily CBS News mail pouch. When
I read her letter, I was surprised. *Maybe we're being cavalier,* I thought. *Have to
choose my words more carefully from now on.* I respected Socolow and didn't
want to offend him, but I thought he was hopelessly square. I didn't know
that cables to the foreign editor were copied and read by management at all
levels.

Marsh Clark, the Saigon bureau chief of TIME-LIFE, met Clevenger and
me for lunch at the Atterbea Restaurant. Clark had been Tim Page's boss in
1969 when he got his fourth and most serious wound. Page was accompanying a foot patrol when the soldier in front of him triggered a booby-trapped
artillery shell. The explosion killed the soldier and blew away a large hunk of
Page's skull. Clark said it was a miracle Tim survived. Half of his body was
still paralyzed. 'That was the last of war for Page,' Clark said.

Another of TIME-LIFE's freelance photographers, Sean Flynn, was in
Bali and was unlikely to return to Vietnam. Flynn too had been pacified, he
said. I was sorry to hear that. My hope had been to get Flynn and his film
camera on the team with Kay and Stone.

After supper, I sat at the desk in C-2 and typed a letter to Joy:

Saigon is already driving me crazy. Very elegant after 7 or so, many parties
and social functions (press activity included). Met some characters in bureau
who don't take this war business as seriously as the number of times they get
on the air (with whatever pictures and text), and their comfortable lives in
Saigon. (I was told by a TV wife that she's lived better, more luxuriously in

Saigon for past two years than she did in the States.) Jimmy and I are now going up to the 9th floor roof of the Caravelle, light up, and watch the show. (It's midnight).

Getting ready to go out into the field, I made the usual rounds the next day. At the Saigon central market, women with black-stained teeth sat behind stands overflowing with U.S. Army supplies, enough to outfit an infantry battalion. Prices were cheap, and a few dollars got all the gear I'd need: government-issue green fatigues, canteens, web belt, inflatable air mattress, poncho liner—all new, still in containers. Handing over the money, not even trying to bargain, I wondered whether GIs in the field had gear like this. *Don't bet on it,* I thought. At the CBS bureau, a considerate Vietnamese technician in the camera shop sprayed several coats of black paint on the shiny aluminum supports of my new backpack and fastened the loose ends with green gaffer's tape. 'Better for you,' he said. 'VC not see you so much.' He smiled. I hadn't asked him to do it; he was being helpful. Vietnamese employees in the bureau treated the American staff like children much of the time, as if we couldn't manage on our own, which was often true. They were always courteous, never condescending, only occasionally patronizing. I once gave a small ivory Buddha I had bought in Thailand to a bureau secretary who insisted on getting a proper chain for it so I could wear it around my neck; but she never got the chain and never gave back the Buddha. At the PX, I bought several bottles of Scotch, one of bourbon, a carton of cigarettes and two decks of cards. On the phone to Phuoc Vinh, J. D. Coleman said we were invited to lunch the next day with the assistant division commander. A chopper would pick us up in the morning. The general wanted to hear our ideas for a documentary.

Clevenger and I had lunch in air-conditioned comfort at La Royale with two old friends, Horst Faas and Peter Arnett of the Associated Press. No one knew the story better: Faas in pictures, Arnett in print. Both had been in Vietnam continuously since 1962; both had won Pulitzer Prizes for their war coverage. Faas asked about my brother, Arthur, who had worked for him until he was seriously wounded in 1968. 'You know,' Faas said in his German accent, 'zat picture in the A Shau Valley your brother took, the one of the wounded paratrooper and the officer with his arms up to the sky, up to *heaven—maybe* that's the best picture of this war so far.' I agreed. Art Green-spon's photograph had run on the front pages of American newspapers as a wirephoto, but it more resembled a painting. 'And you know the story?' Faas went on, talking to Arnett and Clevenger. 'Art had to wait two days and nights in the rain to get that picture out of the A Shau. With the camera wrapped up next to his body so the film doesn't get wet. That took a lot of guts, I tell you.' Faas laughed. 'And when he gets to Saigon I pay him the magnificent sum of $25 for zat picture.' His big, heavy frame rocked as he laughed.

I explained to them that Kay, Clevenger and I were looking for a line infantry unit to follow in the field, but we didn't know where to go. I had not been in country for twenty months. They thought for a minute, and then Arnett spoke in his New Zealand twang.

'Basically, you've got two choices,' he said. 'You can go to Chu Lai and cover the American division in I Corps. They're the most screwed up outfit I've ever seen. You know: My Lai, booby traps, local guerrillas, main-force VC, fragging, race problems, drugs. It's a bloody mess.'

'You name it, they're always getting into trouble,' Faas said.

'You'll get a good story,' Arnett said. 'Depends on what you're after. The Marines are still up in I Corps, but the days of big battles with the North Vietnamese look like they're over. Mostly it's a small-unit war again.'

'And you've got za monsoon up there now. Not so easy to get around,' Faas said.

'Or, you can go up to the First Cav, on the Cambodian border, War Zone C,' Arnett said. 'It's the same war between the Cav and the North Vietnamese as it was in '65. They've had some really nasty fights along the border. You know, cat-and-mouse.'

'Except za cats are very big and za mice are not always losing.' Faas's eyes twinkled.

'Nobody's really trying to cover the story up there,' Arnett said. 'Our front office just isn't as interested any more. AP has lost too many people covering combat.'

Faas nodded. The AP had more people killed and wounded in Vietnam, most of them photographers, than any other news organization.

'If you go with the Cav, be careful who you go out with. Some of their battalions are better than others.'

'I wouldn't go in za field mit anything smaller than a company,' Faas said. 'Maybe a good recon platoon.'

When lunch was over, Clevenger and I tried to figure out where to go. If we covered the Americal division, we'd probably get a sensational story, but would it be typical? We were looking for common experiences of common soldiers. Covering the Americal sounded like trouble. No doubt there were good rifle companies with good officers and men, but their war, deadly as it might be, did not sound as interesting as the old-fashioned one on the Cambodian border. Besides, I had a history with the Cav. I was more comfortable with that division than any other. Arnett and Faas had briefed us well.

'I don't believe they told us all that stuff,' Clevenger said, scratching his hair. 'I mean, what the hell was in it for them? Aren't they supposed to be in bed with NBC?'

'They're friends,' I said. 'We'd do the same for them.'

Back at the bureau, I sent a cable to Sean Flynn, care of the Kuta Beach Hotel in Bali, inviting him to join our expedition. I didn't think he'd come, but I wanted to ask.

STONE, KAY, CLEVENGER, LAURENCE WOULD WELCOME YOUR ACCOM-
PANIMENT ON SERIES EXPLORATIONS IN FORTY-TWO CORPS STOP
SAIGON FREIGHT CHEAP STOP IF AGREEABLE CABLE COLNEWS SAIGON
STOP JACK.

"Forty-Two Corps" was a name we had invented at Frankie's House to describe an imaginary war zone somewhere in the wild mountain rainforests of Indochina, a lost haunted jungle of impenetrable mystery and spookiness, a mythical place where the mist never lifted and the VC had helicopters and tac-air and American soldiers and Marines lived like moles in tunnels and caves and came out only at night with camouflage paint on their faces. Forty-Two Corps was where journalists like us could cover both sides freely, without hassle. Forty-Two Corps was where the ears and noses of the briefing officers grew larger when they lied, until they all looked like elephants, and, of course, where everyone smoked dope.

On Sundays in Forty-Two Corps, troops on both sides gathered in giant stadiums around the country and watched while two generals, one from each side, fought with their bare hands until one of them, bloodied and exhausted, gave up. The American generals usually won because they were bigger, but the Vietnamese generals never gave up, just kept taking the punishment, throwing a punch when they could, ducking and weaving and backing away the rest of the time, always trying to inflict pain on their opponents. Months went by, a month of Sundays, and when all the generals had punched themselves out, the soldiers took a vote to decide whether to continue the war by bringing in the bird colonels to fight or to add up the score and declare one side the winner. That would be the end of the war. 'Far out,' we'd say, sitting in Page's room, our heads in a cloud. The best thing about Forty-Two Corps was that it was a fable that never ended. Someone in the room would be telling a true story about the war when someone else would interrupt and say, "Well, man, that's not the way it happened in Forty-Two Corps," then start a new, fictional chapter taking the true story to absurd heights. Someone else would pick it up, adding more ridiculous detail, and then another and another until everyone in the room had added so much weird fantasy the point of the original story was forgotten. Flynn and Page were best at it, crazier than the others, always ready to take it to another fantastic level. 'Oh, man,' someone said many times, 'one of us has got to write a *book* about that place someday.' Years later, General Westmoreland and his staff created a new military corps in the northern part of South Vietnam, including the A Shau, Que Son, the DMZ, Khe Sanh—all the spookiest places—set up a command, put an army lieutenant general in charge and called it "XXIV Corps." Though it was short of forty-two, it seemed as if our fantasies were coming true. Unfortunately, the generals' imaginations went no further than that.

MARCH 19, 1970

Phuoc Vinh

At first light, as Saigon came awake, Clevenger and I flew from Tan Son Nhut to Phuoc Vinh on the chief of staff's courier helicopter. The flight took less than an hour. The air was still cold. Phuoc Vinh had become the new headquarters of the First Cav late in 1968, after the Tet Offensive, when it began moving down from I Corps. Compared with An Khe, the base seemed subdued. Fewer helicopters were visible than in the early days of the war when the division operated in the Central Highlands. It had gone north to reinforce the Marines but now its three brigades were spread along the Cambodian border. Its battalions and rifle companies were dispersed over a wide area of the surrounding countryside, running patrols in search of North Vietnamese, being hunted themselves.

We were welcomed at the public information office by Major J. D. Coleman. He shook hands and slapped me on the back with one of his giant's hands. 'Good to see you, old-timer,' he said, his six-foot, six-inch frame rising above me. 'Saw your stuff on TV a couple of years back. Thought you weren't going to make it out of some of those places in I Corps.' We had not seen each other in four years. Coleman no longer dressed in a paratrooper's full combat gear but his size was still imposing. I gave him two decks of pinochle cards and a bottle of bourbon.

'Come on in and I'll give you a briefing,' Coleman said. His office was crowded with the paraphernalia of a publisher. Dusty boxes of magazines, film, paper and printing materials were stacked on the plywood floor. Coleman said his staff was responsible for writing, photographing and printing all the newspapers, magazines and yearbooks for the division. It amounted to a small industry. At the same time, the information office ran a commercial store where soldiers could buy First Cav memorabilia such as T-shirts and stationery embossed with the division's black and yellow logo. The operation was known euphemistically as the "First Cav Gift Shop," though you could also pick up an AK-47, an SKS rifle or other war souvenir if you had the cash or something to trade. The word around Phuoc Vinh was, "You can get anything you want at J.D.'s gift shop."

Standing at his desk, Coleman brushed a layer of fine brown dirt off his briefing map and opened it.

'Now, here we are in Phuoc Vinh,' he said, pointing on the map to the rectangular symbol of a division headquarters. He moved his finger to the left and up a few inches. 'Now, here on the border is War Zone C,' he said. 'First Brigade is in there looking for Charlie. They've got their headquarters at Tay Ninh,' indicating the town nearby. 'First Brigade is supported by the 11th ACR and, just south of them, 1st Brigade of the 25th.' He looked up. 'Got that?'

'No,' Clevenger said, scratching his hair. 'What's the ACR?'

'Eleventh Armored Cavalry Regiment. Tanks and APCs. They do with tracks what we do with helicopters, only slower. They're a tough bunch of ass kickers, believe me.'

'And the 25th?'

'Infantry division. Ground pounders.'

'Gotcha,' said Clevenger, writing it down.

'Okay,' Coleman continued, pointing to the map. 'Now, just across the border in Cambodia, in this area here, is COSVN. Jack, you remember what COSVN is. Headquarters for the whole NVA/VC operation in the south.'

'What does COSVN stand for?' said Clevenger.

'Central Office, South Vietnam. We would dearly love to go in there and bust some caps, tear those people a new asshole. But Washington says no. So be it.' Coleman looked at us. 'Our mission is to block the enemy's infiltration into Vietnam, hit them up here before they can attack the populated areas down near Saigon. And we're doing it. We tearing the *hides* off those people.'

'What are you up against?' I asked.

'Well, basically, you've got three NVA divisions operating in Cambodia at the moment: the 1st, 7th and 9th. They come across the border, run an attack or two, and beat it back over, treat their casualties, regroup and rest. The 9th used to be a VC division but it took so many casualties in '68 they filled it back up with North Vietnamese replacements. They've also got a number of independent VC and NVA regiments. So we figure an overall enemy order of battle of 40,000, including support troops.'

'What's the terrain like?' I asked. 'I've never been up here before.'

'Pretty flat, which is a good thing. Double and triple canopy. Some open places, elephant grass, the usual. Not as bad as I Corps, from what they tell

me. Or II Corps either. Charlie's built a lot of heavy bunkers, tunnels and firing holes all along the border area and covered 'em real good. They're
experts at camouflage. You can get half a battalion right in on top of him
before you find out he's there. And then there's hell to pay. So we don't try
and assault 'em head-on the way we used to. Our tactics have changed a lot
since '65. Now we make contact, pull back if we can, and dump air and arty
on him. Lose fewer men. Also, we set a lot of ambushes at night. That's
become very important. We don't take casualties like we did before.'

'What it's like for the grunts?' Clevenger asked.

'The rifle companies generally spend about three weeks at a time in the
field. They carry a three-day supply on their backs—their basic load—then
get resupplied every fourth day. Not many hot meals in the field anymore.
Every five to seven weeks they get a few days at a VIP center in Bien Hoa.
Clean up and cut loose a little.'

'How's morale?'

'Outstanding. I'm amazed at how good it is. Everybody knows the Cav
will be the last to leave Vietnam, but these guys keep on driving. We get a lot
more college kids now and they're smart. They know how to fight and
maneuver. Since the division came down here in '68, we figure we've
stopped those three enemy divisions from getting near Saigon. We think
we've beat him up here.'

'Really?'

'Well, don't quote me on that; you never can tell what Charlie's got up his
sleeve. First of the Ninth made contact in the Dog's Head area recently.
That's this promontory here that pushes into Cambodia; you can see it looks
like the head of a dog. This is the first time we've gone in there. Just got the
AO from the 25th. We've got two battalions in there, 2/8 at Firebase
Illingsworth, and 2/7 at Firebase Jay. You can see here where they are on the
map. They're up against the 272d Regiment.'

Clevenger and I wrote the names of the units and the firebases in our
notebooks. Coleman showed us where the other two brigades of the division were located. He also spoke about combined operations with the South
Vietnamese airborne battalions, how impressive they were, how aggressive
compared with other ARVN units. When he was finished, Coleman sat
down and lit a cigarette.

'So, what can we do for you?' he said. 'Need a little bang-bang for the producers in New York?'

We laughed. It was not surprising, given his friendships with TV correspondents, how much J.D. knew about the inner workings of network television news.

'We're looking for a squad,' I said, 'maybe a platoon. Spend some time with them. Maybe a month or two. Live out in the boonies with them. Get to know them. Not just to get combat, but in a real combat zone.'

'You really want to spend that much time in the bush?'

'It's the only way we'll get what we're looking for.'

'Well, I would suggest 1st Brigade. Second of the Eighth or Second of the Seventh. That's our paratroop brigade, or it used to be. Good officers. Good soldiers.'

'Weren't those battalions in Ia Drang?'

'That's right. With 1/7 and 1/5.'

'One of them got pretty much wiped out, didn't it?'

'Well, 2/7 took some pretty heavy casualties in that one. At LZ Albany. I think the final count was 153.'

'Killed.'

'Yes.'

'In one afternoon. . . .'

'That's right. Their C Company got overrun.'

'Is the 7th Regiment the same as the old 7th Cavalry?' Clevenger asked.

'Roger that,' Coleman said. 'The old horse cavalry.'

'Weren't they at the Little Big Horn?'

'Yup. And a lot of other places.'

Coleman looked at his watch and got up. 'Come on. We're due for lunch with the ADC in a few minutes. Better not keep the Old Man waiting.' We left the PIO shop and walked to the division headquarters area.

Following Coleman, we took off our hats before going inside the general officers' mess—a spotless air-cooled room with plywood paneling and military decorations on the walls. The room was furnished with one long table, chairs, tablecloth with napkins, silverware. It was like an Army base in the United States. The assistant division commander, Brigadier General George Casey, was waiting. Mid-forties, ice-blue eyes, ruddy skin, Casey had a Boston Irish face. He shook our hands with a firm grip and offered us iced tea served by an Army waiter.

'When did you gentlemen arrive in country?' he said.

'A couple of days ago. We're still getting accustomed to the weather.'

'I don't think I've ever got used to this climate,' he said. 'What I really miss is the New England autumn. Where are you from in the States?'

'Connecticut,' I said.

'New Jersey,' said Clevenger.

'Well, happy to have a couple of fellow northeasterners with us today,' he said, smiling.

We sat down and waiters began serving. The food was fresh, as good as the American food in Saigon.

'Ever been over here before?' Casey asked.

'Twice,' I said. 'This is my third tour.'

'Jack and his crew helped us cut the grass for the Golf Course back in An Khe,' Coleman said. 'They did a story on the advance party. General Shoemaker took 'em out on their first operation, Shiny Bayonet.'

Casey nodded. As assistant division commander for maneuver, he worked closely with Brigadier General Shoemaker, the other ADC. Casey had been selected to take command of the division in the spring and with it would go his second general's star.

'What brings you back to the Cav?' he asked.

I explained our plan to find one small infantry unit, stay with the men for a month or two, get to know them, show how they lived and fought. 'We want to show the true face of war,' I said, 'the life your soldiers really live, not the condensed, two- or three-minute version you see on the evening news.'

As he listened, Casey did not eat, though his plate was full. His eyes were sharply focused, bright and intense, his attention concentrated on my words. The only expression on his features appeared to be skepticism. On the way to the dining room, Coleman had described Casey as one of the smartest officers he'd ever worked for—Harvard, West Point, Silver Star in Korea. When I said we wanted to improve on *The Anderson Platoon,* Casey's face brightened.

'That was an outstanding program,' he said.

'We think we can do better.'

'Very good.' He smiled and thought for a moment. 'Can't have the French taking all the documentary honors, can we?'

'Well, from my experience,' I said, 'I'd say our chances of getting a good film with this division were excellent.'

'What are you going to do when the men you're filming get into a fight? It may not be simple.'

'My cameraman and I have been in combat before,' I said. 'With the Cav and with the Marines. I think we know how to work without getting in any-body's way. At least no one's ever complained. And the stories came out well. Just not long enough to tell all the story.'

'I've never been shot at,' Clevenger said, 'but I'll do whatever these guys tell me to do.' He smiled.

The room was silent for several minutes as Casey ate his food. When he finished, he wiped his mouth with his napkin, put it back in his lap and said, 'You and your camera crew are welcome to come in with us and make your film. J.D. says you know what you're doing and that's good enough for me.'

'Thank you, sir.'

'Thank you very much,' said Clevenger.

The waiters collected the empty plates and brought ice cream, fruit salad and coffee.

'We'll need some help with resupply,' I said, 'getting film in and out of the field to Saigon.'

'I'm sure we can manage that.'

'Do you want us to choose the unit?'

'You can go with anyone you'd like,' Casey said. 'I'd say our 1st Brigade is your best bet at this time, but 2d is also a fine brigade. Either of those two would be an outstanding choice. I think 1st may have more enemy contact.'

I looked at Clevenger. 'Shall we go with 1st Brigade?'

Jim nodded, 'Fine by me.'

'Excellent,' said Casey. 'I'll call Bill Ochs and tell him to expect you tomorrow. He's a fine officer. I'm sure he'll look after you.'

'Thank you, sir,' I said.

'Major Coleman will take care of arrangements. I think what you are doing is a very noble idea. I don't believe people at home fully appreciate what's involved in soldiering over here. You have a chance to put that right. The lives of the men in the line are what we care about most—accomplish-ing our mission and taking care of our men. We'll give you all the support we can, Mr. Laurence. I look forward to seeing your film.'

'Thank you, sir.'

'Good luck to you and your team.'

We shook hands with Brigadier General Casey and left the officers' mess. Outside, Coleman said, 'Jack, you're really in luck. The division doesn't let the press in bed with us like this very often.' His voice was enthusiastic, hearty.

'It's all thanks to you, J.D.' I said.

In Saigon when we got back, big news was breaking. A government coup had just taken place in Phnom Penh, capital of Cambodia, 125 miles to the northwest. A coalition of right-wing generals and politicians had seized power from Prince Norodom Sihanouk, the Cambodian leader, and installed one of their own, General Lon Nol, in his place. It had happened the day before while Sihanouk was on vacation in France. The new group was rigorously anti-Communist. American generals and diplomats in Saigon were said to be delighted with the change. At the MACV briefing, a senior officer said, "This makes everything a whole new ball game."

MARCH 20, 1970

Tay Ninh was a garrison town, headquarters for four American and South Vietnamese army brigades. Sixty miles northwest of Saigon, it was halfway along the main road to Phnom Penh, not far from the border with Cambodia—a big dusty city sprawling over several square miles of flat scrub plain. Tay Ninh was a gateway, a jumping-off point, the nerve center for military operations into long-held NLF sanctuaries of War Zone C. The city stood in the shadow of Nui Ba Dinh, a thirty-two-hundred-foot mountain that looked unlike any land formation Americans had seen. It was shaped like a giant cone, out of place on the otherwise flat tropical plain, like a tank in the middle of a rice field. The peak and foot of the mountain were controlled by friendly forces, but the tunnels and caves in its sides were held by the VC. They hid in them on the jungle-covered slopes observing military activity in Tay Ninh and the area for miles in all directions.

Driving around the city in a jeep, you got a sense of American military humor: "NIXON'S HIRED GUNS" was painted on the side of a 25th Division armored personnel carrier. "Draft Beer, Not Students" was written on the cover of a soldier's helmet. Another had written, "Blow your mind— Smoke Gunpowder." On a barracks of A Troop, 1/9 Cav, someone had painted, "SNOW WHITE WAS A HEAD."

We flew up from Saigon early. Keith Kay was with us, still recovering from his cure for jet lag. At the brigade PIO office in Tay Ninh, a large GP tent with open sides and a wooden floor, we waited to meet the commanding officer of 1st Brigade. I was reading a book by Ernie Pyle, the American newspaper correspondent who covered World War II in Europe and the Pacific before he was killed by a sniper.

'Listen to this,' I said to Kay and Clevenger. I read aloud: "The ties that grow between men who live savagely together, relentlessly communing with Death, are ties of great strength. There is a sense of fidelity to each other in a little corps of men who have endured so long, and whose hope in the end can be so small."

'When was that?' Kay said.

'Early 1944.'

'Save it. Maybe you can use it.'

'As long as you give him credit,' Clevenger said.

'Nah,' said Kay, 'why spoil it? Pretend it's your own.'

We all laughed. In truth, Kay was a purist, a fundamentalist of photo-journalism. He refused to shoot anything that had been staged or set up. When he suspected someone was acting for the camera, he switched it off and walked away. If you weren't quick enough to capture an event on film as it happened, Kay believed, you were out of luck. Better to wait for your next chance. He tried to get as close as he could to the natural way of things. To suggest that I steal a quote was Kay being facetious. I wrote the words in my notebook. I had decided to carry that one book, *Brave Men*, by Ernie Pyle, in my field pack, though it weighed more than a pound.

Kay, Clevenger and I were escorted up the steps and into a modern house trailer occupied by the 1st Brigade commander, Colonel William Ochs Jr. He had a complete office inside: desk, chairs, flags, phones, pictures, briefing map, air-conditioner, all the modern conveniences. Colonel Ochs was a tall distinguished-looking Tennessean in his early forties, friendly and polite. He told us he came from the family which owned the *New York Times* and that he had almost become a reporter himself. One branch of the Ochs family, he said, had always gone into military service, and others went into journalism.

Ochs told us he had taken command about a month earlier, on February 15, and was now settled in. Most of the brigade's area of operation along the Cambodian border was a free-fire zone where no civilians lived or dared to travel. 'Anything that moves out there that isn't friendly is the enemy,' he said.

The recent coup in Phnom Penh had created a new politico-military situation, Ochs said, opening up possibilities that had not existed before. It was no secret that the U.S. Army wanted to go in and clean out Communist sanctuaries across the border, particularly COSVN. Otherwise, he would say no more about Cambodia.

'What can we do to help you?' he asked when he had finished briefing.

'We'd like to find a squad to follow,' I said.

'Why don't I take you out to Second of the Seventh?' he said. 'Bob Hannas is an outstanding battalion commander. He's at Firebase Jay.'

'Would it make any difference if we went with Second of the Eighth?'

'Well, I don't think that will be possible at this time. Second of the Seventh has some very fine company commanders. Alpha or Charlie Company would be excellent for your purpose.'

'What's wrong with Second of the Eighth?' Kay said.

'Nothing, really. I just don't think that battalion would be suitable at this time.' Ochs, who had polished the command presence of a gentleman-warrior to perfection, seemed slightly uncomfortable. 'I trust you'll respect my recommendation,' he said.

'Second of the Seventh is fine with us,' I said.

'Good. I'll tell Bob Hannas to expect you tomorrow. You can ride out with me in the afternoon.'

What's going on with 2/8? I wondered. *Be sure and check that out.*

'We're going to need help getting our supplies sent out to the field,' Kay said. 'Fresh batteries and film.'

'We'll link you up with the supply people and they'll manage it for you.' There was a pause in the conversation. 'Will that be all, gentlemen?' Ochs said.

We thanked him, shook hands and left.

At battalion supply we met the sergeant in charge, Jeff Buck, who told us he was from New Jersey, like Clevenger. When he learned we were sent by the brigade commander, he offered us every conceivable kind of gear we might need and more: a two-quart water bag, lightweight ponchos and liners, new air mattresses, heavy-duty socks, insect repellent, halizone purification tablets, freeze-dried field rations.

'These are the new LLRP rations,' he said, pronouncing it *lurp*. He held out a small package the size of a paperback book wrapped in dark fabric and plastic containers. 'Much better'n Cs,' he said. 'Tastier, not as heavy to carry. The grunts don't get these.'

'Why not?' Kay asked.

'Not enough to go around, I guess. The quartermaster general must have a million cases of Cs to get rid of. At least they've used up all the crap from the '50s. That shit was really bad,' Buck said.

An army travels on its stomach, I thought. *Maybe we'll do a story on field rations, how the GIs eat tasteless junk when better food is available.* I recalled the lunch in the generals' mess.

Clevenger asked for a military wristwatch with a compass on the strap, like the one officers wore. 'That I'll have to order,' Buck said. 'Come back in a week or two.'

Walking out of the supply stores, Kay looked at Clevenger and me in amazement. 'Man, what did you guys *do* up here yesterday? They're treating us like *royalty.*'

'Major Coleman set it all up,' Clevenger said. 'He's a friend of Jack's.'

'I let him beat me at pinochle,' I said. I didn't tell them J.D. was a better player.

Outside the supply post, a group of soldiers waited on the back of a truck. They seemed unhappy.

'How's it going?' Kay said.

'It's going like it always goes,' one of the soldiers said, 'hurry up and wait.'

'Where are you going? I mean, *when* you get going?'

'Second of the Seventh. We're new guys, replacements.'

Each of the men gave us his name, rank and hometown: PFC Bill Rose of Leesburg, Virginia; PFC Larry Tollardo of Oakland, California; PFC Carl Winston of Chicago; and a few others. All of them came from the 1st Infantry Division. The Big Red One was due to return to the United States in a month.

'Aren't you supposed to be going home?' I said.

'Yeah, that's what we thought,' one of them said. 'Until they told us we had to stay and serve out the full tour. What a drag.'

'The division's not going home,' another said, 'only the colors are. And guys with close to 'zeroes.' Sixty, sixty-five days or less left on their tours. Only the brass and shield go home. The men stay here.'

'Our people are being sent all over the country as replacements. Like us. Don't seem right.'

I turned to Kay. 'Think this might be a story?'

'Yeah,' he said, picking up his camera. 'Let's follow 'em right out to their company in the field. Make a good introduction to the battalion.'

We climbed into the back of the truck, passed the camera and equipment up, and plugged it all together. Kay rolled film. With his left hand, Clevenger held the microphone—a long sensitive instrument known as a "shotgun mike"—and with the other tried to adjust sound levels. He watched the VU meter on the MA-11 to keep the levels even. As each soldier spoke, Kay panned quickly from one face to another. Often the microphone got caught in the picture frame.

'Jimmy, watch the mike,' Kay whispered.

PFC Tollardo said he had been drafted after a year and a half of college. It was all the schooling he could take. Now that he was being transferred to the

Cav, he felt out of place. "It's like starting all over again, like when I first came to Nam. Everything seems new and different. Got to get used to a new environment altogether."

The truck started up and drove off. Kay rolled film along the way. When the truck stopped, the soldiers talked among themselves. "What I heard is it's bad stuff up here near the border," one said. "Wish I were down near Lai Khe, like before."

The men picked up their rucksacks and climbed off the truck. A sergeant gave them a handful of forms. When he had filled his in, PFC Tollardo said, "It's a hassle, man, it's a hassle. They made us fill out a lot of postal cards. I filled out about twenty. Only need four or six. That was a hassle."

'Be sure and write down the name and address of your next of kin,' the sergeant said. When he heard that, PFC Paul Gerrits, a combat medic who had been in country six days, winced. Kay was rolling on his face.

'Now, when you get in the field,' the sergeant said, 'don't worry if the grunts call you FNGs or cherries for a few days. It don't matter. Okay?'

'What's an FNG?' Gerrits said.

'Fuckin new guy,' the sergeant said.

March 21—Tay Ninh

A day in the life of the new guys. PFC Carl Winston had decided to reenlist in the army for three more years. His military specialty was office clerk but the First Cav redesignated him 11-B, infantry rifleman, which meant he was bound for the line. The troops called 11-B "Eleven Bush." By reenlisting, Winston would get his clerk's job again and the relative safety of being in the rear, out of the bush. He was also promised early rotation home, where he had a wife in Chicago with a baby on the way. Sitting with a group of other replacements, Winston spoke as Kay rolled film:

"It's clerk or nothing," he said. "I want to reenlist back into being a clerk. If I end up bein that again, it's just that. They ain't gonna get nothing more out of me. So I just reenlist as a clerk and probably no more time over here. Nothing ain't gettin me back."

"What's that mean?" I asked. "'Nothing ain't gettin me back?'"

"I'm just going back (home). If I get back, there's no bird, no plane gonna get me here again. I'll stay in the States."

I looked at the other soldiers. "Anyone disagree?"

"No," they said, shaking their heads.

"What do you miss most about not being at home?" I said.

"Well, I miss my wife," Winston said. "I miss the States. The cold weather. Chicago. Snow. Baseball. That's what I miss."

Kay said he was out of film and switched off the camera. We thanked the soldiers and said good-bye.

'I wonder if these guys know what they're doing out here,' Kay said later. 'You know, whether they can see the big picture.'

'Good idea,' I said. 'Let's ask them tomorrow.'

Back in the PIO area, I saw that Clevenger's face and arms were red from the sun. He had fair skin but had not used protective lotion. No one did. Everyone burned at the beginning of their tours, then peeled and tanned until their skin was brown as betel nuts. I could see that Clevenger was going to suffer.

'Jimmy, you might want to keep your sleeves rolled down for a few days,' Kay said. The sun did not seem to affect him.

'Yeah, good idea,' Clevenger said. 'I haven't had this much sun since I was a kid.'

'Where was that? Plainfield?'

'Nah. Atlantic City.'

'No VC there.'

'Not yet.'

Later, thinking about what the GIs had said to us, I was surprised by their candor. They were talking honestly to us, complaining openly in ways I hadn't expected. All soldiers gripe, but usually not in front of a film camera. The stoicism of the line troops I recalled from earlier in the war seemed to be changing.

MARCH 22, 1970

Firebase Jay

Colonel William Ochs flew his command helicopter over the flat unvarying rainforest northwest of Tay Ninh until he saw an oval-shaped clearing about twenty miles from his brigade headquarters. The clearing was the size of a small sports field, barren and dry, no vegetation, a brown hole torn out of the jungle. The location was a mile from the Cambodian border, part of a fifty-square-mile area of dense, uninhabited forest known as the Dog's Head. Ochs landed the Huey just outside the perimeter of a battalion command post in the center of the clearing. A berm—a dirt wall two to three feet high —formed the perimeter of the base. Beyond the berm, barbed wire stretched across the ground in concentric rolls that were interlaced with claymore mines and trip flares fixed in the ground with metal stakes. Large holes were dug along the berm every ten to twenty yards to make a firing line. Light and heavy machineguns were poised on platforms made of wooden ammunition crates filled with dirt. A battery of 105 millimeter artillery guns was positioned at one end of the camp, silent muzzles pointing at the sky. In the middle of the base were several large bunkers made of sandbags and wood with long slender radio antennas on top sticking in the air. Everything in the camp was dirt brown, slightly reddish, the color of the earth. Soldiers walked around with their shirts off. Some worked on their fighting positions, others rested in the shade of ponchos and tent halves, writing letters, reading, dozing. The temperature was well above one hundred degrees.

The new guys being transferred from the 1st Infantry Division arrived in another helicopter at the same time as Colonel Ochs. Walking in from the LZ just outside the perimeter, they were greeted by the battalion executive officer, Major Harry Bacas of Washington, D.C. Kay put the camera on his shoulder and rolled film. Bacas showed the soldiers a map of War Zone C and spoke in a loud precise voice.

"Gentlemen, welcome to Firebase Jay," he said. "When I say firebase, what I am talking about is a base with the ability to provide you with fire support for maneuver. The battalion is not involved in pacification or Vietnamization. We *are* involved in the standard mission of the infantry: to destroy the enemy within an assigned area of operation."

Major Bacas looked at them. Their faces told him nothing.

"When I say destroy," he continued, "I don't mean close, hand-to-hand fighting. I mean find, fix and destroy him with the fire support available." The men shifted the weight on their feet. From the other end of the camp an artillery gun fired.

The group was joined by the battalion commander, Lieutenant Colonel Robert Hannas. Bacas introduced him to the new guys. 'I'm assigning you to C Company,' Hannas said to the men. 'You've got firebase security for a couple of days and then you're going out in the field. Good luck to you.' He shook hands with each of the replacements and watched them walk away to join their new platoons. Colonel Ochs introduced us to Hannas, wished us luck and said good-bye. He turned and walked to his helicopter.

'Welcome to Second of the Seventh,' Hannas said. He smiled with the warm easy manner of a veteran infantry officer. The smile seemed natural. 'Sorry we can't show you much in the way of hospitality,' he said, nodding his head at the camp, 'but the coffee's hot and it's free.' Hannas had dark skin and a broad chest and shoulders, carrying himself with a confident relaxed air that gave the impression of a man of power. When he smiled, the expression illuminated his face, lighting up his mouth and eyes. I saw why Colonel Ochs had taken us to this battalion. Hannas was a winner.

'So you're going to show the folks back home what we're doing out here,' Hannas said, 'Is that right?'

'That's about it,' Kay said.

He smiled. 'Well, they sent you to the right place. Things are starting to get interesting around here. Glad to have you aboard.'

I asked him to tell us a bit about his background and wrote the details in my notebook as he spoke. Hannas said he was born and raised in New York City, attended Brooklyn Tech High School and then City College of New York, and had a master's degree in education. At one stage in his Army career he taught school. His family now lived in Pebble Beach, California. As commander of Second Battalion, Seventh Cavalry, his radio code name was "Scalp Six."

'You guys never forget the Little Big Horn, do you?' Clevenger said.

Hannas laughed. 'I hope not. I hope we never do. The day we forget a defeat like that is the day we're no longer a good battalion.'

He opened his tactical operations map. 'We're here, at Jay, a few clicks from the border. This is as close as anyone has operated up here before. I've got Alpha Company working this area, Bravo over here, and Delta out here. We know the North Vietnamese are in the area. Signs all over the place. As it happened, we came in and opened up Jay the same day the generals took over in Phnom Penh.'

'Is there a connection?' I said.

'I don't know. Maybe. You can read what you want into that.'

I wondered. Washington was withdrawing some American troops from Vietnam, but the Army still had several hundred thousand in-country and was engaging the North Vietnamese with relentless pursuit. From time to time, the hollow rumble of bombs could be heard exploding in the distance, dozens of bombs going off at the same time, the ground quaking faintly underfoot. B-52s, I thought when I heard them. The noise came from the north and west, the other side of the border, inside Cambodia, but it was hard to tell how far in the dense forest.

Kay was anxious to see what was happening with the new guys. We excused ourselves. 'Come back when you're finished and I'll take you to meet the company commander,' Hannas said.

Walking away, Kay said, 'It's gonna be great working with that guy.'

'He's so friendly,' Clevenger said.

'Yeah, I really like him,' I said.

The three PFCs, Winston, Rose and Tollardo, sat on the berm telling their new comrades about their time with the Big Red One. Winston stood with a group of soldiers nearby. When Rose saw Kay rolling film on his dusty sweat-streaked face, he turned away from the camera.

'What's the matter?' Kay said, turning off.

'I don't want my folks to see how grubby I am,' Rose said. 'Just one day on a firebase and I'm filthy.' He poured water from a five-gallon can into his helmet and washed his face.

'This ain't Hollywood, you know,' Clevenger said.

'Could've fooled me,' Rose said.

When his face was clean, I asked, "Any idea what you're doing up here?"

"Yeah," Rose said, "get the enemy, that's what it's for."

"Do you get the big picture?"

"Yeah."

"What is it?"

He smiled, an awkward contortion of muscles. "I can't say. I don't know. I don't know why. All I know is I'm here." Laughter.

Tollardo sat in his shelter, cleaning his M-16.

"Do you get the big picture?" I asked.

"Well, you go out and find bunker complexes, pull back and get the artillery." I waited while he tried to think. "We're out to find the enemy, that's all."

"How do you like your job?"

He laughed. "Just a job, I guess." Big smile.

"Got a girl back in the world?"

"Yeah. Well, I did, but we broke up before I came to Nam. The reason being I figured I might not come back." Tollardo looked down at his rifle and continued cleaning it.

Kay saw Winston climb over the perimeter berm with a grenade in his hand. Signaling Clevenger and me to follow, he ran after him with his camera.

'What's up?' Kay called.

'Practice,' Winston said. He stepped over the barbed wire and looked around to see if anyone was in the open. Pulling the stiff wire pin out of the fuse mechanism, he threw the grenade toward the treeline about thirty yards away. It was a good long throw, an outfielder's peg, and the spoon flew away from the grenade high in the air. Everyone ducked. The grenade exploded with a sharp angry sound, *splaat*. Kay got the sequence on film.

'Might make a closing shot for the piece,' he said.

Lieutenant Colonel Hannas appeared and took us to another part of the camp. He walked up to a blond-haired captain wearing baggy fatigues and sitting on a pile of sandbags. The captain stood up but not to full attention when he saw the colonel approaching. He was bareheaded in the heat. Hannas introduced him as Bob Jackson and said he was commander of C Company. Jackson shook hands one at a time, repeating our names individually, calling each of us "Mister." Hannas said, 'I'll let you gentlemen get acquainted. If you need anything, let us know,' and walked away.

Captain Jackson invited us to sit with him on a row of sandbags piled next to his company command post, a shallow bunker with overhead cover set inside the perimeter. Kay, Clevenger and I put down the equipment and sat. Jackson had a deck of playing cards in his hands.

'A Vietnamese Army colonel taught me some tricks,' he said, 'on my first tour.'

'When was that?' Kay said.

'Sixty-six and sixty-seven. We were stationed in the highlands, about fifty miles northwest of Nha Trang. Infantry battalion. The colonel was a wise old guy. He taught me a lot about the VC too. How to keep your people from getting killed.'

'What casualties have you had?' I said.

'Very few. Two killed and twelve wounded in the time I've had the company. Five months.'

'That's pretty low.'

'Yes it is. Lowest of any company in the division. But we're not avoiding contact. We also hold the division record for the most NVA kills in an ambush. Eleven. That was a few weeks ago, March third as I recall. We set a lot of ambushes at night out here.'

Jackson spoke in a soft southern voice. Five feet eight or nine inches tall, fair-haired and slender, he had a manner that gave the impression of calm maturity. His eyes were modest, gentle. *How many American officers*, I wondered, *have bothered to learn about war from the Vietnamese?* The First Cav officer who had given us permission to start filming the documentary, Brigadier General Casey, had sent us to his best brigade commander, Colonel Ochs, who had taken us to his best battalion commander, Lieutenant Colonel Hannas, who had introduced us to his best company commander, a young captain from the American South who had learned about war from a wise old South Vietnamese colonel. It was as if the general had chosen Captain Jackson himself and here was Jackson telling us he had learned how to keep his soldiers alive from an officer in the ARVN.

A young lieutenant, one of Jackson's platoon leaders, walked up and handed him a canteen cup of water.

'It's warm,' Jackson said.

'The bet didn't say it had to be cold,' the lieutenant said, smiling.

'You're right. Well, I thank you. You're a gentleman and a scholar.'

'No, you're the scholar,' the lieutenant said, then turned and walked away.

"You measure your wealth in water out here," Jackson said. "A serious bet is a canteen of water."

'What was that about?' I asked.

'Oh, he bet I didn't know the number of feet below sea level at which the pressure per square inch doubles.'

'How many feet is it?' Kay said.

'It'll cost you a cup of water to find out,' he said. His eyes flashed for a moment. We laughed. Jackson poured the water slowly into his canteen.

'Where are you from?' I asked.

'Sheffield, Alabama.'

'Family?'

'I have a wife and two children there.'

'How old are you?'

'Twenty-nine,' he said. 'Going on fifty.' He laughed.

'Tell us a little bit about yourself, please.'

'Well, there isn't a whole lot to tell. I went to school in Alabama. Played college ball. I was the kicker. Got a degree in biology. Joined the Army six and a half years ago. Ranger school. Airborne. I was a platoon leader with the 82d. Did twelve weeks in the Dominican Republic in '65.'

'I was there too,' I said.

'Were you?' He smiled. 'I thought the TV coverage there was real fine.'

'I was there for radio. But I worked closely with the TV people. Learned a lot from them. What's your call sign?'

'Team Six. The truth is, running a rifle company is a bit like managing a football team. I mean, team spirit is very important. You can't work too hard to improve it.'

'Tell us about the situation up here on the border.'

'Well, at this time we're getting set to fight the 95-C regiment,' Jackson said. 'We killed one of their soldiers up north—not us, I mean the division got one—and they found a map on him which had a trail system marked on it. His orders said the regiment was supposed to arrive in this area on the nineteenth.'

'Three days ago,' Clevenger said.

'I didn't think they could get here that quickly,' Jackson said.

'Maybe they can't,' said Kay.

'If they're not here yet, they probably will be soon.'

We told him our plan to spend a month or two with a squad.

'They warned me you might be coming. Actually, I like the idea. I understand you can take care of yourselves if things get busy.'

'Don't worry,' I said, 'we won't get in the way.'

'Good,' he said, standing up. 'Come with me. I'd like you to meet my best squad.' He walked to a fighting hole on the berm, a shallow ditch with sandbags around it. Several soldiers sat on the ground, cleaning weapons, talking.

'Gentlemen,' Jackson said, 'I'd like you to meet Sergeant Dunnuck. He is in temporary charge of second squad, second platoon. Some people call him "Killer." Don't worry about that though.' Dunnuck stood up, a thin spidery figure with long arms and loping shoulders. Intense eyes.

'Gene, this is Mr. Laurence, this is Mr. Kay and this is Mr. Clevenger. They're from CBS television.' Dunnuck stood up and shook hands. 'They're going to spend a little time with us in the field,' Jackson said. 'I'd like you to look after them. Take care of them like your own.'

'You're giving me a pretty big squad, Cap'n,' Dunnuck said, smiling. 'Can I make a fire team out of 'em?'

Jackson laughed. 'They're going to have their hands full as it is,' he said. 'But they'll know what to do if we get in the bad stuff.'

A soldier approached and said it was almost time for the mad minute. 'Any of you guys want to shoot the fifty?' he said, looking at Kay and Clevenger.

'Yeah,' said Clevenger, standing up. 'I'll give it a try.' His face was bright red from two days in the sun.

'C'mon with me,' the soldier said. He took Clevenger to a .50-caliber machinegun mounted on a stack of sandbags, shoulder high. Clevenger was not tall enough to see clearly over the top of the weapon so the soldiers brought a wooden ammo box for him to stand on. He got up on the toes of his boots and looked along the barrel, trying to line up the sights. The soldiers showed him how to hold the gun handles and squeeze the trigger in bursts. When the order for the mad minute was given, a hundred weapons opened fire at once—M-16s, M-14s, machine guns, grenade launchers, pistols —a raucous calamitous explosion of noise and flame, one long continuous outpouring of gunfire. Clevenger's fifty made the heaviest sound of all, *duh-duh-duh-duh-duh-duh . . . duh-duh-duh-duh-duh-duh,* the bullets hissing into the forest with an evil-sounding *sssssshhhuussssssshhhhh.* Each time he fired, the gun recoiled sharply with a series of jerks, like a jackhammer, pulling his body upward and lifting his feet into the air, holding them there for an instant, dangling him like a marionette. Elbows out, skinny arms flapping, hair flying, body bouncing up and down, Clevenger screamed *"hot shit!"* into the ear-shattering din.

In a minute, the madness was over. The air was thick with burned gunpowder. The sun hurried away and the sky dissolved to dusk. Kay, Clevenger and I put our gear in a pile near the center of the perimeter and spread ponchos on the earth to get ready for the night. The evening brought some relief from the heat and humidity, but our bodies were hot and dirty and there was no chance of a shower. My own stale sweat mingled with the raw stink of the jungle and the firebase. I poured a little water onto a towel and wiped my hands and face with it and forgot how filthy the rest of me was.

Lieutenant Colonel Hannas came by to see how we were doing. When he saw Clevenger's crimson face and neck, he said, 'I want you to see the medics about that sunburn.' The tone of his voice allowed no misunderstanding. It was an order. One of the colonel's aides went away and within a minute an older man appeared, a sergeant first class wearing a rumpled fatigue jacket outside his trousers and flip-flops on large bare feet. He introduced himself as Bob Burke and said he was the senior medic. He examined Clevenger quickly.

"I've got just the right thing for that sunburn," Burke said in a New England accent. "You come with me." He took Clevenger away to another part of the camp.

Lieutenant Colonel Hannas said, 'You don't want a heat casualty on your first day out.'

After chow, the temperature dropped twenty degrees and the firebase went at ease. Music played. Cans of beer fizzed open. Bottles of bourbon wrapped in towels appeared in the hands of NCOs who sipped them politely, arching their little fingers in the air as if drinking tea. A few joints passed from hand to hand among the enlisted men. Kay and I sat on our ponchos with our boots off and smoked cigarettes, watching. Two soldiers from 3d Platoon came over and asked if we wanted to share their pipe. We welcomed them and they sat down and filled the pipe with brown marijuana and tobacco.

'Do you guys always make so much noise?' Kay asked.

'Nah,' one of them said. 'Normally we keep real quiet in the bush. Sometimes Charlie gets fifteen meters from our night position and sets off a trip flare. That's how quiet we are at night. But not here on the firebase.'

'Yeah,' the other soldier said, 'Charlie knows we're here, so why pretend?'

'This is our first time out of the bush in three weeks, man.'

'Yeah, guys're cuttin loose a little.'

In celebration, the firebase lit up with noise and light. Muzzle flashes, music tapes, outgoing tracers, transistor radios, long bursts of machinegun fire, major and minor explosions filled the air. No one went outside the wire; nothing could survive out there. The random firing seemed to reassure the soldiers of their lethal might. Gradually, the camp became a kaleidoscope of fire and sound: cooking fires, gunfire, flashlights, cigarettes, voices, shouts, silhouettes, rock 'n' roll, laughter, and, above everything, the slow white fire of parachute flares—swinging, hissing, squeaking, smoking down through the busy sky.

Someone fired a grenade into the treeline *phoooot . . . splaaat!* and a GI shouted, *'Git some!'*

Every few minutes artillery guns boomed out H and I, popping ears with the sudden pressure of the explosions, the shells spinning away with an air-splitting *rrrrruuuuusssssshhh,* a low hollow sound like the breath of death. Just outside the wire, a wall of jungle was visible in the twilight, near silent, all-seeing, a black brooding mass that rose high up off the ground and enveloped the firebase in a large black cloak. At night you could see that the rainforest was the main player in the war, a huge malevolent presence, alive and waiting, infinitely patient, as deadly as anything concocted by the enemy. The forest swallowed artillery shells like drops of rain—shells, bombs, soldiers, prayers, dreams, everything.

'Man, I don't believe this,' Kay said, shaking his head.

'Whoooo would imagine?' I said.

'Let's make a tape and send it to Mike,' Kay said. Some of the freakier moments of the war had been described by our friend Mike Herr in his *Esquire* magazine articles, but this went beyond that. I agreed. A little natural sound might help him with his book, move the rocks around for him a little.

I took a blank cassette out of my pack, put it in the little Sony and pressed record. "LZ Jay," I said, "March 22, about 9:15."

The tape recorded the voices of the soldiers around us: slow southern drawls, midwestern twangs, nasal New England inflections, laid-back West Coast funk, jazzy ghetto jive. Aggressive voices, authoritarian voices, angry voices, violent voices, passive voices, the accents and dialects of a large warrior tribe, U.S. Army voices.

A senior NCO: "Anytime you're ready."

"Awwhl right!"

"Fire in the hole!"

"Fire in the hooooole!" repeated down the line.

A pause.

"Which way?"

"Straight out."

"Right out in front of you God damn it!" A sergeant's voice. Angry.

"You dumb motherfucker!"

"On the motherfuckin *whisky* side." Laughter. ('Whisky' meaning west, but also what they were drinking.)

"Ah'll drink to that." A southern NCO voice, slightly drunk.

"Get your God damn head out of your asshole."

"What's he gonna blow?"

"Fu-gas."

"Got a whole tank."

The jellied gasoline known as "fu-gas" was buried in the ground as an enormous land mine. It had been put there years ago, but now it was unstable and dangerous. Everyone got close to the ground and waited for the explosion. Time passed.

"They can't even get that shit to blow."

"What they got out there?"

"Fu-gas. Paris is the one who hooked it up."

"Hey, it might not go off. 'Cause it was Paris is the one who hooked it up."

"Hey, Paris! Take a match out there."

"Don't tell him. He might do it." Laughter. Their mingled voices sounded like a gang of teenagers all talking at the same time, interrupting each other's sentences, two or three conversations overlapping.

"You can see the fuckin fu-gas. It's right out there. See where it's between those two tall trees out there?"

"You know that explosion that went off a while ago? There's a big fuckin piece of tree—that long and that big around—that came out from that blast. Came right over the top of us. I got it right over the bunker, right here. Could'a killed somebody deader 'n hell."

The radio squawked.

"Wait a second, God damn it." An angry sergeant.

"Six-six Delta. Blow that fucker."

"Tell 'em to hold it up."

"Awwwww."

"Six-six Delta says blow it and he says check with Timberclap."

"I'll bet it won't go anyway."

"Timberclap tried to blow it last night and couldn't."

"Aww, Timberclap, he couldn't fuck in a wet dream."

An artillery piece fired, a big noise from a 105, echoing away.

"Fire in the hole!"

"On the whisky side!"

"Let it blow!"

KAABOOOM!!!

A great explosion struck the camp, compressing the air, rocking everyone and everything, shaking the earth, creating a fireball of flame and smoke a hundred meters outside the wire that shot up in the sky and formed a red-orange cloud the shape of a giant mushroom.

"*Ahhhhh-haaaaaa!*" Whistles and shouts.

"*Dig it!*"

"*Awww right!*"

"That's a show!"

"Good show, Paris."

"*Diiigg-iiitt!*"

All around the firebase, hands clapped.

"He would be roasted. He would have his pants hot." Laughter.

"Think, man. What would a gook think, comin through the wood line? And it'd been real quiet, and all of a sudden the whole damn world blows up on him, man."

"Concentrated Fourth of July."

"That's it for him."

A crackling noise came from the area of the explosion, like firecrackers popping.

"Man, that sounds like a fuckin AK burst."

"Yeah."

"Sounds funny, don't it?"

"Wood burnin?"

"Maybe the guy's just sittin there twitching with his finger on the trigger." Laughs.

"Click it on safety, man."

"Naw. That's just his rounds goin off, hooked to his belt."

"Shit, a fuckin gook couldn't live through that."

More rapid explosions.

"Wooooo! Fuckin dig it!"

Kay and I looked at each other and shook our heads. In our travels over the past five or six years in Vietnam, we had not seen soldiers behave like this.

'Far out, man,' he said.

'Nobody's gonna believe this,' I said.

In the spooky half-light, half-stoned on drugs and booze, Firebase Jay was as psychedelic as anything in the States, a true blowout of a party, real and surreal at the same time, bizarre and disconnected as a dream, the wartime military expression of modern American culture, 150 soldiers living it up for one wild night in the heart of War Zone C.

Kay put on a cassette tape of a new Rolling Stones album called *Let It Bleed* and pushed the play switch. The music blended easily with the noise of the camp, as if the two tracks had been orchestrated for each other.

Mick Jagger sang the opening bars of *Midnight Rambler* in his most sinister voice.

A loud low whooshing noise rushed overhead, a fast-moving rocket, close.

"Where the fuck do they fire that thing?" A soldier's voice.

"Got a nice fire going."

"Hey! Nice shot, William Tell." Cynical laughter.

"They're goin over to Cambodia with it."

"Tryin to give Tay Ninh a little 'lumin."

A machinegun fired, long bursts into the bush.

"Dig it."

"Guy knows how to work out with that sixty."

Then the .50-caliber: *duh-duh-duh-duh-duh-duh-duh-duh*, slow, heavy, loud, the stream of bullets *shhhhhhssssshing* into the bush.

"You fired enough, God damn it!" a sergeant cried. "Don't fire no more!"

"Gimmie the ass."

"Shut the fuck up."

BOOOM! Another explosion.

"Hey, half and half. Make the next bowl half and half."

"Wow!"

"Hey! Let's not kill hippies. Let's kill fuckin Indians." A northeastern voice, hip, full of dope.

"Help stamp out reality."

"Fuck up the Indians."

Jagger sang of knives and murder, violence and bloodshed, as if on cue.

"Oh, wow, man."

Most of the GIs had not heard "Midnight Rambler" before. It definitely wasn't being played on Armed Forces Radio.

BOOOOM!

"Two percent of the American population is Indian," the northeasterner said in a fast voice as if he'd told this one before. "Therefore we should give em two percent of the American land. Therefore, give em Death Valley and log em every three days. Right?"

The GI's around him listened as though they'd heard this story before.

"Dig it. Hate them fuckin Indians. Peace-freak God damn peyote-smokin fucks. Fuckin Indians!" Shouting now. "God damn right, man! There ain't a fuckin good Indian. Custer had it fuckin right, man. He was kickin ass on the Indians. It's a good man. Fuckin Indians."

Noise of explosions diminishing.

"They better not be fuckin up my war. Fuck up my war, I'll be pissed off. Fuckin Indians wore headbands and beads and shit. Trinkets. Anybody stupid enough to get jewed out of New York Island, Manhattan Island, for $24, man, they deserve Death Valley. Give em Death Valley."

"You better be glad somebody's goin, God damn it." A black-skinned soldier joined the group.

"Now you're gonna tell me *you're* Indian, right?"

"Dig it."

"Hey, right, man. Here's a fuckin Indian right here. Full fledged, watermelon-eatin Indian. He's gonna burn a cross on my front lawn, I'm gonna burn a watermelon on his. Right, brother?"

"Dig it."

"What's that you're smokin?"

"One hundred percent."

"I'm gonna crash, man," another soldier said.

The party was finishing. The last of the flares fizzled out and the guns stopped firing. The camp became quiet. Soldiers took off their boots, unrolled their poncho liners, stretched out on the ground and closed their eyes. A radio hissed. In the distance, someone snored peacefully. Our first day in the field with Charlie Company, 2/7, was coming to an end at Firebase Jay. I lay on my back and looked at the stars. *How truly bizarre,* I thought, *to find such a strange mix of war and booze and music and dope in the middle of the jungle. So much noise and light. Maybe this is what they do to chase away the evil. Or maybe it's their way of joining it. What they do to convince themselves how bad they are. Whatever happens, we'll get a good story with these guys.* Lying there, getting ready to fall asleep, I had a sense of well-being, of feeling secure and comfortable in the cool air. I was beginning to believe that the three of us belonged here, civilians among soldiers, as if all the time we had spent in Vietnam covering the war had prepared us for this. Right down the line, from General Casey to Sergeant Dunnuck and the privates, the soldiers had tried to make us feel welcome, as welcome as anyone could feel in the circumstances. *And that is the Army's way of seducing you,* I thought, treating you like a gentleman, not as harshly as one of their own, taking you into the secret heart of their war and giving you a sense of the stakes involved and at the same time the impression that all their modern weapons and fighting skills will protect you, insulate you from whatever is going to happen next.

"Where's Jimmy?" Kay said. I looked around. There was no sign of him among the sleeping GIs. Clevenger hadn't come back after he left with the senior medic hours earlier. We had forgotten. Quickly, I put on my boots, got up and went to look for the first aid station. It took a while. The medical bunker was in another part of the camp. I opened the closed flap of the tent half and went inside. A light was on. First Sergeant Burke sat on a large picnic cooler without a shirt, sweating, a can of beer in his hand. Clevenger sat across from him, sweating hard, a neat stack of empty cans on the ground between them. Burke offered me a can of cold beer and I took it. His face was as red as Clevenger's.

'We were starting to get worried,' I said.

'Nah, nuthin ta wurry about,' Clevenger said, slurring. 'I'm in the vury capable hands of the You-nided Shtatsh Army medical corps. Ishn't 'at right sergeant?'

Burke nodded and smiled. "I told you I had the right thing for that sunburn," he said. He slapped the side of the cooler with the palm of his hand. "Did I lie?"

"Absholutely not," said Clevenger. "Don't feel a thing."

When Clevenger and I got back to Kay, we unrolled our ponchos, took off our boots, got under the poncho liners, and stretched out. The stars were bright. Kay lit a joint and passed it.

'Do you think the officers let the grunts pick the name of this firebase?' I said.

MARCH 23, 1970

Firebase Jay awoke at dawn still feeling euphoria from the night before. Memories of the party lingered lightly in our heads, ephemeral as the morning mists that rose from the jungle floor and melted in the glowing early light. Waiting for the sun to come up so that we could start work, I conveyed my feelings to Joy in a letter, conscious of how concerned she was for our well-being.

> We're up on the Cambodian border with a superb unit of the 1st Cav. They just don't ever seem to get hurt. So don't worry about us. The life is dirty and hard, but not so bad for us when it only is for 2 months. We want to stay in the field the entire time. Jimmy is having the most exciting time of his life, digging the light shows every night. Keith is trying to make this series into a documentary. We are REALLY going to show it as it is, and it is amazing!

Kay, Clevenger and I spent most of the day finishing the story about the new guys. We followed them around, interviewed them, observed how they were adjusting to their new lives. Now, after three days of work, almost all of our film and battery power were used up. We had arranged for the CBS bureau in Saigon to send us fresh batteries and more film directly into the field, but nothing had arrived. In order to continue, we needed to go to Saigon to get fresh supplies, write and record the narration for this first story, and ship it. Everything was made more urgent because Charlie Company was going to make a combat assault the next morning. If we were not with the company when it went out, we would have to wait four days until it was resupplied, and if the company made contact with the North Vietnamese in that time, we would miss it. We had to make our way to Saigon and back to the firebase by dawn. Normally the journey would take most of two days, one to get down to Saigon, the next to get back to Tay Ninh and out to the base. We had to do it in twelve to fourteen hours. It was now midafternoon.

'Can't make it,' Kay said.

'Yeah, we need a miracle,' I said.

'What the hell,' said Clevenger, 'let's give it a shot. What have we got to lose?' Of the three of us, Clevenger had spent the least time in the field and was not experienced with the unpredictability of military transportation and the long waits that went with it.

'I've got an idea,' I said.

'What's that?'

'Ask Colonel Ochs for one of his choppers. He's got plenty.'

'Never happen.' Kay said. 'Brigade commanders don't just frag choppers for journalists, no matter how much they like them. What if he needed the bird for an emergency or something?'

'Yeah, but nothing's happening. The whole AO is quiet,' I said. 'Besides, he's got a hundred other choppers.'

'There's no way, man.' Kay shook his head.

'Jack, you're whistling Dixie,' said Clevenger.

But I thought Ochs might help. He had been told by General Casey to cooperate with us on the documentary and was already doing everything he could to get us settled in with 2/7.

'What'll you bet?' I said.

'Bottle of Scotch,' Kay said.

'Okay,' I said. 'A bottle of Scotch says we can get to Saigon and back in time to make the operation tomorrow.'

'You're on.'

'I'll hold the stake,' said Clevenger.

'No you won't,' Kay said. 'If we let you hold the stake, you'll drink it.'

Late in the afternoon, Colonel Ochs flew to the firebase to talk with Lieutenant Colonel Hannas, a one-on-one session between brigade and battalion commanders. I sensed that something important was being planned, though they were not telling us. After his meeting with Hannas, I told Ochs about our problem. I did not ask him for a helicopter. He listened and said nothing for several seconds, pondering. Then he said, 'You gentlemen can take my C and C ship for an hour or two. I'm not going anywhere this evening. Just drop me off in Tay Ninh on your way down to Saigon.'

'Thank you, sir,' I said. 'We really appreciate this.'

'Glad to be of help,' he said.

Kay and Clevenger looked at me with expressions of wonder. I was almost as surprised as they were.

'Laurence,' Kay said, 'you still know how to make daily miracles, don't you?'

'What's a daily miracle?' Clevenger asked.

'What just happened,' Kay said.

A few minutes later, preparing to leave the firebase, we said good-bye to Captain Jackson and some of the soldiers in C Company. We had not told them we were taking the colonel's chopper.

'See you tomorrow,' I said.

'You'll never make it back in time,' one of the soldiers said.

'It takes *days* to get to Saigon, man,' another said.

'Yeah, and a *lot longer* to get back.' They laughed. No one hurried back to the field.

'Have fun anyway.'

'Yeah, say hi to the girls on Tu Do Street for me.'

At Tay Ninh, Colonel Ochs told his helicopter commander to take us to Saigon, wait and bring us back. The crew was from A Company, 229th Aviation Battalion, a unit that called itself the Black Bandits.

'Saigon is normally off-limits to us,' said the pilot, Warrant Officer First Class J. W. Smith, 'so this is a treat.' The aircraft commander was Warrant Officer First Class McGowan, the crew chief was Bill Meyer, and the door gunners were Specialist Fourth Class Smith and Specialist Fourth Class Davis. The crew was young and friendly, happy about making the unexpected trip to the big city.

At Tan Son Nhut, they parked the chopper at the Hotel III landing pad and rode into town with us in big American sedans provided by the bureau. Kay and Clevenger took the crew to dinner at an air-conditioned restaurant downtown while I went to the bureau. At first, Dave Miller, the bureau chief, didn't believe me when I told him how we got down to Saigon.

'We sent your film and batteries to Tay Ninh two days ago,' Miller said, 'and they promised to get it out to you at the firebase.'

'It never made it,' I said.

'It must be sitting around somewhere. Try and find it when you go back up.'

I sat down to write the narration. At the top of the page I typed:

NOTE TO EDITORS: This story represents the first
of a series (we hope) on Charlie Company, 2/7, 1st Cav,

and the men in it. We plan to stay with them continuously
or until Clevenger's sunburn reaches third degree.

We wanted viewers of the story to see Charlie Company through the
eyes of the replacements, the new guys who were joining it for the first time.
It would be the viewers' introduction to the company as well. Kay, Clevenger and I also wanted to show that the new guys were completely
unaware of the "big picture," the strategic forces at work in the war on the
Cambodian border. Keeping in mind Kay's pictures of the new guys riding in
the back of the truck at the base in Tay Ninh, I wrote the first paragraph:

> Tay Ninh, the gateway to War Zone C, and a truckload of replacements that veter-
> ans call FNGs: friggin new guys. At this stage, they are unaware of the role they are
> to play in the larger context of what may be developing into the second Indochina
> War.

By speculating about a second Indochina War, I was suggesting that the
situation in War Zone C was worth attention, that something was happening to make it important. It was only an informed hunch, but I was trying to
signal to viewers who knew the history of French Indochina that the present
ground war might soon be expanded to include Cambodia. The unexpected
change of government in Phnom Penh, the information we had gleaned
from military briefings in Vietnam, and recent deployments by the First Cav
and other American and South Vietnamese units close to the Cambodian
border led me to believe that far-reaching military moves were being
planned, though I did not know the details. Almost every senior U.S. officer
we had talked to in Saigon, Phuoc Vinh and Tay Ninh had expressed a desire
to attack the North Vietnamese with ground forces in Cambodia. The NVA
had used Cambodia as a sanctuary for the past five years, attacking American
and South Vietnamese troops in Vietnam and then withdrawing back across
the border to their refuge. The wishes of American officers to retaliate created pressure within the military that passed up the chain of command to
MACV in Saigon, where General Creighton Abrams had replaced William
Westmoreland as commander. Abrams would pass the recommendation up
to his superiors in Hawaii and the Pentagon, and they would study and take
it to the White House for a decision. President Richard Nixon was more
receptive than his predecessor to suggestions by his senior military advisers.

Who could tell what was going to happen? Pushing the ground war into Cambodia seemed a serious possibility.

The rest of the narration told the personal stories of the four PFCs—Gerrits, Rose, Tollardo and Winston. Scenes in the film showed them going through the bureaucratic hassle of filling out forms before joining Charlie Company in the field, meeting Major Bacas and Lieutenant Colonel Hannas, joining their squads, talking to us on-camera. I did not identify Firebase Jay by name or indicate its position, other than to say it was near the Cambodian border, censoring myself to protect the battalion's security. The final line of the script said we would meet some of the veterans of C Company in our next report. We hoped to establish a continuing series about the company.

When the writing was finished, Kay and Clevenger recorded the voice-over narration and prepared the cans of film for shipment. At the last minute, I dropped in the note to Joy that I had written earlier and a dub of the audiotape of the night party from Firebase Jay.

'What's that?' Kay said.

'The tape we made for Mike Herr,' I said. 'Joy will give it to him.'

Kay laughed. 'That ought to blow his mind.'

'Maybe he can use it,' I said. 'You never know.'

We asked Miller for permission to take Dana Stone with us to Tay Ninh. 'New York will kill me,' he said, 'but I'll take the heat.' Stone had just returned from Laos. He had changed from the quiet, inquisitive still photographer we had last seen two years before. He and his wife, Louise, had left Vietnam in 1969 to make a long driving expedition around Asia. Now he was back and determined to establish himself as a television film photographer. "I want to be rich and famous," he said, half joking, to friends, "and this is the fastest way to do it." It was unlike his usual modest self, but Stone had become more ambitious. He was more serious about his work, more willing to discuss it, more anxious to get a staff job at CBS News. As a freelancer, he was earning $250 a week from CBS, enough for Louise and him to live comfortably in Vietnam. Otherwise, Stone was his same mischievous self: slightly sardonic, witty, perceptive. He had bought a pair of wire-rimmed glasses to replace the broken plastic frames of his former pair, but the bridge of the new ones slipped down his nose as usual.

By the time Kay, Clevenger, Stone, the chopper crew and I got to Hotel III at Tan Son Nhut, it was after ten o'clock at night. The base was quiet, largely deserted. Colonel Ochs's helicopter crew had been given more than a good dinner. One of the pilots got out of the car and tried to take a step but could not find the ground to put his foot on. When he did, he slid gently down the side of the car and sat on the tarmac and smiled. His eyes were solid glass. We carried the crew chief and one of the door gunners into the waiting room where they went to sleep on the benches. The landing pad and buildings were empty. The pilot, who was slightly more sober than the others, instructed the rest of us to wait in the ops shack while he made a quick test of his flying coordination.

'If I can get it to hover a little,' he said, 'I'll be okay to fly. If I can't, well, I don't want anybody on board if I fuck up.' His eyes were runny red.

The young warrant officer walked slowly down the flight line, climbed carefully into the helicopter, switched on the ignition, then the running lights, and started the engine. Each function took two or three times longer than usual. The turbine engine whined—shrill sounds of compressed fuel and air igniting—and the rotor blades turned slowly on their axis. When they were spinning fast, the pilot tried to lift the machine a few feet off the tarmac. It wobbled unsteadily for a few seconds and dropped to the ground with a hard bump. Watching from a hundred yards away, Kay, Clevenger, Stone and I turned to look at each other. A minute later the pilot tried again. Then again. After several attempts, he held the big Huey in a hover for more than a minute, moved it forward and backward a few feet, tilted the nose up and down, and landed again gently. He got out and waved his arm at us to come aboard. We carried the crew chief and door gunner, still unconscious, out to the chopper and strapped them into their seats. When everyone was ready, the helicopter lifted slowly off the ground, dipped its nose, pulled itself over the perimeter fence of the landing pad and gained several hundred feet of altitude. The pilot followed the long straight highway out of Saigon to the northwest toward Cu Chi and Tay Ninh, keeping under a thousand feet. The weather was clear. Below us, lights along both sides of the highway were clear and bright, glowing with color. People sat in cafes, eating and talking and drinking tea. In the chopper, Kay lit a joint, took a deep drag and passed it around the inside of the cabin. Stone abstained. The tensions of the long busy day floated away with the smoke.

Laughing, Clevenger reached into his pack and pulled out a bottle of Chivas Regal. 'Jack, you win the bet,' he shouted close to my ear. Holding the bottle by the neck, he unscrewed the top and took a long drink. Then he put the open bottle on top of the communications console in the center of the passenger compartment—a stack of radios the size of two large television sets—and left it there. Kay and I took turns drinking from the bottle and put it back on the commo deck where it balanced, the top still off. In front, the pilot held his course, following the lights along the highway. Behind us, the door gunner who was still conscious watched the display of casual indulgence with wonder, astonished by our irreverent frivolity. Then he smiled, as if in approval. Stone was quiet. Finally, he shook his head from side to side and shouted over the noise of the engine and the passing wind, "This is something you're only supposed to read in *war novels.*"

At Tay Ninh, a brigade PIO officer was waiting with two jeeps and drivers at the LZ. It was eleven o'clock. The PIO staff gave us cots for the night. Before going to sleep I opened two letters from Joy, the first I received since arriving in-country. On one she had drawn

Cat says hello with a bite. He got to go downstairs with me tonight while I was doing some laundry—his big adventure! He's been acting a little strange since you left . . . sneezing more than usual and never leaving me alone. I think he misses you.

MARCH 24, 1970

The night passed in peace. By 7:30 in the morning the sun was low and bright and casting long shadows across the firebase. The air was cool and still. Life came awake with the morning light and infused the forest with noise and movement. Tiny birds sang. Monkeys squawked. Insects chirped. The sweet fragrance of wildflowers floated on the clear blue air. It felt like the best time of day.

Outside the wire, 110 soldiers of Charlie Company sat or stood in the open field outside the firebase waiting for lift ships to take them into the bush. The slicks were late but there was no hurry. The longer the men were at Jay the better, the less humping they had to do later. They were still at ease, laughing with each other, cheerful, happy for the few days of easy duty they'd had at the firebase. When Kay, Stone, Clevenger and I landed in an early morning supply chopper from Tay Ninh, they were surprised to see us back so soon.

'Aw, man, I don't believe you went all the way to Saigon last night,' one of them said.

Kay told them about the C and C ship and the crew of the 229th getting drunk in Saigon and the pilot flying to Tay Ninh anyway.

'Just imagine that, man,' another soldier said. 'Four of you in the Old Man's chopper. *At* night, *drunk* pilot, *drunk* copilot, *drunk* crew chief, door gunner tied to his seat.' Shaking his head. 'You guys are *definitely* crazy.'

'Told you we'd be back this morning,' Kay said.

'And we didn't think you could,' the soldier said.

'Neither did he,' I said, turning to Kay. 'You owe me a bottle of Scotch, by the way.'

'Jimmy drank it,' Kay said.

'Hey, that was *my* bottle we drank last night,' Clevenger said.

We introduced Dana Stone to Captain Jackson, Sergeant Dunnuck and the soldiers in 2d Squad. They said hello and asked him where he was from and how long he'd been over here and he told them, 'I'm from Vermont, been in Vietnam since '65, more or less, just can't seem to keep away from this place,' laughing a little. Stone looked as much like a grunt as any of them (he was far more experienced in Vietnam), but he was modest with them. He asked Kay to show him how the sound camera worked and they went off for a lesson. Waiting for the helicopters, the group from 2d Squad sat on their packs on the ground and talked about Saigon, which was the subject of the moment.

"Ever been to Saigon?" Sergeant Dunnuck asked one of the newer men in the squad. The soldier shook his head, no. "You owe it to yourself," Dunnuck said. Lean and relaxed, his Virginia voice animated, Dunnuck spoke as the other soldiers listened.

"Dig it. Last time we's down there—twice—got caught by the MPs second day down there." The veterans in the squad laughed, recalling the trip, breaking the rules forbidding them from the city. "Everytime you turned around, MPs lookin at you. We got stopped about ten times. I told him I was going to see a friend at the hospital. He said, 'I ain't gonna doubt your word.' He says, 'But youse are grunts.' He knew we were *line,* man." Dunnuck said the word "line" with pride, drawing it out for emphasis, as if it were sacred.

"Cav ain't even supposed to be down there," another soldier said. "We walkin down the streets, Cav patches on, laughing, just a little bit obvious."

"Couldn't even say you weren't a grunt, man. Everybody had their CIBs on." The squad laughed.

The subject changed to what the soldiers had won and lost in card games the night before, what they were going to do when they went on R and R. In the background, artillery shells boomed toward the patch of jungle the company would soon assault.

"How about this operation you're going on," I asked, "this combat assault?" A field gun fired, *Booom!*

"Tell you when we get there," a soldier said.

"Man, don't even talk about that." Another explosion.

"The more you talk about it, the more I worry. The less you talk, the less I worry."

"This is supposed to be the first time anyone's been out there," I said.

"That don't mean nothin. That place in February there wasn't supposed to be anyone there either. There was beaucoup gooks."

"Supposed to be a whole *regiment* of gooks surrounding the LZ where we're going." Laughter, less comfortable now.

"Sure glad I ain't on that first bird, I know that. They probably *shoot* him down." More laughter.

"Don't worry. If they do, we'll have to go git him. They'll get us in there to find out who shot him, you know that. If I rappel I gonna just hit the ground with a bounce."

"If you don't jump out, they'll kick you out," Sergeant Dunnuck said. All the men laughed, even the new guy. "Dig it. Throw your ammo can right down on top of you." Laughter. "Hit ya on the head with that sixty . . ." Loud laughter.

Sitting with the soldiers of his squad around him, listening to his stories, Dunnuck appeared to be more than an army sergeant in charge of twelve men. As their squad leader, he gave them orders and saw that they were obeyed. They gave him obedience, deference and trust. They seemed to accept his judgment, as they would surely have to do in a firefight, but they also enjoyed his company, liked his way of telling stories, looked up to him as a man. Dunnuck was their leader in every way. He had led them in battle and won their respect. He was the head of their little band of warriors, the leader of their gang, their tribal chief.

I asked him if he would answer a few questions. 'Nothin better to do,' he said, 'fire away.' His first name was "Lyman," he said, but the guys called him "Gene," sometimes "Killer." I decided not to ask why. He was twenty-six years old and came from Alexandria, Virginia. Like everyone in 2d Squad, Dunnuck had been drafted into the Army. His face was long and gaunt like the rest of him—thin and hard, not much more than bone, muscle, skin and dark brown hair. His arms were exceptionally long, sloped at the shoulders like a wrestler's. Though his body moved with casual ease, his eyes were quick.

"What do you think about the fighting?" I asked.

"Doesn't bother me too much," he said easily. "Got a job to do. Might as well do it for my year I'm over here." The others listened and nodded their heads in agreement. Dunnuck brushed an insect away from his face. "I got drafted. Gotta do my thing. Get me some gooks. I got twelve people I got to make sure get back to the world. And as long as I get them back, get myself back, I'll be satisfied. Get this war over so my brother won't have to come over here." He said he had a wife and baby daughter back in Virginia.

The lift ships arrived at 9:30, two hours late. Stone put the sound camera on his shoulder and pointed the lens at the troops as they climbed onto the helicopters with their packs and weapons. Kay stood next to him, advising softly. Clevenger and I waited for him to make the shot. Suddenly, the camera stopped. Stone could not get it to start again.

'What do I do now?' he asked Kay.

'Oh, just call the repair shop and they'll come and fix it,' Kay said. 'Got a dime?' Stone laughed.

Kay put the camera on the ground and opened the side flap to expose the threading mechanism. He unwound the film, opened the shutter gate, blew hard into the metal workings, rethread the strip of film around the stainless steel sprockets, tightened it, closed the side flap and pressed the start switch. Nothing happened. 'It might be the cables,' Kay said. 'Or the batteries.' The muscles in his face were tight. 'Shit, it could be *anything*.' The four of us looked at the camera on the ground. The Arriflex was nicked and scratched and dirty, as if it had not been cleaned for months. Though they produced fine quality images on the 16 millimeter film, Arri-BLs had a reputation for being unreliable in the heat and grime of the jungle, temperamental, like M-16s. Few news photographers used them in Vietnam.

'Dana's going to have to shoot silent for us,' Kay said. 'Jimmy can do wild sound on tape.' Stone had a small silent film camera, a Bell and Howell Filmo driven by a hand-cranked spring. Clevenger got his tape recorder out of his pack and put in a cassette to record natural sound. Kay lifted the thirty pounds of dead camera onto his shoulder and threw himself on one of the helicopters, angry.

The first wave of lift ships took off and flew toward the Vietnam–Cambodia border. Still on the ground at LZ Jay, Captain Jackson spoke on the radio to one of his platoon leaders who was in the air with the first lift.

"When they announce whether they've got a red or green LZ," he said (meaning safe or not), "let me know."

"Crew chief said they spotted a bunker complex," the radio operator shouted, "two hundred meters from the lima zulu."

"First lift?" Jackson said. "Keep a close ear on it."

Stone moved around to get a better camera angle.

"Okay," Jackson said. "When we unload from the aircraft we'll move to the west. Pretending that north is the direction we go into, we'll be going in at nine o'clock. Follow me and I'll lead you over to the nine o'clock position." He paused, smiled. "Looks like it's green."

The helicopters returned for the second lift and landed in the field outside the firebase. Jackson, his radio operator and first sergeant climbed aboard. Stone, Clevenger and I followed. The helicopters took off. The ride to the LZ was short.

On the ground, the troops jumped down and moved toward the edge of the trees. Gunfire cracked sporadically but none of it was incoming. The choppers flew away. The only noise was the slapping of rotor blades against the air, fading in the distance, and the closer chirps and whistles of wild birds. Sergeant Dunnuck and his squad walked into the wood line, then stopped and waited for orders. The men crouched on one knee without taking off their packs and looked into the thicket of trees, elephant grass, vines, brushes and bamboo. Jungle noise dominated: shrill, high-pitched, cacophonous. The sun was up full.

Captain Jackson waited for the third lift to bring in his last platoon. The mission, he explained, was to assess damage from a B-52 strike that had gone in a few days earlier about seven hundred meters from the landing zone, and search it for enemy bodies. It was called a "bomb damage assessment." The third lift arrived and when the men were on the ground and in place, Jackson gave the order to move into the forest. One of the rifle platoons took the lead, then came the headquarters group followed by the mortar platoon, then the two other rifle platoons. The men at the point of the column cut a path through the bush and 108 other soldiers in the company followed, single file, moving slowly. All along the line there was silence.

I walked behind Sergeant Dunnuck. After about ten minutes, the column stopped while the point men hacked into heavy brush. I turned on the tape recorder and whispered to him, "Is this the way to do it?"

"Right," he whispered back. "That's the only way you *can* do it." His eyes opened wide in the dim light of the dark jungle shade and scanned the surrounding brush from side to side.

"You don't want to go too fast," he said softly. "You're liable to walk right into it. Take it easy, you know, just probe along. You don't want to walk down no trail. You won't be comin back."

On previous tours, many of the American patrols I had accompanied went along the routes of least resistance: footpaths, rice paddy dikes, jungle trails, roads. Some of them had been ambushed.

Dunnuck wore a dark green T-shirt with his dog tags tucked in at the neck. His fatigue jacket was draped over the back of his pack, the sleeves folded inside. On the bicep of his arm was a tattoo, "SUE."

"Who's Sue?"

"That's the girl back home," he said, whispering. "I got a little over six months left. Hope about three in the field. There it is."

A small scout helicopter flew above the trees. A few minutes later shells whooshed overhead and crashed in the ground with loud cracking noises several hundred yards ahead of the column.

"The low bird probably spotted some bunkers up ahead," Dunnuck said. "So they're gonna put some artillery in before we go on ahead."

Brraaack! Brraaack!

"That's the way you do it?"

"Yeah, go on artillery at first. So we shake 'em up a little bit."

"They ever miss?"

"Yeah, a lot of times. A lot of times it doesn't help anyway. The gooks, when they build a bunker, they get three and a half, four feet of overhead on it. A 155 doesn't even hurt it. When you come in, they're still waiting for you."

Dunnuck wiped sweat from his face with the end of a green towel that hung over his neck and shoulders.

"Ever been out of War Zone C?"

"Nah. Been here the whole time. About six months. It's rough, real thick. Bamboo's worse than what this is. But most times you got to crawl through it, you know. And then the gooks, they, uh, like to build their bunkers right in the bamboo. It's hard to get em. Probably see beaucoup of em. We's up here last time we saw quite a lot." He thought for a second. "Killed a few," he said casually.

When the order came, Dunnuck and 2d Squad stood up under their packs, picked up their weapons and began to walk, one man behind the other, three to ten yards apart. Their bodies hunched forward under the weight on their backs, sixty, seventy pounds. They put one foot in front of the other and followed the fresh-cut trail in the footsteps of the man ahead, heads down, eyes on the ground. Where the brush was thin the column moved fast and distances between the men lengthened, then shortened again where the bush became thick, the line of soldiers expanding and contracting like a long snake. The men moved deeper into the forest. The heat was strong and sweat came fast.

Stone, Kay and Clevenger moved forward to take pictures of Dunnuck and the men in the squad as they passed: wide shots, close-ups, pans, tracking shots, rear-angle and low-angle shots. Kay and Stone stayed close, discussing the framing and angles, teacher and student. Kay humped the dead camera and let Stone do all the shooting on the little Bell and Howell.

Captain Jackson ordered the column to halt. One of his platoon leaders called on the radio.

"Seen somebody walking," Jackson's radio operator said, handing him the handset.

"You saw somebody walking, you say?" Jackson spoke in a low voice on the radio.

"Yes," came the reply. PFC Rose, one of the new guys, had seen something.

"Okay, just keep your eyes open," Jackson said. "Do you know which way he was going?"

"Onto another trail. . . ."

"Say again?"

"Parallel to the trail. . . ."

"Parallel to the trail." Jackson thought for a moment. "Play it cool," he said in a soft voice and gave the handset back to his RTO. His expression did not change. He remained calm, seemingly relaxed.

The radio hissed and was silent. No one moved except to look around. Farther up the line, Stone made close-ups of soldiers' faces—tense and alert, not frightened. Everyone waited. Time passed. Jackson held the company in place and when nothing happened after five minutes he ordered his three rifle platoons to send out small patrols. Each group walked into the bush and searched the area around them for about a hundred yards, making a clover leaf around the company headquarters. The rest of the men sat down, slipped their arms out of their packs and fell back against them. They called it "crashing." Some took sips of water from their canteens and lit cigarettes. A few fell asleep. All but the most exhausted took off their helmets and wiped the sweat from their faces. The heat settled in around them. The tension passed.

I sat with a group from 2d Squad.

"Tell me, what do you do to pass the time while you're just waiting?"

"Play cards. Play chess," one of the soldiers said. "Some guys passin the time sleepin and eatin. Talkin. A lot about home."

"Time goes by pretty fast in the boonies," another said. "Because, you know, you hump a lot."

"Right. The time goes by a lot faster out here. Pretty near everybody'd agree they'd prefer to stay out here in the boonies most of the time."

"As long as we don't hit anything hard."

"Just playing chess and cards?" I said.

"Passin the time and B-Sing around."

"If we get near a river, we go swimming. Or a bomb crater. We been swimmin in bomb craters several times."

"So you've got a whole system worked out to kind of entertain yourselves while you're in the field, huh?"

"Yeah, I guess you can call it a system. Just comes natural. Whatever we can think of to help pass the time more quickly, we do it."

A soldier at the edge of the group took a letter from a plastic wrapper in his pocket, unfolded it with slow delicate movements of his fingers, and began to read. The letter was old and worn and the folds were very fine.

"Like to be sittin in the rear somewhere drinkin beer, gittin drunk," a soldier said.

"We all look forward to VIP,' another said. 'Go to VIP every six or seven weeks. Everybody gets bombed, loaded. They spend all their money, a couple hundred dollars. Send presents home, stuff like that."

"It's the only real fun we have over here is VIP."

"VIP's something like another Christmas, you know. You go back there and relax. More than you do out here, I guess."

"Don't have to do no detail."

"It's the only time we get over here to hang up our weapons, throw our pack in the corner, and get a bed to sleep on."

"Yeah, *a bed*. There it is."

"*A bed!*" a soldier said with wonder.

"With a mattress, sheet."

"And a *white sheet!*" he said, whispering the words with reverence, as if the subject were holy.

The patrols came back and reported all clear, nothing out there. Captain Jackson called ahead on the radio and told the platoon leader at the front of the column to press on. The squad sergeants called out, "Saddle up!" and the soldiers hooked their arms in their packs, strained to stand up, wobbled on their feet for a second then steadied, shifted the weight on their backs and adjusted the straps. All this was done in a single motion, automatically, without looking, like hitching up their belts. The soldiers lifted their rifles and machineguns and grenade launchers and ammo belts off the ground and walked forward, one after another. In a few minutes the line was absorbed by the jungle.

The column marched for hours. In my vision, the forest became a blur of indistinct shapes—green and black forms pressing in from the sides of the trail, no sunlight except for infrequent beams of dappled white-yellow light that filtered through the vegetation. The air was dense, damp. Breath came in short gasps. Sweat fell over my eyebrows and stung my eyes. Much of the strength went out of my legs; each step felt like walking under water. Heat was a hard steady pressure beating on my chest and head, the helmet a heavy metal oven, the backpack pulling me down from behind. The noise was a shrill unrelenting scream. The smell in the air was of decaying vegetation. Dizzy, faint, I could not understand what was wrong with me. Patrols had not been this hard before.

The column arrived at the area of a B-52 strike and stopped. I collapsed on the ground. A medic came up and took my pulse and told me to start drinking more water or I was going to get heat stroke. I drank half a canteen. In a few minutes the dizziness passed.

Jackson ordered the company to spread out and search for NVA bodies. One of the soldiers, PFC Samuel Kuehn, tried to climb over a downed tree trunk on the edge of a bomb crater, but his boot slipped on the wet surface and he fell over with his heavy pack and turned his ankle. Kuehn, who was from Tomball, Texas, and was twenty-one years old, got up at once and tried to walk but could not. The pain in his ankle was excruciating. As soon as Jackson heard about the injury he ordered a work party to chop down enough trees to make a one-ship landing zone and called on the radio for a medevac. The soldiers made a small clearing in the midst of the forest in an area surrounded by trees rising over a hundred feet. Within a short time, medevac pilots arrived above the forest. The helicopter came down vertically from a great height, slowly. PFC Kuehn was carried aboard and the helicopter lifted back up through the trees, then turned and flew away. Jackson spoke to the pilot on the radio.

"We sure do appreciate your coming in," Jackson said. "We know it was a toughie." The pilot said something in reply.

"Roger," Jackson said, "we'll see you. Thanks again. Same to you."

The noise of the departing helicopter faded.

"What'd he say to you?" I asked.

"He said that was a tight one. That's the way he liked em. Said it's a lot of good practice for them." Jackson looked at the hole in the trees where the helicopter had landed. "That's one of the tightest ones I've seen. I really didn't think he'd come in. Cause he had two big trees there. He could have easily got a blade strike. Out here in the middle of nowhere, that'd mean he'd be here to stay."

"But they got your boy out."

"That's the main thing. Those medevac pilots are worth their weight in gold. They never let us down. They're great."

Sergeant Dunnuck looked around. "This area here's been bombed out," he said. "Lot of trees laying across the trails. People trying to walk across, slip off em. Might twist an ankle, break an arm or something. You know, can't be helped."

The platoon leaders reported that no bodies had been found in the area of the B-52 strike.

"Think we wasted a lot of bombs," Jackson said. "The strike was premature." He decided to camp for the night in the nearby wood. The soldiers spread out in squads and platoons and formed a large, irregular circle. They cleared the brush and built firing positions facing out at the jungle. The idea, Jackson said, was to hide as much as possible in the thickest part of the wood. He set up his command post near the center of the circle: radio operators, forward observers, NCOs, medics and other staff close by.

It was midafternoon, about three o'clock. Dunnuck told the men in his squad where to dig their foxholes and set their weapons for the night but they already knew what to do. Shirts off, the soldiers got out their machetes and entrenching tools, cut away the brush and bamboo and started to dig holes in the earth. They put the dirt from the foxholes into sandbags and piled the sandbags into low walls in front of the firing positions. All the digging and cutting of brush disturbed the ants and other insects in the area. They fell out of the nearby trees onto the backs and arms of the men and bit them. The soldiers swatted the bugs and tried to brush them away with their hands but there were too many of them and the biting stung.

"Red ants, man, all over the place!" one of the soldiers said.

Stone took pictures of the men setting camp and fighting insects and when he had covered everything he could, he stopped and watched them work.

"How about a high shot?" I said.

Stone looked up at a tree. "Yeah," he said, "I guess I should have thought of that myself." He climbed the tree with his camera and made the shot.

Just before dark a few of the men went into the bush outside the perimeter and set claymore mines and trip flares. I took out a bottle of Scotch whisky I had been carrying in my pack and gave it to Dunnuck. He smiled and thanked me, took a drink and passed the bottle to the soldier next to him. The bottle went around the squad from hand to hand and came back in a minute, almost empty, one swallow left politely at the bottom.

Kay and Stone unrolled their rubber air mattresses and started to blow them up.

'Let's have a race,' Stone said, a mischievous expression on his face. 'Bet I can blow mine up faster than you.'

'Oh, yeah?' said Kay.

Hearing the challenge, the squad gathered around. I got out my stopwatch and zeroed it. Kay and Stone stood facing each other in the center of the clearing. Each held the end of an inflatable mattress, the hard rubber airhole near his mouth, plug out, ready to start.

"Go!" said Clevenger.

The two men inhaled deeply and began to blow hard and fast. In a few seconds Kay's air mattress was beginning to inflate. Stone showed less progress. Kay had stronger lungs. Stone blew as hard as he could but fell behind. After twenty-eight seconds, Kay's air mattress was inflated. He took his mouth away, pressed his tongue onto the end of the blowhole and started to push in the plug with his fingers. At that moment Stone jumped in the air and landed with both feet in the middle of Kay's mattress. The air *whooshed* out of the rubber blowhole with a concentrated rush and blew hard in his face. Kay turned away with a groan and dropped the air mattress. Stone laughed. The soldiers in the circle around them laughed together as one, loud rollicking waves of laughter that bent them at the waists and caused them to lose their breath. They held their sides and grasped one another's shoulders for support. When they stopped looking at Kay and Stone, they looked at each other with expressions that seemed to say, *how crazy can you get?*

'I'll get you for that, Dana,' Kay said. Stone smiled and said nothing, standing away from Kay a few steps out of range.

MARCH 25, 1970

War Zone C

The company was awake before first light. The ground was wet with the residue of the night. Men got into their fighting positions and looked into the bush, rifles ready, and waited. Captain Jackson said he was determined that his company would not be caught unprepared in the dangerous hour before dawn. A monkey in one of the trees above 2d Squad screeched with alarm, again and again. Otherwise, the hour passed in silence. When the sun came up, the men made breakfast and packed their gear. A Vietnamese scout known as a "Kit Carson" climbed the tree with the noisy monkey in it and shook the tree until the monkey fell to the ground. One of the soldiers caught it and held it up for the others to see. The monkey was small, the size of a chipmunk, with brown fur and large black eyes wide with fright.

"How cute," someone said. "A gook monkey."

"It's a *baby* gook monkey," another said.

The soldiers got out their machetes and cut down the tree where the monkey had its nest. One of them decided to keep the animal as a pet and wrapped it in a piece of ground cloth. Then he put it down on the ground near his pack. A few minutes later, without knowing, someone stepped on the cloth and squashed the monkey.

"Awww," a soldier said with fake despair. "You killed our pet monkey."

They left the corpse next to the tree.

Sergeant Dunnuck said he hadn't got much sleep. 'You kept me awake with your snoring,' he said.

'Really?' I said. 'I didn't know I snored.'

'Man, you snore like a herd of elephants,' he said. 'You'd have given us away if any gooks were around.'

I didn't believe him. 'I'll try not to snore so loud tonight,' I said.

'Get it on,' came the word and the troops pulled on their packs and rifles and prepared for the day's march. Waiting to start, one of them asked to try on my pack.

'Gee,' he said when I adjusted the brace and belt for him, 'it puts a lot of the weight on your hips. I could get used to that.' They all tried it on. 'Lot better than our GI issue,' one said.

'It balances the weight a lot better,' another said. Each soldier carried between sixty and eighty pounds on his back, depending on how much food and ammunition he had.

'You'll never see Army-issue packs like that,' someone said.

'Yeah, too comfortable.'

The company set a course due west, directly toward the Cambodian border, about two and a half kilometers away. Dana Stone asked if he could take point, as much to keep a safe distance from the avenging Kay as to be up front in case of contact. Point was his favorite place on patrol, where his experience could be helpful. Stone was a lifelong woodsman. After about fifteen hundred meters, Kay complained that he felt tired, that the camera and pack felt heavier than usual.

'Maybe I picked up a bug,' he said, 'tropical virus or something.' He was out of breath.

Kay had my sympathy. My own pack felt as heavy as ever. If I sipped water at every rest break, the dizziness did not come back. The routine was relentless, hour after hour, one foot in front of the other, following the steps of the man ahead, trying to keep my mind off the monotony of the march, the heat, the discomfort. Seeing my exhaustion, one of the medics gave me a handful of salt tablets. 'Take two of these,' he said, 'and drive on.'

Clevenger looked like he might faint at any time. His fatigue shirt was black with sweat and his sandy hair wet and matted. He did not complain. He seemed determined to pull his weight, whatever the discomfort, carrying an extra roll of film and one of the spare batteries in addition to the sound gear and his own food and water. He was not accustomed to long marches but he wasn't going to quit this one. Up ahead, Stone led the company as if he had always been its point man.

The rest breaks came every half hour or so. At one of them, four soldiers from 2d Squad sat down for a game of cards: Sergeant Larry Harrington, 21, of Lincoln, Nebraska; Private First Class Gordy Lee, 23, from San Diego; Private First Class Robert Teschker, 20, of Trenton, Michigan; and Specialist Fourth Class John Schultz, 20, from Lynwood, California. I got my tape recorder rolling and asked them about life in the bush.

"You're all draftees. Have you learned or changed, gone through changes about the war and what you're doing here? And how you feel about it? The rough job, the work, the fact that you're here at all?"

"I never believed it'd be like this," one of them said. "No matter what they tell you back in the world, you'll never understand what it's like until you've been here. I can't describe it."

"The way they describe it in basic and AIT is something that you go out every day and you have contact or somebody's getting killed," another said. "And it's not like that. Its absolutely different. To me, I'd rather spend it here than spend it there."

"Why?"

"Because, well, it's a hassle with the lifers back in the States. And here they pretty much leave you alone. You have to keep on your toes just to keep yourself alive. And you're concerned about your other buddies too."

"Do any of you like being in the Army?"

"Negative. I think you'll get a negative from everybody. We don't like being here. But we know we have to serve our time in the service. So, you can't beat it. You have to go along with it the best you can. You're going to have your ups and downs."

"Everybody has their own reason for fighting over here, I guess. People back in the world don't really know what it's like. But the way I look at it, after you've been over here a while, you feel patriotic about it. And you feel proud when you go back to the world that you did fight over here and that you were in Vietnam. And you have strong friendships after you do."

"Tell me about camaraderie and friendships in the squad."

"It's really great. This is the closest you'll ever be to anybody besides your immediate family, while we're over here together. I think this is the closest that anybody could ever be. Except your brother."

"I think the attitude, back in the world, whether you admit it or not, there's a lot of prejudice, you know. When I first got over here, I met a black-hatted FTA. And, he says, the first thing to do when you get out in the field is make friends with the soul brothers. He says, you're out there at night, they can't see that soul brother, they can see you. So, he's going to protect your hide more than you're going to protect his. And when you get out in the field, he says to say, 'How are you, soul brother? I'm with you all the way. Where you going? I'm right behind you.'"

"So, there's no racial prejudice?"

"Negative, negative. You're covering each other's—excuse the expression

—you're covering each other's asses. And, so, man, there's no room for it, no room for it at all. You're protecting him and he's protecting you. And that's what you're both here for."

At the time, there were no black-skinned soldiers in 2d Squad. The 2d Platoon radio operator, L. T. Winfield, usually sat with the squad on rest breaks because his friends were there but he was not assigned to it. Private First Class Winfield had a handsome boyish face and seemed shy. He was twenty years old and came from Jackson, Mississippi, where his daughter, Evelyn, would be five years old in a few days. After three and a half months in the field, Winfield had earned the respect of those around him, black and white, officers and enlisted men. On his helmet cover he had printed "LOVE."

"Sometimes (at home) you feel like you're not wanted in certain places," Winfield said. "But it doesn't bother me. That's the way it seems, you know? It's not really like that, but, you know, you get that impression. Over here, everybody seems to be very nice. We all work together. Doesn't seem to be any racial problem over here. We all work together, sleep together."

Winfield said he was drafted on July 6. "It was something I didn't want to do, but I had to come in."

"Why?"

"It's really hard to say. I didn't want to come into the Army because of leaving my family, my loved ones. Before I left I figured I'd be comin to Vietnam and that's somewhere I didn't want to come. I didn't really have an exact reason. I just didn't want to come. Being a year away from my mother, my girl—I didn't want to come."

In the afternoon, the company came upon an enemy base camp. Stone saw it first. Walking point with the lead fireteam, he noticed a bulge in the ground and called in a low voice for the others to hold up. The camouflage above the mound was old and dry and he could see through it that the bunker had not been used for a long time. Looking around, Stone spotted interlocking firing positions in the nearby bamboo, close-fitting wooden beams covered with hard-packed earth and narrow slits for firing ports. He detected the communications trenches and spider holes and hidden fields of fire and felt the ghostly emptiness of the place, as he told us later. Stone stood up and walked forward calmly, watching the ground, careful where he put his boots, concentrating hard. No one spoke. The soldiers saw that he knew what he was doing. He had been on patrols like this for so many years he couldn't remember them all; they had merged together in his memory.

He had seen so much combat—set-piece battles, ambushes, hot LZs, hand-to-hand, sniper attacks, artillery exchanges, distant skirmishes, lost patrols, friendly fire, fast retreats—that he was as canny as a wild animal. He learned to sense danger by the most subtle signs of change in the forest: a new sound, a strange smell, a footprint, a branch out of place, an animal call, a silence—until it was instinctive with him. If anyone could read the jungle wind, it was Stone. I told one of the soldiers with him on point that up north, in I Corps, some of the Marines called him "Supergrunt." But here Stone saw there was no danger, the North Vietnamese had gone.

One by one, the rest of the company came forward and looked at the labyrinth of bunkers, trenches and tunnels. It was a large enemy base complex with lines of defense, sleeping quarters, kitchens, assembly areas and the command center for a regiment. The tops of the tallest trees had been pulled over and tied together with vines to form an umbrella of shade and camouflage over the camp. There were more than a hundred bunkers and an elaborate trench system that measured almost two thousand meters. None of it had been used recently. The Vietnamese scouts with Charlie Company said the camp had not been lived in for at least a year.

'It might have been an R and R center,' Captain Jackson said. 'Or a staging base. Nobody from our side has been in this area for a long time. Too far from support.'

The camp was pockmarked by shell holes and broken trees from the B-52 strike. There were no tracks in the earth; the camp had long been abandoned, and nothing of value was left.

Stone discovered a human cage. He called the rest of us, including Jackson, to come and see it. A jail cell, about seven feet high, was anchored deep in the ground. The bars were made from bamboo poles notched together and fastened with vines. It looked like a cage for animals.

'Look,' Stone said, pointing. 'They've got two bunks inside. See how long they are? Must be six feet. Too long for Vietnamese. I bet they had a couple of American prisoners.' Though none of us had seen anything like it before, Stone had found it, examined it, recognized what it was, and figured out what was important. There were few secrets of the jungle he could not decipher, little his Vermont childhood or his years in Vietnam had not prepared him for. Poking around the NVA camp was like sneaking into the empty house of your enemy and discovering his secrets.

Stone had the enthusiasm, playfulness and sincerity of a boy from the backwoods of New England, and also the naïveté. Standing beside the two-man jail, his eyes filled with wonder, he looked up at the rest of us and said, "Isn't that something?"

The troops had counted over a hundred bunkers when Jackson ordered them to stop searching and pull back. He said the day was wearing on and he wanted to be outside the base camp when night came.

"We don't want to set up our NDP in an open area," he said. "Their B-40s are deadly at sixty to seventy meters."

The company moved on without exploring the camp completely. The soldiers covered another twelve hundred meters, still moving west. They came upon a trail, six feet wide, with fresh tracks heading toward the northeast. When his command group came to the trail, Captain Jackson examined the footprints of the rubber tire sandals carefully. "This is the first sign of life we've had," he said. "These slick tracks are no more than a day old."

'Could it be the 95th Charlie?' I asked, recalling the NVA regiment supposed to be in the area.

'Could be,' Jackson said.

'Does that concern you?'

"It concerns me but it doesn't worry me. One squad in this company can put out more firepower than a whole enemy company."

The radio squawked. Lieutenant Colonel Hannas called from Firebase Jay to say that 2d Battalion, 8th Cavalry, was in heavy contact not far away in the Dog's Head. With the dense air and trees, we had not heard the shooting.

'This is their fight,' Hannas said, 'but be on guard. Never know what you might run into.'

Trying to think ahead, Jackson wondered whether he might have to call in artillery support if he got in a serious fight with the North Vietnamese. "The situation is in a state of flux," he said. "We're working closer to the border than we've ever worked. They can fire artillery from over in Cambodia. We can't use artillery ourselves because we're within two thousand meters of the border and our ground rules say we can't fire in here."

Jackson decided the company had gone far enough. The men had been marching for six hours. If the battle between 2/8 and the North Vietnamese spilled over into his area, or his company was ordered to reinforce, Jackson wanted his men to be rested. He ordered them to stop and set up a night defensive perimeter. The troops found a stream and filled their canteens with muddy water.

Kay fell down exhausted. He had carried the useless camera all day and felt sick from the strain. He opened his rucksack to get something to eat and found the bottom of it was full of C ration cans, ten or twelve of them, worthless heavy meals like date pudding and ham and lima beans that no one could eat. He had not put them there.

'*That's* why I've been so tired all day,' Kay said. He handed the rucksack to Clevenger and me, saying, 'Feel that.' It was ten to fifteen pounds heavier than normal.

'Fucking Dana,' Kay said, looking around. 'If I catch that little sonofabitch, I'm gonna kill him.' Stone was not in sight.

At twilight, Jackson and his first sergeant came to 2d Squad's position to look at the defenses. When they finished, the captain asked if I would mind spending the night at the CP.

'Yes, of course,' I said, flattered to be invited to stay with the command group.

'We heard you snoring last night,' he said. 'Probably best if you stay with us. 'Top' here will take good care of you.'

The first sergeant took me to the headquarters area and pointed to a space on the ground to put my bedroll. His name was Luther O'Neal, a short thickset man in his late thirties with a stern silent manner, seemingly without humor. O'Neal said he had been in the Army since he was sixteen and had fought in Korea. Measuring the space between two trees, he got out a green mesh hammock and tied it in place. The hammock was just above and slightly to one side of my bedroll. O'Neal got in the hammock, draped his right leg over the side so that it almost touched the ground, adjusted the height of the hammock, and asked me to move my air mattress to a precise position below him. I did.

Stone appeared at last light. I had not heard his approach, just felt his presence at my shoulder. He asked if Kay was angry about the C rations in his pack and I suggested that he stay away from him until the morning.

'He'll forget he was angry by then,' I said.

Kay was the model for Stone's ambition to become a network photographer. He admired Kay and considered him a friend. Both had studied forestry and loved the outdoors.

'Why do you need all those?' he said, indicating my pill case. I was trying to find a tranquilizer.

'A doctor in New York told me to take one of these at bedtime,' I said, holding up a yellow five milligram tablet of Valium. 'I take one after every meal. They're supposed to help me to relax, cut down on my drinking.'

'A lot of good that does,' Stone chuckled. 'How long you been taking them?'

'Oh, about four years. Since after my first time over here.'

'Every day?'

'Yup.'

'Does it help you sleep?'

'Yes. But I think they make me snore.'

'Can I try one?'

'Sure.' I gave him a few of the valium pills. Stone put one in his mouth and swallowed it without water.

'Where you spending the night?' I said.

'Over there with 1st Platoon,' he said, departing. 'Don't tell Keith.'

MARCH 26, 1970

War Zone C

Waking up in the woods was painful. Cold bones, stiff joints, aching muscles, swollen feet, backache, you always woke up sore. But I woke up this morning in a world of agony. Everything ached. My left side hurt all along the ribcage. My kidneys burned. My left hip and thigh were sensitive to touch. My arm was in pain. *Must have slept in one bad position all night,* I thought, *or on a tree root.* It felt like I'd been in a fight.

'Mornin,' First Sergeant O'Neal called down from his hammock overhead. His voice was unusually animated.

'Mornin,' I said.

'How'd you sleep?'

'Not good,' I said. 'Kept waking up.' A dim memory pushed in toward conscious thought. 'Did I snore?'

'Not for *long*, you didn't.' A trace of triumph was in his voice.

I struggled through the morning; made breakfast with a sore arm; tried to find a way to sit comfortably with an aching hip. Finally I popped a Darvon to numb the pain. On inspection, I discovered a line of welts up and down my left side, from knee to shoulder. Bruises were forming. Each appeared to be about the size of the toe of a boot. Then the memory came. O'Neal had slept with his right leg hanging over the edge of the hammock, boot on, bent at the knee. Every time I snored in the night, he must have swung his leg and kicked me in the side. Kicked me wherever I happened to lie: shoulder, arm, ribs, kidney, hip, leg—the boot was mercilessly indiscriminate. After a while, all it took was the suggestion of a snore, just a vibration of my vocal cords, the slightest stirring of the soft palate, a flutter of the uvula, one little *honk* and I got the boot. Obviously the bastard had done it to snorers before. He could probably kick in his sleep.

Stone came by to thank me for the Valium. "Best night's sleep I've had in ages," he said. 'That's a great little pill.'

'Don't snore or you'll be on Darvon.' I told him what the sergeant had done.

'That's why he's in the Army,' Stone said. 'He gets a kick out of hurting people. He's a lifer.'

After breakfast, Charlie Company moved out. This was the third day of a four-day patrol. Most of the soldiers were out of water and cigarettes and low on food. Moving north along the border, the column came upon a small stream. The men filled their canteens with green brackish water, added hali-zone tablets, shook their canteens a few times, and drank it, making grotesque faces as they swallowed. The water tasted poisonous. Someone told Captain Jackson and he said he would try to get in some decent water by chopper later in the day.

The troops traveled light, carrying only necessities in their packs: a can or two of C rations, poncho and liner, rifle cleaning kit, letters from home, pen and paper, towel, extra pair of socks, knife, maybe a machete, heat tabs, matches, string, insect repellent, a field dressing, spices and sauces, Kool Aid, something to read, a few photographs, good luck charms, playing cards, a lit-tle money, maybe a small transistor radio. Everything else was weaponry. No luxuries. No alcohol or dope. Carrying four days' worth of food was so heavy that many of the men packed only enough rations for three days and went hungry on the fourth.

They seemed to share everything: food, water, cigarettes, gum, candy, gun oil, toilet paper, magazines, books, comics, hopes, problems, dreams, even their deepest and most private fears—when they knew what they were.

PFC Carlton Dudley, a thin black-haired rifleman from Newberry, Florida, said survival was the most important thing.

"Just do my part to stay alive," he said, drawling the words in a slow southern voice. "And help guys out in the company, mostly the squad. Just share everything with them, food and your water. Our squad is real close. Everybody knows their stuff, up tight. It gives you a feeling of security. Just like being at home with your family. A bunch of brothers—brothers and sis-ters. Folks at home."

Some of the others talked about the postal strike in the States. So far it hadn't affected delivery here.

"They'll hear about it when we don't get mail," one said.

"They'll be demonstrations," another said, laughing.

"Yeah, frag the post office."

Captain Jackson said Second of the Eighth was still in contact with the NVA five kilometers away. The fight had gone on all night. All the helicopters in the brigade were committed to the battle. 'We need water resupply,' Jackson said, 'but we can't get a log ship.'

Lieutenant Colonel Hannas called on the radio and said half of C Company, Second of the Eighth, was dead or wounded. Tanks and APCs from other units were trying to reinforce.

"Their C/O put the world in on 'em," Hannas said, "five batteries of artillery, Spooky gunships, ARA . . . everything." The battle was only three miles away but we could not hear it, only the shriek of jet planes and the bombs exploding. Turning to his headquarters group, Jackson said 2/8 had taken so many casualties in recent weeks it might have to be pulled out of the line. *So that's why Colonel Ochs wouldn't let us make the documentary with Second of the Eighth,* I thought.

The only contact made by Charlie Company, Second of the Seventh, was with wild bees. PFC Leroy Bowman was cutting brush for the line of march when he hit a hornet's nest and one of them stung him on the hand. Bowman, 21, from Mount Airey, North Carolina, watched his right ring finger swell up. 'Last week,' one of the medics said, 'the company took so many bee stings we had to have *multiple* medevacs.'

The column crossed another wide trail with fresh tracks. Jackson ordered a platoon to set an ambush along one side of the trail while the rest of the company waited. Far down the line, PFC Gordy Lee sat with 2d Squad. Blond-haired, friendly, Lee had more formal education than anyone in the squad and was considered a character. He had been a part-time student at San Diego State College and was working as a busboy in a restaurant when he was drafted and sent to Vietnam last September. He got married in August just before leaving.

"You're out here waiting for Charlie," Lee said. "You don't know when he's coming or how many of them are coming. And that's part of the horror of it all. Sometimes you wait and hope that he comes. In the back of your mind, you hope it will be a two- or three-man group. And other times you hope that he doesn't come at all—as long as you're over here."

I asked him how the men in the company rated Captain Jackson as a soldier.

"We have a classification," Lee said. "If you're a typical lifer, is what we call it, ones who are always, we feel, hassling you, the ones that want a rifle inspection out in the firebases, out in the boonies. You know, this is no place to go and do a back-in-the-world type inspection. Whereas Captain Jackson, we classify him as a *career* soldier. He's a lifer in a sense, but he's an *okay* lifer. And you can't call him a lifer if he's okay. He's a good man."

An hour passed. And another. Jackson sat with his radio operator and command group several hundred yards from the ambush site. I asked if he would mind answering a question or two. 'No, go ahead,' he said, 'but we might have to stop in a hurry.' I pushed the record button on the tape recorder and held the microphone under his chin.

"Captain, after five months in the field, two tours here, what have you learned?"

"What have I learned? That's a toughie. My first tour, of course, was MACV. And I didn't really have an appreciation of the American soldier. I mean I had a different one. But these people are amazing. They're fantastic. They're the best soldiers in the world. They'll do anything for you. They may not agree with everything that is being done, the recent things that are being done, but they go ahead and do them and they do a good job. And they watch out for each other. And there's good morale and good cooperation amongst them. And if anybody gets in trouble, there's never any hesitation of people going in and getting him out of trouble. Or doing everything they can. For example, if someone's wounded, it's fantastic like that. They're making stretchers and things while the firefight's going on. The NCOs, they just get people squared away and get them pulled back to the rear." I looked down at the VU meter on the tape recorder to check that it was recording properly.

"Your men have a real appreciation for the fact that you take fewer casualties than most companies," I said.

"I think so. At least it appears that way to me. They know that we don't take unnecessary chances. There's no real reason to take unnecessary chances because there are right ways and wrong ways to do things. And there's three ways to make contact with the NVA. One is on your terms. One is on nobody's terms. And one is on the gook's terms. And we go to great lengths to avoid the last one because there's no percentage in it. You get people hurt. And you really don't gain that much from it. If you're just more stealthful and work a little bit harder, then you can bring things around on your terms. And a lot of this comes from experience." Jackson looked around the command group. His RTO and a few of the others listened.

"We have some real good people, real good trackers. We have a lot of people from rural parts of the States and they can read trails and read signs

just like the proverbial Indian in the West. They can tell you how many people came by, when they came by. They can tell you—we have never walked
on bunkers and not known it, just walk up on bunkers. There's always signs,
and they've always told me about it. And we go into our extra-precautionary
measures of go on line and get real extremely cautious and check the area
out thoroughly."

"Casualties?" I asked.

"We've taken casualties. The people in the company, I'm sure, realize
that, that we take a lot less casualties than other people. And they see reasons. Like, we don't use trails. We try to do things with logic. And, if you
want to find gooks, there's no problem in finding the enemy. You can just
walk down a trail and you'll eventually find him. But it will be on *his* terms."
Jackson paused for a second and continued.

"So, it's just the way we operate. And that, I think, is the reason we take
fewer casualties than a lot of people. And the people in the company, I think
they realize it, and they have an appreciation for it." He looked down at his
feet and picked a twig off the jungle floor.

"Now it just kills me if one of my people gets hurt. And they may get
upset because I make them work a little harder or move a little farther. Or
move a little later. But, like I say, I'm supercautious when the time comes to
be cautious."

I thanked him and switched off the tape recorder, got up and walked back
down the line. Dana Stone was sitting alone. Sunlight fell through the trees,
bright light speckled by shade. I told him about the interview with Jackson,
suggested we would need covering shots on film. While we were talking, an
insect landed on Stone's arm and crawled along his skin. Gently, he picked it
up between his thumb and forefinger, held it delicately, and placed it on a
large flat leaf in the sunlight. A few moments later, he looked over to see that
it was safe.

'I don't even kill mosquitoes anymore,' he said, smiling.

'I do,' I said. 'It's them or us.'

'Yeah, but you never really know what you're killing, do you?'

'Oh, you mean it might be somebody special? Reincarnated as a bug?' My
tone was sarcastic.

'Special or not, it's got a right to live too.'

I said nothing.

'Besides,' Stone said, 'there's been enough killing around here already.'

We were squatting on our haunches like Vietnamese, feet flat on the ground, face-to-face, talking in whispers. Most of the time Stone's face had an earnest, interested expression, like a student's. He was not easily distracted. He concentrated carefully on conversations he held, as if he expected to learn something important or find truth in them. I must have said something self-serving or ridiculous because he smiled his devil grin and put a finger in my chest and pushed me gently backward. My balance went. He had measured my center of gravity and tipped it over. Helpless, I fell slowly onto my back.

As I fell, Stone got up and walked away. 'You'll never make a good Vietnamese, Laurence,' he said. 'You don't know how to squat.'

Jackson ordered the ambush to break down. When the platoon was ready, the soldiers crossed the trail and pressed on north. In the afternoon, the company came to an area that had been heavily bombed. The soldiers cleared a landing zone and waited for a helicopter to bring water. An hour passed. Two. When it was apparent no chopper would come, Jackson called it a day. A night defensive perimeter was established in the trees. I found a place to sleep, as far away as possible from First Sergeant O'Neal.

MARCH 27, 1970

At daybreak, Captain Jackson called battalion headquarters on his radio and was told to hold the company where it was. "No plans for us yet," he said with mild frustration. The company was due to be resupplied and possibly lifted to a new location in the forest, but Lieutenant Colonel Hannas did not want to move the company without approval from brigade. Other infantry and some armored units were engaged in heavy, continuous combat in the area and the move might interfere with them. Hannas, at Firebase Jay, could not see beyond his limited area of operations, and brigade was too busy supporting 2/8 to worry about 2/7. The entire brigade area of operation, covering a big part of War Zone C, was in turmoil. Jackson did not know what was going on. The big picture was out of his sight.

I wrote in my notebook: "Wandering around like lost children."

How different everything is, I thought. The First Cav of '65–'66 would have sent out a hot breakfast by now, probably water and mail as well. Might have sent Charlie Company to reinforce 2/8. Might have got them ambushed too. Soldiering is so much more cautious these days. Five years of war have taught the Cav a lot of survival lessons. Like beware where you walk. Walking where the NVA expect you—on trails, roads, rice paddy dikes, paths, ridgelines—is inviting an ambush.

Kay was anxious to return to Saigon and get his camera repaired. Stone had shot several rolls of silent film of the patrol and Clevenger had recorded all the natural sound we would need. We wouldn't know how good Stone's camera work was until the film was screened in New York.

'It's Dudley's birthday tomorrow,' one of the soldiers in 2d Squad said.

'How old?' I asked.

'Twenty,' Dudley said. He spoke easily, the same way he moved—slowly, without effort. I asked him what he had done before he was drafted and Dudley said he was laying electrical cable for the city of Gainsville, Florida. He arrived in Vietnam the week before Christmas. He was planning to extend in-country for an extra forty-six days. In return, the Army would end his enlistment when the tour in Vietnam was over.

"What about your birthday?" I said.

"Just another day in the Nam," he said.

The order came to saddle up, the company was moving. Looking at Kay's camera and pack—they weighed close to a hundred pounds—I offered to help get them on his back. 'No, thanks,' he said. 'It's better if I do it myself. Got it pretty well worked out.'

Kay sat on the ground and pushed his back against the inside of his ruck-sack. The Army-issue pack rested on the ground next to a tree. His sound camera leaned on its shoulder brace against the pack. Kay put his arms into the straps of the rucksack, pulled them tight against his shoulders, bent his legs underneath him, and lifted the brace and camera onto his right shoulder. He paused a moment and took a deep breath. He was going to rise off the ground with one strenuous push of his legs and jerk the pack and camera up with him. The tree would prevent him from falling backward. The movement would require a singular effort of great strength.

"*Aaaarrrrgggghh,*" Kay cried, jerking the weight of the rucksack, camera, batteries and canteens off the ground. Three hundred pounds of man and equipment lurched upward in a mighty vertical heave. Halfway up, Kay was stopped suddenly, as if he had been shot. Stone, standing nearby, made a muffled chortle. Kay collapsed on the ground and did not move. His back and legs were in shock. He had almost reached a standing position when he was jerked back by the pack. Stone giggled. Slowly, Kay put down the camera, unfastened the shoulder straps and turned around. '*Ah-hah!*' he said, untying the straps of his pack that Stone, sometime in the night, had fastened securely to the trunk of the tree.

'Stone,' he said, 'you are a fucking sadist!'

'Just wanted to see if you could lift that tree,' Stone said. 'Guess you can't.'

The soldiers looked at each other quizzically, with incomprehension, as if they could not imagine inflicting such pain on one another, even in fun. One or two of them laughed. Stone stood away from Kay when the company got in file and started the day's march.

The men walked back to the LZ they had cut the day before. A helicopter arrived with water cans. Kay, Stone, Clevenger and I said good-bye to Captain Jackson and the men in 2d Squad and got aboard for the return flight to Tay Ninh. At the last minute, First Sergeant O'Neal climbed on as the chopper took off. As soon as he settled in, O'Neal unholstered his sidearm, a Colt .45, felt for the safety, and prepared to disarm. He held the pistol with the muzzle pointed at my head, the clip still in the handle, and looked directly in my eyes, a mean narrow smile curling his mouth, eyes glowing. I reached toward him, put my hand against the barrel of the .45 and pushed it away. (The first time I had been allowed to hold a gun, as a nine-year-old growing up in rural Ohio, I was told that I must never point it at anyone, whether it was loaded or not.) O'Neal said, "Don't worry. I won't shoot you," and smiled wickedly.

The chopper stopped at Firebase Illingsworth, not far from Jay in the Dog's Head. Illingsworth was headquarters for 2/8, the battalion now in contact. Artillery fired continuously toward the border. A young officer carrying a map case got aboard for the flight to Tay Ninh. His face was haggard, as if he had not slept for days.

At the PIO shop, one of the brigade information officers, a captain, took us aside.

'Major Coleman has a request,' he said. 'Will you mind if the division replaces Captain Jackson as commander of C Company? They want to know whether it will interfere with the continuity of your film. If it does, they'll keep him out there 'til you're finished.'

'No, not at all,' I said, surprised that we were being asked. 'We really don't want to affect the natural order of things. Believe me.'

'We don't stage things,' Kay said.

Stone held up his silent camera and focused the lens on the captain. 'Would you just look at the tree line over there?' Stone said, pointing. 'That's it. Now would you mind ducking and running for cover?' Everyone laughed.

'That's great,' the captain said. 'I'll tell J.D. It's not going to happen for a while.'

'What is it with Jackson?' I said.

'Don't know. They've got a job open at division, I think. He's due to rotate out of the field in a couple of weeks anyway.'

We told the captain to expect us back in a day or two to catch the next supply log to C Company. He said he would set it up. We returned to Saigon in a crowded courier chopper with five other passengers.

At the bureau, a stack of cables and letters from New York was waiting. Each cable the organization sent out began with a five-digit number that showed the date and time of day the message was sent. For example, 25153 meant the cable was sent on twenty-fifth day of the month (March in this case), at fifteen hundred hours, thirty minutes (3:30 P.M.), eastern standard time.

> 25153 MILLER PLEASE ADVISE KAY/CLEVENGER THEY INTERMITTENTLY LOST SOUND ON THEIR FNGS IN WAR ZONE C STOP PLEASE CHECK CAMERA AND AMPLIFIER STOP ALSO EXERCISE MORE CARE WITH SHOTGUN MIKE STOP MANY TIMES IT PROTRUDES THREE QUARTERS WAY INTO SCREEN AND ACTUALLY NOT NECESSARY BE THAT CLOSE TO SPEAKER THANKS REGARDS VANBERGEN

Charles Vanbergen was a technical expert in the New York camera department, a kind friendly man who helped identify mechanical problems in the field by analyzing pictures and sound in the edit rooms. Kay, Clevenger and I were dismayed to learn of the sound problems with the first shipment. Then we read a cable from Russ Bensley, the senior producer who supervised the editing of Vietnam stories for the Cronkite News:

> 25163 MILLER FOR LAURENCE/KAY/CLEVENGER HAVE SCREENED YOUR MAIDEN OFFERING AND WILL CUT TOMORROW STOP YOU HAD AUDIO PROBLEMS ON FIRST FEW REELS DASH SOUND CUTTING OUT ENTIRELY ON INTERMITTENT BASIS STOP THIS MOST SEVERE ON ROLL ONE WHICH HAD VIRTUALLY NO TRACK AT ALL STOP YOU APPEARED UNAWARE OF AUDIO PROBLEMS DASH WERE YOU MONITORING RECORDED TRACK QUERY ANYWAY THERES ENOUGH MATERIAL FOR GOOD MOOD PIECE STOP HANG IN THERE BENSLEY

A second cable from Bensley had arrived the following day saying he had blocked out on paper "AN IMPOSSIBLY LONG CUT ON NEW GUYS" which he planned to complete in a day or two. The message included a detailed list of problems: lack of a picture shot list, no identification of some of the soldiers, the sound problems, no film to cover some of the interviews on quarter-inch audiotape:

> . . . EYE GOT ABOUT AN HOURS WORTH OF QUARTERINCH SOME OF WHICH DUPLICATES FILM TRACK AND SOME OF WHICH DOES NOT SEEM

TO RELATE TO FILM AT ALL DASH ROCK MUSIC AND SO FORTH STOP IS
THERE ANY WAY TO LIMIT QUARTERINCH SHIPPED WITH FILM TO
APPROPRIATE MATERIAL QUERY AN HOUR OF AUDIOTAPE IS A LOT TO
PLOW THROUGH STOP EYE DONT REALLY THINK WE CAN SAY FRIGGIN
ON TELEVISION AND IF NOT EYE GOT A PROBLEM STOP ITS HARD TO
EXCISE BECAUSE OF INFLECTIONS STOP WILL OVERCOME AND THINK IT
WILL MAKE FINE PIECE BUT WANTED TO PASS ABOVE ALONG FOR YOUR
GUIDANCE BENSLEY

Reading the cables, Kay, Clevenger and I felt a serious letdown. It had
taken four days to find the new guys, follow them, record and write the story,
and now the whole effort appeared to have been undone by technical problems. We felt like failures. The only encouragement was that Bensley thought
it would make a piece anyway. We walked across the street to the Continental Hotel and ordered drinks. No one bothered to wash or change clothes.
Taking our order, the waiter kept a distance, as if we might be infectious.

"We've got to get our shit together," Kay said after a long silence.

'Technically and editorially,' I said. 'What made me think I could say
"friggin" on the air?'

'Frig 'em if they can't take a joke,' Clevenger said.

The drinks appeared.

'Do you think we've got enough for a story this time out?' Clevenger asked.

'No way,' Kay said, determined. 'Let's not even ship this stuff until we get
the Arri working up there.'

'We have to ship it,' I said. 'But I won't write a narration. I'll ask them to
hold it for part two."

We made a pact. One hundred percent effort next time out. No sound
problems. No camera failures. No sloppy writing.

'Let's show 'em we're not out here for two months just for fun and war
games,' Clevenger said.

'Let's show 'em there's a war on,' Kay added.

'Can you imagine how we'd feel if we'd made contact out there and our
gear didn't work?' I said.

'I don't even want to think about it,' Kay said.

Clevenger stood up and shouted, 'Waiter, bring us another drink.'

Two letters from Joy were waiting. She had shipped them through the office mail pouch with a box of homemade brownies. They had taken only two days to arrive. I saved the letters to read until I got to my room.

March 24, 1970

Dear Jack,

The enclosed box of brownies—straight by the way—is actually a box full of chocolate love. . . .

Mèo is staring at me wondering why I don't turn out the light and go to sleep. He did tell me earlier tonight that he wishes you would tell all his VC comrades hello. He also says he would only bite you a little bit if you would just come back home.

A newspaper clipping was included, an ad for a new Broadway musical called *JOY*. The O in JOY had a peace symbol drawn in the middle of it. I got my helmet and wrote on the thin elastic strap that secured the cloth cover,

MARCH 28, 1970

Cambodia and its people were hurled into a vortex of violence, intrigue, instability and death. The right-wing military government that had seized power from Prince Sihanouk ten days earlier let loose a riot of nationalist bloodletting across the country. Hundreds of ethnic Vietnamese who had lived and worked in Cambodia for generations were hunted down by local Cambodian mobs and murdered. At the same time, angry demonstrations in support of Sihanouk took place in several provincial towns and cities and more blood was shed in clashes with promilitary nationalists. Sihanouk himself had flown from France to Beijing, where he condemned the United States for its part in the coup and aligned himself with the Chinese Communists. Rival forces in Cambodia, including Communists, maneuvered to exploit the unstable situation. North Vietnamese military units moved inland, away from their bases along the border with Vietnam, and advanced into the Cambodian interior, fighting with government forces around Phnom Penh. The North Vietnamese and their Cambodian allies, the Khmer Rouge, appeared to be preparing for an offensive to capture the capital and overthrow the new leadership. The Cambodian military was believed by Western experts to be too weak to defend the country against the well-armed and disciplined North Vietnamese. The U.S. government announced its support for the new regime and, in a clandestine operation organized in Vietnam, began to ship captured Communist weapons from Saigon to Phnom Penh. Direct American intervention seemed unlikely because of the negative reaction it would cause in the United States. Some reporters in Phnom Penh were predicting an imminent invasion of the capital. Firsthand accounts said the situation was extremely dangerous. Like the battlefields around Charlie Company just across the border in War Zone C, Cambodia was in violent flux.

At the Saigon bureau, CBS News correspondents and camera crews packed their gear and collected airline tickets for the forty-five-minute flight from Saigon to Phnom Penh. The bureau was sending a large staff of combat veterans to cover the story. One of them was Dana Stone.

'But you can't take him away from us now. We've just started,' I protested to Dave Miller.

'It's New York's decision, not mine,' he said.

'If it wasn't for Dana,' I said, 'we wouldn't have had any film at all on our last trip with Charlie Company.'

'Paskman is adamant,' Miller said. 'You can't have Kay and Stone. He says one crew is enough.' As far as Miller was concerned, that was final. You could argue with Little, the foreign editor, but not with Paskman, the manager of news, whose judgments could be as harsh as his temperament. He sent a cable to Saigon:

> MILLER IF YOU ARE SO NEEDY OF CAMERAMEN THAT WE HAVE TO IMPORT JOE YUE FROM HONG KONG WE CERTAINLY CANNOT AFFORD TO HAVE DANA STONE WORKING AS SECOND CAMERAMAN WITH LAURENCE STOP LAURENCE ALREADY HAS AT HIS DISPOSAL THE MOST EXPENSIVE CAMERA CREW IN THE FIELD FOR CBS NEWS AT THIS TIME STOP IT IS A COMPLETELY OVERBUDGET ITEM AND WE SIMPLY CANNOT AFFORD TO ADD TO THIS EXPENSIVE BANDWAGON WITH STILL ANOTHER AMERICAN CAMERAMAN STOP NO OTHER CORRESPONDENT IN VIETNAM NEEDS TWO CAMERAMEN TO GET A STORY DONE AND WE ARE NOT GOING TO ESTABLISH THAT PRACTICE STOP IF LAURENCE TEAM CANT DELIVER FIRST CLASS PRODUCT AT THESE PRICES THEN WE WILL HAVE TO REPLACE THEM INSTEAD OF PROVIDING A CRUTCH PASKMAN

Reading the message, Kay, Clevenger and I were offended. We would miss Stone on our team, but it would not cripple us. What hurt was Paskman's language. Phrases like "expensive bandwagon," "have to replace them" and "providing a crutch" were mean, meant to wound. He didn't understand what we were trying to do or how much Dana was contributing to it. And he had no idea how serious the war was up by the border. By his use of language, Paskman was making us his enemies. *So be it*, I thought.

I took my case to Stone at his Tu Do street apartment. He and Louise were packing.

'You've got a choice,' I said. 'You're a freelance. You can take either assignment.'

'I'd rather go back up to Charlie Company with you guys,' he said.

'Then come,' I said. 'This is going to be a much better story than any-thing you're going to get running around Cambodia.'

'Yeah, I know,' he said. 'But I don't want to get in trouble with New York for not obeying orders.'

'Let me deal with them. I know how to handle it.'

'Yeah, you'll get me fired.'

'Dana, I promise, you will always get work if I'm around.'

'Sure, then you go home in a couple of months and I'm out of a job.'

'Never happen. Believe me, when this film is finished it'll make you famous.'

'But it won't make me *rich*,' he laughed. 'And it won't get me a staff job.'

We argued, politely, for the rest of the morning. At times it seemed he had made up his mind to stay and work with us, though he did not stop pack-ing. Louise was neutral, commenting on the advantages and disadvantages of both options but without suggesting an opinion. Keith Kay came to the apartment and suggested that Dana stay in Vietnam, but he did not force the point. 'It's your call, man,' he said. Finally, Stone chose what he considered to be the most sensible option for his future. He would obey his orders from New York and go to Phnom Penh. I was disappointed. To me, the more important story was with the Americans, not with the Cambodians and Viet-namese. Cambodia was a sideshow. The main event was up on the border. I was coming to the conclusion that Dana, the tough-minded Yankee individ-ualist who had always followed his own star, was becoming a company man.

'The guys in the squad are going to miss you,' I said.

'Well, tell 'em not to get ambushed and all shot up before I get back,' he said, eyes laughing.

How unpredictable, how uncertain, how incalculable are the conse-quences of the choices we make, even when they seem to be simple. Dana made his choice and the consequences of that choice were that it would be the end of him. There are no minor decisions in wartime, no easy choices.

Sean Flynn appeared in Saigon the same day.

Unannounced, he flew in from Indonesia and went straight to his old room in the Stone's apartment at 104 Tu Do street. 'Just here for a few days to pack my things and move,' he said. 'Paris next.'

Four years had passed since I'd seen Flynn. Though we had kept in touch by postcard and letter and the global brotherhood from Frankie's House, I was surprised by the change in him. The confidence was still there, and the modesty that went with it, but he was much quieter, more gracious, serene. His self-assurance came, I suspected, from his long period with the Special Forces—he was one of the few journalists accepted by that organization of xenophobes—and the resolution that came from his experience of war. He had long since surpassed in real life the reckless heroics of the screen idols his famous father portrayed, and in so doing, he had become more than just his father's son.

Flynn had a sweet unassuming smile—mystical, mysterious—as if he inhabited a world that was happier than everyone else's. It was a smile I had seen on the faces of Buddhist monks at one with the moment. His style of dress came from the cultural underground: sarong, baju, sandals, bracelets and beads, light yellow hair to his shoulders. He looked like a hippie. Soft-voiced, meditative, peaceful, Flynn had gone native in Bali.

"Did you get the telegram I sent?" I asked.

"No, what did it say?"

"Come and join us in Forty-Two Corps."

He smiled. I explained our project with Charlie Company and invited him to work with us.

"No thanks," he said. "I'm not covering war anymore." He opened a bag of grass and began to roll a joint. "Besides, I don't need the bread."

Flynn was twenty-eight years old, going on twenty-nine. He lived simply but comfortably on a small income his parents gave him. He had been in Indonesia for nearly nine months, alternately living at the home of Joe and Theresa Galloway in Djakarta and near Kuta Beach in Bali, where he was in love with a local woman. For the first time in his life he had become health-conscious. In Bali he got up with the sun, ran five miles along the seashore, ate vegetarian food, practiced yoga on the beach, and, at the end of the day, meditated in a lotus position as the sun went down. He planned to live with his Balinese lover permanently.

"You know, man," he said, "Bali is the most beautiful place in the world. And the people, the people are the most *amazingly* beautiful."

He put the lighted joint on a copy of Mao's "Little Red Book," which was worn and spotted with candle wax. Holding the book in the palms of his hands, he offered it to me as though he were passing something precious, as part of a ritual. At the same time he looked at my face with an intense stare and smiled. Something inside the look was mischievous, challenging. I did not understand what it meant but smiled in acknowledgment as if I did. *What's going on?* I wondered. *Is this how they pass the grass in Bali? Has Flynn gone Communist?* (He was a most unlikely Marxist.) *Maybe this is a test*, I thought, *a game he's playing, like the ones he used to play with Page at Frankie's.*

As soon as we finished one joint, Flynn rolled and lit another. After the third, I worried when it would end. The grass was particularly strong and the cumulative effect was becoming powerfully hallucinogenic. Hours went by, some of the time in silence, but the joints did not stop coming for more than a few minutes. I thought Flynn was testing my tolerance for dope, which was not great, or maybe indulging a passion of his own. My thoughts drifted in and out of dreams. I tried to hang on to my conscious awareness but it was a struggle.

"I don't do much dope at home," he said. "I get high on carrot juice and vegetables."

Flynn seemed to have become an Asian in mind, body and spirit. The nail on the little finger of his left hand was over an inch long, perfectly straight and not curled, the custom of an old leisure class. The Buddhist altar he had constructed years before still decorated the room of the second-floor apartment. Overhead, the fan turned slowly. The moving blades shifted the smoke and incense in a soft breeze. We talked of old friends, new places, ideas, plans for the future. I told him the story of Mèo and how he had settled with Joy in New York. The war still fascinated him. As the afternoon flowed imperceptibly into evening and the nighttime noise of traffic on Tu Do street bustled outside the window, the idea of joining Charlie Company became more attractive to him.

"We're starting where *Anderson Platoon* left off," I said.

He recalled scenes from the film. 'I ran into those guys while they were shooting around Bong Son,' he said. 'I think one of them got hurt.'

'You may be thinking of Vallop, my soundman.'

'Could be. But I remember the French team. They were excited about the stuff they had.'

'Well, we're going to try to improve on that.'

'Might be interesting. I haven't done much photography lately. What kind of deal do you think CBS would give me?'

'Let's find out,' I said. We got up and went downstairs and turned right up Tu Do street and walked to the CBS News bureau. My legs were unsteady. I worried about appearing in the bureau stoned. Normally, I did not mix work and pleasure like this. We asked Dave Miller what he could pay Flynn to work with the team. It was a generous sum, more than Flynn expected.

'Paskman may have my balls on a plate for this,' Miller said, 'but I respect what you guys are doing.' He did not react to our appearance.

'Okay, count me in,' Flynn said. 'When do we leave?'

'Tomorrow morning,' I said, 'at dawn.'

'I'll be ready.'

'Good luck up there,' Miller said. 'Keep your heads down.'

MARCH 29, 1970

When we arrived at Tay Ninh in the early morning, the heliport was already jammed with traffic. Gunships, medevacs, scout birds, ammo logs, lift ships and command choppers flew in, took on fuel and supplies, and went spinning away in a hurry. Firebase Jay was under attack.

The preliminary North Vietnamese bombardment had begun at 0420, a few hours earlier. Lieutenant Colonel Hannas was asleep on top of his command post in the cool night air outside the bunker when a salvo of mortars and rockets whooshed over the camp and burst inside the perimeter with sudden screaming explosions. In the mayhem of the first minute, one of the rounds hit the CP and spewed white-hot shrapnel into the command group. Both of the battalion commander's legs were severed. The medical team led by the battalion surgeon and First Sergeant Burke struggled to stop the bleeding and save Hannas's life. Farther out in the Dog's Head, Charlie Company was camped about six miles from Firebase Illingsworth. Captain Jackson received a terse message on the radio. "The C/O lost everything," it said.

As soon as the mortar and rocket barrage lifted, an estimated six hundred North Vietnamese assault troops from the 95-C Regiment charged across the open fields outside the camp firing AK-47 and RPG-7 rounds, crawling through the smoke toward the perimeter, their moving khaki figures illuminated in the night air by flares falling in the sky. The camp was enveloped in shattering noise and confusion. Fire, smoke and gunpowder choked the men's lungs. In the first few minutes of the assault, battalion headquarters of 2/7 Cavalry was in danger of being overrun. U.S. troops from Alpha Company fought with machineguns, M-16s, M-79s and beehive rounds fired directly from the lowered barrels of the artillery guns. In ferocious close-quarters combat, NVA sappers broke though the barbed wire perimeter at the far end of the base, planted satchel charges next to the U.S. artillery pieces, set them off and destroyed three field guns.

The American camp received volley after volley of supporting fire from artillery, helicopter gunships and tactical aircraft, forcing the North Vietnamese finally to withdraw. The battalion from 95-C left behind seventy-four dead but managed to evacuate all but a few of its wounded. Fourteen American soldiers were killed and fifty-two more, including Lieutenant Colonel Hannas, were evacuated to hospitals. Alpha Company had suffered 60 percent casualties and was crippled. Firebase Jay, one of the first American positions in the Dog's Head, would have to be abandoned. It had been there eleven days. Three bags of mail due to be delivered to Charlie Company were destroyed. The day was Easter Sunday.

I tried to add up the results and figure out what they meant. In the past four days, one battalion headquarters and two U.S. rifle companies had been decimated during battles in the Dog's Head. One of the American battalions in the area—2/8—was now seriously under strength because of its losses from several recent engagements. American intelligence had accurately predicted the movement of the 95-C Regiment into War Zone C and had given commanders adequate warning, but no one anticipated the immediacy or ferocity of its offensive. Clearly, the North Vietnamese intended to inflict serious losses on the Americans even though they came at heavy cost to themselves. NVA commanders were not going to allow the First Cav to establish itself along the Cambodian border without a fight.

Kay, Clevenger, Flynn and I caught a chopper out to the base. Charlie Company was still in the bush and was not due to be resupplied for two more days, but we wanted to be close if they had an emergency. The firebase was a wreck. Shell casings, spent cartridges, shrapnel, shell holes and a vast assortment of debris from the battle were scattered over the scorched earth. Survivors were trying to put the firebase back together— filling sandbags, repairing damaged bunkers, cleaning and loading weapons. Arriving helicopters brought a constant supply of ammunition into the camp. The men were silent, their faces black with dirt and smoke. Some of them slept. Some wore bandages. Some sat alone with their faces in their hands. One or two wandered through the camp as if walking away from a car crash.

'Do you want to shoot this as a story?' I said to Kay. His camera had been repaired in Saigon.

'No, let's not,' he said. 'It's all aftermath.'

'Yeah, but it's *good* aftermath.'

'I'd rather save the film and batteries for Charlie Company.'

That was our dilemma. Every minute Kay shot in noncombat circumstances left him with that much less film and battery power available for use if Charlie Company got hit. There was no way to know.

Outside the wire, three wounded North Vietnamese soldiers surrendered. They were tired, thirsty, in pain. Under interrogation they confirmed they were from 3d Battalion, 95-C. Flynn shot a hundred feet of them and then took pictures of the bodies of the dead in the field around the camp. Bodies were everywhere.

"I'd rather be out in the field than here on the firebase," a young lieutenant from Charlie Company said. He introduced himself as First Lieutenant Ray Martinez, twenty-two years old, the leader of 2d Platoon. Martinez, holding a can of beer in his hand, said he was trying to get back to C Company from R and R.

'Firebases are not a good place to be,' he said. 'No real cover, no place to maneuver, no chance to flank the other side.' Martinez, from Oceanside, California, said he had been in Vietnam almost continuously since 1965, starting as a seventeen-year-old private, E-2. He said he was due to rotate back to the States in a few weeks and would be promoted to captain by the end of the summer. Then he was coming back with Special Forces, perhaps as an A team commander. His face looked older than twenty-two years.

The brigade executive officer, Lieutenant Colonel John Hettinger, came to Jay to command 2/7 until a replacement for Hannas arrived. Hettinger said that nothing was flying out to C Company today. We could wait if we wished, he said, but the firebase was moving soon. 'No sense in giving Charlie another chance to hit us,' he said. 'Their mortars were ranged on this place perfectly this morning.'

We decided to return to Tay Ninh for the night. Waiting for a ride, Kay and Clevenger went to find a meal. Flynn and I sat down at one of the perimeter bunkers to pass the time. Soldiers worked nearby, clearing up and packing for the move to a new firebase. Bright sunshine burned the earth and kept the air hot. Some of the GIs stopped work, came over and talked to Flynn. They stared at his long yellow hair and handsome face.

"You know," one of them said, "I've seen you somewhere."

Flynn said nothing. GIs sometimes recognized him from one of the B movies he had made but couldn't put a name to him. He never mentioned his father to strangers.

The soldier made conversation while he tried to remember where he had seen Flynn.

"I got it!" he said, pleased with himself. "Man, you look exactly like *Peter Fonda!*"

Flynn smiled, embarrassed, and did not speak. I tried not to laugh out loud. After a few minutes, the soldiers went back to work.

'I won't tell anybody,' I said.

'Promise?'

'Yeah, promise. I swear.'

'Peter's a friend of mine.'

I took out my pen and notebook. 'What's his address?'

Flynn laughed. 'You wouldn't, would you?'

At brigade headquarters in Tay Ninh, there was no entertainment for visiting journalists. We were not interested in drinking and chatting at the officers' club. Nothing to do but smoke and tell stories. One of the public information officers, Lieutenant Richard Tuck, an intelligent, cheerful young journalist, saw we were bored and offered to take us on a tour of the camp. We agreed. The four of us climbed in his jeep and set off, Tuck bright-eyed and sober at the wheel, the rest of us happy and high. The night air was cool, not especially humid.

Tay Ninh brigade camp was spacious and orderly. It had paved streets, rows and rows of barracks, and work facilities for about thirty-five hundred military personnel. From the back of a jeep it appeared endless. After a few minutes the tour was becoming boring.

'How well do you know the base?' I asked Tuck.

'Like the back of my hand,' he said, driving ahead.

'Okay, let's see if we can get you lost.'

'You can't do it.'

'Let's find out, okay?'

'Okay.'

'If we tell you to turn, you have to turn. Immediately. Okay? Then, when we end up somewhere way out of the way, you have to find your way back to the PIO shop. Okay?'

'Okay,' he said. 'But I'm telling you, you won't get me lost.'

We tried. At random, each of us ordered Tuck to turn the jeep right or left. Haphazardly. In and out of roads and streets around the camp. Sometimes abruptly. Sometimes into dead ends. Some commands overlapped, some countermanded one another. At times Tuck was making one maneuver when he was ordered to reverse it and make another. He slowed down or

speeded up on command. He was a good driver and it was difficult to confuse him. Faster and faster we ordered him to go, careening around corners,
trying to avoid accidents in the darkness. At each new surprise, the lieutenant laughed with us, enjoying the anarchy of the game, but he always
found his way back to the main road. We called it "Tuck's Wild Ride."

'Just pray the MPs don't see us,' Tuck shouted, squealing around a corner, 'or we're in deep shit.'

'What are they going to do?' Kay said. 'Take away your license?'

'Yeah, send you back to Fort Benning?' said Clevenger.

The jeep came down a narrow alley and stopped at a dead end. A group
of GIs were standing outside a small club for enlisted men, smoking and
talking. Kay said he was hungry. Tuck waited in the jeep while the rest of us
went inside. The club was small, a single room with a short bar and no frills.
Hot dogs and beer were being served. The only decoration was a sign,

SNOW WHITE WAS A HEAD.

Flynn, Kay, Clevenger and I were dressed in GI fatigues with no insignia.
The soldiers assumed we were visiting grunts. They formed a circle around
Flynn to get a close look at his long hair and beads. They wore beads them-
selves but had short hair.

"Hey, man," one of them said, "how'd you manage to get away with all
that hair?"

"Oh," Flynn said, casually, "I've got this real cool C/O, dig, and he just
let's us do anything we want."

"No shit," one of them said.

"Far out."

"Dig it."

We ordered hot dogs and beer and ate them. Lieutenant Tuck found his
way back to the PIO shop flawlessly.

Later that night, I wrote to Joy describing our arrival and early days in
country:

March 29, 1970

Our first story was too rushed, really! We did not have our equipment carefully checked out and Jimmy was trying sound for the first time. I thought
we had a fine first effort. We worked hard—spent the first night in the field

on ponchos and air mattresses that anyone in the Saigon bureau could remember. Most people covering the war go to dinner parties and social functions in the evenings in Saigon now. It is not at all like '65–'68. You would be amazed at how much old flabby, late-sleeping Laurence is getting into shape. Almost naturally high with the excitement of this story. (I've spent exactly three days in my bed in the Continental—got good old room C-2 back again and Keith is next door like old times.)

War Zone C is in a serious state of combat. About 15 1st Cav soldiers were killed today and 50 wounded in the single action at Fire Base Jay. A sister battalion has taken roughly 100 percent casualties this month and is being pulled out of the War Zone for relief. It is not exactly like our discovery at Con Thien, but there are striking similarities in the lack of press coverage. I have met only one other war correspondent up here, except for CBS. . . . It is much different and more difficult now. Units use ambush tactics learned from the enemy. Arty and gunship support is heavier, but most importantly, some if not all units no longer assault enemy positions. They make contact, withdraw, and call in the air and artillery. I am told by the C Co Commander that he would rather let "six gooks get away than have one of his men hurt." (The enemy, however, is still assaulting.) It seems that every other soldier is wearing a peace symbol. Not all for the same reasons. Why? To aggravate the 'Lifers,' regular army types who push the grunts around. Enlisted men tell their sergeants to 'fuck off' when they think they're wrong. Morale is amazingly good in C Company, which has had relatively little contact in six months. They are expecting more now, but the soldiers say they're better fighters than the enemy—and since they're here, they have to do their job (some—not all).

News of the attack on Firebase Jay was a lead story from Vietnam in the United States. The *CBS Sunday News with Roger Mudd* ran five minutes and thirty-six seconds of our report on the new guys in Charlie Company, which Bensley had cut and left over the weekend. For all the grief, our first effort had not been a failure. The line about the second Indochina War seemed to be coming true.

MARCH 30, 1970

The battalion built a new command post in the Dog's Head, a crude firebase
the men carved out of the forest and code-named "Hammer." It was still
close to the Cambodian border but a long distance from Firebase Jay, abandoned now and left behind with the ghosts of Charlie Company's wild party
and the fearsome battle of Easter morning. Kay, Clevenger, Flynn and I
waited outside the berm on the LZ, checking with the flight crews of each
inbound helicopter to find out where it was heading, hoping to catch a lift to
Charlie Company. A young captain also waited. He introduced himself as Al
Rice and said he was heading out to Charlie Company to take over from
Captain Jackson. Rice, who was twenty-four years old and came originally
from Kingsport, Tennessee, said he was nervous about assuming command.
"This is a big opportunity for me," he said. He knew about the documentary
we were making and said he would cooperate in every way.

The LZ was crowded with soldiers and equipment. As each supply chopper landed or took off, its rotor blades blew up a storm of dry clay dust and
dirt, stinging faces and arms with tiny fragments of stone. The soldiers on
the LZ turned their backs and bent over with their eyes closed to shield themselves from the swirling dirt. During one of the landings, when everyone was
turned away, I saw Flynn pull open a wooden crate on the ground, take out
one of the hand grenades in the box, and slip it quickly into a pocket.

We waited for several hours but it became apparent that Charlie Company was not going to get a chopper today. Kay, Clevenger, Flynn and I
returned to Tay Ninh for the night. Flynn was fascinated with the hand
grenade, examining its round green shape, turning it over in his hand like a
new toy, trying to figure out how to unscrew the top and remove the fuse
mechanism without detonating the powder.

"I saw one of these in I Corps a few years ago," he said. "They were pro-
totypes. They gave them to the Marines. Just like the Pentagon to try 'em
out on the Marines. Some of the grunts didn't get the word that these were

quick-fuse grenades. You pull the pin to throw it and it goes off behind your ear." Flynn laughed heartily at that.

March 31—Tay Ninh

It was cold and damp in the unheated barracks in the hour before dawn. I woke up to see Flynn sitting cross-legged on his cot with a GI blanket around his shoulders, hunched over an old issue of *Stars and Stripes*, reading by flashlight. The headline of the main story on the front page said,

NVA ADVANCE ON PHNOM PENH

Flynn read the article again and again.

'Don't bet on it,' I said.

'Yeah, but what if it happens?' he said. 'NVA tanks in the streets? House-to-house fighting? Can you imagine how far out that would be?'

'The NVA are too smart to fight on two fronts. They've got the Cav gunning for them on this side, remember.'

Flynn stared at the front page. After a long silence he said, "I've got to be there."

I said nothing.

'Jack, would you forgive me if I pulled out and went back to Saigon?' His voice was supplicating. 'I mean, I'll stay if you need me. I haven't even gone out to the company yet and I feel guilty as hell. If you want me to stay, I'll stay for a week or two. But I really want to go to Pnompers and link up with Dana. It'll be like old times.'

I was disappointed. Flynn was a strong addition to the team. He and Kay got along well. At the same time, I knew it would be wrong to try to keep him.

'Don't worry about it, man,' I said. 'If you want to go, it's okay.'

'I'm really, really sorry. I hope you understand.'

'Of course I do,' I said. 'Don't worry about it.' I was sorry to lose him. The shooting of the story would suffer if Charlie Company made contact, but I respected his wishes.

When Kay and Clevenger got up, we had breakfast and drove Flynn to the helipad for a flight to Saigon.

'Keep your head down, man,' Kay said. 'The Cambodian Army isn't exactly the First Cav.'

'That's a Rog,' Flynn said. 'Dana and I will figure out something. Organize our own wheels.'

'I think I can guess what that'll be,' Kay said.

'Rent bikes or something.'

'Just remember you're not in Bali,' Kay said.

'Tell Dana we want you both back as soon as possible,' I said. 'Tell him it's getting hotter up here.'

'I'll do that,' he said. 'Good luck with the film. See you in a couple of weeks, maybe.'

Maybe. Four years after taking Flynn into the field on his first military operation in Vietnam, to the graveyard in 1966, I had taken him on his last. I had seen him arrive in Saigon with a tennis racket, a new camera and his father's name as baggage, and now I watched him go, a cool veteran of the war with Balinese peace beads around his neck and a hand grenade in his pocket.

Kay, Clevenger and I made it out to Charlie Company later in the day. The soldiers were surprised to see us. L. T. Winfield, the 2d Platoon RTO, was startled when we got off the helicopter.

'They told us you guys were on Jay when it got hit,' he said. 'We thought maybe you got blown away.'

'No, we went out by way of Illingsworth. Didn't get to Jay until it was over.'

'You guys are lucky.'

The welcome from the squad was especially friendly. After all the technical difficulties on our first patrol, soldiers in other squads had bet we wouldn't be back.

'Where's that funny little guy with glasses?' one of the GIs asked.

'Yeah,' another said, 'where's Dana?'

'Gone to Cambodia,' Kay said.

'Cambodia, huh?'

'Hell, we're practically *in* Cambodia.' Looking at a map, Phnom Penh was sixty miles west of the Dog's Head, the border just a mile away.

'Might just be meetin up with him 'fore long, ya never know.'

'He sure is a funny little fucker, that guy.'

'Most assuredly had his shit together.'

A flight of helicopters arrived to take the company on a combat assault, its second in a week. Kay insisted on riding with the first chopper so he could take pictures of the men as they deployed. The LZ was an empty field that had once been an ARVN firebase. As the ships landed, Kay ran ahead and got into position to film the men jumping out of the Hueys. He got a perfectly framed picture of Clevenger stumbling off the chopper, his pack and equipment dangling around him awkwardly, and falling over onto the ground.

There was no opposition. Captain Jackson sent out patrols to secure the LZ and consulted with Lieutenant Martinez about the objective that headquarters had ordered them to secure. It was several kilometers away through heavy bush. Martinez, holding a can of beer in his hand, looked doubtful.

'It's too far to walk in one day,' he said.

"They must be dreaming," Jackson said. Captain Rice stood close to him, listening.

"What we're working on now," Jackson said to Rice, "we have two workdays and a log day. And a log day's just a wasted day. It takes most of the day and you've got to move out to take your logs." Looking around at the scattered trees and scrub, Jackson said, "This is definitely mortar country. They can set up a tube anywhere."

The soldiers of 3d Platoon were ordered to test their weapons. The men lined up and fired their M-16s across the field at the tree line opposite them. Jackson checked each rifle to make sure it had not jammed. Several had. The bullets started a fire in the dry brush and the flames soon reached the height of a man. Jackson ordered the company to move out toward the objective, taking them through the fire. The heat from the flames raised the temperature well above a hundred degrees and the company was soon covered in sweat . As the men left the LZ, the fire burned out of control.

I walked with Rice. He was due to take command in a few days and I wanted to know him. He was five years younger than Jackson and had been in-country one year less. Rice had spent six months as the leader of a long-range reconnaissance patrol unit, a LLRP. "I've got to take what I've learned and put it to use," he said.

Rice portrayed himself as an adventurer, wild and rebellious. His father, a Marine Corps NCO, had raised him in strict military style. As a teenager, he said, he rebelled by running bootleg liquor over backwoods Tennessee roads. He also got into gang fights. His friends were tough. He was a popular student, played football in high school and college, got a degree in engineering. The local sheriff once caught his wife embracing Rice in a car and threatened to kill her. But not him. "I weighed 210 pounds at the time," he said laughing.

Rice confided that he wanted to pull a practical joke on a friend of his, a fellow officer in Vietnam. "His wife wants to meet me in Hawaii four days before *he's* supposed to arrive." He laughed at the idea. "I'll wear the bitch out before he gets there."

'What do you plan to do with Charlie Company?' I asked in a more serious moment.

Rice was emphatic. "When you've got a company sitting this good," he said, "you don't make changes." He talked about Captain Jackson's abilities as a commander and how much he wished him well in his new job at Division. Still, he said, "Jackson is kind of cautious."

On the radio, the company heard that one of the Cav's gunships, a Huey Cobra, had just been shot down by a 37 millimeter anti-aircraft gun, a weapon associated with regimental-size NVA units. The North Vietnamese were raising the stakes.

Our first day back with the company passed quickly. The film ran through Kay's Arriflex without jamming. Clevenger was more comfortable with the shotgun mike, keeping it out of the frame during interviews and conversations. Kay made a variety of shots of the patrol, moving up and down the line, rolling film as the soldiers passed. The men seemed to accept our presence. The novelty of having a camera crew had passed. No one took much notice of us. The monotony of the march, boredom and fatigue were more central concerns.

By three o'clock in the afternoon, Jackson decided the company had moved far enough. He and Rice discussed where to locate the night defensive perimeter and called in the map coordinates to battalion. The men cleared the brush and tall grasses in a thick wood and set up their defenses. Jackson dropped his pack and sat down to compose a letter to send to Lieutenant Colonel Hannas at the field hospital in Tay Ninh. He spent an hour writing. When he finished, he came around to each platoon with the letter. He told the men Hannas would probably be going to Japan soon and then on to the United States to recuperate. He read the letter aloud and the men listened carefully:

To Scalp Six.

Needless to say, we were shocked at the news of your being wounded on Easter morning. We could not get a full read-out on the action. However, the initial report was that you were being medevac'd with no pulse. It was a grim day for us all because we did not hear otherwise until late that night when Colonel Conrad called us on radio secure. Everyone said all day that you were too hard to die. You know how we feel about you and we appreciate all the things you did for us. It was good to have a leader like you with us because we knew you'd never let us down. There is really not much we can say except thanks. Best wishes from the best. Hope to see you again soon.

"What I'd like you to do," Jackson said to his men, "is have everyone sign this letter, if you'd like. If there is some reason he might know your call sign or something like that, go ahead and put that beside your name, so he'll know who you are. Okay."

Signing the letter, some of the soldiers recalled that Hannas had visited each of the rifle companies in the field when he first took command of the battalion. On his day with Charlie Company, he had walked point.

'I'll never forget that,' one of the soldiers said, 'the Old Man on point, cuttin the bush like a grunt.'

'Sweatin something fierce,' another said.

'Said it was the only way for an old man like him to get in shape.'

'I know the feeling,' Kay said.

"God, I just hope for his sake he didn't lose his balls," a soldier said.

"Radio message said he lost everything."

APRIL 1, 1970

As soon as he woke up, Captain Jackson knew he had to leave the field at once. Two days earlier, the morning after he learned of the attack on Firebase Jay, he awoke feeling a tightness in his chest, as if something strong was holding him in its grip. His arms were numb, his stomach nauseous. He felt frightened and exhausted. Although he was not scheduled to leave the company for another day, he decided he had to see a doctor as soon as possible.

Jackson called Kay, Clevenger and me aside. "I'm going to leave today," he said. "Is that okay with you guys?"

'Of course,' we said. 'Is anything wrong?'

Jackson described what had happened. 'My father had three heart attacks and he had the same symptoms,' he said. 'But I don't think I've had an actual heart attack. I'm twenty-nine years old and in perfect health.'

'Better to see a doctor and be sure,' I said.

"I've never had a sick day in my life," he said.

Jackson decided not to tell the troops about his medical condition. Instead, he said the time had come to start his new assignment as commander of Headquarters Company at division, an administrative job. Waiting for a helicopter, Jackson walked through the lines and said good-bye to each of the men. He had commanded most of them for more than five months. He shook their hands, addressing them by name.

The soldiers in 2d Squad shook hands with the captain and watched him walk along the line until he was out of sight. Kay kept the camera on his shoulder rolling.

"Just like our father, to our big family," said Specialist Fourth Class John Schultz. Schultz was tall and blond-haired, from Lynwood, California, and had been with Charlie Company for nine months, all of it in the field. "I don't know. Its just when you get used to the way of one man and then you have to change all over again. It's, I don't know, it's sort of like moving, like one house to the other, and having a different father. It just doesn't work right for a long time." Schultz was spending his twenty-first birthday in the field.

"The guys really grooved on Captain Jackson," said PFC Gordy Lee. I mean, they know that he's, he's one of the guys. He's not, he's not away up above everybody else. And, when you go to VIPs, he's one of the first ones drunk. And, you get a C/O that gets drunk with you and gets the ass with you, man, it's just uptight. And we're going to lose him. In my opinion, I don't think we'll ever get another C/O as good as he is."

"Maybe it's just luck or fate," Lee continued, "but out of the whole battalion, since we got Captain Jackson, we have been the company that's been hit, made the least amount of contact. And if we *do* make contact, we're coming out the best. Since Captain Jackson took over we've only lost two guys—actual KIAs—whereas the rest of the companies of the battalion have been losing quite a few more. And it seems like with Captain Jackson, we just kind of lead a charmed life. And, boy, I'm not for knocking that."

"The safety of his men," said Bob Teschker, a lanky twenty-year-old PFC from Trenton, Michigan. "I think he thinks more about the safety of his men than going out and maybe having to kill a lot of gooks. You know, 'cause he'll think about his men, too. There's always gooks around. And you can get, I mean, you'll always run into them. But, like I say, as long as I've known him, it was always safety for the men."

The soldiers in the squad seemed to share common feelings about the change of command: sadness, regret, some foreboding.

Lee said, "There'll be what you would call a trial period. In other words, a lot of us guys, you know, we're been out in the field with Captain Jackson's whole tour out here, the second time around for him. And, like Bob said, we've grown accustomed to his ways. And we like his ways. Mainly we agree with him all the way. I mean, he takes us someplace, it could be contact all over. But if we're behind Captain Jackson, we're not even worried. And, it's going to, it's going to take a little getting used to—getting used to a new C/O."

The battalion executive officer, Major Bacas, arrived in a command chopper to collect Jackson. Bacas got out and talked at length with Captain Rice. The expression on his face was severe, all business.

'Illingsworth got blown away this morning,' he said. 'Second of the Eighth has had it. I think they're coming out of the field.'

Kay, Clevenger and I looked at each other and at Major Bacas without speaking. *The whole battalion? Out of action? Six hundred and fifty men? Incredible,* I thought. None of us had imagined before coming to War Zone C that the war would be so intense that an American infantry battalion would be withdrawn from the field because of heavy casualties. *Who's next? Firebase Hammer? Charlie Company?*

We decided to go back with Bacas and Jackson to the battalion aid station to cover Jackson's medical check. Leaving his company, the modest Alabama officer's face looked sad. "Never thought I'd see this day," he sighed. "I'm gonna miss these people." As the helicopter took off, some of the soldiers on the LZ held up their index and middle fingers in a V. Some of the men in the helicopter returned the sign.

At Firebase Hammer, the battalion surgeon examined Jackson and said he had probably suffered a mild heart attack. "All the symptoms are cardiac," he said. "I doubt that it's serious, but he needs an EKG." Jackson was told to get his heart tested at division headquarters in Phuoc Vinh. We shook hands, wished him good luck and said good-bye. Kay, Clevenger and I got aboard a Chinook flying to Bien Hoa. The pilots went out of their way to take us at Tan Son Nhut, a courtesy that First Cav air crews were making for us now as a matter of routine. The story of our hospitality to the crew of the 229th in Saigon the week before had gone around the division. We could not have been more grateful for the lift.

'I don't believe our luck,' Clevenger said when we landed.

'Daily miracle?' Kay said.

'That wasn't the daily miracle,' I said.

'What the hell was?' Clevenger asked.

'Not being at Illingsworth this morning.'

We learned later that twenty-four Americans were killed and fifty-four wounded at Illingsworth. The battle lasted a little over two hours.

In Saigon, the U.S. military command reported its version of the battle at Illingsworth. A morning news release, number 92-70, was printed on Office of Information stationery with the red, yellow and white MACV shield at the top:

At approximately 0220 yesterday morning (1 April), an element of the 1st Brigade, 1st Cavalry Division (Airmobile), at a fire support base 34km (22 miles) north-northwest of Tay Ninh City and five miles from the Cambodian border, received about 200 mixed 120mm mortar and 82mm mortar rounds, 15 mixed 107mm and 122mm rockets and a ground attack by an estimated two enemy companies. The enemy employed small arms, automatic weapons and rocket-grenade fire. The troopers returned fire with organic weapons supported by helicopter gunships and artillery. As action continued, an element of the 11th Armored Cavalry Regiment, in tanks and armored personnel carriers moved to the area and reinforced the troops in contact. Fighting continued until about 0430 when the remaining enemy withdrew. No enemy were reported to have penetrated the perimeter. In a search of the battle area, the bodies of 54 enemy soldiers were found. In addition, 28 individual weapons were captured. U.S. casualties were 24 killed and 54 wounded. Materiel damage was light to moderate. (The name of the fire support base was FSB Illingsworth.)

Reading the handout, I thought the language captured the American high command's view of the war precisely. The battle was described almost exclusively in statistics: military designations, units of men, numbers of kilometers, miles, millimeters, hours, minutes, numbers of killed and wounded, numbers of weapons, calibers, times, distances, sizes, quantities, amounts. Looking at the statistics, what I saw was a cold, impersonal, detached accounting of what had happened during those two hours of hell at the firebase, devoid of any sense of the human cost. How else for an establishment of obsessive number crunchers and quantitative analysts like Robert McNamara to describe a battle? Attrition, the number of enemy soldiers killed in each fight, meant more to them than anything, even as the total number of America's own killed and wounded had grown itself over the years to a monstrous statistic.

Of course, the news release did not try to describe the horror of the battle, the avalanche of noise, the anguish, the confusion, the fright, the cries of the wounded, their calls for help. No mention of trauma or shock or paralysis or the burning pain in their bodies as they bled and died. No mention of courage. (I could only imagine the thoughts of the 11th Armored Cavalry Regiment troops as they raced through the forest at night to join the battle.) No mention of the consequences of the battle on U.S. operations in War Zone C. No suggestion that with so many of its men killed and wounded, and so many others who survived in shock, 2/8 was crippled, too understrength to stay in the field. The MACV handout told a lot about numbers but nothing of the fury and heartbreak of the fight. The battle was sanitized with statistics.

No civilian journalists had been at the base. No firsthand accounts of the battle were filed by the press. If Americans at home read anything about the encounter at Illingsworth, they got short summaries taken from MACV's already abbreviated description in their newspapers the next day. Or they heard a few lines on radio and television. Days later, a more descriptive story would appear in *Stars and Stripes*, the military newspaper read by the troops, and that too was largely secondhand. Soldiers in Vietnam read more about the fight than people at home. Much of the war was reported that way. Agony-filled battles like Illingsworth were reduced to one-paragraph summaries in statistical shorthand. MACV knew no other way to report the war. It passed on its point of view to the public without heart.

Sitting at the old wooden desk in C-2, the window open, a cup of coffee next to the typewriter, I wrote two stories on a portable Olivetti typewriter. The first was "Charlie Company on Patrol." I tried to write to the pictures Dana Stone had shot on the first patrol and Kay's film from our most recent trip. The story introduced some of the soldiers from the squad: Sergeant Dunnuck, Gordy Lee, Carlton Dudley, Bob Teschker and John Schultz. The scenes included the soldiers' bull session before the first combat assault, the helicopters landing in the LZ, the long patrol, rest breaks, card games, the discovery of the enemy bunker complex, the squad digging in for the night (including Dana's high shot from the tree), and the red ant attack. Each scene was meant to be accompanied by a comment or two taken from the interviews with the soldiers. If the story worked as planned, it would show scenes of life in the field with personal descriptions by the men and with a minimum of voice-over narration by me.

At the end of the script I sent an editorial note, not for broadcast, to producers in New York:

One of C Co's sister companies was heavily engaged defending FSB Jay on Easter Sunday when the battalion commander lost his legs. Their sister battalion was defending FSB Illingsworth, which suffered 24 killed. That battalion has suffered approximately 80–90% casualties in the month of March and has been taken out of the field, no longer an effective fighting force. We get the impression there's a war going on all around C Company and it cannot long avoid becoming engaged.

The second piece was called "Captain Jackson's Heart" and told the story of the company commander's love for his men and the apparent heart attack he suffered in the field. It pointed out that Charlie Company had suffered the lightest casualties of any company in the division, while, at the same time, inflicting a high number of casualties on the enemy. The script explained the reason:

> Captain Jackson never takes his men down trails. He learned in his first tour in Vietnam, as an adviser to a Vietnamese battalion, that marching along a trail—which is the easiest way to move—may also lead to an enemy ambush. The men say their captain would rather wait along the trails for the North Vietnamese, and he has set the most successful ambushes of any company in the First Cavalry Division.

Jackson's concern for the welfare of his men was illustrated by his quick evacuation of PFC Sam Kuehn when he injured his ankle. Also included in the story were comments by Jackson on the tactics he employed ("There are three ways to make contact . . .") and assessments of him by soldiers in the squad. The script introduced Captain Al Rice as Jackson's replacement and said the transfer was taking place ahead of schedule because of Jackson's heart condition. But the change of command worried the men, exemplified by John Schultz:

> Just like our father, to our big family . . . It's sort of like moving from one house to another . . . and having a different father. It just doesn't work right for a long time.

The last line of narration said:

> Second squad and the others in Charlie Company remain in the field under their new company commander, who believes that Captain Jackson may have been too cautious.

I gave the first draft of the scripts to Kay and Miller, who read them closely and suggested a few changes. When the narration was recorded, both stories were shipped to New York. Most of the technical problems seemed to have been solved, but the film had to be developed and screened before we would know.

A cable from Russ Bensley had arrived, commenting on Stone's film of the first patrol. Stone had made a few candid shots of Kay and Clevenger digging in for the night.

31150 HAVE SCREENED FILM OF CHARLIE COMPANY PATROL AND PIC-
TURES GENERALLY FINE STOP . . . TELL CLEVENGER EYE NEED SOME DIG-
GING DONE IN MY BACK YARD AND MAYBE KAY CAN HELP PRUNE THE
MAPLES BENSLEY

Bensley's cable relieved some of the tension we had felt with manage-ment in New York. Being this far away from the front office was a blessing in some ways but a handicap in others. The fluctuating moods of CBS News managers were difficult to judge from this distance. We wanted to know our chances of getting stories on the air, what their reactions to them were, and whether our hopes for an hour-long documentary were still valid. One good source of information was Joy Baker. At the end of the day I wrote to her:

Jimmy is becoming a first class soundman—extremely alert. It is very important to him now to prove his ability . . . We are—all three—truly working as
a team, and I am pleased. People in the company are getting used to the
camera poking into their incredible lives in Nam and thoughts, occasionally.
Slowly, we are being accepted, and they are more relaxed and honest around
us. Yours faithfully has been 'jes' fine—thank you! Drinking 3–4 quarts of
water a day (it's the dry period and we sweat a lot), taking his salt tablets,
vitamin pills (2 kinds), tranquilizers, and eating one hot meal a day and a lot
of fruit. My legs are in excellent shape. My back is getting used to the heavy
pack without much grief. Otherwise, a little tired from all the travelling.
How are you, Cat and the rest of the world?

APRIL 5, 1970

The log ship flew above the trees on a straight line from Tay Ninh to the Dog's Head. The sun was bright, the air clear and cool. Five thousand feet below, the forest lay in a long unbroken blanket of foliage all the way to the horizon, endless and unvarying, green leaves and branches at the tops of the trees woven in a solid mass. Descending toward the LZ, the pilot held the helicopter in a tight grip. Wisps of yellow smoke filtered up from the jungle floor and dissolved in the blue air above. The pilot cleared the opening through the tops of the trees and dropped into the dark space, narrow and deep, as if descending a mine shaft. The chopper cut a clean vertical hole in the humid air, the tips of its blades spinning a few feet from the branches of the trees. The downdraft blew everything below with hot wind. Coming down out of the sunlight, shapes of men appeared on the ground—small shadowy forms in dark green fatigues, their faces upturned, watching us drop slowly into their dark underworld.

Landing, the log ship off-loaded water, rations, mail, radio batteries and several soldiers. The helicopter was supposed to leave, return to the log base and come back immediately with hot food but it did not. There was no explanation. Captain Rice was angry. The company sat in the forest around the LZ and waited. By late morning the heat was scorching.

Four days under the command of Captain Rice and the soldiers were unsettled. There was an edginess among them that had not been there before, an irritability, as if Captain Jackson had taken their confidence with him. The men welcomed us back politely, but when the novelty of our return was over they stopped smiling.

'LZ's too fuckin tight,' one of them said.

'He takes the whole God damn day to get the log done,' said another.

'And now there ain't enough daylight left to hump out of here.'

'It'll be dark 'fore we get the NDP set up.'

'And Charlie knows right where we are.'

'Prob'ly get mortared tonight.'

'Maybe worse.'

'Flaky, man.'

The company had no orders, no mission. Battalion was still waiting for the arrival of a permanent replacement for Lieutenant Colonel Hannas and had issued no instructions. Nor had Brigade, where Colonel Ochs represented the only continuity in command between Charlie Company's platoon leaders and division. The other veterans in the chain of command—Hannas and Jackson—were gone. A one hundred man U.S. Army rifle company waited alone in the wilds of War Zone C with no clear sense of purpose and with North Vietnam's 95-C Regiment patrolling around them.

'Don't know what we're supposed to do,' Rice said. He shrugged his shoulders, then smiled. 'Never mind. I'll think of something.'

An hour later the log ship returned with the meals but they were cold. Ham, stewed tomatoes, sweet potatoes—all cold. Also Kool Aid (warm), grapefruit sections (bitter), iced tea (defrosted long ago), and a sweet gloopy substance that might once have resembled peach cobbler. The troops drank it.

PFC Bob Picano, a cheerful twenty-year-old from Philadelphia with a long oval face, offered each member of the squad a shake from his bottle of hot sauce. Picano was the squad gourmet and was called "Fatty," though he was not fat.

"They ought to send me back to the rear to cook," he said. "I'd make sure you guys get your chow hot."

'You just want to get out of the field,' someone said.

'You bet your ass.'

"I don't normally eat," said Sergeant Dunnuck, "but I ate today. Pretty good." Dunnuck traveled lighter than anyone. Except for his flashlight and extra ammo, his rucksack was virtually empty. He went days with an empty stomach.

'Alpha Company's in contact,' the company radio operator said in a low voice. 'Sounds heavy.'

Everyone around him turned to listen to the battalion net. Word of the contact flashed through the line. Mortar and artillery shells cracked and crumped a few kilometers away, the sound muffled by the brush.

'OK,' Rice said. 'Everybody stay on your toes.'

There was nothing to do but wait for orders. The men finished the meal and opened letters. The mail was the first in more than a week. Some mail had been delayed by the postal strike and three of the bags had been lost in the attack on Firebase Jay. No mail arrived for Lee Boling. "So, I'll just clean my weapon," he said, holding his heavy, long-barreled M-14. Boling was twenty-one years old and came from Chehalis, Washington. He was the only man in the platoon who used the older, semiautomatic .30-caliber rifle. Boling knew guns. He had grown up with them and was a keen marksman. He cleaned the M-14 every day. He had no use for an M-16. He said it was unreliable, jammed for no reason.

"When you don't get mail," I asked him, "do you ever feel sorry for yourself?"

"Well, no. I don't feel sorry for myself," Boling said. "I'm kind of mad at the world. Like about two-odd days ago, some of our mail was burned up on one of the LZs. And usually every log day I get at least one letter or two. And I didn't get nothing. So, it was six or eight days without mail and I get pretty mad. I think I was just mad because it was burned on the LZ."

L. T. Winfield, the platoon radio operator, also got no mail. He was expecting a letter from Jackson, Mississippi, from the woman he wanted to marry.

'Maybe she wrote and the letter got blown away on the firebase,' Winfield said.

'Maybe she didn't write,' one of the soldiers in the squad said.

'Yeah, maybe she's got a new man,' someone else said, 'a soulmate.' Laughter.

'Not even,' Winfield said, his expression timid.

'Don't worry, L.T.,' Gordy Lee said, 'she'll wait for you. You're too good-looking.'

Winfield laughed, reassured.

PFC Jorge Rivera sat alone with his back against a tree and opened his mail with infinite care. He had six letters, the most he'd received in one day, and he read them slowly. Rivera was a small man with fine bones and light brown skin and dark eyes, twenty-nine years old, the oldest man in the squad. He was born in Puerto Rico but raised in New York City and the farthest he had been away from Manhattan was a family trip to Niagara Falls when he was a kid. "Now look at me," he said.

Kay suggested an interview with Rivera and got in position low on the ground facing him. The camera rolled. Rivera said he had spent ten and a half months in the field, his entire tour except for sixteen days in the hospital with a shrapnel wound he got from a B-40 in one of the firefights. Now he was short and all he thought about most of the time was getting home alive.

"When that plane lands," he said, "I'm gonna get the fastest taxi in New York to take me home to my wife and daughter." His voice was strained, tense. "Every time I write, I ask her to pray for us—all of us."

"You told me you were a little worried about making it the last couple of months," I said.

"Yeah, when you get short like that, you kind of get started to worrying. You worry when you go walking down the bush. You worry about getting hit. For me, I worry about getting hit *again*. I don't intend for that to happen. But, you never can tell." He paused. His voice was weary.

"You feel that there's somebody after you. Specifically. Just you. Because you're short. They don't want anybody else. Just you. And it gets pretty scary. It's very dangerous to do that, to be like that, in that position. Very dangerous." Rivera shook his head.

"Usually, when you're not worried about going home, you just hear a shot and you hit the ground immediately. But when you start thinking and looking around, you're not thinking of getting down. And, wow, it's pretty dangerous. *Spooky*. It's really something."

He looked at the ground between his feet and said nothing. Kay panned the camera down to the open letter in Rivera's hands, held it for a few seconds, then turned off. We thanked Rivera for talking to us.

'He was great,' Kay said softly as we walked away.

'How close were you?' I said.

'Head and shoulders.'

'God, he was honest.'

'Yeah, I feel sorry for him.'

We looked across the small open space where the squad sat huddled under ponchos to protect them from the sun. Some read copies of *Stars and Stripes*. Bob Teschker was reading a letter. Teschker had a gentle, friendly disposition. Kay started rolling.

"Who's it from?" I said.

"Its from my fiancée."

"Good news?"

"Well, yeah, there's some things that I don't like to hear, but mostly it's good. It always cheers me up. It's one day I always look forward to."

"What's the news?"

"Well, she's got a brother who's in the service, too. But he's back in the States. And just writing about him and things she's been doing. And she got a raise at work, so, she's kinda happy about that. Clothes she's buying for the summer coming up. Main thing, wishing I was there with her."

"What do you wish?"

"Oh, I wish the same thing!" A big smile brightened his face. "But I'm getting along. I'm used to the idea." He paused. "Mainly, I just keep writing and hope she keeps writing me."

The radio operator said it sounded bad for Alpha Company. 'They're calling for medevacs,' he said, listening to the traffic. 'Seven KIAs.'

'Ours or theirs?' Rice said.

'Ours.'

No one spoke.

That explains the disappearance of the log ship, I thought. *And the lack of orders. Battalion and brigade were preoccupied with Alpha Company.* It was the second time in seven days the company had been in a serious fight. Alpha had been defending Firebase Jay when it was attacked.

Rice ordered his men to move off the LZ. The soldiers formed a column and walked until they came upon an area of scattered shrub where the trees were spread wide. Rice told them to hold up. Squatting on the ground with his first sergeant, he studied his map, trying to locate the position and decide on a place to camp for the night. Darkness was coming on. 'Hell, let's stop here,' he said. Grumbling, the company set its perimeter. Rice radioed his coordinates to battalion.

There had been a sprinkling of rain during the evening and the air was heavy. Kay, Clevenger and I joined two ponchos together, propped them with branches to form an overhead cover and spread the third poncho on the ground. There was not enough daylight left to dig in. We ate a meal in the dark.

Kay slept on my right side and Clevenger on the left. The night was hot, oppressive. Lying on my back, I opened a canteen and sipped a small amount of water, drawing it into my mouth with air, cooling it, holding it on my tongue, wetting the back of my throat. The water moved around in my mouth, and changed form, separating into droplets and joining together again. I savored the taste of it and swallowed slowly, feeling it slide down my throat. The taste was soothing, refreshing, like nectar. *How relative pleasure is,* I thought. *Out here on the edge of nowhere, having nothing helps you understand the true value of things. That was the best drink of water of my life.* I vowed to be more grateful for simple comforts: food, shelter, water, a bed to sleep on. A woman to love and be loved by. How grateful I felt to have a partner waiting at home. I turned on the tape recorder and listened again to "Our House" by Crosby, Stills and Nash and thought of Joy in New York. In a minute the melancholy covered me.

The first round of incoming exploded two to three hundred yards away. *Splaat!* Birds flew off in a flurry of flaps and squawks. Then silence. The second round whistled over and crashed with a loud bang. Closer.

'What the fuck is that?' Clevenger said.

'Sounds like rockets,' I said. 'One-twenties.'

'Definitely rockets,' Kay said on the other side. We reached for our helmets and put them on.

The company was silent. No one moved. Radios still. Another round came in and crashed, still closer. *Whizzz-bang!*

'What do we do if there's a ground attack?' Clevenger whispered. His voice was not afraid.

'Stay where you are,' I said.

'Pray,' said Kay.

A shell shrieked overhead and exploded near the edge of the perimeter. *Craaack!*

'They've got the range,' Kay whispered. 'Now they're bracketing us.' The leaves of the trees fluttered as shrapnel fell on them. Small pieces landed near the shelter.

'Check fire! Check fire!' the company radio operator called to battalion. His voice was urgent.

Three rounds exploded in the next few minutes and then the shelling stopped. None landed inside the perimeter, but shrapnel tore through ponchos and tents and several soldiers were grazed. A big chunk of hot steel hit one of the men in 2d Platoon on his helmet but he was not hurt. Seven rounds had come in.

'Jesus,' Clevenger said. 'What next?'

'They know we're around here,' Kay said. 'But they don't know exactly where.'

'Charlie's idea of H and I,' I said. Kay laughed.

'Well it sure *harassed* the hell out of me,' Clevenger said.

Time passed. Around midnight we heard the sounds of soldiers walking past our position. They were close, perhaps fifty yards away. Each sound was individual and distinct. Feet tramped on soft earth. Cloth rubbed against cloth. Small metal objects like canteens and mess gear clinked against one another. No voices. A column of North Vietnamese soldiers with full packs moved along in the dark at a brisk march. Hundreds of men. Charlie Company held its breath. No one moved or spoke. *Weird,* I thought. *We know where they are but they don't know we're here. Otherwise they'd be silent. It's usually the other way around.* Fifteen minutes passed. The tail end of the enemy column went by and moved out of hearing. Then quiet, absolute silence.

'Might have been the ones who got into it with Alpha Company,' Kay whispered.

'They were moving pretty fast,' I said.

'Must be a trail over there.'

'Probably a battalion.'

'They move like they own the place,' Clevenger said.

'They *do*!' Kay said.

'Might be heading for the border,' I said.

'Too bad we weren't set up for an ambush,' Clevenger said.

'We wouldn't have got it on film,' Kay said. 'It's too dark.'

After a minute, Clevenger said, 'I just don't *believe* that. The whole thing with the incoming and then all those God damned NVA going by. I mean, that was *incredible*!'

'Welcome to the bush, Jimmy,' Kay said.

Now, in the minute before falling asleep, I hated being here, despised it, wished I were somewhere else. *Nothing is safe, no way to cover the story, not enough water, no Captain Jackson to figure out what to do.* For the first time with Charlie Company I felt vulnerable. Alone. Lost in a dreadful wilderness with no sense of security. From what they had been saying, I got the impression the soldiers were having the same thoughts.

APRIL 6, 1970

'Guess what? Kay said.

'What?' I said.

'You didn't snore last night.'

'No kidding.'

'No kidding.'

'Maybe I'm cured.'

'Maybe you didn't sleep.'

The company was awake and on its feet by 0630, but the sky was black with rain clouds and it was too dark for the troops to bring in the trip flares and claymores. So the men cooked breakfast and waited for light. They complained about the incoming the night before. Most assumed it was friendly fire.

'Sounded like 155s last night.'

'C/O gave the wrong location to the arty.'

'Man's got his head up his ass.'

'Don't know where we are.'

'Shit, *nobody* knows where we are.'

Kay and I thought the incoming was North Vietnamese rocket fire. The whooshing sounds were distinctive, familiar to us from Con Thien and Khe Sanh. 'Maybe Charlie was telling us to keep our heads down,' Kay said.

The soldiers listened. 'You sure about that?' one said.

'Pretty sure,' Kay said.

Then one of them said, 'Yeah, Charlie did *not* want to fuck with *us* last night.'

'Not *even*.'

'Man, I did not want to fuck with him *either*.'

Captain Rice agreed that the incoming sounded like rockets but he wasn't sure. 'I've called every battery in the AO and nobody was firing last night at that time. We called a check-fire over the entire Dog's Head but they still kept coming in.' He lit a cigarette. 'I was worried, I'll tell you. Good thing they stopped.'

The soldier who was hit in the head by shrapnel showed everyone the dent in his helmet. "I know where I'd be if I didn't have my helmet on," he said. "In the hospital." *Or worse*, I thought.

The unexpected darkness at dawn caused the company to move out over an hour late. At 7:35, Sergeant Dunnuck took point at the head of 2d Squad and walked into the bush heading south-southeast. The squad had been given company point for the day. The order from battalion was not urgent, so the late departure was not regarded as a problem. Rice was told to locate a trail a few hundred meters away from the NDP and determine whether it was wide enough for a landing zone. If so, the company would be extracted by helicopter and taken on a combat assault. There was no hurry. Kay and Clevenger went up front to film with the squad.

Within a few minutes, Dunnuck arrived at the trail. Cautiously, he stepped out of the jungle and looked down the length of it, both ways. The trail was six to ten feet wide and perfectly straight. There was no movement in either direction. Looking down, Dunnuck saw footprints in the soft red dirt. The trail was covered with footprints, dozens of tracks made by sandals and boots of North Vietnamese infantry. Fresh tracks, heading northeast.

Dunnuck shook his head. Not enough room to get a bird in. Thick foliage and trees grew right up to the edge of the single-lane track. Perfect conditions for an ambush. A helicopter flew over, swiftly. In the open sunlight of the trail, the heat was strong.

Dunnuck walked back to his platoon leader and told him the trail was no good for an LZ. The lieutenant listened. He was new to the company. He had taken command of the platoon a few days earlier and was inexperienced in the jungle. He called Captain Rice on the radio and said the trail would not make a good pickup point. Rice called battalion and told the C/O. Almost at once the answer came back: get your men on the trail, turn left and walk until they come to a bigger LZ. Move northeast.

Rice radioed the new order to the platoon leader, who told Dunnuck to get on the trail and move to an LZ. Thirteen hundred meters. Three quarters of a mile. Dunnuck bristled.

"That's a fuckin *road*," he said. "I ain't goin to walk down there. My whole squad ain't walkin down there." He turned and moved away from the road. The squad followed. The lieutenant said nothing. At that moment an artillery shell screamed over and exploded on the other side of the road. The men in the column dropped to the ground.

'Friendly,' someone said, cursing.

'What the fuck is going on?' another said.

Dunnuck and his squad walked away from the road and the rest of 2d Platoon turned and followed.

I started my tape recorder and walked along the line of men. Apprehension showed in their faces. Some of the newer GIs turned their heads from side to side in fear. Others, like John Schultz, were more in control.

"What's the problem?" I said.

"We just don't want to walk on the road," he said in a steady voice. "This is one of the things that I told you about, when we were wondering what the new C/O was going to be like. And these are the kind of things which you *don't* want him to be like."

The squad stopped for a moment.

"Someone gave an order," Schultz said, "so we have to follow it."

"What do you do?"

"You follow it. And you work it out the best way you can. You fudge on it to protect yourself. Just like everybody else here. Nobody wants to walk it. So we'll fudge on it as much as you can. These guys have been here too long to want to play around."

"You guys really don't want to go."

"You're not kidding." His face made a grim half smile and turned away.

Gordy Lee was next in the line. "After eight and a half months in the country," he said, "I haven't walked down a fucking trail. Yet they want me to walk down *a road.*" He shook his head in exasperation.

"First time we'll be walking down a road," another GI said.

"Like a duck in a shooting gallery," Schultz said.

George Rivera's eyes were nervous, his body tense. He was the most experienced soldier in the squad.

"Rivera, what do you think of this operation?" I whispered.

"This thing is crazy. It's senseless, walking down a road like that." He thought for a moment. "But I guess we'll just have to wait and see what happens."

Another soldier said, "The Old Man wants to walk down the middle of this road and there ain't nobody else wants to go along with it. So, he's got the ass now."

"You mean he's angry?"

"Yes."

Captain Rice moved to the front of the line.

"What's going on?" I said.

"I don't know what to do," he said. "I've got a *mutiny* on my hands." He looked around. "I hope I'm doing the right thing."

Rice called his three platoon leaders away from the rest of the company. Kay stood outside the small huddle of men and rolled film. The officers did not appear to notice him.

"We're gonna move out on the road up ahead," Rice told the platoon leaders. Each word was emphatic, part of an order. "Now we're going to move out and they're going to be left behind. Or, I'm going to take the point and they can follow me if they want to." Rice put his hands on his hips and took a breath. "Now it's that simple. We've got a job to do and we're going to do it. It's not half as dangerous as doing some of the crap that we've done out here in the boonies. At least we can see what we're doing."

Rice spoke to each of the lieutenants in turn. The leader of 2d Platoon tried to argue the case for waiting but Rice cut him off. His voice was insistent, commanding.

"Now, either move out, or else I move out and they sit on their butt right here. It's that simple. All right. Now let's move out. Tell 'em to either make up their mind—they'll sit here and then I'll send some people back for them, which won't go over too big at all. Okay. We can't have this. This is extremely safe. This is the safest thing we've done."

Rice assembled his command staff of six men, including the first sergeant and radio operator and two platoon leaders, and walked to the edge of the road. He stopped and looked back at the waiting troops.

"If an old man like me can walk point," he called to 2d Platoon, "you guys can follow." Then he waited. No one moved to follow. Rice turned and led his command group out onto the road. Slowly. Alone. Flies buzzed around their helmets in the heat. The radio hissed. A helicopter flew nearby, turned and banked away. The sun was very bright.

Rice walked slowly along the road for about fifty yards and stopped. The radio squawked his call sign. The battalion commander called with new orders. Rice listened and radioed back to confirm.

"All right now to move down the Romeo," Rice said into the handset. "Whiskey to Romeo." (Whiskey, for W, meant West; Romeo, for R, meant the road.) "Get in a three-shipper in a hurry," Rice added. He was confirming the order to turn around, go back along the road to the west, cut a three-ship landing zone as fast as possible, and get the company lifted out.

Rice walked back to the rest of the company and explained the new orders. Go three hundred meters the other way and get out as fast as possible. The men nodded their heads.

"Okay. We'll move out and they'll be okay," Rice said.

"No good sitting here," one of the lieutenants said.

"That's right," Rice said, "the longer we sit here the worse it gets." He looked around at the men. "Everybody going? Okay. Let's go."

First Squad, 2d Platoon, took the point and moved down the road in two columns, widely separated. Second Squad followed. Dunnuck clicked the fire switch on his M-16 to automatic and held it ready. The men walked slowly. Their eyes scanned the dense brush on both sides of the road. They could see only jungle in the wild tangle. The soft dirt road was full of footprints. Just to the side of the road the soldiers passed a deep slit trench which had been dug recently.

"It's flaky today," a soldier said in a low voice.

"What does flaky mean?" I asked.

"Flaky means everybody's scared and they don't know what they're going to do. Just like you're walkin down this trail, could be gooks on both sides of it. Gooks always stay on the big trails like this. They always watch it."

"There's tracks all up and down this morning," another soldier said. "We got to stay spread out this morning."

"Bad," one said.

The faces of the men were intense, their eyes angry. They kept their M-16s close to their hips and held them with both hands. Their right hands held the pistol grips of the rifles and their index fingers rested against the trigger guards. Their expressions were flat, muscles tense, skin drawn tightly along the bones. They cursed the C/O in whispers. Their eyes moved from one side of the silent bush to the other. The road ahead looked like the open jaws of a trap. A long accurate line of machinegun fire would waste them all.

Walking with 2d Squad, I felt the exaggerated heat of the sun in the still air, a suffocating closeness magnified by fear. It felt like trying to breathe underwater. My body buzzed with a tingling lightness that wanted me to freeze in place, not go another step. The inside of my stomach was empty and sick, like the low point of a fever. Weak, defenseless, scared, my heart beat in the temples of my head. I moved down the road in a state of purest instinct, alarmed, alert, a primordial being in a primeval forest. Every sense said run away, flee as fast as you can, dig a hole in the ground and disappear. But I held my instincts in check, tried to act unafraid. My sight focused on the side of the road, picking out places to take cover when the shooting started—a tree, a fallen trunk, a shellhole—any indentation in the ground. Every ten yards or so I picked a new place to dive behind. Looking for safe places became a mental exercise, a point of concentration, something to think about other than the danger. The rainforest seemed to close in from both sides of the road and hold us in its dark heart.

A long time passed.

The point reached a place where two bomb craters had cleared the trees on one side of the road. The soldiers took out their machetes and started to cut a landing zone out of the remaining brush. They uncovered an antiaircraft gun position—a round hole in the ground for an NVA .51-caliber—possibly the target of the original air strike. A Huey Cobra zoomed above the road, low and fast, its guns aimed at the bush along the sides.

Without warning, the air exploded like a string of firecrackers, a long rumbling run of heavy explosions. The earth trembled. Some of the soldiers dropped to the ground.

'Arc-light,' someone said.

'B-52s?' Clevenger asked. We nodded our heads.

'Awful damn close,' a soldier said.

'Ain't heard one that close before,' someone else said. The men chopped at the surrounding brush with new urgency. I looked at my watch. It was 11:05.

Waiting for the LZ to be cut, Rice called his platoon leaders together. The anger in his voice was controlled.

"I can't run around and kick everybody in the butt," he said. "I can't run around and tell everybody what to do. You have to back me up. If I say something—and believe me, if it's bad I'll know it's bad—and you'll have to make it out for what you can." He looked at the faces of the lieutenants. "Any questions? Okay. Let's get this LZ built and get the hell out of here. I'm glad we didn't have to walk it."

The lift ships came in one at a time and carried the company away. It took almost an hour to move the hundred men to LZ Wood, command post of 5th Battalion, 7th Cavalry, the third battalion in the brigade along with 2/7 and 2/5. Landing at Wood, the spirits of the men lightened. They spread out in an open field outside the camp, sat down and lit cigarettes. As soon as they were counted and organized in squads and platoons, they were scheduled to go on another combat assault. It would be their fourth mission in thirteen days. This one was to secure a new CP for the battalion. In the distance, a military band played marching music. Eight-inch howitzers fired. The company was back in some sort of civilization.

The squad sat in a circle and waited. Kay, Clevenger and I knelt on the ground next to them and rolled film.

Gordy Lee said, "The road was a suicide walk. Right there. This road was about maybe six, seven feet wide. Big enough for a vehicle. And on both sides of the road there was nothing but thick brush. You could have had [NVA] a good three feet inside the wood line and you couldn't have seen him for love or money."

"What about the C/O's decision?" I asked.

"In my opinion," Lee said, "if he was a little more cautious, he wouldn't take us down the trail. The slit trench is a day or two old. The trail is used quite often. You can see the tracks all over it." Lee shook his head.

"He doesn't know his stuff," Lee said. "He ain't been a captain but maybe two weeks, three weeks. And he's got a lot of stuff to learn before he can command a company like Captain Jackson did." Lee paused for a moment.

"That is about the flakiest thing that I have ever done since I've been in the army. And I won't do it again. Come hell or high water, I won't do it again."

"Was there a rebellion today?"

"You might call it that. Back in the world we call it a rebellion. Here, it's just downright refusal. We, the whole company, the C/O says, 'Okay, we're going to walk through it,' the whole company says, 'No, negative.' We've heard of too many companies, too many battalions want to walk the road, and that's why they aren't what they are now. They just got blown away." A helicopter flew over low and blew dirt off the ground into the squad. Lee grimaced and turned his face away from the wind.

"Today we found out what happens when a whole company refuses to do something," he continued.

"What happens?"

"It puts everything in a big fat bind. And I'll tell you, somebodies' heads are going to roll when this whole thing is over with. I don't know whose. It may be mine. But heads are going to roll. And it's about time. You can't do what we did this morning and get away with it. We happened to be lucky. But I'm not going to try that one again. I just don't feel that lucky."

John Schultz spoke up. "We don't know what's going to happen. It doesn't really make any difference. We're just going to refuse to do it. You may be in jail but you won't be dead. He's used to being in charge of a lurp team, that's only six guys, and he wants to run a company like that. And it can't be done. It's impossible."

"What do you think, Dudley?" I asked Carlton Dudley.

"I don't know. If he told me to do it again, and I was walking point, I'd just flat refuse. They can send me to LBJ (Long Binh Jail) and that's all there would be to it. They'd bust me, of course. But that don't mean nothing either. All it is, is money. I'm just in the Army to spend my time and get out. I ain't got no use for the Army."

"I got a wife I'm going to go home and see," said Lee. "And he's pulling stuff like that, he's downright, in my opinion, he's telling me that you *ain't* going home. Because that's what it amounts to."

We thanked the soldiers for talking to us and left. From LZ Wood, we got a ride to Tay Ninh. Going through the PIO shop on our way back to Saigon, I told Lieutenant Tuck in passing that we had a good story and were taking it back. "The generals aren't going to like it," I said. Tuck nodded his head in acknowledgment.

On the flight to Saigon, Kay, Clevenger and I discussed the story.

'I think we've got a winner,' I said.

'Maybe,' Kay said. 'It depends whether Cronkite's used the piece on Captain Jackson.'

'Yeah,' said Clevenger. 'How's anybody going to know why they wouldn't walk the road otherwise?'

'Let's hope they've already put it on the air,' I said.

'If they haven't, this story's going to make all those guys in the company look like a bunch of cowards,' Kay said.

In Saigon, David Miller told us that the Cronkite news had not used the story on Captain Jackson. I typed out a message to advise New York what we had from this latest trip and to promote "Captain Jackson's Heart."

LAURENCE KAY CLEVENGER RETURNED TONIGHT FROM MOST RECENT FIELD TRIP WITH CHARLIE COMPANY (OVERNIGHT) AND UNIQUE STORY OF MINOR REBELLION BY GRUNTS, NNCCOOS AND SOME OFFICERS

AGAINST NEW COMPANY COMMANDER. TROOPS FEEL STRONGLY THAT
RECENT LOSS OF CAPTAIN JACKSON, WHO THEY TRUSTED, AND REPLACE-
MENT BY MILITARILY OBEDIENT NEW CAPTAIN LED TO NEAR DEBACLE
AND QUOTE SUICIDE MISSION UNQUOTE DOWN TWO TRACK ROAD COV-
ERED WITH FRESH ENEMY FOOTPRINTS. NO COMBAT. NATURAL SOUND
OF ROCKET ATTACK ON COMPANY NIGHT POSITION TO BE USED AS DIS-
EMBODIED MEMORY OF NIGHT BEFORE OVER SHOTS OF TROOPS HUMP-
ING. STORY INCLUDES ARGUMENTS BETWEEN NEW CAPTAIN AND
GRUNTS, AND STRONG INTERVIEWS AFTER MISSION WITH TROOPS FROM
SECOND SQUAD. OUR GUYS FEEL STRONGLY THAT REBELLION STORY LESS
MEANINGFUL WITHOUT CAPTAIN JACKSONS HEART IN ADVANCE CAUSE
THATS WAY IT HAPPENED AND THAT WAY TROOPS FELT IT.

APRIL 7, 1970

Colonel Ochs called from Tay Ninh. His voice was strained, urgent. The poor quality of the military phone line made him sound farther away than he was, but there was distress in his voice, unusual tension in it. He chose his words with care, shouting them down the line syllable by syllable.

'We want you to come up and discuss what happened with C Company yesterday,' he said. 'There is a lot more to the story than what you saw. You need to understand the larger picture. Ah, I can't spell it out to you on this line but there are, ah, certain facts you need to know. Ah, very important details.'

'I understand,' I shouted back. The story of the rebellion was already written. The film was due to be shipped soon.

'We would appreciate it if you hold your film until we've discussed the matter.'

'Understood. We will wait until you talk to us,' I promised.

'Thank you. I appreciate that,' Ochs said. 'I'll send transportation. When can you come?'

I said nothing. With the film and narration ready to be shipped to the States, a holdup in Tay Ninh could delay the story getting on the air as much as a day. Timing was crucial. I didn't want to be at the mercy of military transportation back to Saigon.

'If it's all right with you,' I said, 'I'd prefer to meet halfway, at Bien Hoa or Tan Son Nhut, if that's acceptable. Everything would be more simple.'

Ochs did not reply. A roar of static hissed down the line. After a short time, he spoke again.

'We'll meet you at Tan Son Nhut. Hotel Three. Twelve hundred hours. Do you understand?'

'Affirmative. Yes, sir, thank you. We'll be at Hotel Three at Tan Son Nhut at twelve o'clock. I'll bring Mr. Kay and Mr. Clevenger. We'd like you to tell us what happened on-camera. You can give us the big picture if you like.'

'I'll think about that,' he said. 'Over.'

Dave Miller, Kay and Clevenger were listening to my part of the conversation.

'He'll probably try to get you to kill the story,' Miller said. 'He'll argue that it's bad for morale.'

'He says he wants to fill us in on the larger picture,' I said.

'What does he mean by that?' Kay said.

'I don't know. We'll find out.'

'It might be a trick to get us to change the story. You know, something they've made up.'

'I don't think they'd do that,' I said. 'They might twist the facts to suit themselves, but I don't think J.D. would invent a complete lie. He's an honest journalist.'

Another call came in from Tay Ninh. It was one of the enlisted men from the PIO shop, but he would not give his name. He said Lieutenant Tuck had just been relieved as a brigade PIO officer.

'The L-T is gone,' he said. 'They're punishing him for not telling anyone about your story right away.' He said Tuck had waited until the regular morning briefing before bringing up the rebellion story, quoting me as saying, "The generals aren't going to like it." 'The brass went berserk,' he said. 'Major General Roberts, the division commander, knows about it and is furious. Brigade staff is in a panic. Tuck expects to be sent to a rifle platoon in the field. He's already gone. Just thought you guys should know the shit's really hit the fan up here,' the soldier said and hung up.

Miller said, 'I think we should ship the film as it is and update it later if we have to. We can always send an audio tape to Tokyo or Hong Kong and feed it on a music circuit.'

'What the hell's that?' Clevenger asked.

'A fine-quality phone line,' Kay said.

We decided to send the story on the first flight to the United States after we had met with Colonel Ochs.

A cable came in from Russ Bensley of the *Evening News* in New York:

MILLER FOR LAURENCE KAY CLEVENGER HAVE SCREENED WEEKEND SHIPMENT AND GENERALLY OKAY EXCEPT FOR SOME SOUND PROBLEMS STOP MAIN PROBLEM IS LOUD ALMOST OVERRIDING BACKGROUND NOISE STOP SOUNDS LIKE THOUSAND HYPERTHYROID CRICKETS HOGGING MIKE STOP THOUGHT AT FIRST IT WAS EQUIPMENT PROBLEM BUT

SAME SOUND SHOWS UP ON PORTION OF QUARTERINCH DASH JACKSON
READING LETTER TO COLONEL HANNAS STOP COULD YOU BE PICKING
UP INTERFERENCE FROM SOMBODYS ELECTRONIC GEAR QUERY EYE BAF-
FLED STOP BENSLEY

And another:

06191 MILLER FOR LAURENCE KAY CLEVENGER CRONKITERS USED FOUR
MINUTES FIVE SECONDS OF FINE CAPTAIN JACKSONS HEART STOP
WOULD BE INTERESTED TO KNOW FOR TELL PURPOSES IF DIAGNOSIS OF
HEART ATTACK SUBSEQUENTLY CONFIRMED STOP MIXTURE OF ONCAM-
ERA INTERVIEWS AND DISEMBODIED VOICES SEEMS TO BE WORKING
WELL SO LETS KEEP IT UP STOP GIVES THE SERIES A STYLE STOP WOULD
NOT MIND SEEING CORRESPONDENT ONCAMERA ONCE IN A WHILE STOP
NOT PUSHING UNDERSTAND DASH JUST WHENEVER IT SEEMS APPROPRI-
ATE STOP DECKS NOW CLEARED FOR YOUR INCOMING PIECE WHICH WE
EAGERLY AWAIT BENSLEY

At noon, Kay, Clevenger and I rode to the airport. An officer from the
First Cav took us inside the VIP lounge. The room was large and spartan
without rugs or decorations, furnished with 1950s modern French armchairs, tables and sofas. Air-conditioners hummed. Colonel Ochs arrived at
12:15 accompanied by his brigade sergeant major and a captain from his
headquarters staff. Also in attendance were Major Coleman, the division
public information officer, and Captain Rice, the Charlie Company commander who was brought in out of the field. Tall and erect, Ochs shook
hands and introduced the men around him. They addressed us with stiff formality, cool and correct. Coleman, the largest man in the room and normally the most ebullient, was subdued. We sat facing each other: Kay,
Clevenger and I on the couch, the soldiers across from us in chairs.

Ochs asked what we were going to report about the incident. I said we
were calling it a rebellion.

'Is your story written?'

'Yes,' I said.

'Have you run it by New York?' Coleman asked.

'No. They know what it's about, though.'

Ochs moved in his chair but did not speak.

'Jack, I know it's against your code of ethics,' Coleman said, 'but how about reading us what you've written? Just this once? We've been entirely open and honest with you, I think you'll agree. Now we'd like you to do the same for us. At least so we'll know what we're up against.'

I looked at Kay and Clevenger.

Kay shrugged his large shoulders and said, 'Might as well.'

'I think this is a special case,' Clevenger said.

I felt uncomfortable. To read the full written story of a covered news event to the people who took part in it or might be affected by it would make us vulnerable to pressure to change the story before it was broadcast. In ten years as a journalist, I had not done it before. But I also had a responsibility to hear their arguments if they could show the reporting was inaccurate. Or biased. Reluctantly, I got the script from the pocket of my jacket and unfolded the pages. 'I'll trust you not to tell anyone,' I said.

Ochs, Coleman, Rice and the others leaned forward in their seats. Kay and Clevenger sat to the side.

'This first scene took place the day before yesterday,' I said, 'during resupply.' I took a breath and read aloud in a flat voice:

"Charlie Company had been on patrol in the field since March 24, and as the men were being resupplied this time it was becoming apparent that no one knew clearly what they were doing now or what their mission was."

I took another breath and continued.

"The helicopter assigned to bring in food, water and mail disappeared for more than an hour in the middle of the afternoon, angering the leaders of Charlie Company who were anxious to move on and dig in for the night."

Ochs turned his head and looked at Rice for an instant.

"The men were glad to get a hot meal instead of C rations, their normal diet for the three days between resupply. Today, it was ham, stewed tomatoes, sweet potatoes, grapefruit, peaches, tea and Kool Aid."

"Privately, the men were complaining about the seeming lack of organization and coordination Charlie Company was now experiencing since the loss of its former commander, Captain Robert Jackson, and the critical injury of its battalion commander, Lieutenant Colonel Robert Hannas. In the combat and chaos of the past two weeks, two firebases had been fiercely attacked, at least forty American soldiers killed, and the tempo of the fighting in War Zone C had increased considerably."

I looked up and saw Coleman nod his head, listening.

"As the men ate their hot chow, one of their sister companies was in heavy contact nearby, in a battle which would cost seven more American lives.

"'Flaky' was the word heard most often now, a GI expression meaning that the company and the battalion did not seem to be operating as efficiently as before."

Ochs winced. The faces of the others were cold, without expression. I explained that the next sequence was about mail call and was not controversial. 'I think we can skip this part,' I said.

'Go on, Jack,' Coleman said.

"By the time Charlie Company got its orders to move out, it was already an hour later than the troops normally begin setting up their defensive positions for the night. All along the column they were complaining about 'things getting flaky.'"

"The men pride themselves on their professionalism as soldiers, their cleverness in ambushing and killing the enemy, and the extremely low number of casualties they have taken themselves. The first signs of concern were becoming evident."

I looked up from the script and explained to Ochs and the group that the time now shifted to the following morning.

"The next day, as 2d Platoon moves out, the memory of the previous night's accident—and near disaster—is on most of the men's minds."

'Here I've suggested that the producers play the audio tape of the incoming explosions,' I said. Ochs looked puzzled.

"It was explained later that an artillery battery fired seven shells dangerously close to Charlie Company's position. Even though the company called a cease-fire throughout the entire area of operation, the shells kept coming in. To other observers, who had experienced more severe shelling in Vietnam years ago, it sounded frighteningly familiar to an enemy rocket attack."

'Why wasn't that reported to me?' Ochs said, looking at Rice.

'I definitely reported it,' Rice said. His tone was defensive. 'I checked every gun unit in the AO. It was a 105 battery. He said he stopped when he received my check-fire.'

'I don't think we heard about it from battalion,' said the staff captain.

'I see,' Ochs said. 'Carry on, Mr. Laurence.'

"The new company commander receives orders to move his men nearly a mile this morning, the plan calling for them to be picked up by helicopters to make a combat assault. The orders also say to move down a road, something the veterans in Charlie Company had been taught by their former commander never to do.

"Second platoon—in the lead—refuses to walk down the road. To them, it is too

"flaky"—too risky, too much of an opportunity for the North Vietnamese to ambush them.

"The men hit the ground as a shell—an American shell—crashes in nearby. Second platoon turns back, to argue against taking the road. One or two have begun to panic."

'Here I've suggested they use the interviews we did at the time with men from 2d Squad.' Ochs looked uncomfortable, somber.

"But Captain Rice has received orders from higher up in the command to move down the road. He is confused by the rebellion of his men.

"Even the officers are in disagreement, trying to work out a safer way to complete their mission. No one in the company is quite sure what to do when more than one hundred men—almost all of them combat veterans and normally well-disciplined—refuse to obey.

"Captain Rice, who has already served one tour in Vietnam and is an experienced officer himself, decides to exercise his authority. He takes his own small command group and starts down the road—alone and on point.

"'If an old man like me can walk point,' he says, trying to lead his men, 'you guys can follow.' But no one follows. . . ."

'Here we pause to show the faces of the soldiers who do not follow.' I looked at Rice. He sat alone behind the others leaning over with his arms folded across his legs and his head down.

"Suddenly, as the captain stops along the road, a solution appears. A helicopter pilot spots a possible landing zone closer to Charlie Company's position, about three hundred yards down the road in the other direction.

"Captain Rice changes his orders. The rebellion begins to recede, and reluctantly Charlie Company moves out down the road. The men are angry now, and afraid. Three hundred yards down an open road, with thick bush on both sides, is long enough—if the enemy is waiting—to ambush an entire company.

"The dirt road is covered with fresh footprints of North Vietnamese sandals.

"But the enemy is not waiting, and second platoon, in the lead, reaches its destination, and begins clearing the brush around two bomb craters for the helicopters to come in and take them out.

"The mission accomplished, Captain Rice calls a conference among his platoon leaders and the other officers, and a discussion about discipline under orders. He says he hopes he did the right thing."

I looked up from the script at Colonel Ochs. 'At this point,' I said, 'we show the discussion between Captain Rice and his officers, and then some interviews we did later with 2d Squad.' I didn't want to tell him what the troops said, particularly Gordy Lee, lest their strong remarks get them in trouble.

'Is there any more or is that it?' Coleman asked.

I had written a strongly worded conclusion and didn't want them to hear it. But there was no way out, other than to lie to them. I read quickly, without inflection:

"If there is another dimension to the minor rebellion of Charlie Company, it is that a hundred experienced soldiers—most of whom believe in the biggest picture of all, the political reasons for the Vietnam War—veteran soldiers who are not afraid of combat, normally brave and obedient men—would not walk down a road that, to them, was symbolic of the way 40,000 other GIs had gone before."

No one spoke. I did not look up for a few moments, just folded the script and put it back in a pocket. Ochs, Coleman, Rice and the others looked at one another without speaking. Their faces were hard and angry, warrior looks.

Ochs spoke first. 'I'm not sure I would characterize what happened 'a rebellion,' as you do, Mr. Laurence. I think a more accurate description of the incident would be a, ah, temporary reluctance to follow the order. The men didn't actually rebel, as you said in your report. The order was changed before an actual rebellion took place.' He thought for a moment. 'You know, rebellion is a very, ah, *emotive* word, much stronger than what happened. Rebellion has a connotation to it that implies an insurrection, an uprising.'

'Well, I did tone it down in the final paragraph by calling it a 'minor rebellion,' I said.

'Yes, I appreciate that,' Ochs said.

'*God damn it*, Jack, we don't think it's fair to use the word rebellion at all,' Coleman said, angry. 'You make it sound like a God damned revolt!'

'Well, J.D., it stands by itself,' I said. 'When people see the film of what happened they can make up their own minds whether it was a rebellion or a mutiny or a temporary reluctance to obey orders.'

'You know damn well it depends on how you set it up in your narration,' he said. 'People are going to react to what you say on the film. And how it's edited. That's what matters.'

'Well, we think it *was* a rebellion. So do the troops.'

'Mr. Laurence,' Ochs said, 'there were other factors bearing on the situation. The reason for the order to move along the road to the pickup zone is that a B-52 strike was about to be delivered to that area and we had to get the company out of there in a hurry.'

This was a surprise.

"One side of the target box was fifteen hundred meters from the company's position," Ochs said. He turned to his aide, the staff captain, and asked for his briefing map. "See here. Anything closer than fifteen hundred meters is within the margin of error for an arc-light."

'Why so close?' Kay asked.

"We were expecting an attack on Firebase Blonden at any time. All the brigade's attention was focused on stopping that attack."

'When were the strikes scheduled?' I said.

"One at 10:45, then another at 1100," the staff captain said.

'Your map has got the times wrong,' I said.

'So it has,' the captain said.

'And this location,' I said, pointing to C Company's position on the map. 'It's not correct.' Usually, the brigade commander's war map was a model of precision.

'If you ordered the arc-light, you must have known it was on the way,' I said. 'Why didn't you move the company earlier?'

'I don't order B-52 strikes. I hear about them from higher up. They didn't tell me about this one until the morning. It was too late for C Company to walk out of there. We had to lift them out in a hurry.'

Kay spoke. 'Why didn't anyone tell Captain Rice what the problem was, why he had to go down the road?'

"I have to admit it," Ochs said, "we fouled up at this end. There was a definite breakdown in passing information down to lower levels. But it must be realized that there were strong indications that there was about to be an attack launched on Blonden. All units in the area were involved in stopping that attack."

The sergeant major spoke for the first time. "Sometimes you have to throw caution to the wind. We had to get the men out of there quickly. You can't go around explaining every little detail to every soldier who's got a question or you'd never get anything done. This *is* still the Army."

'We heard a B-52 strike while the men were clearing the LZ,' I said. 'It was very close. A couple of clicks.'

'Are you certain?' Ochs said.

'Yes. The time was 11:07. I wrote it in my notebook.' Rice, Kay and Clevenger confirmed the strike.

'I wasn't told about that,' Ochs said, puzzled. (Not he, nor I, nor anyone in

War Zone C knew about Nixon's ultrasecret bombing of Cambodia. It had been underway for more than a year but few people in Vietnam knew, even in the U.S. military.)

'The whole foul-up was a matter of only about thirty minutes,' the staff captain said. 'If the company had been able to get out of there a half hour sooner, everything would have been okay.'

Ochs said, "One of the reasons we're so sensitive about this matter is that this story reflects not only on Charlie Company but also the battalion, the brigade and the division."

'I appreciate that,' I said. 'It's not our intention to criticize the division.'

'We're not even criticizing the company,' Kay said. 'We're just telling it like it is.'

"No you're not," Coleman said. "This is just a microcosm. But you're going to give the impression that one platoon's reluctance reflects on the entire division."

'That's not correct.'

"Why didn't you check with brigade at Tay Ninh to get the reasons for ordering the men down the road?" Coleman was furious, his temper gone. "Jack, I hate to say this but your responsibility as a journalist is *impugned*. You should have tried to get the big picture. The story should be seen in the context of the old company commander leaving and the new one having problems."

'Well, I thought that was made clear,' I said. 'I didn't check with brigade because there was nothing to check. How were we supposed to know about the B-52 strike?'

"Look," he said. "When we let you guys into our bedroom, you have to understand that all kinds of things happen. And you're seeing everything that happens, the bad with the good. And we want to be able to handle the bad in our own way. We want the dirty linen to come out clean."

Astonished, I didn't know what to say.

'J.D., really, you can't expect us to do PR for you.'

'I damn well can. When we give the kind of cooperation we've given you, you bet we can.' His face was red.

I turned to Colonel Ochs. 'Would you be willing to go on-camera and explain why the company was ordered to go down the road? Give us the big picture?'

Ochs looked at Coleman. 'What's your advice, J.D.?'

Coleman thought for a moment. "I don't think it's in your best interests to go on-camera," he said. "There's a chance that this thing will blow over. There may be a way to smooth things out." Coleman looked at me. "Here's the situation. The public forgets. No problem. But it's within house the generals don't forget. They never forget. Reputations are affected. Promotions are affected."

So that's it, I thought. *They want us to cover up the rebellion because it will hurt their chances for promotion. No wonder they've gone to all this trouble to meet us.*

'When the four-stars in the Pentagon see your story,' the sergeant major said, 'they'll go into orbit. They'll come down on General Roberts like a ton of bricks. And he'll come down on us twice as hard for making him look bad.'

'A whole lot more is at stake than the reputation of just one company,' Coleman said. 'You have to understand the way the Army works.'

'Yes,' I said, 'I understand. Will we be able to go back to Charlie Company?' I said.

"That's up to General Roberts," Coleman said. "It's his decision."

'We've heard that Lieutenant Tuck has been relieved,' I said. 'Can you tell us why?'

'How do you know that?' Ochs said.

'We got a call,' I said.

"We have to deal with these matters on an urgent basis," Coleman said, "just like we deal with the enemy."

'But Tuck isn't your enemy.'

'*You* may not think so,' Coleman said.

"I didn't hear about this incident until 7:30 this morning," Ochs said.

'But he's a perfectly responsible public information officer. Very professional. He helped us a lot over the past couple of weeks.'

"Just like Captain Jackson," Coleman said, "we like to meet the enemy on *our* terms."

The meeting ended. It had lasted ninety minutes. I told them we would amend the story to take into account the information about the B-52 strike. The mood was still tense.

"Good luck with the new company commander," Rice said to us with a bitter smile.

The film was shipped without change. Late at night, back at the bureau in Saigon, I sent a cable to New York:

07235 FIRST CAV DIVISION GENERALS AND STAFF GRAVELY CONCERNED ABOUT OUR STORY CHARLIE COMPANY'S REBELLION AND APPLYING STRONG PRESSURE TO CHANGE TONE OF NARRATION. TODAY, BRIGADE COMMANDER, COLONEL WILLIAM OCHS, DIVISION PPIIOO, MAJOR J.D. COLEMAN, THEIR AIDES AND SERGEANT MAJOR, AND, SURPRISINGLY, CHARLIE COMPANY'S NEW COMMANDER, CAPTAIN AL RICE, CHOPPERED OUT OF FIELD IN WAR ZONE C TO SAIGON AT NOON FOR DYNAMIC HOUR AND HALF ATTEMPT TO GET US TO DELETE WORD REBELLION BEFORE WE SHIPPED FILM. WE OFFERED TO INTERVIEW COL. OCHS ABOUT LARGER PICTURE OF YESTERDAY'S EVENTS, BUT HE DECIDED IN LAST HOUR BEFORE WE SHIPPED STORY THAT HE WOULD NOT COMMENT ON CAMERA. CCBBSS POLITELY EXPLAINED WE WERE STICKING WITH STORY AS FILMED AND REPORTED. DIVISION GENERALS MOST CONCERNED ABOUT PENTAGON GENERALS REACTION. BRIGADE PPIIOO ALREADY RELIEVED AND TRANSFERRED BACK TO INFANTRY FOR NOT INFORMING HIS HIGHER UPS ABOUT OUR STORY SOONER THAN HE DID. WE TOLD HIM, LT. RICHARD TUCK, YESTERDAY WHEN WE CAME OUT OF FIELD AT 1400 HOURS. HE BROUGHT IT UP AT THIS MORNING'S BRIGADE BRIEF-ING, 17 HOURS LATER, TOUCHING OFF MILITARY TRAUMA THAT IMMEDI-ATELY REACHED DIVISION LEVEL AND LED TO TODAY'S EXTRAORDINARY CONFERENCE IN SAIGON, TUCK'S LOSS OF A JOB, AND CAPTAIN RICE'S BELIEF THAT HE, TOO, WILL BE RELIEVED.

OFF CAMERA AT TODAY'S CONFERENCE, BRIGADE COMMANDER OCHS EXPLAINED THAT SOMEONE MADE SERIOUS MISTAKE IN NOT INFORMING GROUND TROOPS OF URGENCY TO MOVE DOWN WIDE ROAD. BUT, HE AND AIDES EXPLAINED THAT TROOPS WERE BEING RUSHED TO NEAREST LLZZ TO GET THEM OUT OF B-52 STRIKE IMPACT AREA. (STRIKE, THEY SAY, WAS CANCELED.) IF TROOPS HAD KNOWN THESE FACTS, THEY BELIEVE, THEY WOULD HAVE WILLINGLY OBEYED ORDERS AND THEIR QUOTE TEMPORARY RELUCTANCE TO FOLLOW CAPTAIN RICE UNQUOTE WOULD HAVE BEEN AVOIDED. THEY SUGGEST YOU TAG OUR STORY WITH THAT.

WE SUSPECT CONTRADICTIONS DUE TO FACT THAT TROOPS WERE FINALLY RUSHED TOWARD IMPACT AREA STEAD OF AWAY FROM IT AND B-52 STRIKE DID GO ON IN ALMOST SAME TIME ABORTED STRIKE WAS SCHEDULED. BOMBS FELL NEARBY DURING EXTRACTION OF TROOPS. TIME 1107 HOURS. ALSO NOTICED, AND AIDES ADMITTED, ERRORS IN

TIME OF STRIKE AND ABORTED STRIKE ON COLONEL'S USUALLY IMPEC-
CABLE WAR MAP.

OTHER MILITARY QUOTES TODAY, NOT FOR AIR BUT INFORMATIVELY,
WERE QUOTE SOMETIMES YOU HAVE TO THROW CAUTION TO THE
WINDS UNQUOTE. ALSO QUOTE WHEN WE (THE FIRST CAV) LET YOU
INTO OUR BEDROOM, WE EXPECT THE DIRTY LINEN TO COME OUT
CLEAN UNQUOTE. WHEN I BEGGED THEM NOT TO RELIEVE THE BRIGADE
PPIIOO, WHO WAS MOST COOPERATIVE IN OUR EFFORTS PAST TWO
WEEKS, WE WERE TOLD QUOTE LIKE CAPTAIN JACKSON SAID, WE DON'T
WANT TO FIGHT ON THE ENEMY'S TERMS UNQUOTE.

DON'T WANT TO SOIL LINEN ANY MORE THAN IT ALREADY IS BUT
HONESTLY BELIEVE WHAT TROOPS, NNCCOO'S AND PLATOON LEADERS
SAID, WALKING DOWN THAT ROAD WAS CRAZY. NEW COMPANY COM-
MANDER WAS TOLD TO OBEY ORDERS AND DID NOT QUESTION THEM.
MORE EXPERIENCED MEN, PARTICULARLY GRUNTS, REBELLED.

WE ASKED IF WE COULD CONTINUE TO GO OUT WITH CHARLIE COM-
PANY AND WERE TOLD QUOTE THAT WILL BE DECIDED BY THE COM-
MANDING GENERAL UNQUOTE. EYE WAS TOLD THAT BY DIVISION PPIIOO
I'VE KNOWN SINCE SIXTY-FIVE. HE AND OTHER OLD FRIENDS FROM THE
CAV HAND-PICKED CHARLIE COMPANY, SECOND OF THE SEVENTH, AS
ONE OF THEIR FINEST UNITS, AND SENT US OUT WITH THEM ORIGI-
NALLY.

YOU MAY EXPECT HEAVY FLAK FROM PENTAGON TOO. WHATEVER
THEY SAY, CHARLIE COMPANY REALLY IS ONE OF FINEST AND MOST FAS-
CINATING GROUP OF SOLDIERS WE'VE MET. WE STILL WANT TO STAY
WITH THEM THE FULL TWO MONTHS. SO, I SUSPECT, WOULD DANA
HAVE WISHED. LAURENCE

The news was coming in from Cambodia: Dana Stone and Sean Flynn
had failed to return to Phnom Penh the night before. They had last been
seen traveling on motorcycles near North Vietnamese and Khmer Rouge
lines east of the capital. They were presumed to have been captured.

APRIL 8, 1970

Stone and Flynn were truly missing. Two days after riding into the no-man's-land of eastern Cambodia, they had not come out. Everyone supposed they had been captured. Details of what had happened came in from Phnom Penh. Other journalists who had seen them the morning they disappeared said they were riding motorcycles along a deserted stretch of Route 1 about ten miles from the South Vietnamese border. Flynn led the way, Stone following at a distance. Nothing else was on the road, no vehicles, no one walking. Like everyone else, they knew the North Vietnamese were in the area and had blocked the road to stop traffic from entering their zone of operations. The two Americans drove around the barrier and went into the forbidden area. At that point, Route 1 cuts across the flat farmland of Svey Rieng Province in a long straight line connecting Phnom Penh with Saigon. On a map, the territory juts into South Vietnam and forms the outline of the head, neck and beak of a large bird. Journalists and military people called it the "Parrot's Beak." Twenty miles north of it, just across the border, was Tay Ninh City.

Several foreign reporters who had ventured into the eastern Cambodian countryside in recent days had been detained by Viet Cong and North Vietnamese troops but released without harm after a few hours. In some cases, the North Vietnamese gave interviews and allowed their pictures to be taken. When they got back to Phnom Penh, the captured journalists were instant celebrities. Dramatic stories of their few hours with the enemy were filed. Other reporters gathered around them at the swimming pool and bar of the Hotel Royale, the journalists' camp, to listen to their stories. All of those who had been captured were European or Asian. By driving into the danger area, Stone and Flynn appeared to be trying to become the first American journalists to be taken and released by the other side. They rode rented Honda motorcycles and wore civilian clothes: floppy bush hats, short-sleeved shirts and jeans, still cameras around their necks. With his long hair and mustache, Flynn's appearance reminded other journalists of the Peter

Fonda character in the film *Easy Rider*. When they teased him about it, Flynn laughed and said the danger made him feel more like "queasy rider."

Trying to get captured and released was an option most journalists in Phnom Penh had considered. The risks were great but so were the rewards. A successful venture would give them reputations as aggressive young reporters willing to risk their lives for a good story. Home office executives and foreign editors would be impressed. Careers would be enhanced. The more daring members of the press corps drove their cars or jeeps to the end of the area of Cambodian government control and waited to be picked up by Communist soldiers, expecting to be released by the end of the day. What they did not know, and were slow to realize, was that the North Vietnamese policy of friendly accommodation toward captured journalists had changed. The initial polite hospitality turned to cold, impersonal hostility. The North Vietnamese began to hand captured foreign reporters and photographers over to the Khmer Rouge.

On April 5, three French journalists were seized on Route 1 and taken into the bush on foot. Their rented car was burned and left behind. The next morning, another French reporter and two members of a Japanese television crew who were traveling together were taken prisoner at the same spot where Stone and Flynn disappeared a few hours later. Their car was left beside the road, empty. None of those six non-American journalists had come out.

In Saigon, we worried.

'They'll come back,' a friend said, 'you'll see.'

'Oh, sure,' another said. 'They're just working on their stories.'

'Yeah, don't worry. They'll make it. They always do.'

Stone and Flynn had worked together often and stories of their adventures in the field were becoming legend. Years earlier, during a small unit action in Vietnam, they had come under fire with a U.S. Special Forces team made up mostly of ethnic Nung mercenaries. The team leader, an American soldier, had been seriously wounded and was pinned down ahead of them. The Nungs did nothing to help him. Flynn decided to take the initiative. Crouching above the ground, he shouted at the Nungs to follow, stretched his right arm out behind him and waved them on. Then he stood up and ran forward to help the wounded Special Forces soldier. It was a daring act, full of risk. Bullets were buzzing overhead at a rapid rate. Flynn could easily have been shot. At the beginning of the charge, at the moment of most danger,

Stone lifted his camera and snapped a picture of Flynn waving the Nungs forward. Other accounts later confirmed that Flynn's action saved the American's life. The episode secured his bond with the Special Forces. But in Saigon later, at Frankie's House, his friends teased him about the photograph.

'Hey, Sean, tell us again how you saved the Special Forces guy,' Page said.

'Yeah, c'mon, Flynn, give us the play-by-play.'

'I hear they're gonna put you in for a medal.'

'Yeah, Distinguished Acting Star.' Everyone laughed, including Flynn.

'Have you sent that snap to your agent yet?'

Stone teased him more than anyone. 'The only reason I took that shot was I thought you were gonna stop one and I wanted a picture like Capa got in Spain.'

'Why didn't you just ask him to fall backward?'

'He'd have done it, right Flynn?'

'Yeah, didn't they teach you that in acting school?'

Flynn smiled in embarrassment but did not defend himself. 'Aw, you guys are just jealous . . .' was the most he said.

Now, news of their release in Cambodia was expected at any time. Kay and I consoled each another with fantasies of what was happening behind the lines.

'I can just see Dana debating small unit tactics with some NVA major,' Kay said, laughing.

'Who would be teaching who?' I said.

'Or Flynn trying to get out on one of their operations, to film it.'

'Yeah, probably against Charlie Company.'

'Oh, man, wouldn't that be something?' Kay said, eyes alight. 'If Dana and Sean came out with footage of the NVA in action? Man, oh man, what a hell of a documentary that would make.'

In Los Angeles, Tim Page was interviewed for a story in *Newsday* being written by Perry Deane Young, a friend of the missing two. "Flynn always wanted to get captured," Page said. "He used to drive his motorcycle into those [Vietnamese rubber] plantations looking for VC to capture him."

A reporter for the Canadian Broadcasting Company, William Cunningham, told me later that he had been with Stone and Flynn at the roadblock in the hour before they disappeared. Several journalists were standing around the barrier waiting to see what happened farther along the road. Cambodian villagers came out to them and said that they had seen Vietnamese troops coming their way, that they were in danger. All of the journalists except Flynn decided to drive back toward Phnom Penh to safety. According to Cunningham, who had been captured and released earlier that week, Stone wanted to go back to the safety of the rear with them. He argued with Flynn about the wisdom of getting captured.

"I've got a wife waiting for me back there," Stone said. "I don't want to spend the next two years rotting away in some POW camp." Cunningham said they were still arguing when he and the others left. Stone remained with Flynn.

Kevin Buckley, a reporter for *Newsweek* magazine, also saw them that morning. According to him, Stone and Flynn had been on a reconnaissance down Route 1 a few hours earlier. They drove past the roadblock where the journalists had disappeared the day before and continued several hundred yards into North Vietnamese–held territory. Then they turned around and rode back to a restaurant where Buckley and other journalists waited. At about midday, a Cambodian colonel informed them that the Japanese TV crew and the Frenchman had just been captured. Stone said he and Flynn had been in the same place where it happened.

"We stuck our heads in the lion's mouth and got out safely," Stone said, according to Buckley.

"It can be a bad trip out there," Flynn said.

"I don't want to get shot and I don't want to spend two years in jail," Stone said. Then he smiled and said, "But I *do* want to be rich and famous."

In Los Angeles, Page recalled Dana's penchant for practical jokes. "Yeah," he said, "the first morning, Stone will stick his finger in some [NVA] colonel's egg and that will be it."

Perry Deane Young concluded his *Newsday* story: "A wire service friend says he will be working the cable desk all night 'and I'll call you as soon as we get anything new on Flynn and Stone. But, listen, man, I wouldn't worry . . .'

"'Don't worry?' I laughed. 'I wish to hell I were with them.'"

Correspondents who covered the war had a code of conduct that they always understated the dangers they faced and the risks they took. It didn't matter whether they were writing a story or telling one; they did not talk about their own courage, nor did they suggest it. Boasting in any form was considered tasteless egotism, unworthy of respect. It was enough to be covering the war. Everyone knew what that involved. No matter that some reporters rarely went into the field to report the fighting while others virtually lived out there; that many stayed in the safety of Saigon and played tennis at the Cercle Sportif while others risked their lives routinely to get stories in the field. Anyone who bragged about his exploits, no matter what he had done, was not cool. The code was never spoken, never defined, never taught. A new arrival to Vietnam learned (or did not) by observing the behavior of old hands, veterans who had picked it up in their early days from those who were there before them. And so, presumably, it had always been, since the days of the Roman Empire and the wonderfully self-deprecating poetry of Horace, and long before him, to Homer's time and earlier. You went to a war to learn, and one thing you learned was that the virtue that best accompanies courage is humility.

So when news of the disappearance of Stone and Flynn reached Saigon, the only way their friends knew how to discuss it was within the boundaries of the code. They played it down, joked about it, laughed over it, even ignored it. Stone and Flynn, they believed, would surely come back in good health with fantastic stories to tell and the same self-effacing nonchalance they took with them into the lion's mouth. They had to come out. Why worry? Alternatives were not seriously considered. That Stone and Flynn might be locked in bamboo cages and exhibited like zoo animals for VC and Khmer Rouge cadre to look at, that they might be starved and terrorized and tortured into submission—the idea was too painful to contemplate. Any of us could have been with them on the road.

Rigorous efforts began at once to obtain their release. The Communists had to be persuaded not to kill them or the six other missing journalists. Given the time Flynn and Stone had spent with the U.S. military, they were in danger of being executed, even though both opposed the political motives that started the war and kept it going. Friends, colleagues and families of the journalists contacted organizations and individuals who might be able to influence the North Vietnamese, NLF and Khmer Rouge. Left-wing and antiwar political connections were pressed. At the top of the list was Prince Sihanouk in Beijing. Phone calls were made, letters written, discreet inquiries pressed, telegrams solicited. An informal network of friends and colleagues sprang up and worked to save the journalists' lives.

By the end of the day, April 8, a European camera crew from NBC News had disappeared. Now ten were missing.

Louise Stone traveled back and forth between Phnom Penh and Saigon trying to gather information about her husband and the others—sending cables, meeting diplomats, writing letters, making phone calls, interviewing journalists, working with obsessive dedication. By the time she returned to Saigon and the communal flat on Tu Do Street, she was exhausted. Her eyes, normally calm and bright, were dark and nervous, and there were blue-black sacs beneath them. She came to the CBS office at the Caravelle, and after we talked she asked me to come with her to the flat for her first night back in Saigon.

'I'm scared,' she said. 'It was all right when Dana was in the field and I was on my own. I knew he'd always come back, sooner or later. But it's different now. I don't know where he is. I don't feel like I've got it together anymore. It's like I'm not a whole person. You know? Like part of *me* is missing.'

We sat in the flat and talked and drank whisky. An hour or two before dawn, we unrolled a couple of sleeping bags and camped on the floor. Before she put out the light, Louise produced a revolver and handed it to me.

'It's Dana's,' she said. 'He kept it at the bottom of his pack.'

'I never knew Dana carried a gun,' I said.

'Well, not always, but some of the time.'

'He never talked about it.' I recalled that Dana protected insects, never killed them.

'He worried that he might get in a situation where he had to use it. To save his own life. Or somebody else's.'

I said nothing.

'I don't know how it works. Will you show me?'

I showed her how to load the revolver and engage the safety.

'Don't point it at somebody unless you're going to fire it at them,' I said, giving it back to her.

'Thanks. I don't want to shoot anybody. I'll just feel better knowing I have the protection. Just in case.'

Louise turned the pistol over in her hand with the barrel down, checked the safe switch, put it under her pillow and turned out the light.

APRIL 9, 1970

Kay, Clevenger and I flew to Tay Ninh to meet Colonel Ochs and his staff at brigade headquarters. Ochs was in a cordial mood, friendly again, no sign of irritation from the argumentative meeting at Tan Son Nhut two days earlier. He said he was happy to let us continue our work with Charlie Company. The report on the rebellion had not been broadcast yet. We flew on to Phuoc Vinh and saw J. D. Coleman at division headquarters. He was not worried about the rebellion incident. Everything would depend, he said, on how the generals in the Pentagon reacted when they saw it. Back in Saigon at the end of the day, I sent a message to New York summarizing our meetings in War Zone C.

BENSLEY TODAY'S DISCUSSIONS WITH FIRST CAV OFFICERS AT BRIGADE AND DIVISION LEVEL INDICATE THEY WAITING TO HEAR PENTAGON'S REACTION TO REBELLION STORY BUT ARE CONFIDENT THEY CAN SURVIVE FLAK. CAPTAIN RICE HAS RETURNED TO FIELD AND IS STILL IN COMMAND OF CHARLIE COMPANY. CCBBSS INFORMED THAT BEDROOM DOOR STILL OPEN, DIRTY LINEN AND ALL, AND WE AS WELCOME NOW AS WE WERE MARCH TWENTIETH. EVERYTHING BUDDY-BUDDY AGAIN, AT LEAST UNTIL STORY AIRS AND THEY HEAR FROM WASHINGTON.

THEY STICK TO STORY THAT URGENCY TO GET OUT OF B FIFTY-TWO AREA REASON FOR LACK OF COMMUNICATION TO TROOPS AND NOT UNCOMMON IN TIMES OF WAR. EYE NOW BELIEVE THAT FIRST STRIKE WAS ABORTED BUT WILL DOUBLE CHECK WITH AIR FORCE AND ADVISE WITHIN TWELVE HOURS.

NO ONE AT BRIGADE OR BATTALION LEVEL CERTAIN THAT SUNDAY NIGHT INCOMING WAS ARTILLERY OR ROCKETS. BEST SOURCE, WHO WAS WOUNDED DURING RECENT ROCKET ATTACK, AN HONEST OFFICER, THINKS IT MORE LIKELY CHARLIE COMPANY HIT BY ENEMY ROCKETS THAN FRIENDLY ARTILLERY, BASED ON OUR DESCRIPTION.

CAPTAIN JACKSON HAS HAD FIRST EEKKGG, DOCTORS ORDERED

ANOTHER, AND WE CHECKING MEDICAL ANALYSIS. JACKSON APPEARED
HEALTHY AND ROBUST YESTERDAY AT FIRST ASSIGNMENT AS NEW COM-
MANDER OF DIVISION HEADQUARTERS COMPANY.

PLEASE DO NOT MAKE OUR TRIBULATIONS PUBLIC AS SUSPECT
THERE'S STILL CHANCE TO KEEP SERIES GOING, EVEN IF ROAD GETS
ROUGHER.

The Air Force confirmed that one of its B-52 missions was aborted on
April 6 in the area where C Company was on the ground. The reason for the
cancellation was the proximity of ground troops to the target. A second B-52
strike took place fifteen minutes later just outside the danger area. That
might have been the bombing we heard shortly before Charlie Company
was lifted off the road. I sent another cable to New York suggesting a tag, a
few lines of voice-over by the anchor to follow the rebellion story:

HIGH RANKING OFFICERS OF THE FIRST CAVALRY DIVISION EXPLAINED
LATER THAT CHARLIE COMPANY WAS ORDERED TO MOVE DOWN ROAD
BECAUSE OF AN URGENT COMBAT SITUATION IN THE AREA. TROOPS HAD
TO BE EVACUATED IMMEDIATELY TO GET AWAY FROM SCHEDULED B-52
STRIKES THAT MORNING. ORDERS WERE ISSUED TO COMPANY WITHOUT
EXPLANATION DUE TO URGENCY OF MISSION, A COMMON PRACTICE
ACCORDING TO MILITARY OFFICIALS, UNDER COMBAT CONDITIONS.
THEY BELIEVE THAT INCIDENT WAS ONLY A TEMPORARY RELUCTANCE
TO MOVE, THAT TROOPS FINALLY OBEYED THEIR ORDERS, AND MISSION
WAS ACCOMPLISHED.

An incoming cable from New York had been sent the day before:

08125 MILLER FOR LAURENCE KAY CLEVENGER HAVE JUST SCREENED
REBELLION STOP WOW EXCLAIMER BENSLEY

April 10, 1970

The telephone rang in room C-2 before breakfast.

'You've got a couple of cables from New York,' the voice said without
greeting or introduction. Coming awake, I recognized it as Dave Miller. I

could see him through the window of my hotel room sitting in the CBS News office just across the square. 'Want to hear them?' he said.

'Yeah, sure.' I was still half asleep.

'Here's the first one. From Bensley. Cronkite used your rebellion story last night.'

'What's it say?'

'The slug is oh-nine-one-nine-one,' Miller said, and continued, "MILLER FOR LAURENCE KAY CLEVENGER CONFIRMING CRONKITERS USED SIX MINUTES FORTY OF REBELS STOP KAY AND CLEVENGER CREDITED BY SUPER BENSLEY."

'Good of them to give Keith and Jimmy a credit.'

'They *never* give credits to camera crews.'

'Sometimes,' I said, recalling Wilson and Funk.

'There's another one. Want me to read it?'

'Please.'

Miller read, "09192 LAURENCE CHARLIE COMPANY REBELLION FIVE MIN-UTES BENTI MORNING NEWS AND SEVEN MINUTES TEN CRONKITE DRAWING HUZZAHS FROM ALL HERE TONIGHT STOP CONGRATULATIONS FOR EXTRAORDI-NARILY SENSITIVE REPORT TO YOU KEITH JIMMY AND ANY OTHERS INVOLVED THIS UNIQUE JOURNALISTIC EFFORT REGARDS MANNING."

'Manning, huh?'

'The man himself.' Gordon Manning was vice president of CBS News, second in command to Richard Salant, the president.

'Guess they liked it.'

'Are you kidding? They *loved* it.'

'I'll go wake Keith and Jimmy. See you a little later. Anything going on?'

'No it's quiet. When are you going back up?'

'Probably tomorrow. Wait for the Pentagon to react.'

At breakfast in the Continental garden, Kay and Clevenger read the cables from New York.

'I hope they send us a kine,' Kay said.

'Yeah,' said Clevenger, 'I want to hear what the sound's like.'

'Probably wall-to-wall crickets,' said Kay, smiling.

'I wonder if there's such a thing as a cricket filter.'

'Why don't you invent one?'

'Yeah, a one-way ticket to the Mojave Desert.'

We learned later that the story had been introduced on the air by Harry

Reasoner, who was sitting in for Walter Cronkite. When the film was over, Reasoner tagged it:

> Later, high-ranking First Cavalry officers told Laurence that Charlie Company was ordered to go down the road in order to move quickly out of the way of an impending B-52 strike. The officers added there was no time to explain why to the soldiers, because of the urgency of the mission.

That was it. No judgments. No analysis. No comment. And no immediate reaction from the Pentagon.

The congratulatory cable from Manning suggested that CBS News executives were happy enough with our work. It seemed like a good time to suggest an hour broadcast on C Company to the powers that be. I wrote a memo to Ernest Leiser, executive producer of *Special Reports*. Leiser had been a *Stars and Stripes* reporter in World War II.

> It has taken us, so far, about three weeks to produce our first meaningful story from Charlie Company, 2/7, First Cavalry Division, a crack unit handpicked by the division staff for us to cover. Fortunately, the company's men turn out to be fairly representative (I am guessing), and not unlike most other units we might find in the field. They include a few RA's, but most are draftees, and come from all parts of the country. Most of the kids we've talked to (they average about 20 years-old) dislike Army life, are extremely cautious about being killed or walking into an ambush, joke and jive among themselves, fight with one another occasionally, and love to talk to us. Keith, Jimmy and I—while we've practically become part of second platoon by now —have become the butt of many cracks for not carrying weapons and using C4 (a dangerous explosive) to cook our meals, when they say it's too volatile and dangerous to carry around.
>
> I am aware of the fine hour-long broadcasts on the inner details of an American soldier's life in Vietnam already filmed. "Anderson Platoon" and Gene Jones' "Face of War" were my favorites. But we believe we can get closer to the men, bring out their deepest feelings (if they're aware of them), and give CBS News a more truthful (perhaps less impressionistic) and as emotionally powerful story, fully produced by CBS News. I am not certain such an effort would appear to be oriented toward the current withdrawal of

American forces, because no one in the Cav deludes himself about being sent home before all other infantry divisions have left. It is still very much of a war for Charlie Company and the rest of the Cav.

I don't know if you've seen our work to date, but it includes five visits in the field with them, one dramatic incident, three group interviews, Mail Call, resupply, two combat assaults, card games, working, patrolling and a number of taped interviews about personal feelings. Most of the draftees believe in fighting the war; some are emotionally fierce and unforgiving toward wounded and captured enemy soldiers. There are, at the same time, a smaller number of soldiers who oppose the war, but are unwilling to oppose the draft. And so they serve, reluctantly.

There is so much personal activity, emotional drama and some suspense that go on in the company that I don't remember seeing them in news films, but only in serious books and articles, and (as you know from personal experience), in other wars, as well. In the weeks ahead, you may expect as we do, Charlie Company is going to get itself into combat. We intend to be with them.

Please let me know if we have a chance for something special. We are progressing with our series of shorter reports for Net 1st and spirits fine.

I showed the memo to Kay, Clevenger and Miller and put it in the pouch to New York.

A letter arrived from Joy expressing her concern—and that of our colleagues at CBS News in New York—for Dana and Sean.

"Baby I'll close now," she wrote at the end. "I'm fine..the cat is the same..mean as ever."

April 11, 1970

Lieutenant Colonel Edward Trobaugh took command of 2d Battalion, 7th Cavalry, replacing Lieutenant Colonel Hannas, who had been wounded in the attack on Firebase Jay two weeks before. Another officer told us that Trobaugh had been given only a day or two to prepare for his new assignment and flew straight to Vietnam from his desk job at the Pentagon, then right on to his command post at a new firebase, Rohr, in the Dog's Head. He was jet-lagged. His skin was pale, as if he had been indoors for months. He was built like a prizefighter: broad shoulders and back, short neck and legs, hard muscular arms, quick eyes. A calm intelligence was suggested by his eyes—calculating, wary.

A twenty-year Regular Army officer, Trobaugh greeted us with cool reserve, polite but formal, measuring us with a degree of detachment that I had not noticed among First Cav officers before. His eyes did not smile. Our former acceptance as part of the battalion was gone. Our permission to rejoin C Company had been approved at division level or higher, and Trobaugh appeared to be following orders. We were visitors to his battalion but not as openly welcome as before. No one said it directly but the message seemed to be that if we behaved, if we did not broadcast any more critical stories, we would be allowed to continue our work about the lives of GIs in the field. Now, however, we would be watched closely. The world of Charlie Company was changing. In Tay Ninh, all the officers on the brigade PIO staff had been replaced.

At Phuoc Vinh, Major J. D. Coleman packed his belongings at the end of his one-year tour and prepared to go home. We met to say good-bye. 'I've got the feeling I'm getting out of here just in time,' J.D. said, smiling. Then, taking me aside, he said, 'Jack, we've known each other a long time. Five years in a war is a long time. Let me give you some advice. From here on in, you and your crew better keep your heads down. That's all I can say. Be careful.'

APRIL 12, 1970

In the morning, Kay, Clevenger and I waited at the helicopter supply point in Tay Ninh for a log ship to take us out to Charlie Company. The air was hot on the open tarmac, the sun baking everything soft, no breeze. Kay found a two-foot-square block of ice melting in the sun. Clevenger scrounged an old rubber duffel bag and I added a case of soda from the PX. We took off for the field hauling the bag full of ice and soda. Arriving at the LZ, soldiers were sitting in their T-shirts under the trees trying to shield themselves from the light. Captain Rice welcomed us and shook hands, no animosity about the rebellion story. His fear of being relieved of command appeared to have passed.

Kay, Clevenger and I distributed the cold sodas to the men in 2d Squad and the command group.

'Hey, it's Christmas!' one of them said.

'You guys are somethin else!' another said.

'Where'd you get this stuff?'

'Cold, too.'

The soldiers opened the sodas and sipped them gratefully. No one mentioned the incident on the road. Gordy Lee left on the departing log ship to start the first leg of his R and R to Hawaii, where his wife was meeting him. The leader of 2d Platoon, the young lieutenant who had tried to persuade Captain Rice not to take the company down the road during the rebellion, was gone. The soldiers told us Rice had relieved him.

I sat down beside a fallen tree and wrote in my notebook. A soldier came over.

'Got any of that soda left?'

'Sorry, it's all gone,' I said. 'Got some ice if you want it.'

I held out the rubber bag. He reached in and took a chunk of wet ice in his hand, bit off a piece and chewed it.

'Hey, thanks man, that's almost as good as a cold soda,' he said. 'You guys didn't have to do that, you know, lug that stuff out here. The guys really appreciate it.' He was a short, round-faced young man with a soft voice and dark curly hair.

'Where you from?' I said.

'You mean back in the world?'

'Yeah.'

'Indiana. Bloomington. If I ever get back there.'

'How much longer you got?'

'Oh, forever. Seven months. They'll keep me in the field the whole year.'

'Why's that?'

'Cause I hate it. The war, I mean. The lifers know it. They don't like me. Try to make my life miserable.'

Around us, soldiers were getting to their feet and preparing to move.

'What's your name?'

'Doc. Doc Howe,' he said. He seemed shy, self-conscious. He did not carry a rifle. He had a canvas medic's bag on a strap over his shoulder with medicine and bandages and drugs in zippered pockets. He slapped the bag with his hand as he got up.

'My tool kit,' he said.

'Take the ice,' I said and handed him the canvas bag.

'Thanks, man,' he said. 'I'll give some to the other guys.' He walked away through the trees.

By 3:30 in the afternoon the log was complete. Orders came from battalion to make a combat assault. This was something new from Lieutenant Colonel Trobaugh, and the men grumbled about making another move so late on a log day. It would be their fifth helicopter assault in nineteen days. The company took off and flew to a place closer to Cambodia than it had been before, less than a mile from the border, near the top of the Dog's Head. Second Platoon went on the second lift. The landing zone was undefended. The terrain was new and unfamiliar, the jungle slightly thinner, trees spread farther apart. The soldiers moved with extra caution. They knew the North Vietnamese were just across the border, a few hours march away.

The artillery prep had set fire to the brush around the LZ and the flames rose six to seven feet in places. Smoke swirled into the sky. The dry foliage burned quickly and produced a fast-moving inferno of flame, heat, smoke and the noise of cracking brush. Smiling, Sergeant Dunnuck led 2d Squad into the flames. "Let's go get us some gooks," he said to the men around him.

In the aftermath of the rebellion, Dunnuck wanted to prove that his squad was ready to fight. Stories had gone around battalion that C Company was not what it used to be, some guys had refused to walk down a road, they had gone soft, scared to obey an order. No one said it to Dunnuck's face but he knew. Captain Jackson heard the gossip at division headquarters. Charlie Company, 2/7, had lost its reputation as the best rifle company in the division and Dunnuck was determined to get it back.

In the confusion caused by the fire, one of the platoons got separated from the main body of the company. Captain Rice got on his radio and called the platoon leaders, trying to maneuver them into position. It was an intricate, dangerous process because in the confusion of the flame and smoke, one of the platoons might mistake another for an enemy patrol and open fire. One nervous soldier could set Charlie Company at war with itself. It took considerable skill by Rice and his platoon leaders to get the company linked up and moving in a single column.

Rice called frequent rest breaks on the march, more often than Captain Jackson had done, and moved the men slowly. At one stop, Rice sent word that he wanted to talk to me. I found him sitting on the ground cleaning his M-16.

'I really appreciate that Coke you brought in,' he said.

'It was Keith's idea,' I said. 'Anyway, it was our pleasure.'

'How y'all doing?'

'It's good to be back. That business about the road kept us away too long.'

'Well, we've got that pretty much settled now, I believe.' Rice smoked a cigarette and wiped the metal parts of the rifle with a rag. "The whole thing's blown over," he said. "No hard feelings."

'Any feedback from the Pentagon?'

'None that's reached me. The way I see it, what happened, happened. No way around that. We did have a temporary reluctance to move down the road. But we got out of it okay. It might have been easier if 20 million people didn't get to see it, including a lot of generals, but that's that. We've made some adjustments around here. And there will be more. You and your crew can finish what you started.'

I thanked him and returned to Second Squad. Kay was on his feet, searching the forest as if he had lost something. He picked up an old C ration can, examined the bottom of it and threw it away.

'What did you lose?' I said.

'Nothing,' he said, concentrating hard.

'How about setting up here for an interview with Dunnuck? I want to ask him how he got the name Killer.'

Kay lined up a shot of Dunnuck sitting on the ground with the men in his squad around him. His helmet was off and he wore a green T-shirt and dog tags. One of the soldiers rested his feet on a log beside Dunnuck's head. The film rolled.

'Tell us about life out here. What's the routine?'

"You come out here for eighteen days," Dunnuck said, "and you don't see anything. Sort of makes you mad. But if you can get a couple of gooks, eighteen days you're out here, nobody gets mad at all. Makes it seem worth-while anyway, to be out here."

"What does it accomplish?"

"What does it accomplish? Well, actually, what we're doin out here now is we're tryin to catch 'em when they come from Cambodia. We're tryin to catch 'em before they get to the big cities, before they put mortars in on 'em and everything. And, uh, must be working because not too many places get-ting mortared now. We been gettin quite a few of them. And their resupply's way down. They don't have anything. We catch 'em humpin a lot of food and that hurts em. Second of the Eighth got about two thousand pounds of rice the last time they's up here. So, there'll be a lot of gooks runnin around hungry."

"A ton of rice?"

"Yeah. We've hurt 'em, hurt 'em bad. They don't have the men anymore, you know, they don't have the men to fight a big war. I think what they're gonna try and do is fight it on a small scale and out-last us."

Dunnuck said he respected the North Vietnamese. "They're very hard. They'll go ahead and fight you. They just don't want to give up. They think they're doin right. They think they've got a good cause. And we think we've got a good cause. So they'll probably keep on fighting. French fought for twenty-five years over here and they didn't win. So, we're liable to be here a long time."

"What about yourself?"

"I'm gonna go home the same way I came over—in one piece. Puncture proof." He smiled. Friendly artillery shells cracked ahead.

"I guess we got to be here to help these people get their freedom, you know. And I think that Communism—I wouldn't want to live under Communism, you know. So, I think they don't want to live under it either. So, we're here to help them out. Nothing you can do. I hope we'd hurry and get it finished, though. Get it over with. I don't want to see my brother over here."

"How old is he?"

"Nineteen. Can't even be seeing him over here. I think he'll be all right."

"You take your job seriously. Is that how you got the nickname?"

"Well, you have to take it serious when you got your life and somebody else's to worry about, you know. If you have an attitude where you just don't care, you might not go back, you know. So you have to do your job. And I've got people I've got to worry about besides myself. I make sure all of them get back, I get back myself, I'll be satisfied."

"Your nickname is Killer. What's your feeling about killing?"

"I don't have any. Don't mean nothin. Just, I guess you could say it was a job to do, that's all. Either you get killed or you kill him. So, better him than me, any day. You really don't have no feelings about it, you know. You see a dead gook, it don't mean anything. The only time you really feel anything is when you see a GI messed up. Then it sort of hurts you, you know? But the gooks, it don't bother you none. Don't mean anything."

"How did you get your nickname?"

Dunnuck smiled. His white teeth flashed in his mouth. "Killer? Killed a couple of gooks in a bomb crater one time. Claymores. Blew a couple of claymores over 'em. Put a few sixty rounds into them." A soldier behind him said something softly. Dunnuck smiled. "Dig it. They was taking a— they was taking a bath." He chuckled. "Just proves not to take no baths in the field." He looked around at the faces of the men in the squad. Most of them smiled.

The company got up and walked another kilometer into the steaming bush. I thought about what Dunnuck said. He had been surprisingly honest. Usually, soldiers only say what they think is acceptable for the public to hear. We rarely got this much truth. I recalled Major Beckwith at Plei Me, the Marines fighting in Hué, Lieutenant Colonel House after A Shau, the young Marines at Khe Sanh singing "Where Have All the Flowers Gone." Their honesty had produced powerful news stories. I wondered why news reporting from World War II and Korea had not been as candid. *Because it was unpatriotic to report the truth?* How senseless it seemed, how unpatriotic *not* to report what was happening. *How can a country send its young people to fight and die,* I wondered, *and then hide from the public at home what happens to them?* Then I thought, *You weren't there. You might have seen it differently.*

At the next break, Bob Teschker held his hand over his left eye. It was swollen and red, a grotesque lump that distorted the side of his face.

'Probably got bit by a spider or something,' Teschker said quietly. 'Happened once before. Must be allergic.'

'Man, I'm allergic to this whole fuckin jungle,' another soldier said.

'Allergic to the Army, man.'

'I'm fuckin allergic to Vietnam.' Laughter.

'There it is.'

Doc Howe checked Teschker's eye and said if it gets any worse they might have to call a medevac. He put skin cream and a dressing over the swelling. When he was finished, I asked Howe if we could do an interview and he agreed.

Kay and Clevenger set up the equipment. Howe said he was one of four medics with the company. The last time they got into a fight, he and Sergeant Dunnuck went up the line under fire to get the point man who had been shot and drag him back. They patched him up and got him on a medevac, but he died in the hospital three days later. "That made it worse," Howe said, "cause we were hoping for him, and he did finally die. Such a pity, too, cause the whole place ain't even worth a person's life. Ain't even."

In Bloomington, where he grew up, Howe said he was an apprentice tool and die maker but his real ambition was to go to Indiana University and become an art teacher. "That would be a ball," he said, "to teach in high school."

'Do any sketches out here?'

"Nah, doesn't interest me at all."

'Got a girl back home?'

"Yeah. Her name is Joanna Settle. We've been engaged for seven months. We're getting married when I get out."

'When's that?'

"November 20."

'How'd you get to be a medic?'

'Well, I told them I didn't want to go around shooting anyone,' he said. "I put in for dental assistant. They gave me this."

Before he left for Vietnam, Howe said, his parents had something important to tell him. They told him they were not his true parents, as he had
always believed. His actual parents left him at an orphanage at birth. His fos-
ter parents had raised him from the age of four. Knowing that, Howe said,
gave him a greater appreciation of life.

Kay and Clevenger signaled they were ready. The camera rolled. Howe
did not change the way he talked.

"How do you feel about being around 120 other men who believe in
killing? Or most of them?"

"Well, I don't think any of them really do. I think that [if] they're confronted, put in a situation where they absolutely have to or die, they'll do it
of course. But I don't think anybody in their right mind grooves on killing.
At least nobody I know around here. Like, if we get in a firefight, I mean, it's
a thing, you or the other guy. And I guess most of them will fight."

"How about you?"

"Not unless I absolutely—I don't know. It scares me. I don't know. I like to
say that I won't fire, or won't shoot anybody. But then you've always got that
little thing in the back of your mind. Well, what if all of a sudden one day
there's a gook and he's got this AK pointed at you? I mean, *Wow!* If I ever do
have to kill somebody I think I'd go insane afterwards. Because of the conscience thing. I killed somebody! *Wow!* I just hope it never happens." Howe
turned his head and looked around as if to see whether anyone was listening. His eyes were wide.

"And you're twenty?"

"Yeah, twenty. Too young to be out here."

"How did you get to be a medic?"

"They stuck me in it, you know. I put in to be a dental assistant, you
know, and they stuck me in the medics for some reason. I don't know why."

"Do you like it?"

"Yeah, I dig it. Because you don't have to kill nobody this way. It's kind of
nice. You get to patch people up."

"What's your thoughts on killing?"

"Pardon?"

"What are your thoughts on killing?"

"Oh, wow. There's no doubt about it. It's wrong. You know, I mean, the
Bible says, 'Thou shalt not kill . . .' It doesn't say, 'Thou shalt not kill' paren-

theses 'Unless there's a war or you hate somebody.' It says that thou shalt not kill period. You know, I think that goes for everything. Putting on a uniform doesn't give you a license to kill somebody. You know?"

"Why did you put on a uniform?"

"Well, I had a nice choice: six years in prison or Canada or here. It might as well be here, you know?"

Howe swept his hand across the air in front of his face, chasing a bug away.

"I think my gripe is that we're supposed to be withdrawing, right? And, well, I figure that since we're going home in the long run, why don't we just sort of take it easy, you know, don't go out looking for trouble. Just sort of maybe sit down and if they come to us we'll fight. But going out looking for trouble and wasting more lives just for time's sake, to me is just absurd. I don't know, maybe I'm wrong. It could be."

"Killing's wrong."

"There it is. I think there's a better way. You know, a better way to living. Maybe we can all get together and coexist with each other some day and it would be nice. It's just a dream. Maybe it'll never happen."

Kay shut off the camera and smiled. Clevenger switched off the amplifier and took his headphones off. I thanked Howe.

'When's it going to be on?' he said.

'Three or four days after we get out of here,' I said.

'Wow. I hope my folks and girlfriend are watching.'

'Give us your phone number. I know someone in New York who'll call and tell them when you're going to be on.'

Doc Howe smiled and told me his number at home. When he was gone, I asked some of the men in 2d Squad what they thought of him.

'Doc? He's all right,' one of them said.

'Yeah, last time we's in it, him and Killer went up and pulled a wounded guy back.'

'Got 'im patched up real good.'

'Medevac'd 'n everything.'

'Too bad he died.'

'Yeah, Doc Howe's got guts.'

'There it is.'

APRIL 13, 1970

In the low gray light at dawn, with the forest cold and wet with the night, a soldier called in from one of the OPs outside the perimeter. His voice was a whisper. *"Enemy movement to my front. Wait one . . ."* Then silence. Captain Rice and the command group did not move. The jungle twitched in the still air. Word went around the line and the men got into firing positions, moving slowly without making noise, pointing their M-16s outward into the brush, eyes and ears straining to pick up strange shapes or sounds in the dark light. Nothing moved. Kay climbed a small mound of earth near the command group, put the camera on his shoulder and waited on one knee. Everyone held his concentration. After a while Rice got on the radio. There was irritation in his voice. "Eight-one Delta. You were supposed to give me a read-back. I have not, yet to hear from him. I'd like to know. Over." Rice looked up, rolled his eyes once, and shook his head from side to side.

Negative contact. Someone said it must have been a fucking new guy or maybe a monkey or, yeah, possibly a gook scout. No sense worrying about it. The men relaxed. Charlie Company ate breakfast, policed the area and moved on. The march was stiff at first with aching bones and muscles but the air was still cool and the vegetation smelled fresh and the weather was not yet brutal. The heat rose slowly, degree by degree. The men began to strip off their fatigue jackets and then the march became another long hot walk in the sun.

After an hour, Rice ordered a halt. The men dropped to the ground and rolled out of their packs, put their rifles and weapons next to them and lit cigarettes. I went for a walk along the line. The air was heavy in the heat. Two GIs played chess on a folding board on the ground, their heads bent in concentration, studying the position. One of the soldiers had taken off his shirt and sat hunched over the board, his legs crossed in front of him. He wore a metal peace symbol on a chain around his neck and a red bandanna tied around his forehead to catch the sweat. The other soldier was Grady Reynolds from 2d Platoon.

'Hi there,' Reynolds said. 'Say hello to Glenn.' I shook hands with the soldier who wore the peace symbol and sat down.

'Who's ahead?' I said.

'He's winning this time,' Reynolds said, 'but I might pull it out.'

'Helps kill the time,' Glenn said.

'Yeah, we got all the time in the world.'

I took out my notebook and pen and asked, "Tell me your name, would you?"

"Glenn Hindley." He spelled it.

"Rank?"

"Spec-Four."

"Where you from?"

"Monticello, New York."

"How long you been over here?"

"Nine months."

"How long in the field?"

"Nine months." Hindley's voice was deep, guttural, laconic, as if he was too tired to speak up. He moved his arms and head with the slow resignation of one who had lost all optimism, who had passed the point of positive imagination.

"How old are you?"

"Twenty-one."

Kay and Clevenger came into the group and rolled film on the chessboard. I asked Hindley to tell us about himself.

"Well, right now I'm in a mortar platoon. I'm sort of a bystander. I sit back and watch most of the stuff. We don't really get involved. We just sit back. We never use the gun or anything. So, that makes it nice. And, right now, I'm in a gun squad. I'm a gun squad leader." He laughed. "I think I'll make it a rule that we don't have to fire the gun. I haven't fired my gun since I've been here. I like it that way."

"How do you get away with that?"

"Just don't fire it. In mortar platoon you don't see anything anyway. We sit back and just about watch everything that's going on. So, it's kind of nice. Lot better being an observer instead of a participant, I guess." There was a pause. I was amazed by what he was saying, that he dared to say it.

"What's wrong with the war," I asked.

"People die. I guess that's the main thing." I waited for him to explain but he said no more.

"What are your feelings about being here in the war and all of it?"

"Well, it's just the war itself. The idea of killing people and having your friends get wounded or killed themselves, just don't make any sense to me. There's beaucoup people in Saigon and back in the rear making a lot of money off this war—people in Washington, and it's not, it's just not worth the human life. I don't think. Just so somebody can make a few extra dollars, or a few million dollars. Money just doesn't mean anything."

"Why are you here?"

"They sent me here. I didn't even want to come. But I know if I didn't come here I would have to stay in Sweden or Canada for the rest of my life and not be able to see the people back home. So I came over here and stuck it out so far. And I hope to make it the rest of the way."

"Does it get into a dilemma being here, being part of an infantry company that goes out looking to kill people and having private feelings that are directly opposite?"

"I'm against everything because I just don't believe in anything that we're doing out here. So I'm fighting a sort of conflict within myself and against the whole army, it just about seems. Because I don't like anything that's going on. And the lifers are shoving all this shit at me." Hindley paused while he thought about what to say next.

"The lifers are, well, they're playing their games and I don't like to play their games. They don't give me rank, they don't give me rear jobs." Another pause. "Be myself and say what I want to say. And they're just holding me back, I guess. You know, the best way they know how to hold me back. I do my job ti-ti. But maybe they're afraid. They're afraid of what's happening, I think. They're afraid of the movement coming to Vietnam. Because what I read in TIME and *Newsweek,* that they're beaucoup scared. The army is really paranoid about all of the people coming over here. Not that they're a lot different than they used to be, like World War II–type people or the old Vietnam people. It's the Woodstock generation coming to Vietnam."

"Is back home really Woodstock?"

"Well, it's about two miles away—Monticello. It's a small, dinky little town. But Woodstock's a big nation. So I'll go back to Woodstock. I plan on going cross-country when I get back, because I'll see the people that I know over here, plus I'll be able to talk to a lot of other people, maybe convince them that killing for peace just doesn't make sense."

Hindley looked at the chessboard. Kay panned the camera down from his face to the peace symbol dangling from his neck, zoomed into a close-up and changed focus.

We thanked Hindley, shook hands and walked back to 2d Squad.

'Man, I don't *believe* these guys,' Kay said, smiling.

We shared the same thought: the interviews with Hindley and Doc Howe would go off in America like a grenade. Nothing we had seen or read in previous coverage of the war had been so outspoken, so defiant. Hindley was *resisting*.

'That's one way to get out of the line,' Clevenger said.

'How so?' Kay said.

'Get yourself locked up for insubordination.'

'Never happen.'

'They used to shoot guys for less than that in World War I.'

'Times change,' I said.

'The worst punishment is leaving him out here,' Kay said.

'Yeah, humping that baseplate.' (The baseplate of a mortar is the heaviest piece of equipment carried in the field.)

Kay rummaged through his pack, got out his black changing bag, and began to reload a magazine of film.

'This is our next to last roll,' he said. 'Don't know how much battery life I've got left.' In one day and night we had gathered enough for a story. The interviews with Hindley, Doc Howe and Sergeant Dunnuck would form the heart of it.

The men mounted up and moved on, one soldier at a time, one foot after another. The elephant grass and wild brush in front of them formed an impenetrable wall. The soldiers on point cut into it with machetes and threw their bodies against it a foot at a time. The heat was still rising.

After two hours, the company stopped. The men dropped to the ground where they stood, exhausted. After taking a drink of water, I went forward so see what was going on. Near the front of the column someone was calling for a medic. Doc Howe went past in a sprint. At the point, a soldier lay on his back, gasping for breath, his whole body convulsing, eyes bulging in his head. Howe poured a few drops of water on the point man's face, unfastened the buttons of his fatigue shirt and exposed his chest and stomach to the air.

He took a towel from around his neck and used it to fan the point man's face and chest. Another soldier knelt on the ground beside the heat-struck man and whispered to him, 'You're gonna be all right, Puge. Hang in there.'

'Loosen his laces,' Howe said. 'And his belt.' He sprinkled water on the man's chest, waved the towel above him, and after a short time the convulsions stopped. The point man's eyes receded and the panting ceased. His face was chalk white.

I ran down the line to find Kay and Clevenger.

'Point man's got heatstroke,' I said. 'Hurry.' We ran back up the line and found the soldier still on his back but conscious and talking to the others. Doc Howe had stopped waving his towel. I asked him his name and he said it was Steven Puget, that he was a PFC, eighteen years old, from Crescent City, California.

"You're the point man, is that right?"

"Yes, that's right."

"Describe what happened."

"Just can't walk through that kinda stuff all day. Just can't do it."

"What does it do to you?"

"Well, try to name something it *doesn't* do to you." Puget thought for a moment. "My partner, Marsh, walked through after I slithered out there— just blacked out. Woke up, all this stupid junk." He looked around. "Just can't hack that stuff all day."

Doc Howe said, "We all deserve a rest. Been through too much. Too bad it takes this to get one. He'll be all right, though."

"You just stand up and fall over," Puget said. "Stand up and fall over. Over and over again. Tears the hell out of a person."

Captain Rice walked up and asked what had happened.

'Point man here, Puge, went down with heatstroke,' Howe said. 'He's dehydrated pretty bad.'

'Okay. Let's get him out of here.' Rice took the handset from his RTO and called a medevac. Then he walked back to the center of the column and ordered some of the men to clear a landing zone out of the elephant grass and low trees. The helicopter arrived within fifteen minutes and landed. Friends carried Puget to the LZ with his arms around their shoulders. Supervising the evacuation carefully, Rice said, "He'll be back within forty-eight hours."

Kay, Clevenger and I said good-bye and good luck again and got on the medevac with Puget. With the heatstroke incident, we had enough for a story. Anyway, we were running low on batteries and film. As the helicopter lifted off, we waved to the troops on the ground. Several of them held up their fingers in peace signs.

Saigon was dark by the time we got to the Continental Hotel. A few hours later, when Kay, Clevenger and I had drunk a few beers and gone to sleep, NLF troops fired four rockets into downtown Saigon. One of them crashed on Tu Do Street two blocks from the hotel. I was too deeply asleep to hear the explosion. Someone told me about it the next day.

APRIL 14, 1970

Writing the story was straightforward. Kay, Clevenger and I sat around a bamboo table in the garden of the Continental, drank coffee and talked about how to put the piece together. We would call it "Charlie Company on Patrol—Part Three" to distinguish it from film of earlier patrols. How to start it was the first question. We could open with pictures of the helicopter resupply and general shots of the troops. An option that might be more visually interesting was the combat assault and brush fire on the LZ. Scenes from the patrol were another possibility. Kay said his shots of the combat assault were probably better than those of the resupply, and the patrol itself would look like most of the other patrols. We decided to open with the helicopter landing at the burning LZ, follow it with Captain Rice and the OP alert, then the interviews with Dunnuck, Howe, and Hindley, and close with Puget's collapse from heatstroke.

When we finished, Kay said, 'Don't forget to remind everybody those poor bastards are still out there humping it.'

'While we sit around drinking French coffee and Courvoisier,' Clevenger said, holding up his saucer and cup.

'Maybe that's the close,' I said.

'Be interesting to see how you work it in,' Kay said. He and Clevenger walked across the street to the bureau to prepare the film for shipment. I went upstairs to my room and wrote the voice-over narration. The words came quickly.

CHARLIE COMPANY ON PATROL (PART III)
Laurence / Kay / Clevenger
War Zone C
April 12–13, 1970

1. COMBAT ASSAULT

It was the fifth combat assault for Charlie Company in nineteen days—the deep-

est penetration into what the First Cav calls the Dog's Head of War Zone C—
and the closest to the Cambodian border, within one mile . . .

2. TROOPS MOVING OUT FROM CHOPPERS

3. "KILLER" SGT. GENE DUNNUCK, 26, ALEXANDRIA, VIRGINIA, LEADING HIS SQUAD ON LZ

Sergeant Gene Dunnuck, the leader of second squad, second platoon—known
to the company as 'Killer,' was anxious to 'get me some gooks' on this patrol.

4. MEN MOVING THRU FIRE AROUND LZ

The first problem was getting through the fire touched off by the artillery barrage before the combat assault. The flames encircled the landing zone, burning
up the dry leaves and bush, baked by the Southeast Asian sun for the months of
the dry season.

5. MEN MOVING INTO JUNGLE

The men were getting along better with their new company commander after
the brief rebellion the previous week. He was careful to call frequent rest breaks
and exercise caution.

6. SOF (sound on film) OF CAPTAIN AL RICE, 24, KINGSPORT, TENN. TALKING ON RADIO ABOUT MOVEMENT OUTSIDE

("Eight-one-Delta. You were supposed to give me a read-back. I have not—yet to
hear from him. I'd like to know, over.")
Captain Rice is talking to his men on observation. They have spotted movement
nearby and he is advising them.

7. DUNNUCK

Sergeant Dunnuck sits nearby, waiting for an opportunity to engage the enemy.

8. INTERVIEW WITH DUNNUCK ABOUT WAR, REASONS, AND KILLING GOOKS.

("What are your feelings about killing?
Don't have any, don't mean nothing. I guess you could say it was a job to do,
that's all. Either you get killed or you kill him. So better off him than me any day.
You really don't have no feelings about it, you know. You see a dead gook it don't

mean anything. The only time you really feel anything is when you see a GI messed up. Then it sort of hurts you, you know? But them gooks, it don't bother you none."

How'd you get the nickname?

Killer? Killed a couple of gooks in a bomb crater one time.

How?

Claymores. Blew a couple of claymores over them. Put a few 60 rounds into them. Dig it. They was taking a—they was taking a bath. Just proves not to take no baths in the field.")

9. MEN PUSHING THROUGH BUSH, FOCUSING ON
   TWO MEN:

   1) PFC RICHARD (DOC) HOWE, 20, BLOOMINGTON, INDIANA,
   2) SP/4 GLENN HINDLEY, 21, MONTICELLO, NEW YORK.

Not all of the men in Charlie Company are as enthusiastic about fighting the war as some of the others. Doc Howe, one of the four medics, is opposed to killing. Yet, as the men say, Howe has guts. He and Sergeant Dunnuck ran up to the point to bring back a wounded buddy the last time Charlie Company was in contact, braving bullets to help the GI who died three days later.

DOC HOWE

("That made it worse 'cause we were hoping for him. And he did finally die. Such a pity too. 'Cause the whole place ain't even worth a person's life. Ain't even. . . .")

10. INTERVIEW WITH DOC HOWE

("I like to say that I won't fire, or won't shoot anybody. But then you've always get that little thing in the back of your mind. Well, what if all of a sudden one day there's a gook and he's got his AK pointed at you? I mean, wow! If I ever do have to kill somebody I think I'd go insane afterwards. Because of the conscience thing. I killed somebody. Wow! I just hope it never happens.")

11. CHESS GAME WITH HINDLEY

Others in Charlie Company, only a few, are unwilling to fight at all. Chess is the most serious contest Glenn Hindley will engage in, for he has not fired a shot in his nine months in the field with Charlie Company.

12. INTERVIEW SOF WITH HINDLEY

("Well, right now I'm in a mortar platoon. I'm sort of a bystander. I sit back and watch most of the stuff. We don't really get involved. We just sit back. We never use the gun or anything. So, that makes it nice. And, right now, I'm in a gun squad. I'm a gun squad leader. I think I'll make it a rule that we don't have to fire the gun. I haven't fired my gun since I've been here. I like it that way.
How do you get away with that?
Just don't fire it . . . I plan on going cross-country when I get back, because I'll see the people that I know over here, plus I'll be able to talk to a lot of other people, maybe convince them that killing for peace just doesn't make sense.")

13. MEN CLEARING BRUSH FOR MEDEVAC LZ

Charlie Company has suffered a casualty. The point man, exhausted from push-ing all day against the thick jungle bush, has collapsed from the heat. The con-vulsions have stopped now, but he must be evacuated.

GI WHO's HURT IS: PFC STEVEN PUGET, 18, CRESCENT CITY,
CALIFORNIA

("Just can't walk through that kinda stuff all day. Just can't do it.
What does it do to you?
Well, try to name something it doesn't do to you. My partner, Marsh, walked through after I slithered out there—just blacked out. Woke up, all this stupid junk. Just can't hack that stuff all day.")

14. MEDEVAC.

Puge, the point man, will be able to rest for a day or two . . .

15. OTHER SOLDIERS HUMPING

. . . but for a hundred other men in Charlie Company, the long exhausting days of pushing through War Zone C, the physically punishing work, and—always—the eventuality of combat and killing, will continue.
JL, CBS News, in War Zone C.

We recorded the narration and shipped it with the film to New York. At lunch we decided to return to Tay Ninh the next day, hoping to get back in with Charlie Company on the resupply scheduled for that morning.
Later, I wrote to Joy:

There is so much to write about and so much to save to tell you. All kooky, crazy, insane, wild, hairy, scary, funny, and occasionally delightful moments. Mostly waiting or humping or crashing, as the troops say. But not dull. It gets boring for me most in Saigon. Don't want to write letters, to answer them, chase local-breaking stories like fire engines, or anything but get the story shipped, talk to you this way, get stoned and catch the next plane back to Charlie Company. They are all better people than you would ordinarily meet in New York and they are treating us as friends. We carry the cache of cassettes into the field with us, being polite enough to share the headphone with each other after each side. Swap tapes with the people in C Co, too. Beatles cassettes the most difficult to get, but we could dub a 1/4 inch onto a cassette, if we had any recent Beatles stuff. They would dig it, as they say. The crew as a unit (us crazy three) have chosen OUR HOUSE by Crosby, Stills & Nash as our favorite. Maybe because we're nostalgic already. Not much we can do about Dana and Sean. My influence probably not worth much. I think they'll be released, soon, without their film.

APRIL 15, 1970

The new First Cav public information officer did not hide his hostility. His manner was brusque, curt, ill-mannered—none of the old-world charm that career infantry officers observed. He was a young major of fair complexion and short stature who said that his predecessor, J. D. Coleman, was too slack with the press, too cooperative, too chummy. 'The first thing we're going to do,' he announced to his staff of reporters and photographers at Phuoc Vinh, 'is close down that damn *gift shop*.' He stood up straight to his full height of five feet seven inches, narrowed his eyes and frowned with his round flabby face. 'That place is a *disgrace*,' he said. 'You can buy *anything* in there.' The enlisted men exchanged brief smiles. (*Of course you could,* their eyes said, *that was the whole idea*.) The new major was as officious and hostile as Coleman was easygoing and friendly. We disliked each other immediately.

"From now on," he said to Kay, Clevenger and me, "I am going to escort you people in the field."

'You can't be serious,' I said. The idea of a division PIO following us in the bush, monitoring every interview, advising the troops what to say and what not to say, telling us where we could go or could not, was ludicrous. It would be anathema to in-depth reporting. It would be like covering the White House.

'If you're going to look over our shoulder every time we do an interview,' I said, 'the troops are never going to talk straight to us. They'll be intimidated.'

'That's right,' the major said. 'That's the whole idea.'

'Then how are we supposed to report the truth?'

'That's your problem.'

We argued. I said we had a mandate from the assistant division commander, General Casey, to show the lives of the GIs as realistically as possible. The major said we could film as much realism as we wanted, but only with an escort. I argued that he would outrank the company commander,

Captain Rice, and cause confusion among the troops. He said he would only be commanding the three of us. He was adamant. It became obvious the order had come from higher up, probably the division commander, and would not be revoked. As soon as we were out of the major's sight, Kay, Clevenger and I picked up our gear and walked out of the PIO area. We did not say where we were going. The new brigade PIO, a captain, pretended not to notice. We hitched a ride to the supply helipad and then caught a lift to Firebase Atkinson, the new command post for 2/7. Atkinson had been established three days earlier and was located within three miles of the Cambodian border, the closest yet for a battalion fire support base.

Atkinson was built in an open field of low grasses surrounded by heavy jungle. Bravo Company, 2/7, was spread along the oval-shaped perimeter in groups of two, three and four men: shallow firing holes, fresh sandbags, heavy weapons positions, a few low bunkers with overhead cover, dirt plowed into a berm two to three feet high. The men were digging holes, laying barbed wire in front of the gun positions, setting claymore mines and trip wires. A unit of 105 millimeter artillery—Bravo Battery, 2/19—was stationed at one end of the camp, its guns pointing at the sky. Dark red dust lay over the camp like a rough coat of paint.

The battalion commander, Lieutenant Colonel Trobaugh, said we were too late to get out to Charlie Company today. The last chopper left ten minutes ago. Tomorrow would be the earliest. Kay, Clevenger and I debated whether to spend the night on the base.

'Probably better to get a good night's sleep in Tay Ninh,' I said.

'The guns'll keep us awake all night here,' Kay said.

'There's cold beer in Tay Ninh,' said Clevenger, his face brightening. Trobaugh was not unhappy to see us leave. We went back on the first departing chopper. It had been an unproductive day, frustrating, no daily miracle. We ate at the officers' mess and drank beer before going to sleep. At midnight, the new PIO officer for the brigade, Captain Ken Benton, came into the press billet and woke us. Atkinson was under attack, he said.

'It a big one,' he said. 'Maybe a battalion. Some of them are inside the wire.'

I looked at Kay. His face was impassive, brain still asleep.

'Any word on casualties?' I said.

'Yeah. One chopper shot down. Pilot's KIA. Just outside the perimeter. Rest of the crew made it. They haven't been able to get a medevac in yet.'

'What about resupply?'

'A few birds are getting ready now. As soon as the heavy stuff lifts a bit, they'll go in.'

'How's Trobaugh?'

'I heard in the TOC that he got hit a couple of times but he's okay. He's real cool, running the show.'

No one spoke. An image of the firebase came to mind: the low berm around the camp sparkling with muzzle flashes, shells exploding in and outside the wire, flares swinging overhead, Bravo Company soldiers firing full clips on automatic, reloading fast, firing again, Vietnamese troops moving forward in a low crouch, firing, throwing grenades, clouds of dust and dense smoke and cordite in the air, men running, shouting, falling, Lieutenant Colonel Trobaugh in the thick of it days after arriving in-country, fearsome noise, blood, war-fighting.

'What's the chance of us getting in?' I said.

'Zero,' Benton said. 'CBS isn't allowed anywhere near Charlie Company.'

'Since when?'

'Since four o'clock this afternoon. Orders from division.'

'Why?'

'Well, the major got pissed off when you gave him the slip. Going to Atkinson without his permission.'

'Hey, man,' Kay said looking at me. 'We don't need to go out there tonight. We can't shoot anything in the dark.'

'There'll be flares,' I said.

'The damn light'll be shitty. You know what flarelight's like. We've tried it before. It comes and goes too much. Can't get a decent exposure.' Kay lit a cigarette. 'Listen. If they're still fighting in the morning, we can go then.'

'Gentlemen,' Benton said, 'I've told you the orders. You do not have permission to visit Atkinson.'

'We understand that,' I said.

'If you choose to go out there, it is without my knowledge or permission.' Overemphasizing the point.

'Understood.'

Benton had not been in-country long and was more like J. D. Coleman than the new major. We did not know him well, but he seemed to be an intelligent officer, clear-headed, thoughtful.

'Listen,' he said. 'The first ammo resupply will be leaving from the log pad any minute now.' The resupply helipad was a half mile or so away. 'You did not hear that from me, okay?'

'Can we get a lift over?' I said.

'Are you going out there?' Benton said.

'Yes,' I said, looking at Kay. 'At least *I* am.'

Benton thought for a second. 'Then I'll have to go with you. If I can't stop you from going out, at least I can escort you.'

I looked at him.

'Don't worry,' he said, 'I won't get in your way. I haven't seen any action since I've been here. Just try not to get me in too much trouble.'

'Be ready in a minute,' I said. I started to put my gear together.

'You're out of your mind,' Kay said. 'What are you going to do out there, man? Make a fucking audiotape?'

'It's our first chance to get in combat with these guys,' I said. 'It won't hurt to show the flag.'

'You're going to get your head blown off.'

'Maybe.' I considered what he said. 'Look, Keith, I have to go. You guys can come out in the morning.'

'Jack, you're crazy,' Clevenger said.

'Thanks,' I said. 'I'm doing this one for myself. Consider me off duty. Maybe I'll get some good tape. If anything's still going on.'

'Just don't expect any sympathy from us when you're sitting in a hospital bed with your balls blown off,' Kay said. He climbed back into his poncho liner, pulled the edge abruptly over his shoulder, and turned over on his side with his back to me.

'Hey, Jack, what are you trying to prove?' Clevenger said.

'Nothing.'

'Well, it sure as hell *looks* like you are.'

I walked outside, got into a jeep with Benton and rode toward the resupply point. I was sorry Keith and Jim weren't coming but I couldn't challenge their decision. There was no sense in getting shot at for no reason. The attack on Atkinson might have little to do with our story on Charlie Company, but after being in the field for nearly a month without combat, I was anxious to get something. If the closest I could get to the war was Charlie Company's battalion CP, I wanted to be there. It seemed right.

Riding in the open jeep through the cool night air, I felt liberated. Working alone was less complicated than working with a camera team. No worries about getting pictures or having equipment breakdowns. I could concentrate simply on getting the story. Filming for television made daily journalism so much more difficult than straight reporting. Without Kay and Clevenger, it would be easier to observe and report. Notebook, pen and tape recorder were all the equipment I needed.

At the resupply pad, a large group of men in T-shirts worked under the illumination of flares and kerosene lamps. They moved quickly, their faces intense, loading crates of ammunition onto a Huey. The helicopter was almost full. Long wooden boxes of M-16, .30- and .50-caliber ammunition sat on the floor of the slick. The pilot stood by the open doorway.

'Going to Atkinson?' I said.

'Yeah. They're low on bullets.'

'Got room for one more?'

He looked at the tape recorder over my shoulder. 'You Press?'

'Yes.' I introduced myself.

'I know about you. You're one of the guys who took the Old Man's C and C ship to Saigon a little while back.'

'That's us.'

'Wined and dined the crew. We heard *all about* that mission.' He took off his glove and shook hands.

'Glad to meet you,' he said.

The pilot was a member of 229th Aviation, one of those who had been flying us in and out of War Zone C.

'Anybody get in yet?' I asked.

'Not yet. I'm leaving with the first load shortly.'

'Can I come?"

The pilot looked at me and smiled. 'If you really need to get in there, sure. But you'll have to wait. I want to go in with just my crew once or twice before I take passengers. It's just that little bit lighter without you.'

He stepped on the skid and climbed into the pilot's seat, strapped himself in, switched on the ignition and started the engine. The big turbo whined and then growled. The rotor blades turned heavily on the central axis of the main column and began to rotate slowly, turning hard against the inertia and force of gravity, then turned faster and faster until they spun so fast they were invisible. I put a fresh cassette into the tape recorder, plugged in the microphone, set the level, and pressed record. I took a breath and spoke in a loud voice into the microphone over the noise of the engine: *"The date is*

April sixteenth. It is shortly after midnight. A battalion headquarters of the First Cavalry Division is under attack."

I paused to let the sound of the engine establish itself on the tape and to allow myself a moment to think of what to say next.

"The helicopter motor is revving up, about to bring the 'Black Bandits,' the 229th Aviation helicopter team, in on an emergency ammunition resupply. One helicopter has been lost already. One pilot is known dead. The enemy is believed to be inside the perimeter."

Another pause for natural sound. The helicopter blades whirred at high speed.

"The fire support base under attack is code-named Atkinson. It was the head-quarters for the battalion where Charlie Company has been operating in the field since late last month. We visited it earlier today and the men of Bravo Company, Charlie Company's sister, were busily engaged building bunkers, putting out their wire, setting their flares, preparing for the eventuality of the attack that has become reality tonight."

The engine revved, the blades whipped the air and the helicopter wobbled on its skids. In the next moment it pulled itself off the ground and hovered a few feet above the tarmac. The pilot put the nose down and started forward, slowly at first, then accelerated and lifted swiftly over the buildings of the brigade camp and flew toward the west and the black forest of War Zone C. Finally the running lights of the helicopter disappeared in the night sky and the sound of it was gone.

At the log pad, one of the radios squawked.

"Three-one Zulu, this is Four-seven November, I got you loud and clear." The voice of a supply sergeant at brigade calling Atkinson. "Roger, a second load of bullets is on your way at this time, over." Then a pause. "Roger. A second load of class five is inbound your location. Should ETA about zero-five, over."

BANG! A mortar tube popped a flare into the air.

"Hey, Gene!" one of the soldiers on the supply pad called to another. "How much more fifty you want?"

"They wanted about twenty cases," came the answer.

"Twenty cases. We got two, four, seven, eight—eight sent out. They need twelve more."

Speaking into the microphone, I said, *"Dozens of men are now working on the log pad, which is the area where resupply begins. Helicopters come in one at a time. There are very few now. One Cobra gunship has been shot down in this attack. . . ." POP! "A flare burst overhead, just lighting the area enough so that the men can see, all working in small clusters, dragging crates and cases of ammunition to support in defense of the firebase."*

Someone on the radio reported that the first resupply chopper had landed at Atkinson and dropped off the ammo. Then it picked up some of the most critically wounded and took them to the field hospital in Tay Ninh.

"The first report reaching the base at Tay Ninh," I said into the mike, *"is that six Americans have been killed, and at least twenty wounded."*

The second time the pilot of the resupply slick returned to the log pad, he signaled for Benton and me to get aboard. I climbed into the middle of the passenger section and sat on a crate of ammunition. There were no seats or seat belts. The crew chief squatted on the floor talking into the mouthpiece of the microphone connected to his flying helmet. Men on the tarmac loaded crates of ammunition, one after another, and the long wooden boxes slid in easily. The metal floor of the helicopter was slick with blood.

I looked ahead into the space between the pilot and copilot as the helicopter shuddered into the air.

"We are taking off now in one of the third lifts of ammo resupply, heading for the firebase where a few helicopters have been able to land so far. I'm sitting on a case of .50-caliber ammunition flying through the darkness after midnight from Tay Ninh to Firebase Atkinson under attack."

Racing over the dark forest, trying to describe what was going on and keeping my voice under control took all my concentration. It was necessary to identify images, organize them into logical thought, and translate that into a coherent description of what was happening. Fortunately, five thousand feet up was an ideal vantage point. The combination of work, danger, excitement and fear produced a powerful sense of purpose, a calm inner feeling that whatever happened was going to be all right.

"Heading toward the firebase, one begins to see flares overhead. No sign of tracers. It may be a momentary lull in the attack, since it's so early in the evening. The enemy usually assaults positions such as these at about four o'clock in the morning. This came extraordinarily early."

Arriving over Atkinson, we saw the sky sparkling with light and movement. Strangely, I could hear no sound.

"One can see ground activity near the firebase—the flash of tracers, slowly, red, glowing, heading up toward the helicopter. We're still some distance from the fire-

base. *The sky around the firebase is illuminated by flares. The firing seems to have subsided.*

"*Now there's more flashing, the muzzle flashes of gun bursts. It's difficult to see at this distance if they're going in both directions.*"

The noise of the helicopter engines and spinning blades droned on.

"*We're making a wide swing around the base. There're yellow flashes and red flashes from the tiny landing zone in the woods where the Second of the Seventh Battalion of the First Cav Division had placed its artillery position and battalion headquarters.*"

"*There're several flashes from the perimeter but it's impossible to tell from here whether they represent enemy fire or our own outgoing.*"

No sounds of gunfire reached the helicopter yet.

"*We're circling in now for an approach. Quite close to the camp. A helicopter that had planned to go in before us circled around and turned away, as we are doing, too, now. One can see only small red lights on the ground. Other helicopters are flying directly overhead. The brigade commander, Colonel William Ochs, is hovering overhead, trying to direct his troops on the ground, his men who are in a tight circle.*"

"*One can see the Cobra gunships working out around the edge of the perimeter, firing rockets and machinegun tracers into the area from which the North Vietnamese launched their attack.*"

"*Now one can see the tracers coming up toward the helicopter itself. It's ground-to-air fire chasing away the helicopters. More flares are fired overhead. The camp looks like a deserted brown patch of clearing in the jungle bush. Now one can see firing in both directions. The enemy is still very much active around the perimeter of Firebase Atkinson and shooting at the helicopters as we try to bring in more ammunition.*"

Far, far above—bright yellow-white against the black sky—the moon was shining. And as the helicopter turned, it came into full view.

"*There's a clear almost cloudless sky and a three-quarter moon, and just a touch of irony that as we move in toward the firebase and the tracers come up toward the helicopter, in the other direction three American astronauts are heading for that same moon providing the illumination for this evening's battle.*"

It was Apollo 13.

"*One can count the flashing red and white lights of nine other helicopters hovering over the firebase: command officers making decisions, coordinating supply and resupply, medevacs bringing out the dead and wounded in the brief lull in the shooting back and forth. Several small fires are burning on the base and a huge cloud of dust hangs over it, as we make another of our passes waiting for an opportunity to get in and get the ammo supply down on the ground."*

I looked at my wristwatch.

"It is about one o'clock in the morning now and there is much time remaining for continued enemy attacks. The helicopter we are riding is now beginning to make its descent from twenty-five hundred feet, two thousand . . . the wind noise rushing past the helicopter. It's a very steep dive. Sixteen hundred feet . . . Circling again, still dropping steeply. Banking sharply now. A thousand feet . . . The jungle—dark and gray below—comes into appearance. Nine hundred feet . . . six hundred feet . . . Down to five hundred and a single flare overhead. No sign of the base. The pilots looking anxiously out the window for signs of the tracers of the .50-caliber machine-guns. Now we're at treetop level. The speed is sixty five to seventy knots. Two hundred feet and roaring in over the tree tops. . . .

"A green flare goes off overhead. The moon is partially hidden now by a bank of clouds, but an illumination round marks the helicopter. All that can be seen of the fire-base is heavy smoke. Dust up ahead. We're directly over the firebase now. A small green light flashing on the ground below marking the position where we could be land-ing. The helicopter dropping very quickly now and banking sharply from left to right."

The chopper hit the ground with a hard jolt. Soldiers appeared out of the dark and seized the ammunition crates with gloved hands and lifted them onto the ground in a rush. Benton and I jumped out and knelt a short distance away beneath the two long rotor blades beating the air. In a few seconds the helicopter was gone. My ears adjusted to the altitude and strange sounds.

Explosions cracked the air. *WHOOOSH! BAANG!*

"Okay. You got civilians with you now," I shouted to one of the soldiers on the LZ.

"Hey man," one of them said, "do me a favor and get behind the berm. Please." His voice was steady. The noise and concussion of artillery shook the ground.

"Okay. Where shall we go?"

"I'll take 'em over here," a young soldier said. "Follow me."

"Are we inside the perimeter?"

"That's a negative. We're outside. Come on over here. We'll get you over here by that hootch that got blown away."

We ran low. A team of men called "Blackhats," who were trained to receive and deliver resupply, shouted at one another as they worked, giving and taking orders and instructions, trying to get the ammunition distributed inside the base. Shells exploded. There was no panic, only urgency in the movements of the men.

"Hey, y'all come around this side and git in the bunker," a soldier shouted.

"Might as well," I said, out of breath.

"The Blackhats have invited us to share their bunker with them," I said into the microphone.

"I *lost* my black hat," the young soldier said. Laughter.

A big explosion burst. I asked another soldier to describe the attack. He was short and skinny and had a thin, high-pitched voice. He spoke rapidly, without emotion, casually.

"Uh, when they first came in they just started pouring it in and they kept it goin for, damn, I don't know how long. The first round nobody knew what was coming off and they had this shit coming in for at least an hour solid, just kept pumping it in. We got out all the bodies. We got out, uh, one whole medevac full of KIAs, and we got 'em out. We had this one bird that came in here and he crashed. I went out there to get those people off that bird and I got three of them in. I tried to get the pilot out and when he jumped out the rotor blade hit him in the head. And so he's still out there. They can't get him in. He's uh, he's dead." The soldier shook his head slowly and looked at the ground.

A shell exploded in the treeline outside the perimeter and echoed across the firebase.

"What's your name, rank and hometown please?"

"Ah, Roger. My name is Frank Rippe. I'm from Wapato, Washington. I'm a PFC."

"How old are you?"

"I'm twenty-one."

A soldier I remembered from the party on Firebase Jay, a sergeant from the South, shouted in a loud voice, "Get some lights out there! Bird coming in!"

"I'll go back out there," said Rippe.

"He's coming in! North to south!"

CRACK! CRACK! CRACK!

I took a deep breath and spoke into the tape recorder:

"The sounds of activity can be heard all around now as another helicopter brings

in supplies. Men in dusty dirty black forms, their M-16s carried in their hands, are pushing small mules, four-wheel jeeps, carrying the ammunition boxes up to the men on the line, the berm as they call it, so that they can reload."

KAH-BOOOM! A huge blast shook the ground and air.

"The explosions you hear now are all outgoing, from Bravo Company, Second of the Seventh. Another helicopter is brought in. My watch says it's twenty minutes after two. The helicopter is blowing dust, the dust that accompanies every firebase that is installed in War Zone C, kicking up the red dirt and filling up one's eyes with it."

"Tell 'em to be standing by for a Hook with some railroad flares," the sergeant shouted. More explosions.

"The men are setting off heavy explosions along the treeline that surrounds this base. The trees are only less than a hundred yards from where the positions are and the enemy was able to penetrate very closely. Now everyone is awake."

BOOOM!

"Heavy outgoing fire is being pushed out now to keep the enemy off balance if possible, trying to prevent a second attack. For it is still early in the morning and several more hours of night to go."

"Hey Rip!" called the sergeant who was working the field radio.

"Right here."

"We got to have continuous illumination."

"Okay."

"Hey they got gooks out there? In the open or anything."

"Have they got em out there?"

"In the open."

"Gooks?"

"Are they taking fire on the LZ at this time?"

"No, not at this time."

"Okay." He went back to the radio.

Small and large explosions echoed around the firebase.

"Men are standing, working everywhere, refilling sandbags, piling up their bunkers, loading up on new ammunition . . ."

"Did any get inside here?" Captain Benton asked.

"No, not inside," Rippe answered. "We kept em outside there. They had .51-cals over here. Is what shot down that bird over there." Rippe pointed toward the edge of the perimeter. "The first one went over there and a piece of shrapnel hit me in the side of the head and it knocked me out."

"We gotta get flares out here ASAP," the sergeant interrupted. "You're gonna have to tell these people to get us about twenty flares."

"I need at least two red flares right now," another soldier said.

"Two red flares?" said Rippe.

"Get 'em, Rip."

Men shouted at one another and gunfire rattled out from the berm and explosions cracked in the jungle.

"The biggest job now is for the Blackhats, the men who see that the infantry is resupplied, given enough ammunition to withstand any more serious ground attacks the enemy might launch. We are located. . . ."

"IGNITERS!" a soldier shouted, and suddenly a great explosion ripped the air and shook the ground. Quiet followed for a few seconds, then automatic weapons cracked in the distance, *Pap-pap-pap-pap-pap-pap-pap*.

"Sounds like a little AK fire out there," Benton said.

"Apparently the enemy remains in the area, but to what extent and what his plans are unknown here."

Another helicopter approached. Explosions thundered. Gunfire cracked. The Blackhat sergeant lit a cigarette, took a full breath and said in a lazy drawl, "Oh, ain't nothing like a hot night in Vietnam."

"Say again?" I said.

"There ain't nothin like a hot night in Vietnam," he said again. "Make all our little draft dodgers at home somethin to march in the streets about." His voice sneered with cynicism.

"What's your name, rank and hometown?" I said.

"Sergeant Ralph Wilson from Mobile, Alabama."

"Ralph Wilson, Mobile, Alabama, a man who is kneeling on top of his bunker holding a radio, guiding the helicopters that are bringing in resupply to Bravo Company and Second of the Seventh."

"I wonder how many of 'em would be marchin in the streets if they knew what was goin on over here now," Wilson said.

I got down from the top of the bunker and walked toward the battalion aid station where the medics would be. I could see clearly. The sky above the camp was a multicolored lightscape.

"It is now almost as bright as daylight. Large flares going off overhead, rocket artillery being fired from the gunships flying above."

Bob Burke, the senior battalion medic, sat in the aid station bunker. He looked more disheveled than on our first day at Firebase Jay, when he treated Clevenger's sunburn with a case of beer.

"Hi, Doc!" I said. Burke smiled, surprised to see me. I asked him his age and hometown and he said he was thirty-seven years old and his home was Honolulu though his accent was from New England.

"Doc, this is the second one for you in about two weeks. You were on Firebase Jay when it was hit and here you are again."

"Right."

"Did you get all the wounded out?"

"Uh, yeah, most of the wounded are out. Just the small stuff is staying back here. Small frags that can be treated out here."

"Doc, is this getting tiring?" I smiled. "Or wearing you down?"

"Oh, no, this Army's great." He laughed. "How are you going to act?" He paused to think. "No, not really. It gets monotonous after a while. Have to have something. If I wasn't doing this I'd be out of a job."

Vooom! A big shell exploded outside the perimeter.

"How about your medics? How'd they perform tonight?"

"Oh, *outstanding.* I've already been approached by some of the platoon sergeants who want to put people in for medals again." *Craash!* "We only had one slightly wounded, one of the medics slightly wounded. Well, two of them, in fact. Slightly wounded. But they all come through fine."

"All the support the First Cav can provide its isolated tiny outpost near the Cambodian border is coming in flashes and flames and great roars. The men of Bravo Company have held their position. They fought fiercely at the berm with the attacking waves and now, at 2:35 in the morning, there is a lull."

I turned to Sergeant Burke.

Phooot! Splaat! An M-79 shell exploded in the treeline.

"Doc, uh, you've been around a lot longer than most of us. How'd it go out here tonight?"

"Well, it was rough. Nobody likes to be running around out in that stuff. But everybody *was,* actually. We've had a lot of help from the grunts, picking up wounded, draggin wounded back with us and, uh, diggin people out. This was a big team effort. Artillery was hauling people for us. One of those things. Everybody was doing their job. Even these choppers comin in now, dropping resupplies for us. It gets kinda hairy for them jokers."

"Did you see any outstanding activity?"

"Yeah, the guy that was riding that minigun jeep. The first couple of rounds that come in, he was right there. Stopped the jeep, jumped around in back and fired the minigun. That minigun goes off, it'll really stop 'em. Stopped them cold. I don't know who it was, but somebody was in it."

"How about your own men? Going up to the line, helping the wounded."

"They all did. They was all up around it. Like ants, all over the place."

A large helicopter flew low over the camp.

"Another huge Chinook helicopter bringing in resupply for the artillery which has been firing constantly all night, kicking up another huge orange-colored red cloud of dust that colors everyone's face, everyone's skin. All the faces are darkened now. It's difficult to distinguish the faces of friends and people one has known in the month spent with Second of the Seventh Battalion. It is understood at this point that minor wounds were received by the battalion commander and his operations officer but they've continued to work under fire."

Turning again to Burke, "Think it's over?"

"I hope so." He laughed.

An explosion boomed.

"Yeah, I think so. You never can tell though."

"Bravo Company, which has defended this firebase throughout about a one-hour attack, is now standing ready for any eventuality that may come, settling down somewhat, a cold can of soda being opened by some of the men sitting around the medical bunker. In discussing the developments of the last few days, as the First Cav moves its firebases from position to position throughout the jungles of War Zone C, the enemy tries . . ."

Craack! A 105 fired at the treeline, *Chuuhhh!* a half second later the explosion shook the camp.

"Direct fire," the medics said in low voices, explaining the thunder.

". . . and has launched successive attacks on three firebases within the past three weeks. This is the latest. Bravo Company, which held this firebase, taking casualties, giving more, had engaged the enemy just three days ago, had killed twenty-one and had not taken any casualties itself. Bravo Company is holding firm."

I put a fresh audiotape in the recorder. It was five minutes to three.

The battalion doctor came into the aid station. He did not appear to be busy. I asked if he would talk.

"Doc, you're going to have to tell me your full name all over again, rank and age and hometown."

"It's Tom Hildebrand, twenty-seven, captain, Medical Corps."

"You're the doctor for the battalion."

"That's right."

"You were here when it hit."

"Yeah, I was right down here in the bunker."

"Would you give me a kind of running description of how it started and. . . ."

"Well, I'm sitting down here reading the local newspaper I just received today, and, uh, the first indication I had that something was wrong was when, uh, Sergeant Ralph White made a hasty entrance into the bunker. And this was just after we'd heard a loud explosion. And until I saw Sergeant White come down into the bunker I thought this was fu-gas, which is a normal occurrence around the LZs here. And then the explosions and so on started."

"How long did it last?"

"Well, real hard to say. We stayed in our bunker probably for the first five or ten minutes. The main incoming rounds lasted about that long. And then when the main burst was over, the medics started going out and policing up the men that were wounded."

"How about their behavior?"

"I gotta admire these medics. It takes a lot of bravery to go out there in the open and police up these wounded men."

"Is this your first combat experience?"

"Right. It is."

"I know you haven't had much time to reflect on it, but what are your first impressions?" A loud explosion went off nearby. Outgoing.

"Well, as you say, I haven't had too much time to reflect on it, ah. . . ."

A heavy machinegun rattled, *Chutt chutt chutt chutt chutt.*

". . . I really couldn't gather my thoughts about it, it's . . . of course, it's a terrible thing to see men . . ." *Booom!* ". . . that have been wounded and then die. And, unfortunately, I had to watch two or three of them die down here tonight because we just, we don't have anything to help them out here on the fire support base. Uh, just a terrible experience is all I can say."

Ka-crack!

"Did we lose many men?"

"At the last count we have six or seven killed and we had about twenty-four wounded."

Another machinegun fired a long, continuous burst. Then another.

"You said terrible experience."

"Well, it's just terrible to see young men die," he said, looking away. No one spoke. Noise of a heavy machinegun overrode other sounds. An M-79 round exploded near the treeline. More machineguns and M-79s fired until a storm of gunfire, explosions and the echoes of both swept across the base.

Burke, the old medic, laughed and said, "Ah, just like the Fourth of July. Listen."

When the firing subsided for a second, I said, "Why are you out here, Doc?"

"Repeat the question, please." The shooting started again.

"Why do you choose to be here?"

"Well, I don't really choose to be here," Hildebrand said. "This is my initial assignment in Vietnam. And as a battalion surgeon it's my duty to be where the main bulk of the battalion is. So the main bulk of the battalion happens to be here at this fire support base now."

"Do you choose to be in Vietnam?"

"No, I don't choose to be here." His voice was low, a note of resignation in it. Outgoing shells echoed in long hollow bursts around the firebase, cracking among the trees. I stopped the tape recorder.

A minute later the battalion commander, Lieutenant Colonel Trobaugh, came into the aid station. He looked surprised to see me. I turned on the tape recorder and held up the microphone.

"Sir, what's your first name, please?"

"Edward." His voice was sharp, authoritative.

"And your age and hometown?"

"My hometown is Kokomo, Indiana, and I'm thirty-seven years old." Outside, the firing became intense.

"The battalion commander who directed the defense of the firebase and secured it, is now being treated for . . ."

"Is this your third wound tonight?"

"Fourth."

A loud explosion.

"The colonel has been wounded four times in the attack and now his right hand is being treated by the medics."

"You stayed on duty all that time?"

"Roger. It wasn't that bad. Hell, it was just some nicks, that's all."

"Well, your face is all covered with bandages, your eyeglasses somehow fit over it, you've got a bandage under your chin and blood running down your neck. Uh, Colonel Trobaugh, it's extraordinary under the circumstances to see you still in command."

"I'm not hurt, though, you know? If you're not hurt you just get on with it. No problem." Trobaugh turned to the medic, Burke, working on him. "What'll it take, two stitches, Doc?"

"I don't know. How many stitches, Ralph?" Burke said.

"Ah, maybe three, four. What do you say, Doc Hildebrand? Three, four?"

"What?" said the surgeon.

"Stitches."

"We didn't put any in," Hildebrand said in a low voice.

Trobaugh changed the subject. "How'd you guys get out here?"

"Ammo log," I said.

"Oh, really?"

"Yeah."

"No shit." He chuckled, then thought for a moment. "It was a good fight, I'll tell you that, babe."

"Give us a quick rundown while they're patching you up?"

"Well, it started out with incoming rounds. I know for sure at least one 107. We've got one dud round down there that looks like a 107 round, but the head on it's much bigger than a 107. Uh, it was followed immediately by a ground attack. Apparently, B-40s, and, uh, our people returned fire immediately. In fact, it was almost simultaneous. We thought we had some movement around the perimeter and we'd been using our thump guns out there, doing a little H and I fire about the time we got hit. I'm reasonably sure they were taking casualties before they ever kicked off their assault."

A helicopter came in over the camp and hovered above the aid station. Trobaugh continued. "Right now, I don't know how much damage we did to 'em. We've counted at least eleven bodies outside the wire. Nobody got inside the wire while the fight was going on." He winced as a medic closed the wound in his hand.

"How were you wounded, sir?"

"Well, I was down at the far end of the perimeter when the fight started and it was a pretty long run back, and I just got hit." He laughed softly. "I don't know, just some kind of an indirect round, I guess."

"You be able to stay out here till morning?"

"Oh, yeah. No problem. I'll stay out here, no problem there. We had real good support. And I think pretty well tied together. We put tac-air in 'em. We knew which way they were withdrawing because I had a unit to the south of us in an ambush position. These guys kicked a trip flare off so we knew they were down there. So we put one air strike in with napalm. Then we shifted our ARA down to the south of that position. We also had a Shadow on station with a minigun. And we put him south of the road and the ARA north of the road so we didn't get that balled up. And, uh, and, uh, we just worked out."

A big gun went off nearby. "I guess that's about it," Trobaugh said.

Guns from the camp fired and the shells from the guns exploded in the treeline outside the wire and in the forest beyond the treeline. The noise of the shooting cracked and shrieked and boomed in the cool air and the ground twitched with each concussion. The night was bright with the illumination of flares and flashes from the muzzles of the guns.

I walked to the edge of the perimeter and came to a hole in the ground. The hole was three to four feet deep and the bottom of it was filled with broken sandbags piled on top of one another at random. The hole appeared to have been a fighting position with overhead cover but the sandbags were covered with shell casings and other debris. A soldier sat on the ground beside the hole.

"Hi, how ya doing?" I said.

"Yeahhh," he said in an easy drawl. "I'm doin all right." He spoke slowly, drawing out the syllables of each word.

"Where you from?"

"I'm from North Carolina."

"What's your name?"

"Dock Brewington." He spelled it.

"What's your rank?"

"PFC."

"How old are you?"

"Twenty-one."

"And what hometown in North Carolina?"

"Goldsboro, North Carolina."

"You been out here on the berm all night?"

"Yes, sir."

A loud explosion, close. I ducked my head. The soldier looked at me and smiled. His eyes were tired.

"Uh, you got your thoughts together?"

"Yes, sir."

"Give me the scoop. What happened?"

"Well, we was sittin down there, me and Maybrey, we just sittin there and messin around, talkin, you know. And that's when the first round hit, right there. So I low-crawled up to my hootch, grabbed my weapon and run out to the berm. By that time we were openin up on fire, you know."

A sergeant interrupted. His voice was sharp, authoritative. "We'll probably have a mad minute around 4:30. So just hang tight. And if you see anything moving, go ahead and burn 'em."

Brewington continued. "So, it seemed like it was all there was to it. At the time, I didn't realize what was happenin. I thought we had fire, you know, right around the perimeter. And then after that, I've told the major, 'Incomin,' so he run up here, you know. I stayed down there about fifteen minutes. So I crawled up here with him, you know. Grabbed my weapon, moved out, just opened up. Sixteens shooting. We got five gooks right there, you know. They was out there sittin up, so I'm kinda jivin, don't know what it was when they got 'em. So they shot 'em down. Seemed like that was all there was to it, you know."

"What did you see and do yourself, personally? Did they come toward the wire?"

"Yeah. They was moving this way. They was comin. We got 'em right outside the wire. It's not too far out there."

"They still out there?"

"Yes, sir. They're layin hard away out there. We had a bird get shot down, cut a couple guys up."

Another soldier came over.

"What unit is this?" I asked.

"Ah, Bravo, 2/7," he said.

"I mean what platoon? What squad?"

"Ah, this is the 1st Squad, 1st Platoon," he said.

A machinegunner nearby fired several long bursts into the treeline and the shells cracked rapidly one after another like an even string of firecrackers, *dit-dit-dit-dit-dit-dit*, then the rounds made that long *shhhuusssshhing* noise as they whizzed into the bush. The compressed sounds of speeding, hissing bullets echoed back on one another and reverberated around the camp.

"It hit hardest right around here, didn't it?" I asked the new arrival.

"Uh, yes it did. This bunker here is what really got it. He got a direct hit, I guess."

"Were you here?"

"No, this is my bunker but I was over in the chow line." The machinegun fired again. "And I came back after it had been hit, things quieted down a little bit, I got back here. And was just a big mess. I started puttin out all the fire I could."

"Would you describe the mess?"

"I don't even want to. Something I don't want to see again and I don't even want to talk about it. That's how bad it was. One big mess."

"People?"

"Yeah. There were three people."

"Three people from your squad?"

"Yes. They were in there." He turned his head toward the ground.

"Was there much you could do for 'em?"

"No, there was nothin at all. They were gone when we got here. They got the other two out and they were pretty bad off but they got em medevac'd. And they say they're gonna be all right."

I spoke into the microphone, *"Here where we're sitting on about a three-foot high pile of dirt, the dust and rest of it covering everything, ammo everywhere, M-79 rounds just all over the place, boxes piled on top of one another, sandbags all caved in where the bunker collapsed . . ."*

I looked at the soldier. "Did it take a direct hit?"

"Yeah."

I asked him his name and he said it was Specialist Fourth Class Paul R. Wright, that he was twenty-one years old and was from Hampton Beach, New Hampshire.

"Once you got up here what did you see? What was going on?"

"Oh, everybody was trying to, you know, cover themselves. They were shootin every which way they could, trying to suppress the enemy fire, and eventually that's what we did."

"What was coming in?"

"Oh, it was small arms when I got here, but before I got here it was pretty big stuff that was comin in. Pretty hot stuff. I was over in the chow line and stuff started hittin and we saw it hittin around the perimeter so I dove into a 105 pit and started helpin 'em load the 105s." He laughed lightly. "Then when things let up a little bit, I got back here to see what I could do for these people and, uh, there wasn't much I could do when I got here."

"Did you see the enemy?"

"I saw maybe one or two of em, but they weren't close enough and they weren't good enough targets that I could have shot 'em anyway. We were just shootin to suppress their fire and drive 'em back if we could."

"And you did."

He laughed. "I hope we did. I hope they don't come back tonight."

"It's quarter to four in the morning and there's still plenty of time."

"Right, this is the time they usually hit."

A huge volume of outgoing fire burst from the camp. I got to my feet and moved to another bunker. A sergeant shouted over the noise, "Hey! Inbound chopper comin in!" The word went around and in a few seconds the firing ceased.

"Hi! Jack Laurence, CBS," I called to the sergeant.

"Okay. Sergeant Ferry. I'm platoon sergeant for this group here. As you can see, it's a mess."

"What's your first name?"

"Frank."

"How old are you?"

"Twenty."

"Where you from?"

"Mount Clemens, Michigan."

"How are your people holding up tonight? And how about yourself?"

"We're real good. We're in good shape right now. Morale factor's pretty high for what we took. We're in good shape. We got enough ammo." He spoke in a rapid, confident voice. "It's just a mess what happened around here. But we're in good shape."

A big gun fired and the shell exploded in the bush.

"We're just hangin in here till the morning and police call starts and we get our ass out of here."

"It's quite a mess right now."

"Well, what can you expect when you're taking 82s and 107s, 102s and that good stuff. RPGs on direct fire. Can't expect too much. We're lucky this time. Last time we had a firebase hit we lost the colonel and everything else. Came out pretty good on this one. Casualties were light, real light."

"You're pretty calm."

He laughed. "It's over with. Ask me a half hour ago."

Sergeant Perry excused himself to go and check on his people. Outgoing fire continued. Soldiers worked in the erratic light of the flares, slow-moving shadows, their faces and hands covered with dust, their fatigues saturated with it. Single rifle shots ricocheted off something hard to the front.

"The men from Bravo Company, their fatigues covered with the dust from the fighting of the night, are, uh, leaning up against the berm—just a few men scattered out along the line, and an empty hole where the bunker was blown away."

I walked over to a young soldier who was sitting on a sandbag. He was slightly built under his helmet with a thin face and long fingers that held a single bullet for an M-16. He turned it over and over through his fingers.

"What's your name, please, and your rank," I asked.

"Eugene Manning, PFC," he said and spelled it. His words came out in a rush.

"How old are you?"

"Twenty."

"From where?"

"Saint Augustine, Florida."

"What about tonight?"

He smiled a half smile. "Hmmff," he said. "Well, it was rough. Ain't too much to say about it. Be glad when it's over with, glad to see daylight. I know that'd be the longest day I've had in Vietnam."

"How did it go for you."

"Aw, it was pretty rough. I seen, uh, you know, one of the buddies I finished AIT with, he was on the bunker next to me and he took a direct hit. Shook me up pretty good. I'm thinkin about re-uping. Can't take it no more. Six months is enough.

"You've had six months out here?"

"Yes. I'm thinkin about givin it up now. Re-up. I can't take no more of that." Guns cracked next to him. "No more of this stuff."

"You're holding a bullet in your hands, kinda playing with it. You nervous?"

"Yeah, you could say I'm still kind of shaky. And my back hurts a little bit. And I'm cold, too, for one thing. That's it. Tryin to stay calm. I don't have any cigarettes, so I just play with the bullet, you know, to keep myself together."

I gave him my pack of cigarettes, lit one for him and turned to the soldier sitting next to him.

"How do you feel right now?"

"Well, I feel pretty good," he said in an easy voice, as relaxed as Manning was tense.

"Why?"

"Well, you know, I feel like the man goin to kill me, I gotta kill him. So, there ain't no need of me bein scared. I'm over here for a reason. To kill. That's the only way I can see it. So, just do the best I can. Get back home, you know. Got a son back in the world, waitin for me. If I do my job, I get back there. That's the only way I can feel about it."

"You really had a hard night's work tonight."

"Yeah, it was pretty nice. But they hit us at the wrong time, though. I figure they hit us at the wrong time, 'cause everybody was awoke, you know. And, messin around. See, when they throw the jive, then everybody know what it was, so they just took quick reaction, you know, started moving in on the line."

I turned back to Manning. "How 'bout yourself?"

"I sort of have the same viewpoint on it. First off, we's all standing around this bunker here that took a direct hit. At first we thought some guy in the bunker blew a claymore. And then about six or seven seconds behind it, we ran down here and the bunker right there took a direct hit. And there it was. Everything just started happenin at once. Couldn't see nothin. All you were doin was in your hole with your weapon up over your head, started firin it. That was it."

A .50-caliber machine gun pounded on the line.

"It was a rough night," Manning said.

"So, you're going to re-up, huh?"

"Yeah, I got to re-up. I can't go back out to the field. I got six more months and I can't hike them bushes. Too rough."

An M-60 fired two long bursts into the treeline.

"About three nights ago, we was about eight hundred meters from the Cambodian border and we made contact that night about 10:30 and we had gooks about three meters from our hole, you know, throwin Chicoms and everything. We were lucky we got them before they got us. Too many breaks like that when you make it through, you know, you figure your luck bound to run out somewhere down the line. Two incidents like this, back to back, you figure your luck bound to run out, sooner or later."

"So you put in another three years in the Army to get out of the field?"

"First I'm gonna try to converse with some of the higher authorities and try to see about it. I don't really want to put, you know, go back through three more years, cause I get out of the Army in June, and I don't want to be, you know, puttin three years in. But I'd rather put three years in the rear somewhere and be alive instead of bein in the boonies for six more months. That's it."

"That's it."

"I figure six months in the field should be enough for any man. But when you have to stay out there ten, eleven months, that ain't no good. You'd never be all to yourself afterwards."

Wow, I thought. *'You'd never be all to yourself afterwards.'*

Manning was quiet for a second. Then he said, "You see all kind of different things. Seein all your buddies hollerin and stuff. A man just can't take all that stuff too long."

The easygoing soldier next to him spoke with the same slow southern accent.

"We was sittin over there playin cards, you know, earlier today, before all of this happened. All of us sittin around socializing. Then after a while things started scattering out. All of it piled in on us. So, nothing for us to do then until the jive cooled down to try to get em out of the hole. After we tried to get em out of the hole all of em were dead, 'cept two." He winced and looked at the ground.

"What do you think about the whole big mess?" I asked Manning.

"Well, Vietnam, period. I'm not sayin I'm against it and I'm not sayin I'm for it. I'd rather'd fought over here than be back home in the world, and see my brothers and sisters and wife and kids and stuff, runnin around, runnin for their lives. I'd rather have it over here. Stay over here and do my tour. And try to make it back."

Manning leaned over toward the microphone. "If we let 'em take over here, they'll be in the world next. People don't realize it though, but, I, in a way I can see why I'm over here fightin, you know? Cause if they take over here, they'll get to Hawaii and from there on, just try to take all over, see."

I thanked them and stopped the tape. Time passed. Guns fired and shells exploded. Suddenly, the camp was filled with the most brilliant light.

"A flare just dropped inside the perimeter. Men are rushing to put it out, rushing into the flames to put it out, hoping it doesn't hit any ammo. Their faces are diving back and forth, afraid that it might hit some ammo and explode it."

I moved to find cover.

"Men are standing around the flare, trying to put it out. Not much luck. They're just letting the flare burn itself out. Not much else they can do. It's extremely bright."

A helicopter flew low over the camp. I walked back to the aid station. Sergeant Ralph Wilson was standing outside. "It's a flare," he said. "It was either dropped from the bird, or a 105 tube shot it. And it didn't function properly. If it's from the flare bird, it's a 2 million candlepower."

"Lights it up like daylight when it hits the ground."

"It sure does."

"Good thing it didn't hit no ammo," another soldier said.

"That's lucky, huh?"

"That's a Rog."

"There's a fire burning now from the flare that dropped inside the perimeter."

"That must have been from that flare bird," Wilson said. "The chute probably didn't work."

"Everybody standin around lookin at it," Doc Burke said. "Gook sniper could have a field day now."

"He sure could," Wilson said.

"Look at the TOC wire." Burke pointed to the chain-link fence around Colonel Trobaugh's command post. The wire was designed to stop rocket propelled-grenades and other direct fire, but it was in pieces.

"Boy, they tore that apart, huh?" Burke said.

"Wow," said Wilson.

Eventually, the fire from the flare went out.

A jet bomber flew high overhead, the hollow roar of its engine vibrating in the air.

"Give em hell, tac," a soldier said.

"Yeah, just hope it's not a MiG," Burke laughed.

The mad minute took place at 4:30 and the noise was overpowering. It seemed that every gun on the base was firing in unison. When it was quieter, I spoke into the microphone.

"Bravo Company opened up with a heavy barrage of fire, timed and coordinated in advance. A lone artillery shell is fired, the muzzle pointed almost directly upward. It's been that close tonight."

It was two hours before dawn. Sergeant Burke offered me a cold beer and I took it gratefully. No one bothered to sleep.

APRIL 16, 1970

By dawn, the noise and chaos of the night had dissolved and the firebase was calm. The sun hid behind the horizon and the air was moist from the damp earth that held the humidity of the day before. No individual or crew-served weapons were being fired, no helicopters came or left, the artillery guns at the end of the camp were silent. Sleepless men bent over the scorched ground working with slow, weary movements like pickers in cotton fields, policing up pieces of debris and throwing them on one of the fires that filled the camp with the smell of burned gunpowder. Some of the soldiers stood with their hands on their hips and spoke with friends they hadn't seen since the start of the battle the night before, shaking their heads slowly from side to side as details flashed in their minds, gesturing with their hands in exaggerated animation like children telling a story, high on feelings of having survived. A few soldiers sat apart from the others, alone, staring at the tree line or the ground between their dirt-caked boots.

The camp was torn and burned by the forty to fifty rounds of incoming that exploded inside the wire. The earth was strewn with detritus of the battle: shell casings, broken boxes, live ammo, commo wire, field dressings (some with dry blood on them), blackened shell holes, shell fragments, scraps of cardboard and paper, torn fatigue cloth, shattered timber, sandbags, canvas, and a solitary combat boot with its laces untied. More layers of dark red dust had given the camp another coat of grit. It was a Friday, though few of the soldiers knew that. Days of the week had no meaning in the bush, only the date of the month and the number of days until their DEROS.

Lieutenant Colonel Trobaugh sent word he wanted to see me. He stood outside his CP with dusty white bandages on his face. His neck and hands were spotted brown with blood. His eyes were fresh, ready.

'I'd be grateful,' he said, 'if you don't report that I've been wounded. They're only superficial and I don't want my family to worry.'

'That's fine by me,' I said.

'I signed a waiver so my wife won't be notified if I'm wounded but not hurt seriously. The idea is even if you get a Purple Heart, your next of kin doesn't worry.'

'I was hoping we could do an interview with you when Keith and Jimmy get here,' I said. 'Your wife might see you on TV all bandaged up.'

'That's a problem.'

'If you'd like, I can arrange for someone from CBS to call and tell her not to worry when she sees you like this.'

Trobaugh thought for a few seconds and said that seemed a good idea. 'The Pentagon won't be calling her anyway,' he said, 'so if you just say I'm okay and still in command that should do it.' He gave me his wife's name and phone number in the States and I made a note to pass it on to Joy in New York. Then he turned away from the men standing around the TOC and put his face close to mine so that no one else could hear him.

"Look," he said, "as far as Al Rice and I are concerned, the road incident is forgotten. Okay?" He said division headquarters had not heard from the Pentagon about the rebellion and the Army seemed to be treating it as an aberration. "You guys called it as you saw it," he said. I agreed. We shook hands. I did not tell him that film of the rebellion would be shown again if we got approval to do an hour-long documentary.

Kay and Clevenger arrived just after dawn.

'Well, how was it?' Kay said. 'Get some good audiotape?'

'Yeah, I think so,' I said, 'It was noisy. Cause of all the outgoing. They had a hell of a fight before I got here.'

'Yeah, yeah,' Kay laughed, 'you should have been here an hour ago.' I told them what happened.

'How many got killed?' Clevenger asked.

I looked at my notebook. 'Seven U.S. Twenty-five wounded. Three guys got killed in a bunker that took a direct hit. It's a mess. I'll show you.'

'What about the other guys?' Kay said.

'So far, it looks like anything up to a hundred NVA dead. Three wounded prisoners. They got the rest of their wounded out.'

Kay looked around the base. 'Any chance of breakfast?' he said. 'I haven't had anything this morning.'

We got into the chow line and ate breakfast and drank coffee and then we set out to build a story around the aftermath of the attack. Kay shot scenes of the policing up, the downed helicopter, the bunker where the three GIs died. I did interviews with a group of soldiers who were judged to have shown conspicuous gallantry: Sergeant Tim Letcher, 21, of Washington, D.C. (recommended for a Silver Star); Specialist Fourth Class Margarito Aguilar, 21, from Alice, Texas; Sergeant Chris Gallagher, 20, of Westchester, Pennsylvania; and Second Lieutenant Mike Moon, 26, a red-headed officer from Middletown, Ohio. They described the battle and what they had done in modest words.

'What did you think about during the fighting?' I asked Aguilar.

"I don't know," he said, shaking his head. "It's just no feeling until after it's all over with. It's one big nightmare in a way which you don't realize. Everything's happening so fast yet when it's all over you stop to think what happened. Then you get a little shaky."

Seven men from Bravo Company, from the battalion headquarters group, and from the artillery battery, 2/19, were recommended for Silver Stars.

The battalion chaplain held a memorial service for the dead. The troops stood with their helmets off and their heads bowed in front of seven rifles fixed in the ground by their bayonets, the dead soldiers' helmets resting on the stocks of the rifles. The chaplain, Captain Dale Messersmith, 30, from York, Pennsylvania, recited from the Psalms, "He maketh me to lie down in green pastures. He leadeth me beside . . ." At the end of the service a firing party fired a volley of shots in the air and the soldiers fell out of formation and went back to their positions.

With the daylight came the body count. Bravo Company sent patrols outside the perimeter to police the battlefield for dead and wounded NVA soldiers, weapons, explosives and documents. A few of the troops were in a mean-tempered mood. When they came to bodies of dead Vietnamese, they tucked the toes of their boots under the hips and turned them over roughly. A patrol went inside the tree line and soon we could hear short bursts of riflefire coming from their M-16s. The body of the pilot who was killed by the rotor blade of his helicopter was placed in a rubber bag and flown away.

Lieutenant Colonel Trobaugh walked into the jungle to inspect the battlefield. The foliage was scarred black by fire and heat and the ground was churned by shell holes. Metal fragments, weapons, ammunition, bodies and pieces of bodies were scattered through the woods: bodies with a single wound and no other marks on them, bodies without heads or feet, bodies with faces frozen in pain and shock, bodies with no apparent wounds as if their hearts had simply stopped, bodies on their backs with faces looking upward at the sky in expressions of sublime peace, as though relieved in their final moments to be released from such rueful lives. As he stepped over each body, Trobaugh counted it. He came finally to a figure of sixty-six.

A North Vietnamese soldier in dirt-covered brown fatigues lay on his back looking up at a group of American soldiers who stood unmoving above him. He was a small man with strong shoulders and arms and a brown solid face dark with dirt. His eyes were cold and hard and did not blink. The look in his face was fear. A stomach wound had been treated and dressed by Doc Hildebrand. The battalion operations officer, Major Bacas, squatted beside the wounded man and asked him questions in Vietnamese. Bacas's words were fluent but he had difficulty understanding the wounded man's northern accent. Kay rolled film on the exchange between them. The soldier said his company marched for seven hours the night before (almost certainly from Cambodia) and arrived at the firebase shortly before the start of the attack. He fought until he was wounded. Bacas said the soldier was angry at being left behind when the others withdrew. The fear in his eyes showed that he expected to be killed at any time.

Bacas sifted through the soldier's wallet and studied the papers inside. "We think he's from the 95 Charlie and he's definitely an old soldier," he said. "He's got a couple of awards here. And he's been in battle before."

Bacas stood up. "It's unfortunate, I think. They've lost, they've probably lost a hundred men out here in this weak line. It's just loaded with people. It's loaded with weapons." He shook his head as if trying to comprehend his enemy's logic. "It's unfortunate that these people came in equipped as they did because it's almost a suicide type of thing that they attempted to do here."

"In fact it *was* a suicide mission," Lieutenant Colonel Trobaugh interrupted. "We can tell by the number of bodies we found out there."

Bacas arranged for the wounded North Vietnamese soldier to be evacuated to Tay Ninh by helicopter and treated at the American field hospital. 'He's a tough old veteran and he knows a lot,' Bacas said. 'He could be a big help if we can get him to talk to us.'

Kay and Clevenger stayed at the firebase to finish filming. I decided to go back to Tay Ninh. A helicopter came in and shut down. The wounded soldier was lifted aboard and placed on his back on the metal floor. Three young GIs from the firebase got aboard and sat down to wait for the helicopter crew to come back and start up. I did not recognize them. The wounded soldier looked up at me and spoke in a weak voice.

"Nook," he said.

I did not understand.

A few seconds later he said it again,

"Nook."

His eyes looked into mine. He repeated the word every few seconds.

"Nook."

He spoke the word with great effort but I did not understand him. The look on his face had changed to despair. I looked at the American soldiers and shrugged my shoulders. Their faces were angry. After a minute, I put my head down near the deck of the helicopter and listened to the wounded soldier. He said it again, just a low whisper.

"Nook."

What is he trying to say? I wondered. *Nook?*

A moment later it registered.

"Nuoc." Water!

Of course. He's thirsty. I reached for my canteen. As I unsnapped the buckle of the case I remembered it was not wise to give water to a man with a stomach wound. I looked closely. The bandages were more on his side than his stomach but I couldn't tell where the damage was. I imagined how dry he must be after all night under that almighty bombardment the firebase had put out.

I poured a few drops onto his tongue. He choked at first but then he swallowed with difficulty and when he had drunk about a small cupful I put the canteen away. The soldier looked at me with his head on the floor of the helicopter. A brief faint smile crossed his face. I smiled back and got up into my seat.

'Goddam gook,' one of the American soldiers said. 'What you do that for?' His eyes were black.

'He's thirsty,' I said. 'How would you feel?'

'I feel like shootin that motherfucker right here.' He pointed his M-16 toward the wounded soldier and slipped the safety. The expression in his eyes was homicidal. I did not speak.

'No sense givin water to a dead man,' one of the other soldiers said and laughed.

'He's lucky if he makes it to Tay Ninh,' the third one said.

'Might jes have a accident on the way.'

A chopper crewman climbed aboard with a canteen cup of coffee and sat

down. Then another crewman and then the pilot and copilot got into their
seats and strapped in and started the engine. The first GI clicked his rifle back
on safe and rested it between his legs. The helicopter took off for Tay Ninh.

From time to time the three GIs looked at the wounded soldier and me
with anger but otherwise they sat and stared out at the forest as it passed
below.

The chopper landed a hundred yards from the field hospital. There was
no one to carry the wounded soldier to a medical tent. The crew lifted him
onto the ground and left him on the edge of a field. I wanted to get to the
PIO area and arrange a flight to Saigon as soon as possible but didn't want to
leave the wounded soldier alone with the three GIs. I felt awkward and
uncomfortable, standing there, not speaking. The wounded soldier squinted
his eyes in the bright light and tried to cover his face but his arms were limp
with lack of strength. No one spoke. The GIs waited. After a few minutes
one of them said, 'No sense standin in the sun,' and walked away. The others
followed. When they were out of sight I walked to the hospital and told an
orderly there was a wounded man outside. A stretcher crew came out and
carried the North Vietnamese soldier into the emergency operating tent. I
waited around until I found one of the doctors and asked him if he would
take care of the NVA sergeant, make sure no one killed him. The doctor said
he would, 'Just like one of ours, don't worry.'

APRIL 17, 1970

After the long night at Firebase Atkinson, it was a pleasure to be in Saigon. The steamy old city seemed more civilized, more attractive, almost elegant in its fading fashion. Spring flowers were in bloom. Mail from home waited. Bed and pillow beckoned: a shower, clean sheets, cool air, cold drinks. Kay complained that we had been working for over a month without a break so we decided to take a day off and get caught up. Much had happened in our absence. The heavy heat of the approaching summer monsoon baked the streets and sidewalks like an oven, holding the city in its hot embrace.

The trip to Atkinson had been worth the effort. We had shown up in combat with the battalion and managed not to embarrass ourselves. Though our story of the aftermath of the attack might not get on the air because it lacked dramatic pictures, our willingness to be there had been observed. Senior officers saw that we were determined to finish the documentary. At the bureau, we shipped the story with small hope it would be broadcast.

A copy of *Stars and Stripes*, the armed forces newspaper, was in the office. A full-page headline read:

TROOPS PRAISED FOR BALKING AT CO'S ORDER

The April 16 issue reported the rebellion by Charlie Company ten days earlier and included the first official reaction by a military official.

The story filed by the Associated Press said:

A company of American infantrymen who balked at a battalion commander's order to move down a narrow jungle road were praised Monday for showing "common sense."

Praised for showing common sense? This was not the reaction we had expected. Lieutenant Colonel Robert Drudick, deputy commander of 1st Brigade, was quoted:

Thank God we've got young men who question. The young men in the
Army today aren't dummies, they are not automatons. They think.

Drudick said the men involved would not be punished because "it was
not the order itself they questioned, it was its execution."

The story explained the urgency to get the company out of the area
because of an impending B-52 strike. Drudick aborted the mission two minutes before the bombs were dropped because Charlie Company was three
hundred yards from the edge of the strike zone. Drudick said he did not
warn the company commander by radio because the transmission might be
intercepted by the North Vietnamese. "There hasn't been a war in which the
troops didn't question certain judgments," Drudick said. "It happens time
and again—it's nothing new." The article pointed out that the incident was
filmed and broadcast by CBS News, which certainly *was* new.

Reading the story, Kay, Clevenger and I were surprised. We hadn't seen
the U.S. Army in Vietnam react to a controversial story in an enlightened
way before.

'Do you believe this?' I said.

'They're getting smart,' Kay said. 'A couple of years ago they would have
claimed it never happened.'

'Not with our film of it, they wouldn't,' Clevenger said.

'Well, at least they didn't try to cover it up,' I said.

'Yeah, and the grunts aren't gonna have to pay,' Clevenger said.

'Don't be too sure about that,' said Kay, the Army veteran.

There was no solid news about Stone and Flynn, still missing in Cambodia.
Rumors and speculation circulated in the press corps, particularly among
reporters returning from Phnom Penh, but there was no verified information. Zalin Grant, a freelance reporter who had worked for TIME magazine
and CBS and was a friend of Dana and Sean, was on his way from the United
States to investigate. Zip was a scrupulously thorough journalist.

Mail had arrived. I kept a letter from Joy unopened all day, waiting until
evening when I could sit alone and read it slowly. The letter felt warm and
inviting in my pocket. We were planning to meet, possibly in Hawaii, when I

could get away for a few days. The idea of a reunion, with all its attendant fantasies, made Saigon more bearable. In the letter, written on April 12, she described her bedtime routine:

> Cat and I are having our cookies and milk . . . and thinking a HELLUVA LOT about you. I can't really speak for Mèo—I'm not ever sure of what he's thinking.

I pictured the cat sitting on the window sill, watching the nighttime New York traffic out the window, tracking it.

April 18, 1970

The overnight broadcast log from New York came in on the office lease line. The story we called "C Company on Patrol (Part III)" had been broadcast on Cronkite the evening before for five minutes. It was an unusual length for a piece made up mostly of the interviews with Sergeant Dunnuck, Doc Howe and Glenn Hindley. I wondered how the staff at the White House and Pentagon reacted when they saw Howe, the hero-pacifist, and Hindley, the peacenik, on national television.

A cable arrived from Ralph Paskman, manager of news, the dour disciplinarian who rarely communicated:

> 17163 MILLER LAURENCE ANOTHER SOCKO CHARLIE REPORT HAS US WONDERING HOW WE LUCKED INTO GETTING WITH THAT OUTFIT IN THE FIELD STOP APPRECIATE FULL DETAILS ON HOW YOU DID HAPPEN TO CONNECT WITH CHARLIE COMPANY STOP WERE YOU STEERED TO THEM BY THE MILITARY AND IF SO WHY OR DID YOU PICK THEM OUT AND ASK TO ACCOMPANY THAT SPECIFIC UNIT QUERY IF THATS HOW IT HAPPENED WHAT CALLED YOUR ATTENTION TO CHARLIE COMPANY AS THE OUTFIT TO STAY WITH QUERY STOP APPRECIATE BACKGROUND CABLE ON HOW THIS MARRIAGE HAPPENED REGARDS PASKMAN

My reply said the assistant division commander, Brigadier General Casey, approved our original proposal to live with a squad for two months or more and report on the daily lives of the GIs. I told Paskman that Casey sent us down the chain of command to his 1st Brigade commander, Colonel Ochs, who took us to meet Lieutenant Colonel Hannas, the 2/7 Battalion commander, who handed us over to Captain Jackson, who introduced us to Sergeant Dunnuck and his squad. It was all straightforward, by the book. We got the unit the Cav selected for us. It was one of the best squads in an excellent infantry company.

Paskman's questions puzzled me. For someone who had been so critical of the project until now, his sudden interest seemed hypocritical. Why did he need to know the background? Why was he supporting us after being so obstructive? Part of the answer came in a letter he wrote on April 14. He was writing, he said, to apologize for his angry cable earlier (the "expensive bandwagon" message) reprimanding me for taking Dana Stone into the field as a second camera. Now he wrote:

What prompted me to blow my stack was that your request for a second cameraman to work with you Keith and Jim was the FIRST word I had that this had previously been suggested and was possibly not only desirable but necessary. . . . I got the feeling that I was being nickeled and dimed to death and was being presented un fait accompli. Also at that time we had yet to see anything concrete in terms of output but there had been quite a bit (of) communications back and forth about sound trouble. It appears my worst fears were being realized—that no matter how good the intentions it is still necessary to know something about the equipment to be a good technician so that when there is trouble, as there is likely to be with things electrical under such conditions, there is at least a possibility of fixing it. I was very leery about the idea of having a soundman who had never handled sound. Then to be told after the unit finally was launched—that more manpower was needed—hit that nerve made raw by the fact that every cent expended by your team is over budget. But we made the decision to do it even though your presence and the presence of your crew in Vietnam is not provided for in the budget. You can hardly expect me to jump with joy at the idea of increasing that coverage. Even so, Jack, I will admit that my response was excessive and I do apologize for that.

April 19, 1970

A message from New York said our story of the attack on Firebase Atkinson had been broadcast on the *CBS Sunday News with Roger Mudd* for almost four minutes. We figured it must have been a slow news day or maybe the producers were becoming genuinely interested in what was going on in War Zone C. That evening, Kay and Clevenger took me to dinner at a good French restaurant. We drank, ate and laughed. Life seemed good again. I had not learned the wartime lesson that one hour of peace and happiness is not always followed by another, that your world can change in a moment, that this moment is all we have.

April 20, 1970

Colonel Ochs sent a message from Tay Ninh to the bureau saying he wanted a meeting to discuss the future of our project with C Company. The message was specific: 'The Colonel will see Mr. Laurence alone tomorrow.' No time was suggested, no other details. It was puzzling. Dave Miller said it sounded bad. He called the new division PIO, Major Melvin Jones, and asked what was going on. Jones said he was establishing new ground rules for covering the Cav. Reporters and camera crews would begin each visit by reporting to Phuoc Vinh and picking up an escort officer who would take them into the field. At the end of the day they would return to Phuoc Vinh. If they wanted to return to the unit the following day, new transportation would have to be arranged.

We knew that it would be unworkable. There was no way to chopper in and out to Charlie Company every day. In effect, Jones was making it impossible for us to complete the documentary.

Miller suggested that we test the new ground rules. He chartered a private plane to take us to Tay Ninh the next morning. There we would try to get aboard a helicopter and fly out to Charlie Company. It was a log day and the men were scheduled to be resupplied. A second camera crew would film a confrontation if it happened. Miller called Jones's office and left a message saying we were going back in with C Company tomorrow and asked for an acknowledgment.

In the evening, a phone call came from Tay Ninh: 'You know who this is?'

a young man's voice said. Static crackled. The voice was familiar—our enlisted man friend from the PIO office.

'That's affirmative,' I said.

'Tomorrow's meeting between you and the Old Man?'

'Roger.'

'Be careful. The brigade staff made us give them a tape recorder last night. A Tango Romeo. Got that? Over.'

'Gotcha.'

'They're gonna hide it someplace in the room so it records everything you say. Do you copy? Over.'

'That's affirm. Tomorrow's meeting will be taped.'

'I think they're hoping you'll say something incriminating. Or lose your temper. They're gonna try to provoke an argument. So they can discredit you, personally. Understand? Over.'

'Yes. I understand. Thanks much. Anything more?'

'Yeah. Division sent two guys from military intelligence to spy on the PIOs in Tay Ninh. To investigate a so-called security leak.'

'Spooks?'

'That's a Rog.'

'What next?'

'God knows. All I know is that they're gonna bug the meeting tomorrow. So watch your ass, Jack. And be cool. Over and out.' The line dissolved to static and hiss.

April 21, 1970

A twin-engine charter took off from Tan Son Nhut at dawn with six men from CBS News aboard: Miller, Kay, Clevenger, film photographer Skip Brown, his sound tech, Joe Yue, and me. Miller and I were sleepy. We had been awake all night in the bureau waiting for a call from Major Jones that never came. The plan was simple. At the logistics pad in Tay Ninh, Kay, Clevenger and I would try to get on the resupply helicopter to Charlie Company. If someone tried to stop us, Brown and Yue would film it for broadcast later. Miller would observe. We were not going to accept Major Jones's restrictive new ground rules without a fight.

From the airport, we hitchhiked to the PIO shop. Along the way, we met an officer from Charlie Company who recognized us and stopped to talk. He said an extraordinary investigation was under way. All the company's records were being checked, he said. 'Don't ask me why,' he said, 'but thought you should know. Something's up.' The officer said an article about the rebellion in the current issue of *Newsweek* really angered the top brass. He wished us well.

At the PIO office, the staff greeted us with friendly courtesy. Miller said we were ready to log in again with Charlie Company. After a wait, Major Jones appeared. He said Colonel Ochs wanted to see me alone, now. The six of us walked to the portable trailer home Ochs used as an office. Brigade staff officers standing outside the door allowed me to go inside but not the others. When I went in, I told Ochs my bureau chief was waiting outside. 'Bring him in,' he declared. Miller joined the meeting. The one other person in the room, Lieutenant Colonel Drudick, the deputy brigade commander, stood in the back while everyone else sat.

I looked around the office for a tape recorder or microphone but did not see one. I took my own tape recorder out of the small medic's bag I carried, placed it on my lap and pressed the record button. Miller also started a tape recorder and put it on a table. We were relaxed but cautious. Ochs was formal, tense. Drudick, standing behind us, did not speak or sit.

Ochs held a copy of the April 20 Asian edition of *Newsweek*. A one-column story without a picture was headlined:

JUST DOWNRIGHT REFUSAL

I had read it earlier. The text was made up of quotes from the TV report on the rebellion that had been broadcast on the Cronkite news. Sitting behind his desk, Ochs started the meeting.

"I've viewed this article in *Newsweek* which is titled 'Just Downright Refusal,' and it mentions Mr. Laurence and also quotes Captain Rice and some soldiers. And this article of course is distributed to troops throughout the fire support base. And in light of the article and under the circumstances, I've reevaluated the CBS project in Charlie Company—in the light of its impact on the efficiency of the company and also on the ability of Captain Rice to exercise command responsibility. I've talked this over in considerable detail with the battalion commander and, in fact we talked for some time about the crew being down there and the impact of the article had on the uh . . .."

"Did the article have an impact on the unit?" I asked.

"It has on the fire support base," Ochs said. "The unit [C Company] is in the jungle now so they haven't. But I've come to the conclusion I think it's time to discontinue the project—uh, CBS covering Charlie Company as it has in the past."

Miller and I said that we considered the conversation to be on the record. Ochs nodded.

"I think that it is time that Charlie Company get on," he continued. "Let the new company commander exercise his command without the presence of the TV camera continually around him. I think it is in the best interests of the overall efficiency of the command. I think it's in Captain Rice's best interests that you discontinue. I recognize your position but I think the interest of the company, the interests of the company commander are overriding. They have a mission. And I think that they should be permitted to accomplish the mission without continuously being in the spotlight, think they're being spotlighted."

"How do you mean spotlighted?" I asked.

"Well, having a camera crew in the company area continually, can't help but feel the presence—the company commander [is] certainly mindful of the presence of the camera crew in his company area continually. And I think you've had ample opportunity to cover Charlie Company. I believe it's in the interest of the company, interest of the commander now, uh, to discontinue the program."

"Why the abrupt change after the initial understanding? That we will be with Charlie Company for two months?" I said.

"Well, as I said, the *Newsweek* article has caused me to reevaluate the, uh, desirability of continuing the program."

"We had nothing to do with the publication of that article."

"The fact remains that the article quotes you and the article is made available to the troops. And I just feel that it's in the overall best interests of the company that we let them, uh, permit them to accomplish their task without the presence of the CBS crew."

I asked Ochs if he would repeat what he had just said for the record in front of a camera crew.

"No. I have no desire to make a statement for the camera. This is my decision and I will prefer not to make it part of a TV series."

"Can I make sure that I heard your quote exactly?" I asked, starting to write his words in my notebook. "'The reason for discontinuing. . . .'"

Ochs bristled. *"All right!"* he said in a loud voice. "My reason for discontinuing the program is that I feel that it's in the overall best interests of the company, and in Captain Rice's interests as a commander. I'm primarily concerned with the efficiency of the company, and Captain Rice's proper discharge of command responsibility."

"'. . . primarily concerned with the efficiency of the company?'"

"Right."

"'. . . and Captain Rice's . . .' I'm sorry, sir."

"Proper discharge of command responsibility."

"How were we interfering with that?" I asked.

"I feel that the TV crew has been with the company long enough, and that their presence no longer serves the best interests of the unit or its company commander. That's all I wish to say."

"And on that basis we are denied permission to log in with Charlie Company today or in the future?"

"That is correct."

I realized even as we argued that there was no way to convince Ochs to change his order. All that was possible to do now was try to find out where the decision had been made, at what level, and by whom.

"We are in the middle of a series, sir, on Charlie Company," I said. "And we are ending, I mean, abruptly, suddenly, chopping off in the middle of a projected series, a continuing story on the development of Charlie Company, its days in the field, all the things we talked about when we first met. And, uh, that's not clear enough an answer, in all honesty. 'The presence no longer serves the best interests of the unit or the company commander.' How? Why?"

"Well, I've got no further comment to make, Mr. Laurence. I feel that Charlie Company has, ah, been available, ah, as the object of your stories long enough. I feel that it's time to discontinue, that's. . . ."

"But there's no reason."

"I don't have any. . . ."

"You mentioned the *Newsweek* article, but, uh, that's not our product. Do you have a morale problem? Do you . . ." I wanted Ochs to tell us the true reason for the expulsion.

"I've got nothing further to say on the matter, for the record or otherwise. I think the decision has been made. The, uh, project should be discontinued."

"This is your decision? And you are accepting responsibility for it?"

"I've consulted with the battalion commander. Ah, I'll accept responsibility." Ochs stood up from behind the desk. "Well, thank you very much."

Dave Miller spoke for the first time. He did not stand. "Excuse me, sir. I would like to ask you a few questions now if I may."

Ochs sat down again. "Yeah."

"First, I want to make clear that I am the bureau chief of CBS News in Saigon and I have followed the military activity in Vietnam with some interest. As I have been here for a year and a half now, this makes me just about, I think, the senior bureau manager in Saigon, more or less, I suppose. This leads me to the first question that I have while listening to you speak. That is, have you personally seen any of these pieces on television?"

"Yes."

"Which one, sir?"

"I saw the ah the one which, ah, where there was a disagreement about going down the road."

"That was the only one you saw?"

"That's the only one I saw."

"Did you by any chance see transcripts of the other stories?"

"No, I don't recall that I did."

"Would you be interested in seeing them?"

"Ah, no, not particularly."

"Doesn't logic dictate that if you are so intimately involved in a project like this that you would like to see the output?"

"Well, I understand that there have been four or five favorable stories on, ah, in connection with Mr. Laurence's project."

"But you are not interested in seeing the transcripts?"

"If they were available, of course, but I would not go to any great lengths to see them. I've got a job to do."

"Have you discussed this question with your superior officers? Not with your lower officers, with your superior officers? I mean at the general staff level?"

"Mr. Laurence's presence down here is, of course, common knowledge at every echelon in the division."

"No, but has this specific subject—the subject of this morning's meeting—been discussed at a higher level?"

"I don't think there is any need for me to discuss, ah, the issue at higher level. I think the matter is that I accept responsibility, ah, and made the determination of that, ah, project should be discontinued, ah, of the Charlie Company."

"Have you discussed this with division?"

"I've discussed it with the PIO of division."

"Have you discussed with non-PIO of division?"

"Of course it's been discussed. And no project of this nature [would not have] been discussed. The decision and responsibility is mine and I think that is [a] simple point to convey."

"Did you discuss it with the chief of staff?"

"I don't see why I have to be subject to all these questions. I think these are matters which are, ah, of really no concern to you as a. . . ."

"They are of great concern, sir, because we like to see how things develop, and how they develop as a military officer, sir. I'm sure that you are really interested in tactics and the grand strategy and the movement and the development and growth and concepts. I think these are of vital interest to you in your field. They are certainly of vital interest to us in our field. Was this question raised with the general of the division?"

"Just ask the other question. I have to get on with my job here."

"This represents the . . ."

"I have informed you of the decision," Ochs said. "I see no further need to go into the details, background. I gave you my reasons, indicated that I accept responsibility. I've discussed it with the battalion commander, and we're taking this action because we feel that it's in the interest of the company." Ochs stood up again.

Miller stood up in front of him. "Well, you can't just dismiss us like this. I think that we are entitled to some of your time here. I've come from Saigon with the specific purpose, sir, of finding out about this project. I don't think I can be thrown out of your office when you're finished with me."

"No one is going to throw you out of this office."

"Well, I would like to continue the conversation."

Ochs sat down. "I, ah, think that if we get into this sort of discussion I prefer to have a public information officer who is more expert in discussing these matters than I. I'm not technically, ah, competent to, ah, conduct a discussion of this nature. A PIO of my, ah, I would like to have a PIO present."

Miller sat down. "Sure," he said.

"For advice," said Ochs.

"Well, did MACOI, the MACV Office of Information, have any influence in this decision?" Miller asked.

"As I say, these are questions you should ask the PIO."

There was a pause. I asked, "Have we in any way interfered with the tactical operations of your battalion? Of your company? Have we in any way disturbed the normal functioning of that unit as a fighting unit?"

"That would be hard to assess. Ah, I think that you're being in the company obviously gives the company commander an additional responsibility in exercising command—the presence of other than the members of the company. Ah, so it is an additional mission to them to handle you can't overlook."

"Have we interfered?"

"I would have to consult the battalion commander before I answered that."

"Well, you indicate that you and Colonel Trobaugh, ah, concur in this decision."

"Right."

"A month ago we sat in this office, sir, and I outlined what our program was and that is precisely what we have done. We have broadcast six stories on Charlie Company—ah, excuse me, ah, five stories on Charlie Company and one on the battalion at Atkinson that had the fight. And if you can give me one logical reason why you've made this decision—we're asking what did we do wrong and you're not giving us an answer."

"Well, as I said before, my answer is I think that it's in the best interest of the company and best interest of the company commander. And I think that's a sufficient answer. You make a decision upon what is best for the organization, what is best for its commander. You have a new commander and, ah, I feel that, ah, your presence in the company no longer serves his interest or the company's interest, and I must make that determination on the basis of what's best for the company. I appreciate your, ah . . ."

Miller broke in. "Colonel, what do you think personally of Mr. Laurence? And Mr. Kay and Mr. Clevenger? You've seen them in action. What do you think of them?"

"I, ah, said before I don't think I have any further comment to make at this time. I, ah . . ."

"This is a comment you would make of men who have shared combat with your troops? Is that it?"

"I think, ah, ah, I think I have treated Mr. Laurence as a gentleman and he has treated me as a gentleman."

"But you have no opinion of them?"

Ochs said nothing. No one spoke.

"I'm sorry," I said finally and stood up.

"Good luck to you," Ochs said. He smiled and resumed his command presence, offering his hand. It was as if our former relationship had not been changed by the preceding exchange, as if the colonel had only been carrying out an order.

"Thank you," I said, shaking hands.

"Mr. Miller, take care," Ochs said, reaching out, shaking his hand. "Nice to have seen you."

The meeting had taken twenty-five minutes. As we left, I spotted a tape recorder concealed on a table behind Lieutenant Colonel Drudick, who was still standing. Walking out of the cool shaded office trailer, the light and heat of the day hit our faces like a desert wind.

We explained what had happened inside to Kay, Clevenger, Skip Brown and Joe Yue. Miller did not appear to be worried. 'The fight begins,' he said. I was less confident. Kay and Clevenger were shocked. It took several minutes for the weight of Colonel Ochs's decision to make itself clear. As far as the Army was concerned, we were finished with Charlie Company. Kay, Clevenger and I walked back to the PIO shop and told the officers and enlisted men on the PIO staff what had happened. They said they were sorry but had seen it coming.

'You guys tried to tell it like it is out there—like it *really* is,' one of the EMs said.

'Yeah, whenever *we* write a story like that they cut it out of the paper,' an Army reporter said. There was a long silence.

'We're gonna miss you,' another said.

'Those grunts in Charlie Company are gonna miss you too.'

Kay and I sat and looked at the floor, not speaking. Clevenger was defiant. He held up a can of beer he had scrounged somewhere.

'Fuck the Army!' he said.

'You can't,' one of the soldiers said. 'The Army always wins.'

'Tell that to the VC,' Clevenger snapped.

I went outside the PIO office and sat on the ground. Miller went away to organize transportation back to Saigon. Overhead, the sun was a flaming fireball, a glowing yellow disc high in the sky. I felt nothing. I had no idea what we were going to do next, what was going to happen. Time passed.

A loud rushing noise whooshed overhead and crashed in the brigade camp with a terrific *SPLAAAAT!* The power of the explosion sent shock waves through the earth. The ground trembled. *Rockets!* I thought. *Three hundred meters.* Someone shouted, "Incoming!" and ran. I turned over on my hands and knees and looked around. Nothing moved. In a moment the camp was quiet. It seemed deserted. Dust blew in the wind. *God,* I thought, *they're trying to kill us. Blow up the PIO shop so it looks like combat. All they'd need is a grenade.* Kay and Clevenger had disappeared. Alone on the ground in the middle of an open field, I heard a second rocket scream over and burst on the ground near the same place. Dust rose in the distance.

I looked for cover. The PIO office was too exposed. A hundred yards away was a small building with radio antennas fortified by neat rows of sandbags five to six feet high. I got to my feet, ran across the field and ducked inside. The building was crammed with radio receivers and electronic equipment stacked up from the concrete floor to the roof with a narrow aisle between. Three soldiers wearing military fatigues with no markings were sprawled on the floor. They looked up in surprise.

'Mind if I take cover with you?' I said, kneeling.

'Not a bit,' one of them said.

'Make yourself right at home,' said another.

'Welcome to the wonderful world of radio,' the third said.

Another rocket shrieked over and exploded.

'Sounds like 122s,' I said. The men did not seem worried.

'They'll need a direct hit to hurt us,' one of them said.

'They haven't got direction-finding gear.'

'Not yet.'

'They're probably after the TOC,' one of the soldiers said.

'Yeah, it's probably the gook who washes the Old Man's laundry.'

'Didn't get paid this month.' The men laughed.

When no rockets came in for a few minutes we stood up and shook hands. I introduced myself. The men said they were from the radio listening section of military intelligence and were assigned to monitor VC communications in the area. They did not mention the security leak in the PIO shop, but it appeared they might also be tapping the phones and offices across the field. Several large reels of tape turned slowly on their recorders.

'How long you been in-country?' one asked.

'This is my third tour,' I said. 'Started in '65.'

'What d'you like it over here or something?'

'No, I hate it. It just keeps pulling me back.'

'Guess you seen some shit.'

'A little. Rockets are the worst. You can't tell where they're going to hit.'

'Neither can the VC.' They all laughed.

I thanked them and left. Outside, paranoia got a tight grip on me. I wanted to get away from Tay Ninh as soon as possible.

Kay, Clevenger, Miller, Brown and Yue were waiting in the PIO office.

'Where the hell were you?' Kay said.

'Over there,' I said, pointing. 'In that bunker. You'll never believe what they're doing.'

'What?' said Clevenger.

'Tell you later,' I said, pointing to the ceiling.

As we were leaving, one of the enlisted men in the PIO shop appeared with a bunch of tiny red wildflowers. He put one of the flowers in the lapels of each of our fatigue jackets. He and the other soldiers seemed sincerely sorry that we were going away and not coming back.

As we flew to Saigon in a helicopter, Miller took still pictures of us sitting in the open back. Kay was dark, unshaven, his black hair unfurled and waving in the wind, the white patch on the side prominent, his face in deep melancholy. I appeared in the photograph, head down, as if mourning a death. Clevenger was red-faced, sunburned, holding a can of beer. As Miller snapped the shutter, Clevenger smiled wickedly into the lens, giving it the finger.

APRIL 22, 1970

The full impact of the expulsion hit like a hammer blow. Overpowering, humiliating, crushing—like losing a fistfight. I felt empty inside, lost, without purpose. Our dream of making a documentary about the lives of ordinary soldiers was dead. We had tried to show the war as it truly was but the generals and public relations managers had shut us down before we finished. The truth was dangerous to them. The generals must have known, better than we, that when good soldiers argue openly about the wisdom of fighting a war, as they had in Charlie Company, the war is lost.

'Wonder where they are now,' Kay said at breakfast in the garden of the Continental.

'Still in the Dog's Head,' Clevenger said. 'The L-T at the log pad said they were on the border.'

I looked at my watch. 'Probably humping by now.'

'Wonder if Gordy got back from R and R yet,' Kay said.

'God, I hope they don't get hit,' I said.

'Not without us.'

'Can you imagine if they get hit and we aren't there?'

'Aw, man, don't even say it.'

Clevenger had been listening carefully. He said, 'Do you realize what you just *said*?' We looked at him. He shook his head. 'You guys are totally *crazy*.'

Being unable to finish the work was bad enough; being banished from 2d Squad was worse. We had become attached to them: Dunnuck, Lee, Teschker, Rivera, Boling, Dudley, Howe, Winfield and the others. And we missed them. We did not miss the long patrols or the pack weight or the bugs or the sore bones or cold ground, but we missed the guys. Our attachment to them had become more than professional interest in what happened, more than personal concern for their well-being. The connection was deeper. In our way, we had become part of the squad. We weren't soldiers and we didn't pretend to be and we wouldn't fight in combat with them, but we were honorary members of their team, at least part of the time. We were civilians who had been accepted by them. No matter that we didn't carry weapons and didn't have to obey orders, we did most everything else with them and they respected us. We were a link between them and the world back home, the guys who covered the war and got it shown in the States. As far as the squad was concerned, we were Keith and Jim and Jack and we were okay. We had been in the war a long time and were still there. We wanted to see this period through with them, with their squad and their rifle company, however it ended. To us, the danger of getting shot seemed less important than being there to go through the experience with them and record it on film. (The idea of getting hurt was always an abstraction, a possibility you couldn't think about seriously until it was about to happen, or until after it had.) Now it was as though we had been separated from our family. A gray enduring gloom enveloped us like a fog.

I tried to keep busy. Details of what happened had to be communicated to New York. Long cables and transcripts of the meeting with Ochs were sent. The more information we cabled, the more questions New York asked. It became an investigation. We tried to find out how and why the decision to expel us was made. A few First Cav officers and enlisted men called or came to the office in Saigon to tell us what they knew. Other journalists did interviews. They seemed sympathetic, especially James Sterba and Gloria Emerson of the *New York Times,* and sent messages to their editors in New York. No one could recall a case of a reporter being forbidden to visit an American infantry unit in the field on routine operations. We were being censored.

Within twenty-four hours, Kay and Clevenger were reassigned by CBS. The network was producing an instant special on the gathering crisis in Cambodia and needed every camera crew it could get to shoot it. Kay and Clevenger would go to Phnom Penh. Clevenger was sorry to leave Charlie Company but excited about going to Cambodia. Compulsive traveler and sightseer, he wanted to get to Angkor Wat before the war did. North Vietnamese forces had advanced to within twenty miles of Phnom Penh and government troops seemed powerless to stop them. The United States was shipping weapons and equipment to Phnom Penh urgently and South Vietnamese troops had staged several armed raids across the border. The future of Cambodia was being decided.

I stayed in Saigon. If there was any chance of getting back with C Company, I needed to be there.

Lieutenant Tuck, the friendly PIO from Tay Ninh, called to say he believed our expulsion was decided by general officers at division headquarters in Phuoc Vinh. Moreover, he said, the order was approved in Saigon by the Information Office of the U.S. Army, Vietnam.

Tuck had managed to get a job in Phuoc Vinh at the division press office. "We sent a message down to USARV-IO," he said on the phone, "informing them of our decision. And the decision was made in conjunction with the generals here and Colonel Ochs."

"Who's responsible?" I said.

"Division. It came from, you know, as high as you can go."

"The commanding general?"

"Yeah, the generals. That article in *Newsweek* really pissed them off." (How ironic: to be banned because of a follow-up story rather than our own report.) "That and the thing about showing that guy as a heat casualty."

"You mean Puget, the point man?"

"Yeah. I guess his parents first saw it; the first thing they heard about it was on television." I didn't know that the Cav did not report heat causalities to next of kin. Puget's parents had been given no warning their son would be seen on *The Evening News*. It was a mistake.

"So who decided to kick us out?"

"The decision came from at least division level. It had to be concurred from higher than us. It had to be concurred from USARV."

"Do you know for sure that it wasn't Colonel Ochs's decision?"

"I don't know for sure, but I'd say it wasn't his. He may have concurred, but the final decision was not his. It came from even higher."

I asked him how the troops in the field were taking the decision. Tuck handed the phone to the top enlisted man in the division PIO office, a reporter named Bob.

"Most of the grunts understand the reasons used by the Army," he said. "That is, that the efficiency of the unit would be hampered. And they believe those reasons to be silly. I was out there with Charlie Company today. They said they didn't mind you out there at all. They said they really grooved on it. The captain [Rice] was standing right next to them when they said it."

"What did he say?" I asked.

"He took it really good. Because he was even laughing, joking with the guys, you know, when they got letters and stuff."

An officer named Larry called from Tay Ninh. "Charlie Company at present has got very bad morale problems," he said. "For one reason, they know what's going on. You can't fool these guys. Part of the company is taking one side and part of the company is taking the other side [about the rebellion]. They're fighting among themselves. The company is just, you know, struggling. About what was right and what was wrong. Some guys thought they should have gone [down the road] and the Old Man was right, and other guys say, 'No, never,' and 'They're not walking.'"

Cable traffic between Saigon and New York became busy. Bensley pointed out that he still had a long scene of Charlie Company's mail call that we had filmed on April 5 but had not been used on the air. He had screened all the footage, blocked out a structure and wanted to use it for a finale.

With Bensley's outline, writing the narration was straightforward. I had to hurry because a flight to the States was leaving in a couple of hours. I wrote quickly:

CHARLIE COMPANY'S LETTERS
Laurence / Kay / Clevenger
War Zone C
April 5 and 22, 1970

1. MAIL BEING HANDED OUT (NATURAL SOUND)

2. LAURENCE V/O:

> Mail call. Once every four days—along with the fresh supply of food and water—Charlie Company gets letters from home.
> (Natural sound)
> Mail call means more to a soldier—spending part of his life in an Asian jungle on orders to kill and be killed by other men—mail call means more than anything else . . . except perhaps that he is still alive. And four days shorter, four days closer to what the military vocabulary calls DEROS, the day a man gets out of Vietnam, what the line troops call 'going back to the real world.'
> (*Sound*)
> The days are counted as carefully as the words of the letters are read.
> PFC Bob Teschker was expecting a package but believes it was burned up with the other mail in the attack on the battalion command post. This day he got four letters, one for every day he went without one.
> (*Teschker interview*)
> PFC Lee Boling decided to clean his rifle while his friends in 2d Squad read their letters. He received none.
> (*Boling interview*)

PFC George Rivera got six letters—the most ever at one time in the ten and a half months he's been in the field in Vietnam. He figures it's because he's getting so short, so close to going home—and his family knows he has been badly wounded once and that he is really worried now about surviving the final days.

(*Rivera interview*)

But we will not know whether PFC George Rivera makes it home safely . . . or what happens in the weeks ahead to the rest of the men of Charlie Company, for it can no longer be reported by the CBS News camera team of Keith Kay, Jim Clevenger and me. High military officials have decided that the series must stop. The explanation given is that our reports are no longer believed to be in the best interests of the company or its commander.

John Laurence, CBS News, and our last letter from Charlie Company in War Zone C.

We recorded the narration and shipped it. Then we fed another copy of the voice-track on the daily PTT audio circuit to New York, enabling Bensley to start cutting the piece to the voice-over before the broadcast-quality narration reached New York by plane. The next day he cabled:

23175 LAURENCE CHARLIE FINALE RUNS FIVE FORTY FIVE AND WORKS FINE STOP YOUNG ASSOCIATE OF MINE NAMED GOULD SUGGESTS ONE POSSIBLE FOLLOWUP STORY WHAT EVER HAPPENED TO CAPTAIN JACKSON QUERY IS HE AVAILABLE OR OFFBOUNDS TO YOU QUERY EYE NEVER DID HEAR HOW HEART TESTS CAME OUT STOP ANYWAY IF JACKSON AVAILABLE IT MIGHT MAKE USEFUL PIECE TO SHOW HIM AT NEW JOB AND DO INTERVIEW ON WHAT HE THINKS OF WHATS BEEN HAPPENING STOP WHAT THINK QUERY BENSLEY

A cable from Paskman arrived.

MILLER LAURENCE STOP BENSLEY HOPES HAVE ANOTHER CHARLIE COMPANY PIECE ASSEMBLED FOR CRONKITE USE AT WHICH TIME WE WILL REPORT THAT YOU NO LONGER PERMITTED COVER CHARLIE COMPANY STOP HAVE YOU ASKED FOR PERMISSION TO COVER ANOTHER OUTFIT ONE WHERE COMPANY COMMANDER FACTOR CANNOT BE USED AS REASON FOR NOT ALLOWING CBS TEAM TO ACCOMPANY UNIT QUERY SURELY THERE MUST BE ANOTHER UNIT AROUND AND IF THEY SAY NO THEN IT

WILL BE QUITE OBVIOUS THAT YOU HAVE BEEN PROSCRIBED COM-
PLETELY ALTHOUGH FROM YOUR MESSAGES TODAY COLONEL OCHS HAS
NOT ACCUSED YOU OF ANY WRONG DOING OR FAULTED ACCURACY OF
YOUR REPORTING STOP WE CURIOUS AS TO WHAT HAPPENS NEXT IN
YOUR PURSUIT OF THE GRUNT STORY REGARDS PASKMAN

Miller called Major Jones in Phuoc Vinh and spoke with him at length.

"Your crew cannot go back in with 2/7," Jones said. "They can go to another battalion but not on the same basis. We can get you out there in the morning with a unit and if you want to go in with a company you can come back to Tay Ninh and they will get you back there the next day. And you can go back with the unit and so forth."

"You mean they cannot overnight in the field with the units?" Miller said.

"Yeah. I think this thing has probably killed it for everybody—ABC, NBC, Laurence, everybody—to just go down with a unit like that. The business of going out with one unit and staying out there, that's gone."

I cabled New York with details of the conversation and continued:

PASKMAN YOUR 21175 . . . HIS EXPLANATION FOR THIS SWEEPING NEW BAN
ON WHAT HAS BEEN A RARELY-USED BUT TRADITIONAL PRIVILEGE OF
PRESS TO STAY WITH ANY UNIT AS LONG AS DESIRED IS QUOTE THE PEOPLE
DOWN THERE ARE GETTING THE CLIPPINGS BACK (LETTERS FROM HOME).
THE PARENTS ARE MAD AND THEIR BUDDIES ARE MAD AND THE GUYS ARE
MAD TOO. THEY ARE ALL MAD. UNQUOTE. ANOTHER SPOKESMAN FOR
BRIGADE SAYS ALL HELICOPTER CREWS HAVE BEEN ORDERED NOT TO FLY
CCBBSS CREWS TO SECOND OF SEVENTH, NOR ANYWHERE ELSE WITHOUT
BEING ESCORTED BY MILITARY. THAT'S IT OFFICIALLY.

The cable went on to tell about the reports we had received of morale problems in Charlie Company, Captain Rice's relaxed attitude toward CBS News, comments of the soldiers and other details. The message continued:

YOU SHOULD BE ABLE TO SEE THE CONTRADICTIONS BETWEEN WHAT WE ARE
BEING TOLD OFFICIALLY AND WHAT PEOPLE ARE TELLING US FROM FIRST
HAND CONVERSATIONS AND OBSERVATIONS. ANYWAY, THE MILITARY HAS
SLAPPED WHAT EYE REGARD AS THE MOST SEVERE RESTRICTIONS ON PRESS
COVERAGE IN MY EXPERIENCE IN VIETNAM. NOT EVEN UNDER THE MOST
INTENSE COMBAT EMERGENCIES KHE SANH AND BATTLE OF HUE AND CON

THIEN AND PLEI ME AND ALL OF THE TET OFFENSIVE HAVE WE BEEN SO RESTRICTED, ESPECIALLY AFTER BEING GIVEN FULL PERMISSION TO GO ANY-WHERE WITH THEM LAST MONTH. MILITARY MAY MAKE ISSUE OF FOLLOWING INCIDENTS:

ONE THAT THE ENTIRE COMPANY DID NOT REBEL AND CBS NEWS WAS WRONG. EYE HAVE TOLD THEM THAT EYE WENT DOWN THE ENTIRE LINE OF THE COMPANY WHILE IT WAS ON ROAD AND INTERVIEWED MEN ON TAPE AND NONE OF THEM SAID IT WAS A WISE DECISION. ONE PLA-TOON LEADER WAS TRANSFERRED OUT OF CHARLIE COMPANY FOR NOT SUPPORTING CAPTAIN RICE. THAT WAS TOLD ME ON BACKGROUND BY BATTALION COMMANDER, LT. COL. TROBAUGH.

TWO THAT PARENTS OF P.F.C. STEVEN PUGET, OF CRESCENT CITY, CALIFORNIA THE POINT MAN WHO WAS THE HEAT CASUALTY IN "PATROL PART THREE" COMPLAINED TO PENTAGON THAT FIRST THEY KNEW OF HIS HEAT STROKE WAS WATCHING IT ON TELEVISION. ARMY SAYS HE WAS NOT A CASUALTY AND THEREFORE PARENTS WERE NOT INFORMED. WE BELIEVE THAT IT WAS OBVIOUS FROM FILM THAT HE WAS NOT A SERIOUS CASUALTY AND WE STATED HE WOULD BE BACK WITH UNIT IN COUPLE OF DAYS.

THREE THAT LT. COLONEL TROBAUGH'S WIFE FIRST LEARNED OF HER HUSBAND'S WOUNDS FROM CBS NEWS, NOT THE ARMY. SHE RECEIVED PHONE CALL FROM CBS NEWS AS WE REQUESTED. HER NAME, ADDRESS AND PHONE NUMBER WERE GIVEN TO ME BY TROBAUGH HIM-SELF, AND HE ENCOURAGED ME TO CALL. HE HAS SIGNED ARMY WAIVER, ALLOWING MILITARY NOT TO INFORM NEXT OF KIN WHEN WOUNDS JUDGED TO BE NOT SERIOUS, AND HE WAS CONCERNED SHE MIGHT WORRY IF HE APPEARED IN FIRE BASE ATKINSON STORY ALL BANDAGED UP.

THAT'S ALL WE KNOW NOW. WE HAVE UNCHALLENGABLE RECORD OF QUOTES ABOVE. WE FEEL LIKE WE BEING OVER-RUN IN FIRST SKIR-MISH. HOW ABOUT SOME HEAVY ARTILLERY FOR SUPPORT QUERY.

REGARDS, LAURENCE

I assumed that the military and civilian agencies of the U.S. government tried to monitor all cable traffic between Saigon and the outside world, for its own security and for intelligence gathering, but I ignored it. I made no attempt to encode the information in our communications with New York. I thought the generals in Vietnam and Washington might learn a little about the case from our reporting of it. It wouldn't harm us for them to know how seriously we planned to fight their decision.

The struggle would be fought on several fronts. In Saigon, Dave Miller had some influence with the MACV Office of Information and the U.S. embassy. As bureau chief for CBS News, he had access to senior military and civilian officials and could argue our case with them for reinstatement with Charlie Company. Miller also decided to press the issue with the commander of the First Cav, Major General Elvy Roberts, who was due to complete his assignment shortly. Miller arranged to have lunch with him.

In the United States, pressure could be applied to senior officers at the Pentagon through the Washington bureau of CBS News. In an environment where information, influence and favors were exchanged by reporters and public officials daily, the Washington front was an important one. Public relations officials at the Defense Department did not wish to be accused of muzzling the press without good reason, and CBS representatives would remind them of that.

But the most important front was the public. The military might decide what went on in the war, but the networks determined what went on the air. Bound by traditions of honesty and fairness, CBS News editors, producers and executives decided carefully how to play the story of our expulsion. "Charlie Company's Letters" went on the air April 22 with an introduction by Walter Cronkite. The foreign desk sent a transcript:

THIS EVENING, WE HAVE ANOTHER VIETNAM REPORT FROM JOHN LAURENCE ON CHARLIE COMPANY. AND IT TERMINATES — THOUGH NOT VOLUNTARILY — ONE OF THE MOST PRODUCTIVE NEWS ASSIGNMENTS OF THE LONG WAR. FOR WEEKS, CORRESPONDENT LAURENCE AND A CBS NEWS CAMERA CREW COVERED THE ARMY UNIT IN WAR ZONE C. AT ONE POINT, THERE WAS A NEAR REBELLION BY THE GIS . . . WHO QUESTIONED THE WISDOM AND LOGIC OF A FIELD ORDER BY A NEW COMMANDER. THAT ISSUE WAS QUIETLY RESOLVED AND THE UNIT WENT ON WITH THE WAR. TONIGHT, THIS FINAL LAURENCE REPORT ON COMPANY C, 7TH CAVALRY, FIRST CAVALRY DIVISION:

After the report on Charlie Company's letters, Cronkite said:

. . . FURTHER COVERAGE OF CHARLIE COMPANY BY THE CBS NEWS TEAM WAS BANNED BY THE BRIGADE COMMANDER, COLONEL WILLIAM OCHS.

AT NO TIME DID HE CHARGE THAT THERE WAS ANYTHING WRONG WITH
THE TEAM'S REPORTING. HE SIMPLY SAID THAT ANY FURTHER LAURENCE
REPORTS WOULD NOT BE IN THE BEST INTEREST OF THE COMPANY.

The broadcast was followed by silence. Nothing happened. No public
outcry, no phone calls, no letters of outrage, no apparent reaction at all. The
transmission seemed to float into the ether and vanish. Days passed. Kay left
Saigon for a brief holiday in Indonesia and Clevenger prepared for his trip to
Cambodia. The war went on. The military situation along the Cambodian
border became more active, particularly in the Fishhook and Parrot's Beak,
where the ARVN buildup progressed. Vietnamese student protests against
the government's support of the new military leadership in Cambodia took
place in Saigon. I covered the demonstrations but with little motivation. My
heart was in the field. Idle, without prospects, separated from the squad, my
melancholy deepened.

Then, this reaction to the final report came in:

24152 LAURENCE INTERESTING AFTERMATH TO MAIL CALL STOP WE
BEEN FLOODED WITH CALLS FROM PEOPLE WANTING TO KNOW HOW TO
WRITE LETTERS TO BOLING STOP HE IS ABOUT TO SET NEW INCOMING
MAIL RECORD FOR CHARLIE COMPANY. BENSLEY

A letter from Joy, written on April 16, arrived. Part of it said:

> Our house is a very, very, very fine house
> With two cats in the yard,
> Life used to be so hard,
> Now everything is easy 'cause of you.
> Mèo is lying on my tummy and he says he is sure glad you chose that
> song—because he really thinks it's great. He told me he's sure you like it
> 'cause it talks about pussycats.

I wrote back:

Dearest Joy,
    I got three letters today and I feel better than Rivera getting six and
thinking about going home. No more humping the boonies now, thanks to
the Army. Although we are bitter at being interrupted in the middle of our

effort, there's a bit of relief that accompanies getting out of the field. Keith left today—for a weekend in Singapore and then on to Pnompers to shoot the instant special on Cambodia with Jimmy. No signs of Dana or Sean. Zalen Grant is doing a fantastic job trying to track them down, very discreetly. Louise Stone (Dana's wife) is a strong woman and is holding up well. Best thinking now is that if they're still alive (???) they've been moved north, but how far and how safe it may be (???). Their best chances are being released through the Cambodians' resistance, the Khmer Rouge, not by NLF or NVA, who don't admit officially to their presence in Cambodia. But the situation there is so fluid, no one can be certain who will be running the country in the next month. Dana's friends are settling in for a long wait— maybe months—until solid information about their fate can be definitely determined. I hope the *Newsweek* letter gets printed and does some help.

[Several other reporters and I had written a letter to *Newsweek* to protest its portrayal of Flynn and Stone as reckless adventurers.]

I was sorry to see Keith go, and with Jimmy leaving in two days, I won't have my best friends around anymore. Got the tapes and THANK YOU, they were a Godsend for my spirits. Anything helps. Literature, music.

I expect I have no more than ten days left here, mostly in Saigon, and then I'm taking off. If Ernie [Leiser] doesn't need me then, or Russ thinks it's wise, a week or two in Europe or Hong Kong will get me back into better spirits. I'm reluctant to leave only because Dana and Sean are still out there somewhere, and I want to know what's happening.

Bensley, a master of understatement whose highest accolade was usually "it works fine," cabled:

MILLER FOR LAURENCE KAY CLEVENGER FURTHER THOUGHT RE CHARLIE COMPANY COLON ALTHOUGH WE SHARE YOUR DISAPPOINTMENT AT UNTIMELY DOORSLAM DO NOT BE TOO DISMAYED STOP SERIES IN PRESENT FORM IS ONE OF PINNACLES OF VIETNAM WAR REPORTING AND IN VIEW OF THIS UNPREJUDICED OBSERVER IS GUARANTEED MULTIPLE PRIZEWINNER STOP WE ARE TREMENDOUSLY PLEASED AND IMPRESSED WITH DISTINGUISHED JOB YOU HAVE DONE BENSLEY.

I carried a copy of the cable around and read it often. It gave me strength. The days passed slowly. A letter from Joy, written on April 23, arrived: "Mèo wrote you a letter," it said.

The second page was torn in two places by sharp cat's claws. Next to the holes in the paper, Joy wrote, "Page 2 of Mèo's message" and drew an arrow pointing to the claw marks. "Before Mèo bites me one more time I'm going to turn out the light and try to go to sleep."

Ernest Leiser sent word that he would soon screen the twelve thousand feet of accumulated Charlie Company footage and see if there was enough for a half-hour documentary. The idea of doing thirty minutes instead of an hour was disappointing, but it seemed better than nothing. At least they were interested.

The president of CBS News, Richard Salant, joined the battle by writing a letter to the Defense Department's assistant secretary of defense for public affairs, Daniel Henkin. The foreign desk sent a transcript:

IT IS WITH GREAT REGRET AND CONCERN THAT WE LEARN THAT CBS NEWS CORRESPONDENT JOHN LAURENCE COMMA AND HIS CAMERA CREW COMMA HAVE BEEN DENIED PERMISSION TO CONTINUE REPORTING THE ACTIVITIES OF COMPANY C 2ND BATTALION SEVENTH CAVALRY FIRST CAVALRY DIVISION IN VIETNAM STOP FORMAL NOTIFICATION OF THIS RESTRICTION WAS GIVEN TO CBS NEWS IN SAIGON ON APRIL 23, 1970, BY A SPOKESMAN FOR THE FIRST CAVALRY DIVISION STOP MR LAURENCE WAS ALSO TOLD THAT HE AND HIS CAMERA CREW WOULD NOT BE PERMITTED TO REMAIN OVERNIGHT IN THE FIELD WITH ANY UNIT OF THE FIRST CAVALRY DIVISION STOP

THE PURPOSE OF THIS LETTER IS TO REQUEST I) CLARIFICATION FROM THE DEPARTMENT OF DEFENSE CONCERNING THE REASONS FOR THIS DECISION AND 2) RECONSIDERATION AND WITHDRAWAL OF THE DENIAL STOP

THE SIX REPORTS BY CORRESPONDENT LAURENCE CONCERNING COMPANY C WE HAVE INCLUDED IN OUR NEWS BROADCASTS HAVE AROUSED GREAT AND FAVORABLE PUBLIC REACTION AND INTEREST STOP I BELIEVE THAT THEY HAVE CONSTITUTED SOME OF THE MOST DISTINGUISHED REPORTING OF WHAT THE WAR IS REALLY LIKE, AND MORE IMPORTANT, OF THE NATURE AND CHARACTER OF OUR MEN IN COMBAT STOP THE REPORTS HAVE REFLECTED THE FULL RANGE OF INDIVIDUAL SOLDIERS AND OFFICERS AND HAVE MIRRORED THE CHARACTER OF AMERICA ITSELF STOP

HOWEVER, BRIGADE COMMANDER COLONEL WILLIAM OCHS ON APRIL 21, 1970, TOLD MR LAURENCE AND DAVID MILLER, THE CBS NEWS

BUREAU CHIEF IN SAIGON, THAT FURTHER COVERAGE OF C COMPANY
WAS BEING PROHIBITED QUOTE IN THE BEST INTEREST OF THE COM-
PANY AND THE BEST INTEREST OF THE COMPANY COMMANDER
UNQUOTE COLONEL OCHS DID NOT EXPLAIN THE PROHIBITION AGAINST
OVERNIGHTING IN THE FIELD BY MR LAURENCE AND HIS CAMERA CREW
STOP THIS INJUNCTION IS A MARKED DEPARTURE FROM THE TRADI-
TIONAL PRIVILEGE OF NEWSMEN TO STAY WITH A UNIT, AT THEIR OWN
RISK, AS LONG AS THEY WANT TO DO SO, PROVIDED THEIR CONDUCT IS
NOT IMPROPER AND THEIR PRESENCE DOES NOT VIOLATE MILITARY
SECURITY STOP THERE HAS BEEN NO ALLEGATION OF IMPROPER CON-
DUCT BY MR LAURENCE AND HIS CAMERA CREW DURING THEIR TIME
WITH C COMPANY STOP

WE BELIEVE IT IMPORTANT THAT THESE REPORTS BE CONTINUED
STOP I HOPE THAT EXPLANATION AND RECONSIDERATION WILL BE
FORTHCOMING.

As April ended, I wrote to Joy:

Writing from bed for first time, as you often do. Good way to end long day
and night. It is 3:20 AM. Holding you—and being held—is a memory that's
getting more vivid as the remaining days get shorter.

Don't quite know how soon, or where, but it will be that same treasured
feeling next to you again—and again—closer. Saigon (and relative safety) for
the next week. Pray—meditate—levitate—anything!—for our missing
friends.

A photocopy of an official U.S. Army letter arrived from New York. The
heading at the top was United States Military Academy, West Point, New
York. The letter was dated 14 April:

I would like to explore the possibility of obtaining a copy of the John Laurence film concerning the change of company commanders (CPT Jackson
and CPT Rice) of Company C, 2 Battalion, 7 Cavalry, 1st Cavalry Division
(Airmobile) (aired during the week of 6–11 April 1970).

The situation CPT Rice finds himself in on assuming command of the
company is a classic and often repeated one for junior officers in the U.S.
Army. The drama you have captured is invaluable. The expressions of anxi-

ety and fear would allow the cadets to feel an empathy for the situation that is lacking in our current instructional material.

If it is possible to obtain the film, I would show it to our junior year cadets during the leadership and management classes. The film would complement the series of tapes and skits that are now used to provide the cadets with an understanding of the complexities of assuming command of a unit.

Sincerely,

JOHN H. DORF
Major, Infantry
Assistant Professor of Military Science

CBS News sent him the film.

MAY 1, 1970

The voice of President Richard Nixon cut through the airwaves in bursts of tightly written rhetoric—somber, strident, heavy with consequence. "To protect our men who are in Vietnam," the voice declared, "and to guarantee the continued success of our withdrawal and Vietnamization programs, I have concluded the time has come for action!" *As if five years of bombing and killing Vietnamese has been inaction*, I thought. Nixon's voice on the radio sounded righteous, as though trying to find a balance between authority and sincerity, but it came over as portentous and arrogant, as Commander in Chief Nixon.

It was just after ten o'clock, Friday morning, Saigon time. In Washington, where Nixon was addressing the nation live on television, it was nine o'clock Thursday night. I sat in the bureau office listening on Armed Forces Radio, separated from the voice by thirteen time zones, an ocean, two continents and a night of darkness. Nixon's words dominated the office.

"Tonight," he said, "American and South Vietnamese units will attack the headquarters for the entire Communist military operation in South Vietnam."

Dave Miller and I looked at each other across his desk.

'Jee-sus!' he said. 'Cambodia. We should have seen it coming.'

'They're going after COSVN,' I said. 'Far out.'

'The generals are gonna love this,' Miller said. 'What a story!' He looked on the wall at his list of bureau personnel and assignments. 'How the hell are we going to cover this fucking thing?' he said. 'I've got everybody down in the Parrot's Beak with the ARVN. You're the only correspondent I've got.'

I wondered how long it would take to get Kay and Clevenger back from Phnom Penh. The phone rang on Miller's desk. It was the semiofficial Tiger line.

Miller identified himself. The voice on the phone said, "Go to Bu Dop," and hung up.

Miller's face was blank, eyes unfocused. He lifted his large body out of the chair, walked around the desk and put his face close to mine. "That was my main contact at the embassy," he said in a low voice. "All they said was, 'Go to Bu Dop.' Where the hell is that?"

'On the border,' I said, 'past Loc Ninh. Special Forces camp.' I got up to locate it on the large-scale map hanging on the office wall. Bu Dop was almost due north of Saigon, about eighty-five miles away, right on the Cambodian border.

'Okay,' Miller said, picking up his phone. 'I'm gonna try and organize a charter and see if they can get us in there. There'll be other reporters but it'll be our pool. You'll be in charge. We'll try to leave in an hour. I can give you Skip Brown and Dan. You better go get ready.'

'I wish Keith and Jimmy were still here,' I said. Willis (Skip) Brown was a fine cameraman from San Francisco and had an excellent reputation. But he was Richard Threlkeld's regular partner and we had not worked together. Pham Tan Dan, my old friend from Con Thien days, would be doing sound.

I crossed the street and went to my room, put on a pair of fatigues and filled my canteens with water. The room boys stood at the open door and watched. They could sense my excitement. Who knew what was happening in Cambodia? Who knew how close we would get to it? There were so many variables, so many uncertainties, and all I could focus on was the next thing to do. I put fresh batteries in the tape recorder and filled the battered pewter flask with cognac. The room boys watched and smiled and chattered in Vietnamese. When I got my gear on my back, I hurried past them, pointing to my chest. 'Kampuchea!' I said, and they smiled and nodded their heads as if they understood perfectly. I ran down the steps. This might be as big a story as the Tet Offensive over two years ago. The possibilities were infinite. I was excited by the challenge of trying to cover it, the mystery of what might happen, the alluring risk.

An hour and a half later, I stood with a group of reporters and still photographers on the tarmac at Tan Son Nhut watching two American pilots from Air America take an old unmarked C-47 through preflight, checking the engines and wings closely. The pilots were civilian. Later I discovered that the company was run secretly by the CIA. Dan looked worried. About a dozen members of the Saigon press corps climbed aboard. NBC and ABC had not been invited.

The flight to Bu Dop took about an hour. The pilots circled the airstrip in a steep bank at a thousand feet and dropped onto the dirt field with no final approach. The place was deserted. Tufts of grass grew in the rusty ground.

We got out and stood in the dazzling light. It was just after one o'clock. The airstrip was built on a narrow plateau which sloped away on the other side of a single-track dirt road that ran along the edge of the field. The pilots kept the engines running. 'We're not waiting here,' one of them shouted.

'Can you come back for us later?' I said. Miller had said the latest we could ship film out of Saigon today was six o'clock.

'That's part of the deal.'

'Okay. Come back at four o'clock,' I said. 'Whoever's here can go back with you.' The other reporters nodded agreement. It would give us about two and a half hours to work on the story.

'Will do,' the pilot said.

'Don't wait any later. If any of us get stuck over there,' I motioned toward Cambodia, 'we'll get back on our own.'

'See you at sixteen hundred,' the pilot said. Turning, he got aboard the C-47 and closed the door. We watched the plane take off. Then silence.

Fifteen of us stood on the low ridge and looked out at the terrain: dry scattered scrub, low trees, a modest range of mountains to the east. No sign of military. No troops, no helicopters, no civilians, no smoke. Nothing moved, not even the wind. We had been dropped onto an uninviting tropical plateau beyond the edge of civilization and were absorbed immediately in its wild sweep.

'Who was it told Miller to come up here?' a reporter asked.

'Somebody from the embassy,' I said.

'Which embassy?' a second reporter said sharply. '*Hanoi's?*' Laughter.

'You sure they knew what they were talking about?' the first reporter said.

'No,' I said.

'Neither am I.'

The journalists stood in small groups and inspected the land. I looked north through a pair of binoculars. Nothing but wilderness. No sign of human life. A still photographer snapped a picture. No one showed his fear.

A vehicle approached from the other side of the shelf. Out of sight, all we could hear was the sound of its engine. We stopped talking and looked toward the sound. One of the photographers ran down the side of the shelf, his still cameras bouncing off his chest and shoulders, and took cover in the low scrub.

'No sense trying to hide,' someone said. 'If that's Charlie, we've had it.' Everyone stood still. The atmosphere became electric: insects, heat, engine whine, fright, sweat.

A radio antenna, then the top of a windshield, then helmets, then the faces of two young GIs in an open-top jeep appeared over the hill and drove toward us on the dirt track. The soldiers had black horses' heads on the shoulder patches of their uniforms and rifles resting on the backseat. One of them stood up in his seat and squinted at the group of civilians, some of whom wore sport shirts and slacks, waiting beside the road. The jeep stopped.

'Boy, are we glad to see you!' a reporter said.

'What y'all doin here?' one of the GIs said.

'We're here to cover the operation,' I said.

'Well, you're just in time,' he said. 'Whole bunch of brass down the road a way. An lots a choppers.'

'Will you take us?'

'All of you?'

'Well, we can't hang around here.'

'Okay,' he said, turning to look at the other soldier.

Five of us climbed into the back of the jeep, bodies and equipment packed in an awkward crunch. We promised the others to send the jeep back for them. It traveled along the narrow road for several minutes, climbing over undulating terrain until it came around a corner and revealed a vast open field of helicopters—dozens and dozens of stationary Hueys with their engines idle and rotor blades tied down—spread out on clear ground just below the edge of the plateau. The crews sat in the shade beneath the choppers and read magazines or slept or worked on their weapons. The sight of so many helicopters in such a remote place was spectacular, projecting power and violence, as if the old Golf Course at An Khe had been reconstructed and transposed to this field. The reporters were surprised the choppers weren't already in the air, ferrying troops and supplies into Cambodia.

'Didn't Nixon say the operation had already started?' one of the journalists said.

'What the hell does he know?' another said.

'Probably blew it. The surprise element, I mean.'

'You can bet they were listening in Hanoi.'

'And at COSVN.'

'Gentlemen,' one of the older reporters said, 'Never underestimate the machinations of Mr. T. Dick. He will surprise you every time.'

'Yeah,' a younger one said, 'watch out for the trick.'

Either the operation is late getting started, I thought, *or this is part of a second strike.*

The jeep drove along the edge of the plateau and stopped at a corner of the shelf where the high ground jutted into the valley. A group of senior officers with Cav patches and stars of rank on their shoulders stood over a large map on the ground and listened as one of the younger officers gestured with a pointer, checking details. When they saw the journalists and photographers, the officers stood up and straightened their backs and smiled, as if surprised. It was unusual to see so many high-ranking officers bunched in one place—the senior commanders of the 1st Cavalry Division: Generals Elvy Roberts and Robert Shoemaker. *One round'll get 'em all,* I thought, very privately.

'How did you gentlemen find us?' General Roberts said when we approached.

'We had a clue something might be going on up here,' I said, protecting Miller's source. I introduced him and his staff to the reporters. Everyone tried to shake hands at once. It was awkward, three generals trying to shake hands with a group of civilians at the same time. Tiring of the effort, Roberts stepped back and waved to the remaining journalists and the other officers followed. The photographers snapped pictures of the command group.

'Well, since you're here, you might as well know what's going on,' Roberts said. His voice was confident, relaxed. The other officers stood next to him, attentive. 'As you probably know,' Roberts said, 'we're going into Cambodia shortly.' He turned to one of his staff and said, 'Do you think we can arrange a briefing for these gentlemen?' A young officer stepped forward. For once I was grateful to be getting a briefing.

'Major Benton is our G-3 and he'll see that you get the information you need,' Roberts said. 'He'll take you to our briefing tent. Then you can return and we'll try to find room for you on the assault. C Company, 2/7, is going in first.'

C Company? Our C Company?

'Excuse me, sir,' I said, feeling awkward. 'We haven't been back in with Charlie Company since the, ah, incident on the road.'

Roberts had steady eyes. 'Well, I'll look into that, Mr. Laurence. I'm sure we can work something out. Perhaps one of the other companies.'

By now all the journalists had been ferried down the road from the airstrip and we filled them in with what we knew. Major Benton commandeered a truck and took us to a large tent that appeared to be a forward command post. No other reporters were present, just soldiers and officers working urgently: carrying messages, listening and talking on radios, giving and receiving orders, coming and going in jeeps. The forward base showed signs of having been constructed in haste.

The fifteen journalists entered the tent and sat in rows of portable chairs that faced a series of large-scale contour maps of Vietnam and Cambodia standing upright on easels. The maps had plastic overlays and were covered with roll-down fabric for security. Soldiers turned down the flaps of the tent and two stone-faced MPs stood outside with M-16s at their sides. Several officers waited at the front and rear of the tent.

'Gentlemen, this will be on background,' Major Benton said. 'Anyone have a problem with that?' The reporters looked at their notebooks, wrote "background" and said nothing. Benton was poised, confident, as if he had given the briefing before. He said the order to prepare the operation against North Vietnamese sanctuaries in Cambodia came from higher headquarters ten days ago.

'We were told to come up with a concept for the attack on April 24 and submitted our plan on April 27,' he said. 'Then, on April 29, we got the order to go in forty-eight hours.'

The journalists wrote as fast as they could. The usual atmosphere of confrontation and sarcasm that characterized the daily MACV briefings in Saigon was not present. Benton and the others were field combat officers, not rear area people who briefed for MACV. Something important and violent was about to happen.

"Our orders were to neutralize COSVN," Benton said. He pointed to a rectangular symbol with three red crosses marked on the map in grease pencil that designated an enemy headquarters. "Our latest intelligence put it here in the Fishhook region at grid coordinates X-ray Tango four four niner six." I wrote in my notebook, "COSVN at XT 4496."

"We are to conduct coordinated operations to neutralize the COSVN base area and destroy enemy installations," Benton declared.

'How certain are you that COSVN is there?' a reporter asked.

'You can never be certain. In fact, we have indications, don't ask me what, that COSVN may have had advance warning of the operation and already moved out, further west. They move all the time. There's no way to keep something like this a secret, though we have tried our best. Please don't quote me on that.'

'How many people are involved?' a reporter asked.

'Altogether, about twelve thousand infantry,' Benton said. He indicated on the map where each of the units was moving. Most were going into the Fishhook. He said the units were the 3d Brigade of the 1st Cavalry Division with one battalion, 2/7, attached; the 11th Armored Cavalry Regiment; two armored and mechanized battalions; the 3d ARVN Airborne Brigade; the 1/9 Cavalry Squadron of the Cav; and supporting artillery, helicopter and other units. The ARVN Airborne and 11th ACR were already in Cambodia and fighting was reported.

'We had six B-52 strikes that went in early this morning,' Benton said. 'They were followed by an hour of artillery preparation from a total of eighty-two guns in nine bases from 0600 to 0700. Zero hour was 0730.'

'How big is that overall, in terms of other operations?' someone asked. By now, several middle-ranking officers had entered the tent and were standing at the back.

'I am told,' Benton said, 'that it is the largest battlefield preparation of the Vietnam War.' The reporters looked at one another for confirmation. No one could remember a bigger one.

'What about civilians?' I said.

'We have done everything possible to strike nonresidential areas. Most of this region is very lightly populated. We're staying away from the population centers.'

'Does this operation have a name?'

'It does. It is called "Toan Thang 43,"' Benton said.

'Total Victory.'

'That is correct.'

'For the forty-third time.' Mild laughter.

'I don't give names to these things,' Benton said, 'I just help plan 'em.'

'Any casualties so far?' a reporter asked.

"So far, contact has been minimal. Two light observation helicopters have been shot down. I don't know if the pilots have been picked up. The operation so far has been marked by an absence of enemy antiaircraft activity. We had expected much heavier fire."

"Why is that?"

"The reason? Well, one, either we surprised the hell out 'em or, two, they knew we were coming and left."

The reporters asked a few more questions, then closed their notebooks and walked outside the tent. I asked Major General Roberts if he would give us an on-camera interview and he agreed. A tall man, Roberts stood erect and repeated many of the facts that Benton had mentioned in his briefing. He added that this was the initial phase of an operation that would go on for some time, the full consequences of which could not be predicted. When the interview was finished, Roberts said, 'We weren't expecting you gentlemen from the press to find us so quickly. But I've arranged for two helicopters to take you in with us. Try not to get in the way, will you?'

'Yes, sir.'

'Mr. Laurence, you will go in with one of the other companies, not C Company. Is that acceptable?'

'Yes, that's fine. Thank you, sir.' We shook hands. I figured I was covering the invasion of Cambodia, not Charlie Company.

'We'll be getting airborne in about fifteen minutes. Good luck to you.' He could not have been more cordial.

Skip Brown, Dan and I went to a corner of the camp and prepared to shoot a stand-up. If we failed to get any pictures in Cambodia, or if we got stuck there, or if the equipment failed, or worse, at least the on-camera would be there to ship. Hopefully, it would tell the basic story. I made a few notes in my notebook and looked into the camera. Dan handed me the mike. Skip rolled film.

"This was D day," I said, "for the military operation President Nixon ordered against North Vietnam Headquarters in Cambodia. It was launched at 7:30 this morning. The first American troops crossed the border within minutes after the president concluded his address to the nation. The target is the Central Office for South Vietnam—COSVN—which has operated just inside the Cambodian border for the five years of this war and controlled Vietcong and North Vietnamese operations in South Vietnam." I looked down at my notes for a second and continued.

"A combined American and South Vietnamese task force involving thousands of crack airborne and infantry units has been striking across the border all day. So far, there has been insignificant contact with the enemy. The massive task force is trying to encircle and trap the North Vietnamese/Viet

Cong headquarters and destroy it." Lowering my head to consult the notebook again, I went on.

"Military sources indicate, however, that the North Vietnamese command may have had advance knowledge of the operation and moved out of the area before today. At this stage, that is not known. If the North Vietnamese choose to stand and fight or become encircled, one of the major battles of the war may be impending.

"One design of this operation is to put severe pressure on the North Vietnamese command now directing forces toward Phnom Penh.

"Coincidentally, the American task force now driving and air-assaulting into Cambodia includes the men of Charlie Company, of the First Air Cav, whom we had come to know before."

I signed off at "task force headquarters near the Cambodian border." Brown put the exposed film in a film can and sealed it. He handed it to me and said, laughing, 'If I get shot, make sure this gets on the air.'

The reporters were driven back to the edge of the plateau. Helicopters were loading troops and starting engines. General Shoemaker took me aside.

'They're calling this thing "Task Force Shoemaker" because I supervised the planning. It's a little embarrassing.'

'I won't mention it on the air,' I said and smiled. 'Do you remember Shiny Bayonet?'

'I sure do,' he said, thinking for a moment. 'The war's come a long way since then.'

'So have you,' I said, looking at the single black stars on his helmet and collar. Just five years ago, Shoemaker was a battalion commander, the lieutenant colonel who accidentally called artillery on top of his own position and nearly got us all blown away. Now he was a brigadier general.

'You and your crew can get on that bird over there,' he said, pointing to one of the helicopters in the field below. 'It's not going in with C Company. Good luck.'

Brown, Dan and I walked down the embankment and introduced ourselves to the chopper crew. They greeted us politely, as if they had flown us before. There were no troops on the flight, just us. My heart beat harder. With engines and rotors racing, the helicopters took off from the low field and lifted above the trees and then the valley and the forward base with the generals watching from the plateau below and joined formation in a swarm of fast moving ships that bobbed up and down in the brilliant blue sky.

Crossing into Cambodia from the east, the helicopters dropped down close to the ground and skimmed over the trees at a hundred knots. This was to avoid (or at least surprise) the anti-aircraft gun crews of the North Vietnamese, but no one was firing at the choppers. The foliage became less dense. Roads appeared with thatched-roof houses along them and fields of rice and groves of rubber trees. The terrain was flat. On the flanks of the invasion force, Huey Cobras flew nose-down and fired long bursts of cannon and rockets at the fields ahead.

The helicopter landed in a rush of whirling blades and swirling dust and running soldiers—a confusion of men and machines and dirt and wind moving swiftly in all directions. The soldiers ran for the treeline with their heads low, the heavy packs bouncing on their backs, and dropped to the ground behind a row of narrow rubber trees. As soon as all the soldiers were off, the helicopters lifted up from the ground and flew away. Brown rolled film and Dan stood beside him without bothering to take cover, concentrating hard on getting the sound. The only gunfire was the buzz of the Cobras on the margins of the LZ. The company had landed at the edge of a rubber plantation, the trees spread apart in neat rows, hollow tubes embedded in their trunks, the ground cleared of foliage. I looked into the shade of the trees and recognized the familiar shape of Sergeant Dunnuck crouched behind a tree, alert, staring ahead. *Dunnuck? What's he doing here?* I felt a strange dizziness, disorientation. I was confused. Dunnuck was organizing the men of 2d Squad into fighting positions behind the trees, telling them where to line up fields of fire.

'Skip, this is Charlie Company!' I whispered into Brown's ear as he rolled film. 'I don't believe this!'

'No shit,' he said. Dunnuck saw us and nodded his head for a moment. Then he turned back to his squad.

'I'll point out the key guys,' I said to Brown. 'Maybe you can give us some close-ups, okay?'

He switched off the camera and looked at me. 'How close?' he said.

'Close as you want.'

'Gotcha,' he said. He put his eye to the viewfinder, pointed the camera at Dunnuck, focused the lens and switched on.

'That's Killer,' I said. 'We need plenty of him.'

Brown kept rolling. Dunnuck and the men in the squad looked out from behind the rubber trees at the terrain ahead. The ground was perfectly flat. A road ran along the forward edge of the plantation from left to right, and beyond the road a few Cambodian farmhouses stood. It was quiet. The air was heavy with the heat. Most of the company was in place. Brown shot pictures of the squad from several angles and switched off. I went up to Dunnuck and said hello.

'Didn't expect to see *you* here,' he said.

'Neither did we.'

'Where's the other guys?'

'Phnom Penh. They split us up.'

'Too bad,' Dunnuck said and wiped the sweat from his face with a green towel around his neck. 'How long you staying?'

'Just a few minutes. We've got to get this on the air tonight. You guys are big news today.'

'Don't see why. Ain't done nothing.'

'You're the first into Cambodia.'

'No shit.'

'It's a big operation. Twelve thousand people. Where's the CP?'

'Over there.' Dunnuck pointed to a cluster of men in the trees.

'We gotta go,' I said. 'See you in a day or two.'

'Say hello to Keith and Jim if you see 'em.'

I got up and looked at Brown and Dan and they followed. Walking low through the trees toward the command group, I recognized the members of Charlie Company, silent impassive young men and NCOs with expectant worried faces. Some of them smiled as we went past but no one spoke. At the CP, Captain Rice was squatting on the ground with his helmet off and a radio handset in each hand, talking and listening, an unlighted cigarette in a corner of his mouth. He looked calm, under control, working. He had the company around him and was trying to maneuver it into good fighting positions. He was in a hurry. Another company was on the way in choppers, and the assault force was most vulnerable when it was split like this. Rice was trying to keep in contact with all the elements, talking to his platoon leaders on the company net in one hand and battalion with the other.

"This is Two-nine," Rice said on the radio. His words were rapid-fire, commanding. "Negative. Move down here with the unit where the yellow smoke is and set up through the six. Okay we took ground-to-air about two hundred Mikes (meters) to the Sierra Echo (southeast)."

Rice listened to the reply. The earpiece of the other radio handset crackled with simultaneous transmissions.

"Okay. You see where all the people are down here?"

He turned his head and looked over his left shoulder for an instant. The radio squawked.

"Well, down here towards me!" he shouted. "Come to the left!"

A soldier next to him flicked open a metal lighter and lit Rice's cigarette. "Come down to the Sierra Echo!" Exasperated, his forehead showed sweat. Brown tightened his lens closer. Helicopters flew, far away.

'You okay?' Rice said.

'Yes, thanks,' I said.

'Where's your other crew?'

'About a hundred miles that way,' I said, pointing west. 'In Phnom Penh, covering the war from that end.' Rice shook his head slowly once, listening all the time to his radios. Brown and Dan walked to the edge of the plantation and photographed a family of Cambodian civilians walking on the road with a their possessions on their backs. Refugees. *Like Vietnam,* I thought.

'Where are we?' I said.

Rice handed the radio handsets to his RTO and opened a simple, hand-drawn map of the area. He pointed to a spot about six kilometers inside Cambodia, near the town of Mimot. It was marked "X-Ray."

Rice looked up. 'You know about X-Ray?' he said.

'Yes,' I said.

Who could forget X-Ray and the Ia Drang? X-Ray and Albany where this same 7th Cavalry that Rice was now a part of had fought for a week in November 1965 and 234 American soldiers had died. The first big battles of the war between the Americans and North Vietnamese. Was this the Cav's way of planning some payback? I wondered. Helicopters chopped the air in the distance, coming closer.

Rice said, 'That's B Company, coming in behind us. Another battalion.' Both his hands were back on the radio handsets, the cigarette dangling from his mouth.

'We've got to get out of here,' I said. 'We'll catch that lift back. With any luck, you'll be on the news back home tonight.'

'No kidding?'

'Yeah. We're gonna try to make it to Bangkok. They've got a new satellite station. Never been used.'

'Well, good luck. Hope you make it.'

'Sorry we can't stay longer. Good luck. See you again.'

The helicopters landed in whirling droves and the soldiers of B Company jumped off and ran for cover. Brown, Dan and I climbed onto one and rode back to the forward command post in Vietnam. It was four o'clock. The pilots of the C-47 from Air America were waiting at the airstrip at Bu Dop. The tension of the early afternoon was gone. We flew to Saigon with a small group of other journalists, some of whom had not gone into Cambodia but stayed at the task force CP to gather information and write their stories. They asked what we saw in Cambodia and we told them and they wrote it down. The plane landed on the civilian side of Tan Son Nhut and taxied to a stop, nose high in the air. On the tarmac, Dave Miller and what looked like half the bureau's Vietnamese staff were waiting. One of my suitcases stood next to him.

'You've got to hurry,' Miller shouted. He was sweating hard. 'See that?' He pointed to a large passenger jet with Air France markings near the main passenger terminal. I nodded.

'It goes to Bangkok in half an hour. We've got to get you through customs and emigration fast. Here's your passport. Got enough money?'

'No.'

'Take this.' He handed me an envelope jammed with hundred dollar bills.

All of us—Miller, Brown, Dan, bureau secretaries, shipper, driver—ran toward the passenger terminal entrance. One of the office secretaries took my passport and disappeared. The terminal building was not crowded; nearly everyone who was booked on the flight was already aboard. A few passengers from an incoming flight searched for their baggage. The atmosphere was less laconic than usual, less weary, excitement in the eyes of the Vietnamese. News of the invasion of Cambodia was all over Saigon, though there were few details of how it was going, and people worried and gossiped about what might happen. The operation had already created a national sense of adventure.

'Skip will edit the piece for you,' Miller said. I looked surprised. 'Don't worry, he knows how. Just give him a little more time. Here's the address of the lab. They can only process it as black and white. Make sure they run a test first. They know you're coming. And here's where you go to feed.' He handed me a sheet of paper with Bangkok addresses and telephone numbers written on it. 'Nobody's ever fed a bird out of Thailand before. They're opening the satellite station for us ahead of time. You'll be the first to use it. Did you see NBC or ABC?'

'Not a sign.'

'Great. We might have this one to ourselves. What did you get? Any action?'

'No, but you won't believe this. We went in on the first lift with—guess who?'

'I don't know.'

'You won't believe it.'

'Who, for fuck's sake? General Abrams? Jane Fonda?'

'Charlie Company.'

'No shit.'

'Yeah. I don't know how it happened but we got them going in, hitting the ground, setting up in a rubber plantation, Rice on the radio. Lots of stuff.'

Miller shook his head. 'I don't believe it.'

'It's true.'

'Daily miracle,' Dan said, smiling politely.

'I'll say,' said Miller. 'You're gonna need another one to get it on the air tonight.'

'We also shot a stand-up in Vietnam, as a backup. Can you ship it?'

'*You're* the shipment,' Miller said. 'This is the last flight out of here today. Maybe you can transship from Bangkok. New York will help. I'll tell them you're on the way.'

The Vietnamese from the CBS bureau walked Brown and me through customs and emigration formalities, but there were delays with my passport. The names on the ticket and the passport did not match. Bureaucratic, indolent, a small group of civil servants refused to allow me through. Skip went ahead with the film. We tried to bully our way past the officials.

'Tell them it's a matter of life and death,' Miller shouted at one of the secretaries. 'They have film of the operation in Cambodia! It's very important!'

Looking through the terminal, I saw Brown standing at the top of the steps that led to the forward cabin of the Air France plane. He held the onionskin bag of film in one hand and the metal railing of the ramp with the other. The ground crew tried to pull the tall ramp away from the plane. Brown had one foot inside the plane and the other on the steps. The Air France crew tried to close the door of the cabin, but Brown held fast. I could see them arguing and gesturing, but their voices were obliterated by the whine and whoosh of the jet engines.

One of the CBS staff handed me my passport and ticket. 'Okay, Jack, you go now. Please, you must hurry!'

I took the documents, made a little bow of thanks, turned and ran through the terminal and out the exit, showing my ticket a final time to an agent wearing a clean blue Air France uniform by the low fence leading to the tarmac.

Two hundred yards away at the top of the stairs, Brown struggled with the cabin staff.

'Hurry! Hurry!' the Air France agent said. His cold-eyed look showed disdain, as if he wondered what insanity this last-minute arrival in sweat-stained combat fatigues and jungle boots was doing getting on his clean orderly flight to Bangkok.

I ran. I ran with my field pack and tape recorder over one arm, tickets and passport in hand, and the small suitcase in my other. My legs wobbled under the awkward weight. 'Come on, Jack! Don't stop,' Brown cried from the gangway. His voice seemed to come from a distant place, as if through a tunnel, hollow, disembodied. Two members of the cabin crew gave his arm a mighty pull and he stumbled into the front of the aircraft and disappeared. Immediately, the ground crew started to wheel the tall steel ramp away from the plane. I ran harder. A member of the cabin crew looked out the open door and shouted in French to the ground crew and pointed toward me. They stopped to look. I ran. My heart beat in my head. My legs moved up and down like pistons, the heavy boots hitting the tarmac and rolling away behind me into the air and back again in front of me. Each fraction of time was a distinct moment, clear and precise. Slow speed, light and heavy at the same time, flowing across the hard ground, lungs heaving, heart pumping. Then my feet hit the first steps of the ramp and the momentum of the long run carried me up in a few big strides to the top and across the gap to the plane and I was inside feeling cold air on my face and seeing the clean fresh cabin and curious faces of the other passengers. The crew swung the door behind me and slammed it closed with a bang.

MAY 1–2, 1970

Bangkok was another world. There were bright colors and smart fashions, new cars and neon lights, polite manners and cheerful efficiency. The contrasts with Saigon made everything seem more civilized. Modern buildings were being built. The telephone system worked. Air conditioners kept things cool. People appeared to be well-nourished. No soldiers in battledress with rifles and grenade launchers peered from the shadows of sandbagged bunkers, no suspicious looks followed your back and hung in the air behind you, no wounded war veterans in tatty uniforms looked up from the sidewalk, no war widows with babies, no refugees, no incoming. Thai society appeared to be one of gentle grace. Just off the Air France jet and still only an hour out of Saigon, Skip Brown and I felt like we'd been lifted out of a hot wild corner of hell and transported in cool heavenly comfort into a world of peace.

We went to work in a spare office at the airport operations center. Thai authorities were extremely solicitous, waving us through immigration and customs, finding a desk and phone for us, bringing us a beer, being polite and helpful in every way. They seemed to sense the regional instability set off by the big American-Vietnamese military adventure among their Cambodian neighbors to the east. They behaved toward us as if we all belonged to the same team: U.S. Army, South Vietnamese government, American press corps, Kingdom of Thailand, Bangkok airport authority. Brown and I were still wearing combat fatigues and boots and I felt self-conscious about my appearance in the busy airport but didn't bother to change clothes. The unmarked American uniforms gave our presence a suggestion of drama. Everyone knew where we had come from.

New York was on the line. Working from a similar small office halfway around the world, Bob Little had to make a big decision: how to get the story on the air in the next nine or ten hours without fail? Where in Asia would be the best place to feed? Tokyo? Hong Kong? Manila? Bangkok? Risks were apparent in each case. The Tokyo bureau had the most experience working satellite feeds but was farthest away and would have the least time to process and edit the film. Hong Kong was closer, but there were no scheduled flights going there until morning. A charter would have to be arranged, if one could be found. Manila was unreachable at this hour, and the staff at the satellite facility was inexperienced and therefore unreliable. Bangkok seemed most logical, but its television and film facilities were basic and its technicians least experienced. Little had a tough call to make. He already had CBS News staffers awake and working in a dozen places in Asia and America. It was now about nine o'clock in Bangkok, just after nine in the morning in the States. If we tried to make a satellite transmission from Bangkok, we had about nine hours to process and edit the film, write the narration and try to feed from Thailand's new ground station. There would be plenty of time. But, other than make test transmissions on their new satellite equipment, the Thais had not used it in commercial service before.

Little worried. 'Something is sure to go wrong with the ground station,' he said. 'We've got a real throw of the dice ahead of us.'

Technically, the process was complex. Once we had the story ready to feed, the edited film had to run through a telecine projector that converted visual images into electronic signals. The signals went by landline from the Bangkok TV station to the new ground facility in the Thai countryside. From there, the signals were modified and transmitted into the atmosphere to a commercial satellite in orbit over the Pacific Ocean. And from there they had to be bounced from the satellite to a receiving station in the United States and then to CBS News in New York, where they were converted back into visual images for broadcast over the airwaves. All this happened at the speed of light.

Scores of technical connections and adjustments had to be made. One plug in the wrong place, one crossed wire, one switch not thrown, one sleepy technician and all the work and expense would be wasted. Waiting in the airport office, we were told that there were no pilots or planes available to charter out of Thailand. The decision had been made for us. We were stuck in Bangkok.

'You folks just come out of Saigon?' I recognized the voice over my shoulder as American. I looked up. A man in his mid-thirties smiled. He wore a Pan American Airways uniform, his tie loose at the neck.

'How'd you guess?' I said, looking at the dirt on my boots.

He laughed. 'How're we doing over there?'

'You mean today or long-term?'

'Today.'

'So far, it's pretty quiet,' I said, drinking from a bottle of Thai beer on the desk. 'The armor got in a fight today—11th ACR—but not much contact otherwise. The North Vietnamese may have bugged out. I think the COSVN group probably got away, but you never know. It's too early to tell.'

'Sounds like it might get bigger.' He had the presence of a pilot: easy manner, soft scratchy voice, quiet confidence. The features on his face came together at sharp angles, his jaw and cheekbones set in square lines. He reminded me of my uncle, a brave handsome pilot named Arthur E. Herman who flew bombers out of Lakenheath in World War II and then B-47s for SAC and, more recently, reconnaissance planes over Vietnam. He was in Thailand too, but not in Bangkok.

'Would you like a beer?' I asked.

'No thanks. I'm scheduled to fly out pretty soon. Deadheading back to Tokyo.'

'Cargo?'

'That's the stuff.'

I thought for a second. *Could this be a miracle in the making?* On an impulse I said, 'Will you take us with you?'

'Sure,' he said. His eyes became less laconic. 'Why do you need to go?'

'We went in to Cambodia this afternoon and we're trying to get our film on the air tonight. Tokyo's the best place to feed. We've got a bureau there.'

The Pan Am pilot thought for a moment. 'Okay. I'll have to check my office, but I don't see why not.'

We got back on the phones. Little said it was a great idea. He'd make arrangements with Pan Am in the States. Brown and I shook hands with the pilot, thanked him profusely, ordered another beer. Two hours later, he came back.

'I can't take you,' the pilot said in a defeated tone. 'We don't have a license to carry passengers on this route.'

'Couldn't you sneak us aboard without telling anyone?' I said. 'The Air Force flew us into the Philippines a few years ago. No problem.'

'I wish I could. I really do. But I can't break the rules, even in this case. I'd lose my job.'

I called Little and told him the news. The line was silent for ten, fifteen seconds.

'See if he'll stop in Hong Kong on his way back to Tokyo.' Little said. 'We'll charter him.'

'You want to charter a 707?' the pilot said.

'Why not?'

'Do you know what that costs?'

'No.'

'A fortune.'

'Are you willing? In principle, I mean.'

'Yeah, why not?'

Little said the story was big enough to pay for a charter to Hong Kong. 'Give him the stand-up and we'll feed it from Hong Kong. You and Skip cut the Charlie Company landing and feed it to us on the bird. Okay?'

'Got you,' I said.

'Go to it, Tiger.'

It made sense. If the satellite feed from Bangkok failed, at least New York would have the stand-up to broadcast. Brown gave the pilot a black and yellow shipping bag with the roll of unexposed film inside. In the United States, CBS News agreed to pay Pan American $10,000 for diverting its cargo plane to Hong Kong.

Now it was the middle of the night. A Thai employee of CBS drove Brown and me into town to find the film processor. It was located in a remote part of the city with unpaved roads and no traffic lights and took an hour to find in the dark. A tired young man in his nightshirt took the film with a yawn and promised to deliver it to the TV station in an hour or so. He disappeared into an alley lined with bamboo houses. Brown and I were skeptical.

'Don't worry,' the bureau employee said. 'He'll be there. Just hope he doesn't have a problem with the machine.'

What an operation, I thought. *If we make this it'll really be a miracle.*

At the Thai television station, a guard let us inside and showed us a room with a desk and a film-editing machine. Brown turned it on and looked at it.

'This is going to be interesting,' he said, looking at the equipment. 'I haven't cut a spot in ages.'

I opened my typewriter case and set it on the desk, put in a sheet of paper and looked at my notebook. One by one, I tried to imagine each scene on the film. I wrote:

CHARLIE COMPANY IN CAMBODIA
May 1, 1970

1. CHOPPERS

Charlie Company made a combat assault deep into Cambodian territory today—part of the massive task force of American and South Vietnamese soldiers trying to encircle the North Vietnamese command headquarters.

2. LOW CHOPPERS

The helicopters flew for miles—mostly at treetop level—over the flat, quiet countryside that exploded this morning.

3. COBRAS FIRING (SOUND UP FULL)

4. CHOPPERS LANDING

The first American troops in the assault force crossed the Cambodian border within minutes after President Nixon announced the operation to the nation.

5. TROOPS ON GROUND

Charlie Company landed in an open farmyard and moved into the neat rows of rubber trees in a nearby plantation. There was no immediate opposition.

6. MEN RESTING — FACES

Most of the men had no idea they were going across the border until this morning. Some were apprehensive and uncertain. . . .

7. RICE ON RADIO

Captain Rice, the company commander, was efficient, confident, and completely in command . . ..
(SOUND UP FULL)

8. MEN PUT ON PACKS AND MOVE OUT

The men move quickly on orders now. They are in a strange and mysterious new war zone . . . behind enemy lines . . . in Charlie country, as they call it, and certain they will soon be fighting.

9. DUNNUCK

Some, like Sergeant Dunnuck, are looking forward to the action . . . intrigued by
a military offensive designed to destroy the North Vietnamese headquarters . . .
if it is still in the area.

DUNNUCK (SOUND UP FULL: "Let's find some gooks and I'll kill em.")

10. GEN. ROBERTS SETUP

The commanding general of the 1st Cavalry Division assesses the initial phase of
his operation:

11. INTERVIEW ROBERTS (SOUND UP FULL: ". . . as the days will develop.")

12. REFUGEES

One of the first developments: refugees. . . . Cambodian farmers and their families . . . quickly caught up in the war that spread suddenly to their villages this
fateful morning.

JL, CBS News, near Mimot, Cambodia.

I read the narration to a stopwatch, timed the sections, and wrote the
number of seconds for each section in the margins of the script.

The developed film arrived. Brown cut the pictures and natural sound to
my timings of the narration. The editing process was slow. The timings were
approximate. In order to save time, I would have to read my voice-over narration live as the edited film was being fed on the satellite, a "hot switch" as
we called it.

An hour before the scheduled transmission, Thai technicians began to
arrive at the station and turn on their equipment. Their eyes were dark with
sleep and their shoulders drooped, but they moved across the wide control
room floor with what appeared to be a sense of responsibility, communicating with each other briskly, seriously. When Brown or I asked them a question, they smiled politely and bowed gracefully but it was soon apparent that
none of them spoke more than a few words of English: "yes" and "no,"
"okay" or "no okay" and "maybe." Communications with New York were
worse. We had not spoken to Little or anyone else for several hours. International phone lines were down.

Brown cleaned the edited film with a white cloth and thread it onto a projector. The scheduled time for the feed was approaching. I was taken to a small studio room with soundproofed walls and a rectangular glass window looking out. The control room was forty feet away. I could not see Brown or the technicians. A microphone, a small TV monitor and a telephone sat on the table in front of me. The time of the transmission arrived. My heart was racing. The first beams of sunlight appeared outside the window.

Nothing happened. No one told me to speak into the microphone. I waited. Outside the booth, technicians hurried back and forth across the control room floor and shouted instructions at one another. Nothing seemed to be working. The thirty minutes of scheduled transmission time passed quickly. It was almost over. I walked out to the control room. 'What's going on?' I asked.

'I don't know,' Brown said, tense. 'We keep feeding picture but we don't know if they're getting our signal in New York or not. We haven't got a fucking co-ord. The phone lines are still down. And you haven't fed your narration.' For someone who never panicked, Brown was close to despair. He put his hands through his long hair and looked at the floor. 'Jack, I think we're fucked.'

I went back to the studio room and sat down. Suddenly I felt exhausted. Every muscle went slack at the same time. My head hurt. All that work, all that running around, all those risks, all that adrenaline for nothing. *What a way to make a living*, I thought. *This sucks*. The black telephone on the table rang. Startled, I reached for the receiver.

"Hello," I said.

"*Get your frame in the gate!*" A faint distant voice, shouting, as if from the moon. It was Sandy Socolow in New York.

I put down the phone and opened the door of the studio. "Get a frame in the gate!" I screamed.

A moment later, Socolow shouted, "*We see you! We see you! Go! We have speed. Go now!*"

I put the phone receiver on the table and shouted out the door, "*Roll film!*" I sat down at the table and inhaled. I closed my eyes and exercised my voice, "Doe, doe, doe, doe, doe . . ." as low as it would go. Then "me, me, me, me, me . . ." as high as possible. A picture appeared on the monitor. The film rolled. I read the voice-over narration from the script carefully, line by line. *Don't fluff*, I thought as I read. *This is your only shot. No second feed.* The scene changes on the monitor seemed to be hitting in synch with the narration. Time passed as an instant. Four minutes and five seconds later it was finished. I picked up the phone and shouted, "Did you get it?" There was no answer. The line was dead.

After a few hours' sleep on clean sheets in a modern hotel in downtown Bangkok, Brown and I got up, ate a meal and rode back out to the airport. A shower and change of clothes had been refreshing. Bangkok was a dream in the daylight, alive and colorful, so much more prosperous than Saigon. But I felt out of place. I needed to get back to Vietnam. The invasion of Cambodia was an ongoing story. *God knows what the reaction's going to be in the States,* I thought. Landing back at Tan Son Nhut, I realized that our trip had taken less than twenty-four hours. A message from Little was waiting at the bureau. It said the piece we fed from Bangkok had been the lead story on the *CBS Evening News* the night before, May 1. No other network had news film of the invasion out of Cambodia. With the support of dozens of CBS staffers and technicians around the world, Brown, Dan and I had delivered a scoop. We felt proud of what we had done. Little's message added that there had been a bad storm over Hong Kong the night before. The Pan Am cargo plane chartered by CBS had been unable to land. It arrived in Tokyo too late to feed the roll of film with the stand-up.

MAY 3, 1970

The invasion army rumbled over the border and into the green rolling countryside of Cambodia. Fifty-ton tanks, tracks, trucks, APCs, jeeps, ACAVs, rocket launchers, artillery guns, gunships, slicks, jet bombers, A-1Es, and thousands of soldiers laden with rifles, radios, mortars, machineguns and grenades swooped onto the land and attacked it with swift furious might. American and South Vietnamese forces drove inland with the armed strength and aggressive belligerence of a NATO assault on Eastern Europe. South Vietnamese troops attacked into the Parrot's Beak area of Svey Rieng Province two days ahead of the Americans and fought running battles for several days. Moving by foot, helicopter and armored vehicles, the Allied Army occupied the jungles, hills and farmland of eastern Cambodia in its search for the North Vietnamese command center. The result was really no contest. Except for a few units ordered to stay behind and delay the advance, the mainforce North Vietnamese fighting battalions packed up quickly and withdrew to the west and north. Their commanders were ordered to retreat rather than fight in conventional combat against such superior force. Nothing was to be gained by it. COSVN, ever elusive, vanished.

The expedition pushed the North Vietnamese Army off balance, forcing its units to flee from its usual areas of operations, and it upset any immediate plans to seize Phnom Penh and install a Khmer Rouge government. The mission also interrupted its military operations in War Zones C and D in Vietnam, driving its troops so far into the Cambodian interior they were unable to continue cross-border raids against First Cav firebases.

Journalists measured the operation's success against the goal set by the commander in chief. President Nixon had stated that the objective was to get COSVN, which appeared to have failed. Senior U.S. commanders were grateful that Nixon had finally allowed them to chase the North Vietnamese out of their Cambodian sanctuaries, but some were critical of the way he announced the operation. They said privately that he gave away too much information in his TV address, telling U.S. enemies what to expect and making it easier for them to get away and regroup. Some thought Nixon was obsessed with self-importance and his commanding role in the operation. They pointed out that experienced military officers prefer to tell the enemy nothing or, if anything, to deceive them. In this case, it may have made no difference. Later intelligence revealed that at least some North Vietnamese commanders knew of the impending operation by April 27 or 28, probably through their spies in Saigon, giving them three to four days to make their retreat.

I wanted to get back to Charlie Company and 2d Squad to finish the documentary and see how the men were doing, but the division PIO still refused permission. No reasons were given. Dave Miller offered to speak with Major General Roberts, the division commander, and try to persuade him to let us back in. Miller sensed that Roberts, now nearing the end of his one-year tour, was softening on the issue. He thought it might soon be possible to get back with the company. CBS had put a lot of pressure on the Pentagon. Anticipating our return, I tried to reconstruct the team that had started the project. Keith Kay, who was visiting his family in the United States, was asked to return to Saigon. Messages were sent for Jim Clevenger, who was vacationing somewhere in Asia and was out of touch. In the meantime, Miller said, take another camera crew and cover breaking news. He suggested linking up with the 11th Armored Cavalry Regiment, the only American unit to make serious contact so far.

I was assigned to work with a new freelance camera crew. We flew to the headquarters of the 11th ACR in Quan Loi and then forward into Cambodia. The regiment was laagered deep in the jungle near Mimot, its tanks and tracks drawn up in large circles, their guns pointed toward the surrounding bush. The unit had been the spearhead for the U.S. ground assault on D-Day and fought a two hour battle in which fifty-two North Vietnamese and two U.S. soldiers had been killed. Sitting on the tanks, APCs and ACAVs in dusty green fatigues with their shirts off, reading old newspapers, taking makeshift showers in the heat, the troops waited for orders.

A soldier was reading a copy of *Stars and Stripes*. A headline said:

NIX ARMS CAMBODIA

It was a cute headline. The main story quoted officials who denied the United States was sending weapons to Cambodia, though the South Vietnamese were doing so covertly.

"That's pretty good," one of the soldiers on an APC said. "They won't send *arms* over here, but they'll send *people*."

"Roger that," another GI said. The men laughed.

"How long we supposed to be here?" one said.

"Eight, six more days."

"Nope, five."

"Supposed to be here eight days," one of them said with authority. The others could not confirm that he was right or wrong. In fact, other than what they could see before them, none of them knew what was going on. The big picture was made up of dozens of fragments of information—an incident here, a firefight there, a prisoner taken in some other place—so that not even senior commanders knew what was happening overall. The one certainty for the troops of the 11th ACR was the shortage of food. They were almost out of field rations.

"They find that hospital, it'll be all right," a GI said calmly. A search was under way for a main NVA field hospital. "I'd like to go in there and blow it all to pieces, find a bunch of gooks and stuff."

"Yeah."

Privately, I despised the word "gook" and never said it. It came out of the Korean War and was used to describe any Asian. In Korean, I was told, "gook" means "person." Here it was a term of belittlement, usually racist.

I asked if the GIs would mind answering a few questions for the folks at home. No one objected.

Spec-4 Daniel Ludwig sat on a can of ammunition, bandoleers of machinegun bullets beside him. He said he was eighteen years old, came from St. Louis.

"How's it going?" I asked.

"They may starve us half to death," he said, "but we ain't gonna run out of *bullets*." He laughed. "Man, I think it's about time they started doing something like this. Instead of just messin around. Come up here and get 'em where it hurts 'em. That's the only way you're gonna win the war."

PFC Joseph Stallings, who was twenty-one and from Pekin, Illinois, said, "Personally, I'll be glad to get back to Nam, myself." The others laughed.

"What's your feeling about moving into Cambodia?" I asked. PFC Dennis Van Alstinn, eighteen, of Roosevelt, California, answered, "If we're doing our job right, gettin 'em out of here, fine and dandy. Run 'em back into South Vietnam, we'll just have to take care of 'em back there."

"Most of the guys in the outfit feel the same way?"

"I don't know. You'll have to ask them. I imagine they dig it. It's better than just waitin around for the dinks, I guess."

The men said they were part of Echo Troop, 2d Squadron. When the interview was over they introduced me to their commander, Captain Fred Kyle, a twenty-seven-year-old from Norfolk, Virginia. Kyle said his men were presently searching the jungle around the camp and trying to find evidence of an enemy headquarters. So far they had uncovered a bunker complex with a cache of rice, dried food, bicycles and documents but no weapons and no evidence of COSVN. Kyle said his unit had captured four North Vietnamese soldiers who told him a lot of their comrades wanted to surrender but didn't know how to do it without getting shot.

"They say they knew about our operation on the twenty-eighth [of April]," Kyle said. "One way or another, they knew we were coming. Nixon told 'em what we were doing. So they started moving right away. I think the command group is long gone by now. Our expectations are to search the jungle for weeks if necessary to find their CP and destroy it."

"Do you think the enemy's still in the area?"

"They may not be in the immediate area, but they're close enough that they can get here in a hurry if they have to. They're not too far away."

Kyle took us to meet the regimental commander, Colonel Donn A. Starry. He shook hands and smiled. 'Glad to see you talking to the men,' he said. 'Not all the reporters we've seen out here bother to do that.' I explained that most print journalists had to file copy from Saigon and were spending most of their time getting to and from the field, all day in some cases. Time was too short to do many interviews.

Starry said he was forty-four years old and came from Kansas City, Kansas, though his wife was living in Springfield, Virginia. Tall, taciturn and with an intense command presence, Starry seemed, in manner and appearance, the personification of a warrior chief. Higher command, he said, was convinced that if the COSVN complex was anywhere, his regiment was sitting on it.

"What we're doing here now is—we've come in here on a rather narrow corridor and we're trying to expand this and get into the base areas, see what we've really got on our hands."

"What would you say are the odds, relatively, of finding the complex?" I asked.

"Well, if it's here, we'll find it," he said. "Uh, I dare say that by the time we do, the birds may have flown the coop. There's nothing very stealthy about a cavalry regiment coming through the jungle. So, he's had plenty of warning now. But the mission is to get in and destroy his base complexes, communications systems, his rice caches and so forth, and eliminate his logistics support base in here."

"From the three days of the operation so far, would you estimate that the enemy has fled the area?"

"I really can't say. We know we outflanked what I would estimate to be one battalion on the first day. He may have gone away to another part of the base area where he's holed up waiting for us or trying to decide what to do. He may have withdrawn. It's not like him to withdraw. These are regular NVA forces. They're tough, well-trained, well-armed. They like to fight and, ah, I expect we'll meet him again."

"If *you* were surrounded by a ten to fifteen thousand man fighting force, ah, would you choose to stand and fight, do you think?" I asked the question expecting "no" for an answer.

"I think so," he said. The words came without hesitation, the pupils of his eyes cold black dots.

The answer surprised me. Then I figured it out. *There's no other answer he could have made. It isn't false heroics or male pride or boastfulness. It's part of his military breeding, his warrior soul.* For an American armored cavalry officer trained to fight World War III on a battlefield in Europe, Starry had no choice. Of course his regiment would stand its ground. Maybe not to the last man (officers know the prudence of withdrawal), but not before taking heavy casualties. *The difference between Starry and Vo Nguyen Giap*, I thought, *is that Starry sees war in the light of the experience of the Battle of the Bulge. Of course he would try to hold his position, even at the cost of having his regiment destroyed. Giap would run and hide and be able to fight for another five, ten, twenty years.*

A short time later a powerful tremor swept the camp. Tanks and tracks wobbled on their platform trailers. The air howled with close explosions. Soldiers ducked their heads and put on their helmets. Some dived for cover. A long string of bombs from a B-52 strike burst in the near distance, a kilometer or two away. Then, much closer, the loud cracks of individual air strikes.

The crew and I got the film back to Saigon just in time for a shipment to the Philippines and a satellite feed the same day. It was close. We were pleased with ourselves for the hot dirty work and the fortunate timing. It was a simple unspectacular piece, just enough to advance the ongoing story of the invasion. That evening, after work, I accompanied Gloria Emerson of the *New York Times* to dinner. She had recently arrived in Saigon and we were becoming friends. We had a pleasant, informative conversation. I admired her knowledge of Vietnamese history and her determination to cover the war closely. She wanted to get into Cambodia with an American unit but MACV was making it difficult. She suspected it was because she was a woman. I promised to take her with us on our next trip in a day or two and she was delighted.

An overnight cable from New York said a technician at the film laboratory in Manila had made a mistake during the processing and destroyed our film from Cambodia.

MAY 4, 1970

April 28, 1970

Dear Jack,

Hi—Lying in bed—just a sheet on—the weather is warm enough that you don't need more than a sheet. We've really had lovely weather the last 4 days—spring has sprung. Wish you were here to enjoy it. The tree across the street in front of the church is budding and getting greener every day. And, I think our cat has spring fever—in other words—he's acting weirder than usual. He's been unusually docile—a real pussycat . . . that is, everyday but today. He managed to put a 2 inch scratch on my face (because I was reading and he wanted me to pay attention to him) and—imagine this—fell head-first into the toilet. I was running my bath water and he was doing his "crazy dance" and slipped and fell right into the john.

He did a funny thing last night . . . He slept in his box (you know, the one in the corner), the first time he's done that since you went away. The least I could say about him is he's fascinating.

May 4, 1970

Dear Joy,

I love you. I should send you a postcard every day and say it. I miss your company, and affection. I want to come home and sleep with you and all the other things we do together.

There is no one else in my thoughts.

MAY 5, 1970

The whole regiment was watching the duel. Thousands of men stood or sat near a long column of tanks and other armored vehicles parked along the road and stared into the distant sky to see the show. Up ahead, where the column would soon be headed, an Air Force light observation plane was doing loops and rolls and ninety-degree breaks between bright lines of anti-aircraft fire rushing up from the ground. The plane was a single-engine Cessna, an O-1 Bird Dog, and the pilot handled it with quick graceful ease, twirling the control stick like a ballet partner, blue open sky for a stage, dancing between the bullets. The North Vietnamese gunners on the ground were trying to get an accurate lead on the plane, black and green in its camouflage paint, vulnerable as a bird. They fired long bursts of tracers that swept up and across the sky in slow red luminescent lines, burning and flashing like streams of water from a garden hose sparkling in the sunlight. Each time the gunners fired in front of the plane, the pilot turned and dived out of the way, disappearing for a time and then circling back to taunt them again. His skill would have been impressive on its own, even without tracers stabbing the sky, but the gunfire made it a duel. Soldiers on the tracks watched with dread and delight, transfixed, waiting to see what happened.

'Jeees! Will ya look at that jive!' one of the soldiers on an APC said, wonder in his voice.

'Why does he *do* that, man? I mean, why doesn't he just di-di the fuck outta there?'

'He's havin fun, man, showin his stuff.'

'He's getting a good fix on where they're at,' an officer watching with them said. 'So we can go in there and clean 'em out.'

'He's gonna get his ass waxed. Any second, you'll see.'

No one looked away. Up and down the long column soldiers stood on the hulls and turrets of their tanks and tracks mesmerized by the simple gracefulness of the duel, the ageless spell of combat, one to one. They could have been watching a bullfight in Spain, or gladiators in Rome.

'Oh, I'm telling you, man, Charlie has got *all* his shit together today,' a soldier said. Everyone knew the tracers came from the place they were going next, a rubber plantation a few kilometers ahead. They knew that anti-air-craft batteries firing .51-caliber bullets usually accompanied regiments of North Vietnamese infantry.

To someone watching from a distance, with no accurate depth of field, it looked like the line of tracers and the path of the plane were intersecting. *That thing could trail smoke any moment,* I thought, *just roll over in one more lazy turn like that and not come out of it.* The air was silent, radios hushed. Men held their breath. Occasionally, some of them sighed '*ooooooh*' and '*aaahhhh*' when the plane escaped, as if watching a circus high-wire act. The pilot flew around again, turned and climbed, and the sparkling red stream of tracers floated after him like a beacon, chasing. As a spectacle the display was splen-did, elegant, immediate, played on a stage of endless sweeping sky, blue and eternal. The show lifted us out of our modest mortal lives and into a world of timeless terrible beauty.

'Ahhhh!' one of the GIs said as the plane passed through the tracers. 'I thought he had him that time.'

'It's an illusion,' the officer said, looking through binoculars. 'We're only seeing it from one angle. It looks flat to us, like that triple A is a lot closer. But they're fifty, sixty meters away from the plane. That sky jockey can see it in all three dimensions. We can't.'

'If I was up there, man, I'd be lookin at four, five dimensions,' a GI said. 'An all of 'em spooky.'

The armored column was over a mile long. It sat dead in its tracks, the vehicles scattered in loose defensive alignment on and off the paved two-lane road known as Route 7. The regiment, the 11th Armored Cavalry, had charged up the road at maximum speed, chasing a retreating force of North Vietnamese, covering thirty-five miles in two days. The tactics belonged to World War II. So did the hazards. The drive had come to a sudden stop a few hours earlier at a river crossing where the bridge was blown. The other bridges along the road had been left intact but this one was gone. The North Vietnamese got away on the other side. Army engineers were trying to put a new temporary bridge in place, a big heavy M4T6 that was hoisted in by a Flying Crane helicopter, but it was going slow. The terrain was flat farmland, hard-baked earth at the end of the dry season, a few simple bamboo houses by the side of the road, rice fields in the background. Seven miles ahead was

Snoul, a crossroads town where the North Vietnamese were presumed to be dug in and waiting. The regiment sat and watched in the white heat of the afternoon Cambodian sun.

The Bird Dog made a final pass above the anti-aircraft guns in the rubber plantation, rolled over on its wing and dived at the ground. A white phosphorous rocket shot out from under its wing, trailing a straight line of smoke in front of the plane, and exploded in the trees. Then the plane flattened out low and flew east, disappearing in the distance. The shooting stopped. GIs got down from their vehicles and tried to find shade.

'Do you *believe* that?' one of them said.

'No, man, I truly don't,' another said.

'Oh, man, that was just a *movie*,' said a third GI.

'Ain't never seen that one before.'

'And I don't wanna see the ending either.'

A group of Cambodian farm families walked along the edge of the road carrying baskets of food and cooking pots on their shoulders and in two-wheeled carts. They walked north toward Snoul, away from the area just occupied by American and South Vietnamese troops. They had not been exposed to American soldiers before and tried not to look at them as they walked past. The GIs shouted at them and held out their hands with cigarettes, chewing gum and candy from their C ration boxes. At first they gave it to the children, who were less afraid and took it innocently. The GIs smiled at them, then laughed with them, inventing games, being silly, behaving like children themselves. Finally the adult refugees stopped and smiled and thanked the soldiers politely.

A Marine Corps major walked over to the group of villagers and asked in Khmer what they had seen of the North Vietnamese. The villagers said they saw many, many Viets with uniforms and weapons moving north along the road in the past few days.

'There were big men with them,' the villagers said, 'from way north, beyond the mountains. Chinese maybe. They are in Snoul.'

'How many?' the major asked.

'Maybe a thousand, maybe two, three thousand,' the villagers said.

One of the Cambodians said he had lived in Snoul until recently.

'What happened there?' the major asked.

'A week to ten days ago,' the man said, 'soldiers from the Cambodia National Army arrested all the Viets in the area, about twenty to forty people who worked around here. The soldiers said they were Communists. Then they killed them,' he said, 'all of them. Then Viet soldiers came into Snoul and surrounded the National Army camp. They shot all the officers and sergeants and took the regular soldiers away. About three hundred of them. No one knows what happened to them. The Viets told us that if the Americans came into Snoul they would kill the men and rape the women and burn down our houses.'

The major walked across the road to the command track of the regimental commander, Colonel Starry, and told him what the civilian had said. Starry listened closely, grateful for every bit of intelligence he could get to plan his assault. He was frustrated by his inability to get the regiment across the river and into the attack quickly.

'Our mission has changed in the past twenty-four hours,' Starry said. 'We're no longer trying to find COSVN. We want to get to Snoul and take it by this afternoon. We've covered fifty to sixty kilometers in the past two days and we're almost there. That bridge the NVA blew is the only thing holding us up.'

Everyone waited for the engineers to put the new heavy bridge in place. Starry decided to look for an alternative crossing himself. In a short time he found one. He ordered a small portable bridge to be laid across the river and tested it with an APC. The bridge held. In less than an hour, the lead elements of the regiment went across the river and advanced on Snoul along the main road, Route 7.

Upon reaching the outer edges of the town, still a mile or so out, Starry called a halt. To the right of the road was a dry streambed or wide irrigation ditch that ran at right angles to the road. Beyond that to the north was a large rubber plantation. Starry held the column in place to allow his two squadrons to tighten up and gather for attack. Cambodian civilians nearby said the North Vietnamese had prepared an ambush along the main road ahead. Starry decided against a frontal attack up the road. Instead, he ordered his 2d Squadron to turn right off the road and drive along the dry streambed to the east, then wheel around to its left and attack the city from the southeast. Third Squadron was to sweep west of the city and attack it from there. The regiment would surround Snoul on three sides while an air cavalry unit of helicopter gunships screened North Vietnamese escape routes to the north. The regiment waited for all the elements to get into position.

About a half dozen reporters were present, including Gloria Emerson, who had come with me, and James Sterba of the *New York Times*. Starry decided to disperse us through the regiment. He assigned the CBS team to 2d Squadron and handed us over to its commander. Lieutenant Colonel Grail Brookshire was thirty-seven years old, from Stone Mountain, Georgia, and was all business. He greeted us with cool indifference, preoccupied with his preparations for the attack, sizing us up quickly.

'You can go with G Troop, Captain Menzel,' Brookshire said in dismissal, giving me a smile, as if he knew something that I did not.

The radios came alive. Brookshire called in his troop commanders to brief them on the attack. He stood over a map of the area.

"This is a recon-by-force to find out what's in there," he said. "And also, if possible, to take the town. Without destroying it. I want everybody up tight, weapons and flak jackets, helmets on. And when you take fire, shoot. Try to avoid shooting into crowds of civilians. In other words, if you're taking light fire and there are civilians in the area, try to return the fire without losing all the fucking civilians."

"That's what I'm worried about," one of the captains said. "Going through that village."

"Look," Brookshire said, "if we've made contact by then, I'll probably have different instructions."

Different instructions? *God*, I thought, *this could be a mess*.

He pointed to his map. "Now, if we can get around these fuckers, we may have them bottled up down in this end of the rubber. Because they're probably expecting us to come right up [the] highway. The village people down here say they've broken the highway somewhere between here and there and they undoubtedly have. We'll try to find a way around it. We can always shove up through the rubber and come up this side of the draw."

After the briefing, 2d Squadron started its engines and drove along the bottom of the dry streambed, moving quickly in single file—tanks, armored personnel carriers, attack carriers and other vehicles—churning up dirt and dust. G Troop was near the end of the column. Captain Menzel, the troop commander, sent the CBS team to accompany the forward observer of G Troop, First Lieutenant Earl Zerbach.

Zerbach was twenty-six years old from Mount Gilead, North Carolina. As soon as he saw how much room the three of us took up in his APC, he told the camera crew to move to an APC behind us, a medics' track.

'Don't worry,' Zerbach said, 'we'll all be together.'

When the column had moved about a mile east of the road, the tanks and tracks turned left and maneuvered into a line of attack at the edge of the rubber plantation. The narrow rubber trees were widely spaced across twenty to thirty flat acres, cool-looking in the shade. The radio crackled. It was Brookshire, call sign "Battle-Six."

"Three-Six, maneuver on my left flank. Get down on the edge of the rubber. One-Six-Six, get down on my right flank." The transmission hissed. "Roger," Brookshire said, "get down here on my left flank, on the outer edge of the rubber there."

The soldiers on the forward observer's track put on their helmets and flak jackets and pulled back the bolts of their machineguns to load the first rounds on their ammunition belts. Lieutenant Zerbach stood at the right front of the open-top APC behind a .50-caliber machinegun mounted on the hull. Below and forward of him were the driver, PFC Armando (Moose) Dicenso, aged twenty, from Boston, Massachusetts, and the front gunner, PFC Dean Shoemaker, also twenty, of Portsmouth, Ohio. Three quarters of the way down the right side of the track, near the back, PFC Patrick Reid, aged twenty-one, from Chicago, operated an M-60 machinegun on a mount.

I turned on my tape recorder and spoke to Reid.

"What do you think at a time like this?"

"I don't know what to think, to tell you the truth. Just keep on goin in column until we get to the village and then we'll see what happens from there. That's about it."

"Anything special you think about when you know there might be a real heavy force up there?"

"Yeah. I just hope there ain't." He smiled. "If they are, I just hope they're bad shots." He laughed and then looked away, as if embarrassed.

"Hope I make it to live to the next battle," Reid added. "Tomorrow will be my twenty-second birthday."

The radio squawked. Zerbach received orders to take his APC and two more, including the medical track, into the rubber trees. Zerbach told Moose Dicenso to drive forward at speed. The three tracks raced their engines, clanked into gear and charged toward the plantation, bouncing over the rutted earth, rattling metal on metal, their engines whining, churning up dust. I looked around at the APC just behind and saw the camera crew trying to hang on. Now I realized why Brookshire looked sinister. He had put us on point.

PFC Reid opened fire first and surprised everyone—a long angry burst to the right front, *craak-craak-craak-craak-craak-craak-craak!* The sudden extreme noise of the machinegun made sharp shocking explosions in my ears. Immediately, the other automatic weapons opened fire and then the machineguns on the tracks on both sides. The APC was a hothouse of explosions, smoke, vibrations, and the bitter smell of burning gunpowder. The tracks raced forward through the rubber plantation with their guns firing long sweeping bursts through the trees. About a hundred yards ahead, just outside the tree line, was a thicket of brush eight to ten feet high. Light sparkled from the brushline, bright orange and red flashes twinkling in the distance. The dirt ahead of the APC jumped and spit and then exploded in geysers of earth. The patrol halted. All the machineguns fired nonstop into the brush, the men behind them aiming and holding on like helmeted robots, mechanical extensions of the machines that carried them. I stood at the center of the APC with my head and shoulders out the top watching in all directions, especially to the rear, which was not covered. From time to time I spoke into a tape recorder. Zerbach turned and screamed.

'Gimme water! The barrel's burnin up!' There was fire in his eyes.

I froze. No idea what to do.

'Over there!' he jabbed with his finger. I looked down inside the track and saw a five-gallon water can strapped to the side of the hull.

'Now!' Zerbach screeched. Impulsively, I reached for the can, unfastened the straps and lifted it up. Zerbach seized it with a jerk, unscrewed the top and poured water over the barrel of the machinegun. Steam sizzled off the metal. In a moment he was firing again.

Reid called for ammo, shouting at me over his shoulder to grab a can from the back of the track. I turned and saw a metal box marked "7.62mm" on the floor. Without thinking, I opened it and passed a belt quickly up to him. Everything was enveloped in the fury of noise and vibration, happening fast, no time to think. I looked around. *What next? What needs to be done?* Zerbach called for .50-cal. I found him a belt and handed it up. Taking it, he flashed a brief smile at me from his perch, turned and loaded it into his machinegun. This was the first time I had been truly engaged in combat, being useful, doing something constructive, even part of something so wildly destructive. With the camera crew in the other track, there was nothing else for me to do except watch. Helping the crew gave me a sense of purpose. I felt energized. Fear and excitement were there but were under control, subdued by supremely heightened alertness, watching out, working. I felt part of the team. Every minute or so I took a quick look out the back where no one else was looking but saw no one there. I was conscious of what happened to the Marines on Operation Starlite in 1965, moving fast, ambushed from behind. At my feet, dozens of spent shell casings from the outgoing machinegun rounds fell and bounced on the floor of the track. The brass was slippery underfoot and I reached down to clear them away. Touching them with my bare hand, I felt sharp pain go through my fingers and palm. Fat blisters came up at once.

"Let's go, Moose!" Zerbach shouted at Dicenso. The track lunged forward, picked up speed, headed toward the brush line.

"A damned RPG just hit right in front of us!" Zerbach screamed, aiming and firing the fifty into the woods.

Explosions, gunfire, engine whine, transmission changes, clanking treads, radios, shouts, screams—the three tracks drove blindly into the brush and found themselves in the midst of a fortified North Vietnamese bunker complex. Muzzle flame and tracers flashed everywhere.

"*The APCs are rolling directly over the tops of the bunkers, plowing right through them,*" I spoke into my tape recorder.

"Move down to the east and the south, over," the radio squawked. Heavy gunfire. Explosions.

"They just captured two POWs and one .50-caliber machinegun," another voice shouted.

The tracks trundled over the bunkers and out the other side of the brush. At a clearing they stopped, guns still firing. I looked over at the APC next to us. No sign of the camera crew. *Probably got their heads down,* I thought. *Just hope they're getting some of this on film.* Our luck together was not good. It was the same freelance crew whose film had been destroyed in the lab in Manila.

Abruptly, the shooting stopped. The three tracks were in a wide clearing with another line of brush ahead and the copse of trees over the bunker complex behind them. I looked back. All clear. Then, from behind one of the trees, a slender figure, almost a shadow of a man, stepped slowly into the open and raised his rifle, an AK-47, lifting the muzzle up from the ground to fire at the back of our track. Zerbach, Reid and the others were facing forward, concentrating on what was ahead. My sense of time and place stopped, suspended, fracturing into the slowest fragments of visible motion. All my senses became superalert. The soldier raised the rifle slowly, as if lifting a great weight. He was forty or fifty feet away and I recognized him as North Vietnamese at once: mustard-colored khaki uniform, raven black hair cut with a bowl around the sides, rubber-tire sandals on his feet, a teenage boy's face, smudges of dirt on it. *How young he is!* It was the same figure I had seen a hundred times, the soldier in the garden behind the house in Hué, the same one who had been trying to kill me in and out of my dreams for years. And here he was finally in the flesh. The barrel of his rifle rose upward in infinitesimally fine slow calibrations of speed and movement and pointed toward us.

Without a thought I reached over and seized PFC Reid from the back by his shoulders and forced his body around to the right hard and in the same instant I shouted, *"Gook!"*

Reid turned immediately, swinging his .30-caliber machinegun with him. As soon as he was clear of the APC at our side, he pulled the trigger and the machinegun jerked in his hands, rattling with exploding cartridges, spitting a stream of hissing missiles that kicked the dirt in a moving line of earth toward the figure of the soldier with the AK-47 raised up fully pointed at us now and tore into his shadow form with invisible spite. His body shuddered for an instant as the rifle flew away from his hands and hung in midair and his head bent slowly forward, bowing to us, as his arms went slack and the rifle tumbled and his body fell backward onto the ground in a fractured heap.

At the same moment, the APC lurched forward, all guns firing. Reid swung around to face ahead. I was conscious of feeling numb. Life moved at regular speed again, as if reality had been interrupted for the few moments of the killing and was now back to normal. On the radio, Captain Menzel ordered Zerbach to swing around and make a 180-degree turn and come back to the main body of G Troop waiting far behind in the rubber plantation. Riding through the brush and the trees, guns silent, the tension lifted.

Zerbach looked down from behind his machinegun.

"I got a couple of more gray hairs on that one, I think." His tone was casual, relaxed, as if talking to a friend. The other soldiers on the track began to talk excitedly about what they had seen and done. Their mood was light, relieved, almost merry. Reid told them about the North Vietnamese soldier behind us.

"Did you see him?" one of the others asked.

"Yeah, he was close," Reid replied.

"If you saw him, you got him."

Reid looked down.

"Probably scattered from the rest of his unit," he said. "I don't know, man. Hope he wasn't a farmer or something." He seemed genuinely concerned.

I watched the ground on the way back, looking for him. The body was there, though not where I had expected. He was five feet five or so, a loose brown clump of arms and legs splayed at awkward angles where they touched the ground. No blood, no obvious wounds in him, no torn up body parts, no agony on his face. The track moved directly past him. Death had kissed his eyes and he had fallen. It was difficult to comprehend that he had been a living presence, a mortal threat to my life, minutes before. The big round baseplate for one of the anti-aircraft guns lay beside him. The AK-47 was gone. In a minute he was out of sight. The three tracks rolled back through the rubber plantation and then came to a long iron gray line of Sheridan tanks massed for the full attack on Snoul and passed between them to go to the rear, our reconnaissance mission completed.

MAY 6, 1970

Why didn't he stay behind the tree? He was safe there. No one could see him in the shadows. We would have rolled by and in another minute he could have got away. The heavy tanks and other tracks were a kilometer behind. Why did he come out and expose himself? Wasn't he afraid? Did he think he could kill us? Did he hate us that much?

The questions went with me. They asked themselves. When no answers came they repeated themselves. I heard them in my ears, felt the weight of them in my mind, stomach, heart. The answers didn't come. There were no answers because there was no logic, in my mind, for what he had done. He committed suicide when he could have escaped. In the night I woke in a sweat with his ochre-colored face in front of me: composed, inquiring, an expression of supreme melancholy on it, a look that said, 'Why did you do that?' I couldn't answer. The truth was too painful to admit to myself. I was a killer.

I wished it had not happened. A vision of the moment popped in and out of my consciousness—vivid, frightening, real—as powerful as the moment itself. Each time his figure appeared, my nerves twitched and I felt a jolt of fear like an electric shock. He was there much of the time, a severe presence, reminding me of what we had done. He stared at me so deeply, so scornfully, that the punishing gaze seemed to invade the most secret part of me. I tried to keep busy by making the usual rounds of Saigon—attending briefings, feeding radio spots, writing memos, meeting friends for lunch and dinner, writing home. I tried to behave normally. But there was always a vague sense of uncertainty, as if the ground underfoot was unstable. Friends and colleagues saw my usual outer self: polite, civilized, unthreatening. Inside I was insecure. The contradiction made me crazy. The killing had let loose, if only for an instant, the darkest part of me, a part I hated, a killer-beast I did not want to accept. Thoughts terrified me. In the evenings I drank heavily. I fell asleep in a stupor but did not rest. Guilt was in everything. How could I have done that? For me, a civilian, to take part in the killing of a soldier was as shameful as a soldier killing a civilian. Though my own survival had depended on it, I knew it was wrong. I tried to tell myself it was an instinctive reaction to protect myself and the APC crew, that it was kill or be killed, but it was no good. I had become a participant in the war. Until the moment of his appearance, I had been comfortable playing my part in the battle, enjoying the camaraderie and teamwork, feeling the excitement. At the instant of supreme involvement I had shouted a word I considered obscene, "gook," condemning the man with my word and deed. His blood was all over me. Taking a life had killed the best part inside me, my sense of humanity.

I told no one.

MAY 7, 1970

Life went on. The freelance photographer who had been working with me during the attack on Snoul said he had got most of the fighting on film. We went over each scene, one by one. He assured me he had it all.

'Did you see a North Vietnamese soldier behind us?' I asked.

'Oh, yeah. Saw that, mate. Got him,' he said confidently. 'It's all there.'

I wrote the narration and the film was shipped to New York. When it was screened a couple of days later, Bensley reported that he had received only a hundred feet of usable images on the film and no combat, not enough to make a story. The photographer had spent much of the time huddled for cover in the medical track. *All that for nothing*, I thought.

On the street, I met Peter Arnett of Associated Press. He had gone into Snoul with the attacking force of the 11th ACR and had seen a family of Cambodian civilians who had been hit by an American tank shell and burned to death. Their bodies were frozen together, he said, *fused* by the heat of the explosion, grotesque expressions of agony on their faces. Arnett said it was the worst thing he had seen in his nine years in Vietnam. He said he was leaving Southeast Asia forever. "I've had enough," he said. "I've got to get out of here before I lose my mind completely."

Brigadier General Robert Shoemaker, the task force commander, was asked in an interview about the loss of civilian life in Snoul. He said, "The actions were taken by the commander on the ground to protect his force." *Against civilians?* I thought. "Sherman said it best," Shoemaker added. "'War is hell.'"

Word arrived from Tay Ninh that Colonel Ochs, the brigade commander, had been relieved of command. No reason was given publicly. Being relieved in the field meant the probable end of Ochs's military career. Later, when we asked if the decision had anything to do with what happened with Charlie Company, we were told that it did not. A senior division officer said, 'He doesn't know what's going on in his AO.'

Captain Jackson settled in as headquarters company commander in

Phuoc Vinh. When I visited him, Jackson said his heart was okay; the doctors had cleared him of medical problems. In Cambodia, I had bought a captured North Vietnamese officer's pistol with its holster and web belt. Keith Kay and I gave it to Jackson as a souvenir.

A few days later, Major General Elvy Roberts ended his tour of duty as commander of the First Cav and prepared to return to the United States. Skip Brown filmed the change of command ceremony. When it was over, Roberts said we could return to Charlie Company. He had spoken with the battalion commander, Lieutenant Colonel Trobaugh, and we were welcome to come back and finish the documentary. Dave Miller, who had made the arrangements, said there was no connection between the favorable story I did on Roberts's end of tour and his decision to let us return to C Company.

On May 17, five members of CBS News, including correspondent George Syvertsen, photographer Tomoharu Ishii, sound recordist Kojiro Sakai, producer Jerry Miller and second photographer Romik Lekhi, disappeared in Cambodia. They had been driving down a road outside Phnom Penh that a British colleague, who had been captured and released the day before, had told Syvertsen was safe. A three-man team from NBC News, including veteran correspondent Wells Hangen, also went missing. In all, twenty-three foreign journalists were in the hands of the North Vietnamese and Khmer Rouge. Dana Stone and Sean Flynn were still missing, with no word of their whereabouts.

It took another ten days to get back to Charlie Company. By now, the company was out of Cambodia and patrolling outside division headquarters at Phuoc Vinh. The company was divided into nine squads of about ten men each who were patrolling separately eight to ten miles outside the base perimeter. The duty was called "palace guard" and it was relatively easy. Without officers or platoon sergeants to enforce discipline, the soldiers did more or less what they wished, regardless of orders.

Keith Kay was back in-country and working with a new soundman, John Steinbeck, son of the author. Steinbeck had served a tour in Vietnam in the Army and was comfortable in the field. He was young and rebellious and eager to learn about television news documentary production. We got along well. Jim Clevenger returned to New York with a serious case of dysentery. When he recovered, he was given a job as an associate producer on the Cronkite broadcast. He had finally got the job he wanted most: to work on stories in the field. With Charlie Company, we interviewed Captain Rice and more of the men in 2d Squad. The tension over the rebellion had diminished

but was not gone. A few of the other members of the company, outside of
2d Platoon, let me know that they were not happy with my reporting of the
incident on the road. None of them had seen the TV story, but they were
angry that the men of C Company might have been portrayed as cowards.

In New York, the network decided to provide airtime in July for a special
one-hour broadcast on Charlie Company. Russ Bensley was the producer.
He asked me to record an on-camera open to accompany scenes we shot in
March and April of the GIs in 2d Squad humping the bush. One morning
when the troops were sitting around their small camp, not going anywhere,
I decided to write it. Since it would be recorded on film, it was the only part
of the narration that could not be changed later. I had to get it right. There
were too many distractions in the camp, so I decided to walk a hundred
yards outside the perimeter. One of the soldiers gave me his M-16. Even
though I wasn't experienced using it, it made me feel more secure out there
on my own. I sat with my back to a tree facing some low scattered bush
away from the camp and wrote:

> Spring, 1970. After five years of killing, the gears of the Vietnam death
> machine were grinding more slowly in the months before the invasion of
> Cambodia. After five years of war, the lives of the line infantrymen—the
> grunts—were practically the same: young men with guns tramping around
> the tropical jungles, living like the other animals, occasionally engaging in
> the death game the first grunts were sent here for in 1965.
>
> But there did appear to be some change in their attitudes in 1970—a cer-
> tain sense of independence, a reluctance to behave according to the mili-
> tary's insistence on obedience, like pawns or puppets. Sometimes there was
> open rebelliousness.
>
> It was an internal conflict within the American Army among the soldiers
> themselves. Some called it the war between 'the lifers' and 'the grunts,' a
> rumbling resentment, usually verbal but sometimes violent, involving some
> of the older men making careers of military work, and the young draftees
> committed to a year of military service in Vietnam.
>
> The grunts were determined to survive. Since they were forced to endure
> the most extreme physical hardships, they insisted on having something to
> say about the making of decisions that determined whether they might live
> or die. It happened, among other units, in Charlie Company.

When it was written, Kay insisted that I read it aloud to the squad while he rolled film. The soldiers sat in a group and listened. When I finished reading it to them they said it was true, that's the way it was, there it is.

In early June, Charlie Company regrouped as a single rifle company and made a helicopter assault back into Cambodia. Kay, Steinbeck and I went with the soldiers into a region of steep hills, dense underbrush and difficult patrols. During rest breaks, Kay searched outside the camp for any sign that the North Vietnamese might have taken American prisoners through the area, inspecting the bottoms of old cans, scraps of paper, anything that might have an initial or two scratched on it.

We were staying with the company continuously now in order to be with the troops if they made contact. We set up a rotation. Kay and Steinbeck spent four days in the field and left with their film on the resupply chopper. They were replaced the same day by a young Australian freelance named Norman Lloyd, a delightful, dark-haired photographer who was new to television news and Vietnam. He made up in hard work and absolute courage what he lacked in experience. Working as a photographer for less than a month, he had already distinguished himself by getting dramatic combat footage in Cambodia. When Lloyd had spent four days with the company, Kay and Steinbeck came back to replace him. I stayed in the field throughout. The summer monsoon had started and it rained much of the time.

On June 18 the company was withdrawn from Cambodia. Gordy Lee was promoted to specialist fourth class. I asked him how the troops were getting along with Captain Rice. "We're getting along a lot better than we were. We're still not jelling properly, but we're getting along better than we were before. He's starting to give us more breaks, which helps us, and then we're more ready in case we do hit something. And we're stopping earlier now and running patrols, this kind of thing. We're starting to get back to the old Charlie Company."

Sergeant Dunnuck said, "I think everything's squared away now. He's getting a little better now anyway." Dunnuck had four months left on his tour and had given up hope of getting out of the field before then. He and Rice did not get along.

One afternoon in the field I became ill: dizzy, weak, sick to my stomach. I felt more fatigued than ever before. It wasn't the heat because the weather was cool, raining lightly. Steinbeck and Lloyd got me out of the field and onto a C-130 to Saigon and into the Air Force dispensary at Tan Son Nhut. As I waited on a stretcher to be seen by a doctor, an older nurse leaned over and said in a confidential, maternal voice, "Have you been taking drugs, son?" I shook my head no. I wondered whether they were being inundated with drug overdose cases. Someone stole my medic's bag with my notebook, tape recorder and tapes, probably because they thought it had morphine inside. Steinbeck told the admissions clerk, "Take good care of him. He's Walter Cronkite's nephew." I was admitted promptly.

JUNE 18, 1970

Doc Dempsey was a joker. Everything was funny to him—the war, the Army, the heat, the rain, the Vietnamese, the doctors and nurses at the hospital where he lay, his wounds—it was all riotously funny to him. He couldn't help seeing the irony, the contradictions, the insanity, the nonsense, the stupidity, the utter absurdity and waste of the war without pointing it out to others and laughing about it. He didn't take the war seriously because the war wouldn't take *him* seriously. It kept trying to kill him. To give in to the war, to accept its crushing power over everyone, was to be defeated by it. So, for the sake of his sanity, Doc Dempsey played it as farce, the final pathetic phase of a great ironic tragedy.

'You know,' he said from the clean white linen of his hospital bed, propped up by pillows, talking fast, 'the Vietnamese are like the Irish. Yeah, that's right, man, the Irish. I know, 'cause I'm Irish. They've been fucked over so long they think there's something wrong with 'em.'

He laughed, a short, shrill Irish laugh, *Hahahaaah!* and went on without pause, 'Look at 'em, man! They act like they *deserve* all the shit we're givin 'em. Like they had it comin. *Hahahaaah!* And maybe they do! *Hahahaaah!*' Doc Dempsey had a point. Sometimes the Vietnamese were so stoic, so stupefyingly passive, you could mistake their Confucian fatalism and humility for self-hate.

Dempsey was a combat medic. He went up Shakey's Hill in Cambodia with 5th Battalion, 7th Cavalry—poor old hard-luck 5/7—when they fought over it with the North Vietnamese for ten slow suffering days in the middle of May. He was at the front most of the time treating wounded. Norman Lloyd was there for CBS News and Doc introduced him to the guys, showed him how to low-crawl and scramble up to the line, warned him when to keep his head down. Lloyd was new to battle and did not know how to work under fire, so he stood up once behind a tree with AK rounds coming in from the other side of the tree on both sides and pointed his camera down into the faces of GIs who were taking cover and got close-ups of their expressions. When the film was seen on TV, the word went around Saigon that Lloyd had no fear, that he was going to be special.

Dempsey's first name was James but everyone, including the officers up to the Old Man, called him "Doc." He was black-haired and swarthy with a square Irish face that looked older than his years. He was from North Babylon, Long Island, and now he was waiting for a flight to Japan and eventually the ride home.

'No more war for this old man,' he said, lying on his back in a bed of the intensive care unit of the 377th Air Force hospital in Saigon, a big wound in his chest.

'Laurence,' he shouted across the aisle, 'there's nothing wrong with you that a few minutes on the air won't fix. That right? Get your ass out in the boonies again. Get into a nice little firefight, not too big, pick up a little bang-bang on film and you'll be fine. Right? Get Lloyd, that crazy fucking Australian, to shoot it. Right? Fuckin-A right. I know. Norm told me about you guys. Five minutes on Cronkite is what the doctor ordered.' And he laughed, a high manic half scream that filled the ward with waves of hysteria and stopped at the end of a low cough that sounded like it came from a sick old man with something terminal. Some of the other soldiers also laughed—those who weren't in oxygen tents or breathing through tubes—but theirs was the laughter of young men. I laughed too, hard, until I felt too weak to laugh any more.

The hospital was the main dispensary for Tan Son Nhut. It had been designed to treat routine injuries and illness but it also took serious casualties on their way to the big military rehab hospitals in Japan and the Philippines and looked after them overnight. The ward was at the end of a corridor with two rows of five beds and a low ceiling and air conditioning but no windows. The patients had gunshot and fragmentation wounds and burns and needed surgery and long-term care out of the environment. Some of them were in shock. Most were on morphine.

They brought me in after the examination and put me in a bed at the end of a row next to the nurses' desk with an intravenous needle in my arm, a saline and glucose solution dripping *plop, plop, plop*. The doctors ran tests and waited for the results, but they didn't know yet what specific illness I had. Dempsey was in the opposite bed next to the door. He stopped talking only to close his eyes and slip into a short sleep every hour or so. Then he was awake again and talking to everyone in the ward.

'Hey! You on the end! Yeah, you! What's your name?'

He was shouting at a soldier with a head wound and a large white bandage covering most of his head and face in the last bed. The soldier's eyes were open but that was all. He moved his mouth without making a sound.

'What's that?' Dempsey shouted. 'Bob? Okay, Bob, we're gonna call you Bob. Whatever your name is. Okay Bob?' The soldier seemed to smile though it was hard to tell with the bandages.

'What are you doing in here, Bob? Huh? Say you got a headache? Is that right, Bob? Hey, man, lemme tell you about *my* headache. Nine months and fourteen days on the line, Bob. Continuous. The lifers hate me 'cause I won't kill for 'em. It's true, man. They don't dig my *attitude*. Say I've got a problem. They were tryin to get *me* killed. That's right. As punishment for not being like them. Now, ain't that a headache?' The other soldiers in the ward who could laughed.

'Hey, Jones!' he shouted at another. The soldier looked at him. 'Yeah, you. No malingering in the ICU. If you got a dose of the clap you're in the wrong place.' More laughter. 'Is that what that dressing's for? Yeah, the one on your balls. Huh? You got gonorrhea, boy? Next ward, please. This ward is for psychos only.' He laughed. 'Is that right there Blooper-Man?' He turned to the soldier next to me. 'Stop playin with yourself. I see you. No hard-ons allowed in this ward. Believe me, if the nurses see you with a hard-on they'll take you straight into surgery. Get the surgeon to cut it off. Am I right? Oh, man, the nurses around here are so fucking frigid, I swear, they got no sense of humor at all. Don't let em see a rise in the sheets when they walk by or it's surgery for you. You'll be a *real* short-timer all right.' The young men in the ward laughed.

'Oh, man, I'm so short I'm not even *here* anymore,' Dempsey cried. 'Dig it. I already miss this place.'

A nurse came into the ward and asked him to be quiet. 'For your own sake, James. You know you've got a very serious wound. You need to save your strength.' She spoke with compassion and looked up at the rest of us in mild frustration.

'Oh, yeah! Thanks a lot. She tells me I've got a serious wound. Tell me something I don't know, darlin. This hole in my chest was suckin like a carburetor a couple hours ago. You should've seen me treatin myself in the bush. Weirdest case I ever had. Didn't know whether the patient or the medic was gonna pass out first. *Hahahaaah!* You get it?'

He looked at one of the soldiers. 'Stop laughing there no-nuts, it ain't good for your health. Nurse's orders. No more laughin on the ICU. Only screamin. Let's hear a few *screams* for the nurses. Make em feel right at home. *Aaarrrrgggghhh!*' Some of us laughed until it hurt.

Late in the night when it was quiet, in the early early hours, Dempsey spoke softly across the aisle. He said this was the second time for him, his second bad wound and his second evac.

'A suckin chest wound is God's way of tellin you you're not welcome in this place,' he said with a smile.

He was against the war in every way—political, moral, religious, philosophical—you name it.

'We've got no right to be over here, man, no right at all. Killin people for so-called democracy and freedom. Drivin em off their farms. Stealin their rice. Burnin their homes. Screwin around with their women. And *shootin* em, man. For what? For fucking free enterprise? The American way of life? Ain't that a joke. These people don't want our big cars and rock 'n' roll and Johnny Carson, man. They *definitely* don't want Richard Nixon and Henry Kissinger. All the Vietnamese want is a little peace and quiet. So's they can get on with their lives, makin boom-boom, makin families, growin rice, watchin their kids grow up, teachin em how to live. Like it should be. And what do we give 'em? *H and I*, man. *Air strikes*. Fuckin *arc-lights*. Oh, what a laugh.'

In 1965, Dempsey said, he ran away to Canada to escape his draft call. Canada was boring but okay, he said, and when he went home to Long Island for a visit the police picked him up and put him in jail for a while and brought a case against him. Draft evasion. In court, the judge gave him a choice: a six-year hitch in the Army or a six-year stretch in prison. 'Hell of a choice that was, wasn't it?' he said, laughing. 'That wasn't a choice, it was a *sentence*.' Dempsey went into the Army and because he refused to fight and kill, the Army made him a line medic. No one doubted he had guts. 'You'd be surprised how many medics are COs,' he said. 'Conscientious objectors, man. Best damn people in the Army. I'm tellin you I never did any more than anyone else would have done. Saved a few guys, that's all. Anybody would've.'

At first I thought he was crazed, a total casualty of the place, but after a while I figured it out. What we were seeing and hearing on the ward was the Doc Dempsey Show. It was an act, though it didn't seem like one, and Doc was the host. Though wounded himself, he went on playing his role as medic to the troops. He was the Doc. He didn't know how else to act. His jokes and wisecracks, his nonstop stream of banter, were helping the others get their minds off themselves and their uncertain futures. To have laid back and accepted his condition would have been to give in to the war. He was too rebellious to stop joking. All of us on the ward loved it, felt ourselves in the presence of a strange and wonderful entertainer, maybe a saint.

The next morning, Friday, June 19, I woke up and saw the empty bed. The sheets had been replaced and were stretched tight. His gear was gone. I hadn't expected him to leave without saying good-bye. The nurse who had been on duty the day before came in, cold, businesslike.

'Did Doc Dempsey get off to Yakoda all right?' I asked.

She looked at her clipboard.

'He didn't make it,' she said, no feeling in her voice, no emotion at all.

'What?' I was shocked. Guys like Dempsey *had* to make it.

'He died in the night,' she said.

That was all. No questions, no postmortems, no letters to his family to praise his fine soul, his noble bearing, his fatal unselfishness, his humor. James (Doc) Dempsey from North Babylon was just another casualty of the war, another lost cause, like America's honor. My eyes tried to cry for him but could not make the tears.

PART FIVE

1970–PRESENT

All wars end; even this war will some day end, and the ruins will be rebuilt and the field full of death will grow food, and all this frontier of trouble will be forgotten. When the trenches are filled in, and the plough has gone over them, the ground will not long keep the look of war.

JOHN MASEFIELD
The Old Front Line (1917)

THE PRESENT

I am old now. All the life of the time between is gone, flown, fleeting as the memory of a long night's dream. I am a different person. I no longer crave adventure, not as before. War and courage and the lessons of what happens in war interest me less. Vietnam is far away. My memories of those wild wartime days are deteriorating, slowly, one by one, washing away like sand castles on the shore, lost to the unconscious. It doesn't matter. I don't need them anymore. Thinking about the old days, some of the stories are hard to believe. Did I really do that? I wouldn't do that now, not with what I know. Writing about the war has taught me how fragile we are—all of us, those who made it through and those who fell along the way. Many of my friends have fallen along the way. Others are wounded, some of them badly. There is hope for them, and for me. That I have survived this long is a miracle, and it is repeated, daily.

So, what can I tell you about this journey of mine, this long voyage into the past, this catharsis? What have I learned? How has it changed me? Can someone who's made the trip say something worthwhile to someone who hasn't? We'll see. First, let's finish the story.

JUNE 22, 1970

After four days in the hospital my strength came back. I woke up that morning feeling refreshed, alert, ready to go back to the world outside the intensive care unit. The experience of being brought in on a stretcher and put in a bed and treated as if I were wounded was like being taken to the edge of a place where people go when they are about to die and then being brought back to life. I didn't want to die and I had no intention of allowing myself to die, but I also knew that it was not entirely my choice. The loss of Doc Dempsey was still a weight on my heart. Lying in bed at the end of the row next to the nurses' station, I watched a procession of wounded Americans arrive and depart, day and night, young and old, light and dark, alive and then, sometimes, dead. The whole war was in the ward.

Gordon Manning, the CBS News vice president, came to visit. I saw him first. He walked into the ward looking cheerful and bright. But when he saw me on the bed with my pale skin, hollow face and an IV in my arm, his expression turned sympathetic, concerned, almost sorrowful. It surprised me to see his emotion. Manning's normal manner was brisk, ultra-alert, as tightly wound as a clock spring. I expected him to act tough the way he usually did: tough on his correspondents (as he was to me), tough on his subordinates, tough on himself. But here he was in a hospital ward showing concern. Genuine as it was, it seemed out of character.

Manning had come from New York to find out what happened to the five CBS journalists who were missing in Cambodia. In Phnom Penh, he hired a company of Cambodian Army soldiers to provide security while he and a team from CBS News searched the area outside the city where George Syvertsen, Gerald Miller, Tomoharu Ishii, Kojiro Sakai and Ramnik Lekhi had disappeared on May 14. The region was still under the military control of the Khmer Rouge and North Vietnamese. Manning, Kurt Volkert, David Miller, Stuart Witt and Skip Brown risked their lives to recover the bodies of Syvertsen, Miller and Lekhi. Local villagers said the guerrillas had ambushed Syvertsen's military-looking jeep when it drove into the area. Unarmed, in strange territory, the CBS journalists had no chance to fight back or escape. The guerrillas shot everyone in the jeep and then buried the bodies with their knees sticking out of the ground away from the road.

Manning's mission was the most dramatic expression of concern from CBS News management for its people in the war. Executives did not ordinarily display much care for their employees in Southeast Asia. Everyone was expected to be tough. Throughout the war, CBS producers urged correspondents and camera crews to go into the field and get dramatic combat stories to show on CBS News programs. In communications that were carefully worded to avoid the appearance of giving direct orders, they made it clear they wanted *bang-bang*. Those of us who covered the Tet Offensive in 1968 remembered the bizarre instructions from the New York foreign desk ordering CBS News personnel into Khe Sanh during the very worst of the siege. 'We want Khe Sanh covered around the clock!' was the command at a time when the Marine combat base was taking as much incoming artillery as the old front lines in World War I, hundreds of rounds a day. CBS News management created a culture of aggressive, even reckless coverage of the war, especially the big battles, and most of us who worked for them answered the call. In New York, the foreign editor kept a bulletin board hanging in his office with the names of everyone from CBS News who had been to Southeast Asia, either to work or to visit. Some of the names had red or orange Xs marked on them. An orange X signified that the CBS employee had been wounded. A red X meant he had been killed. (Russ Bensley had *two* orange Xs over his name, one of them from Khe Sanh.) The foreign editor was proud of his board. 'Other than the Associated Press,' he said, a manic look in his eye, 'we've taken more casualties than anybody else in the war.'

Manning's visit and expression of concern helped me recover. On the morning of the fourth day in the hospital, I checked out. A doctor said I should stay longer but that he wouldn't keep me against my will. I looked at my medical chart. The symptoms noted were dehydration, malnourishment, fatigue and fever. Treatment had consisted of rest and rehydration but a diagnosis had not been made. It may have been an unidentified tropical disease, something gastrointestinal, or it may have been fatigue. Skinny as usual, I had lost weight in Cambodia and now weighed less than 125 pounds. The Air Force presented a bill for $159.00 and I paid with a check. As I was leaving, I confessed to the nurses that I really wasn't Walter Cronkite's nephew. They laughed and said they already knew that, good luck back in the world.

I went around Saigon and said good-bye to everyone I knew and liked. We had already made our farewells to the troops in Charlie Company. The soldiers in Second Squad seemed genuinely sorry when we left them and asked if there was anything they could do for us. One of them wrote a letter to Walter Cronkite to say how grateful they were that we had spent the time with them showing how they lived in Vietnam. Though we had not been in combat with them, we had been in the war with Second Squad.

Keith Kay, Norm Lloyd and John Steinbeck gave me a party and, after recovering from that, I flew home. Joy was waiting at the airport in New York. When we met in the terminal, her eyes filled with alarm. She was shocked at how emaciated I looked. We held each other for a long time until I felt the warmth and softness of her body come through the clothing into mine.

At home in Manhattan, Mèo paid no attention to me. He sniffed each inch of my baggage closely, inspecting it as though it reminded him of something he couldn't quite put his claw on. I gave him a toy I had brought from Saigon but he ignored it. He went into his bunker and retired for the rest of the springtime afternoon. In the evening, as I slept, Joy said that he climbed on the bed and sat near my head and stared at my face for the longest time.

A few weeks later, on July 14, *The World of Charlie Company* was broadcast on the CBS television network. Russ Bensley, the film editors, Jim Clevenger and I had worked on it tirelessly, fine-tuning the words and pictures, trying to make it as accurate as we could. Ernie Leiser supervised the overall effort as executive producer and thought up the name. But so few people saw it on the night of broadcast (the baseball All-Star game was showing on NBC at the same time) that the network decided to air it again three weeks later. The one-hour documentary made some viewers uncomfortable. Though we did not show combat as we had expected to do (Charlie Company was not in battle while we were with it), the film showed the conditions of American line troops in War Zone C realistically and allowed the soldiers to speak honestly about the war and how they coped with it. Other veterans who had been in the field saw the program and wrote to thank us for telling it the way it is.

Joy, Mèo and I shared a one-bedroom apartment on the third floor of an old brownstone on the West Side. Mèo was irascible, cantankerous and feisty, though not all the time. Occasionally, he set ambushes: leaping onto my head from the top of the kitchen cabinets, springing from behind doors, scratching and biting without provocation. Maybe he thought I was invading his territory and he had to defend it. But his ambushes seemed to be designed less with malice than play in mind. The old spirit of vengeance was gone, or at least in remission. Mèo appeared to know his side was winning. When journalist friends from Vietnam came to visit, he sprang at them without warning. When they leaned over to pet him, he bit their hands as hard as he could. It was as though he saw all American men as his enemies and was letting them know whose side he was on. One, two, three, many Vietnams, I imagined him thinking. 'What a wicked cat you've got here,' guests remarked.

That summer and autumn, Keith Kay and I worked on a series of documentaries called *Generations Apart,* exploring the attitudes of young people and their parents. It was the era of the so-called generation gap in the United States, when parents and their children disagreed strongly on issues ranging from the Vietnam War to sexual freedom, and CBS News wanted to look at it in detail. Working with field producers Helen Moed and Bernard Birnbaum, Kay and I had as much enjoyment working on these documentaries as we had difficulties making *Charlie Company.* Leiser, the executive producer, allowed us to follow our journalistic instincts as we had done in Vietnam: getting to know our subjects before interviewing them, allowing scenes to develop naturally, not arranging anything for the camera. Working in and around Boulder, Colorado, we had almost unlimited freedom to find the story. There was one major distraction. Almost every day during this period, Kay received a telephone call from the office of a feature film director who kept asking Kay to fly to California and talk with him. The director had seen his work on *Charlie Company* and was seriously considering him for the job of cinematographer on his next film. Kay declined, politely at first, forcefully at the end. He told the person calling from California that he was having too much fun working on documentaries for CBS News. Finally, the phone calls stopped. Two years later when he saw the film, Kay realized what he had missed. The director was Francis Ford Coppola. The film was *The Godfather.*

My future appeared secure, though I didn't think about career advancement. I was getting challenging assignments. Producers seemed pleased with my work. The pay was good. I got to travel around the country and meet people involved in interesting activities. Joy and I enjoyed our social life. After hours, we drank and ate with friends at The Slate. We saw Mike, Keith, Jimmy, Stanhope, Art, Tim, Jeff and the Rudds regularly. The cat was reasonably contented. He seemed less at war with the world. Joy had soft-ened some of his rough edges. She had a similar effect on me. By her nature, she personified the virtues of honesty, intelligence, beauty (she was truly beautiful) and peacefulness. She was helping to heal us both.

In time, though, I began to miss the excitement and adventure of Viet-nam. The thoughts occurred only occasionally, but I longed for the challenge of working on a big, breaking story in that environment. The importance of the news and the danger of covering it made life more interesting, more challenging, more rewarding. It may have seemed perverse to others, but wartime life elevated the experience of every day. Some of my colleagues at CBS whispered that I had a death wish, that eventually I was going to kill myself and whomever I was working with, but I didn't believe that. I saw myself as an experienced reporter who was cautious in the field but man-aged to get frontline stories on film. To me it was a matter of calculating the risks. My deeper impulses may have been reckless and self-destructive but my conscious motives were less complicated. I wanted to do the work well, something that had been taught to me by teachers and parents since child-hood. Secretly, I desired to recreate those happy, scary times with friends in Vietnam. Life was brighter, more intense, more enjoyable when you took the risk of losing it and then nearly lost it and then survived to have it back. It was like being told you have an illness with an unknown time to live and are forced to focus your attention on what is most important in life.

Close friends from the war got together regularly in Manhattan and drank, smoked, ate, laughed and talked, sometimes all night. We celebrated our common experiences in journalism and war, our appreciation of litera-ture and art, our attitudes toward politics and life. Hughes and Ann Rudd, veterans who had met in World War II, were exceptional hosts. The group gathered often at their apartment on Central Park West and talked the night and morning away. After a few months, however, our gatherings became less inspired, less wonderful than they had been at the Continental and Caravelle and, in my case, at Frankie's House. We didn't know it but we missed the danger, uncertainty and the opportunity to be courageous that we had in Vietnam. The drama of New York was not the same as Saigon's. In time, friends argued. Rivalries developed. Joy and I stayed friendly with everyone but the group fractured, fell apart.

At work, the rewards of covering domestic news felt limited. I got good stories to cover, worked hard with the producers and camera crews, and helped to get the stories on the air, but it was not like working on the big one. I needed to show my skills in dangerous places, to prove myself again. Though I did not want to go back to Vietnam, that idea was too repellent, something had been left unfinished there. More needed to be done, although I was not sure what. I began making an outline for a book. The title suggested itself immediately. Of course it would begin with my meeting with Mèo.

My craving for excitement was disguised, hidden from conscious awareness, too deeply buried to recognize. More consciously, I felt uneasy with the status quo. I needed a change. Memories of the war had infiltrated my dreams, found refuge there, appearing in similar scenarios night after night. The faces of the dead were part of them, haunting, more alive in my sleep than when I had last seen them in life, cautioning me. Another part of me wanted to go back to Vietnam and undo some of the terrible things I felt responsible for doing there (helping shoot the North Vietnamese soldier, for one) and erase the anguish in my conscience. It was as if I was replaying my memories of the war over and over in my dreams in the expectation that eventually they would end differently.

I found a replacement, at times, in alcohol and drugs. They had the curious effect of calming me down and making me excited. Drink and drugs brought relief from the tension of everyday fears, making exciting ideas possible, or what appeared to be exciting ideas. Drink and drugs were other means of risk taking. They caused my mind to open up to new ideas, to think more creatively, to explore areas where it had not been before. Then, on the extreme edge of conscious thought, it struggled for control. Sometimes it was simply the challenge of consuming more than anyone else and trying to stay focused, like the afternoon with Flynn at the apartment on Tu Do Street. The difficulty of trying to tell a story without losing the thread, or speaking without slurring my words, or driving a car without crashing, was somewhat like maintaining calm attention under fire, making the right moves, hanging on. Sometimes it was like riding the back of a tiger. The challenge of doing something difficult, or even something impossible, had to be attempted. I did not always succeed. Sometimes I made a fool of myself, said something stupid, missed the point. Drinking may have been no more than a substitute for adventure, but the buzz was real. It was also addictive. Of course, I didn't realize that I was also trying to escape my nightly haunting by plunging into a chemical whirlpool. At times it was the deepest of dives.

Late that summer, in the middle of the night, Joy and I were awakened by sounds of a commotion in the alley behind the apartment. The windows were open to the heat.

"Halt!" an authoritative voice shouted. "Halt or I'll shoot."

A second later there was gunfire. Then quiet. We looked out the open window to see a policeman standing over the body of a man in the backyard. More policemen arrived, lights went on, an ambulance came. The body did not move. A suspected burglar had been shot and killed. Afterwards, Joy and I could not sleep. For me, it was like being back in a combat zone. The next day and for the rest of the summer, fear of being attacked followed me in the streets. Though it was not the worst period of violence in New York City (that would come later), it was too much for me. I drank more heavily, falling asleep only if drunk or nearly drunk, though the difference would have been hard to measure. Heavy drinking became a primary part of my existence, a habit. I persuaded Joy it was in our interests to move away, to find some other place to live, somewhere we wouldn't be frightened of everyday life on the streets. At about the same time, a job became available in London. Morley Safer had been chosen to join the team at *Sixty Minutes* and was leaving his position as chief of the London bureau. I asked to go as his replacement and, after difficult negotiations with management, was given the job. Mèo came too.

Joy and I found a place to live in West London, married and started to raise a family. Two daughters were born, Jessica and Rebecca, in the 1970s. Mèo spent six cold, damp months in quarantine at a kennel in the suburbs. He reacted with fierce resistance, as if a prisoner, though he did not escape. Joy and I visited him on Sundays and brought him treats, but he never forgave us for his imprisonment. Upon his release, he was wilder than before. He tore around the apartment like a demon. When a friend brought her German Shepherd to visit, she was genuinely worried he might hurt the cat. She offered to leave the dog in the hall. 'Don't worry,' I said, 'Mèo can take care of himself.' By the end of the evening, the cat was prowling the apartment like a lion, full of arrogance and pride. We found the dog, which was five times the size of Mèo, cowering in the bedroom, trying to hide beneath the bed.

Tim Page moved in around the corner and resumed his old rivalry with Mèo. Having been paralyzed on one side by his last wound, it was surprising how agile Page could be when dueling with the cat, if only in self-defense.

Mèo sensed Page's disability, always approaching from his weak side, attacking him where it was most difficult to defend. In the late 1970s, Mike and Valerie Herr moved to a nearby apartment. When they came to visit, Mèo left them pretty much alone except to sit occasionally in one of their laps and purr, no doubt because they were gentle and loving.

I was sent to Northern Ireland, East Pakistan, Israel and other places where there were wars. I worked with Keith Kay in the war between India and Pakistan in 1971. Kay taught camera work to his young sound tech, David Green, and also how to take pictures in combat without getting killed. Both of them had extraordinary vision, 15/15, enabling them to anticipate harm before it struck. In Dacca, Kay showed Green how to watch the wing tips of Indian Air Force MiG 17s as they lined up to make their bombing runs on the city. He taught him as it was happening how to see the wings flatten out at the top of the dive indicating that the plane was going to fire at them. Kay showed Green how to get out of the way by running away perpendicular to the bombing line. When Kay decided to run for cover, suddenly Green was pulled behind him by the sound cable. An accomplished club runner in London, Green was as fit and fast as anyone in Dacca. But he swore he had never seen anyone sprint so fast as Kay getting out of the way of an Indian MiG. From then on, I worked mostly with Green. He proved to be as resourceful, talented and fearless as Kay and went on to become one of the world's most distinguished photojournalists, ranking with the best still and film photographers. When the war was over in Southeast Asia, Kay moved to Paris for CBS News as its bureau chief. Clevenger joined the London bureau as a producer. All of us were involved in covering wars for CBS. There were many.

During and after the civil war in Angola, with its paranoia and hostility toward non-Marxist foreigners, my nightmares became horrific. I drank to blot them out but the booze stopped working. A bout of drinking left me more troubled than I had been before it started. Finally, I realized I had to do something. A friend who knew I was struggling with the bottle sent me a book, *Living Sober*, published by Alcoholics Anonymous. After reading it, I decided to give up all drugs—alcohol, dope, Valium (I had been taking twenty milligrams a day for eleven years), even cigarettes. I stopped without joining AA or NA or going to meetings. The consequences were worse than the nightmares. I didn't realize that my brain was accustomed to being drugged every night with booze or dope (usually both), so that I now found it impossible to sleep for more than a few hours at a time. I woke up at three or four o'clock in the morning feeling energized, slightly euphoric, and went to work at my desk. Each day, around the middle of the afternoon, my energy diminished. Gradually, I began to see, hear and imagine things that weren't there. I heard voices plotting my death. I was convinced that I was being stalked by powerful enemies who intended to kill me. Other than Joy and my closest friends, I trusted no one. Mike Herr tried to help. "It's all in your mind, Jack," he said. I knew he was right but it didn't take away the fear. I tried everything I could think of to stop the paranoia. I hid away from the outside world. My doctor prescribed major tranquilizers that were no help. After months of considering all possible ways to end the distress, I saw a news report from Northern Ireland. IRA prisoners were claiming to have been tortured by the British Army, which used a technique called "sleep deprivation" to make them talk. Lack of rest had caused the prisoners to become paranoid. *That's it,* I thought. *Maybe I'm not getting enough sleep.* I stopped myself from getting up in the middle of the night and tried instead to go back to sleep. Eventually, it worked. Within a few nights of sound sleep, the worst of the symptoms went away. I began to feel normal, although a residue of paranoia remained.

At about the same time, I quit CBS News. I had become disillusioned with the foreign desk. As a serious news organization, CBS changed in the mid–1970s. The foreign desk and other departments were taken over by young managers who had no experience in their jobs and who had been put there by a new member of senior management. This administration seemed to be more interested in saving money for the company than in covering the news well. It seemed to get the balance wrong. Major breaking stories went uncovered in their early stages. CBS News, once the most competitive network of the three, got badly beaten, again and again, because of cost-conscious indecision by the new management. The effect on the foreign staff was demoralizing. I quit to get away from covering wars and the pressures that went with the job, and to stop working for people I considered incompetent. It was 1977. I had spent twelve years at CBS.

A year later, after starting work on this book, Joy and I ran out of funds. The writing had started well but became blocked, mostly because of my lack of experience writing for the printed page. It was something I needed to learn gradually, over a longer time. I put the unfinished work in a drawer.

ABC News was becoming competitive with NBC and CBS and was looking for experienced correspondents to strengthen its staff. Roone Arledge, the new president, hired me to work in the London bureau. After a few months at ABC, I realized that I was working for a news organization with a heart. Correspondents were treated with respect. The atmosphere was professional and competitive without being merciless. No one ordered me to cover wars. I was asked, politely. And I declined, politely, at least for the first year or so. David Green became a freelance and we were able to work together, particularly for *Nightline,* which was then getting started. We were fortunate to work with exceptional *Nightline* senior producers Tom Yellin and Elizabeth West. *Nightline* exemplified the virtues of calm, mature, professional news gathering. No one there insisted on changing the reports we sent in. My family life and work flourished. I didn't take a drink or a drug of any kind for more than four and a half years. Most days life felt worth living. The reckoning came later.

1971–1980

After the war, Mèo settled into a life of mature comfort in London. He would have preferred a warmer climate but the high humidity and regular rain were just like home. He sneezed a lot, especially in the winter when the sun rarely shone. He had meals at least twice a day, more often if he found himself alone with food in the kitchen. He had graduated from fish heads and rice to canned meat and fish, though he would eat almost anything except dog food. He despised dogs and everything associated with them. They made his hair stand on end. Jessica, who was four, spoiled him with cat treats between meals. In return, he slept with her at night, curled up beside her on (or under) the covers.

Much of the time he slept, though not always peacefully. From time to time he twitched. Then his whole body convulsed fitfully, as if he too were wrestling with ghosts. He chose the most secluded places to sleep, preferably with overhead cover. When Rebecca was born, he howled outside the door to her room at five or six o'clock in the morning until she woke up and started to cry. Then he was quiet. The baby's cries woke Joy, who got up and fed her and, while she was at it, the cat as well. Mèo got what he wanted in ways that were not apparent.

One day, I got a phone call from Abbie Hoffman, the antiwar political activist whose trial in Chicago I had covered in 1969 and who was wanted for jumping bail in the United States. Hoffman asked if he could come to visit. Mèo welcomed him like a long lost comrade from the wars, curling up in his lap, sniffing the air from the marijuana he was smoking, fawning over him all evening. Abbie saw the world as his stage, and himself as a leader, though he seemed unusually nervous and vulnerable that night. Mèo would have followed him anywhere.

Every morning, the mail arrived through a slot in the front door to the apartment. Mèo observed this phenomenon and determined that the hand pushing the mail through the slot belonged to one of his enemies. He waited on the other side of the door until he heard the brass flap open and, as the letters were being pushed through one day, leapt up and scratched the mail carrier's fingers. The mail carrier said he had been attacked by a wide variety of dogs in his career but Mèo was the first cat to draw blood. From that day on, the mail arrived through the letter slot in a quick, heavy burst.

In the late 1970s, friends asked us to care for their cat while they lived in the States for a year and we agreed. He was a big, friendly black-and-white European house cat with a strong body that was fitted with what must have been one of the smallest brains in creation. His name was Sylvester. He did not grasp the way things worked in his new environment easily. He was accident prone. He was a slow learner. Innocently, he joined us in our fifth floor apartment without realizing that he was entering an active war zone. From the first day, Mèo made his life as miserable as he could. Until it was clearly established that he was the dominant animal in the flat, Mèo attacked Sylvester regularly, repeatedly, routinely, leaping out at him without warning, digging into his fur with his claws, biting him on the back of the neck as hard as he could. Although Sylvester was younger and stronger and could have won their encounters, Mèo forced him into submission with his superior fighting skills and tactics. Sylvester lived much of the time in fear. Compared to Mèo, he was a wimp.

One Sunday afternoon, returning from a visit to the countryside, Joy, Jessica and I could not find Sylvester. A search of the place failed to turn up any sign of him. Mèo was sleeping. I noticed that the apartment windows were open to the warm summer air. Suspecting the worst, I went downstairs and looked in the bushes that decorated the ground floor edges of the apartment building. A faint cry came from one of them. Beneath the foliage, I found Sylvester resting on his side on the ground, panting heavily, one of his back legs twisted awkwardly, his head a mass of cuts and scratches. We rushed him to an animal hospital. Sylvester's broken bones were set and his leg cast in plaster. We took him home a few days later. He began to recover. Mèo left him alone.

In the months that followed, we told friends that Sylvester "fell, jumped or was pushed" from the fifth floor window by Mèo. We had no proof, of course, and Mèo wasn't confessing, but he behaved as if he had achieved a higher level of superiority over Sylvester, ignoring him in his heavy white cast limping around the apartment. From then on, we kept the windows of the apartment closed.

Months later I was sitting in the living room, reading, when Mèo and

Sylvester came racing through, one after another. They tore into the room and out again in a few seconds. It was their favorite game. Mèo led Sylvester on a wild chase through every room of the apartment and up and down the long corridor. They ran at top speed, across the tops of beds, cabinets, dressers, tables and chairs, behind drapes, onto radiator covers, windowsills, tearing through the flat as if possessed by devils.

Hearing them come back down the hall again toward the living room, I looked up. In a blur of speed, Mèo raced across the carpet like a cheetah. Sylvester was no more than a few inches behind him, nose to tail, in a gallop. Mèo leapt about three feet up onto a painted wooden cover over a radiator close by the main window and, at the top of the jump, turned abruptly to his right. It was a pirouette, a difficult maneuver at that speed, and obviously planned. Sylvester, in full flight, came up behind him and, unprepared to make the quick right turn, collided headfirst with the closed window. The force was so great that Sylvester lost consciousness for a second, fell over and then staggered onto his feet, shaking his head. Mèo watched him, seemingly without interest. The game was over. That was when I knew how it had happened that Sylvester went out the open window months before. He hadn't learned.

Late at night, when everyone else was in bed, Mèo and I drank together. He liked cognac, served to him on the end of my finger a few drops at a time. He enjoyed the taste and the effect. A few times during these drinking sessions I saw him stagger. And he saw me, more than a few times, stagger to bed. I think we had come to respect each other's skills as survivors. There was no doubt that his limited number of lives allotted had been used up long ago, so that every new day he lived was a bonus. Also, he seemed wise. He knew. We had become friends. Our long, angry, loving relationship had come to symbolize in some way the bond between our countries, drenched in each other's blood, locked in an unbreakable embrace of life, suffering and death.

At the age of thirteen, Mèo got pneumonia and, this time, failed to recover. I suspect that what finally got him was the English climate.

Remembering Mèo, I think of him alone in the night, wandering through the far end of the apartment, making a cry that was unlike any other sound he made, unlike a sound I had heard any animal make. It seemed to be the call of an animal taken out of the wild, or out of its home, or away from its family. It was more of a wail, a long powerful howl, not a scream or a meow or an ordinary cat cry, but a call from the deepest part of his soul, the wail of the forest. The only time Mèo cried like that was when the home was quiet, usually when everyone was asleep, when he thought he was alone. It was a call for no one but himself.

JUNE 23, 1982

The telephone rang at home in London.

'Jack, how'd you like to go back to Vietnam and do a story or two?' It was Jeff Gralnick, my old friend from Saigon and New York. He too had quit CBS News and was now executive producer of the evening news for ABC.

'What's happening?'

'The Vietnamese are letting in everybody who wants to go,' Gralnick said in his rasp of a voice. (Since their military victory in 1975, Communist leaders in Hanoi had allowed Western journalists to visit Vietnam only occasionally. I had not been back since leaving in 1970.)

'Sure,' I said. 'What's the story?'

'They're holding a news conference in Saigon next week,' he said. 'Looks like they're trying to draw attention away from Sihanouk, who's going back to Cambodia at the same time.' (Prince Norodom Sihanouk had been living in exile in Beijing since being overthrown in 1970 and was planning a publicity stunt at the Thai border with his homeland. Vietnam supported the Communist government of Cambodia, which was anti-Sihanouk.)

'When do I go?' I was busy trying to write this book.

'Get to Bangkok by the thirtieth and pick up your visa.'

'Okay, I'll get started. Why me?'

'Mark Litke (the Hong Kong correspondent) is getting married next week. I thought we ought to send somebody who's actually been there. You're only in Saigon a week.'

'Sounds good. I've wanted to go back and have a look.'

"Keep your head on your shoulders, Jack. Just remember, you're going through the looking glass."

July 2, 1982

Ho Chi Minh Ville, Ho City, Sin City, the Tarnished Pearl—whatever you wanted to call the place, I knew right away it was the same old Saigon when a hungry street kid picked my pocket the first night in town. He was only nine or ten, too young to remember the American days, so I knew it was nothing personal.

We were drinking coffee and milk shakes at the Cafe Brodard, my colleagues and I, looking out the window from a corner table, chatting with an old Vietnamese friend whom we had met on the street and who remembered us with surprise and affection. He filled us in on who had gone away and who was still around, telling us the gossip and the rumors (Nguyen Cao Ky was out in the bush leading the Resistance)—the city was still a fantasy land of improbable hopes and fears.

Next to the table, polished and gleaming, sat the wonderful old Wurlitzer that once played the hits that helped us clear the jungle cobwebs out of our brains those hangover mornings in wartime. The jukebox was empty and silent now by government decree (no room for decadent Western music in the New Order), just another monument to the old days.

A bunch of smiling street kids stood outside the big glass window giggling and jabbering and pointing at us like animals at the zoo. A twelve-year-old girl in a dirty red sweater with caramel skin and hazel-brown hair cut in bangs waved and smiled, a round-eye like us, no questioning her parentage.

Outside she said, "Please, you buy?" We gave her and her friends dong, just a few pennies worth, and they took them gratefully. Standing on their toes, they fired questions at us, rat-a-tat: "Where-you-from? What-your-name? You buy?" Holding out trinkets, bags of peanuts, anything they could scrounge.

"My name Mai," she said when the noise subsided. "You know American? His name Gary. He my father. No can come back. Gary want but no can come." Then, holding my hand while the fast kid picked my pocket, Mai said proudly, "I American."

Heading back to my hotel a few nights later, Mai appeared, ragged and grubby, out of the shadows along Tu Do Street. "Please-you-give-me-money," she shouted in her rapid-fire way, "I-buy-new-clothes." I gave her a few dollars worth of dong and forgot about it. But the next night when she popped out, unexpected as usual, I didn't recognize her at first. She wore a pretty blue and pink pajama suit, her hair was clean and combed, and her face was shining. She laughed, "Now I feel better," taking my hand in hers. "Thank you, Jack." For a moment there, walking along the tranquil, tree-lined street on the other side of the world, Mai seemed enough like my little girl back home to make me sorry for Gary, wherever he was.

Four of us from ABC made the rounds of Saigon that first night. Y. B. Tang, the photographer, was Chinese. Malet, the sound person, had been born and raised in Saigon and was half Vietnamese. Bill Thomas, the producer, was making his first visit. We walked all around the central part of the city, visiting old haunts, pointing out places of interest, letting our memories take us back to the best of times in that exotic place, asking questions of people in the streets and getting the translations from Malet, sharing some of his special pleasure in coming home.

Everywhere we went, every block or two, a Vietnamese kid called out "Lien Xo" or "Roos" and, from a balcony once, "Hallo Mister Roos." They figured us for Russians, of course, and there was no apparent antagonism, even on streets where you could once measure the level of hostility to foreigners by the number of times the Vietnamese spit on the ground in front of your footsteps.

The Russians were sometimes referred to as "Americans with no dollars," and it was evident that the new advisers to the Vietnamese were as poor as their hosts. At one of the souvenir shops on Tu Do, I watched a Russian who appeared to be a new arrival try to barter for a trinket he wanted. When the woman behind the display case agreed to consider a trade, the Russian withdrew a knee-length woolen sock and offered it to her.

Walking through the old second district, we stood and watched a crowd of Vietnamese standing around a tough-looking young man with dark eyes wearing black pajamas and sandals. As the crowd cried encouragement, a larger man pulled the younger man's shirt up over his head, binding his neck and shoulders, then twisted his right arm behind his back, and finally bent his fingers over the back of his hand so severely that they almost touched his wrist. It was an expert's hold and passersby stopped to watch. Some of them smiled. An older woman with an umbrella declared that the young man had stolen her earring and whacked him hard on the head. Two other men stood in front of the youth and kicked at his groin. The suspect, doubled over and standing on wobbly legs, made no sound. Less than a hundred yards away at the end of the block, five young men wearing khaki uniforms and pith helmets knelt or stood on the steps of the local police station playing a game of cards, shouting and gesturing to one another, taking no notice of the incident with the thief.

We wandered around without aim or plan, generally on impulse, past familiar places: modest villas where we'd lived and visited, network news bureaus where we'd been given our orders, the government offices where the information flowed, the restaurants and cafes and clubs where we'd gone to escape the war and had ended up discussing and debating it anyway—the old hangouts with their reminders. Most of them were closed or converted to other purposes. Frankie's House on Bui Thi Xuan had become a police station.

The elegant rooftop restaurant at the Caravelle Hotel was open for business but it was almost empty. A visiting delegation of East Europeans dining privately behind a screen, bossing the Vietnamese waiters around with the same gruff impatience we Americans had once shown. Arriving in the restaurant, we were greeted by the hotel staff with such unabashed courtesy and fondness, bowing and smiling and weeping in one case, you might have thought we owned the place. (We had, in a way. CBS News took up most of a floor of the Caravelle for years.) The waiters selected the food and wine, delivered it with grace and good manners, and seemed genuinely sad when we left.

Down in the hotel lobby, we inspected the souvenirs for sale in tall glass display cases: beads and bracelets and lacquered bowls, a life-sized ceramic tortoise, imitation ivory earrings, a plastic bust of Ho Chi Minh, and three cans of Budweiser beer. That was a laugh. We told Bill Thomas he'd understand why the Vietnamese put cans of Bud in a glass case if he'd ever tasted *Ba Muoi Ba*, the local beer.

The famous bar on the eighth floor of the Caravelle was closed for business, but we managed to sneak inside and take a peek, an essential stop on our nostalgic tour, the former watering hole of off-duty correspondents and their contacts, where the S-shaped bar with its blue plastic top propped up the elbows of Pulitzer Prize-winners and freelance hacks alike and the war was fought in verbal combat nightly. Nothing had changed: the low checkerboard tables with plastic-covered chairs, the funny 1950s-modern design, an

empty bottle of Cointreau from New Jersey gathering dust behind the bar—
it was all as it had been left, vacant and frivolous. I felt the ghost of Walt
Kelly in the room, glass in hand, jolly and swaying at the bar, proclaiming to
any and all, every few minutes, *"We have met the enemy and he is us!"*

July 3, 1982

Saturday night in Ho Chi Minh City, just after sundown, and the midsummer
heat comes up from the scorched pavement like jungle steam. A group of
orphans, Mai among them, is gathered on the sidewalk outside the Rex
Hotel, twenty children in ragged clothing with the anxious faces of half-
castes, begging and shouting and flashing expressions that range from piety
to malevolence.

"Please-you-buy-peanut?" "Hey-you!" "You-buy!" High-pitched, insistent, demanding voices.

The kids move in a pack, blocking my forward motion on the sidewalk
and surrounding me, reaching up to tug on my trousers and shirtsleeves, trying to make contact with their unblinking eyes, hawking garlands of fra-
grant white *hoa lei* and tiny bags of dwarf peanuts. Only foreigners give
them dong, some of us out of charity, others out of guilt.

The Rex Hotel is as exclusive as ever. The old Marine guard post is gone:
no shotgun muzzles or vigilant eyes in the shadows behind the sandbags, but
everyone obeys the new rules. Only very important Vietnamese are permitted to rest at the Rex these days, cooled in the same sterile, air-conditioned
rooms, tucked into the same freshly laundered linen where the top U.S. brass
once slept.

The new management has closed the rooftop restaurant, the once popular truckstop for drivers of the war machine—T-bone steaks and twenty-cent
beers, fresh ice cream and a live rock 'n' roll band—an authentic American
roadhouse six stories above the Saigon streets.

Most of the old attractions are closed now: the GI strip, the Tu Do bars,
the USO, the Arc-en-Ciel, the sex houses and the dope dens, out of favor and
therefore out of business.

Except!!

On the one night a week when times turns back, when the few who survive in the fast lane of this suddenly slow city are allowed to come out and play, when revolutionary authorities yield to the remnants of a vanishing bourgeois style, when officially discredited Western culture raises its head from the ashes of the burned-out cause—except for Saturday night at the Rex when *dancing* is still allowed.

Seven-thirty and the immaculate tiled floor of the hotel lobby clicks with the heels of arriving guests: Western men with topaz tans just in from the field, mustache-macho Cuban sailors from the ships in Saigon harbor, hard-faced Russians and East Germans from the aid projects and advisory programs, sunshine-haired Scandinavians in baseball caps, all casual and loose in sport shirts and slacks, visiting the big city for the weekend, scrubbed and shaved and ready for the action.

Arriving, the Vietnamese men are more subdued. They are aloof and arrogant like some of the former French colons, their bodies decorated with gold chains and bracelets, open-necked silk shirts, double-breasted jackets with wide lapels, flared trousers and patent leather loafers, ten years out of fashion in every way imaginable. Leaning back on two-inch heels, their hair is longer and they look a lot older than the Western men, trying to give the impression that they've seen it all before and never, ever cared, nonchalant to the last.

An aging Saigon hustler in dated Paris fashions stands in a corner shadow, his face scarred and lumpy, a Marseilles gangster look, gazing out at the passing parade with sinister opium eyes, measuring the possibilities.

The arriving Vietnamese women are young and pretty, their high cheekbones and full lower lips set in apricot-yellow faces framed in black, the color of their hair. Some are dressed in designer jeans and T-shirts with nothing underneath, others in slender dresses and high heels. They walk straight ahead to the reception desk to purchase two-dollar tickets to the Saturday night hoedown in Ho City.

All conversation in the lobby comes to an abrupt halt as a tall, voluptuous Vietnamese woman wearing a close-fitting white *aó dài* enters with an older, modestly dressed woman who appears to be her mother. The young woman's face is powdered white, as white as milk, and her carbon-black hair hangs to her waist. She looks around her at the men standing in the lobby, inspecting each one individually. (Their eyes are riveted now, unable to look away from her.) She searches their faces for one she knows and, seeing none, turns and walks back to the entrance, staring outside for more than a minute. When she turns again, much of her composure is gone. Her expression is disappointed, as if a rendezvous has been broken. The older woman takes her arm and leads her into the nightclub.

The lobby of the Rex is soon empty. The American air conditioners drone away, clearing the air of cologne and perfume. Then the clear glass doors of the entrance swing open and a big European steaming with sweat from heat and booze bursts in ahead of two other men and a demure Western woman dressed in a baggy white blouse and skirt.

"How much dong?" he asks, banging a guitar on the reception desk. The words are English but the accent is Slavic. He is six feet tall, dark and rugged from the sun, wearing a faded blue and yellow T-shirt, denim trousers and low-cut cowboy boots.

"How much dong for three?" he says the words slowly, with difficulty, slurring the words, gesturing toward his friends with an expansive sweep of his arm that brushes the guitar off the counter of the reception desk and onto the floor, cracking the wood. A plastic thumb screw snaps off the neck and spins on the shining tiles.

The young woman behind the desk answers politely. She is frail and fine-featured, delicate as a porcelain doll in her *aó dài*. "You pay in dollars, please."

"*Nyet!*" he bellows. "No dollars! How much dong for three?"

The receptionist recoils from the blast and the breath. She counts the three men and the woman. "One hundred dong for four."

"No pay for woman," he snorts and pulls a tangled wad of notes from his pocket and plops it on the desk.

"One hundred," she insists.

He looks down at her, his eyes narrowed, and then at the money, counting it slowly with thick, uncoordinated fingers, and—*smack!*—slaps the bills on the counter. She backs away, startled. As he sees her reaction, his face broadens into a wide smile.

"Come!" he calls to the others, picking up the broken guitar. "Ve go." And he ushers them toward the nightclub in triumph.

God, were we ever that bad? I wonder. And the answer comes. *Probably.*

There is an awkward silence. The veneer of dignity and decorum in the lobby has disappeared. The receptionist looks down at her feet. A young man who has been observing from the end of the reception desk, a northerner by accent and appearance (in fact the manager of the Rex), speaks now to the young woman, sharply, in Vietnamese.

"Why do you let them do that?"

There is no reply. Her expression is stoic. "You shouldn't let them speak to you like that. Teach them a lesson. Tell them to be polite. *This is our country!*"

"What can I do?" she says, looking away.

Behind the bulky hardwood doors of the nightclub is a big room with a low ceiling and a history as old as the war. Journalists went there once, late every afternoon, for military briefings and battle information, the original *Five O'Clock Follies*. As the war expanded so did the press corps, and the briefings had to be moved to an auditorium. The old briefing room then became an officers club, an off-duty oasis for the American military. It had solid, expensive furniture, polished mahogany tables and chairs with fine leather inlays, upholstered walls, and a long bar with oval mirrors behind it—a room suffused in brown, dark as the inside of a bunker.

And tonight, Saturday night, seven years after the end of the war, the room is exactly the same except for the crowd. The tables are arranged end to end, radiating away from the dance floor. Waiters scurry back and forth from the bar to the tables, filling glasses with vodka, wine and soda. About a hundred guests are clustered around the dance floor, drinking and dancing but rarely speaking, oblivious to the muffled music from a live band at one end of the room. A Vietnamese woman stands at a microphone singing a lifeless version of "Hello Dolly," swallowing the words, barely pronouncing the English. The musicians are listless and bored, playing for no one, not even themselves, off-key and out of tune, all rhythm lost. It is as if they are imprisoned in a postwar time warp and are sentenced to play all the old songs for seven years as punishment for having once entertained the enemy.

The big European has left his guitar on a table and holds the beautiful white-faced Vietnamese woman, clutching her in a bear hug, chest to chest, sweeping her around the floor in a continuous spiral. His left arm hangs stiffly at his waist in imitation 50s camp. The Vietnamese woman's mother watches them closely from a chair.

Overhead, the old spotlights and strobes blink on and off in brilliant colors of white, blue and flame-yellow, pulsating to a rhythm entirely their own. The dancers are going in every direction, out of step with each other and nearly out of control, the men bouncy and bright and trying to show off, the women passive and polite and trying to please, all shaking and swirling together more in drunkenness than in dance, hanging on to one another as if it's the last night of the old order.

Down in the lobby, there is a mural of a forest that covers one of the walls from the floor to the ceiling. It is a photograph of a forest, an enormous wide-angle blowup of tall straight pines and lofty fir trees in the foliage of late fall. The picture had been taken in black and white and was tinted later in pale grayish shades of green and yellow that give the landscape a desolate, surrealistic hue. The murmuring pines could have been New England or the Central Highlands, the Berkshires or the Ia Drang—it was hard to tell. The photograph had been put up sometime in the 60s to remind American officers checking in and out of the Rex Hotel where they had come from or where they were going, but no one appeared to notice the old mural anymore.

Just around the corner, it gets so hot in the nightclub that the windows are open and the doors are closed an hour before the performance begins. It's three blocks from the Rex by foot but five hundred miles from the mood, as far away as Bangkok. Every table is taken every night of the week and late arrivals are stopped at the door.

The Cafe Terria at 80 Dong Khoi Street (formerly Tu Do) is an official government cabaret. There is no dancing, no Western music and few foreigners attend, but the place is wired with energy and excitement. Young attractive Vietnamese couples in casual Western clothes sit at crowded tables covered with starched white linen. The couples are well-mannered and talkative; the men drinking bitter Bierre "33" from pint glasses with ice the size of fists floating in the beer; the women sipping hot tea or cold lemonade from aperitif glasses. The waiters have their hearts in the service, dancing and jinking between the tightly packed tables like running backs on a broken field. "Take it Easy" is printed across the front of a T-shirt worn by one of the women.

During the war, number 80 was a nightclub near Minh the tailor's shop, one of the sleazy split-level joints with two bars, a multitude of mirrors and a blinking Schlitz Beer sign that helped to turn Tu Do into something like Hollywood Boulevard, where desperate Vietnamese women with families to support whispered sexy, suggestive words in the ears of their American tricks and touched the insides of their thighs in exchange for short glasses of Saigon tea for a dollar a shot.

At around 10:30 at night in the old days, just before the curfew, Tu Do was transformed into a carbon monoxide race course of motorcycles and MP jeeps, drunken soldiers and civilian workers trying to make a deal with the bar girls for the night, outmaneuvered by long-haired Vietnamese cowboys on fast Hondas who sped away with their girlfriends and sisters before the broken-bottle brawls, the warning shots from the M-16s, and the nightly arrests.

By 1982, number 80 is a showpiece of propriety. An elderly white-haired man with the humorless demeanor of a political officer sits at an upstairs table close to the front taking notes on the songs that are sung. But the songs are as innocent as the crowd: traditional Vietnamese ballads of love and separation, hardship and hate, anguish and anxiety—reflecting the way things were—solemn and sad, songs the guests still want to hear.

The music is performed by some of the most famous singers and movie stars from old Saigon: Kim Anh, Hong Van, Ngoc Dung—women with graceful, wide-ranging voices and breathtaking beauty that could touch the soul of the most hardened anti-Vietnamese cynic. They are backed by a five-piece band that appears to include "Elvis Phuong" on lead guitar, the legendary Vietnamese Elvis, black stringy hair to his shoulders, hips like a gyro, tight black trousers with an indiscreet bulge in the crotch, and glazed wasted eyes on a long happy face with dark lines in it as deep as tank tracks.

Outside, between sets, Hoa Mi, who is twenty-seven years old and has been singing in public since her teens, catches a breath from the hothouse inside, standing with a young man who is leaning against his motorcycle. She is radiantly attractive in a turquoise *aó dài* and matching eyeshadow.

"I used to sing only in small clubs," she says with some hesitation, a wary eye on the official interpreter. "Now I travel all over, out to the provinces and in the cities, and I serve many people." She smiles brightly.

"Do you ever think of leaving Vietnam?" I ask. "Are you glad you stayed?"

She draws back from me as she hears the question in her language. "I never think . . . about leaving. . . . Vietnam," she says, pausing between the words. "Anyway, my family has no one abroad." She giggles with relief. Then, *"Choi oi!"* (Good grief)!

The interpreter tells her she's allowed to speak openly. "No," she says, "that's enough for me."

It is getting late now. The hour of the curfew is close. From the lower end of To Do, past the new government tourist shops in the butter-yellow buildings the French built, up to the old opera house and across Lam Son Square to the lighted fountain on Le Loi Avenue, past the new monument to the Fifth Communist Party Congress (a massive scarlet and yellow neon-illuminated hammer and sickle, as ostentatious as the old black granite statue of the American and Vietnamese soldiers), and back down the wide boulevard of Nguyen Hué to the river, the streets swarm in a procession of bicycles, motorbikes, pedicabs and pedestrians—all moving slowly around the circuit, past street merchants in stovepipe hats and gaily costumed balloon-sellers, taking it all in calmly and quietly with no outward signs of tension or trouble—the long Saturday night parade passing politely by, cruising in Ho Chi Minh City.

July 5, 1982

Four-thirty in the morning, just before dawn, and the children are already up and playing soccer in the empty streets, getting a jump on the heat. The moon is high and full and softens the sharp shadows of the street lamps. Two bare-chested men in running shorts and sneakers jog briskly along Nguyen Hué, sidestepping around an elderly woman in a straw hat who is picking carefully through a pile of garbage in the gutter.

The bodies in the streets around the central market are huddled together in small groups on the sidewalks and doorsteps, enveloped in straw mats and plastic sheets like battle casualties, silent and still. A child sits up and slowly stretches its arms, breathing in the cool morning air, then lies down again on its side without opening its eyes. There are hundreds of motionless bodies in the streets, sleeping.

Just past the market, near the statue of the warrior on Pham Hong Thai Street, there is a commotion: an angry crowd surrounds a short muscular man who is shrieking for mercy. He is stripped to the waist and barefoot, wearing only shorts. Three older men hold him firmly and drag him roughly toward the market and the police guard post there.

"He stole a watch," someone shouts. "Hooligan!" calls another. The youth screams. His face is flushed and wet with tears. Prison is the least frightening of the possibilities that await him.

An hour later a rooster crows and the sun appears, dominant and fierce even at first light, crawling above the bleached orange-tiled rooftops and burning through the dawn haze. Kerosene cooking fires flicker among families who are stirring on the sidewalks. A line of men and boys stand unselfconsciously at a wall, urinating.

Almost everywhere you look, on balconies and rooftops, in the parks and along the waterfront, men and women of all ages stand erectly, breathing slowly in and out, doing their daily exercises, limbering up in the fresh, rapidly warming air.

A mother and her infant child sleep late in the lee of a locked and shuttered shop front on a street along the river, sprawled in the awkward posture of public sleep, no reason to wake up. The woman appears to be emaciated, bony ankles and wrists, drained and wasted by the demands of motherhood and hunger. The baby sleeps on its back, twitching from the attentions of an oversized black fly buzzing around its face. The infant shows signs of malnutrition, a protruding abdomen on a skeletal frame, its eyes squeezed tightly shut against the growing light of the day.

"Hunger does not exist in Ho Chi Minh City." The speaker is Mai Chi Tho, chairman of the Peoples Committee of Ho Chi Minh City. He is trying to persuade a large group of visiting foreign correspondents that his administration is making important economic and social advances in the southern part of Vietnam despite diabolical opposition.

Tho is a hardened old revolutionary with gray hair and a square jaw. Like virtually all the authorities who hold key administrative positions in the South, he had come down from the North. The reporters have been advised to address him as "mayor," but he is also the chief of State Security for the region and "mayor" seems too modest a title for Chairman Tho.

The briefing is held in the ornate conference room of the old Saigon city hall, easily accommodating Tho and his staff, about fifty reporters and photographers, and a stage set with camera lights, microphones and cables. A few of the older correspondents remember wartime briefings just down the block at JUSPAO, and the old hands might be forgiven for feeling a sense of déjà vu in the room: the fading brown tapestries left behind by the last regime still hanging on the walls, the overhead fans spinning like airplane propellers, optimistic rhetoric from the people in power, a new cast of characters with the same auspicious stories of progress contradicted by evidence in the field.

Some of the reporters have been probing around in their spare time, digging discreetly into the darker corners of the social scene, visiting places like Children's Hospital Number Two and talking with Dr. Hoa, the nutritionist, and concluding, as she has, that nearly half the people of Ho Chi Minh City are undernourished and hungry, especially the children.

Chairman Tho shows a confident smile, parrying reporters' questions with positive statistics and programs, repeating admissions of failure that emerged at the Fifth Party Congress. He says the government is worried about unemployment ("at least 100,000 in Ho Chi Minh City"), slums and homelessness ("a legacy of the old regime"), malnutrition ("Our food ration is lower than in your countries"), and widespread economic failure, with the resulting poverty ("our enemies are trying to bleed us to death"). He lists the recent achievements claimed by the government—new jobs created, houses built, foreign trade increases—all the positive points that ignore the failures of the first five-year plan when Hanoi tried to impose instant collectivization on the people and economy of the South.

Southern resistance to the authoritarianism of its new masters, combined with the inefficiency, mismanagement, corruption and general carpet-bagging of many Communist Party officials (all of which was admitted in the candid criticism of the party Congress: "...opportunists, exploiters, traffickers, speculators, embezzlers, bribe-takers, bullies..." said Party Chairman Le Duan)—all this led to a sweeping purge of the party rank and file.

"North Vietnam won the war and lost the peace." This has been said so often it is becoming a new Vietnamese proverb. The editor in chief of *Nhan Dan*, the Party newspaper in Hanoi, Hoang Tung, said, "In wartime we had enough to eat and we were successful. In peacetime we are hungry and failing."

"So far, the State does not have the resources for satisfying all the needs of the people," says Chairman Tho, flashing the same bright smile we once saw on the face of his older brother, Le Duc Tho, when he won the peace agreement in Paris ten years earlier.

★

At first, going back after twelve years produced a sentimental glow, a pleasure to be among people and places I'd been familiar with, but it didn't take long for the euphoria to fade. A few days into the trip I found myself getting short and counting days, anxious to get away from Ho City, waking up in the darkest hours of the night with the symptoms of short-timer's syndrome: restless and nervous, cold sweats and paranoia, the old wartime fear of losing touch with reality. My body chemistry was in turmoil: short circuits in brain panels from jet lag and stomach bugs, bad water and unfinished food, circadian rhythm out of synch, toxic memories making it back to the surface. Here I was back where I had begun in August of 1965, in a tiny room of the Majestic Hotel on the Saigon River waterfront, unable to sleep, unable to think calmly, edging toward the abyss.

There was no logical reason for the paranoia, but it was no less extreme for lack of logic. The dish-shaped pole poking out of the window of the building across the street was only an old-fashioned TV antenna, not a KGB microphone my mind suspected. The soldiers in the street below were merely on guard, not setting an ambush for me in the morning. But logic and reason were no help to me in that place. Some of the old standby remedies brought temporary relief: yesterday's news on the Voice of America, food from the survival kit, baseball scores from the States, Mozart on the tape deck, and also, for one playing of *We Gotta Get Out of This Place*, the Animals.

Sometime before dawn and the deepest despair, working its way up from unconscious depths and running beside the accelerating depression, a conscious flash cut through the gloom, a bulletin from beyond, a psychic antidote suggesting itself among memories of war madness, a secret to sanity for such moments. The thought was not profound or even particularly enlightened, offering only a small consolation for those of us who had put it on the line in Vietnam. It suggested that those who came here and got away alive, who made it through the bad times (and the good), are stronger than they may think by having survived it, maybe also wise with the knowledge that nothing, ever, anywhere, would be as hard. It was another way of saying that having survived the war, I could survive this night. I held on to the thought, nurtured it, invoked it every time the fear was strong, used it to fight the madness, and, eventually, it got me through.

The next day we left from Ho City and drove into the countryside. The road was a wide, smooth asphalt highway built originally by American engineers and Vietnamese laborers, a road so straight and hard and perfectly paved that airplanes could have landed on it. The expensive highway looked incongruous in the underdeveloped setting. The surrounding brush had been cleared away for a hundred to two hundred yards on both sides of the road and the soil had been sprayed with defoliants to reduce the risk of ambush during the war. Looking at the distant treeline, I was reminded of wartime rides into the same countryside years before, on convoys bristling with troops and weapons, when the fear was sharp in our stomachs. But there was no sense of danger now. I recognized the signs of peacetime among the population along the way: busy market stalls, commerce, children going to school, the absence of soldiers and guns. It came as a deep personal relief. I was breathing normally.

I tried to explain how I felt to our Vietnamese escort, an intense young man from the Ministry of Foreign Affairs. Huynh Chinh had been working with us for a few days and, while he had been perfectly correct in his behavior, his words and actions had seemed controlled, as if he had to think carefully about everything he said. He was surprised when I confessed my fears to him, as if I were revealing too much of myself. The big American car rolled on along the highway out of Saigon toward Cu Chi. There was very little other traffic. Everyone in the car was silent for a long time.

"My mother and father were *Viet Minh*," Chinh said unexpectedly. "My father fought in three wars." His voice was flat, unemotional. "I was born in old Saigon. But my mother and father had to go to the countryside to fight in the revolution. I was in an orphanage. My parents were in Tay Ninh Province. My mother was killed by the bombs in the big American operation, what was it called?" He put his hand on his forehead and closed his eyes. "Junction City," he said softly.

"My father came to visit me in the orphanage in a big black car, like this one. No, it was bigger, with a driver. And nobody knew he was Viet Minh!" He looked up and smiled.

The car traveled on for some time. I thought Chinh had finished his story. "When you were a student," I asked, "did you take part in the demonstrations against the government? In the Struggle Movement?"

"Oh, no! Never! I was always afraid, very afraid that the Americans would discover I was the child of Viet Minh, that my parents were Viet Minh, and kill me!" The faintest sign of a shiver twitched in his chest and shoulders and passed through his hands.

"Anyway, that was a long time ago," he said, "and the war is finished."

★

In the years since Chinh said the war is finished, I have thought about what he said and the way he said it—calmly, resolutely, as if the war, like the past, is not worth any more worry, no matter how much suffering was involved. It can't be changed. The dead cannot come back. Maybe it is time to say our grief has been exhausted. I have a sense that the expression of my own grief may have barely begun. It is there, somewhere, but I have confined it, kept it in check, held it under control for fear that there is too much to allow more than a little of it out. I suspect that in this I may not be alone.

When I learned that the people of Vietnam held no resentments against Americans for waging a war that devastated their country, I was amazed. *How can they not hate us?* I wondered. Or maybe they *are* still angry, I thought, but don't show it. I was projecting what my reactions would be in the same circumstances onto them, and that was a mistake. Of course the Vietnamese don't hate us. They're too busy living their lives, trying to make a little money, raising families, enjoying life. During the war, I worried whether life would be miserable for the people of South Vietnam if the Communists took over and imposed their political and economic system on them. But the more I saw of the war, the less I worried about what would happen when it was over. It didn't matter. The most important thing was that the killing stopped. That's what most Vietnamese believed, and, eventually, most Americans. The greatest blessing for those who suffered through the war years is that it is finished, and that, having survived, they know what they are capable of doing and who they are capable of being in war and in peace.

Long after the war was over, a friend said, "After all, the Vietnam War is about *love*, isn't it?" Laura Palmer had been there in the 1970s and had written about it, quite beautifully, and she said this so deliberately, with such offhand conviction, that I was puzzled. *Love?* How could the war be about love? How could *any* war be about love? I didn't say anything at the time but privately I dismissed what she said as romantic, wishful-thinking perhaps. But I didn't forget it. Now I understand. She meant the profound love of the families and friends for the victims of the war, particularly American victims. She sees their expression of grief as an outpouring of love for those who died, the one great enduring legacy of the Vietnam War, the love for those who were lost.

Anyone who was not there (and maybe some who were) may have difficulty understanding that the Vietnam War is about love now. It's all that those of us who lived through it have left. We've used anger, rage, vengeance, condescension, scorn, deceit, intolerance and just about everything else that goes with violence, and to what end? To hurt one another. And what good did that do?

In the 1990s, I saw an interview on British television with the senior

United States diplomatic official in Hanoi. This was at a time before relations were established between the two governments. The trade representative was a military veteran of the war and he was asked to comment on the boom in foreign investment in Vietnam: joint ventures, tourism, luxurious new hotels, business offices, satellite communications, entertainments. Capitalist enterprises were infiltrating the economy with Communist government approval. The American official looked out the window of his office in Hanoi at a foreign businessman on water skis skimming over the surface of the Lake of Reunification where a young John McCain had fallen after bailing out of his Navy jet during the war. "You know," he said, smiling lightly, "it would have been a lot easier if they had just let us win the war."

I think the best legacy of the Vietnam War would be a deep and sincere love between people of our two countries, a willingness to put each others interests before our own, and a respect for the dignity of the other based on where we have been together, what we have endured, what we have learned. In truth, a great part of the war *was* about love, though most Americans and Vietnamese didn't see that until it was over. I mean the intense wartime love among friends, families, and even strangers who found themselves in distress together. War allows compassion and love on a scale not usually possible in peacetime, and peace between war-making peoples allows compassion and love that was not possible in wartime. We had to go through the war to see the connection. I saw it only after living the war over, day by day, moment by moment, feeling the heat of it in my bones again. Now I understand. After all the hate, all the violence, all the cruelty, the Vietnam War *has* to be about love. Is there an alternative? If making war is about violence and death, the unmaking of war has to be about love and life. I hope that the Vietnam War has shaken some of the arrogance of America's leaders and taught them caution and prudence, maybe even humility, when considering military action against another country. For the rest of us, perhaps the war has given us a stronger sense of our humanity. Americans had to fight and lose the war to find out who we are as a nation. And what we are capable of. And what we are *not* capable of. I think that what we may be most capable of is love and understanding. If we try.

★

Ten years after it was built and inaugurated, I found the courage to visit the Vietnam War memorial in Washington, D.C. It was an emotional time, that tenth anniversary night, cold and quiet. Most of the people who were there at midnight, as I was, were veterans and the families of veterans. Many of them had tears on their faces. It was my first visit. I went alone. I walked around the wall and looked at the names, trying to make sense of how they were organized. The wall had the effect of humbling me, making my life seem insignificant in the presence of so much death. At twelve o'clock I went to a tent on the fringes of the area where a group was meeting and met two young women who were trying to find out what they could about their father. He had been killed in Vietnam. They were too young at the time of his death to have much memory of him, so they had come to Washington and the memorial to learn from others who had been there. I told them some of my story and what line soldiers in the field were like, how they had lived in Vietnam, what happened to them in the war. I gave them as much detail as I could about their father's division, what it was like where he was stationed, and some of the unit's history in the war. The young women asked questions and listened and hugged me when we said good-bye. Big tears were in their eyes. There were some smaller ones in mine. It was the first time in many years I had cried.

I wanted particularly to find one name on the wall. I walked up and down looking for Doc Dempsey's. It didn't appear to be there. I searched around the date we had been in the hospital together in Saigon in 1970 and later. I looked carefully but couldn't find it. (There was no computerized list then to help.) I'm sure his name wasn't there. I didn't think much about it until years later when I was searching the U.S. Army website on the Internet for facts to check and came across the Vietnam memorial page. I entered the name James Dempsey in the search field. Once again, it did not appear. *Is it possible?* I thought. *Did Doc make it out alive after all? Maybe the nurse got him mixed up with someone else. It happens all the time in war.* I did not have time to check with the Army to find out if Doc Dempsey actually did survive the war, but the thought that he might have has helped to sustain my hope that there is justice in the universe, or at least mercy.

Doc Dempsey lives!

I've wanted to shout it for years. *Hey, Doc, where are you?*

In Distrust of Merits

BY MARIANNE MOORE

Strengthened to live, strengthened to die for
    medals and positioned victories?
They're fighting, fighting, fighting the blind
    man who thinks he sees,—
who cannot see that the enslaver is
enslaved; the hater harmed. O shining O
      firm star, O tumultuous
        ocean lashed till small things go
    as they will, the mountainous
      wave makes us who look, know

depth. Lost at sea before they fought! O
    star of David, star of Bethlehem,
O black imperial lion
    of the Lord—emblem
of a risen world—be joined at last, be
joined. There is hate's crown beneath which all is
      death; there's love's without which none
      is king; the blessed deed bless
    the halo. As contagion
      of sickness makes sickness,

contagion of trust can make trust. They're
    fighting in deserts and caves, one by
one, in battalions and squadrons;
    they're fighting that I
may yet recover from the disease, My
Self; some have it lightly; some will die. "Man's
      wolf to man" and we devour
      ourselves. The enemy could not
    have made a greater breach in our
      defenses. One pilot-

ing a blind man can escape him, but
　　　Job disheartened by false comfort knew
that nothing can be so defeating
　　　as a blind man who
can see. O alive who are dead, who are
proud not to see, O small dust of the earth
　　　　　that walks so arrogantly,
　　　　　　　trust begets power and faith is
　　　　　an affectionate thing. We
　　　　　　　vow, we make this promise

to the fighting—it's a promise—"We'll
　　　never hate black, white, red, yellow, Jew,
Gentile, Untouchable." We are
　　　not competent to
make our vows. With set jaw they are fighting,
fighting, fighting—some we love whom we know,
　　　　　some we love but know not—that
　　　　　　　hearts may feel and not be numb.
　　　　　It cures me; or am I what
　　　　　　　I can't believe in? Some

in snow, some on crags, some in quicksands,
　　　little by little, much by much, they
are fighting fighting fighting that where
　　　there was death there may
be life. "When a man is prey to anger,
he is moved by outside things; when he holds
　　　　　his ground in patience patience
　　　　　　　patience, that is action or
　　　　　beauty," the soldier's defense
　　　　　　　and hardest amor for

the fight. The world's an orphans' home. Shall
    we never have peace without sorrow?
without pleas of the dying for
    help that won't come? O
quiet form upon the dust, I cannot
look and yet I must. If these great patient
    dyings—all these agonies
        and woundbearings and bloodshed—
    can teach us how to live, these
        dyings were not wasted.

Hate-hardened heart, O heart of iron,
    iron is iron till it is rust.
There never was a war that was
    not inward; I must
fight till I have conquered in myself what
causes war, but I would not believe it.
    I inwardly did nothing.
        O Iscariotlike crime!
    Beauty is everlasting
        and dust is for a time.

ACKNOWLEDGMENTS

The Cat From Hué was created with the encouragement, advice and love of my family, friends, and colleagues. I would not have finished the book without their faith in me. I am deeply grateful to them for their kindness.

Special thanks to Reed Laughlin who gave me the courage to leave my job and start writing. My daughters, Jessica Laurence and Rebecca Laurence, read the early chapters over Saturday afternoon pizzas and Pepsis, and gave me strength to go on by approving what they read and asking for more. My late mother, Doris Greenspon, was a steady source of encouragement and advice from the days that she first cared for Mèo. Dr. Sidney Crown gave his considerable wisdom and support from the beginning, for which I am sincerely thankful.

I was blessed with friends who became editors and an editor who became a friend, and I am particularly indebted to them. Susan Cope edited the manuscript several times and made it better by using her exceptional skills as a reader, teacher and writer. Russ Bensley, a journalist of gifted ability, edited the intermediate stages. His keen, thoughtful eye for accuracy and detail is much appreciated. Lisa Kaufman, my editor at PublicAffairs, read the book, took it apart, and then helped to put it back together in its present form. She is an editor of extraordinary intelligence. Susan, Russ and Lisa have my lasting gratitude.

Friends read all or parts of the book and made perceptive suggestions for content and style, or provided steadfast support through the writing and editing. My deepest thanks go to Bill Blakemore, Simon Dring, Vicki Feaver, Frances FitzGerald, Leah Freiwald, Joseph Galloway, Arthur Greenspon, Jenny Hare, Sohani Hayhurst, Michael Herr, Steven Herr, John Hockenberry, Keith Kay, Joy Laurence, Robin Pym Mannock, Steve Northrup, David Purt, James Sterba, Martin Stuart-Fox, Terrence Wrong, and Tom Yellin.

To the members of Professor Brian Crossley's writers' group, who listened regularly to these pages over eight years and made many fine suggestions for their improvement, my deepest thanks, especially to Rosemary

Guilding, Peter Curran, Jasmine Davies, Tara Economakis, Vanessa Edwards, Brenda Evans, Joanna Fenwick-Smith, Val Harrison, John Lemmon, Rhodri Powell, Richard Price, Annie Stanley, John Weaver and Linda Webster. May your hard work and dreams become books of your own.

A few good men who served in the U.S. military in Vietnam have helped me to get the story right. I am most thankful to: Lieutenant Colonel J.D. Coleman, U.S. Army (Ret.); Sergeant Bill Ehrhart, U.S. Marine Corps (Ret.); Colonel Robert Thompson, U.S. Marine Corps (Ret.); Lieutenant Colonel Robert (Bud) Marconi, U.S. Air Force (Ret.); Lieutenant Colonel Arthur Herman, U.S. Air Force (Ret.); and the late Colonel Charlie A. Beckwith, U.S. Army. Dr. John Partin of the Special Forces Operations Command was most helpful in checking details of U.S. Special Forces records.

Many others gave their time and knowledge in interviews during and after the war, and I will always be thankful to them.

Peter Osnos, Publisher and Chief Executive at PublicAffairs, is proving that it is possible to publish enlightening nonfiction and to thrive in the modern marketplace. I am proud to have my work in his house. I am grateful to other members of the PublicAffairs team, particularly Robert Kimzey, Assistant Publisher, David Patterson, Melanie Peirson Johnstone and Chrisona Schmidt, all of whom have made important contributions to this work. Special thanks to Amanda Urban for pointing me in the right direction to begin with, to David Halberstam, always, for his kind advice, and to Robert Solomon for his legal wisdom and wit.

To all of you who helped, thank you.

For more information about the people in
The Cat from Hué and what has happened to them since the
author met them in Vietnam, please go to
thecatfromhue.com
on the internet. You will also find further reading,
photographs and other interesting news on the website.

PublicAffairs is a new nonfiction publishing house and a tribute to the standards, values, and flair of three persons who have served as mentors to countless reporters, writers, editors, and book people of all kinds, including me.

I.F. STONE, proprietor of *I. F. Stone's Weekly*, combined a commitment to the First Amendment with entrepreneurial zeal and reporting skill and became one of the great independent journalists in American history. At the age of eighty, Izzy published *The Trial of Socrates,* which was a national bestseller. He wrote the book after he taught himself ancient Greek.

BENJAMIN C. BRADLEE was for nearly thirty years the charismatic editorial leader of *The Washington Post.* It was Ben who gave the *Post* the range and courage to pursue such historic issues as Watergate. He supported his reporters with a tenacity that made them fearless and it is no accident that so many became authors of influential, bestselling books.

ROBERT L. BERNSTEIN, the chief executive of Random House for more than a quarter century, guided one of the nation's premier publishing houses. Bob was personally responsible for many books of political dissent and argument that challenged tyranny around the globe. He is also the founder and longtime chair of Human Rights Watch, one of the most respected human rights organizations in the world.

———

For fifty years, the banner of Public Affairs Press was carried by its owner Morris B. Schnapper, who published Gandhi, Nasser, Toynbee, Truman and about 1,500 other authors. In 1983, Schnapper was described by *The Washington Post* as "a redoubtable gadfly." His legacy will endure in the books to come.

Peter Osnos, *Publisher*